November 2–3, 2015
Palo Alto, California, USA

I0054758

Association for Computing Machinery

Advancing Computing as a Science & Profession

COSN'15

Proceedings of the 2015 ACM
Conference on Online Social Networks

Sponsored by:
ACM

Supported by:
NSF, Facebook, Yelp, Twitter, & Google

**Association for
Computing Machinery**

Advancing Computing as a Science & Profession

The Association for Computing Machinery
2 Penn Plaza, Suite 701
New York, New York 10121-0701

Notice to Past Authors of ACM-Published Articles
ACM intends to create a complete electronic archive of all articles and/or other material previously published by ACM. If you have written a work that has been previously published by ACM in any journal or conference proceedings prior to 1978, or any SIG Newsletter at any time, and you do NOT want this work to appear in the ACM Digital Library, please inform permissions@acm.org, stating the title of the work, the author(s), and where and when published.

ISBN: 978-1-4503-3951-3 (Digital)

ISBN: 978-1-4503-4103-5 (Print)

Additional copies may be ordered prepaid from:

ACM Order Department
PO Box 30777
New York, NY 10087-0777, USA

Phone: 1-800-342-6626 (USA and Canada)
+1-212-626-0500 (Global)
Fax: +1-212-944-1318
E-mail: acmhelp@acm.org
Hours of Operation: 8:30 am – 4:30 pm ET

Printed in the USA

Foreword

People across the world are increasingly connected together through online social networks, and the emergence of these networks has given rise to new and exciting research challenges at the intersection of social sciences and computing. It is our great pleasure to welcome you to the 3rd ACM Conference on Social Networks (COSN 2015), which provides a forum for researchers worldwide to present and discuss original research in this exciting area. ACM COSN 2015 will be held on Nov 2-3, 2015 in the heart of silicon valley at Stanford, California, providing a unique opportunity for academic and industry researchers, and practitioners to come together and share their research insights and experiences.

The COSN 2015 program includes three plenary keynote sessions by eminent academic and industry leaders, a strong research session program, a poster session, and panels. We are fortunate to have Jon Kleinberg, Tisch University Professor at Cornell University, and Alex Roetter, Senior Vice President of Engineering at Twitter as our plenary speakers. The research session will feature 22 high quality research papers where one author for each paper will give a 20-minute presentation followed by a short question-answer session. The poster session will feature seven high quality posters. Together with the panel discussions, we hope that these sessions will spark stimulating conversations and lead to future research. The detailed program will be included in the conference proceedings for your reference. We truly hope that you will find the quality of the program pleasing and intellectually stimulating.

The ACM COSN conference is only possible through dedicated voluntary contributions from many individuals and institutions, all of whom deserve our deepest gratitude. We would especially like to thank our dedicated organizing committee: Balachander Krishnamurthy and Ben Zhao from the COSN steering committee; Matthias Grossglauser and Rakesh Agrawal, program committee chairs; all the voluntary members of the program committee; Jim Blomo, proceedings chair; Hamed Haddadi, publicity chair; Ponnurangam Kumaraguru "PK", web chair; Meeyoung Cha, budget chair; Ashish Goel, awards committee chair; Camelia Simoiu, local arrangements chair; Cerek Budak, registration chair; Reza Rejaie, student travel grant chair; Huan Liu, Alan Mislove, and Evimaria Terzi, poster co-chairs; Lucas Maystre for managing the hotcrp conference management system; and Wendy Tan for all her invaluable help with the conference logistics. We would also like to thank all our generous sponsors who exemplify the strong support we've received for the conference.

Finally, we also wish to express thanks to the many contributors to the conference who are giving talks, submitted papers, posters and participated in the panels. Their contributed content is the heart of the conference. We truly hope that you will find the conference program thought provoking, and that the conference will provide you with a valuable opportunity to connect with fellow researchers and industry practitioners. We wish you have a pleasant time during the conference and hope you enjoy COSN 2015.

Aneesh Sharma
COSN'15 General Chair
Twitter Inc

Welcome from the Program Co-Chairs

Online Social Networks reach a significant and growing fraction of the population of the planet, and increasingly govern society's patterns of communication and information sharing. OSNs are now deeply woven into every major social process, and are transforming how politics, business, entertainment, surveillance, and advertisement operate. Their emergence has opened up new avenues for research at the intersection of computing and the social sciences, thanks in part to the efforts of scientists in curating large-scale behavioral datasets collected from these systems.

In light of these exciting trends, we would like to welcome you to the third edition of the ACM Conference on Online Social Networks (COSN), this year held at Stanford University. The program, featuring the presentation of 22 research papers along with two stellar keynote presentations by Jon Kleinberg and Alex Roetter, represents an eclectic mix of research in privacy, mobility, social epidemics and cascades, social media, network and group dynamics, and advances in the underlying theory, models, and algorithms. We trust you will find the program both intellectually stimulating and practically relevant.

We solicited full papers (up to 12 pages) describing original research in detail, and short papers (6 pages) conveying promising work and high-level vision. We received 82 submissions, of which 65 were full papers and 17 were short papers. We did not try to enforce a target mix of short and long papers, and the final program ended up containing 22 long papers. Interestingly, 9 of the 22 papers had authors from more than one continent. Attributing each paper to the continent with the most authors, the following geographic distribution results: North America: 11; South America: 1; Europe: 4; Asia: 6.

The PC consisted of 26 members (including the two of us). On average, every PC member reviewed around 10 papers and read a few more. We also sought advice from external reviewers for some papers as needed. Reviewing was single blind. The PC co-chairs refrained from submitting papers to the conference. In order to focus reviewer effort on the most difficult decisions, we early-rejected some papers after a first round with two reviews per paper. The remaining papers received at least one additional review. Reviewers were encouraged to use logarithmic scoring (1="bottom 50%", 2="top 50% but not top 25%", etc.) to keep scores from clustering around the average. We were careful to avoid conflicts in the review assignments, taking into account declarations of conflicts from both reviewers and authors. The reviewing process included extensive on-line discussions, followed by a full day face-to-face PC meeting, which took place at Stanford University on July 20th. The face-to-face PC meeting was attended by a large majority of the PC, and benefited from lively discussions and a great team spirit. We also held a one-day workshop on July 21st, chaired by Stelios Paparizos and attended by most PC members and a few invited guests interested in discussing trends and directions in the field. The Professor Ram Kumar Memorial Foundation bestowed several service awards to committee members to recognize their important contributions to the conference: Daniel R. Figueiredo and Krishna Gummadi for their contributions to committee deliberations; Krishna Gummadi for the best presentation during the "Trends and Directions" workshop; and Lucas Maystre for his management of the conference paper submission system.

As Program Co-Chairs, we mostly organized, asked (sometimes begged), facilitated, prodded, synthesized, and summarized. We are greatly indebted to the devoted members of our Program Committee for their hard work. We would also like to thank the Steering Committee, particularly Balachander Krishnamurthy and Ben Zhao; Aneesh Sharma, our general chair; Jim Blomo, our proceedings chair; Hamed Haddadi, publicity chair; Ponnurangam Kumaraguru "PK," web chair;

Meeyoung Cha, budget chair; Ashish Goel, awards committee chair; Camelia Simoiu, our local arrangements chair; Cerek Budak, our registration chair; Reza Rejaie, student travel grant chair; Huan Liu, Alan Mislove, Evimaria Terzi, our poster co-chairs; Lucas Maystre for ensuring the smooth operation of the hotcrp conference management system; and Wendy Tan for meeting logistics and for dealing with all our last minute requests with indulgent patience. Finally, we wish to thank all our sponsors and supporters for making COSN'15 possible.

Enjoy COSN 2015!

Rakesh Agrawal
COSN'15 Program Co-Chair
Data Insights Laboratories

Matthias Grossglauser
COSN'15 Program Co-Chair
EPFL

Table of Contents

Keynote Address

Session 1: Computational Methods and Algorithms

Session 2: Economics Including Advertising and Monetization

Session 3: Privacy

Posters

Session 4: Security & Information

Session 5: Measurements and Experimentation

Session 6: Location

Session 7: Learnings from Operational Social Networks

Session 8: Novel Applications of Social Networks

COSN 2015 CONFERENCE ORGANIZATION

General Chair: Aneesh Sharma *(Twitter, USA)*

Program Chairs: Rakesh Agrawal *(Data Insights Laboratories, USA)*
Matthias Grossglauser *(EPFL, Switzerland)*

Proceedings Chair: Jim Blomo *(Yelp, USA)*

Local Arrangements Chair: Camelia Simoiu *(Stanford University, USA)*

Publicity Chair: Hamed Haddadi *(Qatar Computing Research Institute, Qatar)*

Web Chair: Ponnurangam Kumaraguru *(IIIT Delhi, India)*

Treasurer: Meeyoung Cha *(KAIST, Korea)*

Registration Chair: Ceren Budak *(Microsoft Research, USA)*

Awards Committee Chair: Ashish Goel *(Stanford University, USA)*

Student Travel Grants Chair: Reza Rejaie *(University of Oregon, USA)*

Poster Chairs: Huan Liu *(Arizona State University, USA)*
Alan Mislove *(Northeastern University, USA)*
Evimaria Terzi *(Boston University, USA)*

Steering Committee: Virgilio Almeida *(UFMG, Brazil)*
Jon Crowcroft *(University of Cambridge, UK)*
Balachander Krishnamurthy *(AT&T Labs-Research, USA)*, chair
Ben Zhao *(UC Santa Barbara, USA)*

Program Committee: Rakesh Agrawal *(Data Insights Laboratories, USA)*
Virgilio Almeida *(UFMG, Brazil)*
Ricardo Baeza-Yates *(Yahoo Labs, USA)*
Jim Blomo *(Yelp, USA)*
Kenneth W. Church *(IBM Research, USA)*
Tina Eliassi-Rad *(Rutgers University, USA)*
Daniel Figueiredo *(UFRJ, Brazil)*
Matthias Grossglauser *(EPFL, Switzerland)*
Krishna Gummadi *(MPI, Germany)*
Dimitrios Gunopulos *(Athens University, Greece)*
Emre Kiciman *(Microsoft Research, USA)*
Nick Koudas *(University of Toronto, Canada)*
Hady Lauw *(Singapore Management University, Singapore)*
Huan Liu *(Arizona State University, USA)*

Program Committee
(continued): Kun Liu *(LinkedIn, USA)*

Cecilia Mascolo *(University of Cambridge, UK)*

Alan Mislove *(Northeastern University, USA)*

Stelios Paparizos *(Google, USA)*

Rajeev Rastogi *(Amazon, India)*

Amin Saberi *(Stanford University, USA)*

Aneesh Sharma *(Twitter, USA)*

Subbu Subramanian *(Facebook, USA)*

Evimaria Terzi *(Boston University, USA)*

Panayiotis Tsaparas *(University of Ionnina, Greece)*

Jian Wang *(LinkedIn, USA)*

Ben Zhao *(UC Santa Barbara, USA)*

COSN'15 Sponsor & Supporters

Sponsor:

Supporters:

Platinum

Gold

Silver

Keynote: On-Line Social Systems with Long-Range Goals

Jon Kleinberg
Cornell University
kleinber@cs.cornell.edu

ABSTRACT

Many systems involve the allocation of rewards for achievements, and these rewards produce a set of incentives that in turn guide behavior. Such effects are visible in many domains from everyday life, and they are increasingly forming a designed aspect of participatory on-line sites through the use of badges and other reward systems. We consider several aspects of the interaction between rewards and incentives in the context of collective effort, including a method for reasoning about on-line user activity in the presence of milestones and badges; and a graph-theoretic framework for analyzing procrastination and other forms of behavior that are inconsistent over time.

The talk includes joint work with Ashton Anderson, Dan Huttenlocher, Jure Leskovec, and Sigal Oren.

Categories and Subject Descriptors
E.0 [General]

General Terms
Human Factors

Keywords
On-line social networks; incentives; rewards

BIO

Jon Kleinberg is the Tisch University Professor in the Departments of Computer Science and Information Science at Cornell University. His research focuses on issues at the interface of networks and information, with an emphasis on the social and information networks that underpin the Web and other on-line media. He is a member of the National Academy of Sciences, the National Academy of Engineering, and the American Academy of Arts and Sciences, and has served on the Computer Science and Telecommunications Board (CSTB) of the National Research Council and the Computer and Information Science and Engineering (CISE) Advisory Committee of the National Science Foundation. He is the recipient of research fellowships from the MacArthur, Packard, Sloan, and Simons Foundations, and awards including the Harvey Prize, the Lanchester Prize, the Nevanlinna Prize, the Newell Award, the SIGKDD Innovation Award, and the ACM-Infosys Foundation Award in the Computing Sciences.

COSN'15, November 2–3, 2015, Palo Alto, California, USA.
ACM 978-1-4503-3951-3/15/11.
DOI: http://dx.doi.org/10.1145/2817946.2827355

On Predictability of Rare Events Leveraging Social Media: A Machine Learning Perspective

Lei Le
School of Informatics and
Computing, Indiana University
Bloomington, Indiana 47408
leile@indiana.edu

Emilio Ferrara
School of Informatics and
Computing, Indiana University
Bloomington, Indiana 47408
ferrarae@indiana.edu

Alessandro Flammini
School of Informatics and
Computing, Indiana University
Bloomington, Indiana 47408
aflammin@indiana.edu

ABSTRACT

Information extracted from social media streams has been leveraged to forecast the outcome of a large number of real-world events, from political elections to stock market fluctuations. An increasing amount of studies demonstrates how the analysis of social media conversations provides cheap access to the wisdom of the crowd. However, extents and contexts in which such forecasting power can be effectively leveraged are still unverified at least in a systematic way. It is also unclear how social-media-based predictions compare to those based on alternative information sources. To address these issues, here we develop a machine learning framework that leverages social media streams to automatically identify and predict the outcomes of soccer matches. We focus in particular on matches in which at least one of the possible outcomes is deemed as highly unlikely by professional bookmakers. We argue that sport events offer a systematic approach for testing the predictive power of social media conversations, and allow to compare such power against the rigorous baselines set by external sources. Despite such strict baselines, our framework yields above 8% marginal profit when used to inform simple betting strategies. The system is based on real-time sentiment analysis and exploits data collected immediately before the game start, allowing for bets informed by its predictions. We first discuss the rationale behind our approach, then describe the learning framework, its prediction performance and the return it provides as compared to a set of betting strategies. To test our framework we use both historical Twitter data from the 2014 FIFA World Cup games (10% sample), and real-time Twitter data (full stream) collected by monitoring the conversations about all soccer matches of the four major European tournaments (FA Premier League, Serie A, La Liga, and Bundesliga), and the 2014 UEFA Champions League, during the period between October, 25th 2014 and November, 26th 2014.

1. INTRODUCTION

A large number of case studies have proved that social media like Twitter can be effective sources of information to understand real-world phenomena and to anticipate the outcomes of events that are yet to happen, like political elections [9, 25] and talent shows [6], movies box-office performance [1, 19], and stock-market fluctuations [32, 4]. Even discounting the fact that successful case studies don't tell much about failures, the effectiveness of social media as information source to predict real events may not be surprising: they offer a window on the collective wisdom of a potentially very large crowd of users that can be harvested at the expense of a relatively small technological investment. On the other hand, a number of potential issues may affect such effectiveness: beyond all sorts of biases in the population of users whose tweets are collected, in virtually all cases the opinion of users can not be directly polled to answer the questions at hand. In some cases, there is arguably a strong correlation between the signal collected and the event to be predicted. The Twitter traffic volume about a movie and the revenue it later generates in the opening week, or the valence of political discussions and the outcome of an election are example of such cases. In others, such correlation is, at least in principle, more tenuous (e.g., the overall mood of Twitter conversations and fluctuations in the stock market). In general, the potential of leveraging information from social media to predict the outcome of real-world events is unclear and certainly has not been systematically studied.

Here we propose that an ideal test bed for addressing this issue is to consider team sport events. They offer several advantages: the number of possible outcomes of sport matches is usually limited, they occur continuously, and there is a lot of potentially useful signal to collect: social media are used by millions of sport fans everyday to discuss about their favorite sports, the teams they cheer for and their performance, and the expectations for future games. Another non trivial advantage is that prediction based on social media wisdom can be systematically compared with that implicitly reflected in the odds fixed by bookmakers. Betting odds in fact represent the opinion of experienced professionals. Presumably they also take into account the wisdom of the betting crowd, as quotes are continuously re-adjusted to reflect the influx of incoming bets, which in turn can be regarded as proxies of the bettors opinion.

In this paper we discuss the design, implementation, and validation of a machine learning framework to predict the occurrence of very unlikely (in terms of their betting odds) outcomes in soccer games by leveraging the mood of Twitter conversations relative to such games. The choice of soccer was made because it offers a larger Twitter traffic with respect to other sports. Soccer is the most popular sport in the world[1] with more than 3 billions fans accourding to recent estimates[2]. The official blog of Twitter for example reports that there were 672 million tweets posted related to the 2014 FIFA World Cup tournament, making this the most spoken event online in the history of the platform[3].

As mentioned above, here we focus on games that have the potential for an outcome deemed very unlikely by bookmakers. There are at least two reasons for this choice. On the one hand, these games are those potentially more profitable to bet upon, as one of their results has very high odds. More importantly, they are arguably those for which to "correctly" estimate the odds is problematic both for bookmakers and bettors, and therefore they offer a potential for successfully leveraging exogenous signals as that extracted from social media.

We consider games from six different competitions, including the 2014 FIFA World Cup tournament, and the relative Twitter conversations [14]. We extract separately the average mood in the conversations generated by supporters of both teams for a period of six hours before the beginning of the games, and use its discrete representation to train a machine learning classifier called to discriminate between games whose outcome is the expected result (low-odds), or the unlikely one (high-odds). Our results translate in a simple betting strategy that offers above 8% margin of profit. We interpret this finding as a consequence of both the presence of "wisdom of the crowd" signal in social media conversations, and the difficulty to properly estimate the odds of unlikely events.

Next we present the methodology employed in this study, the procedure used to select the specific games to which our machine learning framework is applied, we introduce the adopted features and then define our classification task. We also offer some intuition on how the selected features, based on the mood of Twitter conversations from the two teams fans, may provide useful information for prediction purpose. In Section 4 we describe in detail the implementation of our machine learning approach and its validation according to standard measures of performance. In Section 5 we assess the economic profit yielded by using our framework introducing a simple betting strategy based of the results of our predictions. We finally discuss further details on data collection and related work in sections 6 and 7 respectively. We conclude with a summary of our results and a discussion of their relevance.

2. METHODOLOGY

We considered games from six different tournaments: *(i)* the 2014 FIFA World Cup tournament, *(ii)* the major four European national tournaments during 2014 (FA Premier League, Serie A, La Liga, and Bundesliga), and *(iii)* the 2014 UEFA Champions League. While for the FIFA World Cup we collect historical data from our Twitter *gardenhose* repository at Indiana University (containing about 10% of

[1] http://mostpopularsports.net/in-the-world/
[2] http://www.topendsports.com/world/lists/popular-sport/fans.htm
[3] https://blog.twitter.com/2014/seven-worldcup-data-takeaways-so-far

the entire datastream), the conversation about the other events is collected using a real-time monitoring algorithm processing the full Twitter stream. In the following, we will consider two datasets: the FIFA, consisting of the games in the the 2014 FIFA World Cup tournament, and one with the games from all other tournaments. We will refer to this second dataset as "Live-monitoring".

While the games in the two datasets could be merged in a single one, we believe that the collection strategies adopted for the FIFA and the Live-monitoring datasets are sufficiently different to necessitate separate treatment. The fact that the FIFA tournament attracts a much larger and more diverse public (the ultimate source of our signal) is a further reason to keep the datasets separated.

We are specifically interested in games that before their starting had a potential outcome deemed as very unlikely. For a generic game g we considered the average odds (the latest available before the start of the match) assigned to that match by multiple bookmakers[4]. We leverage four betting agencies: William Hill, Ladbrokes, Bet 365, and Bwin; these four bookmakers together cover most of the betting market. We define O_{max}^g and O_{min}^g as the maximum and minimum odds assigned to one of the possible outcomes of the game g. We also define O^g as the the odds of the outcome that finally materializes. Of course O^g can coincide with one of O_{max}^g and O_{min}^g. To each game we assigned a *potential upset* score $PU(g)$ that measures the relative likelihood of the most likely outcome to the least one

$$PU(g) = \frac{O_{max}^g - 1}{O_{min}^g - 1}. \tag{1}$$

Note that, in betting, larger odds identify less likely outcomes: from Eq. 1 it follows that the higher the upset score for a game, the more unlikely that outcome was according to the bookmakers. Eq. 1 has lower bound at 1 and no theoretical upper bound: the practical upper bound is determined by how disproportionate the game odds are; in our experience the upset score max out around 100. Correctly betting on games turning into unexpected outcomes could generate the largest marginal profits if correctly bet upon.

The subset of games relevant to our prediction task are those whose PU score exceeds a given arbitrary large threshold θ. We considered various values of threshold, and in this study we report the results for $\theta = 5$; consistent findings hold for other values in the range $3 \leq \theta \leq 5$. We finally define the *upset* score $U(g)$ of a game g as the relative likelihood of the outcome that finally materializes to the most likely

$$U(g) = \frac{O^g - 1}{O_{min}^g - 1}. \tag{2}$$

$U(g)$ can be as small as 1 when the most likely result (minimum odds) materializes and as big as $PU(g)$ if the least likely result occurs. For illustrative purposes, in Table 1 we show the list of all FIFA World Cup games with an outcome different from the most likely ($U(g) > 1$). This happened for 31 games out of 64 played during the 2014 tournament. In the following, we will refer to games with

[4] The odds can be found at http://odds.sports.sina.cn/liveodds/ They are the average of decimal odds rather than Asian Handicap odds from all accessible betting companies. All odds are the last updated ones before the game.

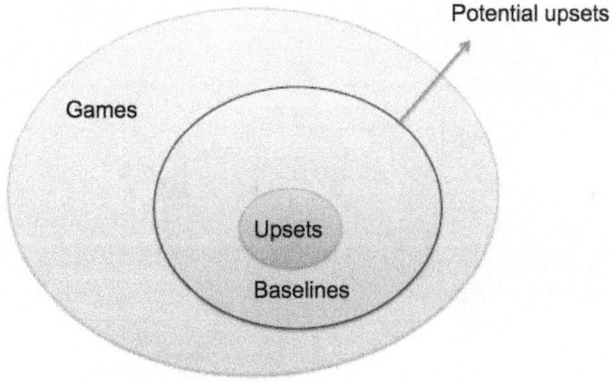

Figure 1: Upsets, potential upsets and baselines.

Table 1: Upset scores for the 2014 FIFA World Cup upset games. *(a.e.t.*: result after extra time)

Game	$U(g)$
Uruguay 1:3 Costa Rica	18.04
Germany 2:1(a.e.t.) Algeria	15.03
Germany 2:2 Ghana	14.06
Brazil 0:0 Mexico	12.87
Italy 0:1 Costa Rica	9.69
Spain 0:2 Chile	7.96
Brazil 3:2(a.e.t.) Chile	6.46
Netherlands 4:3(a.e.t.) Costa Rica	6.22
Argentina 1:0(a.e.t.) Switzerland	5.72
Ecuador 0:0 France	5.09
Spain 1:5 Netherlands	4.86
USA 2:2 Portugal	4.08
Costa Rica 0:0 England	3.79
Nigeria 1:0 Bosnia Herzegovina	3.79
Russia 1:1 Korea Republic	3.17
Greece 2:1 Côte d'Ivoire	3.04
Iran 0:0 Nigeria	2.93
Uruguay 2:1 England	2.86
Algeria 1:1 Russia	2.61
Belgium 2:1(a.e.t) USA	2.39
Brazil 0:3 Netherlands	1.75
Japan 0:0 Greece	1.71
Germany 1:0(a.e.t.) Argentina	1.70
Netherlands 2:4(a.e.t.) Argentina	1.46
England 1:2 Italy	1.46
Ghana 1:2 USA	1.40
Korea Republic 2:4 Algeria	1.31
Costa Rica 5:3(a.e.t.) Greece	1.26
Italy 0:1 Uruguay	1.15
Brazil 1:7 Germany	1.14
Netherlands 2:0 Chile	1.01

$PU(g) > \theta$ as *potential upsets* and to games with $U(g) > \theta$ as *upsets*. Given the definition above, the latter constitute a subset of the former, as depicted in Fig. 1. We will refer to games that are potential upsets but not upsets as baseline games.

From Table 1, the reader knowledgeable of soccer will immediately see that some games with very unlikely scores (for example Brazil 1:7 Germany) are attached with low upset scores: this because our framework ignores goal differences and considers only for the overall outcome of a match. On the other hand, largely unexpected defeats like Uruguay 1:3 Costa Rica and Italy 0:1 Costa Rica, or ties like Germany 2:2 Ghana or Brazil 0:0 Mexico, yield large upset scores.

Note that a potential upset game can be an upset without necessarily resulting in $U(g) = PU(g)$. Consider the following example game between team A and B whose odds are $(2,7,11)$ on the victory of team A, a draw, and the victory of team B, respectively. The game is a potential upset according to our threshold $\theta = 5$, because $PU(g) = (11 - 1)/(2 - 1) = 10 > \theta = 5$. Suppose that the final outcome is a draw. The game is an upset because $U(g) = (7 - 1)/(2 - 1) = 6 > \theta = 5$, but $U(g) < PU(g)$. Interestingly, although this is a possibility, we never observed any such case in our datasets (see Tables 4 and 5).

Our classification tasks will consist in discriminating games that turn out to be *upsets* among all *potential upsets* using features extracted from Twitter conversations relative to such games. We discuss the details about the data collection Section 6. Before turning to a detailed description of our framework and of the features it employs, in the next section we provide some support to the idea that Twitter conversations may reflect important information about a game, which in turn can be leveraged to predict its outcome.

3. INTERPRETING THE GAME SIGNALS

Excluding extra time and penalties, a soccer game usually lasts less than 120 minutes with two 45-minute halves, a 15-minute halftime break, and several minutes of injury time. In this section, we seek to understand how well Twitter reflects the events occurring during a soccer game. For this in-depth analysis, we focus on the 2014 FIFA World Cup matches, and for simplicity we analyze the Twitter conversation occurring during the 120 minutes representing the effective duration of each game, at the minutes resolution.

3.1 Events and Response

We start trying understanding how users respond to important events during a soccer game. We only considered the events defined in the official match report provided by FIFA: "Goal scored," "Penalty scored," "Yellow Card," and "Red Card". By manually analyzing five upsets and five baseline games, we noticed that in both cases, the number of tweets spikes for a few minutes after these events occur. "Penalty scored" is somehow an exception because the number of tweets spikes before this type of events happens, as expected since "Penalty scored" occurs shortly after another unrecorded event, namely "Penalty decision". Fig. 2 shows one example of such collective reactions, for the game "Belgium vs Algeria". Clear spikes of traffic are annotated with in-game events, which also trigger big fluctuations in the collective sentiment scores (the technical details about sentiment analysis are in Section 6.4): the underdog fans' average sentiment is consistently much lower than the favorites' one, and drops drastically twice as an immediate consequence of the favorite team scoring. This type of analysis shows how well the Twitter conversation captures in real time the collective mood of the supporters, in support of our high-level idea that social media signals can be used to sense live events, and possibly even predict rare ones.

3.2 Interaction of Groups

We divided the users tweeting during a game into two groups. One group contains the fans of the favorite team

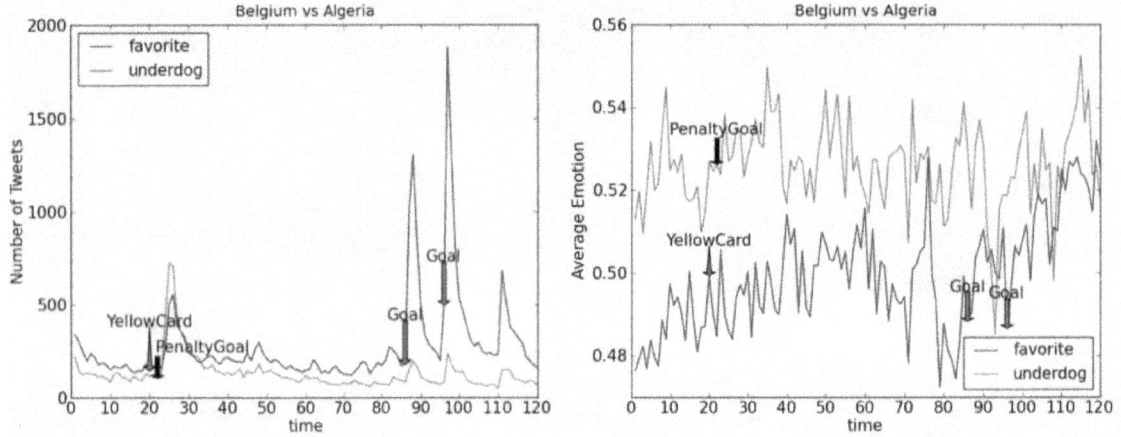

Figure 2: Events and response during games: volume (left) and average emotion (right) of tweets.

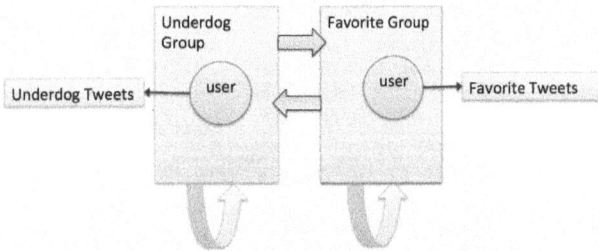

Figure 3: Groups and their possible interactions.

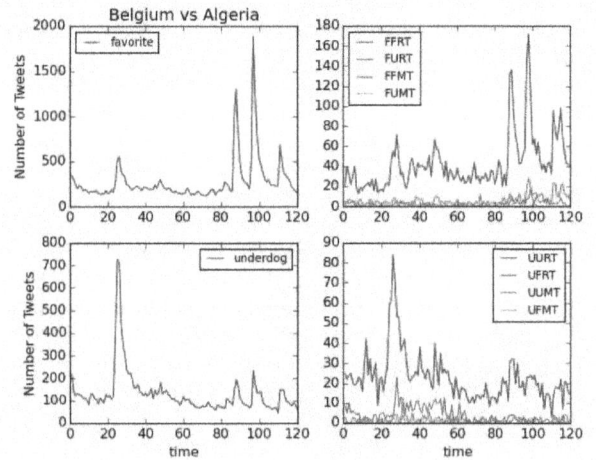

Figure 4: Interactions between and within groups during games. *FFRT/FFMT*: retweets and mentions within Favorite fans; *FURT/FUMT*: retweets and mentions from Favorite fans to Underdog fans. Viceversa, *UURT/UUMT*: retweets and mentions within Underdog fans; *UFRT/UFMT*: retweets and mentions from Underdog fans to Favorite ones.

(users who only tweet using the name/abbreviation of the favorites) while the other contains only supporters of the underdog team (see Section 6 for the details about the data collection). We assume that these two groups represent the two factions of supporters. We want to study the interaction dynamics within and between these two groups. The interaction can be in the form of *retweets* or *mentions* to users within the same group or from the other group. Fig. 3 schematizes this dynamics. Our analysis shows that the volume of interactions within groups greatly outnumbers that between groups: Fig. 4 illustrates this for the example game "Belgium vs Algeria".

4. THE PREDICTION FRAMEWORK

Our framework relies on the intuition that fans' discussion preceding a soccer game might convey useful information to predict the outcome of the game. Here in particular we seek to exploit the temporal evolution of the sentiment extracted from the Twitter conversations of the opposite set of fans to predict the outcome of potential upset games. We argue that sentiment analysis may help uncovering the hopes and therefore the collective opinion about the outcome of the game. The basic assumption is supported by recent social and behavioral psychology studies on social attention [16, 26, 27]: in a situation of perceived advantage, the fans of the favorite team will collectively express more positive emotions and feelings than the fans of the opposing team. Our working assumption is, therefore, that games where such gap in positive emotions is not observed before the game

starts will consistently turn into upsets. Before describing our effort to test such assumption it is worth stressing that choosing mood as single representative feature is here a deliberate choice. In principle, metadata and text could also be helpful for the classification task at hand. Unfortunately our training dataset is limited, and increasing excessively the number of features carries the risk of overfitting. Also, other features that may seem obvious can introduce confusing signal. The volume of tweets from the two teams supporter groups, for example, may reflect more the size of such groups than the fans' opinion on the outcome of the match. Presumably, a human could find helpful information in the text of messages, for example about the players and their overall shape. Information of this kind would be game-specific and hard to extract, making the approach presented here far less general and more complicated. To avoid using game-specific words as features, we conducted an experiment where feature words were selected as the top 50 words (ranked according to tf-idf, excluding stopwords from nltk.corpus) across all the collected tweets. The resulting performance is worse than the best results presented below, even when we add additional metadata such as presence of mentions, hashtags, or urls.

4.1 Testing the significance of sentiment gap

We computed the sentiment score for each tweet produced either by the favorite or the underdog supporter in a 6 hours time period preceding the beginning of the game: tweets sentiment scores range in the interval $[0, 1]$ (see Section 6 for details). For each game, we retrieved the Twitter conversation occurred during the 6 hours before the start, and we broke this period into 12 windows (each representing 30 minutes) and computed the distribution of sentiment score in each window for tweets from the favorite and the underdog supporters, separately.[5]

We finally represented each game with a single vector $P(g) = \{p_1, \ldots, p_{12}\}$, where each component is the p-value of the Mann-Whitney U-test between the distribution of sentiment expressed toward the favorite and the underdog team during the ith time window.

Tables 2 and 3 show the results under the significance level of $p < 0.0001$ for the two datasets (FIFA and Live-monitoring respectively). When one considers early time windows our hypothesis fails, as most of the games don't pass the U-tests, regardless of their final result. However, when one considers later time windows (e.g., time windows 10 and 11, which is 90 minutes to 30 minutes before the games start), the majority of baseline games pass the U-test, while only a small fraction of upsets do (see Fig. 5). This suggests that a significant difference in sentiment distribution between the two factions of fans is discriminative in identifying games that turn into upsets.

Most of the usable sentiment signal is conveyed between 90 minutes and 30 minutes before the games start. For readers knowledgeable of soccer, such information won't be surprising: line-ups are usually announced about 90 minutes before the games. Releasing news on line-ups and other factors of the game, such as last-minute injuries, the weather, etc., may influence the opinions of the fans about the outcome of the game.

4.2 Prediction

As anticipated above, the primary goal of this paper is to describe a machine learning framework that, among all potential upset games, discriminate those that *actually* turn into an upset. In the datasets considered here, based on the odds we collected, any result other than the victory of the favorite team will make the game an upset; therefore, our classification task can be rephrased as discriminating between the victory of the favorite and either a draw or the victory of the underdog.

We considered different classification approaches, all based on the feature vector $P(g)$ defined above.

---

[5]We explored alternatives, including sliding windows with partial overlap and different window lengths. The configuration reported here yields the best performance. We also exclude match-related tweets (those mentioning both teams) to avoid deciding how to attribute that sentiment the teams.

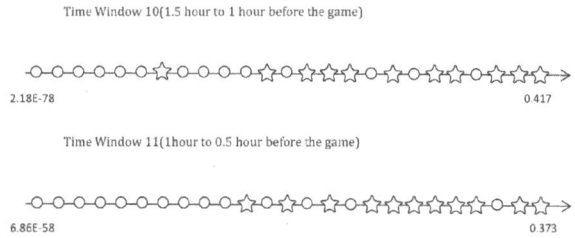

Time Window 10(1.5 hour to 1 hour before the game)

2.18E-78   0.417

Time Window 11(1hour to 0.5 hour before the game)

6.86E-58   0.373

Figure 5: Predictions based on sentiment score gap. Each star/circle denotes a game prediction. Stars denote games predicted as upsets, circles are games predicted as baseline. The axis denotes the p-values.

Table 2: U-test on sentiment scores ($p < 0.0001$) on the **FIFA World Cup** dataset. Ideally, upsets should pass no tests, and baselines should pass all test

Window	Upset (pass/total)	Baseline (pass/total)
1	3/10	5/15
2	3/10	3/15
3	2/10	2/15
4	3/10	3/15
5	3/10	3/15
6	2/10	4/15
7	3/10	3/15
8	2/10	3/15
9	3/10	3/15
10	3/10	10/15
11	3/10	11/15
12	7/10	8/15

Table 3: U-test on sentiment scores ($p < 0.0001$) on the **Live-monitoring** dataset. Ideally, upsets should pass no tests, and baselines should pass all test

Window	Upset (pass/total)	Baseline (pass/total)
1	1/9	0/22
2	5/9	3/22
3	0/9	2/22
4	2/9	7/22
5	0/9	0/22
6	3/9	11/22
7	0/9	2/22
8	4/9	10/22
9	1/9	2/22
10	2/9	14/22
11	2/9	11/22
12	3/9	12/22

We explored the performance of most classifiers available in the Python library scikit-learn [21]: the best performance is provided by Gaussian Naive Bayes. Note that our goal here was not that of finding the best classifier or the best parameter tuning, but to illustrate the feasibility of our method: more advanced machine learning techniques, such as deep learning, might yield even better performance. We use the two datasets (FIFA and Live-monitoring) to train our classifier and then perform a stratified three-fold cross

Table 4: The 2014 FIFA World Cup training set ($\theta = 5$): upset and baseline games

Game	U(g)	PUS(g)	Class
Uruguay 1:3 Costa Rica	18.05	18.05	upset
Germany 2:1(a.e.t) Algeria	15.03	30.2	upset
Germany 2:2 Ghana	14.06	24.47	upset
Brazil 0:0 Mexico	12.88	12.88	upset
Italy 0:1 Costa Rica	9.69	9.69	upset
Spain 0:2 Chile	7.96	7.96	upset
Brazil 3:2(a.e.t) Chile	6.46	9.98	upset
Netherlands 4:3(a.e.t) Costa Rica	6.22	12.04	upset
Argentina 1:0(a.e.t) Switzerland	5.72	9.98	upset
Ecuador 0:0 France	5.1	7.25	upset
Cameroon 1:4 Brazil	1.0	166.25	baseline
Argentina 1:0 Iran	1.0	145.69	baseline
Australia 2:3 Netherlands	1.0	53.59	baseline
France 3:0 Honduras	1.0	41.81	baseline
Brazil 3:1 Croatia	1.0	35.5	baseline
Argentina 2:1 Bosnia H.	1.0	29.43	baseline
Belgium 2:1 Algeria	1.0	25.97	baseline
Nigeria 2:3 Argentina	1.0	19.43	baseline
Chile 2:1 Australia	1.0	18.41	baseline
France 2:0 Nigeria	1.0	17.71	baseline
Australia 0:3 Spain	1.0	17.39	baseline
Honduras 0:3 Switzerland	1.0	12.7	baseline
USA 0:1 Germany	1.0	10.52	baseline
Honduras 1:2 Ecuador	1.0	7.85	baseline
Cameroon 0:4 Croatia	1.0	6.89	baseline

Table 5: The European leagues games training set ($\theta = 5$): upset and baseline games

Game	U(g)	PUS	Class
Dortmund 0:1 Hannover 96	91.66	91.66	upset
Liverpool 0:0 Hull City	14.44	24.07	upset
West Ham 2:1 Manchester City	14.85	14.85	upset
Tottenham 1:2 Newcastle Utd	9.65	9.65	upset
Milan 0:2 Parlemo	15.27	15.27	upset
Arsenal 3:3 Anderlecht	20.47	39.05	upset
Manchester City 1:2 CSKA	44.73	44.73	upset
QP Rangers 2:2 Manchester City	9.44	14.44	upset
Real Sociedad 2:1 Atletico Madrid	6.63	6.63	upset
Southampton 1:0 Stoke City	1.0	12.68	baseline
Sunderland 0:2 Arsenal	1.0	6.60	baseline
Cesena 0:1 Inter	1.0	11.70	baseline
Juventus 2:0 Palermo	1.0	100.00	baseline
Napoli 6:2 H. Verona	1.0	25.18	baseline
Arsenal 3:0 Burnley	1.0	78.57	baseline
Bayern Munich 2:1 Dortmund	1.0	10.97	baseline
Empoli 0:2 Juventus	1.0	27.85	baseline
Granada 0:4 Real Madrid	1.0	84.61	baseline
Dortmund 4:1 Galatasaray	1.0	65.00	baseline
Juventus 3:2 Olympiacos	1.0	42.85	baseline
Malmo 0:2 Atletico Madrid	1.0	35.87	baseline
Real Madrid 1:0 Liverpool	1.0	66.07	baseline
Ajax 0:2 Barcelona	1.0	26.80	baseline
Bayern Munich 2:0 Roma	1.0	67.85	baseline
PSG 1:0 Apoel	1.0	75.00	baseline
Manchester Utd 1:0 Crystal Palace	1.0	42.50	baseline
Roma 3:0 Torino	1.0	18.82	baseline
Dortmund 1:0 Borussia M.	1.0	7.55	baseline
Wolfsburg 2:0 Hamburg	1.0	9.33	baseline
Juventus 7:0 Parma	1.0	92.30	baseline
PSG 2:0 Olympique Marseille	1.0	8.87	baseline

validation to evaluate its performance, which are shown in Tables 6 and 7. Data about the World Cup were collected from the Twitter gardenhose (10% sample), while those in the "Live-monitoring" set from the Twitter Streaming API (full stream). We decided to keep these two sets separate as they exhibit sensibly different volumes of tweets, due to the magnitude of the events and the sampling rate of the Twitter streams.

Let us discuss these two cases separately. Table 6 illustrates the prediction performance with the 25 potential upsets that constitute our FIFA World dataset. Our classifier in this scenario achieves an accuracy near to 79% and a score in terms of AUC near to 73%. The results based on the Twitter gardenhose are promising, but we expect to be able to do even better with live-monitoring the games using the full Twitter stream. Table 7 shows the performance for the 31 potential upsets identified during the period between October, 25th 2014 and November, 26th 2014 in the four major European national tournaments plus the UEFA Champions League.

In the case of live-monitoring games, we can improve our prediction performance scoring an accuracy of 83.63% and an AUC of 78.87%. These results clearly suggest that our framework can be potentially used for early prediction of the games. As a proof of consistency, given the relatively small set of potential upset games, we constructed two randomized versions of the datasets in which we randomly reshuffle the class labels of each game (upset or baseline game) across all games. This process yields a yardstick in which sentiment is disentangled from the actual game results. As Table 8 shows, both Accuracy and AUC in such random model classification exhibit scores near 50%, confirming the presence of predictive signal in our game representation.

Table 6: Classification performance of historical games (2014 FIFA World Cup)

Accuracy	Precision	Recall	F1-Score	AUC
0.7898	0.8512	0.5431	0.6631	0.7286

Table 7: Live-monitoring game prediction performance (2014 European tournaments)

Accuracy	Precision	Recall	F1-Score	AUC
0.8363	0.5833	0.6667	0.6190	0.7887

Based on all results and observations above, we concluded we can make highly profitable predictions on potential upset games based solely upon the difference of sentiment expressed by the fans of the two teams prior to the match. Specifically, in the range between 90 to 30 minutes before the games start, the difference of sentiment scores between favorites and underdogs is usually significant for baseline games and not significant for upsets. We leverage this prediction framework next, to determine what margin of profit we can achieve betting on potential upsets, as compared to other betting strategies not informed by social media data.

Table 8: Classification performance on reshuffle model for baseline comparison

Accuracy	Precision	Recall	F1-Score	AUC
0.5576	0.45	0.3	0.3428	0.5116

5. ECONOMIC PROFIT ON PREDICTIONS

The ultimate test of the effectiveness of the predictive power of our approach consists in determining whether it can return a profit if used systematically against the odds offered by the bookmakers. Such odds are notoriously hard to beat because: *(i)* they are initially set by professional soccer experts, *(ii)* they are continuously adjusted to take into account the incoming flow of bets (and therefore they take indirectly into account the wisdom of the bettor crowd), and *(iii)* they incorporate a systematic profit margin for the bookmakers. In other words, given the underlying probability of an event to occur, the profit for a successful bettor is less than that would be entitled to in a fair bet.

Here, we first estimate the average return of a betting strategy based on our predictions, and then compare it with that achievable with different baseline betting strategies.

Our two datasets combined contain a total of $N = 56$ games (25 potential upsets from the 2014 FIFA World Cup and 31 potential upsets from the live-monitoring European tournaments). We perform 100 rounds of betting. For each round we perform a stratified three-fold cross validation and bet 1 dollar in each of the games in the test set according to the following simple strategy: if our system predicts that the game will not turn into an upset, we bet the dollar on the favorite team; otherwise, we bet half dollar on the victory of the underdog, and half dollar on the draw. In our datasets, both the latter two results —if realized— make the corresponding game an upset and therefore offer a return at least $\sigma = 5$ times larger than the victory of the favorite. We then compute the marginal profit for the given betting round as

$$P = \frac{r - b}{b} \quad (3)$$

where r and b are the total payoff and money bet, respectively. Clearly, if $r < b$, Eq. 3 is negative, which means to incur in a loss rather than a profit ($P < 0$). Finally, we compute the average and standard deviation of the marginal profit across all the betting round. The result is represented in the blue bar in Fig. 6. The average marginal profit of 8.57% is surprisingly high. One possible explanation we wish to exclude is that we consistently classify correctly a single (or few games) with very high return, which would possibly offset and hide a large number of less profitable misclassifications. We therefore performed an experiment analogous to the one described above, but where the three odds relative to game are randomly reshuffled across the games. The average marginal profit is 8.43% and, again, surprisingly high (see red bars in Fig. 6). This demonstrates that our results are not an artifact of a possibly peculiar odds distribution.

We adopted a stratified three-fold cross validation procedure on the 56 potential upset games and evaluated the results of our predictor on the testing set every time. This simple strategy that bets equally on all games, regardless on their potential upset score, provides a systematic advantage

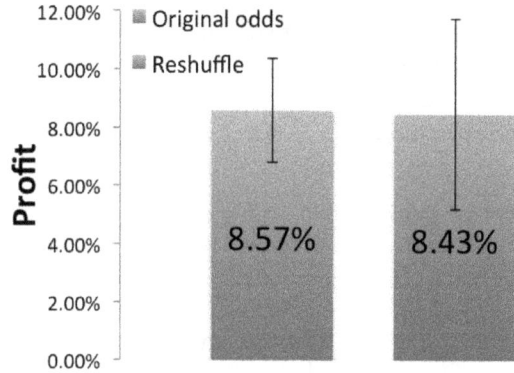

Figure 6: Average profits above 8% yielded by betting according to our predictions.

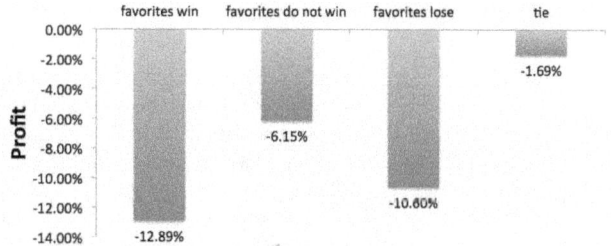

Figure 7: Losses on bets using systematic strategies.

and marginal profit. We tested more advanced strategies (for example betting different amounts based proportional to the odds) finding consistent results although increasing the risks and therefore the fluctuations in marginal profit.

The final comparison is against systematic betting on the following results, independently from the game: *(i)* the favorite team always wins, *(ii)* the favorite team does not win (half dollar bet on a tie, half dollar bet on the underdog winning), *(iii)* the favorite team loses (one dollar on the underdog winning), and *(iv)* the match is a tie. For each strategy we first compute the marginal profit on each game and then compute the average marginal profit (and the relative standard deviation) across all games. The results are shown in Fig. 7: these strategies, once again all yield possibly large losses. Interestingly enough, the safest fixed strategy (that still imposes a loss) is to bet on ties.

All benchmarks demonstrate that betting according to the predictions produced by our machine learning framework yields a consistent, positive and potentially large marginal profit, unparalleled by other systematic betting strategies, even informed by the odds.

6. DATA COLLECTION

We employed two different strategies for the collection of Twitter data relative to the 2014 FIFA World Cup and the other tournaments.

6.1 Twitter data for the 2014 FIFA World Cup

World Cup games attracted much more global attention than any other soccer games before and after (indeed, of any other event ever, as previously noted) providing a very large data base. We systematically collect and store all data

Table 9: Manual validation of the quality of the 2014 FIFA World Cup dataset

Game	Favorite	Underdog	Match
Uruguay vs Costa Rica	94% (Y) 6% (?) 0% (N)	92% (Y) 8% (?) 0% (N)	100% (Y) 0% (?) 0% (N)
Germany vs Algeria	94% (Y) 6% (?) 0% (N)	96% (Y) 4% (?) 0% (N)	100% (Y) 0% (?) 0% (N)
Germany vs Ghana	96% (Y) 4% (?) 0% (N)	96% (Y) 4% (?) 0% (N)	100% (Y) 0% (?) 0% (N)
Brazil vs Mexico	92% (Y) 8% (?) 0% (N)	94% (Y) 6% (?) 0% (N)	100% (Y) 0% (?) 0% (N)
Italy vs Costa Rica	92% (Y) 8% (?) 0% (N)	92% (Y) 8% (?) 0% (N)	100% (Y) 0% (?) 0% (N)

from the Twitter *gardenhose*, a 10% sample of the entire Twitter stream. Focusing our search on the period during which the World Cup occurred (June, 12th 2014 though July, 13th 2014), we isolated all tweets containing any of these keywords: *(i)* the official abbreviation of the game, as recommended by FIFA[6]; *(ii)* one or both of the team names; *(iii)* one or both the official team abbreviations; or, *(iv)* the hashtag combining the team names or abbreviation with "vs" (e.g., "BRAvsGER" to identify the game between Brazil and Germany). This procedure yielded a corpus of tweets for each of the 64 games occurred during the competition.

We isolated the tweets produced during the 6 hours before the beginning of each game and analyzed the frequency of adoption of the related keywords. The results for five representative matches are shown in Fig. 8. We noted that the abbreviations dominated the frequency of keywords adoption in all games. With a maximum limit of 140 characters per tweets, abbreviations are commonly used to save both space and typing time. Besides the team abbreviations, most of the other somehow frequent hashtags are either irrelevant (e.g., #eng in the game of Uruguay vs. Costa Rica) or too general or broad (e.g., #worldcup) to apply to the specific game itself. Therefore, we decided to use only hashtags of team abbreviations. Each game is therefore characterized by three subcategories of tweets: those related to each of the two teams involved in the match, and those related to the match itself (namely, those in which both team names appear). We finally performed a manual validation of the dataset: for all games, we randomly sampled 50 tweets in each of the three subsets and manually verified whether the tweets were correctly identified. In Table 9 we show the results of the validation procedure for five upset games. Essentially all tweets collected with our procedure are closely related to the games. The precision is consistently above 90% for every game in all the three subcategories. The final dataset of games for the 2014 FIFA World Cup contains 658,468 tweets, of which 319,312 are retweets and 28,707 are replies produced by 478,529 unique users.

[6]http://www.fifa.com/worldcup/teams/index.html

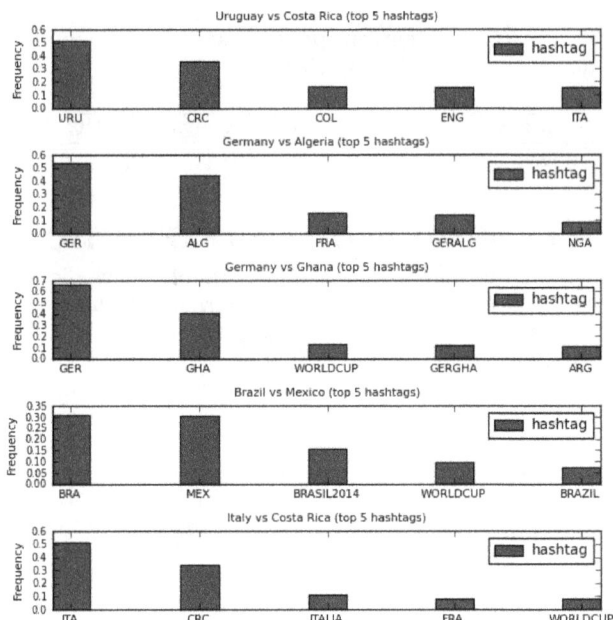

Figure 8: Hashtags distribution for five upset games. The frequency is the percentage the tweets containing each hashtag among all collected tweets for that game. Co-occurrences yield sums larger than one.

6.2 Live-monitoring soccer games data

During the period between October, 25th 2014 and November, 26th 2014 we monitored the odds of all games for four European national tournaments (the English *FA Premier League*, the Italian *Serie A*, the Spanish *La Liga*, and the German *Bundesliga*), and the UEFA Champions League. Our system selected 55 potential upsets with a profitability of at least 5:1 ($\theta = 5$) and we collected in real time tweets about these games using the Twitter Streaming API. As for the 2014 FIFA World Cup games, we selected tweets based on hashtags containing teams' abbreviations. The adoption of the Streaming API ensured that we collected the entirety of relevant tweets, rather than a sample. Some games, however, do not have enough tweets to guarantee a meaningful analysis (for example because the involved teams are not very popular). We therefore filtered out those games that did not collect at least 40 tweets per team per hour. This post-processing yielded a dataset 31 games, of which 9 turned into upsets and 22 into baselines. The final dataset of league matches contains 1,278,485 tweets, including 521,776 retweets and 31,281 replies, produced by 1,009,034 unique users.

6.3 Datasets characteristics

During our experimental evaluation we also considered merging the two data sets. The reason that brought us to finally decide against it is twofold: the datasets are collected using different sampling rates, and they refer to events of different sizes and attracting different audiences. The FIFA World Cup data are collected through the Twitter Gardenhose that provides a nominal 10% sample of all relevant tweets at best. Both the real sampling rate and the method of sampling are essentially unknown. Given the small sam-

Table 10: Sentiment tools performance on STS-test

Algorithm	Accuracy	Configuration
Text-Processing	0.6045	no neutral tweets
Indico	0.7465	no neutral tweets
Indico	0.7088	neutral: between 0.4 and 0.6
Indico	0.8052	neutral: between 0.3 and 0.7

pling rate potential under-sampling issues for a team with few Twitter-fans cannot be excluded. For the other tournaments, the live-monitoring data were collected through the Search API that returns *all* relevant tweets. Also, the FIFA World Cup attracts a much larger and likely more diverse kind of public with respect to the other tournaments, and it is the public that ultimately provides the signal we leverage. We believe that, given the different collection strategies adopted and the somewhat different nature of the games and their public, to keep the datasets separated is the scientifically sound choice. The consistency of the prediction results also hints at the fact that our method enjoys some degree of robustness across different potential sources of bias introduced in the data selection and collection process.

6.4 Sentiment Analysis

The ability to capture and computationally represent supporters emotions and feelings, and how these evolve over time, is a crucial component of our system. In particular, the framework is designed to capture *favorability* from content using sentiment analysis algorithms based on natural language processing [18] and opinion mining [20]. Previous studies have shown that sentiment analysis is able to capture the overall mood of a population and inform predictions about elections and financial markets movements [3, 29, 4].

After benchmarking the performance of the majority of sentiment analysis libraries available, we determined that the most suitable for our system is the *Indico deep learning* sentiment analysis framework, and we adopted the relative Python API[7]. The algorithm returns a sentiment score between 0 and 1 for each tweet. We evaluated its performance using the *Stanford Twitter sentiment corpus* (STS-test)[8], a manually annotated dataset containing 177 negative, 182 positive and 139 neutral tweets [22]. The STS-test is relatively small but it has been widely used to benchmark several sentiment analysis algorithms [22, 23, 24, 13, 28, 2]. As a comparison example we report the performance of *Text-Processing*[9], a sentiment tool trained on both Twitter data and movie reviews[10] adopting a Naive Bayes classifier. The results of the benchmarks are shown in Table 10. Indico outperforms Text-Processing (and all other algorithms we tested) achieving above 80.5% accuracy, the highest ever reported on the STS-test [22], when we label as neutral all tweets with sentiment score comprised between 0.3 and 0.7. Hereafter, we use this configuration.

[7]https://pypi.python.org/pypi/IndicoIo/0.4.7
[8]http://help.sentiment140.com/for-students
[9]http://text-processing.com/docs/sentiment.html
[10]http://www.cs.cornell.edu/people/pabo/movie-review-data/

7. RELATED WORK

This work, to the best of our knowledge, is the first to exploit social media streams to predict soccer matches. However, various recent studies have approached related problems [30], such as predicting the outcome of political elections [9, 25], talent shows [6], movies success [1, 19], stock-market fluctuations [32, 4], political protests [5, 7, 8, 31], and diffusion of information [17, 10].

To prove the idea that social media data convey predictive power, Asur and Huberman [1] designed a system that uses Twitter to forecast the box-office revenues of upcoming movies: simple signals such as the buzz around a given movie seem indicative of its future popularity. DiGrazia *et al.* [9] used a similar framework to show that there exists a statistically significant association between tweets that mention a political candidate for the U.S. House of Representatives and his or her subsequent electoral performance. Bermingham and Smeaton [3] illustrated a similar case study for the recent Irish General Election, modeling political sentiment by mining social media conversations. They combined sentiment analysis using supervised learning and volume-based measures and found that this signals are highly predictive of election results. Bollen *et al.* [4] analyzed the textual content of the daily Twitter stream to show that Twitter mood is predictive of the daily fluctuations in the closing values of the Dow Jones Industrial Average (DJIA). Xue Zhang *et al.* [32] collected Twitter data for six months and found that the percentage of emotional tweets significantly negatively correlates with Dow Jones, NASDAQ and S&P 500 fluctuations, but displays a significant positive correlation to VIX.

Various works called for caution when using social media to predict exogenous events [11, 12]: in such cases, it is important to keep in mind that the usage of machine learning algorithms or statistical models that function as black boxes can yield to results which are not interpretable and misleading [15].

For all these reasons, when we designed our machine learning framework we based it on simple assumptions: the prediction dynamics are entirely explainable and observable in real time. In fact, our model relies only on one single feature (the average conversation sentiment measured over time) and it allows to interpret the predictions in a concise and clear way. Our hypotheses are also rooted on recent advances in social psychology that support the idea that collective attention enhances group emotions [16, 26, 27].

8. CONCLUSIONS

In this paper we presented a machine learning framework that leverages social media signal to effectively predict the outcome of very unbalanced games.

We analyzed Twitter conversations relative to potential upset games to provide evidence that signal extracted from the conversation reflects the sentiment of the large crowd of fan following the game. We showed that our systems achieves a very promising prediction performance, with accuracy and AUC around 80%. We also demonstrated that the predictions yielded by our system can be effectively used to inform betting strategies achieving a positive and not negligible profit above 8%, and compared it with a number of baseline strategies that invariably leads to losses. We deem this as a strict and rigorous test of the effectiveness of our method.

Beating the odds offered by bookmakers is notoriously difficult, and is certainly not by chance that the betting industry is large and very profitable. Professional bookmakers matured great expertise in setting the initial odds, can readjust quotes continuously according to the incoming bets, and grant themselves a generous profit margin.

We believe that the reason for our success relies, in part, in focusing on very unbalanced games, where at least one of the potential results is deemed as highly unlikely. The high unlikelihood of one the result may lead to an increased difficulty in correctly estimating the relative odd. Also the exploitability of very unbalanced games could be the consequence of a general aversion in the betting crowd towards betting on unlikely results: this would lead to enhanced odds for the unlikely result to attract bets that can offset the losses incurred by the bookmaker if the most likely (and most bet upon) result materializes.

We performed experiments with lower values of the upset threshold ($\theta = 3$) therefore considering a set of matches with less unbalanced odds. They returned consistently decreased profitability margin, although still a reasonable profit was obtained.[11] In the limit in which we include all possible games, without any form of restriction, we can safely assume that the margin of profit will continue to decrease. We therefore expect that our method cannot "beat" the odds and produce a profit when no restriction is posed on the rarity of one of its possible results.

Bookmakers do an excellent job at setting the initial odds and adjusting them to the incoming flows of bets. In adjusting the odds they implicitly realize an "opinion market" that efficiently reflects the "wisdom of the betting crowd". We can only speculate why this opinion market is less efficient when rare events are involved. One obvious reason is that it is, almost by definition, much harder to estimate correctly the probability of rare events. Also, if the rare event is not (or is very little) bet upon, bookmakers may have to unduly increase the profitability of such event (by rising its odds) to attract bets that would compensate the loss incurred by the rare event not taking place.

Concluding, we argue that the prediction of rare events doesn't substantially differ from that of more common ones. The reason why we here focus on very unbalanced games is that games with strongly unbalanced odds are the only ones that provide an opportunity to "beat" the odds, the baseline we adopted to measure the performance of our method. For future work, we thus plan to try extend our methods to other prediction problems with well defined baselines, possibly employing techniques such as transfer learning to make our framework suitable to work within other scenarios.

Acknowledgments

EF is partially supported by the DARPA grant W911NF-12-1-0034. AF acknowledges support by NSF Award No. IIS-0811994.

---

[11]The margins of profit ranged between 5% and 6.5%.

9. REFERENCES

[1] S. Asur and B. A. Huberman. Predicting the future with social media. In *Web Intelligence and Intelligent Agent Technology (WI-IAT)*, volume 1, pages 492–499. IEEE, 2010.

[2] A. Bakliwal, P. Arora, S. Madhappan, N. Kapre, M. Singh, and V. Varma. Mining sentiments from tweets. *Proceedings of the WASSA*, 2012.

[3] A. Bermingham and A. F. Smeaton. On using Twitter to monitor political sentiment and predict election results. *Sentiment Analysis where AI meets Psychology (SAAIP)*, page 2, 2011.

[4] J. Bollen, H. Mao, and X. Zeng. Twitter mood predicts the stock market. *Journal of Computational Science*, 2(1):1–8, 2011.

[5] A. Choudhary, W. Hendrix, K. Lee, D. Palsetia, and W.-K. Liao. Social media evolution of the egyptian revolution. *Communications of the ACM*, 55(5):74–80, 2012.

[6] F. Ciulla, D. Mocanu, A. Baronchelli, B. Gonçalves, N. Perra, and A. Vespignani. Beating the news using social media: the case study of american idol. *EPJ Data Science*, 1(1):1–11, 2012.

[7] M. D. Conover, C. Davis, E. Ferrara, K. McKelvey, F. Menczer, and A. Flammini. The geospatial characteristics of a social movement communication network. *PloS one*, 8(3):e55957, 2013.

[8] M. D. Conover, E. Ferrara, F. Menczer, and A. Flammini. The digital evolution of occupy wall street. *PloS one*, 8(5):e64679, 2013.

[9] J. DiGrazia, K. McKelvey, J. Bollen, and F. Rojas. More tweets, more votes: Social media as a quantitative indicator of political behavior. *PloS one*, 8(11):e79449, 2013.

[10] E. Ferrara, O. Varol, F. Menczer, and A. Flammini. Traveling trends: social butterflies or frequent fliers? In *Proceedings of the first ACM conference on Online social networks*, pages 213–222. ACM, 2013.

[11] D. Gayo-Avello. No, you cannot predict elections with Twitter. *Internet Computing*, 16(6):91–94, 2012.

[12] D. Gayo-Avello, P. T. Metaxas, and E. Mustafaraj. Limits of electoral predictions using Twitter. In *ICWSM*, 2011.

[13] A. Go, R. Bhayani, and L. Huang. Twitter sentiment classification using distant supervision. *CS224N Project Report, Stanford*, pages 1–12, 2009.

[14] J. W. Kim, D. Kim, B. Keegan, J. H. Kim, S. Kim, and A. Oh. Social media dynamics of global co-presence during the 2014 FIFA World Cup. In *Proceedings of the ACM SIGCHI Conference on Human Factors in Computing Systems*. ACM, 2015.

[15] D. Lazer, R. Kennedy, G. King, and A. Vespignani. The parable of Google flu: Traps in big data analysis. *Science*, 343(6176):1203–1205, 2014.

[16] W. A. Mason, F. R. Conrey, and E. R. Smith. Situating social influence processes: Dynamic, multidirectional flows of influence within social networks. *Personality and social psychology review*, 11(3):279–300, 2007.

[17] M. Mathioudakis and N. Koudas. Twittermonitor: trend detection over the Twitter stream. In *Proceedings of the 2010 ACM SIGMOD International*

Conference on Management of data, pages 1155–1158. ACM, 2010.

[18] T. Nasukawa and J. Yi. Sentiment analysis: Capturing favorability using natural language processing. In *Proceedings of the 2nd international conference on Knowledge capture*, pages 70–77. ACM, 2003.

[19] A. Oghina, M. Breuss, M. Tsagkias, and M. de Rijke. Predicting imdb movie ratings using social media. In *Advances in information retrieval*, pages 503–507. 2012.

[20] B. Pang and L. Lee. Opinion mining and sentiment analysis. *Foundations and trends in information retrieval*, 2(1-2):1–135, 2008.

[21] F. Pedregosa, G. Varoquaux, A. Gramfort, V. Michel, B. Thirion, O. Grisel, M. Blondel, P. Prettenhofer, R. Weiss, V. Dubourg, J. Vanderplas, A. Passos, D. Cournapeau, M. Brucher, M. Perrot, and E. Duchesnay. Scikit-learn: Machine learning in Python. *Journal of Machine Learning Research*, 12:2825–2830, 2011.

[22] H. Saif, M. Fernandez, Y. He, and H. Alani. Evaluation datasets for Twitter sentiment analysis. In *Proceedings, 1st Workshop on Emotion and Sentiment in Social and Expressive Media (ESSEM)*, 2013.

[23] H. Saif, Y. He, and H. Alani. Semantic smoothing for Twitter sentiment analysis. 2011.

[24] H. Saif, Y. He, and H. Alani. Alleviating data sparsity for twitter sentiment analysis. *Making Sense of Microposts (# MSM2012)*, 2012.

[25] H. Schoen, D. Gayo-Avello, P. T. Metaxas, E. Mustafaraj, M. Strohmaier, and P. Gloor. The power of prediction with social media. *Internet Research*, 23(5):528–543, 2013.

[26] G. Shteynberg and E. P. Apfelbaum. The power of shared experience: Simultaneous observation with similar others facilitates social learning. *Social Psychological and Personality Science*, 4(6):738–744, 2013.

[27] G. Shteynberg, J. B. Hirsh, E. P. Apfelbaum, J. T. Larsen, A. D. Galinsky, and N. J. Roese. Feeling more together: Group attention intensifies emotion. *Emotion*, 14(6):1102, 2014.

[28] M. Speriosu, N. Sudan, S. Upadhyay, and J. Baldridge. Twitter polarity classification with label propagation over lexical links and the follower graph. In *Proceedings of the First workshop on Unsupervised Learning in NLP*, pages 53–63. ACL, 2011.

[29] M. Thelwall, K. Buckley, and G. Paltoglou. Sentiment in Twitter events. *Journal of the American Society for Information Science and Technology*, 62(2):406–418, 2011.

[30] A. Tumasjan, T. O. Sprenger, P. G. Sandner, and I. M. Welpe. Predicting elections with Twitter: What 140 characters reveal about political sentiment. *ICWSM*, 10:178–185, 2010.

[31] O. Varol, E. Ferrara, C. L. Ogan, F. Menczer, and A. Flammini. Evolution of online user behavior during a social upheaval. In *Proceedings of the 2014 ACM conference on Web science*, pages 81–90. ACM, 2014.

[32] X. Zhang, H. Fuehres, and P. A. Gloor. Predicting stock market indicators through Twitter "I hope it is not as bad as I fear". *Procedia-Social and Behavioral Sciences*, 26:55–62, 2011.

Tracking Triadic Cardinality Distributions for Burst Detection in Social Activity Streams

Junzhou Zhao* John C.S. Lui† Don Towsley‡ Pinghui Wang* Xiaohong Guan*

* Xi'an Jiaotong University, China
† The Chinese University of Hong Kong, Hong Kong
‡ University of Massachusetts at Amherst, US

{jzzhao,xhguan}@sei.xjtu.edu.cn, cslui@cse.cuhk.edu.hk, towsley@cs.umass.edu,
phwang@mail.xjtu.edu.cn

ABSTRACT

In everyday life, we often observe unusually frequent interactions among people before or during important events, i.e., people receive/send more greetings from/to their friends on Christmas Day than regular days. We also observe that some videos suddenly go viral through people's sharing in online social networks (OSNs). Do these seemingly different phenomena share a common structure?

All these phenomena are associated with sudden surges of user activities in networks, which we call "*bursts*" in this work. We uncover that the emergence of a burst is accompanied with the formation of triangles in networks. This finding motivates us to propose a new and robust method to detect bursts in OSNs. We first introduce a new measure, "*triadic cardinality distribution*", corresponding to the fractions of nodes with different numbers of triangles, i.e., triadic cardinalities, within a network. We demonstrate that this distribution not only changes when a burst occurs, but it also has a robustness property that it is immunized against common spamming social-bot attacks. Hence, by tracking triadic cardinality distributions, we can reliably detect bursts in OSNs. To avoid handling massive activity data generated by OSN users during the triadic tracking, we design an efficient "*sample-estimate*" solution to provide maximum likelihood estimate on the triadic cardinality distribution from sampled data. Extensive experiments conducted on real data demonstrate the usefulness of this triadic cardinality distribution and effectiveness of our sample-estimate solution.

Categories and Subject Descriptors

J.4 [**Computer Applications**]: Social and Behavioral Sciences

General Terms

Design, Measurement

COSN'15, November 02–03, 2015, Palo Alto, CA, USA.
ⓒ 2015 ACM. ISBN 978-1-4503-3951-3/15/11 ...$15.00.
DOI: http://dx.doi.org/10.1145/2817946.2817955.

Keywords

Social Activity Stream, Burst Detection, Sampling Methods, Data Stream Algorithms

1. INTRODUCTION

Online social networks (OSNs) have become ubiquitous platforms that provide various ways for users to interact over the Internet, such as tweeting tweets, sharing links, messaging friends, commenting on posts, and mentioning/replying to other users (i.e., @someone). When intense user interactions take place in a short time period, there will be a surge in the volume of user activities in an OSN. Such a surge of user activity, which we call a "*burst*" in this work, usually relates to emergent events that are occurring or about to occur in the real world. For example, Michael Jackson's death on June 25, 2009 triggered a global outpouring of grief on Twitter [15], and the event even crashed Twitter for several minutes [31]. In addition to bursts caused by real world events, some bursts arising from OSNs can also cause enormous social impact in the real world. For example, the 2011 England riots, in which people used OSNs to organize, resulted in 3,443 crimes across London due to this disorder [1]. Hence, detecting bursts in OSNs is an important task, both for OSN managers to monitor the operation status of an OSN, as well as for government agencies to anticipate any emergent social disorder.

Typically, there are two types of user interactions in OSNs. First is the interaction between users (we refer to this as *user-user interaction*), e.g., a user sends a message to another user, while the second is the interaction between a user and a media content piece (we refer to this as *user-content interaction*), e.g., a user posts a video link. Examples of bursts caused by these two types of interactions include, many greetings being sent/received among people on Christmas Day, and videos suddenly becoming viral after one day of sharing in an OSN. At first sight, detecting such bursts in an OSN is not difficult. For example, a naive way to detect bursts caused by user-user interactions is to *count* the number of pairwise user interactions within a time window, and report a burst if the volume lies above a given threshold. However, this method is vulnerable to spamming social-bot attacks [10, 14, 32, 7, 34, 6], which can suddenly generate a huge amount of spamming interactions in the OSN. Hence, this method can result in many *false alarms* due to the existence of social bots. Similar problem also exist when detecting bursts caused by user-content interac-

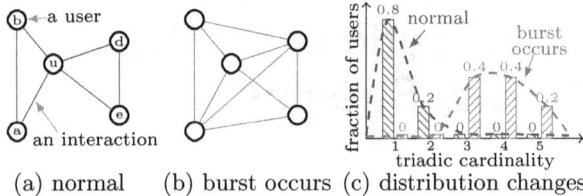

(a) normal   (b) burst occurs (c) distribution changes

Figure 1: Interaction burst and interaction triangle

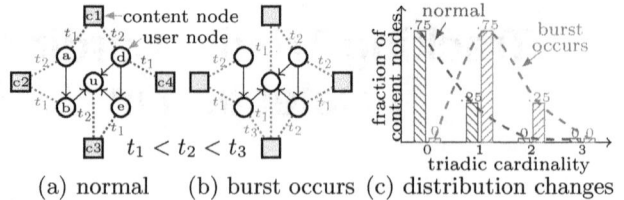

(a) normal   (b) burst occurs (c) distribution changes

Figure 2: Cascading burst and influence triangle

tions. Many previous works on burst detection are based on idealized assumptions [17, 40, 25, 13] and simply ignore the existence of social bots.

Present work. The primary goal of this work is to leverage a special *triangle structure*, which is a feature of humans, to design a robust burst detection method that is immune against common social-bot attacks. We first describe the triangle structure shared by both types of user interactions.

Interaction triangles in user-user interactions. Humans form social networks with larger clustering coefficients than those in random networks [39] because social networks exhibit many *triadic closures* [19]. This is due to the social phenomenon of "*friends of my friends are also my friends*". Since user-user interactions usually take place along social links, this property implies that user-user interactions should also exhibit many triadic closures (which we will verify in later experiments). In other words, when a group of users suddenly become active, or we say an *interaction burst* occurs, in addition to observing the rise of volume of pairwise interactions, we expect to also observe many interactions among three neighboring users, i.e., many *interaction triangles* form if we consider an edge of an interaction triangle to be a user-user interaction. This is illustrated in Fig. 1(a) when no interaction burst occurs, while in Fig. 1(b), an interaction burst occurs. In contrast, activities generated by social bots do not possess many triangles since social bots typically select their targets randomly from an OSN [7, 34].

Influence triangles in user-content interactions. We say that a media content piece becomes *bursty* if many users interact with it in a short time period. There are many reasons why a user interacts with a piece of media content. Here, we are particularly interested in the case where one user *influences* another user to interact with the content, a.k.a., the cascading diffusion [21] or word-of-mouth spreading [28]. It is known that many emerging news stories arising from OSNs are related to this mechanism such as the story about the killing of Osama bin Laden [35]. We find that a bursty media content piece formed by this mechanism is associated with triangle formations in a network. To illustrate this, consider Fig. 2(a), in which there are five user nodes $\{a, b, d, e, u\}$ and four content nodes $\{c_1, c_2, c_3, c_4\}$. A directed edge between two users means that one follows another, and an undirected edge labeled with a timestamp between a user node and a content node represents an interaction between the user and the content at the labeled time. We say content node c has an *influence triangle* if there exist two users a, b such that a follows b and a interacts with c *later* than b does. In other words, the reason a interacts with c is due to the influence of b on a. In Fig. 2(a), only c_2 has an influence triangle, the others have no influence triangle, meaning that the majority of user-content interactions

are not due to influence; while in Fig. 2(b), every content node is part of at least one influence triangle, meaning that many content pieces are spreading in a cascading manner in the OSN. From the perspective of an OSN manager who wants to know the operation status of the OSN, if the OSN suddenly switches to a state similar to Fig. 2(b) (from a previous state similar to Fig. 2(a)), he knows that a *cascading burst* is present in the OSN.

Characterizing bursts. So far, we find a common structure shared by different types of bursts: the emergence of *interaction bursts* (caused by user-user interaction) and *cascading bursts* (caused by user-content interaction) are both accompanied with the formation of triangles, i.e., interaction or influence triangles, in appropriately defined networks. This finding motivates us to characterize patterns of bursts in an OSN by characterizing the triangle statistics of a network, which we called the *triadic cardinality distribution*.

Triadic cardinality of a node in a network, e.g., a user node in Fig. 1(a) or a content node in Fig. 2(a), is the number of triangles that it belongs to. The triadic cardinality distribution then characterizes the fractions of nodes with certain triadic cardinalities. When a burst occurs, because many new interaction/influence triangles are formed, we will observe that some nodes' triadic cardinalities increase, and this results in the distribution shifting to right, as illustrated in Figs. 1(c) and 2(c). The triadic cardinality distribution provides succinct summary information to characterize burst patterns of a large scale OSN. Hence, by tracking triadic cardinality distributions, we can detect the presence of bursts.

In this paper, we assume that user interactions are aggregated chronologically to form a *social activity stream*, which can be considered as an abstraction of a *tweet stream* in Twitter, or a *news feed* in Facebook. We aim to calculate triadic cardinality distributions from this stream. The challenge is that when a network is large or users are very active, the social activity stream will be of high speed. For example, the speed of the Twitter's tweets stream can be as high as $5,700$ tweets per second on average, $143,199$ tweets per second during the peak time, and about 500 million to 12 billion tweets are aggregated per day [20]. To handle such a high-speed social activity stream, we design a sample-estimate solution, which provides a *maximum likelihood estimate* of the triadic cardinality distribution using sampled data. Our method works in a near-real-time fashion, and is demonstrated to be accurate and efficient.

Overall, we make three contributions in this work.

- We propose a robust measure, triadic cardinality distribution, which provides succinct summary information to characterize burst patterns of user interactions in a large scale OSN (Section 2).

- We design a sample-estimate method that is able to accurately and efficiently estimate triadic cardinality distributions from high-speed social activity streams in near-real-time (Sections 3 and 4).

- Extensive experiments conducted on real data demonstrate the usefulness of our proposed triadic cardinality distribution and effectiveness of our sample-estimate solution. We also show how to apply our method to detect bursts in Twitter during the 2014 Hong Kong Occupy Central movement (Section 5).

2. PROBLEM FORMULATION

We first formally define the notion of social activity stream as mentioned in previous section. Then we define triadic cardinality distribution and describe our proposed solution.

2.1 Social Activity Stream

We represent an OSN by $G(V, E, C)$, where V is a set of users, E is a set of relationships among users, and C is a set of media content such as hashtags and video links. Here, a relationship between two users can be undirected like the friend relationship in Facebook, or directed like the follower relationship in Twitter.

Users in the OSN generate *social activities*, e.g., interact with other users in V, or content in C. We denote a social activity by $a \in V \times (V \cup C) \times [0, \infty)$. Here user-user interaction, $a = (u, v, t)$, corresponds to user u interacting with user v at time t; and user-content interaction, $a = (u, c, t)$, corresponds to user u interacting with content c at time t.

These social activities are aggregated chronologically to form a *social activity stream*, denoted by $S = \{a_1, a_2, ...\}$, where a_k denotes the k-th social activity in the stream.

2.2 Triadic Cardinality Distribution

Triadic cardinality distributions are defined on two *interaction multi-graphs* which are formed by user-user and user-content interactions, respectively.

Interaction multi-graphs. Within a time window (e.g., an hour, a day or a week), user-user interactions in stream S form a multi-graph $\mathcal{G}_{uu}(V, \mathcal{E}_{uu})$, where V is the original set of users, and $\mathcal{E}_{uu}$ is a multi-set consisting of user-user interactions in the window. The *triadic cardinality of a user* $u \in V$ is the number of interaction triangles related to u in $\mathcal{G}_{uu}$. For example, user u in Fig. 1(a) has triadic cardinality two, and all other users have triadic cardinality one.

Similarly, user-content interactions also form a multi-graph $\mathcal{G}_{uc}(V \cup C, E \cup \mathcal{E}_{uc})$ in a time window. Unlike $\mathcal{G}_{uu}$, the node set includes both user nodes V and content nodes C, and the edge set includes user relations E and a multi-set $\mathcal{E}_{uc}$ denoting user-content interactions in the window. Note that in $\mathcal{G}_{uc}$, triadic cardinality is only defined for content nodes, and the *triadic cardinality of a content node* $c \in C$ is the number of influence triangles related to c in $\mathcal{G}_{uc}$. For example, in Fig. 2(a), content c_2 has triadic cardinality one, and all other content nodes have triadic cardinality zero.

Triadic cardinality distribution. Let $\theta = (\theta_0, ..., \theta_W)$ and $\vartheta = (\vartheta_0, ..., \vartheta_{W'})$ denote the triadic cardinality distributions on $\mathcal{G}_{uu}$ and $\mathcal{G}_{uc}$ respectively. Here, θ_i (ϑ_i) is the fraction of users (content pieces) with triadic cardinality i, and W (W') is the maximum triadic cardinality in $\mathcal{G}_{uu}$ ($\mathcal{G}_{uc}$).

The importance of the triadic cardinality distribution lies in its capability of providing succinct summary information to characterize burst patterns in a large scale OSN. By tracking triadic cardinality distributions, we will discover burst occurrences in an OSN.

2.3 Overview of Our Solution

We propose an on-line solution capable of tracking the triadic cardinality distribution from a high-speed social activity stream, as illustrated in Fig. 3.

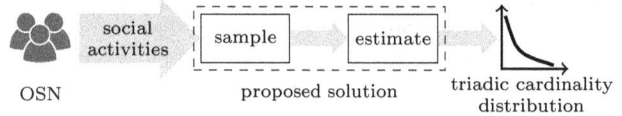

Figure 3: Overview of our sample-estimate solution

Our solution consists of sampling a social activity stream in a time window maintaining only summary statistics, and constructing an estimate of the triadic cardinality distribution from the summary statistics at the end of a time window. The advantage of this approach is that it is unnecessary to store all of the samples in the stream, and enables us to detect bursts in a near-real-time fashion.

3. STREAM SAMPLING METHOD

In this section, we introduce the sampling method in our solution. The purpose of sampling is to reduce the computational cost in handling the massive amount of data in a high-speed social activity stream.

3.1 Sampling Stream with a Coin

The stream sampling method works as follows. We toss a biased coin for each social activity $a \in S$. We keep a with probability p, and ignore it with probability $1 - p$. Hence, each social activity is independently sampled, and at the end of the time window, only a fraction p of the stream is kept. We use these samples to obtain a summary statistics of the stream in the current window, which we describe later.

3.2 Probability of Sampling a Triangle

When social activities in the stream are sampled, triangles in $\mathcal{G}_{uu}$ and $\mathcal{G}_{uc}$ are sampled accordingly. Obviously, the probability of sampling a triangle depends on p. In what follows, we analyze the relationship between triangle sampling probability and p, for an interaction triangle and an influence triangle, respectively.

Probability of sampling an interaction triangle. Sampling an interaction triangle, which consists of three user-user interaction edges in $\mathcal{E}_{uu}$, is equivalent to all its three edges being sampled. Because each interaction edge is independently sampled with probability p, then an interaction triangle is sampled with probability p^3, as illustrated in Fig. 4(a).

Probability of sampling an influence triangle. Calculating the probability of sampling an influence triangle is more complicated. First, we know that an influence triangle consists of two user-content interaction edges in $\mathcal{E}_{uc}$ and one social edge in E. Second, we note that stream sampling only applies to edges in $\mathcal{E}_{uc} \cup \mathcal{E}_{uu}$; edges in E are not sampled as they do not appear in the social activity stream.

In Fig. 4(b), suppose we have sampled two user-content interaction edges uc and vc, and assume user u interacted

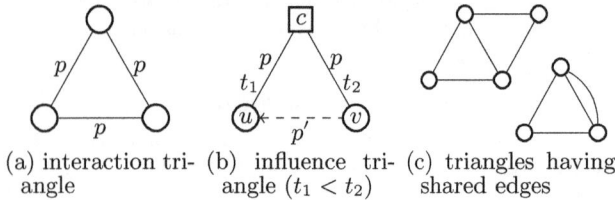

(a) interaction triangle   (b) influence triangle ($t_1 < t_2$)   (c) triangles having shared edges

Figure 4: Sampling triangles. A solid edge represents an interaction, and a dashed edge represents a user relation in E (i.e., a social edge). Figure (c) illustrates two cases of two interaction triangles having shared edges.

with content c earlier than user v. To determine whether content c has an influence triangle formed by users u and v, we need to check whether (directed) edge (v, u) exists in E. This can be done by querying neighbors of one of the two users in the OSN. For example, in Twitter, we query *followees* of v and check whether user v follows user u; or in Facebook, we query friends of user v and check whether user u is a friend of user v.

Suppose we observe n_c sampled users that all interact with c during the current time window, denoted by $V_c = \{u_1, \ldots, u_{n_c}\}$ where u_i interacted with c earlier than u_j, $i < j$. To verify every sampled triangle related to c, we need to query the OSN $n_c(n_c - 1)/2$ times. This query cost is obviously expensive when n_c is large. To reduce this query cost, instead of checking every possible user pair, we check a user pair with probability p'. This is equivalent to sampling a social edge in E with probability p', conditioned on the two associated user-content interactions having been sampled. Then, it is easy to see that an influence triangle is sampled with probability $p^2 p'$.

We summarize the above discussions in Theorem 1.

THEOREM 1. *If we independently sample each social activity in stream S with probability p, and check the existence of a user relation in the OSN with probability p', then each interaction (influence) triangle in graph $\mathcal{G}_{uu}$ ($\mathcal{G}_{uc}$) is sampled with identical probability*

$$p_\delta = \begin{cases} p^3 & \text{for an interaction triangle,} \\ p^2 p' & \text{for an influence triangle.} \end{cases} \quad (1)$$

Remark. Although triangles of the same type are sampled identically, they may *not* be sampled *independently*, such as the cases two triangles have shared edges in Fig. 4(c). We will consider this issue in detail in Section 4.

3.3 Statistics of Sampled Data

The above sampling process is equivalent to sampling edges in multi-graphs $\mathcal{G}_{uu}$ and $\mathcal{G}_{uc}$: an activity edge $e \in \mathcal{E}_{uu} \cup \mathcal{E}_{uc}$ is independently sampled with probability p; a social edge $e' \in E$ is sampled with conditional probability p'.

At the end of the time window, we obtain two *sampled multi-graphs* $\mathcal{G}'_{uu}$ and $\mathcal{G}'_{uc}$[1]. Calculating the triadic cardinalities for nodes in these reduced graphs is much easier than

---

[1] In $\mathcal{G}'_{uc}$, each sampled social edge e' needs to be marked with the influence triangle which e' belongs to, corresponding to the two user-content interactions that e' is checked for.

on the original unsampled graphs. For the sampled graph $\mathcal{G}'_{uu}$, we calculate triadic cardinality for each user node, and obtain statistics $g = (g_0, \ldots, g_M)$, where g_j, $0 \le j \le M$, denotes the number of nodes with j triangles in graph $\mathcal{G}'_{uu}$. Similar statistics are also obtained from $\mathcal{G}'_{uc}$, denoted by $f = (f_0, \ldots, f_{M'})$ (where f_j is the number of content nodes with j influence triangles in graph $\mathcal{G}'_{uc}$). We only need to store g and f in computer memory and use them to estimate θ and ϑ in the next section.

4. ESTIMATION METHODS

We are now ready to derive a maximum likelihood estimate (MLE) of the triadic cardinality distribution using statistics obtained in the sampling step. The estimation in this section can be viewed as an analog of the network flow size distribution estimation [11, 27], in which a packet in a flow is viewed to be a triangle a node belonging to. However, in our case, triangle samples are not independent, and a node may have no triangles. These issues complicate estimation, and we will describe how to solve these issues in this section.

Note that we only discuss how to obtain the MLE of θ using g, as the MLE of ϑ using f is easily obtained using a similar approach. To estimate θ, we first consider the easier case where graph size $|V| = n$ is known. Later, we extend our analysis to the case where $|V|$ is unknown.

4.1 MLE when Graph Size is Known

Recall that g_j, $0 \le j \le M$, is the number of nodes with j sampled triangles in graph $\mathcal{G}'_{uu}$. First, note that observing a node with j sampled triangles in graph $\mathcal{G}'_{uu}$ implies that the node has at least j triangles in graph $\mathcal{G}_{uu}$.

We also need to pay special attention to g_0, which is the number of nodes with no triangle in graph $\mathcal{G}'_{uu}$. Due to sampling, some nodes may be unobserved (e.g., no edge attached to the node is sampled), and these unobserved nodes also have no sampled triangle. We include these in g_0; the advantage of this inclusion will be seen later. Since we have assumed a total of n nodes in graph $\mathcal{G}_{uu}$, the number of unobserved nodes is $n - \sum_{j=0}^{M} g_j$. Therefore, we calibrate g_0 by

$$g_0 \triangleq n - \sum_{j=1}^{M} g_j.$$

Our goal is to derive an MLE of θ. To this end, we need to model the sampling process. For a randomly chosen node, let X denote the number of triangles to which it belongs in original graph $\mathcal{G}_{uu}$, and let Y denote the number of triangles observed during sampling. Then $P(Y = j | X = i), 0 \le j \le i$, is the conditional probability that a node has j sampled triangles in $\mathcal{G}'_{uu}$ given that it has i triangles in original graph $\mathcal{G}_{uu}$. The sampling of a triangle can be viewed as a Bernoulli trial with a success probability of p_δ, according to Theorem 1. If Bernoulli trials are independent, which means triangles are independently sampled, then $P(Y = j | X = i)$ follows a binomial distribution. However, independence does not hold for triangles having shared edges, as illustrated in Fig. 4(c). As a result, it is non-trivial to derive $P(Y = j | X = i)$ with the existence of dependence. To deal with this dependence, we approximate the sums of dependent Bernoulli random variables by a Beta-binomial distribution [41], which yields

$$P(Y = j | X = i)$$
$$= BetaBin(j | i, p_\delta/\alpha, (1 - p_\delta)/\alpha)$$
$$= \binom{i}{j} \frac{\prod_{s=0}^{j-1}(s\alpha + p_\delta) \prod_{s=0}^{i-j-1}(s\alpha + 1 - p_\delta)}{\prod_{s=0}^{i-1}(s\alpha + 1)}$$
$$\triangleq b_{ji}(\alpha)$$

where $\prod_0^{-1} \triangleq 1$. The above Beta-binomial distribution parameterized by α allows pairwise identically distributed Bernoulli trials to have covariance $\alpha p_\delta(1 - p_\delta)/(1 + \alpha)$. It reduces to a binomial distribution when $\alpha = 0$. We have carried out χ^2 goodness-of-fit tests and the results demonstrate that the above model indeed fits well the observed data on many graphs (and is always better than the binomial model, of course).

Using this model, we easily obtain the likelihood of observing a node to have j sampled triangles, i.e.,

$$P(Y = j) = \sum_{i=j}^{W} P(Y = j | X = i) P(X = i) = \sum_{i=j}^{W} b_{ji}(\alpha)\theta_i.$$

Then, the log-likelihood of all observations $\{Y_k = y_k\}_{k=1}^n$, where $Y_k = y_k$ denotes the k-th node having y_k sampled triangles, yields

$$\mathcal{L}(\theta, \alpha) \triangleq \log P(\{Y_k = y_k\}_{k=1}^n) = \sum_{j=0}^{M} g_j \log \sum_{i=j}^{W} b_{ji}(\alpha)\theta_i. \quad (2)$$

The MLE of θ can then be obtained by maximizing (2) with respect to θ and α under the constraint that $\sum_{i=0}^{W} \theta_i = 1$. Note that this is non-trivial due to the summation inside the log operation. In the next subsection, we use the expectation-maximization (EM) algorithm to obtain the MLE in a more convenient way.

4.2 EM Algorithm when Graph Size is Known

If we already know that the k-th node has x_k triangles in $\mathcal{G}_{uu}$, i.e., $X_k = x_k$, then the complete likelihood of observations $\{(Y_k, X_k)\}_{k=1}^n$ is

$$P(\{(Y_k, X_k)\}_{k=1}^n)$$
$$= \prod_{k=1}^{n} P(Y_k = y_k, X_k = x_k)$$
$$= \prod_{j=0}^{M} \prod_{i=j}^{W} P(Y = j, X = i)^{z_{ij}}$$
$$= \prod_{j=0}^{M} \prod_{i=j}^{W} [b_{ji}(\alpha)\theta_i]^{z_{ij}}$$

where $z_{ij} = \sum_{k=1}^{n} \mathbf{1}(x_k = i \wedge y_k = j)$ is the number of nodes with i triangles and j of them being sampled (and $\mathbf{1}(\cdot)$ is the indicator function). The complete log-likelihood is

$$\mathcal{L}_c(\theta, \alpha) \triangleq \sum_{j=0}^{M} \sum_{i=j}^{W} z_{ij} \log [b_{ji}(\alpha)\theta_i]. \quad (3)$$

Here, we can treat $\{X_k\}_{k=1}^n$ as hidden variables, and apply the EM algorithm to calculate the MLE.

E-step: We calculate the expectation of the complete log-likelihood in Eq. (3) with respect to hidden variables $\{X_k\}_k$,

conditioned on data $\{Y_k\}_k$ and previous estimates $\theta^{(t)}$ and $\alpha^{(t)}$. That is

$$Q(\theta, \alpha; \theta^{(t)}, \alpha^{(t)}) \triangleq \sum_{j=0}^{M} \sum_{i=j}^{W} \mathbb{E}_{\theta^{(t)}, \alpha^{(t)}}[z_{ij}] \log [b_{ji}(\alpha)\theta_i].$$

Here, $\mathbb{E}_{\theta^{(t)}, \alpha^{(t)}}[z_{ij}]$ can be viewed as the average number of nodes that have i triangles in $\mathcal{G}_{uu}$, of which j are sampled. Because

$$P(X = i | Y = j, \theta^{(t)}, \alpha^{(t)})$$
$$= \frac{P(Y = j | X = i, \alpha^{(t)}) P(X = i | \theta^{(t)})}{\sum_{i'} P(Y = j | X = i', \alpha^{(t)}) P(X = i' | \theta^{(t)})}$$
$$= \frac{b_{ji}(\alpha^{(t)}) \theta_i^{(t)}}{\sum_{i'} b_{ji'}(\alpha^{(t)}) \theta_{i'}^{(t)}}$$
$$\triangleq p_{i|j}$$

and we have observed g_j nodes with j sampled triangles, then $\mathbb{E}_{\theta^{(t)}, \alpha^{(t)}}[z_{ij}] = g_j p_{i|j}$.

M-step: We now maximize $Q(\theta, \alpha; \theta^{(t)}, \alpha^{(t)})$ with respect to θ and α subject to the constraint $\sum_{i=0}^{W} \theta_i = 1$. After the log operation, θ and α are well separated. Hence, we obtain

$$\theta_i^{(t+1)} = \arg\max_\theta Q(\theta, \alpha; \theta^{(t)}, \alpha^{(t)})$$
$$= \frac{\sum_{j=0}^{i} \mathbb{E}_{\theta^{(t)}, \alpha^{(t)}}[z_{ij}]}{\sum_{j=0}^{M} \sum_{i'=j}^{W} \mathbb{E}_{\theta^{(t)}, \alpha^{(t)}}[z_{i'j}]}, \quad 0 \le i \le W,$$

and $\alpha^{(t+1)} = \arg\max_\alpha Q(\theta, \alpha; \theta^{(t)}, \alpha^{(t)})$, which can be solved using gradient descent methods.

Multiple iterations of the E-step and the M-step, EM algorithm converges to a solution, which is a local maximum of (2). We denote this solution by $\hat{\theta}$ and $\hat{\alpha}$.

4.3 MLE when Graph Size is Unknown

When the graph size is unknown, one can use probabilistic counting methods such as loglog counting [12] to obtain an estimate of graph size from the stream, and then apply our previously developed method to obtain estimate $\hat{\theta}$. Note that this introduces additional statistical errors to $\hat{\theta}$ due to the inaccurate estimate of the graph size. In what follows, we slightly reformulate the problem and develop a method that can simultaneously estimate both the graph size and the triadic cardinality distribution from the sampled data.

When the graph size is unknown, we cannot calibrate g_0 because we do not know the number of unsampled nodes. A node of degree d is not sampled with probability $(1 - p)^d$. There is no clear relationship between an unsampled node and its triadic cardinality. As a result, we cannot easily model the absence of nodes by θ, and this complicates estimation design.

To solve this issue, we need to slightly reformulate our problem: (i) instead of estimating the total number of nodes in $\mathcal{G}_{uu}$, we estimate the number of nodes belonging to at least one triangle in $\mathcal{G}_{uu}$, denoted by n_+; (ii) we estimate the triadic cardinality distribution $\theta^+ = (\theta_1^+, \ldots, \theta_W^+)$, where θ_i^+ is the fraction of nodes with i triangles over the nodes having at least one triangle in $\mathcal{G}_{uu}$.

Estimating n_+. Under the Beta-binomial model, the probability that a node has i triangles in $\mathcal{G}_{uu}$, of which none are

sampled, is

$$q_i(\alpha) \triangleq P(Y = 0 | X = i) = \prod_{s=0}^{i-1} \left(1 - \frac{p_\delta}{s\alpha + 1} \right).$$

Then, the probability that a node has triangles in $\mathcal{G}_{uu}$, of which none are sampled, is

$$q(\theta^+, \alpha) \triangleq P(Y = 0 | X \geq 1) = \sum_{i=1}^{W} q_i(\alpha)\theta_i^+.$$

Because there are $\sum_{j=1}^{M} g_j$ nodes having been observed to have at least one sampled triangle, n_+ can be estimated by

$$\hat{n}_+ = \frac{\sum_{j=1}^{M} g_j}{1 - q(\theta^+, \alpha)}. \tag{4}$$

Note that estimator (4) relies on θ^+ and α, and we can obtain them using the following procedure.

Estimating θ^+ and α. We discard g_0 and only use $g^+ \triangleq (g_1, \ldots, g_M)$ to estimate θ^+ and α. The basic idea is to derive the likelihood for nodes that are observed to have at least one sampled triangle, i.e., $\{Y_k = y_k : y_k \geq 1\}$. In this case, the probability that a node has $X = i$ triangles, and $Y = j$ of them are sampled, conditioned on $Y \geq 1$, is

$$P(Y = j | X = i, Y \geq 1)$$
$$= \frac{BetaBin(j | i, p_\delta/\alpha, (1 - p_\delta)/\alpha)}{1 - BetaBin(0 | i, p_\delta/\alpha, (1 - p_\delta)/\alpha)}$$
$$\triangleq a_{ji}(\alpha), \quad j \geq 1.$$

Then the probability that a node is observed to have j sampled triangles, conditioned on $Y \geq 1$, is

$$P(Y = j | Y \geq 1)$$
$$= \sum_{i=j}^{W} P(Y = j | X = i, Y \geq 1)P(X = i | Y \geq 1)$$
$$= \sum_{i=j}^{W} a_{ji}(\alpha)\phi_i,$$

where

$$\phi_i \triangleq P(X = i | Y \geq 1) = \frac{\theta_i^+[1 - q_i(\alpha)]}{\sum_{i'=1}^{W} \theta_{i'}^+[1 - q_{i'}(\alpha)]}, \quad i \geq 1. \tag{5}$$

Now it is straightforward to obtain the previously mentioned likelihood. Furthermore, we can leverage our previously developed EM algorithm by replacing θ_i by ϕ_i, b_{ji} by a_{ji}, to obtain MLEs for ϕ and α. We omit these details, and directly provide the final EM iterations:

$$\phi_i^{(t+1)} = \frac{\sum_{j=1}^{i} \mathbb{E}_{\phi^{(t)}, \alpha^{(t)}}[z_{ij}]}{\sum_{j=1}^{M} \sum_{i'=j}^{W} \mathbb{E}_{\phi^{(t)}, \alpha^{(t)}}[z_{i'j}]}, \quad i \geq 1,$$

where

$$\mathbb{E}_{\phi^{(t)}, \alpha^{(t)}}[z_{ij}] = \frac{g_j a_{ji}(\alpha^{(t)})\phi_i^{(t)}}{\sum_{i'=j}^{W} a_{ji'}(\alpha^{(t)})\phi_{i'}^{(t)}}, \quad i \geq j \geq 1,$$

and $\alpha^{(t+1)} = \arg\max_\alpha Q(\phi, \alpha; \phi^{(t)}, \alpha^{(t)})$ is solved using gradient decent methods.

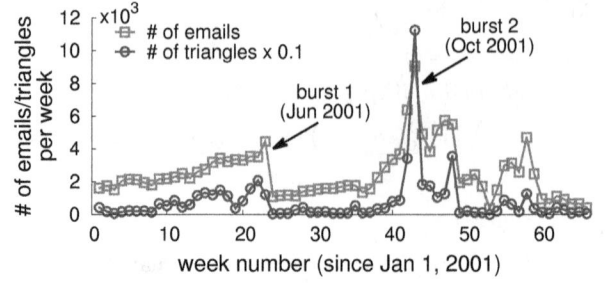

Figure 5: Email and triangle volumes per week

Once EM converges, we obtain estimates $\hat{\phi}$ and $\hat{\alpha}$. The estimate for θ^+ is then obtained by Eq. (5), i.e.,

$$\hat{\theta}_i^+ = \frac{\hat{\phi}_i/[1 - q_i(\hat{\alpha})]}{\sum_{i'=1}^{W} \hat{\phi}_{i'}/[1 - q_{i'}(\hat{\alpha})]}, \quad 1 \leq i \leq W. \tag{6}$$

Finally, $\hat{n}_+$ is obtained by the estimator in Eq. (4).

5. EXPERIMENTS

In this section, we first empirically verify the claims we have made. Then, we validate the proposed estimation methods on several real-world networks. Finally, we illustrate our method to detect bursts in Twitter during the 2014 Hong Kong Occupy Central movement.

5.1 Analyzing Bursts in Enron Dataset

In the first experiment, we use a public email communication dataset to empirically show how bursts in networks can change the triadic cardinality distribution, and verify our claims previously made.

Enron email dataset. The Enron email dataset [18] includes the entire email communications (e.g., who sent an email to whom at what time) of the Enron corporation from its startup to bankruptcy. The used dataset is carefully cleaned by removing spamming accounts/emails and emails with incorrect timestamps. The cleaned dataset contains $22,477$ email accounts and $164,081$ email communications between Jan 2001 and Apr 2002. We use this dataset to study patterns of bursts caused by email communications among people, i.e., by user-user interactions.

Observations from data. Because the data has been cleaned, the number of user-user interactions (i.e., number of sent emails[2]) per time window reliably indicates burst occurrences. We show the number of emails sent per week in Fig. 5, and observe at least two bursts that occurred in Jun and Oct 2001, respectively. We also show the number of interaction triangles formed during each week. The Pearson correlation coefficient (PCC) between the email and triangle volum series is 0.8, which reflects a very strong correlation. The sudden increase (or decrease) of email volumes during the two bursts is accompanied with the sudden increase (or decrease) of the number of triangles. Thus, this observation verifies our claim that the emergence of a burst is accompanied with the formation of triangles in networks.

How bursts change triadic cardinality distributions. Our burst detection method relies on a claim that, when a burst occurs, the triadic cardinality distribution changes.

---

[2]If an email has x recipients, we count it x times.

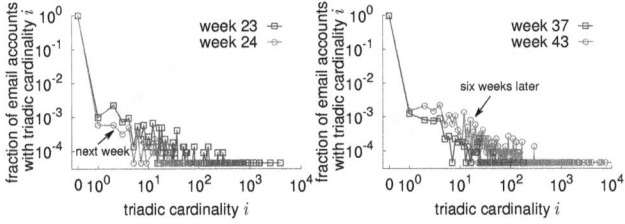

(a) Burst 1 shifts the distri- (b) Burst 2 shifts the distri-
    bution to left.   bution to right.

Figure 6: Bursts change distribution curves.

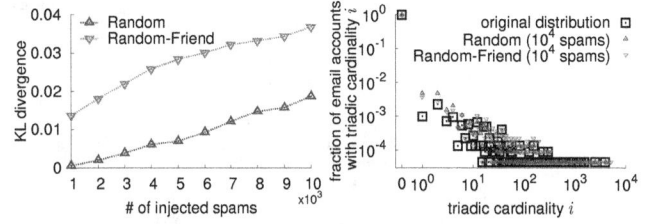

(a) KL divergence   (b) Distorted distributions

Figure 7: Impacts of spam.

To see this, we show the triadic cardinality distributions before and during the bursts in Fig. 6. For the first burst, due to the sudden decrease of email communications from week 23 to week 24, we observe in Fig. 6(a) that the distribution shifts to the left. While for the second burst, due to the gradual increase of email communications, we observe in Fig. 6(b) that the distribution in week 43 shifts to the right in comparison to previous weeks. Again, the observation verifies our claim that triadic cardinality distribution changes when a burst occurs.

Impacts of spam. As we mentioned earlier, if spam exists, simply using the volume of user interactions to detect bursts will result in false alarms, while the triadic cardinality distribution is a good indicator immune to spam. To demonstrate this claim, suppose a spammer suddenly becomes active in week 23, and generates email spams to distort the original triadic cardinality distribution of week 23. We consider the following two spamming strategies:

- *Random*: The spammer randomly chooses many target users to send spam.

- *Random-Friend*: At each step, the spammer randomly chooses a user and a random friend of the user[3], as two targets; and sends spams to each of these two targets. The spammer repeats this step a number of times.

In order to measure the extent that spams can distort the original triadic cardinality distribution of week 23, we use Kullback-Leibler (KL) divergence to measure the difference between the original and distorted distributions. The relationship between KL divergence and the number of injected spams is shown in Fig. 7(a). For both strategies, KL divergences both increase as more spams are injected into the interaction network, which is expected. The Random-Friend strategy can cause larger divergences than the Random strategy, as Random-Friend strategy is easier to introduce new triangles to the interaction network of week 23 for the reason that two friends are more likely to communicate in a week. However, even when 10^4 spams are injected, the spams incur an increasing KL divergence of less than 0.04. From Fig. 7(b), we can see that the divergence is indeed small. (This may be explained by the *"center of attention"* phenomenon [3], i.e., a person may have hundreds of friends but he usually only interacts with a small fraction of them in a time window. Hence, Random-Friend strategy does not form many triangles.) Therefore, these observations verify

---

[3] We assume two Enron users are friends if they have at least one email communication in the dataset.

that triadic cardinality distribution is robust against common spamming attacks.

5.2 Validating Estimation Methods

In the second experiment, we demonstrate that our proposed estimation methods produce good estimates of triadic cardinality distributions using sampled data while reducing computational cost.

Datasets. Because the input of our estimation methods is in fact a sampled graph, we use several public available graphs of different types and scales from the SNAP graph repository (http://snap.stanford.edu/data) as our testbeds. We summarize statistics of these graphs in Table 1.

Table 1: Network statistics

Network	Type	Nodes	Edges
HepTh	directed, citation	27,770	352,807
DBLP	undirected, coauthor	317,080	1,049,866
YouTube	undirected, OSN	1,134,890	2,987,624
Pokec	directed, OSN	1,632,803	30,622,564

For each graph, we sample an edge with probability p, and obtain a sampled graph. We then calculate the triadic cardinality for each node in the sampled graph, and obtain statistics g. Note that the estimator uses g to obtain an estimate of the triadic cardinality distribution for each graph, which is then compared with the ground truth distribution, i.e., the triadic cardinality distribution of the original unsampled graph, to evaluate the performance of the estimation method.

Validation when graph size is known. We first evaluate the estimation method when the graph size is known in advance, as is the assumption of our first method. The first method outputs estimate $\hat{\theta} = (\hat{\theta}_0, \ldots, \hat{\theta}_W)$.

The estimates on the four graphs and comparisons with ground truth distributions are depicted in Fig. 8. For each graph, we set $p = 0.05, 0.1$ and 0.15, respectively. From these results, we show that when more data is sampled the estimate generally improves, but even when $p = 0.05$ is sufficient to obtain a good estimate. The sampled triadic cardinality distribution of g for $p = 0.15$ is also shown for each graph. It is clear to see that the estimator has the ability to "correct" this distribution to approach the ground truth distribution.

We also compare the computational efficiency of our sampling approach against a naive method that uses all of the original graph to calculate θ in an exact fashion. The results are depicted in Fig. 9. Obviously, the naive method is very

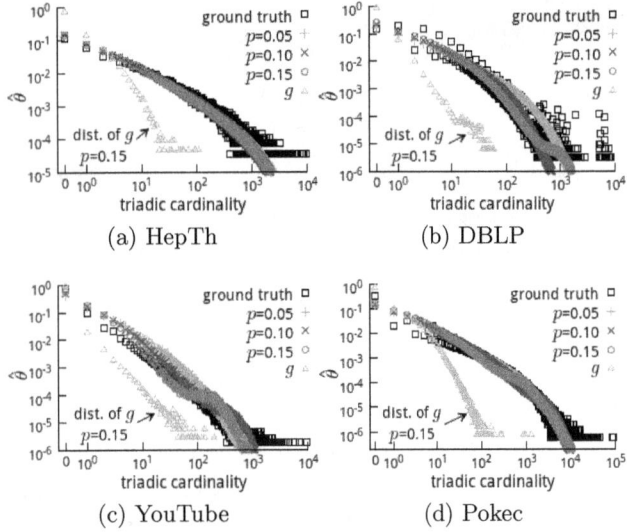

(a) HepTh   (b) DBLP

(c) YouTube   (d) Pokec

Figure 8: Estimates of θ when graph size is known. $\hat{\alpha}$ corresponding to each graph and p is typically small, ranging from 0.00015 to 0.028. $W = 10^4$ and each result is averaged over 100 runs.

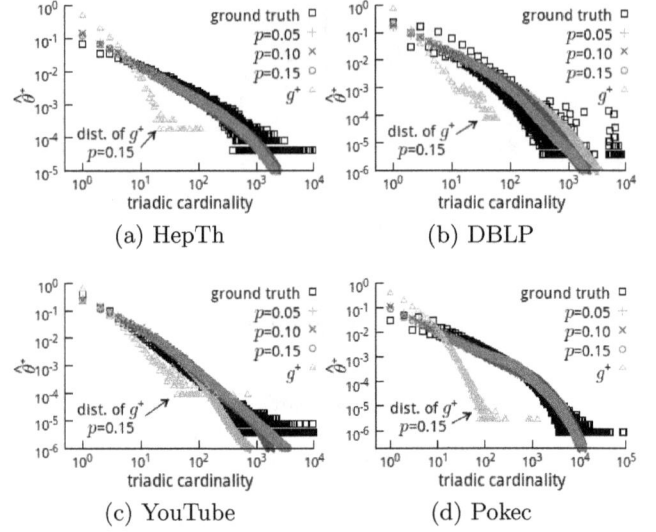

(a) HepTh   (b) DBLP

(c) YouTube   (d) Pokec

Figure 10: Estimates of θ^+ when $|V|$ is unknown. $\hat{\alpha}$ for each graph and p ranges from 0.0001 to 0.01. $W = 10^4$ and each result is averaged over 100 runs.

inefficient and our sample-estimate solution is at least about 50 times faster with $p = 0.3$ on all of the four graphs.

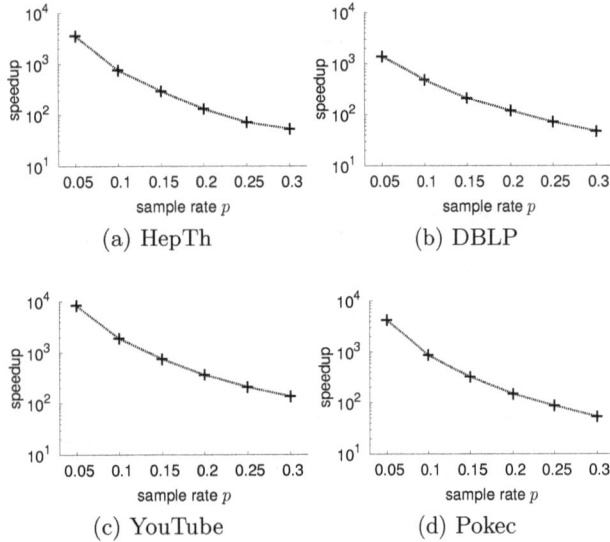

(a) HepTh   (b) DBLP

(c) YouTube   (d) Pokec

Figure 9: Computational efficiency comparison

Validation when graph size is unknown. When the graph size is unknown, the second method in Subsection 4.3 provides estimates for the number of nodes with at least one triangle in the graph $\hat{n}_+$ and triadic cardinality distribution $\hat{\theta}^+ = (\hat{\theta}_1^+, \ldots, \hat{\theta}_W^+)$ for the nodes with at least one triangle.

The results are shown in Fig. 10, using three sample rates $p = 0.05, 0.1$ and 0.15, respectively. It is clear that the second method also provides good estimates. Using a fraction of 5% of the data is sufficient to obtain good estimates.

The computational efficiency is similar to results depicted in Fig. 9.

The estimate of n_+ for each graph is shown in Fig. 11. Because the majority of the nodes have small triadic cardinalities, good estimates of θ_i^+ for small values of i are critical for a good estimate of n_+ using estimator (4). For the HepTh graph, estimate $\hat{n}_+$ is very accurate even with small p. While for the other three graphs, accurate estimates of n_+ require relatively large sample rates, and $\hat{n}_+$ is usually an underestimate of n_+ on DBLP and Pokec due to a slight underestimate of θ_i^+ for small values of i on the two graphs. Nevertheless, using a sample rate $p = 0.3$, the relative estimation error for $\hat{n}_+$ is less than 20% for all four graphs. The design of a better estimator for n_+ is left for future work.

5.3 Application: Tracking Triadic Cardinality Distributions during the 2014 Hong Kong Occupy Central Movement

In the third experiment, we conduct an application study to show that the triadic cardinality distributions change during the 2014 Hong Kong Occupy Central movement in Twitter.

2014 Hong Kong Occupy Central movement a.k.a. the Umbrella Revolution, began in Sept 2014 when activists in Hong Kong protested against the government and occupied several major streets of Hong Kong to go against a decision made by China's Standing Committee of the National People's Congress on the proposed electoral reform. Protesters began gathering from Sept 28 on and the movement was still ongoing while we were collecting the data.

Building a Twitter social activity stream. The input of our solution is a social activity stream from Twitter. For Twitter itself, this stream is easily obtained by directly aggregating tweets of users. While for third parties who do not own user's tweets, the stream can be obtained by following users using a set of Twitter accounts, called *detectors*, and aggregating tweets received by detectors (i.e., detectors'

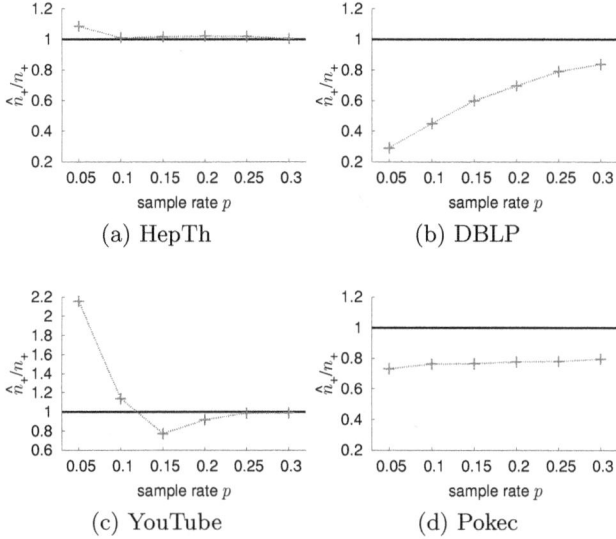

(a) HepTh   (b) DBLP

(c) YouTube   (d) Pokec

Figure 11: Estimates of n_+. $W = 10^4$ and each result is averaged over 100 runs.

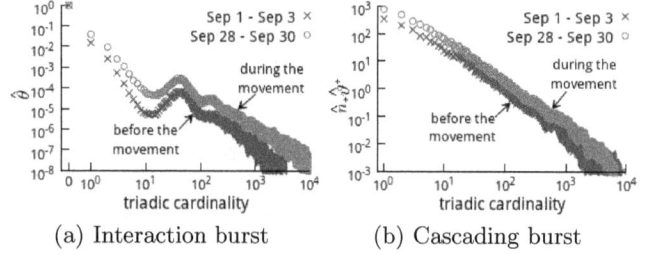

(a) Interaction burst   (b) Cascading burst

Figure 12: Triadic cardinality distributions before and during the movement.

timelines) to form a social activity stream. Since the movement had already begun prior to our starting this work, we rebuilt the social activity stream by searching tweets containing at least one of the following hashtags: #OccupyCentral, #OccupyHK, #UmbrellaRevolution, #UmbrellaMovement and #UMHK, between Sept 1 and Nov 30 using Twitter search APIs. This produced $66,589$ Twitter users, and these users form the detectors from whom we want to detect bursts. Next, we collect each user's tweets between Sept 1 and Nov 30, and extract user mentions (i.e., user-user interactions) and user hashtags (i.e., user-content interactions) from tweets to form a social activity stream, with a time span of 91 days.

Settings. We set the length of a time window to be one day. In a time window, we sample each social activity with probability $p = 0.3$ and check a social relation with probability $p' = 0.3$. For interaction bursts caused by user-user interactions, because we know the user population, i.e., $n = 66,589$, we apply the first estimation method to obtain $\hat{\theta} = (\hat{\theta}_0, \ldots, \hat{\theta}_W)$ for each window. For cascading bursts caused by user-content interactions, as we do not know the number of hashtags in advance, we apply the second method to obtain estimates $\hat{n}_+$, i.e., the number of hashtags with at least one influence triangle, and $\hat{\vartheta}^+ = (\hat{\vartheta}_1^+, \ldots, \hat{\vartheta}_W^+)$ for each window. Combining $\hat{n}_+$ with $\hat{\vartheta}^+$, we use $\hat{n}_+\hat{\vartheta}^+$, i.e., frequencies, to characterize patterns of user-content interactions in each window. For both $\hat{\theta}$ and $\hat{\vartheta}^+$, W is set to be 10^4.

Results. We first answer the question: are there significant differences for the two distributions before and during the movement? In Fig. 12, we compare the distributions before (Sept 1 to Sept 3) and during (Sept 28 to Sept 30) the movement. We can find that when the movement began on Sept 28, the distributions of the two kinds of interactions shift to the right, indicating that many interaction and influence triangles form when the movement starts. Therefore, these observations confirm our motivation for detecting bursts by tracking triadic cardinality distributions.

Next, we track the daily triadic cardinality distributions to look up the distribution change during the movement. To characterize the sudden change in the distributions, we use KL divergence to calculate the difference between $\hat{\theta}$ and a base distribution θ_{base}. The base distribution θ_{base} represents a distribution when the network is dormant, i.e., no bursts are occurring. Here we omit the technique details, and simply average the triadic cardinality distributions from Sept 1 to Sept 7 to obtain an approximate base distribution $\hat{\theta}_{\text{base}}$, and show the KL divergence $D_{\text{KL}}(\hat{\theta}_{\text{base}} \parallel \hat{\theta})$ in Fig. 13.

We find that the KL divergence exhibits a sudden increase on Sept 28 when the movement broke out. The movement keeps going on and reaches a peak on Oct 19 when repeated clashes happened in Mong Kok at that time. The movement temporally returned to peace between Oct 22 and Oct 25, and restarted again after Oct 26. In Fig. 13, we also show the estimated number of hashtags having at least one influence triangle. Its trend is similar to the trend of KL divergence which indicates that the movement is accompanied with rumors spreading in a word-of-mouth manner.

In conclusion, the application in this section demonstrates that the using of the triadic cardinality distribution can track bursts from a social activity stream and the result is consistent with real world events.

6. RELATED WORK

Kleinberg first studied this topic in [17], where he used a multi-state automaton to model a stream consisting of messages. The occurrence of a burst is modeled by an underlying state transiting into a bursty state that emits messages at a higher rate than at the non-bursty state. Based on this model, many variant models are proposed for detecting bursts from document streams [40, 22], e-commerce queries [25], time series [42], and social networks [13]. Although these models are theoretically interesting, some assumptions made by them are inappropriate, such as the Poisson process of message arrivals (see [4]) and nonexistence of spams/bots, which may limit their practical usage.

The topic of event detection is also related to our work. Recently, Chierichetti et al. [9] found that Twitter user tweeting and retweeting count information can be used to detect sub-events during some large event such as the soccer World Cup of 2010. Takahashi et al. [33] proposed a probabilistic model to detect emerging topics in Twitter by assigning an anomaly score for each user. Sakaki et al. [29] proposed a spatiotemporal model to detect earthquakes using tweets. Different from theirs, we exploit the triangle structure ex-

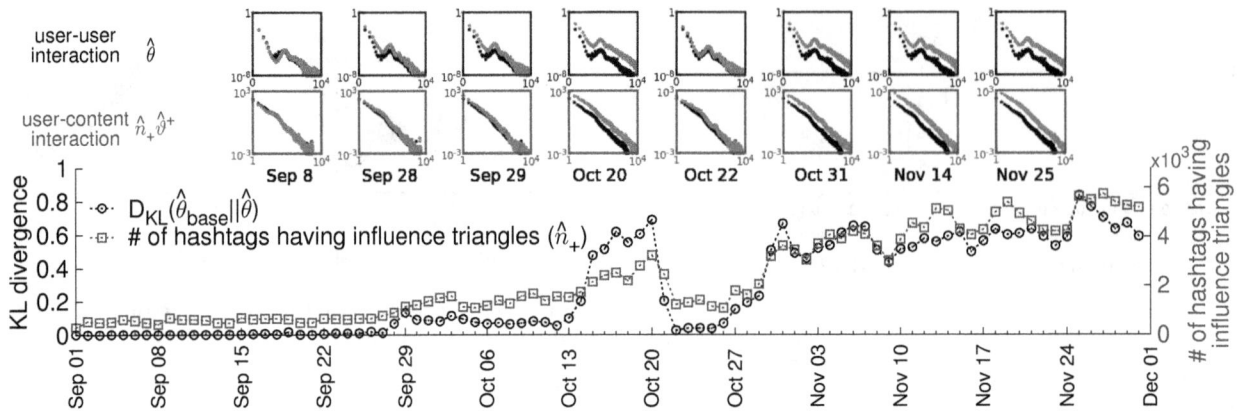

Figure 13: Triadic cardinality distributions change during the 2014 Hong Kong Occupy Central movement in Twitter

isting in user interactions which is robust against common spams and can be efficiently estimated using our method.

The triangle structure can be considered as a type of network motif, which is introduced in [23] when the authors were studying how to characterize structures of different types of networks. Turkett et al. [37] used motifs to analyze computer network usage, and [38] proposed sampling methods to efficiently estimate motif statistics in a large graph. However, both the motivation in [37] and subgraph statistics defined in [38] are different from ours.

Recently, there are many works on estimating the number of triangles [36, 8, 26, 16, 2] or clustering coefficient [30] in a large graph. However, these methods cannot be used to estimate the triadic cardinality distribution. Becchetti et al. [5] used a min-wise hashing method to approximately count triangles for each individual node in an undirected simple graph. Our method does not rely on counting triangles for each individual node. Rather, we use a carefully designed estimator to estimate the statistics from a sampled graph, which is demonstrated to be efficient and accurate.

7. DISCUSSION AND FUTURE WORK

Online social networks provide various ways for users to interact with other users or media content over the Internet, which bridge the online and offline worlds tightly. This provides an opportunity to researchers to leverage online users' interactions to detect bursts that may cause negative impact to the offline world. This work studied the burst detection problem from a high-speed social activity stream generated by user's interactions in an OSN. We find that the emergence of bursts caused by either user-user or user-content interaction are accompanied with the formation of triangles in users' interaction networks. This finding prompts us to devise a new method for burst detection in OSNs by introducing the triadic cardinality distribution. Triadic cardinality distribution is found to be robust against common spamming attacks which makes it a more suitable indicator for detecting bursts than the volume of user activities. We design a sample-estimate solution that can efficiently and accurately estimate triadic cardinality distribution from a high-speed social activity stream in near-real-time.

There are several limitations in this work that offer opportunities for future work. First, in Section 3, we used a triangle sampling method that the probability of sampling a triangle is cubic to the probability of sampling an edge in the user-user interaction graph $\mathcal{G}_{uu}$. This sampling efficiency can be further improved by using other sampling methods such as the recently proposed graph sample and hold method [2] and the colorful triangle sampling method [24], which are more efficient in sampling triangles from networks than the current method. Second, in Subsection 5.1, we studied the impacts of spam through synthetically adding spam interactions to the interaction network, and concluded that triadic cardinality distribution is robust against the Random and Random-Friend spamming strategies. It is also important to verify this conclusion in real world datasets, and we leave this for future work.

8. ACKNOWLEDGMENT

This work was supported in part by the MURI ARO grant 66220-9902 and ARL Cooperative Agreement W911NF-09-2-0053, of US; the National Natural Science Foundation (61221063, U1301254, 61202392, 61103240, 61103241, 91118005), 863 High Tech Development Plan (2012AA011003) and 111 International Collaboration Program, of China. The work of John C.S. Lui is supported in part by the GRF Funding 415013.

9. REFERENCES

[1] London riots: More than 2,000 people arrested over disorder. http://www.mirror.co.uk/news/uk-news/london-riots-more-than-2000-people-185548, Aug. 2011.

[2] N. K. Ahmed, N. Duffield, J. Neville, and R. Kompella. Graph sample and hold: A framework for big-graph analytics. In *KDD*, 2014.

[3] L. Backstrom, E. Bakshy, J. Kleinberg, T. M. Lento, and I. Rosenn. Center of attention: How Facebook users allocate attention across friends. In *ICWSM*, 2011.

[4] A.-L. Barabasi. The origin of bursts and heavy tails in human dynamics. *Nature*, 435:207–211, 2005.

[5] L. Becchetti, P. Boldi, C. Castillo, and A. Gionis. Efficient semi-streaming algorithms for local triangle counting in massive graphs. In *KDD*, 2008.

[6] A. Beutel, W. Xu, V. Guruswami, C. Palow, and C. Faloutsos. CopyCatch: Stopping group attacks by spotting lockstep behavior in social networks. In *WWW*, 2013.

[7] Y. Boshmaf, I. Muslukhov, K. Beznosov, and M. Ripeanu. The socialbot network: When bots socialize for fame and money. In *ACSAC*, 2011.

[8] C. Budak, D. Agrawal, and A. E. Abbadi. Structural trend analysis for online social networks. In *VLDB*, 2011.

[9] F. Chierichetti, J. Kleinberg, R. Kumar, M. Mahdian, and S. Pandey. Event detection via communication pattern analysis. In *ICWSM*, 2014.

[10] Z. Chu, S. Gianvecchio, H. Wang, and S. Jajodia. Who is tweeting on Twitter: Human, bot, or cyborg? In *ASCAC*, 2010.

[11] N. Duffield, C. Lund, and M. Thorup. Estimating flow distributions from sampled flow statistics. In *SIGCOMM*, 2003.

[12] M. Durand and P. Flajolet. Loglog counting of large cardinalities. In *ESA*, 2003.

[13] M. Eftekhar, N. Koudas, and Y. Ganjali. Bursty subgraphs in social networks. In *WSDM*, 2013.

[14] C. Grier, K. Thomas, V. Paxson, and M. Zhang. @spam: The underground on 140 characters or less. In *CCS*, 2010.

[15] M. Harvey. Fans mourn artist for whom it didn't matter if you were black or white. http://wayback.archive.org/web/20100531165925/ http://www.timesonline.co.uk/tol/news/world/ us_and_americas/article6580897.ece, June 2009.

[16] M. Jha, C. Seshadhri, and A. Pinar. A space efficient streaming algorithm for triangle counting using the birthday paradox. In *KDD*, 2013.

[17] J. Kleinberg. Bursty and hierarchical structure in streams. In *KDD*, 2002.

[18] B. Klimt and Y. Yang. The Enron corpus: A new dataset for email classification research. In *ECML*, 2004.

[19] G. Kossinets and D. J. Watts. Empirical analysis of an evolving social network. *Science*, 311(5757):88–90, 2006.

[20] R. Krikorian. New tweets per second record, and how! https://blog.twitter.com/2013/ new-tweets-per-second-record-and-how, Aug. 2013.

[21] J. Leskovec, M. McGlohon, C. Faloutsos, N. Glance, and M. Hurst. Cascading behavior in large blog graphs. In *SDM*, 2007.

[22] M. Mathioudakis, N. Bansal, and N. Koudas. Identifying, attributing and describing spatial bursts. In *VLDB*, 2010.

[23] R. Milo, S. Shen-Orr, S. Itzkovitz, N. Kashtan, D. Chklovskii, and U. Alon. Network motifs: Simple building blocks of complex networks. *Science*, 298(5594):824–827, 2002.

[24] R. Pagh and C. E. Tsourakakis. Colorful triangle counting and a MapReduce implementation. *Journal of Information Processing Letters*, 112(7):277–281, 2012.

[25] N. Parikh and N. Sundaresan. Scalable and near real-time burst detection from ecommerce queries. In *KDD*, 2008.

[26] A. Pavan, K. Tangwongsan, S. Tirthapura, and K.-L. Wu. Counting and sampling triangles from a graph stream. In *VLDB*, 2013.

[27] B. Ribeiro, D. Towsley, T. Ye, and J. C. Bolot. Fisher information of sampled packets: An application to flow size estimation. In *IMC*, 2006.

[28] T. Rodrigues, F. Benevenuto, M. Cha, K. P. Gummadi, and V. Almeida. On word-of-mouth based discovery of the web. In *IMC*, 2011.

[29] T. Sakaki, M. Okazaki, and Y. Matsuo. Earthquake shakes Twitter users: Real-time event detection by social sensors. In *WWW*, 2010.

[30] C. Seshadhri, A. Pinar, and T. G. Kolda. Triadic measures on graphs: The power of wedge sampling. In *SDM*, 2013.

[31] M. Shiels. Web slows after Jackson's death. http://news.bbc.co.uk/2/hi/technology/8120324.stm, June 2009.

[32] G. Stringhini, C. Kruegel, and G. Vigna. Detecting spammers on social networks. In *ACSAC*, 2010.

[33] T. Takahashi, R. Tomioka, and K. Yamanishi. Discovering emerging topics in social streams via link anomaly detection. In *ICDM*, 2011.

[34] K. Thomas, C. Grier, V. Paxson, and D. Song. Suspended accounts in retrospect: An analysis of Twitter spam. In *IMC*, 2011.

[35] A. Tsotsis. First credible reports of Bin Laden's death spread like wildfire on Twitter. http://techcrunch.com/2011/05/01/ news-of-osama-bin-ladens-death-spreads-like-\ wildfire-on-twitter/, May 2011.

[36] C. E. Tsourakakis, U. Kang, G. L. Miller, and C. Faloutsos. DOULION: Counting triangles in massive graphs with a coin. In *KDD*, 2009.

[37] W. Turkett, E. Fulp, C. Lever, and J. Edward Allan. Graph mining of motif profiles for computer network activity inference. In *MLG*, 2011.

[38] P. Wang, J. C. Lui, B. Ribeiro, D. Towsley, J. Zhao, and X. Guan. Efficiently estimating motif statistics of large networks. *TKDD*, 9(2):1–27, 2014.

[39] D. J. Watts and S. H. Strogatz. Collective dynamics of 'small-world' networks. *Nature*, 393:440–442, 1998.

[40] J. Yi. Detecting buzz from time-sequenced document streams. In *EEE*, 2005.

[41] C. Yu and D. Zelterman. Sums of dependent Bernoulli random variables and disease clustering. *Statistics and Probability Letters*, 57(1):363–373, 2002.

[42] Y. Zhu and D. Shasha. Efficient elastic burst detection in data streams. In *KDD*, 2003.

Streaming Graph Partitioning in the Planted Partition Model

Charalampos E. Tsourakakis
Harvard School of Engineering and Applied Sciences
babis@seas.harvard.edu

ABSTRACT

The sheer increase in the size of graph data has created a lot of interest into developing efficient distributed graph processing frameworks. Popular existing frameworks such as GRAPHLAB and PREGEL rely on balanced graph partitioning in order to minimize communication and achieve work balance.

In this work we contribute to the recent research line of streaming graph partitioning [30, 31, 34] which computes an approximately balanced k-partitioning of the vertex set of a graph using a single pass over the graph stream using degree-based criteria. This graph partitioning framework is well tailored to processing large-scale and dynamic graphs. In this work we introduce the use of higher length walks for streaming graph partitioning and show that their use incurs a minor computational cost which can significantly improve the quality of the graph partition. We perform an average case analysis of our algorithm using the planted partition model [7, 25]. We complement the recent results of Stanton [30] by showing that our proposed method recovers the true partition with high probability even when the gap of the model tends to zero as the size of the graph grows. Furthermore, among the wide number of choices for the length of the walks we show that the proposed length is optimal. Finally, we perform simulations which indicate that our asymptotic results hold even for small graph sizes.

Categories and Subject Descriptors

G.2.2 [**Graph Theory**]: Graph Algorithms

General Terms

Theory, Experimentation

Keywords

Streaming Graph Partitioning; Planted Partition Model; Distributed Computing

COSN'15, November 2–3, 2015, Palo Alto, California, USA.
© 2015 ACM. ISBN 978-1-4503-3951-3/15/11 ...$15.00.
DOI: http://dx.doi.org/10.1145/2817946.2817950.

1. INTRODUCTION

The size of graph data that are required to be processed nowadays is massive. For instance, the Web graph amounts to at least one trillion of links [1] and Facebook in 2012 reported more than 1 billion of users and 140 billion of friend connections. Furthermore, graphs of significantly greater size emerge by post- processing various other data such as image and text datasets. This sheer increase in the size of graphs has created a lot of interest in developing distributed graph processing systems [15, 21, 23], in which the graph is distributed across multiple machines. A key problem towards enabling efficient graph computations in such systems is the **NP**-hard problem of *balanced graph partitioning*. High-quality partitions ensure low volume of communication and work balance.

Recently, Stanton and Kliot [31] introduced a streaming graph partitioning model. This line of research despite being recent and lacking theoretical understanding has already attracted a lot of interest. Several existing systems have incorporated this model such as PowerGraph [13]. The framework of FENNEL has been adapted by PowerLyra [6], which has been included into the most recent GRAPHLAB version [3, 21] yielding significant speedups for various iterative computations. Stanton performed an average case analysis of two streaming algorithms, and explained their efficiency despite the pessimistic worst case analysis [30]. Despite the fact that existing established heuristics such as METIS typically outperform streaming algorithms, the latter are well tailored to today's needs for processing dynamic graphs and big graph data which do not fit in the main memory. They are computationally cheap and provide partitions of comparable quality. For instance, FENNEL on the Twitter network with more than 1.4 billion edges performed comparably well with METIS for a wide variety of settings, requiring 40 minutes of running time, whereas METIS $8\frac{1}{2}$ hours.

So far, the work on streaming graph partitioning is based on computing the degrees of incoming vertices towards each of the k available machines. Equivalently, this can be seen as performing a one step random walk from the incoming vertex. A natural idea which is used extensively in the literature of graph partitioning [20, 29, 37] is the use of higher length walks. In this work we introduce this idea in the setting of streaming graph partitioning. At the same time we maintain the time efficiency of streaming graph partitioning algorithms which make them attractive to various graph processing systems [13, 15, 21, 23].

Summary of our contributions. Our contributions can be summarized as follows:

- Our proposed algorithm introduces the idea of using higher length walks for streaming graph partitioning. It incurs a negligible computational cost and significantly improves the quality of the partition. We perform an average case analysis on the planted partition model, c.f. Section 3.2 for the description of the model. We complement the recent results of [30] which require that the gap $p - q$ of the planted partition model is constant in order to recover the partition whp[1], by allowing gaps $p - q$ which asymptotically tend to 0 as n grows.

- Among the wide number of choices for the length of t-walks where $t \geq 2$, we show that walks of length 2 are optimal as they allow the smallest possible gap for which we can guarantee recovery whp, c.f. Section 3.5.

- We evaluate our method on the planted partition model and we provide simulation results that strongly indicate that our asymptotic results hold even for small graph sizes.

- We complement prior work by showing that Fennel's optimal quasi-clique partitioning objective [34, 33] is NP-hard.

2. RELATED WORK

Balanced graph partitioning. The *balanced graph partitioning* problem is a classic **NP**-hard problem of fundamental importance to parallel and distributed computing. The input to this problem is an undirected graph $G(V, E)$ and an integer $k \in \mathbb{Z}^+$, the output is a partition of the vertex set in k balanced sets such that the number of edges across the clusters is minimized. We refer to the k sets as *clusters* or *machines* interchangeably. Formally, the balance constraint is defined by the imbalance parameter ν. Specifically, the (k, ν)-balanced graph partitioning asks to divide the vertices of a graph in k clusters each of size at most $\nu \frac{n}{k}$, where n is the number of vertices in G. The case $k = 2, \nu = 1$ is equivalent to the **NP**-hard minimum bisection problem. Several approximation algorithms, e.g., [9], and heuristics, e.g., [16], exist for this problem. When $\nu = 1 + \epsilon$ for any desired but fixed $\epsilon > 0$ there exists a $O(\epsilon^{-2} \log^{1.5} n)$ approximation algorithm [18]. When $\nu = 2$ there exists an $O(\sqrt{\log k \log n})$ approximation algorithm based on semidefinite programming (SDP) [19]. Due to the practical importance of k-partitioning there exist several heuristics, among which METIS [28] stands out for its good performance. Survey [5] summarizes many popular existing methods for the balanced graph partitioning problem.

Streaming balanced graph partitioning. Despite the large amount of work on the balanced graph partitioning problem, neither state-of-the-art approximation algorithms nor heuristics such as METIS are well tailored to the computational restrictions that the size of today's graphs impose.

Stanton and Kliot introduced streaming balanced graph partitioning. In this setting the graph arrives as a stream and decisions about the partition must be taken online [31]. Specifically, when a vertex with its neighbors arrives, the partitioner decides where to place the vertex "on the fly", using limited computational resources (time and space). A vertex is never relocated after it becomes assigned to one

of the k machines. Fennel generalized the notion of optimal quasi-cliques [33] to k-partitioning and is closely related to detecting large near-cliques [12, 32]. This extension provided well-performing decision strategies for streaming graph partitioning. In the Appendix we prove that FENNEL is NP-hard. Both [31] and [34] can be adapted to edge streams. Nishimura and Ugander [27] consider a variation of Fennel that allows multiple passes over the stream. It is worth mentioning that very recently Margo and Seltzer provided a state-of-art distributed streaming graph partitioner [24]. Stanton showed that streaming graph partitioning algorithms with a single pass even for random stream orders cannot approximate the optimal cut size within $o(n)$ [30]. Stanton [30] analyzes two variants of well performing algorithms on real-data from [31] on random graphs. Specifically, Stanton proves that if the graph G is sampled according to the planted partition model, then the two algorithms despite their similarity may perform differently. Furthermore, one of the two recovers the true partition whp, assuming that inter-, intra-cluster edge probabilities are constant, and their gap is constant.

Planted partition model. Jerrum and Sorkin [14] studied the planted bisection model, a random undirected graph with an even number of vertices. According to this model, each half of the vertices is assigned to one of two clusters. Then, the probability of an edge (i, j) is p if i, j have the same color, otherwise $q < p$. We will refer to p, q as the intra- and inter-cluster probabilities. Their difference $p - q$ will be referred to as the *gap* of the model. Condon and Karp [7] studied the generalization of the planted bisection problem where instead of having only two clusters, there exist k clusters of equal size. The probability of an edge is the same as in the planted bisection problem. They show that the hidden partition can be recovered whp if the gap satisfies $p - q \geq n^{-1/2+\epsilon}$. McSherry [25] presents a spectral algorithm that recovers the hidden partition in a random graph whp if $p - q = \Omega(n^{-1/2+\epsilon})$. Recently, Van Vu gave an alternative algorithm [36] to obtain McSherry's result. Zhou and Woodruff [37] showed that if $p = \Theta(1), q = \Theta(1), p - q = \Omega(n^{-1/4})$, then a simple algorithm based on squaring the adjacency matrix of the graph recovers the hidden partition whp.

Random walks. The idea of using walks of length greater than one [37] is common in the general setting of graph partitioning. Lovász and Simonovits [20] show that random walks of length $O(\frac{1}{\phi})$ can be used to compute a cut with sparsity at most $\tilde{O}(\sqrt{\phi})$ if the sparsest cut has conductance ϕ. Later, Spielman and Teng [29] provided a local graph partitioning algorithm which implements efficiently the Lovász-Simonovits idea.

Theoretical preliminaries.[2] A useful lemma that we use extensively is Boole's inequality, also known as the union bound.

LEMMA 1 (UNION BOUND). *Let $A_1, \ldots, A_n$ be events in a probability space Ω, then*

$$\mathbf{Pr}\left[\cup_{i=1}^n A_i\right] \leq \sum_{i=1}^n \mathbf{Pr}\left[A_i\right].$$

The following theorem is due to Markov and its use is known as the first moment method.

---

[1] An event $\mathcal{E}_n$ occurs *with high probability*, or whp for brevity, if $\lim_{n \to \infty} \mathbf{Pr}\left[\mathcal{E}_n\right] = 1$.

[2] A detailed description can be found in [8, 26].

THEOREM 1 (FIRST MOMENT METHOD). *Let X be a non-negative random variable with finite expected value $\mathbb{E}[X]$. Then, for any real number $t > 0$,*

$$\mathbf{Pr}[X \geq t] \leq \frac{\mathbb{E}[X]}{t}.$$

The following theorem is due to Chebyshev and its use is known as the second moment method.

THEOREM 2 (SECOND MOMENT METHOD). *Let X be a random variable with finite expected value $\mathbb{E}[X]$ and finite non-zero variance $\mathbb{V}ar[X]$. Then, for any real number $t > 0$,*

$$\mathbf{Pr}[|X - \mathbb{E}[X]| \geq t] \leq \frac{\mathbb{V}ar[X]}{t^2}.$$

Finally, we use the following Chernoff bounds for independent and negatively correlated random variables.

THEOREM 3 (MULTIPLICATIVE CHERNOFF BOUND). *Let $X = \sum_{i=1}^{n} X_i$ where $X_1, \ldots, X_n$ are independent random variables taking values in $[0,1]$. Also, let $\delta \in [0,1]$. Then,*

$$Pr(X \leq (1-\delta)E(X)) \leq e^{-\delta^2 E(X)/2}.$$

DEFINITION 1. *Let $X_1, \ldots, X_n$ be random binary variables. We say that they are negatively correlated if and only if for all sets $I \subseteq [n]$ the following inequalities are true:*

$$Pr(\forall i \in I : X_i = 0) \leq \prod_{i \in I} Pr(X_i = 0)$$

and

$$Pr(\forall i \in I : X_i = 1) \leq \prod_{i \in I} Pr(X_i = 1).$$

THEOREM 4. *Let $X = \sum_{i=1}^{n} X_i$ where $X_1, \ldots, X_n$ are negatively correlated binary random variables. Also, let $\delta \in [0,1]$. Then,*

$$Pr(X \leq (1-\delta)E(X)) \leq e^{-\delta^2 E(X)/2}.$$

3. PROPOSED ALGORITHM

Section outline. Section 3.1 introduces our notation and Section 3.2 presents in detail the random graph model we analyze. Section 3.3 provides two useful lemmas used in Sections 3.4 and 3.5. Section 3.4 shows an efficient way to recover the true partition of the planted partition model *whp* using walks of length $t = 2$ even when $p - q = o(1)$, i.e., the gap is asymptotically equal to 0. Section 3.5 shows that when the length of the walk t is set to 2, then we obtain the smallest possible *gap* $p - q$ for which we can guarantee recovery of the partition *whp*. We do not try to optimize constants in our proofs, since we are interested in asymptotics. Our proofs use the elementary inequalities $1 - p \leq e^{-p}$, $\binom{n}{k} \leq \left(\frac{en}{k}\right)^k$ and the probabilistic tools presented in the previous Section.

3.1 Notation

Let $G(V, E)$ be a simple undirected graph, where $|V| = n, |E| = m$. We define a *vertex partition* $\mathcal{P} = (S_1, \ldots, S_k)$ as a family of pairwise disjoint vertex sets whose union is V. Each set S_i is assigned to one of k machines, $i = 1, \ldots, k$. We refer to each S_i as a *cluster* or *machine*. Throughout this work, we assume $k = \Theta(1)$. Let $\partial e(\mathcal{P})$ be the set of edges that cross partition boundaries, i.e., $\partial e(\mathcal{P}) = \cup_{i=1}^{k} e(S_i, V \setminus S_i)$. The fraction of edges cut λ is defined as $\lambda = \frac{|\partial e(\mathcal{P})|}{m}$. The imbalance factor or normalized maximum load ρ is defined as $\rho = \max_{1 \leq i \leq k} \frac{|S_i|}{\frac{n}{k}}$. Notice that ρ satisfies the double inequality $1 \leq \rho \leq k$. When $\rho = 1$ we have a perfectly balanced partition. At the other extreme, when $\rho = k$ all the vertices are placed in one cluster, leaving $k - 1$ clusters empty. In practice, there is a constraint $\rho \leq \nu$ where ν is a value imposed by application-specific restrictions. Typically, ν is close to 1. We omit floor and ceiling notation for simplicity, our results remain valid.

3.2 Planted Partition Model

The model $G(n, \Psi, P)$ is a generalization of the classic Erdös-Rényi graph [4]. The first parameter n is the number of vertices. The second parameter of the model is the function $\Psi : [n] \to [k]$ which maps each vertex to one of k clusters. We refer to $C_i = \Psi^{-1}(i)$ as the i-th cluster, $i = 1, \ldots, k$. The third parameter P is a $k \times k$ matrix such that $0 \leq P_{ij} \leq 1$ for all $i, j = 1, \ldots, k$ which specifies the probability distribution over the edge set. Specifically, a graph $G \sim G(n, \Psi, P)$ is generated by adding an edge with probability $P(\Psi(u), \Psi(v))$ between each pair of vertices $\{u, v\}$. Notice, that when all the entries of P are equal to p, then $G(n, \Psi, P)$ is equivalent to the $G(n, p)$ model. In this work we are interested into graphs that exhibit clustering. The planted partition model we analyze is the same as in [7, 25, 30, 37]: $P_{ij} = p\mathbf{1}(i = j) + q\mathbf{1}((i \neq j))$ for all $i, j = 1, \ldots, k$. We assume that $p > q = \Theta(1)$. For simplicity, we refer to this version of $G(n, \Psi, P)$ as $G(n, k, p, q)$.

3.3 Results and useful lemmas

We prove two simple lemmas that we use in the analysis of our algorithms. We refer to the vertex that arrives exactly after $i - 1$ vertices as the i-th vertex.

LEMMA 2. *For all $i \geq D \log^{1+\delta}(n)$ where $D, \delta > 0$ are any positive constants, there exist at least $\frac{i}{2k}$ vertices that have already arrived from each cluster j whp, $j = 1, \ldots, k$.*

PROOF. Fix any index $i \geq D \log^{1+\delta}(n)$. Define for each $j \in [k]$ the bad event $\mathcal{A}_j$ that cluster j has less than $\frac{i}{2k}$ vertices after the arrival of i vertices. Given our assumption on the random order of the stream, the first i vertices form a random i-subset of $[n]$. Let Y_j be the number of vertices from cluster j among the first i vertices. We observe that the distribution of Y_j is the hypergeometric distribution $H(n, n/k, i)^3$. Therefore, we obtain the following exact expression for the probability of the bad event $\mathcal{A}_j$:

---

[3]Recall, the hypergeometric distribution $H(N, R, s)$ is a discrete probability distribution that describes the probability of choosing r red balls in s draws of balls without replacement from a finite population of size N containing exactly R red balls.

$$\mathbf{Pr}\left[\mathcal{A}_j\right] = \sum_{r=0}^{i/2k} \mathbf{Pr}\left[Y_j = r\right] = \sum_{r=0}^{i/2k} \frac{\binom{n/k}{r}\binom{n(k-1)/k}{i-r}}{\binom{n}{i}}.$$

Even if an asymptotic analysis using Stirling's formula is possible, a less tedious approach is possible. We express Y_j as the sum of i indicator variables $Y_{j,1}, \ldots, Y_{j,i}$ where $Y_{j,l} = 1$ if and only if the l-th vertex v has $\Psi(v) = j$, $l = 1, \ldots, i$. Clearly, $\mathbb{E}\left[Y_j\right] = \frac{i}{k}$. Notice that even if the indicator random variables are not independent, they are negatively correlated. Therefore, Theorem 4 applies, obtaining

$$\mathbf{Pr}\left[Y_j \le (1 - \frac{1}{2})\frac{i}{k}\right] \le e^{-\frac{i}{8k}} \le e^{-\frac{D\log^{1+\delta}(n)}{8k}} \ll o(n^{-1}).$$

The proof is completed by taking a union bound over k machines and $(n - D\log^{1+\delta}(n))$ vertices. Specifically, let $\mathcal{E}$ be the event that there exists an index $i \ge D\log^{1+\delta}(n)$ such that $\cup_{j=1}^{k}\mathcal{A}_j$ is true. Then, $\mathbf{Pr}\left[\mathcal{E}\right] \le (n - D\log^{1+\delta}(n))ko(n^{-1}) = o(1)$. $\square$

LEMMA 3. *Let $\delta > 0$ be any positive constant. After $\log^{6+\delta}(n)$ vertices have arrived, all remaining vertices in the stream have $\log^6(n)$ neighbors which reside in the k machines.*

PROOF. Let $i = g(n) \ge \log^{6+\delta}(n)$, be the number of vertices that have arrived in the incidence stream. Let $\mathcal{E}$ be the event that there exists a vertex v that has arrived after the first i vertices with less than $\log^6(n)$ neighbors in the set of arrived vertices. We obtain that $\mathbf{Pr}\left[\mathcal{E}\right] = o(1)$ using the following upper bound.

$$\mathbf{Pr}\left[\mathcal{E}\right] \le n\sum_{j=0}^{\log^6(n)}\binom{g(n)}{j}\left(\frac{p}{1-q}\right)^i(1-q)^{g(n)}$$

$$\le n\sum_{j=0}^{\log^6(n)}\left(\frac{g(n)e}{j}\right)^j\left(\frac{p}{1-q}\right)^j(1-q)^{g(n)}$$

$$\le Cn\log^6(n)\left(\frac{pg(n)e}{j(1-q)}\right)^{\log^6(n)}e^{-qg(n)} = o(1).$$

$\square$

3.4 Path-2 classification

The main theoretical result of this Section is that we can use paths of length 2 to recover the partition Ψ *whp* even when $p - q = o(1)$. Our algorithm avoids making final decisions for the first B vertices until the end of the process and uses the fact that vertices from the same cluster have more common neighbors compared to a pair of vertices from different clusters. Our algorithm is shown below.

---

1. Place the first $B = \log^{6+\delta}(n)$ vertices in any of the k machines, marked as non-classified. Here, $\delta > 0$ is any positive constant.

2. Let S be a random sample of size $3k\log n$ vertices from the set of B non-classified vertices.

3. Let R be a random sample of $\log^6 n$ vertices from the set of B non-classified vertices.

4. For the j-th vertex, $B + 1 \le j \le n$, do the following:

   - For each $x \in S$ compute the number of common neighbors of j, x in R.
   - Let $M = (p^2 + (k-1)q^2)\log^6 n$. Assign j to the same cluster with a vertex $x^* \in S$ which has at least $M - M^{2/3}$ common neighbors with j. Ties are always assigned to the vertex with the smallest id. Remove non-classified tag from x^*.

5. Perform the same procedure for the remaining, if any, non-classified vertices.

We prove the correctness of the algorithm. The next lemma states that when we obtain the random sample S, there always exists at least one vertex from each cluster of the partition. This is critical since our algorithm assigns each incoming vertex v to a representative vertex from cluster $\Psi(v)$. Among the various possible choices for a representative of cluster c, we choose the vertex u with the minimum vertex id, namely $u = \arg\min\{u \in S : \Psi(u) = c\}$.

LEMMA 4. *Let S be a random sample of size $3k\log n$ vertices from a population of $j \ge \log^{6+\delta}(n)$ vertices. Then, with high probability there exists at least one representative vertex from each cluster of the planted partition in S*

PROOF. First, notice that by Lemma 2 there exist at least $j/2k \ge \frac{\log^{6+\delta}(n)}{2k}$ vertices from each cluster $i = 1, \ldots, k$. Let $\mathcal{E}_i$ be the event of failing to sample at least one vertex from cluster i of the partition, $i = 1, \ldots, k$. We can upper bound the probability of the union $\cup_{i=1}^{k}\mathcal{E}_i$ of these bad events as follows:

$$\mathbf{Pr}\left[\cup_{i=1}^{k}\mathcal{E}_i\right] \le k\left(1 - \frac{\frac{j}{2k}}{j}\right)^{3k\log n}$$

$$\le ke^{-3k\log n/2k} = o(n^{-1}).$$

$\square$

The next theorem is our main theoretical result. It states that the algorithm recovers the true partition Ψ *whp*.

LEMMA 5. *If $p = \Theta(1), q = \Theta(1), p - q = \omega\left(\frac{1}{\log(n)}\right)$, then all vertices are classified correctly whp. The algorithm runs in sublinear time.*

PROOF. Let j be the index of the incoming vertex, $x \in S$. We condition on the event $\mathcal{E}$ that there exists at least one vertex from each cluster of the planted partition in the sample S. Define Y_x as the number of triples (j, u, x) where $u \in R$ and $x \in S$ such that $\Psi(j) = \Psi(x)$. Similarly, let Z_x be the number of triples (j, u, x), where $u \in R$ and $x \in S$

such that $\Psi(j) \neq \Psi(x)$. The expected values of Y_x, Z_x are respectively

$$\mathbb{E}\left[Y_x\right] = \left(p^2 + (k-1)q^2\right)\log^6 n,$$

and

$$\mathbb{E}\left[Z_x\right] = \left(2pq + (k-2)q^2\right)\log^6 n.$$

A direct application of the multiplicative Chernoff bound, see Theorem 3, yields

$$\mathbf{Pr}\left[Y_x \leq \mathbb{E}\left[Y_x\right] - \mathbb{E}\left[Y_x\right]^{2/3}\right] \leq e^{-O(\mathbb{E}[Y_x]^{1/3})} = n^{-O(\log n)}$$

and

$$\mathbf{Pr}\left[Z_x \geq \mathbb{E}\left[Z_x\right] + \mathbb{E}\left[Z_x\right]^{2/3}\right] \leq e^{-O(\mathbb{E}[Z_x]^{1/3})} = n^{-O(\log n)}$$

Furthermore, due to our assumption on $p, q = \Theta(1)$ and the gap $p - q \gg \frac{1}{\log n}$ we obtain

$$\mathbb{E}\left[Z_x\right] + \mathbb{E}\left[Z_x\right]^{2/3} \ll \mathbb{E}\left[Y_x\right] - \mathbb{E}\left[Y_x\right]^{2/3}.$$

The above inequalities suggest that the number of 2-paths between j and any vertex $x \in S$ such that $\Psi(x) = \Psi(j)$ is significantly larger compared to the respective count between j, x' such that $\Psi(x') \neq \Psi(j)$ whp. Let $\mathcal{B}_j$ be the even that j is misclassified. Combining the above inequalities with Lemma 4 results in

$$\mathbf{Pr}\left[\mathcal{B}_j\right] \leq \mathbf{Pr}\left[\bar{\mathcal{E}}\right] + \mathbf{Pr}\left[\mathcal{B}_j | \mathcal{E}\right]\mathbf{Pr}\left[\mathcal{E}\right] = o(n^{-1}).$$

By a union bound over $O(n)$ vertices, the proof is complete.

Finally, the algorithm can be implemented in $\tilde{O}(n)$ time in expectation. Sampling $\tilde{O}(1)$ samples can be implemented in expected $\tilde{O}(1)$ time time, c.f. [17, 35]. Also, checking whether a neighbor of an incoming vertex resides in a given machine can be done in $O(1)$ time by using appropriate data structures to store the information within each machine. $\square$

It is worth noticing that our algorithm is a sublinear time algorithm as the number of edges in G is $O(n^2)$.

3.5 Path-t classification

We conclude this section by discussing the effect of the length of the walk $t \geq 2$. Intuitively, t should not be too large, otherwise the random walk will mix. We argue, that among all constant lengths $t \geq 2$, the choice $t = 2$ allows the smallest possible gap for which we can find the true partition Ψ. It is worth outlining that $t = 2$ is also in favor of the graph partitioning efficiency as well, since the smaller t is, the less operations are required. Our results extend the results of Zhou and Woodruff [37] to the streaming setting. Our main theoretical result is the following theorem.

THEOREM 5. *Let $t \geq 2, t = \Theta(1)$ be the length of a walk. If $p, q = \Theta(1)$ such that $p(1-p), q(1-q) = \Theta(1)$, then $t = 2$ results in the largest possible gap $p - q$ for which we can decide whether $\Psi(u) = \Psi(v)$ or not whp, where $u \neq v \in [n]$.*

To prove Theorem 5, we compute first the expected number of walks of length t between any two vertices in $G(n, k, p, q)$. Because of the special structure of the graph, we are able to derive an exact formula.

LEMMA 6. *Let $G \sim G(nk, k, p, q)$ and $p_t = A_{uv}^t, q_t = A_{uw}^t$ be the two types of entries that appear in A^t depending on whether $\Psi(u) = \Psi(v)$ and $\Psi(u) \neq \Psi(w)$ respectively. Then*

$$p_t = (k-1)\frac{n^{t-1}(p-q)^t}{k} + \frac{n^{t-1}(p+(k-1)q)^t}{k},$$

and

$$q_t = -\frac{n^{t-1}(p-q)^t}{k} + \frac{n^{t-1}(p+(k-1)q)^t}{k}.$$

PROOF. Let A be the (p, q)-adjacency matrix defined as $A_{uv} = p$ if $\Psi(u) = \Psi(v)$ and $A_{uw} = q$ if $\Psi(u) \neq \Psi(w)$ for each $u \neq v \in [n]$. It is easy to check that for any $t \geq 1$ the block structure of the planted partition is preserved. This implies that for any t, matrix A^t has the same block structure as A and therefore there are two types of entries in each row. Let p_t, q_t be these two types of entries in A^t. For $t = 1$, let $p_1 = p$ and $q_1 = q$. Then, by considering the multiplication of the u-th line of A^t with the v-th column of A we obtain

$$p_{t+1} = pnp_t + (k-1)nqq_t,$$

and similarly by considering the multiplication of the u-th line of A^t with the w-th column of A we obtain

$$q_{t+1} = qnp_t + pnq_t + \frac{k-2}{k}nqq_t.$$

We can write the recurrence in a matrix form.

$$\begin{bmatrix} p_{t+1} \\ q_{t+1} \end{bmatrix} = M \times \begin{bmatrix} p_t \\ q_t \end{bmatrix}$$

where $M = \begin{pmatrix} pn & (k-1)nq \\ qn & pn + \frac{k-2}{k}nq \end{pmatrix}$. By looking the eigendecomposition of M, despite the fact that it is not symmetric, we can diagonalize it as

$$M = USU^{-1},$$

where

$$S = \begin{pmatrix} n(p-q) & 0 \\ 0 & n(p+(k-1)q) \end{pmatrix}$$

and

$$U = \begin{pmatrix} -(k-1) & 1 \\ 1 & 1 \end{pmatrix}.$$

Given the fact

$$M^k = U \begin{pmatrix} (n(p-q))^k & 0 \\ 0 & (n(p+(k-1)q))^k \end{pmatrix} U^{-1}$$

and simple algebraic manipulations (omitted) we obtain that

$$p_t = (k-1)\frac{n^{t-1}(p-q)^t}{k} + \frac{n^{t-1}(p+(k-1)q)^t}{k},$$

and

$$q_t = -\frac{n^{t-1}(p-q)^t}{k} + \frac{n^{t-1}(p+(k-1)q)^t}{k}.$$

$\square$

Now, we are able to prove Theorem 5.

PROOF THEOREM 5. Let $p_t = A_{uv}^t, q_t = A_{uw}^t$ where $u, v, w \in V(G)$ such that $\Psi(u) = \Psi(v) \neq \Psi(w)$ and A is defined as in Lemma 6. Also, define $\bar{A}$ to be the result of the randomized rounding of A. By Lemma 6 we obtain

$$p_t - q_t = \frac{n^{t-1}(p-q)^t}{k^t}.$$

Notice that we substituted n by n/k as we G has n vertices, with exactly n/k vertices per cluster. Now, suppose $|A_{uv}^t - \bar{A}_{uv}^t| \leq \gamma$, where $\gamma > 0$ is large enough such that the inequality holds *whp* and will be decided in the following. Then, if $\Psi(j_1) = \Psi(j_2) = \Psi(u)$ we obtain the following upper bound

$$|\bar{A}_{uj_1}^t - \bar{A}_{uj_2}^t| \leq |A_{uj_1}^t - \bar{A}_{uj_1}^t| + |A_{uj_2}^t - \bar{A}_{uj_2}^t| = 2\gamma.$$

On the other hand if $\Psi(u) = \Psi(j_1) \neq \Psi(j_2)$, given that $|x| = |x + y - y| \leq |y| + |x - y| \to |x - y| \geq |x| - |y|$, we obtain the following lower bound

$$|\bar{A}_{uj_1}^t - \bar{A}_{uj_2}^t| \geq |A_{uj_1}^t - A_{uj_2}^t| - 2\gamma = \frac{n^{t-1}(p-q)^t}{k^t} - 2\gamma.$$

Therefore, if $\frac{n^{t-1}(p-q)^t}{k^t} - 2\gamma > 2\gamma$, then there exists a signal that allows us to classify the vertex correctly. In order to find γ we need to upper-bound the expectation of the non-negative random variable $Z = (\bar{A}_{uv}^t - A_{uv}^t)^2$.

Zhou and Woodruff prove $\mathbb{E}[Z] = \Theta(n^{2t-3})$,c.f. Lemma 5, [37]. The proof of this claim is based on algebraic manipulation. It is easy to verify that $\mathbb{E}[Z]$ is dominated by the terms that correspond to two paths of length t which overlap on a single edge. Applying Markov's inequality, see Theorem 1, we obtain

$$\mathbf{Pr}[Z \geq \mathbb{E}[Z]\log n] \leq \frac{1}{\log n} = o(1),$$

This suggests that setting $\gamma = n^{t-3/2}\sqrt{\log n}$ since $|A_{uv}^t - \bar{A}_{uv}^t| \leq n^{t-3/2}\sqrt{\log n}$ *whp*. The gap requirement is

$$\frac{n^{t-1}(p-q)^t}{k^t} > 4n^{t-3/2}\log n \to p - q = \Omega\left(\left(\sqrt{\frac{\log n}{n}}\right)^{1/t}\right).$$

This proves our claim, as for $t = 2$ we obtain the best possible gap.

$\square$

4. EXPERIMENTAL RESULTS

4.1 Experimental setup

We refer to our method as EGYPT (*E*fficient which stands for *G*raph *Par*Titioning). The experiments were performed on a single machine, with Intel Xeon CPU at 2.83 GHz, 6144KB cache size and and 50GB of main memory. We have implemented EGYPT in both JAVA and MATLAB. The method we use to compare against for the 1-path classification is LWD, c.f. [31], the single streaming graph partitioning method for which we have theoretical insights [30]. The simulation results were obtained using the JAVA code. The data streaming application was implemented in MATLAB.

Synthetic data: We generate random graphs according to the planted partition model. We fix $q = 0.05$ and we range the gap from 0.05 until 0.95 with a step of 0.05. This results in pairs of (p, q) values with p ranging from 0.1 until 1. We show the results for $n = 8\,000, k = 4$ as the results for other values of n and k ranging from 2 to 16 as successive powers of 2 are qualitatively identical. Notice that given that $p, q = \Theta(1)$ despite the small number of vertices the number of edges is large ranging from 2 to 9.2 million edges. Parameter B ranges in the interval $\{50, 100, 200, \ldots, 1000\}$. The imbalance tolerance ρ was set to 1, demanding equally sized clusters (modulo the remainder of n divided by k). Since groundtruth is available, i.e., function Ψ is known, we measure the precision of the algorithm, as the percentage of the $\binom{n}{2}$ relationships that it guesses correctly. The success of the algorithm is also evaluated in terms of the fraction of edges cut λ.

Real data: An interesting question is what kind of real-world datasets does the planted partition model represent well? Real-world networks typically exhibit skewed degree distributions which are not captured by power-laws. It is worth emphasizing at this point that despite this fact, heuristics that are shown to work provably well using average case analysis can also be successful on real-world data, e.g., [30, 31].

We explore nearest neighbor graphs of well-clustered point clouds. Specifically, we use a perfectly balanced set of 50 000 digits (5 000 digits for each digit 0,1,..., 9) from the MNIST database [2]. Each digit is a 28×28 matrix which is converted in a 1-dimensional vector with 784 coordinates. The following numerical evidence indicates that the geometric structure of the dataset is strongly reflected in the nearest neighbor graph. Specifically, we create a 5-nearest neighbor graph and we measure the conductance of the sets induced by each one of the digits. Recall, that the conductance of $U \subseteq V$ the conductance of U is defined as $\phi(U) = \frac{E(U,\bar{U})}{\min(vol(U),vol(\bar{U}))}$ where $E(U, \bar{U}) = |\{(u, v) \in E(G) : u \in U, v \in \bar{U}\}|$ and $vol(U) = \sum_{v \in U} deg(v)$. The conductances of the 10 subsets of vertices each corresponding to one of the digits $\{0, \ldots, 9\}$ are 0.0088, 0.0160, 0.0203, 0.0282, 0.0214, 0.0253, 0.0122, 0.0229, 0.0291, 0.0328 respectively.

4.2 Simulations

Figures 1(a) and (b) plot the average fraction of edges cut λ and the average precision versus the gap $p - q$ for LWD and three runs of EGYPT with different seed sizes, $B \in \{100, 500, 1000\}$. We observe that even for a small value of B, the improvement over LWD is significant. Furthermore, we observe that even for $p = 1, q = 0.05$ which

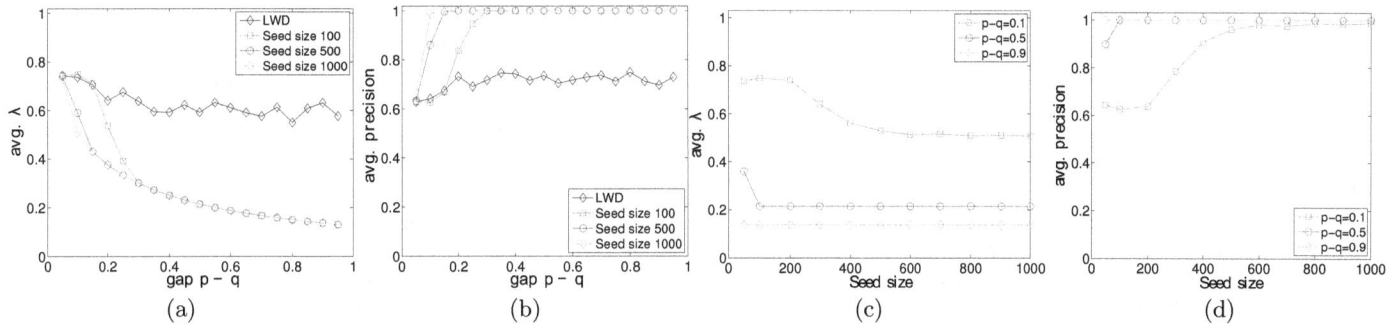

Figure 1: (a) Average fraction of edges cut λ and **(b)** average precision versus gap $p - q$ for LWD and EGyPT for three different B values (seed sizes). **(c)** Average λ and **(d)** average precision, versus B for three different gaps. All data points are averages over five experiments. Observed values are strongly concentrated around their corresponding averages.

corresponds to the 0.95 gap, LWD is not able to output a good quality partition. This shows that the asymptotic analysis of [30] requires a larger n value in order to recover the partition *whp*. Furthermore, as B increases from 100 to 1000 the quality of the final partition improves. It is worth emphasizing that the results we obtain are strongly concentrated around their corresponding averages. The ratio of the variance over the mean squared was at most 0.0129 and typically of the order 10^{-3} indicating a strong concentration according to Chebyshev's inequality, see Theorem 2.

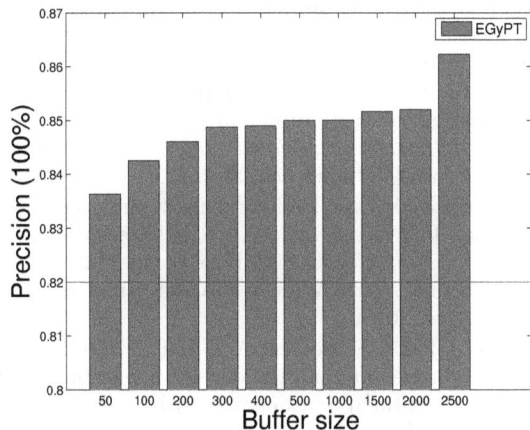

Figure 2: Digits classification

Finally, Figures 1(c) and (d) plot the average fraction of edges cut λ and the average precision versus the seed size B for three different gaps, averaged over five experiments. Again, data points are concentrated around averages. As expected, the smaller the gap $p - q$ the larger the parameter B has to be in order to obtain a given amount of precision. When the gap is large even for a small seed size $B = 50$, EGyPT obtains the correct partition. Notice that LWD cannot achieve this level of accuracy. Finally, we outline that our method is efficient with respect to run times. Indicatively, we report that for $p = 0.15, q = 0.05$ and $B = 50, 100$ the run times are 0.8 and 1.6 seconds respectively. Similarly for $p = 0.95, q = 0.05$ and $B = 50, 100$ the run times are 2.7 and 8.1 seconds respectively. For these run times, the computational overhead of EGyPT is at the order of 10^{-2} seconds.

4.3 Streams of data points

We consider a stream of data points where each data point $x \in \mathbb{R}^{784}$ represents a digit from 0 to 9. Whenever a new data point x arrives, we find its $k' = 5$ nearest neighbors among the B first points. This is a variation of the well known k'-nearest neighbor graph [22]. Figure 2 shows the improvement in the precision of the clustering as parameter B increases from 0.1% (50) to 5% (2 500) of the total number of data points (50 000). The blue straight line shows the performance of LWD. We observe the improvement over LWD even for $B = 50$ and the monotone increasing behavior of the precision as a function of B. While these classification results are not state-of-art in digit classification, they indicate that EGyPT captures the community structure of the underlying graph better than LWD.

5. CONCLUSIONS

In this work we introduce the use of higher length walks for streaming graph partitioning, a recent line of research [31] that has already had a significant impact on various graph processing systems. We analyze our proposed algorithm on clustered random graphs.

An interesting research direction is to perform average case analysis using a random graph model with power law degree distribution and small separators, e.g., [10, 11].

Acknowledgements

The author would like to thank Professor Alan Frieze and Professor Moez Draief and the anonymous reviewers for their feedback.

6. REFERENCES

[1] http://tinyurl.com/pmzmtys.
[2] http://yann.lecun.com/exdb/mnist/.
[3] Large scale machine learning and other animals, http://tinyurl.com/qfn766u, June 2014.
[4] B. Bollobás. *Random graphs*. Cambridge University Press, 2001.
[5] A. Buluc, H. Meyerhenke, I. Safro, P. Sanders, and C. Schulz. Recent advances in graph partitioning. Arxiv 1311.3144.

[6] R. Chen, J. Shi, Y. Chen, H. Guan, and H. Chen. Powerlyra: Differentiated graph computation and partitioning on skewed graphs. 2013.

[7] A. Condon and R. M. Karp. Algorithms for graph partitioning on the planted partition model. *Random Structures and Algorithms (RSA)*, 18(2):116–140, 2001.

[8] D. P. Dubhashi and A. Panconesi. *Concentration of measure for the analysis of randomized algorithms.* Cambridge University Press, 2009.

[9] U. Feige and R. Krauthgamer. A polylogarithmic approximation of the minimum bisection. *SIAM J. Comput.*, 31(4):1090–1118, Apr. 2002.

[10] A. D. Flaxman, A. M. Frieze, and J. Vera. A geometric preferential attachment model of networks. *Internet Mathematics*, 3(2):187–205, 2006.

[11] A. Frieze and C. E. Tsourakakis. Some properties of random apollonian networks. In *Internet Mathematics.* 2014.

[12] A. Gionis and C. E. Tsourakakis. Dense subgraph discovery: Kdd 2015 tutorial. In *Proceedings of the 21th ACM SIGKDD International Conference on Knowledge Discovery and Data Mining*, pages 2313–2314. ACM, 2015.

[13] J. Gonzalez, Y. Low, H. Gu, D. Bickson, and C. Guestrin. Powergraph: Distributed graph-parallel computation on natural graphs. In *Operating Systems Design and Implementation (OSDI)*, 2012.

[14] G. Jerrum, M.and Sorkin. The metropolis algorithm for graph bisection. *Discrete Applied Mathematics*, 82(1):155–175, 1998.

[15] U. Kang, C. E. Tsourakakis, and C. Faloutsos. Pegasus: A peta-scale graph mining system. In *IEEE International Conference on Data Mining (ICDM)*, 2009.

[16] B. W. Kernighan and S. Lin. An efficient heuristic procedure for partitioning graphs. *Bell Syst. Tech. J.*, 49(2):291–307, Feb. 1970.

[17] D. E. Knuth. Seminumerical algorithms. 2007.

[18] A. Konstantin and H. Räcke. Balanced graph partitioning. In *ACM Symposium on Parallelism in Algorithms and Architectures (SPAA)*, pages 120–124, 2004.

[19] R. Krauthgamer, J. S. Naor, and R. Schwartz. Partitioning graphs into balanced components. In *Symposium on Discrete Algorithms (SODA)*, pages 942–949, 2009.

[20] L. Lovász and M. Simonovits. The mixing rate of markov chains, an isoperimetric inequality, and computing the volume. In *Annual Symposium on Foundations of Computer Science (FOCS)*, pages 346–354. IEEE, 1990.

[21] Y. Low, J. Gonzalez, A. Kyrola, D. Bickson, C. Guestrin, and J. M. Hellerstein. Graphlab: A new framework for parallel machine learning. In *Proceedings of the 2009 ACM SIGMOD International Conference on Management of data*, pages 340–349, 2010.

[22] M. Maier, M. Hein, and U. von Luxburg. Optimal construction of k-nearest-neighbor graphs for identifying noisy clusters. *Theoretical Computer Science*, 410(19):1749–1764, 2009.

[23] G. Malewicz, M. H. Austern, A. Bik, J. Dehnert, I. Horn, N. Leiser, and G. Czajkowski. Pregel: a system for large-scale graph processing. In *SIGMOD '10*, pages 135–146, 2010.

[24] D. Margo and M. Seltzer. A scalable distributed graph partitioner. *Proceedings of the VLDB Endowment*, 8(12), 2015.

[25] F. McSherry. Spectral partitioning of random graphs. In *Annual Symposium on Foundations of Computer Science (FOCS)*, pages 529–537. IEEE, 2001.

[26] M. Mitzenmacher and E. Upfal. *Probability and computing: Randomized algorithms and probabilistic analysis.* Cambridge University Press, 2005.

[27] J. Nishimura and J. Ugander. Restreaming graph partitioning: Simple versatile algorithms for advanced balancing. In *ACM KDD*, 2013.

[28] K. Schloegel, G. Karypis, and V. Kumar. Parallel multilevel algorithms for multi-constraint graph partitioning (distinguished paper). In *Proceedings from the 6th International Euro-Par Conference on Parallel Processing*, Euro-Par '00, pages 296–310, 2000.

[29] D. A. Spielman and S.-H. Teng. A local clustering algorithm for massive graphs and its application to nearly-linear time graph partitioning. *arXiv preprint arXiv:0809.3232*, 2008.

[30] I. Stanton. Streaming balanced graph partitioning algorithms for random graphs. In *Proceedings of the Twenty-Fifth Annual ACM-SIAM Symposium on Discrete Algorithms (SODA)*, pages 1287–1301, 2014.

[31] I. Stanton and G. Kliot. Streaming graph partitioning for large distributed graphs. In *Proceedings of the 18th ACM SIGKDD international conference on Knowledge discovery and data mining*, 2012.

[32] C. Tsourakakis. The k-clique densest subgraph problem. In *Proceedings of the 24th International Conference on World Wide Web*, pages 1122–1132. International World Wide Web Conferences Steering Committee, 2015.

[33] C. Tsourakakis, F. Bonchi, A. Gionis, F. Gullo, and M. Tsiarli. Denser than the densest subgraph: extracting optimal quasi-cliques with quality guarantees. In *Proceedings of the 19th ACM SIGKDD international conference on Knowledge discovery and data mining*, pages 104–112. ACM, 2013.

[34] C. E. Tsourakakis, C. Gkantsidis, B. Radunovic, and M. Vojnovic. Fennel: Streaming graph partitioning for massive distributed graphs. *Seventh ACM International Conference on Web Search and Data Mining, WSDM 2014*, 2014.

[35] C. E. Tsourakakis, M. N. Kolountzakis, and G. L. Miller. Triangle sparsifiers. *J. Graph Algorithms Appl.*, 15(6):703–726, 2011.

[36] V. Vu. A simple svd algorithm for finding hidden partitions. *CoRR*, abs/1404.3918, 2014.

[37] H. Zhou and D. Woodruff. Clustering via matrix powering. In *Symposium on Principles of Database Systems (PODS)*, 2004.

Appendix
FENNEL is NP-hard

We show that maximizing the optimal quasi-clique objective

$$f_\alpha(\mathcal{P}) = \sum_{i=1}^{k} \left(e(S_i) - \alpha \binom{|S_i|}{2} \right),$$

over all possible vertex (disjoint) partitions $\mathcal{P} = (S_1, \ldots, S_k)$ is NP-hard. We reduce the k-clique partition NP-hard problem to optimal quasi-clique partitioning: can we partition the vertex set of a graph $G(V, E)$ in k cliques. We claim that if we set $\alpha = 1 - \frac{1}{n^3}$ then the answer to the k-clique partitioning problem is YES if and only if $f_\alpha(\mathcal{P}) > 0$. Notice that the latter inequality is equivalent to

$$\sum_{i=1}^{k} \left(e(S_i) - \binom{|S_i|}{2} \right) + \frac{1}{n^3} \sum_{i=1}^{k} \binom{|S_i|}{2} > 0.$$

Clearly, if we can partition V in k disjoint cliques $f_\alpha(\mathcal{P}) > 0$. On the other hand, suppose that $f_\alpha(\mathcal{P}) > 0$ for a partition $\mathcal{P}$ that does not correspond to a k-clique partitioning of V. Then the first summation term $\sum_{i=1}^{k} \left(e(S_i) - \binom{|S_i|}{2} \right) \leq -1$ and the second summation term $\frac{1}{n^3} \sum_{i=1}^{k} \binom{|S_i|}{2} < 1$. Hence, we derive a contradiction as $f_\alpha(\mathcal{P}) < 0$.

Who Contributes to the Knowledge Sharing Economy?

Arthi Ramachandran and Augustin Chaintreau
Computer Science Department, Columbia University, New York NY, USA
arthir@cs.columbia.edu, augustin@cs.columbia.edu

ABSTRACT

Information sharing dynamics of social networks rely on a small set of influencers to effectively reach a large audience. Our recent results and observations demonstrate that the shape and identity of this elite, especially those contributing *original* content, is difficult to predict. Information acquisition is often cited as an example of a public good. However, this emerging and powerful theory has yet to provably offer qualitative insights on how specialization of users into active and passive participants occurs.

This paper bridges, for the first time, the theory of public goods and the analysis of diffusion in social media. We introduce a non-linear model of *perishable* public goods, leveraging new observations about sharing of media sources. The primary contribution of this work is to show that *shelf time*, which characterizes the rate at which content get renewed, is a critical factor in audience participation. Our model proves a fundamental *dichotomy* in information diffusion: While short-lived content has simple and predictable diffusion, long-lived content has complex specialization. This occurs even when all information seekers are *ex ante* identical and could be a contributing factor to the difficulty of predicting social network participation and evolution.

Categories and Subject Descriptors

G.2.2 [**Graph Theory**]: Network problems

General Terms

Theory, Economics, Measurement

Keywords

Online diffusion; Economics of information; Social networks

1. INTRODUCTION

In social network services, such as Twitter and Facebook, the primary commodity produced and exchanged is content

and information. While, arguably, much of this process is solely hedonic, these social conversations play an increasingly larger role in today's economy. The revenue of content publishers is now primarily driven by audience originating from online social networks [30]; brands increasingly channel their products to a targeted audience alongside content exchange [27]; new business models aim at integrating with peer connections, sometimes competing with traditional firms in providing accommodation, car ride, or financial services [12, 16, 5]. This is unsurprising since decades of empirical studies, predating any online conversation, have shown how individuals rely on their peers or contacts to acquire information before making a choice. It could be to cast a vote [26], to keep up to date with new products [20], or to gather important data in the working place [17].

Our goal is to understand how individual choices govern how *original* information is produced and acquired in today's social networks. We focus on the domain of identification of news content worth reading, where social connections are massively used. As we are all aware, acquiring original information requires effort and some time investment. Social networks benefit users by making the result of this effort available to more people. Previous studies highlighted that most of the population receives original information from a small set of opinion leaders or influentials. To put it bluntly, only a minority of participants add information to those networks, as opposed to simply listening or passing it on (via, e.g., retweets, likes). Many important open questions remain: In a given network, which users have an incentive to produce more original content? Previous studies have shown that influencers are not easy to differentiate from ordinary users. Can we predict the outcome of such a mechanism, where some users specialize? Are there types of content or networks that favor the formation of an elite?

To answer the above questions, we first conduct an empirical study of original information in news diffusion on social media. We then show how they relate to mathematical analysis of a variant of *public goods*. In contrast with some other goods, most online news are tailored for a particular shelf-life. Our results show that this appears to be one of the primary factors which governs both how activity is distributed, and how multiple types of specialization appear in a dynamic non linear public goods model. We show the following contributions:

1. We analyze data from multiple online sources exchanged through Twitter, highlighting the production of original content remains extremely concentrated. Barring institutional accounts, the majority of the orig-

inal content comes from users with mid-range popularity rather than just the just well known people. In fact, counterintuitively, original content production is skewed towards less active and connected people. We also make the following observations: the size of this active minority in proportion to the audience appears to follow primarily from the shelf-life of the content exchanged. Long term content appears to favor a smaller elite, while short-lived information expands the size of active participants. (Section 2).

2. Since the availability of news worth reading in a social network exhibits the property of a public good, we propose a simple model that extend public good theory to accommodate investment made by individual players towards a perishable good. We show that it reproduces previous observations and does correlate with the activity we empirically observed. (Section 3).

3. This model allows us to answer how specialization occurs in knowledge sharing, even where players are *ex ante* identical. We first prove that a unique Nash Equilibrium exists for sufficiently short-lived content, under a condition related to spectral properties of the social network. However, we prove that when content is long-lived, specialization is unavoidable, even with identical players on a symmetric graph. Given the presence of multiple equilibria and sensitivity to initial conditions, predictions are complex. (Section 4).

To the best of our knowledge, our paper is the first example that bridges predictions of the behavior of players in a public good game, with empirical evidence from one of its motivating example: information acquisition. The main novelty of our approach is to model information as a public good with decaying value over time *i.e.*, they are perishable goods. As a public good, the utility of information to a user comes from her own contributions as well as those of her neighbors. This new approach allows theory and practice to qualitatively align, in spite of simplistic modeling of user behavior. Perishable public goods create non-linear best response, which makes the analysis more complex, but we hope that this first step can motivate more work in this area. Our work is also, to the best of our knowledge, the first one that analyzes the characteristics and shape of the group of users with an original contribution. This addresses a critical problem as social media are typically described as full of noise and redundancy. Our results may further inform how to promote and reward users for their participation, and mechanisms to design social media which makes user well informed.

2. WHO IS ACQUIRING NEW INFORMATION?

Early studies consider information diffusion as two-step model of information flow, with large cascades originating at institutional sources, followed by a series of connectors. However, more recent results [21] proved that the vast majority of content is received *directly* from one content originator. Knowledge sharing in social media hence depends on some users to exert effort to acquire *original* information. Original content is obtained externally to the social network, either through search engines, time spent on informal web browsing, or offline conversations. To the best of

our knowledge, little is known about the characteristics of the users performing that task, although one expects them to be a minority.

To better understand these dynamics, we analyze two complementary datasets: **(1) The KAIST dataset** (see [14] for more details) contains the entire Twitter graph from August 2009 and consists of 8m users and 700m links. Taken over the course of a month, the dataset contains 183m tweets. Of these tweets, we considered only those with urls (37m) since those are the tweets that provide an indication of sharing media on twitter. Further, we filtered the tweets by news domains (*e.g.*, `nytimes.com`). The classification of a domain as news was obtained from the Open Directory Project (`http://www.dmoz.org/`), a volunteer edited directly of Web links. Each link in the directory is annotated with a top level categories and multiple levels of subcategories. In our analysis, we only took into account the top level category. We kept all the domains with a reasonable number of posts (> 2000 posts) resulting in 31 domains. We removed domains which did not seem to follow the same definition of news as others (aggregators such as e.g. `news.google.com` and `reddit.com`, weather services such as `weather.gov`, and region specific domains such as `thehindu.com`). While the KAIST dataset provides a holistic view of the media landscape, we complement it with a denser, newer snapshot we collected ourselves: **(2) The NYT dataset** (see [29] for more details) contains all the Twitter posts containing a URL from the nytimes.com domain during a full week of December 2011. In parallel, we crawled the follower-followee relationship at the same time in order to construct the URLs that each user received. The final dataset totals 346k unique users receiving a total 22m tweets with URL (including multiplicity). Of these, there are 70k unique links.

2.1 Imbalanced content creation

Unsurprisingly, in social media like Twitter, a small fraction of users are responsible for a large part of the activity. To quantify this concentration, we use the Lorenz curve [28], or the cumulative share of the top $x\%$ of users as a function of x, in Figure 1. Since some domains only cater to niche groups, the fraction x here is measured relative to the domain's audience size (*i.e.*, anyone who received or sent at least one such URL). A quick glance at the plot confirms that the size of passive and active audience differ by orders of magnitude (*e.g.*, as seen here and in other domains, 99% do not tweet a single URL. Equivalently, 1% of the audience produces almost all the new tweets in the network).

In addition to examining how users post in general (red solid line), we also look at how they acquire original information for the network. We, hence, looked at users who were the first on twitter to post a url link ("global first" represented by the short green dotted line) and users who were the first in their local network, i.e. they did not receive the url from anyone they followed before they sent the url ("local first" represented by the long blue dashed line). Note that in each of these cases, the overall audience remains the same - those who have received the link either directly or indirectly from an originator. Here, in the left figure, 0.1% of the `cnn.com` audience produces half of all tweets. But the same number of people produce 60% of the globally original content and almost 90% of the locally original content. Perhaps unsurprisingly, while only a small minority of nodes

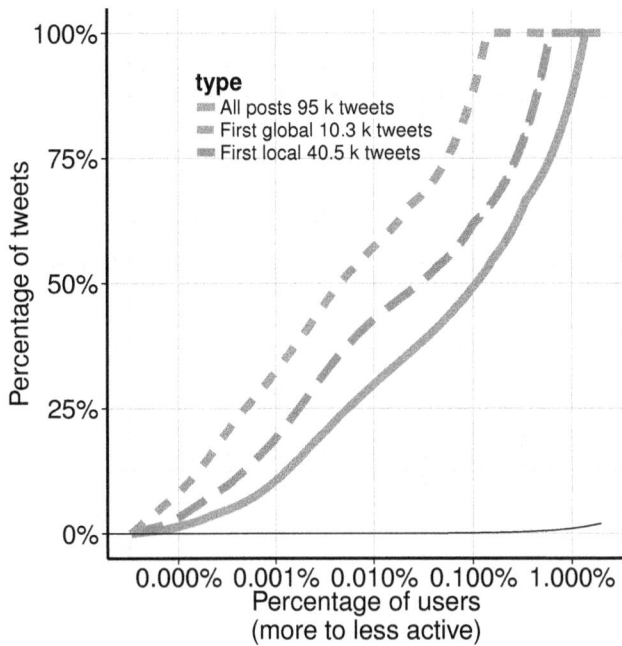

Figure 1: Lorenz curve (*i.e.*, cumulative share of the top x% nodes in the audience seen as a function of x): (top) comparing production of tweets and original content for cnn.com from KAIST; (bottom) comparison of Lorenz curve for "first local" tweets in two different domains.

repost articles, it is an even smaller minority that introduces original content in the network.

Specialization is the phenomenon of users taking extreme positions - in our case, some users expend a lot of effort while others are on the other extreme of expending almost no effort. To help quantify this phenomenon, we introduce the 90%-volume originators measure. This is the fraction of the audience that together produce 90% of the volume. While we later study how this metric of specialization varies with different content type, we first study the minority of originators in more detail.

2.2 Characterizing content originators

It has been shown (see, *e.g.*, [29]) that a user's tweeting activity is strongly correlated with their in- and out-degree. Intuitively, an active online presence is required to gather many followers. Having many followers encourages a return connection by other users. Most Twitter users remain passive in diffusing information, and those promoting original content are a tiny minority. One hypothesis of a simple hierarchy of social media emerges: the content producers responsible for new content creation, the power users and intermediaries who drive the traffic and the passive consumers. As we see here, reality is at odds with this expectation when it comes to production of original content.

Figure 2 (left) presents, for users binned according to their activity on the x-axis, the distribution of the fraction of local first content they produce with median and various percentiles. To help interpretation, we represent qualitatively with a thin solid line the number of users in each bin, where the first bin contains approximately 129k users. On the

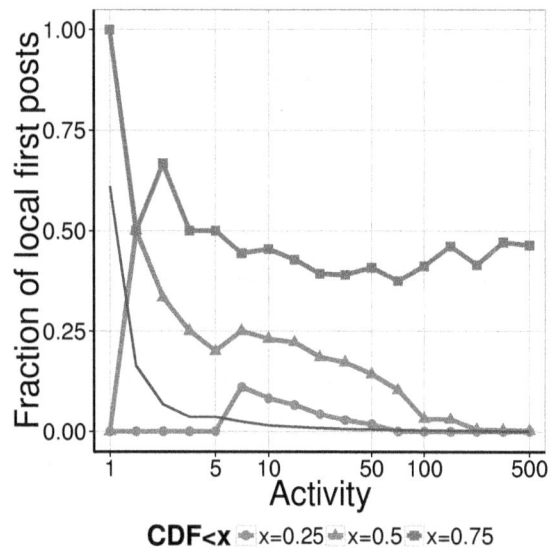

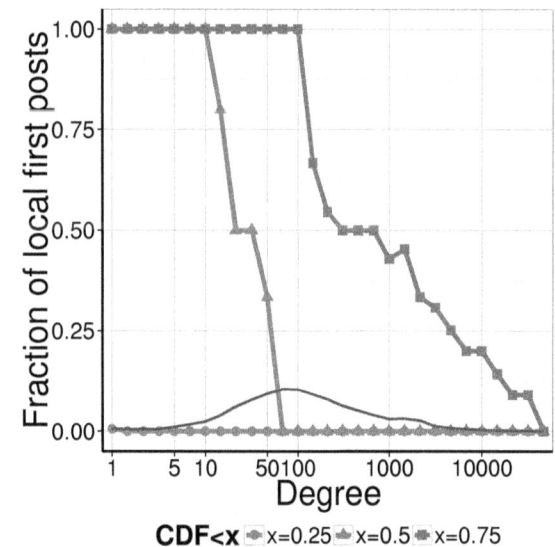

Figure 2: Fraction of locally original activity, presented as percentiles among users population binned according to (top) activity and (bottom) number of accounts they follow.

right we observe the effects of a few heavy nodes: there are in total 90 users posting more than 400 URLs in a month, who are primarily either institutional accounts or professional journalists and are almost always original. However, those are exceptions: among the active users, originators are generally a minority âĂŞ typically the 25% most original âĂŞ chosen across all activity levels. On the contrary, this trend proves that a URL is most likely to be locally original when it is posted by less active users. Equivalently, if the authors of that tweet post approximately 50 URLs in a month, it is likely to be one she has previously received. Another concurring observation, shown in Figure 2 (right), presents the same distribution where users are binned on the x-axis according to the number of people they follow. The trend here is even more pronounced as users belonging to the less connected half are much more likely to produce original information.

While, at first, this trend appears relatively surprising, the theory of public goods offers a simple explanation that we leverage later: that the effort exerted by others creates a disincentive for a well connected player to acquire new information. It seems in particular that 50% of users with larger than average degree rely entirely on the information they receive for their posts.

2.3 Effect of Time

Finally, we study the factors quantitatively affecting specialization. To take an example, first, we show in Figure 3 a comparison between the Lorenz curves for two news media domains: New York Times and The Atlantic. These are different in multiple ways: The New York Times is a daily newspaper with a very large readership while the Atlantic is a monthly magazine with a smaller readership. Within the KAIST dataset, 111k nytimes.com tweets were posted (and an audience of 2.6m users) while 4.7k theatlantic.com tweets were posted (audience of 400k users). Of these tweets only a small fraction are unique links (5917 for nytimes.com vs 891 for theatlantic.com) [31]. When comparing lorenz curves, the Atlantic is more specialized than the New York Times with 0.4% of the audience accounting for 75% of theatlantic.com tweets while 0.8% of the audience accounts for 75% of nytimes.com tweets. This indicates that audiences of different sources specialize in different ways.

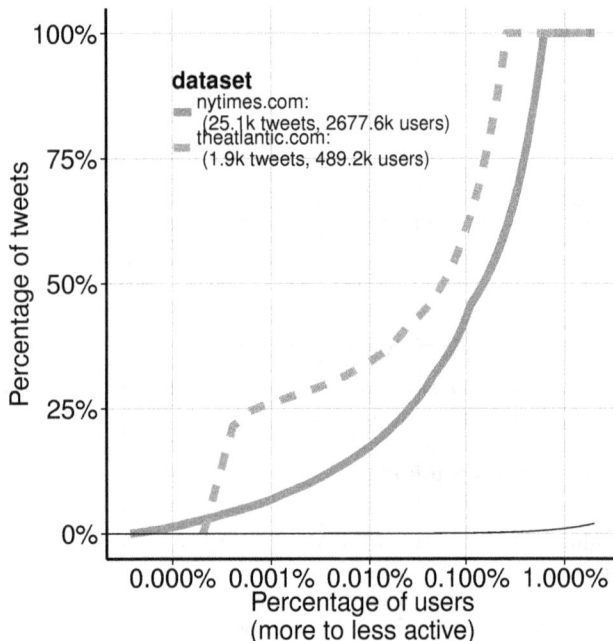

Figure 3: Lorenz curve for "first localâĂŹâĂŹ tweets in two different domains.

Our main observation is as follows: the degree of specialization is related to the temporal dynamics of the content, with remarkable regularity. In the same time period, more new content is introduced by nytimes.com, indicating that the content becomes stale quicker than for atlantic.com. This is consistent with nytimes.com being a daily news source. For every media, we measure its average *shelf life* by using the number of unique URLs produced over a month. We define the shelf life of an article to be the amount of time for which it is relevant *i.e.*, it contin-

ues to be shared among users. This captures the fact that, since all media compete for attention within the same online network, one producing ten times more content expects the content to be renewed ten times faster. Figure 4 shows the 90%-volume originator (*i.e.*, the percentage of the audience producing 90% of tweet volumes) for 31 media sources. There is a fairly large range of shelf life from approximately 2 minutes to over 2 hours. However, we consistently observe that domains with long shelf times tend involve a smaller fraction of the population to produce most of the content. Note that the x- and y-axis are in logscale. This temporal dynamics affects all tweets and original content similarly. After renormalization, this seems not be affected much by audience size, although we did observe the smaller effect of the fraction of active users grows slowly with the audience.

We also examined the effect of different measures of shelf lives in Figure 5. We calculate the diffusion life as the length of time that the article is shared (time of last post - time of first post). The y-axis is a measure of concentration, fraction of locally first posts of the total number of people receiving the article. We normalized by the number of users posting the article, in order to better account for larger cascades. Other measures of concentration, such as the fraction of first local posts by the total number of posts of an article, also exhibit similar trends, albeit in a more muted fashion. We continue to see the trend of articles with longer shelf lives tend to be more concentrated in sharing.

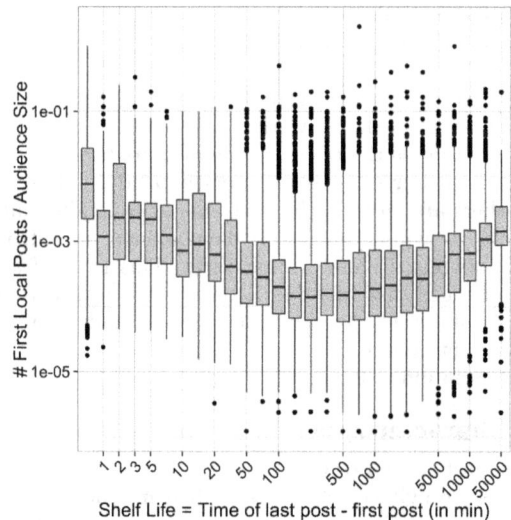

Figure 5: Concentration of sharing compared to the diffusion-life for each article. Each article's diffusionlife is the total active time (in minutes) of the article.

In summary, we have made several observations. (1) The presence of specialization where a small number of individuals are responsible for most of the original content produced on Twitter. (2) These individuals who produce most of the original content are not, as expected at first glance, the most well connected or the highest degree nodes. Rather, they are average-degree nodes in the network. (3) There is a correlation between the shelf life of an article, the time for which it is relevant, and the degree of specialization. To the best of our knowledge, there does not exist a previous model with reproduces these characteristics. In the following section,

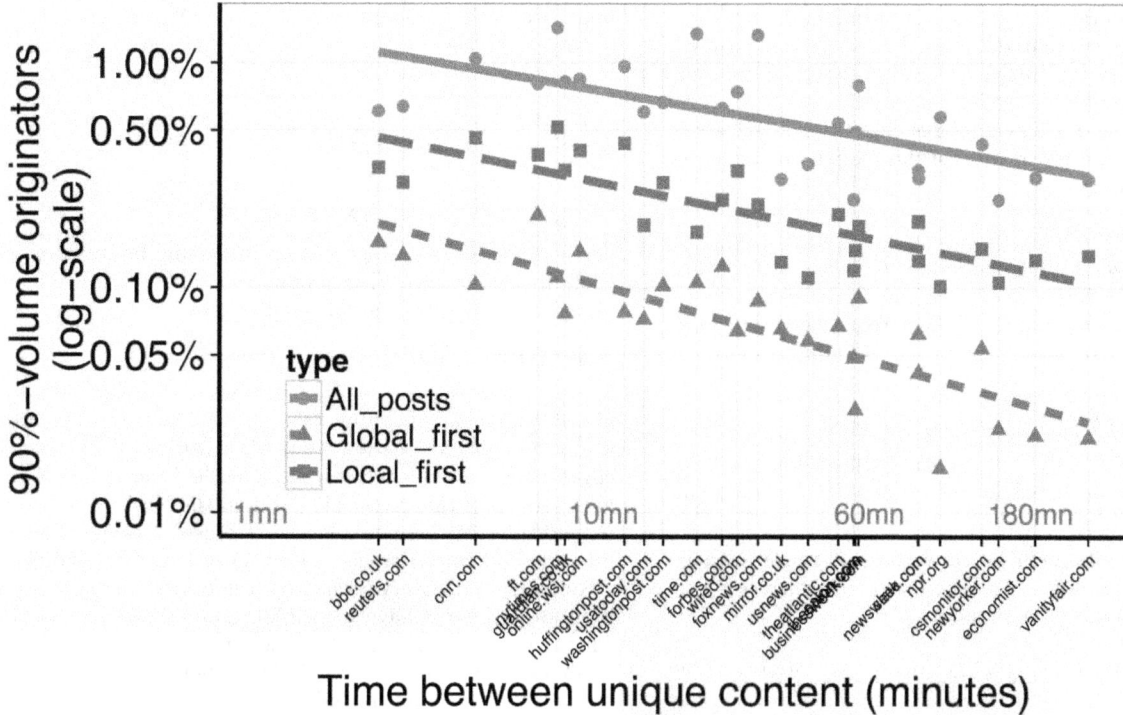

Figure 4: Concentration of sharing compared to the shelf-life for each media source. Each point is the fraction of the audience responsible for 90% of the tweet volume of the media source.

we present an idealized model which retains the flavor of the problem of information search.

3. PERISHABLE PUBLIC GOODS MODEL

While information diffusion on social media is complex and topic dependent, our goal in this section is to provide a simple model with which previous observations of information acquisition can be predicted. We leverage the economic theory of public goods – goods that are non-rivalrous where use by one individual does not reduce availability to others. In fact, in many public goods models, the ownership of the good by on individual has an impact on the utility of his neighbors. Further, we consider news as a perishable good, i.e. a good that needs to be used within a short period of time and bought again (such as milk or produce). While news does not spoil in the same sense as produce does, the value of news does decrease with time due to updated information and later events occurring. In both cases, since the product is short-lived and the demand is persistent, there is a time dynamic to renew it.

3.1 A Public Good Approach to Original Content Production

As content online is vast and not easy to navigate, we assume that player i seeks knowledge at a given rate. This results in content being discovered by her at random times with an intensity y_i, forming a Poisson process of discovery times. The effort of that user to individually achieve a discovery rate y_i has a convex cost $c(y_i)$. This captures the fact that as more effort is exerted, or time is invested, worthwhile information becomes rare and harder to find. The utility of information is represented as being in an informed state. In

this state, a user has an additional unit of return compared to being uninformed. Upon a discovery, a user remains in the informed state for a time τ equal to the shelf time of this item. We assume τ is a constant.

There is a social component to the interaction: users make the results of their work available to neighbors in a social network graph. We denote the adjacency matrix of the social network as $G = (V, E)$ and it can either be undirected (e.g., Facebook) or directed (e.g., Twitter). Without loss of generality, we assume that the effort of a user only affects its direct neighbors. The general case simply requires redefining neighboring relations to include future descendents.

Let us denote $y_{-i} = \sum_{j \in N(i)} y_j$ as the rate of content discovery that a user i in the network receives at no cost from her neighbors. Then, including her own effort cost $c(y_i)$, the average utility received per unit of time can be written as:

$$U(y_i, y_{-i}) = 1 - e^{-\tau(y_i + y_{-i})} - c(y_i) .$$

At time $t = T$, the probability to have received one content item within $]T - \tau; T]$ is the probability that a Poisson process of rate $(y_i + y_{-i})$ creates no point in that interval.

Note here, that discovering multiple content simultaneously creates no additional benefit to the user since the user is already in the informed state. Note also that having content items of various shelf-lives would result in the same dynamics as long as those durations are chosen independently of the discovery process. Finally, while most of the properties of the model we show generalizes to general convex cost, we are primarily interested in polynomial cost $(c : y_i \mapsto \frac{\theta}{\alpha+1} y_i^{\alpha+1}), \alpha > 0$. We can think of θ as the reference time period. A reward of 1 is equivalent to the effort spent to produce content once every θ time. In this work, we assume, in general, that the cost is normalized such that $\theta = 1$hr. This means that the reward exactly compensates for the search effort incurred to produce original content every hour. More general models, especially ones with heterogeneous costs and a matrix of benefits transfer between users, are likely to perfect realism of this model, but we leave them for future work.

3.2 Best Response

We first analyze a single individual response of a player to her neighbors' efforts. Even with non-linear dynamics is non-linear, we can represent this best response action in a simple closed form.

THEOREM 1. *For a node, i, of $G = (V, E)$, the best response to i's neighbors' efforts, y_{-i}, is given by*

$$\phi(y_{-i}, \tau) = \frac{\alpha}{\tau} W(\frac{\tau^{\frac{\alpha+1}{\alpha}}}{\alpha} e^{-\frac{\tau y_{-i}}{\alpha}}), \text{ where } W \text{ is the Lambert}$$

function defined on $[0; \infty[$ as the inverse of the function $x \mapsto x \exp(x)$.

PROOF. For an individual, i, their best response to their neighbors efforts occurs when i's utility is maximized w.r.t. the amount of effort i invests, y_i.

$$\max_{y_i} U(y_i, y_{-i}) \text{ s.t. } y_i \geq 0, \text{ i.e., }, \frac{\partial U(y_i, y_{-i})}{\partial y_i} = 0.$$

This yields $\tau e^{-\tau(y_i+y_{-i})} - y_i^\alpha = 0$.

Hence $\tau y_i = \alpha W(\frac{\tau^{\frac{\alpha+1}{\alpha}}}{\alpha} e^{-\frac{\tau y_{-i}}{\alpha}})$ where W denotes the Lambert function, which proves the result. □

The Lambert function W (Figure 6) is a positive increasing function, that is asymptotically equivalent to the identity near 0 and comes within a negligible distance of the function $x \mapsto \ln(x) - \ln\ln(x)$ as x becomes large. The last two decades has found numerous applications of this function to differential equation, combinatorics, theoretical physics and others. Its computation, both through formal calculus and numerical approximation can be done fast.

Our closed form implies the bound for any $y : 0 = \lim_{x \to \infty} \phi(x) \leq \phi(y) \leq \phi(0) = \frac{\alpha}{\tau} W(\tau^{\frac{\alpha+1}{\alpha}})$.

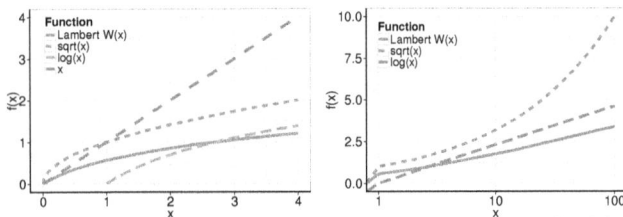

Figure 6: **Comparison of the Lambert function ($W(z)$ where $z = W(z)e^{W(z)}$) to the common function of x, $\log(x)$, and $\sqrt{x}$ in the range (left) [0,4] and (right) [1,100].**

3.3 Nash Equilibrium

We initially focus on analyzing the Nash equilibrium in symmetric graphs.

DEFINITION 1. *A graph G is symmetric if, given any two pairs of edges (u_1, v_1) and (u_2, v_2) of G, there is an automorphism $f : V(G) \to V(G)$ such that $f(u_1) = u_2$ and $f(v_1) = v_2$.*

In a symmetric graph, in a unique Nash Equilibrium, all nodes exert the same amount of effort. Observe that if this were not the case, a transformation of the graph results in another equilibrium.

LEMMA 2. *For a D-regular graph, a symmetric Nash Equilibrium always exists and is given by*

$$y_i = \frac{\alpha}{\tau(1+D)} W(\tau^{\frac{\alpha+1}{\alpha}} \frac{(1+D)}{\alpha}), \forall i.$$

The case of symmetric graphs is interesting because, as we show in Section 4.1, this symmetric equilibrium need not always be a unique or stable equilibrium.

3.4 Model Validation

Real world graphs are, of course, more complex than the above symmetric graph models. We validate our model on a subset of the NYT graph (a random sample of 10% of the edges). We use an iterative update method (described in the long version of this paper [31]) to find the Nash equilibrium numerically. In these simulations, we used a range of shelf-life times ranging from short ($\tau = 1$) to long ($\tau = 1000$).

Matching our observations from the KAIST dataset, users with larger degree have less "information seeking activity". This is reflected in a smaller amount of effort spent in the Nash Equilibrium. Figure 7 (left) shows the correlation of the Nash Equilibrium effort with out-degree of a node ($\tau = 0.5$ on a sample of 0.1% of the NYT graph). Here, we see a very strong relationship between the degree and the amount of effort expended in the Nash Equilibrium. Thus, our model yields predictive power for relation of connection and investment in information search

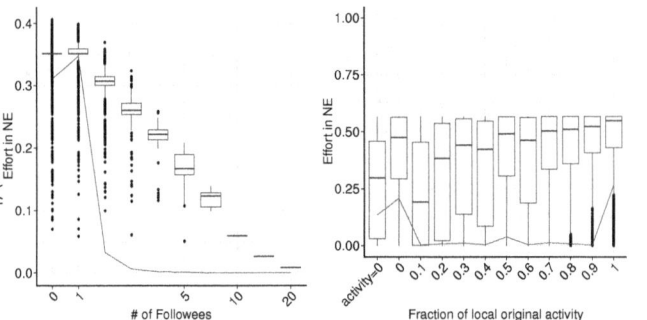

Figure 7: **The Nash Equilibrium (as a function of (left) node degree and (right) fraction of first local activity) in a sample of the NYT graph**

We then observe that the elite in the modeled equilibrium share similar structure to those observed empirically (Figure 8). A small subset of individuals are responsible for a large fraction of the effort spent – mimicking the behavior of individuals with original content.

Lastly, we examine how the effort in the Nash equilibrium of our model correlates to the fraction of local original activity vs total activity observed in the NYTimes dataset (Figure 7 right). Ideally, we would expect to see perfect correlation since the effort in our model captures exactly this, the effort you spent to bring new content to your neighbors. We see that individuals who in the real world had no effort (the left most group) expend low effort in the Nash Equilibrium. Those who posted at least one article expended more effort and the amount of effort steadily rises.

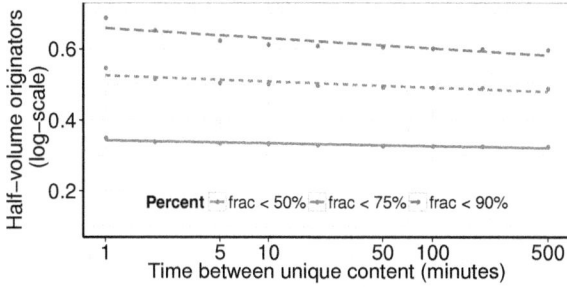

Figure 8: Proportion of population responsible for 50%, 75% and 90% of the effort in the Nash Equilibrium in sample of NYT graph.

4. EQUILIBRIUM AND SPECIALIZATION

4.1 Conditions for a Unique Nash Equilibrium

Different classes of goods exhibit different types of behavior. In economic theory, one of these classifications are that of a *normal good* is a good for which demand increases with increased wealth. Mathematically, if $\gamma : \mathbb{R}_{\geq 0} \to \mathbb{R}_{\geq 0}$ is a differentiable function representing the income elasticity of demand (the responsiveness of the demand to a change in the income), then the good is normal iff the derivative satisfies $0 < \gamma' < 1$. A *network normal good* carries that idea to a networked case where there is a income elasticity of demand function for each player i in the network. The consumption γ_i is defined in terms of the wealth of i (set externally), w_i, and i's "social income", the income from neighbors of i, y_{-i}. A network normal good satifies the condition: $1 + \frac{1}{\lambda_{\min}} < \gamma_i'(w_i + y_{-i}) < 1$ [3]. We can also express these conditions in terms of the best response $\phi(y_{-i}) = \gamma_i(w_i + y_{-i}) - w_i$ as follows.

Fact. In the above notation, a good is network normal iff for every player i, $\frac{1}{\lambda_{\min}} < \phi'(y_{-i}) < 0$.

In our model, there can exist multiple equilibria for the effort that individuals expend. Using network normality conditions, we now give a condition involving the expiration time parameter, τ under which the Nash equilibrium for the system will be unique.

Theorem 3 (Short-Lived Content Exhibits Less Specialization) *Let $\lambda_{\min}$ be the minimum eigenvalue of the adjacency matrix of the network, $G = (V, E)$, and let τ be the expiration time parameter of the system. Then, a unique Nash Equilibrium exists if*

$$\tau < \hat{\tau} =^{def} \Big(\frac{\alpha}{-\lambda_{\min} - 1} \Big)^{\frac{\alpha}{\alpha+1}} e^{\frac{\alpha}{(\alpha+1)(-\lambda_{\min}-1)}}.$$

PROOF. We will prove the theorem by using the previously established connection between network normality of the system and the existence of a unique Nash equilibrium [3, 10, 11, 9]. Hence we only need to show that the network normal conditions hold under the assumptions of the theorem.

We will show that the condition holds for every player, i. For ease of notation, let $\phi = \phi_i$ and $x = y_{-i}$.

Observe that since W is an increasing function, we have $\phi'(x)$ is a non-decreasing function. Hence the derivative only takes values in $[\phi'(0), \lim_{x \to \infty} \phi'(x)] = [-\frac{\tau^{\frac{\alpha+1}{\alpha}}}{\alpha} W'(\frac{\tau^{\frac{\alpha+1}{\alpha}}}{\alpha}), 0]$.

Now, the network normality condition simplifies to verifying

$$\frac{1}{\lambda_{\min}(G)} < -\frac{\tau^{\frac{\alpha+1}{\alpha}}}{\alpha} W'(\frac{\tau^{\frac{\alpha+1}{\alpha}}}{\alpha}) < 0.$$

Simplifying the first inequality, we get:

$$\tau < \Big(\frac{\alpha}{-\lambda_{\min} - 1} \Big)^{\frac{\alpha}{\alpha+1}} e^{\frac{\alpha}{(\alpha+1)(-\lambda_{\min}-1)}} = \hat{\tau}$$

Thus, the network normality conditions holds and a unique Nash equilibrium exists for any $\tau < \hat{\tau}$. $\square$

The quantity $\hat{\tau}$ of G specifies the condition under which a unique Nash equilibrium exists. Table 1 details the value of $\hat{\tau}$ for various regular graphs ([31]).

Table 1: Conditions for unique Nash Equilibrium ($\tau < \hat{\tau}$) for graphs with n nodes ($\alpha = 1$)

Graph	$\lambda_{\min}$	$\hat{\tau}$
Complete	-1	$\forall \tau \ (\infty)$
Cycle (Even)	-2	$\sqrt{e}$
Cycle (Odd)	$-2 + \frac{\pi^2}{n^2}$	$\frac{n}{(n^2 - \pi^2)^{\frac{1}{2}}} e^{\frac{n^2}{2(n^2 - \pi^2)}}$
Erdös-Renyi	$-2\sqrt{np}$	$\big(\frac{1}{2\sqrt{np}-1} \big)^{\frac{1}{2}} e^{\frac{1}{2(2\sqrt{np}-1)}}$
Star	$-\sqrt{n-1}$	$\big(\frac{1}{\sqrt{n-1}-1} \big)^{\frac{1}{2}} e^{\frac{1}{2(\sqrt{n-1}-1)}}$
Complete Bipartite	$-\frac{n}{2}$	$\big(\frac{2}{n-2} \big)^{\frac{1}{2}} e^{\frac{1}{n-2}}$

Our observations on simple regular graphs give us an understanding of the behavior of the Nash Equilibrium in differnet types of settings. We see that for shorter lived information (content with smaller τ), the process of sharing is relatively straightforward. In most graphs, for small $\tau < \hat{\tau}$, there exists a unique equilibrium. In symmetric graphs, this equilibrium is symmetric. In non-regular graphs, the equilibrium response is inversely related to the degree of a node since higher degree nodes can rely on good quality content through their many neighbors. Conversely, lower degree nodes tend to expend more effort since they have few neighbors that they can free ride on.

In general, more balanced graphs (with larger $\lambda_{\min}$) have less sensitivity to the ephemeral nature of information *i.e.*, the conditions for a unique equilibrium encompass a larger range of shelf life values. In more segregated graphs (with smaller $\lambda_{\min}$), the efforts of a few people can be enough for the graph as a whole and the equilibrium is less balanced in nature.

Understanding the dependencies of the equilibrium in real world graphs is a little more challenging. Since these are not d-regular graphs, we do not expect symmetric equilibria to occur. In the case of the real world NYTimes graph, $\lambda_{\min} \approx -70$ (computed with python's sparse matrix package). Considering that the size of the NYTimes graph is $n = 346k$ users, this case more closely resembles a balanced graph, like an Erdös-Renyi graph. For $\alpha = 1$, a case where there is a relatively low cost of finding information, $\hat{\tau} \approx 0.12$ of the reference time period. For $\theta = 1hr$ (*i.e.*, ., assuming readers' utility for content roughly compensate an effort to search every hour for new information), $\hat{\tau} \approx 7min$ which is close to the empircally estimated shelf life of $\tau = 7.30$ min.

4.2 Tuning Shelf Life to Maximize Original Information

A media source would want to encourage users to spend more time on their site. Thus, they might be interested in tuning their parameter to maximize user effort. In a disconnected setting, each person is responsible for finding and consuming their own content. In this case, $y_{-i} = 0$ and the best response simplifies to $\phi(0) = \frac{\alpha}{\tau} W(\frac{\tau^{\frac{\alpha+1}{\alpha}}}{\alpha})$. At the value $\tau = \tau^*$, an individual is incentivized to expend maximal effort.

CLAIM 4. *For an isolated node, i, the effort is maximized at $\tau^* = e^{\frac{1}{\alpha+1}}$.*

In the case of symmetric graphs, there is always a symmetric equilibrium (Lemma 2). We can calculate, for symmetric graphs, the τ^* that maximizes the amount of effort by any node in a symmetric equilibrium.

CLAIM 5. *For an symmetric graph of degree D, the effort in a symmetric equilibrium, y_i, is maximized at $\tau^* = \frac{e}{(1+D)^\alpha}^{\frac{1}{\alpha+1}}$*

4.3 Specialization and Symmetry

We use simulations to examine how these theoretical results translate to various graph families. For each graph family, we look at graphs of sizes ranging from $n = 4$ to $n = 400$ and edge density from $p = 0.0001$ to $p = 0.5$ (for Erdös-Renyi graphs). We then run an iterative algorithm that updates the best response until convergence [31] . The point of convergence (when it converges) is the Nash equilibrium. In the cases that we examined, the best responses converged to an equilibrium within 20 steps (though our algorithm does not guarantee convergence).

Considering, first, the case of symmetric graphs (figure 9), each line in the graph is the effort made by a particular node. Note that since many nodes have the same effort across different regimes of τ, those lines overlapping each other and are hence not visible. In both the bipartite and cycle graph, in the specialized equilibrium, half the nodes overlap and expend most of the effort and the remaining half free-ride on those nodes. We see that, with shorter shelf-lives, individuals are more self-reliant. Conversely, longer shelf lives result in individuals relying on others efforts. Both cycle graphs and complete bipartite graphs exhibit the property that when content is long-term, the equilibria becomes more specialized with some individuals doing the majority of the work and others doing almost no work. Bipartite graphs split into their two partitions where those in one partition do all the work while those in the other do none.

The story is more complex in the case on assymetric graphs (figure 10). In each of the cases, we see a specialized equilibrium emerge. We consider the case of a star graph and an Erdös-Renyi graph, which gives us simple cases without the effect of heterogeneity. We also looked at a 10% subset of a real world graph. In the case of the star graph, the single central node does almost no work while all of his neighbors overlap and have much higher effort.

We see that specialization can occur as a result of the degree distribution (as in assymetric graphs). However, this also occurs in symmetric graphs, when all nodes have the same degree. From lemma 2, we know that a symmetric Nash equilibrium exists, but we observe that the system

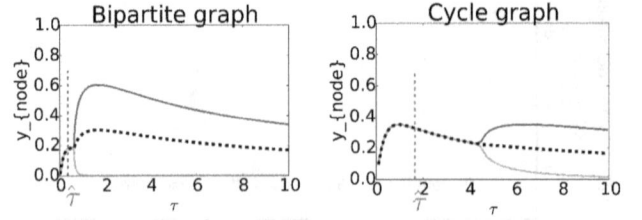

Figure 9: **Differing effort levels in the Nash Equilibrium (y-axis) with different τ (x-axis) in symmetric graphs. Each node (of $n = 20$ nodes) is represented by a line in the figure. The unique equilibrium ($\tau < \hat{\tau}$) is always symmetric. (left) Complete bipartite graph (right) Cycle graph.**

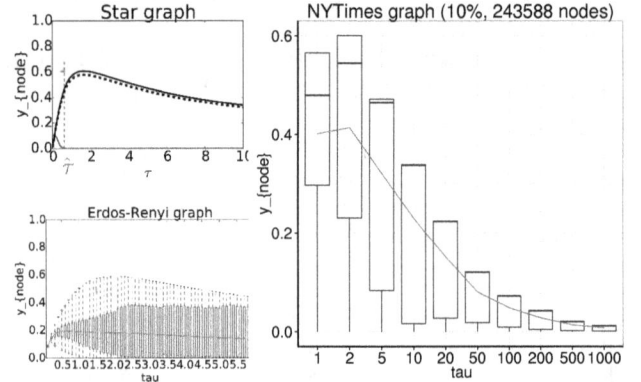

Figure 10: **Differing effort levels with different τ in assymetric graphs. Each bar represents the distribution of the amount of effort by all the nodes. The pink line is the average effort of all the nodes. (top-left) Star graph. (bottom-left) Erdös-Renyi graph ($n = 1000, p = 0.01$). (right) Randomly sampled NYTimes graph with 243k nodes.**

converges to a specialized Nash equilibrium. In the following section, we show that symmetric equilibria are not stable for large τ.

4.4 Theoretical Proof of Specialization

When a unique Nash equilibrium exists, we understand the convergent network configuration. However, when there are multiple equilibria, it is not clear which of these configurations are realized — for instance, some of these Nash equilibria can be unstable and, hence, never realized in practice. Here, we use the same definition of stability as in [10, 11]. A Nash equilibrium is stable if a small change in the strategy of one player leads to a situation where two conditions hold: (i) the player who did not change has no better strategy in the new circumstance (ii) the player who did change is now playing with a strictly worse strategy.

Empirically, we observe that for longer-term content, the equilibrium for a cycle graph and a bipartite graph are specialized (figure 9), *inspite* of them being symmetric graphs. This indicates that the stability of the Nash equilibrium has some dependency on τ.

Theorem 6 (Specialization for Longer Shelf-Life) *There exists an shelf-life τ, such that, for any symmetric graph G of degree $D \geq 3$, the symmetric equilibrium is not stable.*

44

PROOF. The proof follows the outline of the Proof of Theorem 2 in [10]. It has two steps. The first step is a simple observation: If $\vec{y} < \vec{y'}$, then $\phi \circ \phi(\vec{y}) < \phi \circ \phi(\vec{y'})$. This follows because the response function $\phi(y)$ is a decreasing function of y.

The second step is to show that under some small perturbation $\vec{\epsilon} > 0$, we have $\phi \circ \phi(\vec{y} + \vec{\epsilon}) > \vec{y} + \vec{\epsilon}$ (here the vector inequality $\vec{x} > 0$ corresponds to coordinate wise inequality $x_i > 0 \; \forall i$). In other words, with any small change from the equilibrium, the best response moves further away (strictly) from the equilibrium. This shows that the equilibrium is not stable in the sense of [10, 11]. For simplicity's sake, we consider only a quadratic cost function.

Let $\tilde{\mathbf{y}}$ be the symmetric equilibrium in the symmetric graph of degree D. Then, $\tilde{y}_i = \tilde{y}, \forall i$. Note that $\tilde{y} = \phi(\tilde{y})$ because it is an equilibrium. Here, we perturb all the responses by some $\epsilon > 0$

$$\phi(\vec{y} + \vec{\epsilon}) = \phi(\vec{y}) + \nabla\phi \cdot \vec{\epsilon}$$

$$\phi_i(\vec{y} + \vec{\epsilon}) = \phi_i(\vec{y}) + D\frac{\partial \phi_i}{\partial y_j}\epsilon \quad \text{for some } j \in N(i)$$

since $\frac{\partial \phi_i}{\partial y_j} = 0$ if $j \notin N(i)$ and equal otherwise. Similarly,

$$\phi_i \circ \phi(\vec{y} + \vec{\epsilon}) = \phi_i([\dots, \phi_j(\vec{y} + \vec{\epsilon}), \dots])$$
$$= y_i + D^2\left(\frac{\partial \phi_i}{\partial y_j}\right)^2\epsilon \quad \text{any } j \in N(i)$$

To show that the symmetric equilibrium is not stable, we need

$$y_i + D^2\left(\frac{-W(\tau^2 e^{-\tau\tilde{y}})}{1 + W(\tau^2 e^{-\tau\tilde{y}})}\right)^2\epsilon > y_i + \epsilon$$

$$W(\tau^2 e^{-\tau\tilde{y}}) > \frac{1}{D-1}$$

In other words, we want $\tau^2 e^{-\tau\tilde{y}} > \frac{1}{D-1}e^{\frac{1}{D-1}}$. Substituting for $\tilde{y}$ (lemma 2) and simplifying, we get that the symmetric Nash equilibrium is not stable when

$$2\ln\tau - \frac{1}{(D+1)}W(\tau^2(D+1)) > -\ln(D-1) + \frac{1}{D-1}.$$

Setting τ to be a constant (e.g., $\tau = 10$), one only needs to verify that the following holds: $W(D+1) < (D+1)(\ln(D-1) + 2\ln\tau) - \frac{D+1}{D-1}$, which is true for $D > 3$. □

5. RELATED WORK

Our contributions relate and contribute to several directions of research:

(1) Studies of online diffusion of information have previously established the importance of content produced by mass media in online diffusion. They highlight in particular that news typically reaches a large audience not directly but through a set of influencers or connectors [13, 33]. This result confirms the classical hypothesis of a two-step information flow [24], and was shown to have additional benefits, such as broadening the range of opinions seen by a user [4]. However, the dynamics of participation and influence remains elusive. For instance, relying on number of followers to judge an influencer can be misleading [14, 6] and predicting who is successful at an individual level was shown to be generally unreliable [6]. Our work takes a different starting point: We follow evidence that a large fraction of diffusion cascades occur close to a seed node [21]. Hence we focus on

identifying those who contribute in adding *original* content in the network, and how this relates to temporal characteristics of the content being exchanged. Previous studies of temporal properties of diffusion typically focused on leveraging that those are short-lived [15, 32], or on using patterns in the time series for better classification [25, 23, 34].

(2) Analysis of the private provision of public goods, or investments made by players that more generally affect the outcome of others, originally emerged to inform public policy. Its most celebrated result, the *neutrality principle* [9], states that the investment produced by a group is entirely carried by most wealthy individuals, and is insensitive to income redistribution. This, however, holds only for a *global* public good in which all players are equally affected by others, and recently was shown not to generalize beyond regular graphs [3]. The general network case was studied more recently [8, 10, 11], typically in a model assuming that a playerâĂŹs best response follows from other playerâĂŹs actions in a linear matrix form. Even for that simple case, predictions vastly differ: On the one hand, a study of small effects [11] proves that the system converges to a unique equilibrium in which all participate. On the other hand, more general cases prove that specialization is unavoidable, and that multiple equilibria can be attained [10]. Our analysis extends those results by providing the first non linear dynamics for which a similar dichotomy can be proved; in particular, it proves that a simple model of perishable public goods leads to either of these behaviors depending on the product lifespan.

(3) The role of elites in information acquisition has been studied in very different contexts such as social learning [7, 1] and opinion formation [22, 2]. Those results are different in spirit as they typically focus on aggregation of multiple contributions on the same specific topic, either within a social networks or in the presence of a kernel of experts. For that reason, they typically assume specific types of information or interactions. Our model focuses on a simpler model in which information can be produced under some exerted effort, but is free to reproduce within a given network. The work motivated similarly to ours considers a similar process in an endogenous network where players may create new links at a fixed cost [19]. It was shown that these dynamics typically lead to extreme specialization, even among *ex ante* identical players. However, Heterogeneous systems can't be analyzed in the same manner, and networks produced are typically very schematic (bi-partite). Our work proves that specialization emerges in an exogenous network, even without the reinforcing process of strategic link formation.

6. CONCLUSION

Knowledge sharing has been greatly facilitated by social network services. Increasingly, it affects businesses, political debates and public services. Yet, after years of measurements, the structure of online diffusion remains complex and was shown to vary across media and topics. Our results identify, for the first time, how the shelf life of information affects its diffusion. This leads to various types of specialization that can all be described in the unifying theory of public good.

While we empirically observe a remarkable match to the theoretical predictions on a qualitative level, we would like to point out that the current model of public good we introduce is highly idealized, especially as it assumes homogeneous cost of information acquisition. Proving that specialization occurs even in such symmetric cases is, in a sense, a worst-case result. In reality, several other factors contribute to users exerting higher effort in information acquisition including enjoyment [18], which typically varies across users depending on topics. However, our results generalize to heterogeneous perishable public goods to predict, for instance, that a single equilibrium exists whenever shelf life is sufficiently small. The qualitative effect of shelf life should also remain since our empirical observations prove it, even in a large number of very different mass media sources. We do, however, observe some amount of variance within this trend and accounting for other previously identified factors to predict span of content diffusion more accurately seems a promising direction.

Whenever public good theory allows for simple equilibrium computation, i.e. for short lived content, it also yields additional insight on how to locally or globally optimize content to encourage more participation. Ultimately, testing if those insights provide algorithms to design effective incentives to users for enhanced participation offers a way to validate those claims.

7. ACKNOWLEDGEMENTS

We would like to thank Meeyoung Cha for providing access and help on the Twitter Data used for comparison. This material is based upon work supported by the National Science Foundation under grant no. CNS-1254035 and through a Graduate Research Fellowship to Arthi Ramachandran. This research was also funded by Microsoft Research under a Graduate Fellowship.

8. REFERENCES

[1] D. Acemoglu, M. A. Dahleh, I. Lobel, and A. Ozdaglar. Bayesian learning in social networks. *The Review of Economic Studies*, 78(4):1201–1236, 2011.

[2] D. Acemoglu, A. Ozdaglar, and A. ParandehGheibi. Spread of (mis) information in social networks. *Games and Economic Behavior*, 70(2):194–227, 2010.

[3] N. Allouch. On the Private Provision of Public Goods on Networks. *Journal of Economic Theory*, forthcoming:1–34, 2015.

[4] J. An, M. Cha, K. Gummadi, and J. Crowcroft. Media landscape in Twitter: A world of new conventions and political diversity. In *Proceedings of the International Conference Weblogs and Social Media (ICWSM)*, pages 18–25, 2011.

[5] J. An, D. Quercia, and J. Crowcroft. Recommending investors for crowdfunding projects. In *WWW '14: Proceedings of the 23rd international conference on World wide web*. International World Wide Web Conferences Steering Committee, Apr. 2014.

[6] E. Bakshy, J. M. Hofman, W. A. Mason, and D. J. Watts. Everyone's an influencer: quantifying influence on twitter. In *WSDM '11: Proceedings of the fourth ACM international conference on Web search and data mining*. ACM Request Permissions, Feb. 2011.

[7] V. Bala and S. Goyal. Learning from Neighbours. *Review of Economic Studies*, 65(3):595–621, July 1998.

[8] C. Ballester, A. Calvó-Armengol, and Y. Zenou. Who's Who in Networks. Wanted: The Key Player. *Econometrica*, 74(5):1403–1417, Sept. 2006.

[9] T. Bergstrom, L. Blume, and H. Varian. On the private provision of public goods. *Journal of Public Economics*, 29(1):25–49, Feb. 1986.

[10] Y. Bramoullé and R. Kranton. Public goods in networks. *Journal of Economic Theory*, 135(1):478–494, July 2006.

[11] Y. Bramoullé, R. Kranton, and M. D'amours. Strategic interaction and networks. *American Economic Review*, 104(3):898–930, 2014.

[12] J. Byers, D. Proserpio, and G. Zervas. The Rise of the Sharing Economy: Estimating the Impact of Airbnb on the Hotel Industry. *Boston U. School of Management Research Paper (Forthcoming)*, pages 1–36, Jan. 2014.

[13] M. Cha, F. Benevenuto, H. Haddadi, and K. Gummadi. The World of Connections and Information Flow in Twitter. *Systems, Man and Cybernetics, Part A: Systems and Humans, IEEE Transactions on*, 42(4):991–998, 2012.

[14] M. Cha, H. Haddadi, F. Benevenuto, and K. Gummadi. Measuring User Influence in Twitter: The Million Follower Fallacy. In *Proceedings of the International Conference Weblogs and Social Media (ICWSM)*, 2010.

[15] M. Cha, H. Kwak, P. Rodriguez, Y.-Y. Ahn, and S. Moon. Analyzing the video popularity characteristics of large-scale user generated content systems. *IEEE/ACM Transactions on Networking (TON*, 17(5):1357–1370, 2009.

[16] B. Cici, A. Markopoulou, E. Frias-Martinez, and N. Laoutaris. Assessing the potential of ride-sharing using mobile and social data: a tale of four cities. In *Proceedings of the 2014 ACM International Joint Conference on Pervasive and Ubiquitous Computing*, pages 201–211, 2014.

[17] R. L. Cross and A. Parker. *The hidden power of social networks*. Harvard Business School Press, 2004.

[18] L. F. Feick and L. L. Price. The Market Maven: A Diffuser of Marketplace Information. *Journal of Marketing*, 51(1):83–97, Jan. 1987.

[19] A. Galeotti and S. Goyal. The law of the few. *American Economic Review*, 100(4):1468–1492, 2010.

[20] G. L. Geissler and S. W. Edison. Market Mavens' Attitudes Towards General Technology: Implications for Marketing Communications. *Journal of Marketing Communications*, 11(2):73–94, June 2005.

[21] S. Goel, D. J. Watts, and D. G. Goldstein. The structure of online diffusion networks. In *EC '12: Proceedings of the 13th ACM Conference on Electronic Commerce*, 2012.

[22] B. Golub and M. O. Jackson. Naive learning in social networks and the wisdom of crowds. *American Economic Journal: Microeconomics*, 2(1):112–149, 2010.

[23] K. Y. Kamath, J. Caverlee, K. Lee, and Z. Cheng. Spatio-temporal dynamics of online memes: a study of geo-tagged tweets. In *WWW '13: Proceedings of the 22nd international conference on World Wide Web*. International World Wide Web Conferences Steering Committee, May 2013.

[24] E. Katz. The Two-Step Flow of Communication: An Up-To-Date Report on an Hypothesis. *Public Opinion Quarterly*, 21(1):61, 1957.

[25] S. Kwon and M. Cha. Modeling Bursty Temporal Pattern of Rumors. In *Proceedings of the International Conference Weblogs and Social Media (ICWSM)*, 2014.

[26] P. Lazarsfeld, B. Berelson, and H. Gaudet. *The peoples choice: how the voter makes up his mind in a presidential campaign.* Columbia University Press, 1948.

[27] Y. Liu, C. Kliman-Silver, R. Bell, B. Krishnamurthy, and A. Mislove. Measurement and analysis of osn ad auctions. *COSN '14: Proceedings of the 2nd ACM conference on Online social networks*, pages 139–150, 2014.

[28] M. O. Lorenz. Methods of measuring the concentration of wealth. *Publications of the American Statistical Association*, 9(70):209–219, 1905.

[29] A. May, A. Chaintreau, N. Korula, and S. Lattanzi. Filter & Follow: How Social Media Foster Content Curation. In *SIGMETRICS '14: Proceedings of the ACM International conference on Measurement and modeling of computer systems*, pages 43–55, New York, New York, USA, 2014. ACM Press.

[30] K. Olmstead, A. Mitchell, and T. Rosenstiel. *Navigating News Online: Where people go, how they get there, and what lures them away.* Pew Research Center's Project for Excellence, 2011.

[31] A. Ramachandran and A. Chaintreau. Who contributes to the knowledge sharing economy? 2015.

[32] M. G. Rodriguez, D. Balduzzi, and B. Schölkopf. Uncovering the temporal dynamics of diffusion networks. In *Proceedings of ICML*, 2011.

[33] S. Wu, J. M. Hofman, W. A. Mason, and D. J. Watts. Who says what to whom on twitter. In *WWW '11: Proceedings of the 20th international conference on World wide web.* ACM Request Permissions, Mar. 2011.

[34] J. Yang and J. Leskovec. Patterns of temporal variation in online media. In *WSDM '11: Proceedings of the fourth ACM international conference on Web search and data mining.* ACM Request Permissions, Feb. 2011.

Social Visibility and the Gifting of Digital Goods

Jameson K. M. Watts
Atkinson Graduate School of
Management
Willamette University
jwatts@willamette.edu

Yotam Shmargad
School of Information
University of Arizona
yotam@email.arizona.edu

ABSTRACT

One of the defining features of online social networks is that users' actions are visible to other users. In this paper, we argue that such social visibility has a detrimental effect on users' willingness to gift digital goods. The gift giving process often generates substantial anxiety, and social visibility exacerbates this anxiety to the point that it can deter gifting altogether. To study the effect of social visibility on the decision to gift, we analyze a unique dataset from a large online social network that offers users the option of buying a digital gifting service. We find that purchase rates of the service increased with the number of social ties that users kept on the network, but decreased with the extent to which those ties were tied to each other. We argue that the latter effect is due to the fact that, when a user's ties are tied themselves, any gift sent between the user and one tie is visible to their mutual contacts. This argument is bolstered by a stronger negative effect of social visibility for users with larger, less intimate, and categorically diverse networks.

Categories and Subject Descriptors

K.4.1 [**Computing Milieux**]: Computers and Society—*Privacy*; J.4 [**Social and Behavioral Sciences**]: Sociology

Keywords

Privacy, Social Networks, Social Risk, Digital Gifts

1. INTRODUCTION

In August 2014, Facebook shut down a service called Gifts, which allowed users to send digital gift cards to one another over its online social network. The move surprised Wall Street investors and online commentators alike, who only two years earlier had heralded the service as a potential threat to the dominance of the popular online retailer Amazon.[1] Because the gift cards that Facebook sold were digi-

[1] Facebook is Shutting Down Gifts to Focus on its Buy Button and Commerce Platform, TechCrunch, July 2014

COSN'15, November 2–3, 2015, Palo Alto, California, USA.
ⓒ 2015 ACM. ISBN 978-1-4503-3951-3/15/11 ...$15.00.
DOI: http://dx.doi.org/10.1145/2817946.2817966.

tal, not physical, users did not need to know a gift receiver's home address to send a gift. Moreover, since the production and distribution of digital goods take little money or time [17], Facebook's service was ideal for last minute gifting. So why was it unsuccessful?

One of the defining features of online social networks is that users' actions are visible to other users [41, 36]. Rhue and Sundararajan [27] show that such social visibility can alter users' purchasing decisions and, in particular, makes users conform to others' expectations. Of course, gifts are inherently socially visible to the extent that receivers see their gifts. However, in an online social network there is an additional layer of social visibility not often present in the offline world — gifts sent between two users are visible to any mutual contacts they share. The degree to which a gift conforms to the expectations of these observers constitutes what Yadav et al. [41] refer to as "social risk." Given that there is already substantial anxiety surrounding the gifting process [33, 40], we argue that such "third-party" social visibility increases social risk, which can the exacerbate anxiety and deter users from gifting through online social networks altogether.

If the presence of third-parties can deter gift exchange, then services like Facebook Gifts will be less successful in networks where users' friends are friends with each other. When users' friends are friends themselves, gifts sent to one friend will be visible to other friends. On the other hand, in networks where users' friends are not friends, gifts are only visible to their intended recipients, and gifting services should be more successful. In fact, in 2008, Facebook introduced a feature called People You May Know, which encouraged users to form connections with friends of their existing friends.[2] While the feature may have increased the number of connections users had on Facebook, it likely also increased the tendency for users' connections to be connected to each other. The feature may thus have had the unintended effect of increasing third-party social visibility on Facebook, rendering the gifting service unappealing from the moment it launched.

To study how social visibility affects the gifting of digital goods, we analyze data from a large online social network that sells a service which lets users send electronic greeting cards (eCards) to one another. We find that purchase rates of the service increased with the number and strength of ties users kept on the network, but decreased with the extent to which those ties were connected to each other. Moreover, this negative effect of third-party social visibility

[2] People You May Know, Facebook, May 2008

was stronger for users with larger, less intimate, and categorically diverse social networks.

2. THEORETICAL DEVELOPMENT

The behavior of individuals under surveillance, whether social (like users' friends on Facebook) or institutional (like Facebook the company or the NSA) is gaining in popularity as a topic for scholarly attention. For instance, Raynes-Goldie [25] argues that Facebook users are more concerned about privacy from their connections than from Facebook itself or affiliated businesses. Brandtzæg et al. [3] find that Facebook users with many friends feel more pressure to conform when posting information on the platform. Indeed, Rhue and Sundararajan [27] show that users of a social shopping website sometimes alter their buying habits in order to conform to comments received on previous purchases.

Social visibility can also have implications for how users interact with each other online. Gross and Acquisti [11] argue that online social networks engender new kinds of intimacy. This is evidenced by the fact that users regularly share personal information broadly and with many people. Lambert [16] refers to this new kind of intimacy as "group intimacy," and suggests that it may be replacing traditional versions of intimacy—those which are more interpersonal in nature. Geser [9] goes further and suggests that intimacy is completely destroyed in most online settings because individuals are discouraged from revealing information privately to their close social ties. As Gerstein [8] suggests, it is precisely these private disclosures of information that separate intimate relationships from those of a more casual nature.

We follow Wilson et al. [39] and others by taking the view that users of online social networks typically consider the privacy of an interaction when choosing to disclose information. Dinev and Hart [7] refer to this consideration in information exchange as a "privacy calculus." We use their framework in the context of gift giving, and show how social network theory helps to quantify the potential threats to privacy that result from digital gift exchange. We believe that gift exchange is a natural setting to study privacy concerns because, as others have pointed out, gift giving is often the subject of social scrutiny [32, 40].

We present our conceptual model in Figure 1. In this model, we look at the effects of social visibility on the adoption timing of a service that lets members of an online social network send eCards to one another. Social visibility constitutes the potential that an interaction between two individuals (i.e. an eCard) is observed by a third-party. Adoption is defined as a new purchase of the eCard service. The primary focus of our model is on social visibility. However the effect of social visibility on eCard adoption depends on an individual's perception of social risk [41, 40]. The magnitude of this social risk may depend on characteristics of those observing the interaction. Thus, we explore the moderating effects of audience size, type, and diversity. Finally, we control for a number of alternate explanations such as the influence of prior adopters as well as various user demographics.

2.1 Gift Giving Under Surveillance

The anticipation that a gift will be ill-received can generate substantial anxiety for the giver [20, 33, 40]. Researchers have identified two primary sources for this anxiety. The first relates to the uncertainty that a giver may have with regards to the recipient's preferences. When givers are un-

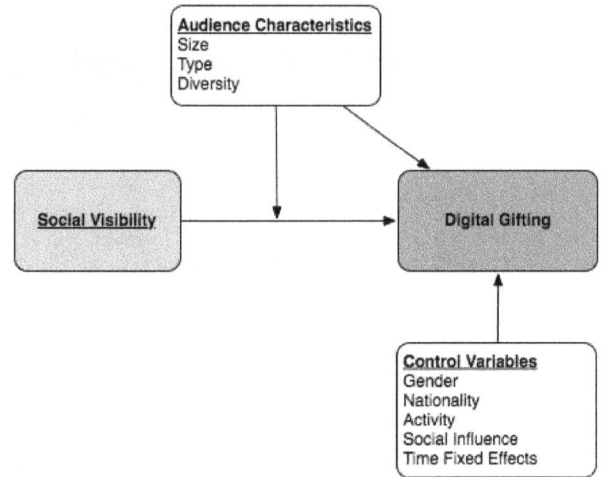

Figure 1: Conceptual model.

sure of these preferences, they tend to experience higher levels of anxiety in the gift selection process [21]. The second source of anxiety is more social in nature. Individuals view gifts as tools to manage impression, and givers get anxious when they are concerned about how they will be evaluated by others who observe their gifting behavior [33, 40]. It is from this latter source of anxiety—that which stems from an individual's social context—that we construct our hypotheses.

One of the defining features of online social networks is that users' actions are visible to other users. As a result, users are attuned to the potential for social surveillance—the monitoring of one's behaviors by other users [3]. For example, Rhue and Sundararajan [27] show that users alter their online purchasing behaviors in response to feedback from other users. Thus, we suggest that the anxiety surrounding online gift exchange will increase when one's gifting behaviors are socially visible to other users.

To capture the extent to which a user's gifting behavior will be visible to other users, we borrow a concept from the social networks literature known as clustering. Clustering measures the extent to which an individual's social ties are themselves also tied. In practice, the concept is sometimes referred to as redundancy by cohesion [5] or the clustering coefficient [37]. When a user's social ties are themselves tied, then any gifts that the user sends to one tie will be visible to their mutual contacts. On the other hand, when a user's ties do not know each other, then gifts will only be visible to their intended recipient. Clustering thus captures the potential for third-party social visibility. For this reason, we hypothesize:

HYPOTHESIS 1. *The time to adoption of a digital gifting service increases with the level of clustering in an individual's online social network.*

2.2 Audience Characteristics

2.2.1 Diversity

The degree to which social visibility poses a social risk is often a function of observer characteristics (Rogers 2002). This is especially true if a potential interaction contains content that is either controversial or has the potential for misinterpretation (Chen and Berger 2013). Often the intent of an interaction must be understood within the context of prior interactions or shared cultural understandings. A third-party observer can misinterpret the meaning of an interaction if that observer is not privy to the context—a communication issue that Fleming et al. (1990) term the 'multiple-audience problem'.

In the present context, some users have online social networks that are fairly homogenous, while others have networks comprised of individuals with varying characteristics. In a broad sense, we expect that individuals who share certain demographic characteristics, are more likely to interpret the meaning of an eCard in the same way. In contrast, a diverse set of individuals may interpret the meaning of an eCard in very different ways. Thus, users with the same level of social visibility, will experience more social risk if their online social network is diverse on some characteristic. We test this argument by calculating the diversity of a user's online social network according to gender, culture and tie type and hypothesize that:

HYPOTHESIS 2. *The effect of clustering on time to adoption of a digital gifting service increases with the level of a) gender b) cultural and c) tie type diversity in an individual's online social network.*

2.2.2 Size

For a given level of clustering, social visibility should be more salient to users with larger networks than smaller ones. This is due to the fact that large networks contain more individuals that can potentially monitor one's gifting behavior. With a large social network, individuals are unlikely to have close relationships with all of their social ties and may find it more difficult to predict the response of every observer of an interaction. Moreover, large social networks make it more likely that audience members differ across a variety of characteristics. Thus, audience size may also be capturing a level of unobservable diversity. Thus we predict that the negative effect of clustering will be greater for individuals that keep larger networks.

HYPOTHESIS 3. *The effect of clustering on time to adoption of a digital gifting service increases with the size of an individual's online social network.*

2.2.3 Intimacy

Individuals often maintain several distinct social groups. For example, social ties in a business setting may have little overlap with ties in a family or friendship setting. Thus, the effect of clustering on the value of a digital gifting service could vary across these distinct groups. Wooten [40] proposes a mechanism driving social anxiety based on the lack of parameters established prior to gift exchange. For social groups that consist of more personal (or intimate) ties, these parameters (rules) may be tacitly agreed upon or even openly discussed. For social groups that consist of less intimate ties, the parameters of gift exchange may be less obvious. Indeed, Sherry et al. [33] provide some empirical evidence that individuals are more anxious about exchanging gifts with relative strangers than they are giving gifts to closer friends and family. While we expect that additional social ties will decrease the time to adoption in general (because there are more individuals with whom one can

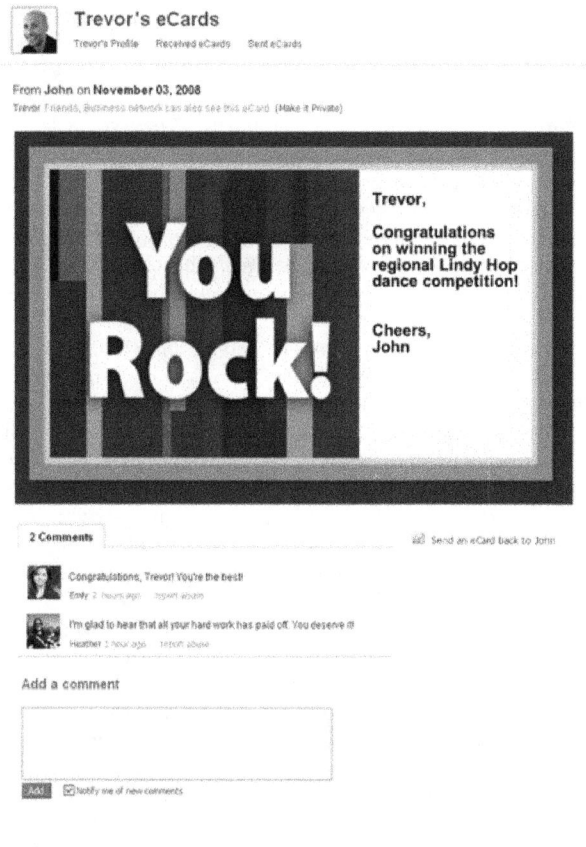

Figure 2: An example of an eCard displayed on a recipient's profile page. Senders and recipients had the option of making these cards private, though the default was to make them public.

exchange eCards), we expect the effect to be greater with increases in more intimate connections. We test this argument by looking at the number of family, friend and business ties in an individuals online social network and hypothesize that:

HYPOTHESIS 4. *Family and friendship ties decrease the time to adoption of a digital gifting service more than business ties.*

If individuals are less comfortable giving gifts to relative strangers, they are likely to also feel less comfortable exchanging gifts in the *presence* of strangers. We test this argument by looking at the effect of clustering in distinct networks comprised of only family, friend or business ties and hypothesize that:

HYPOTHESIS 5. *The time to adoption of a digital gifting service increases more with the level of clustering in an individual's business network than with the level of clustering in an individual's family or friend network.*

3. EMPIRICAL SETTING

3.1 Overview

The dataset that we analyze in this paper originates from a California-based company that launched an email address book management service in 2002. Users of the service could update their contact information, and these updates were then automatically pushed to their contacts' email address books. However, when online social networks like Facebook and LinkedIn started gaining popularity a few years later, the company decided to launch an online social network of its own.

The company launched its social network in 2007. The network allowed users to maintain an online profile, connect with other users, and share messages, photos, videos, and other content with their connections. A unique feature of the network is that it required users to specify the types of connections they had with other users. Connections could be specified as family, friend, business, or any combination of these types, and only the types that were mutually agreed upon by both users were associated with a connection on the network. This feature made it easier for users to share content with each group separately.

We analyze the purchases of a digital gifting service provided by this online social network, which let users send electronic greeting cards (eCards) to their connections. The service cost users $12.95 for a one-year subscription, and the price did not change during the period under investigation. While the service was occasionally promoted to all users of the platform, it was not targeted towards any specific group.

Figure 2 shows an eCard exchange between two users of the online social network. In general, users could choose to make eCards private, which meant that only the sender and receiver were able to see them. However, eCards where public by default, and few users opted to make them private. In addition to being displayed on the receiverâĂŹs profile page, eCards were also visible in the content streams of users who had connections to both the sender and receiver. Thus, users that were not directly involved in an exchange could see and even comment on the eCard.

3.2 Data

Social networks are usually bounded artificially. As researchers, we tend to define what constitues ties between individuals and largely ignore the set of interactions that occur outside of our chosen context. This is often a matter of practical necessity. For example, Nitzan and Libai [22] study a social network based on the occurrence of millions of phone calls between individuals. In their context, it is not feasible to document the set of face to face interactions that may have occurred in concert with the phone communication. In our study, we avoid this concern by focusing on a digital gifting service that requires both givers and recipients to be users of the online social network. As such, the value of the service can be directly linked to the existence of social ties in the online social network, and not to ties by some other definition.

To estimate the effects of users' social network characteristics on purchase of the company's eCard service, we construct a set of network measures for each user by analyzing her ties on the online social network. Our data start in 2007, when the company's social network launched, and ends in September of 2009. We sample the network of connections in this dataset at 12 points in time (i.e. every two months), and only consider users that, at every time point, had at least two ties. This requirement ensures that users' clustering measures are well-defined throughout the timespan of our study.

The network was growing rapidly during the period of our study, and by the end of the two-year window there were 3,702,474 users that met our criteria for inclusion and a total 38,891,294 ties. To calculate network measures, we analyzed all available 6,711,964 users and 39,116,763 ties. In the first time period, approximately 2.25% of all users had a subscription to the eCard service. That number dropped to approximately 1% by the final time period. Table 1 breaks down the number of users, ties, and subscriptions by time period.

Table 1: Usage by time period

Time Period	Users	Ties	Subscribers
11/2007	67,915	432,721	1,454
01/2008	540,850	4,108,562	6,734
03/2008	866,771	6,923,045	9,600
05/2008	1,194,273	9,702,064	11,985
07/2008	1,569,877	12,537,632	15,752
09/2008	2,180,914	19,005,294	21,184
11/2008	2,664,137	24,868,597	25,541
01/2009	2,937,110	28,791,961	29,027
03/2009	3,203,440	32,377,461	31,515
05/2009	3,442,508	35,475,822	33,389
07/2009	3,588,735	37,319,627	33,460
09/2009	3,702,474	38,891,294	32,250

Due to the size of our dataset, it was not feasible to estimate the parameters using the entire population of users. We therefore employed a sampling technique, in which we selected approximately 100,000 – 300,000 users at random and only included their records in our estimations. We used at total of 10 such samples to estimate our models, and results were qualitatively similar across these samples.

4. METHODOLOGY

Scholars regularly use hazard models to examine the duration prior to some event [18, 22, 28]. In our context, the event of interest is the purchase of the company's eCard service. The hazard specification has several advantages over standard regression methods like ordinary least squares and logistic regression. For one, it can handle data that are right-censored, which allows us to include users who do not adopt by the end of our sampling window. Another advantage is that hazard models can capture both time-varying and time-constant independent variables. This allows us to include social network measures that changed from period to period, as well as demographic variables (e.g. gender and nationality), which did not. We address left-censoring by using the date a user joined the social network to define the point at which they become at risk of adoption.

Following Risselada et al. [28], Polo et al. [23] and others, we specify the baseline hazard function using the complementary log-log parametric form. This approach approximates an underlying continuous-time process given data that are grouped into discrete time intervals (e.g. every two months). In this approach, the hazard of user i with individual characteristics x_{it} of purchasing an eCard subscription at time t can be expressed as:

$$h_i(t) = 1 - exp[-exp(\beta_0 + \beta^{'} x_{it})], \quad (1)$$

where $\beta^{'}$ captures the effects of the variables in the vector x_{it} on the hazard rate.

In the standard hazard specification, one assumes that all users will, eventually, experience the event of interest. In our context, actual purchase rates are quite low, which highlights the possibility that many users are never actually 'at risk' of adoption [23, 31]. Digital gifting represents an additional layer of technological complexity above and beyond routine use of the online social network, and for technologically complex products, there is often a significant group of consumers who will resist adoption [24].

To account for the possibility that some users will never purchase the eCard service (i.e. have zero probability of adoption), we estimate both the adoption probability and adoption timing simultaneously. This approach is often referred to as as a 'split-population' hazard model [30, 13], because it weighs the likelihood of each observation by the probability of belonging to the 'at risk' population to begin with. In this way the survival analysis is applied only to the users who are predicted to adopt in the future.

Following the notation of Jenkins [13], we define an indicator A of whether a user eventually adopts or not, where $A = 1$ means eventual adoption, and $A = 0$ means never adopt (i.e. the event of interest never occurs). Using this indicator, we can say that $prob(A = 1) = 1 - c$ (the eventual adopter probability) and $prob(A = 0) = c$ (the never adopter probability). For those with an adoption observed during a given time interval, the contribution to the likelihood is $(1 - c) \times$ (probability of no adoption to end of the previous time interval) $\times$ (probability of the event in the given interval). Censored observations consist of those where $A = 0$ plus those still at risk but not yet observed to adopt. Thus, the contribution to the likelihood from a censored survival time is $c + (1 - c) \times$ (probability of survival to end of the given time interval).

Taken together, we can express the (log)likelihood contribution for person i with a survival time of t periods as:

$$ln(L_i) = d_i \times ln[(1 - c) \times (h_{it}) \times (S_{it-1})]$$
$$+ (1 - d_i) \times ln[c + (1 - c) \times S_{it}],$$

where S_{it} is the discrete-time survivor function and d_i is a censoring indicator that equals 1 if adoption is observed in the current time period and 0 otherwise. Parameters for the hazard portion are estimated along with a value for c using the maximum likelihood methods available in Stata.

4.1 Variables

We extend the notation in Shmargad [34], which accommodates social networks with multiple relation types and multiple time periods. We denote a social network of type $r \in \{Family, Friend, Business\}$ at time $t \in \{1, ..., 12\}$ by $G_t^r(V_t, E_t^r)$. Here, V_t is the set of active users and E_t^r is the set of type r relations among them at time t. We define the set of user i's type r ties at time t as $N_{it}^r = \{j | j \in V_t \text{ and } (i, j) \in E_t^r\}$. We then define $N_{it} = N_{it}^{Family} \cup N_{it}^{Friend} \cup N_{it}^{Business}$ and $E_t = E_t^{Family} \cup E_t^{Friend} \cup E_t^{Business}$, which capture the set of user i's ties and all of the ties in the network, respectively, at time t. To construct variables based on a user's social ties, we also define the following indicator for any two users $i, j \in V_t$,

$$e_{ijt} = \begin{cases} 1 & \text{if} (i, j) \in E_t \\ 0 & \text{otherwise.} \end{cases}$$

4.1.1 Network size

In the social networks literature, degree is simply a count of the number of direct ties, or *neighbors*, an individual keeps. In most naturally occurring social networks, the number of ties individuals keep is distributed according to a power law [see e.g. 2, 38]. To adjust for this skew, we take the natural log of each user's degree. Formally, we define the size of a user's network as $CON_{it} = ln(\|N_{it}\|)$. We also generate variables that capture the size of each type of network (i.e. family, friend, or business), and denote them by CON_{it}^{FA}, CON_{it}^{FR}, and CON_{it}^{BU}, respectively.

4.1.2 Clustering

We operationalize the extent of social visibility in a user's network by calculating their clustering coefficient, which is the number of ties between a user's neighbors divided by the number of possible ties [37]. The clustering coefficient for user i at time t is thus defined as

$$CLS_{it} = \sum_{i \neq j \in N_{it}} e_{ijt} / \sum_{i \neq j \in N_{it}} 1.$$

We also generate this measure for each relation type (i.e. family, friend, or business) and denote these variables by CLS_{it}^{FA}, CLS_{it}^{FR}, and CLS_{it}^{BU}, respectively.

4.1.3 Diversity

We operationalize three diversity measures based on the composition of an individual's network by gender, nationality and tie type. Gender is a self-reported measure that takes on a value of 0 for male and 1 for female. Nationality indicators were created from an individual's self-reported country of origin; however, only the top 10 countries by absolute membership were used in the diversity score. All other countries were lumped together. Tie types were family, friend or business as described above. Our measure uses the Herfindahl index [12, 10], defined as

$$H = 1 - \sum_{j=1}^{d} p_j^2,$$

which is maximized when the probability of randomly selecting two items of the same type at random is minimized. For example, an individual would have a high tie-type diversity score if their network consisted of an equal number of family, friend and business ties. A low diversity score would occur if that individual's network consisted of only business ties.

4.1.4 Control variables

To account for the possibility of social influence in the adoption process [e.g. 28], we include a count of the number of individuals in N_{it} that have already adopted an eCard subscription. Because users send eCards to one another, the existence of prior adopters in a user's social network could indicate additional exposure to the product or a social influence effect. A user's level of activity on the social network could also affect their purchase likelihood. We control for this by including a variable that measures the amount of time since the user last created a tie on the network. Users that have not formed connections in a long time may have lost interest in the online social network altogether.

In addition to these exposure and activity effects, purchase could also depend on demographic and cultural characteristics. For example, females are generally expected to play a larger role in gift exchange [1]. To account for this possibility, we include a dummy variable indicating the user's gender, along with variables that capture a user's age and country of origin. We found no major differences with the inclusion of dummy variables for each of the 229 countries in our sample, and instead use a dummy variable to indicate whether or not users reside in the US.

Finally, we include time period fixed-effects (i.e. monthly dummy variables) to capture factors that affected all users, like mass-media advertising by the firm or its competitors and the popularity of this type of service in the market. Table 2 summarizes our variables and their operationalizations.

Table 2: Summary of Variables

Variable	Description	Formula
$t_2, ..., t_{12}$	Dummy variables indicating the month of the observation period	
CON_{it}	Natural log of count of user's social ties	$ln(\sum_{i \neq j \in N_{it}} e_{ij})$
CLS_{it}	% of actual ties out of all possible between neighbors	$\frac{\sum_{i \neq j \in N_{it}} e_{ij}}{\sum_{i \neq j \in N_{it}} 1}$
DIV_{it}	Diversity score by gender, tie type and nationality for a user's ego network	$H = 1 - \sum_{j=1}^{d} p_j^2$
EXP_{it}	# of neighbors who are subscribers at time t	
ACT_{it}	Negative of time in days since last tie was formed (less negative = more active)	
AGE_{it}	Age in years	
SEX_i	Sex of user (0=male, 1=female)	
US_i	Country (1=USA, 0=other)	

5. RESULTS

5.1 Main effects

From the nearly seven million users in our dataset, we constructed a random sample of 300,000 to estimate the parameters in our hazard model. Of these, 168,801 users had at least two ties, which was required in order to calculate the clustering coefficient. Those with fewer than two connections were dropped from the sample, and were likely users of the company's address book service but not the online social network. There were no other missing variables. Across our two year time window, these users constituted 1,007,915 observations and 1,593 purchases of the eCard service.

Table 3 presents the estimation results for Model 1 (control variables only), Model 2 (main effects) and Model 3 (interaction of network size and clustering). The direction of the estimates from Model 1 are as expected. The hazard of adoption increased with exposure to prior adopters and higher activity levels, and was higher for females and residents of the US. We see that each adopting neighbor is

Table 3: Hazard of eCard Subscription

	(1) Controls	(2) Main Effects	(3) CON x CLS
CON		1.530***	1.663***
		(0.0616)	(0.0774)
CLS		0.331***	0.798
		(0.0529)	(0.223)
$CONxCLS$			0.629***
			(0.0808)
EXP	1.418***	1.193***	1.172***
	(0.0337)	(0.0330)	(0.0330)
ACT	1.006***	1.004***	1.004***
	(0.000366)	(0.000392)	(0.000394)
AGE	1.005***	1.011***	1.011***
	(0.000922)	(0.00105)	(0.00106)
SEX	1.248***	1.404***	1.408***
	(0.0694)	(0.0832)	(0.0837)
US	1.968***	2.054***	2.049***
	(0.121)	(0.133)	(0.133)
Observations	1007915	1007915	1007915
AIC	22732.1	22451.5	22440.7
BIC	22933.1	22676.1	22677.2

Exp. coefficients; Standard errors in parentheses
$^+ p < 0.1$, $^* p < 0.05$, $^{**} p < 0.01$, $^{***} p < 0.001$

associated with an increase of 41.8% in the focal user's hazard of adoption; however this is attenuated to 19.3% once total network size is accounted for. This value is inline with social influence effects reported in other studies of adoption or defection [see e.g. 22].

In Model 2, we also added the measures of network size and clustering. This increased the fit of our model substantially, according to both the Akaike Information Criterion (AIC) and the Bayesian Information Criterion (BIC). Moreover, the parameter estimate of our clustering variable indicates that social visibility hads a significant and negative effect on eCard purchase. This provides support for hypothesis 1.

In Model 3, we introduce an interaction between network size and clustering, which is statistically significant and in the direction predicted. This means that marginal increases in clustering have a stronger negative effect on eCard purchase for users with larger networks, which provides support for hypothesis 3. We depict this relationship graphically in Figure 3. This result also rules out an important alternative explanation for our results—that the negative effect of clustering on eCard subscriptions is driven by new users joining, who are both unaware of the eCard service and whose networks are small and thus highly clustered.

Table 4 Model 1 shows parameter estimates for the effects of the sizes of users' family, friend, and business networks. For example, the estimate of the coefficient for the variable CON^{FA} represents the effect of increases in the size of a user's family network. From the estimated values, it is clear that the hazard of eCard subscription increased most with the size of a users' family and friend networks, and little with increases in the size of users' business networks. If we assume that, in general, family and friend ties are more intimate than business ties, then these results provide support for hypothesis 4.

Table 4 Model 2 shows parameter estimates for interactions of clustering with our three diversity measures. While the interaction is statistically significant for both gender diversity and tie type diversity, it is not significant for the di-

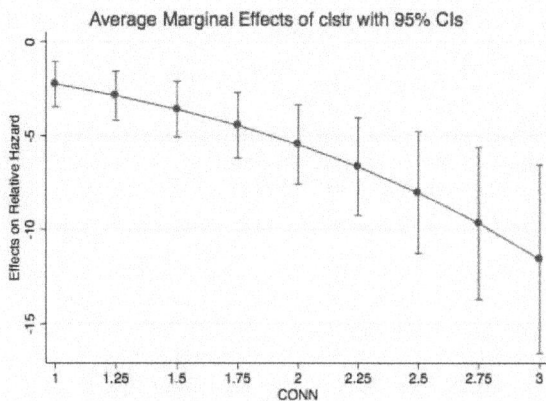

Figure 3: Marginal effects of clustering at different levels of connectivity

Table 4: Scaled Clustering Variables

	(1) $CLSTR^{FA}$	(2) $CLSTR^{FR}$	(3) $CLSTR^{BU}$
CON^{FA}	2.135***		
	(0.381)		
CON^{FR}		2.021***	
		(0.104)	
CON^{BU}			1.338***
			(0.0588)
CLS^{FA}	1.170		
	(0.532)		
CLS^{FR}		1.061	
		(0.443)	
CLS^{BU}			1.373
			(0.557)
$CON^{FA}xCLS^{FA}$	0.611		
	(0.201)		
$CON^{FA}xCLS^{FR}$		0.503**	
		(0.123)	
$CON^{FA}xCLS^{BU}$			0.419***
			(0.0824)
EXP	1.311***	1.236***	1.277***
	(0.0479)	(0.0325)	(0.0362)
ACT	1.006***	1.005***	1.006***
	(0.000652)	(0.000437)	(0.000482)
AGE	1.005**	1.010***	1.009***
	(0.00167)	(0.00110)	(0.00118)
SEX	1.160	1.317***	1.420***
	(0.112)	(0.0838)	(0.0942)
US	1.846***	1.770***	1.998***
	(0.219)	(0.123)	(0.141)
Observations	212486	721712	737247
AIC	7266.2	18898.3	17632.9
BIC	7471.5	19128.1	17863.1

Exp. coefficients; Standard errors in parentheses
$^{+}$ $p < 0.1$, * $p < 0.05$, ** $p < 0.01$, *** $p < 0.001$

versity measure calculated using nationality. This provides support for hypothesis 2a and 2c.

As we noted above, Table 3 Model 3 confirms that the effect of clustering depends on network size. This presents a challenge when trying to compare parameter estimates for clustering within the different network types, which we know differ in size. For example, users in our sample have, on average, just one family tie, but over thirteen business ties. Thus, a more negative effect of clustering in the business network could be due to the fact that business ties are impersonal, or that business networks are generally larger. To address this, we compare the *rates* at which the negative effect of clustering increases as these networks grow, rather than simply the negative effect of the clustering coefficients themselves. In practice, this means that we compare the interactions between network size and clustering for each network type. Table 4 reports the results of this analysis.

While the parameter estimate for the interaction in the family network is not statistically significant (Model 1), it is close ($z = -1.3$) and is strongly significant when we use a larger sample. However, the important feature is that the negative effect of clustering increases as we move from the family to the friendship network, and from the friendship to the business network (i.e. as ties become less personal). As we discussed above, this effect of clustering is independent of network size, and thus provides support for hypothesis 5.

5.2 Robustness

To account for potential unobserved heterogeneity that we could not capture with the demographic variables, we estimate a parametric hazard model with an additional random intercept (or frailty term) to account for the potential effects of omitted variables [28, 35]. Table 5 shows the results of this estimation. Model 1 confirms that all of the hypothesized main effects still hold. In fact, the negative effect of clustering is stronger and the effect of increased connectivity is weaker once we account for unobserved heterogeneity. Model 2 shows that the interaction we predicted in hypothesis 5 also holds under this specification. Though not shown here, we also ran all other models using the new specification, and find that the results are qualitatively the same.

Finally, given that we ran our models on a random sample of users, and not on the entire population, it is possible that our results could be caused by biases introduced by our sampling method. For example, the number of users increased rapidly during the two years in our study. Thus, a purely random sample of users will draw more heavily from users that joined later. To account for this potential bias, we resampled the data by choosing twelve 10,000 user random samples that were stratified on when users joined the network. The results of our model with this sample are also displayed in Table 5. Model 3 confirms that the hypothesized effects are in the predicted directions.

6. DISCUSSION

In this paper, we test how the presence of social visibility influences the decision to gift through online social networks. We analyze a novel dataset from a large online social network that offers users the option of buying a service that lets them send electronic greeting cards (eCards) to other users. We find that purchase rates of the service increased with the number and strength of the ties that users kept, but de-

Table 5: Robustness

	(1) Main Frailty	(2) Inter. Frailty	(3) Stratified
CON	1.433***	1.591***	1.719***
	(0.0869)	(0.108)	(0.0874)
CLS	0.114***	0.430+	0.291***
	(0.0323)	(0.204)	(0.0834)
CON x CLS		0.503**	
		(0.106)	
EXP	1.096***	1.084**	1.002
	(0.0266)	(0.0269)	(0.0167)
ACT	1.006***	1.006***	1.004***
	(0.000506)	(0.000509)	(0.000757)
AGE	1.036***	1.036***	1.004**
	(0.00189)	(0.00189)	(0.00158)
SEX	2.025***	2.037***	1.504***
	(0.210)	(0.211)	(0.125)
US	3.993***	3.937***	1.771***
	(0.456)	(0.449)	(0.161)
Observations	1007915	1007915	360956
AIC	18757.0	18748.6	13181.2
BIC	18993.4	18996.9	13364.7

Exp. coefficients; Standard errors in parentheses
$^+$ $p < 0.1$, * $p < 0.05$, ** $p < 0.01$, *** $p < 0.001$

creased with clusteringExp.-the extent to which users' ties were tied themselves. We argue that social visibility is more prominent in networks that are highly clustered, because gifts sent from a user to one tie can be monitored by any mutual contact they share. Given the well-documented anxieties surrounding the gifting process, such social monitoring can discourage users from gifting digital goods altogether.

The negative effect of clustering we uncover is relatively strong compared to the effects of other variables. After controlling for a variety of individual and environmental factors, we find that the hazard of adoption increases by 53% for every 1 point increase in network size. Since we operationalized network size as the natural log of the number of ties in a user's network, a one point increase here is actually equivalent to a 270% increase in the number of ties. Thus, a 10% increase in the size of an individual's network only increases the hazard of subscription by 1.9% on average. In contrast, the hazard rate *decreases* by 6.7% for every additional 10% of clustering in a user's network and the number is higher for individuals with relatively large social networks.

A key question facing managers of large online social networks is what types of social ties to promote. Companies like Facebook and OkCupid regularly make feature changes that affect the ways in which their users interact with one another [14, 29]. For example, Facebook introduced their PYMK feature in 2008. Since that time, Facebook has twice tried and failed to implement a revenue-generating gifting service for its users [6]. To be successful, managers of products and services that rely on large social networks will have to think more strategically about how they recommend users to connect to each other. Importantly, companies could also benefit from giving users better control over whether or not their online activity is visible to other users. For example, the company in our study allowed users to send eCards in private, but this was not the default option. By making private gifting the default option, the company may have been able to mitigate some of the concerns around social monitoring.

Often, product managers are provided with incentives to increase the number of connections users have in order to encourage more engagement with online social networks. For many of these companies, greater engagement means higher revenue from advertising dollars. However, there can be hidden costs that depend on the *type* of connectivity that drives engagement. For example, in our context, increases in clustering had a large negative impact on eCard adoption when the increases were in users' business networks, but not in their friendship networks. This is because there is more anxiety associated with giving gifts to impersonal social ties, and likely also with giving gifts *in the presence* of these ties. The implication of this finding is that product managers should encourage connections to friends of friends, but not to business ties of business ties.

More generally, our findings relate to the broader issue of practicing intimacy in an increasingly public, online world. Social psychologists have long argued that individuals require private disclosures of information in order to build meaningful relationships with those around them [26, 19]. The public nature of interactions on Facebook could be on of the reasons why the platform is increasingly associated with loneliness and decreases in well-being [4, 15]. This has also created a void which is quickly being filled by competitors like Snapchat and Sup, which give users more privacy in their interactions. If large online social networks and the services that rely on them are to succeed over the long term, managers need to be more strategic about the types of interactions they promote.

References

[1] C. S. Areni, P. Kiecker, and K. M. Palan. Is it better to give than to receive? exploring gender differences in the meaning of memorable gifts. *Psychology and Marketing*, 15(1):81–109, 1998.

[2] A. L. Barabási and R. Albert. Emergence of scaling in random networks. *Science*, 286(5439):509–512, 1999.

[3] P. B. Brandtzæg, M. Lüders, and J. H. Skjetne. Too many facebook "friends"? content sharing and sociability versus the need for privacy in social network sites. *Intl. Journal of Human-Computer Interaction*, 26(11-12):1006–1030, 2010.

[4] M. Burke, C. Marlow, and T. Lento. Social network activity and social well-being. In *Proceedings of the SIGCHI Conference on Human Factors in Computing Systems*, pages 1909–1912. ACM, 2010.

[5] R. S. Burt. *Structural holes: The social structure of competition.* Harvard University Press, 1992.

[6] J. Constine. Facebook is shutting down gifts to focus on its buy button and commerce platform, 07/29/2014 2014.

[7] T. Dinev and P. Hart. An extended privacy calculus model for e-commerce transactions. *Information Systems Research*, 17(1):61–80, 2006.

[8] R. S. Gerstein. Intimacy and privacy. *Ethics*, pages 76–81, 1978.

[9] H. Geser. Exhibited in the global digital cage: on the functions and consequences of social network sites in complex societies. 2008.

[10] J. P. Gibbs and W. T. Martin. Urbanization, technology, and the division of labor: International patterns. *American Sociological Review*, pages 667–677, 1962.

[11] R. Gross and A. Acquisti. Information revelation and privacy in online social networks. In *Proceedings of the 2005 ACM workshop on Privacy in the electronic society*, pages 71–80. ACM, 2005.

[12] O. C. Herfindahl. Concentration in the steel industry. *Concentration in the steel industry*, 1950.

[13] S. P. Jenkins. Spsurv: Stata module to fit split population survival ('cure') model. *Statistical Software Components*, 2001.

[14] A. D. Kramer, J. E. Guillory, and J. T. Hancock. Experimental evidence of massive-scale emotional contagion through social networks. *Proceedings of the National Academy of Sciences of the United States of America*, 111(24):8788–8790, 2014.

[15] E. Kross, P. Verduyn, E. Demiralp, J. Park, D. S. Lee, N. Lin, H. Shablack, J. Jonides, and O. Ybarra. Facebook use predicts declines in subjective well-being in young adults. *PloS one*, 8(8):e69841, 2013.

[16] A. Lambert. *Intimacy and friendship on Facebook*. Palgrave Macmillan, 2013.

[17] A. Lambrecht, A. Goldfarb, A. Bonatti, A. Ghose, D. G. Goldstein, R. Lewis, A. Rao, N. Sahni, and S. Yao. How do firms make money selling digital goods online? *Marketing Letters*, 25(3):331–341, 2014.

[18] V. Landsman and M. Givon. The diffusion of a new service: Combining service consideration and brand choice. *QME*, 8(1):91–121, 2010.

[19] J.-P. Laurenceau, L. F. Barrett, and P. R. Pietromonaco. Intimacy as an interpersonal process: the importance of self-disclosure, partner disclosure, and perceived partner responsiveness in interpersonal exchanges. *Journal of personality and social psychology*, 74(5):1238, 1998.

[20] T. M. Lowrey, C. C. Otnes, and J. A. Ruth. Social influences on dyadic giving over time: A taxonomy from the giver's perspective. *Journal of Consumer Research*, 30(4):547–558, 2004.

[21] C. P. Moreau, L. Bonney, and K. B. Herd. It's the thought (and the effort) that counts: How customizing for others differs from customizing for oneself. *Journal of Marketing*, 75(5):120–133, 2011.

[22] I. Nitzan and B. Libai. Social effects on customer retention. *Journal of Marketing*, 75(6):24–38, 2011.

[23] Y. Polo, F. J. Sese, and P. C. Verhoef. The effect of pricing and advertising on customer retention in a liberalizing market. *Journal of Interactive Marketing*, 25(4):201–214, 2011.

[24] R. Prins and P. C. Verhoef. Marketing communication drivers of adoption timing of a new e-service among existing customers. *Journal of Marketing*, 71(2):169–183, 2007.

[25] K. Raynes-Goldie. Aliases, creeping, and wall cleaning: Understanding privacy in the age of facebook. *First Monday*, 15(1), 2010.

[26] H. T. Reis and P. Shaver. *Handbook of personal relationships: Theory, research and interventions.*, chapter Intimacy as an interpersonal process., pages 367–389. Oxford, England: John Wiley and Sons, 1988.

[27] L. Rhue and A. Sundararajan. Playing to the crowd? how digital social visibility shapes our choices. Working Paper, 2014.

[28] H. Risselada, P. C. Verhoef, and T. H. Bijmolt. Dynamic effects of social influence and direct marketing on the adoption of high-technology products. *Journal of Marketing*, 78(2):52–68, 2014.

[29] C. Rudder. We experiment on human beings!, 7/28/2014 2014.

[30] P. Schmidt and A. D. Witte. Predicting criminal recidivism using 'split population' survival time models. *Journal of Econometrics*, 40(1):141–159, 1989.

[31] D. A. Schweidel, P. S. Fader, and E. T. Bradlow. A bivariate timing model of customer acquisition and retention. *Marketing Science*, 27(5):829–843, 2008.

[32] J. F. Sherry. Gift giving in anthropological perspective. *Journal of consumer research*, pages 157–168, 1983.

[33] J. F. Sherry, M. A. McGrath, and S. J. Levy. The dark side of the gift. *Journal of Business Research*, 28(3):225–244, 1993.

[34] Y. Shmargad. Social media broadcasts and the maintenance of diverse networks. Thirty Fifth International Conference on Information Systems, 2014.

[35] T. M. Therneau. *Modeling survival data: extending the Cox model*. Springer, 2000.

[36] X. Wang, C. Yu, and Y. Wei. Social media peer communication and impacts on purchase intentions: A consumer socialization framework. *Journal of Interactive Marketing*, 26(4):198–208, 11 2012.

[37] D. J. Watts and S. H. Strogatz. Collective dynamics of small-world networks. *Nature*, 393(6684):440–442, 1998.

[38] J. K. M. Watts and K. W. Koput. Supple networks: Preferential attachment by diversity in nascent social graphs. *Network Science*, 2(03):303–325, 2014. URL http://dx.doi.org/10.1017/nws.2014.21.

[39] D. W. Wilson, J. G. Proudfoot, and J. S. Valacich. Saving face of facebook: Privacy concerns, social benefits, and impression management. In *Proceedings of the 35th International Conference on Information Systems*. ACM, 2014.

[40] D. B. Wooten. Qualitative steps toward an expanded model of anxiety in gift giving. *Journal of Consumer Research*, 27(1):84–95, 2000.

[41] M. S. Yadav, K. de Valck, T. Hennig-Thurau, D. L. Hoffman, and M. Spann. Social commerce: A contingency framework for assessing marketing potential. *Journal of Interactive Marketing*, 27(4):311–323, 11 2013.

Identifying Personal Information in Internet Traffic

Yabing Liu
Northeastern University
ybliu@ccs.neu.edu

Han Hee Song
Cisco Systems
hanhsong@cisco.com

Ignacio Bermudez
Symantec Corporation
ignacio_bermudezcorr@symantec.com

Alan Mislove
Northeastern University
amislove@ccs.neu.edu

Mario Baldi
Cisco Systems & Politecnico di Torino
mbaldi@polito.it

Alok Tongaonkar
Symantec Corporation
alok_tongaonkar@symantec.com

ABSTRACT

Users today access a multitude of online services—among the most popular of which are online social networks (OSNs)—via both web sites and dedicated mobile applications (apps), using a range of devices (traditional PCs, tablets, and smartphones) that are connected via a variety of networks. The resulting infrastructure makes these services conveniently available anytime and anywhere, enabling them to become an integral part of daily life. As a consequence, users explicitly and implicitly provide a wealth of Personal Information (PI) that reflects several aspects of their life. Service providers monetize this information by selling to third parties (e.g., advertisers). Unfortunately, today, it remains difficult for end users to fully understand the amount and nature of the collected data.

Our goal in this paper is to bring visibility into PI collected when accessing online services such as online social networks. This is a major challenge because PI is transferred in a proprietary way by each service. We develop a novel method that can automatically discover various types of PI carried within protocol fields of network traffic; the method includes techniques to filter out potential "containers" that do not actually carry PI and extend the set of containers initially found with additional ones. We evaluate the false positive/negative rates of our proposed method and show examples of interesting findings, including what kind of web sites or apps are more likely to transmit PI and which types of PI are most commonly collected.

Categories and Subject Descriptors

C.2.0 [**Computer-Communication Networks**]: Security and protection; K.4.1 [**Computers and Society**]: Privacy

Keywords

Privacy; Leaks; Web sites; Mobile applications

1. INTRODUCTION

People heavily and constantly rely on services accessible through the Internet for professional, personal, and entertainment needs. For example, online social networks (OSNs) are a popular way for individuals to keep in touch, communicate, and share content. These services are accessed not only via web sites, but also via dedicated applications (apps) on mobile devices, thus being accessible through a range of devices (PCs, tablets, and smartphones) and a variety of wired, wireless, and mobile networks. Given that such services are an integral part of users' lives, service providers have a privileged observation point into the habits and interests of their users. Hence, many operate using a similar business model: services are made available for free in exchange for users (allegedly with an informed decision) accepting that service providers monetize on such personal data by selling it to third parties (e.g., advertisers).

Even though users are often provided with privacy controls, these generally only affect flow of information to other users or third-party applications; users today have no option of making their data private *from* the service provider. Even worse, the limited visibility into app behavior coupled with the significant amount of data stored on smartphones makes it even harder for users to understand the extent to which these services are automatically collecting personal data.

In this paper, we address this situation by developing techniques that automatically detect *personal information* (PI) traveling through the network as it is collected by services accessed via web browsers or mobile apps. This phenomenon is hereafter referred to as PI *leaks*. In contrast with related approaches that rely on "rooting" a user's device [4, 6] or instrumenting applications or browsers [1, 17], we instead aim at a solution requiring access only to the network itself, because such an approach significantly lowers barriers to deployment. Moreover, it has the potential to achieve higher coverage since the system can leverage visibility on traffic from multiple users in learning how PI is transmitted (i.e., how it is encapsulated in proprietary ways). Although the approach is general, we choose to focus on HTTP, as this is the protocol on which both traditional web services and a large fraction of mobile apps base their communications.

In designing and evaluating our approach, we make three high-level contributions. First, we underscore the difficulty of the problem of locating PI in network traffic by demonstrating that only a very small fraction of protocol fields actually convey PI, making our endeavor akin to "finding a needle in the haystack" (in § 4.1). We also show that an approach based on simple statistical analysis (e.g., selecting fields that are unique to a user, or common across different services) is not practical as it results in unacceptably high levels of false positives/negatives (in § 4.2).

Second, we develop a novel method based on (*i*) grouping data according to the domain name of the servers it is sent to and the key associated to it for the transmission, called a *domain-key*, and (*ii*) concluding that all of the domain-key combinations in a group are PI "containers" if a threshold subset of them are found to contain PI (§ 5.1). This subset of PI containers are identified through a list of *seed rules* manually crafted to locate PI of different types, including, but not limited to, users' names, genders, email addresses, ages, geo-locations, cities, postal codes, and phone numbers (§ 5.2 and § 5.3). Then the coverage is extended by inferring additional containers by analogy with the seeded ones (§ 5.4).

Third, we evaluate our approach on a network dataset collected from a point-of-presence of a European ISP, covering 13,000 real users. As we do not know the ground truth PI for these users, we establish ground truth by relying on multiple human raters to label domain-keys that contain PI. In § 6.1, we find that our approach is able to identify these rare domain-keys automatically, with a low false negative rate (2.7%) and an acceptable false positive rate (13.6%). We then apply our approach to the entire dataset in § 6.2, exploring the frequency with which web sites and applications transmit PI in practice. There, we discover that different types of Internet service focus on different PI (*e.g.*, CDNs tend to leak physical locations of users while adult services leak age and gender information). We also find that an invasive user-tracking service leaks higher amount of PI than others.

2. BACKGROUND

In this section, we provide a more formal definition of personal information (PI) and describe our assumptions and intended operating environment.

2.1 Personal Information (PI)

There are many different kinds of PI, including a user's name and social security number, their current location when performing a purchase over the Internet, or even rich media information in the form of photos and videos. For simplicity, we focus on a text-based personal information (e.g., names, user identifiers, and locations) collected by web sites and smartphone applications. Further, to discern different high-level characteristics of PI, we classify them along the following three dimensions.

Static vs. Dynamic Static PI does not typically change over time (at least, over short- to medium-length time intervals). Examples include the user's name, gender, phone number, and email address. In contrast, dynamic PI may change over such intervals; examples include the user's geo-location, a user's session ID, or the user's set of personal interests.

Unique vs. Non-unique Unique PI distinctly identifies a single (human) user from others. For example, a user's email address or phone number uniquely distinguishes a user from the rest. On the other hand, non-unique PI may be shared

Personal information	Static?	Unique?	Shared?
Name	☑	☐	☑
Email address	☑	☑	☑
Date of Birth	☑	☐	☑
Geo-location	☐	☐	☐
Username	☑	☑	☑
Tracking cookie	☐	☑	☐

Table 1: Examples of different types of textual PI, and the breakdown of PI along different dimensions.

by multiple users; examples include a user's name, gender, or date of birth.

Shared vs. Distinct The third dimension we consider is PI that, for a given user, is likely to be shared *across services* or distinct. An example of shared PI is mailing address of a user (presuming that the user provides factual information to each site). In contrast, distinct PI is potentially different for each website (or domain name); examples include time the user last logged in or the session identifier in a tracking cookie.

We provide breakdowns of how different examples of PI are classified along these dimensions in Table 1.

2.2 Assumptions, environment, threat model

In contrast to approaches that assume access to user devices (e.g., via browser plugins, "rooting", or operating system modifications), we instead assume that network administrators wish to understand when their users' personal information is being transmitted over the network. Thus, we assume that we have access to traces of network activity from a large group of users, as would be the case at a large corporation or university.

While web sites are constrained by the browser to only using HTTP to communicate with remote servers, smartphone applications are free to use any UDP/TCP protocol. However, as much as 40% of application traffic actually is HTTP [5, 21], presumably to re-use many of the same APIs as web-based services and to avoid certain firewalls. Hence, we only consider PI leaks that occur over HTTP, but our approach could easily be extended to other protocols if given appropriate parsers.

We therefore develop techniques to look for instances of textual PI in certain HTTP fields of the observed network traffic. We assume that applications and web sites are not actively obfuscating transmitted information by hiding PI or obscuring data by using steganography-like techniques. Handling PI transmitted by actively adversarial applications (e.g., malware) introduces significant additional challenges, and we leave it to future work.

Finally, because we do not assume any privileged access to devices, we are unable to gain visibility into HTTPS traffic.[1] While HTTPS and, more generally, any TLS/SSL encrypted traffic, represent an ever increasing fraction of Internet data, we find that a significant fraction of traffic remains in plain

---

[1]We assume that mechanisms to access encrypted content can be put in place independently of our techniques for PI identification. For organizations that provision devices with additional trusted root certificates (e.g., certificates owned by the local administrators), one could leverage techniques for interposing on HTTPS transactions to gain such visibility [14,20], thereby extending our approach to HTTPS traffic as well. However, such an approach would have significant implications on privacy and security, so we do not consider it to be the common deployment scenario.

Observed HTTP transaction

```
GET /foo.html? user_firstname=Alice & id=17  HTTP/1.1
Host:  imagevenue.com
Cookie:  a=293 & g=00s9229daa & age=39 & id=27
ETag:  2039-2dc90ea2-12
Referer:  http://www.facebook.com/? user_id=89
Accept-Encoding:  deflate,gzip

HTTP/1.1 200 OK
Date:  Mon, 23 May 2013 22:38:34 GMT
...
```

Derived domain-keys and values

Domain	Key	Field	Value
imagevenue.com	user_firstname	GET	Alice
imagevenue.com	id	GET	17
imagevenue.com	a	Cookie	293
imagevenue.com	g	Cookie	00s9229daa
imagevenue.com	age	Cookie	39
imagevenue.com	id	Cookie	27
imagevenue.com	user_id	Referer	89

Figure 1: Example query from one HTTP connection, and the derived domain-keys with the associated values.

HTTP. For example, in our *Lab traffic* dataset described in Section 3.2, we find that 62% of the flows are HTTP, and that 44% of the ground-truth user PI is located in these HTTP flows. As a result, even without access to HTTPS traffic, we still can observe a large fraction (44%) of PI transmitted in the traffic.

3. DATASET DESCRIPTION

In this section, we introduce the datasets used for characterization of PI transmission over the network and for evaluating extraction of PI from traffic. While it is ideal to collect traffic traces with ground truth PI on every user, it is unrealistic to be able to collect such data at large scale. Instead, we use two complementary datasets: (i) small scale traffic traces with reliable ground truth collected in a controlled lab environment (*Lab traffic*) and (ii) large-scale traces collected from an ADSL point-of-presence (*ISP traffic*). The *Lab traffic* dataset helps us to obtain preliminary understanding on the mechanisms of PI transmission on the Internet; the *ISP traffic* dataset is then used to build models for PI extraction and test them at scale.

We begin this section by overviewing how we parse out PI from raw traffic, followed by detailed explanation of the *Lab traffic* and *ISP traffic* datasets, respectively.

3.1 HTTP parsing

From Layer-7 flows of user traffic, we extract PI of users from HTTP requests assuming that it is transferred in the form of *key-value* pairs. In order to properly handle these keys, we use the concept of *domain-key* in which we combine a key name with the name of the domain associated to the request. The intuition behind this is that key names will likely be used coherently (i.e., for carrying the same type of information) within the same domain (e.g., google.com may use the keyword "ggender" to collect user's gender regardless the specific Google service). On the other hand, a same key might be used in the context of different domains with a different meanings (e.g., the key `id` may be used dif-

Dataset	HTTP flows	Tuples	Domain-keys
Lab traffic	9,227	20,810	8,372
ISP traffic	40,775,119	51,368,712	3,113,696

Table 2: High-level statistics of our two datasets.

ferent by Google and Facebook). Specifically, we extract the domain from `Host` HTTP header, and derive keys (and values) from three locations: (a) the query string of HTTP GET requests, (b) the query string in the `Referer` HTTP header, and (c) the `Cookie` HTTP header. For each location of potential keys, we divide the contents into key/value pairs using standard formatting rules (e.g., for GET query string parameters, we use the & character; for cookies, we use commas, semicolons, and ampersands). Figure 1 shows an example of a query and domain-keys and values extracted from it.

The use of domain-keys (as opposed to just keys alone) allows us to capture how different domains use keys with the same name. Consider two HTTP GET messages `http://loginradius.com/login?name=alice` and `http://ymail.com/getservice?name=send_mail`. While the query string `name` is the same for both domains, the former domain uses it as a login ID, while the latter uses it the name of the service that the user is requesting. Thus, keeping these separate allows us to identify the former as potentially carrying PI, while the latter is unlikely to.

3.2 Controlled lab environment dataset

In the *Lab traffic* dataset, we collect traffic of a single user who intentionally transmitted a variety of *known* PI (i.e., ground truth) to a number of popular online services. For this dataset, we wanted to be able to examine the TLS/SSL encrypted traffic as well. Thus, we collect data by tapping in to the connections with a middlebox that passes traffic through VPN/Man-In-The-Middle (MITM) transparent setup [15].

Using an Apple iPhone 4 with iOS 7, we ran the top 35 free iTunes apps for 15 minutes each, conducting a variety of activities including service registration, login/logout, message posting, chat message transmission, browsing, etc. Detailed information about the size of this dataset is provided in Table 2. Given that this dataset is highly biased toward one specific user and one device, we use this dataset as an exploratory sandbox, in which we manually inspect how the known PI is transmitted in HTTP/S traffic.

3.3 Real ISP dataset

In order to generalize our PI extraction models with larger scale data, we conducted a large-scale traffic collection from a point-of-presence of an ISP providing ADSL service in a European city. We use a Layer-7 traffic trace, *ISP traffic*, of 13,000 users for 24-hour in August 2011.[2]

We identify over 3 million unique domain-keys and 51 million unique domain-key/value tuples (see Table 2 for more details). While this real-user dataset lacks ground truth information on the user PI, we evaluate correctness of our proposed method by having humans manually inspect sampled domain-keys in Section 6.1.3.

---

[2]Per the privacy policy of the ISP, we anonymized true identities of the users prior to our study.

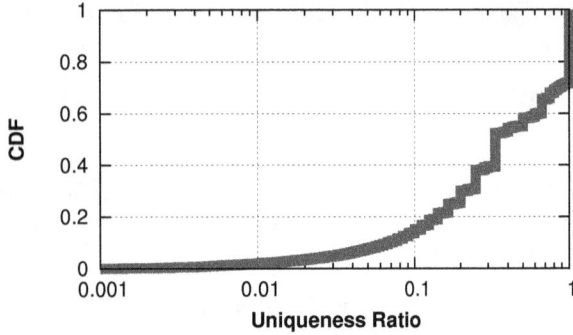

Figure 2: The cumulative distribution of the *uniqueness ratio* of all static domain-keys in *ISP traffic* dataset.

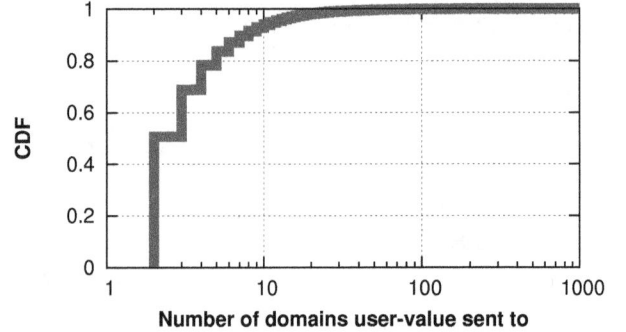

Figure 3: The cumulative distribution of number of domains that each user-value has been sent to in *ISP traffic* dataset.

4. STATISTICAL APPROACH

We begin by measuring the overall level of PI present in traffic, and then explore whether simple statistical techniques (inspired by Section 2.1) might be able to identify PI leaked in large ISP traffic.

4.1 Small scale study on controlled lab traffic

Using the *Lab traffic* dataset, we locate all of the domain-keys present in the traffic; this results in 8,372 domain-keys in total. Because we know the ground truth entered by the user, we search through the values of the domain-keys, looking for information that was provided by the user including the email address, name, city, postal code, gender, age, and geo-coordinates. We find that the fraction of domain-keys with different PI varies between 0.01% (for phone number) to 0.31% (for postal code), but overall, only 1.25% of *all* domain-keys ever contained any PI. Thus, we observe that locating PI in raw traffic is akin to finding needle in a haystack.

4.2 Statistical metrics in discovering PI

Next, using *ISP traffic* dataset, we explore whether we may be able to identify PI in traffic by looking for simple statistical properties of the domain-keys. For example, perhaps values that users upload to different domains may be more likely to be PI than other values. Below, we explore each of the three properties of the domain-keys in the *ISP traffic* dataset based on the taxonomy presented in Section 2.1. Then, we analyze the effectiveness of combining the statistical metrics in discovering the PI leakage.

Static vs. Dynamic Overall, we find that there are 341,179 (11.0%) static domain-keys (*i.e.*, every user has only one value for the domain-key) and 111,664 (3.6%) dynamic domain-keys (*i.e.*, every user has two or more values); the remaining are mixture of both (*i.e.*, some users have single value, some have multiples). This is unsurprising as the vast majority of domain-keys have very few values. Manually inspecting the static and dynamic domain-keys reveals a few candidates for PI, but the majority of domain-keys have no obvious semantic meaning for PI. Thus, while this approach does identify domain-keys that are static or dynamic for users, it is still not precise enough to be useful for pinpointing PI.

Unique vs. Non-unique The second feature we explore is whether each user is mapped to a unique value. We focus on the static domain-keys discovered above in order to use

domain-keys that are likely to map a single value to each user (*i.e.*, examining uniqueness of dynamic values requires careful consideration of the number of online users, etc). We define a new metric *uniqueness ratio* for a domain-key, which is simply the number of unique values in the domain-key divided by the number of users for the domain-key. We show the cumulative distribution of the *uniqueness ratio* in Figure 2. Among all the static domain-keys, 96,375 (28.24%) of them have a *uniqueness ratio* of 1, meaning every user has a unique value.

While the static domain-keys with *uniqueness ratio* of 1 are more likely to contain the static type of PI, such as user's username, and email address, the majority of them are comprised of session identifiers, GUIDs, and the like. Thus, relying on uniqueness alone is also likely to produce too many false positives to be useful.

Shared vs. Distinct Data a user is sharing across domains suggests that the value may correspond to the user's PI (*e.g.*, the same email address used as login account for different websites). Out of 26,453,858 unique user-values, we find 5,923,084 (22.4%) of them have been sent to multiple domains; we show the cumulative distribution of the number of domains for each user-value in Figure 3. There, we find over 7% of user-values have been sent to at least 10 domains.

Among the values sent to multiple domains (*i.e.*, distinct data), we find some meaningful PI (*e.g.*, we find tracking user identifiers that are used across domains). However, the majority of them are common values with no implications on PI such as 0, 1, true, false, etc (*e.g.*, a user sent the value of 1 to more than 100 different domains). Thus, as before, looking only at the values that are shared across domains is simply not precise enough to effectively locate PI.

Combining features We have observed so far that looking for individual features of domain-keys is not precise enough to locate PI. We now briefly explore combining statistical features together, looking for domain-keys that are static, unique to a user, *and* shared across domains. Our selection of these features is to capture PI such as email addresses, which may be used as login information for multiple web sites. This combined criteria leaves with a small set of 262 *pairs* of domain-keys that are unique, static, and have at least 20 users that share the same value in both domain-keys.

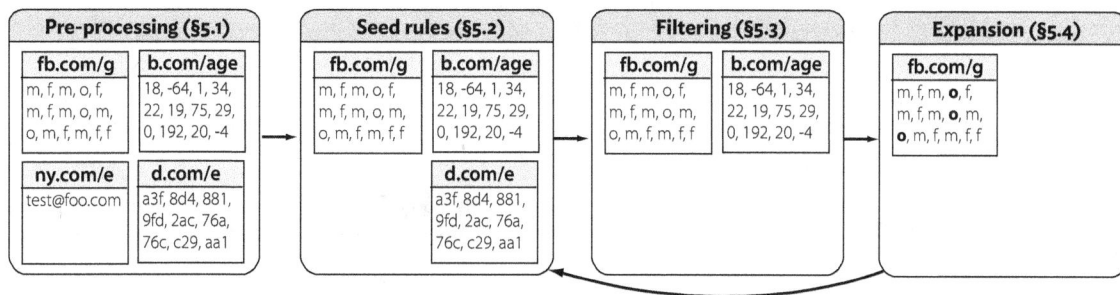

Pre-processing (§5.1)		Seed rules (§5.2)		Filtering (§5.3)		Expansion (§5.4)

Figure 4: Overview of our proposed approach, exemplifying the four steps in identifying domain-keys that may contain PI. In the Pre-processing step, domain-keys with too few values are filtered. In the Seed rules step, different rules are applied to the values in each domain-key; domain-keys with too few matching values are filtered out in the Filtering stage. Finally, in the Expansion step, the newly discovered values are shown in **bold**, and these may be used to help refine the seed rules.

To evaluate whether these domain-keys contain real user PI, several human raters[3] manually inspected each of the domain-keys. Overall, we find that only 33 (12.6%) of the domain-keys were labeled by humans as PI; examples include email addresses, ids, user interest, locations, etc. Taking a closer look at the false positives, we find that they contain values that are related to the users' activities, however, not users' sensitive PI, including dates, timestamps, click tags, referrers, etc.

Summary Applying individual statistical tests in the real *ISP traffic* results in too many false positives; applying a combination of the tests results in too few true positives. In the following section, we propose a more sophisticated technique based on the properties of values of different domain-keys we learned so far.

5. SEEDED APPROACH

This section describes the method we propose to identify PI in network traffic traces, parsing traffic data and distinguishing user PI in an automated fashion. We begin by extracting fields from the various HTTP headers in the manner described in Section 3.1.

As observed in the previous section, in the vast majority of cases, reliance on the statistics of domain-keys fails to reveal values with PI. Hence we shift our focus to the domain-key *values* and propose a novel semantically-based method which we refer to as the *seeded method*. We briefly describe our high-level approach here, and provide more details on each step. First, we have an initial pre-processing step, where we examine all domain-keys of a dataset and filter out those that do not have enough values to produce statistically meaningful results. Second, we apply a number of *seed rules* crafted to find clues of PI *directly from the values* contained in each domain-key. Using these rules, we select candidate domain-keys to be those that have a sufficient level of matches. Fourth, we extend the set of possible values to include those in the candidate domain-keys by adding the missing values into our value pool. A diagram of these four steps is presented in Figure 4.

These four steps are described in more detail in the following subsections. Many of the steps require choices of con-

stants and parameters; when describing each of the steps, we describe our process for selecting the parameters based on observations from the *Lab traffic* and *ISP traffic* datasets.

5.1 Pre-processing

Our approach relies on the format of the values of different domain-keys to select domain-keys that are likely to be carrying PI. Thus, we need a large enough sample of values to be able to produce statistically significant results. To do so, we simply select a threshold n, and only consider domain-keys for which we have observed n tuples (user/value pairs). For example, $n = 5$ can either mean one unique value from each of 5 different users, or 5 different values from a single user.

When applying this pre-processing step, we naturally face a tradeoff between the potential false positives and the coverage of domain-keys where we have few data points. Thus, we briefly explore the *coverage* of domain-keys that different choices of n provide. Using the *ISP traffic* dataset, we plot the cumulative distribution of the number of distinct values each domain-key has (we also plot the number of users and total number of tuples for comparison) in Figure 5. We observe that out of the 3.1M total domain-keys, only the top 270,756 (8.7%) "heavy hitter" domain-keys have at least 10 distinct tuples. However, these heavy hitter domain-keys in aggregate cover 90.8% of all observed tuples; thus, when applying pre-processing, we filter out a significant fraction

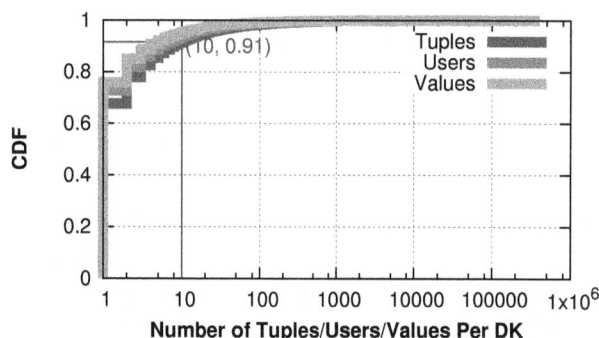

Figure 5: The cumulative distribution of the number of unique tuples, users, and distinct values for each domain-key discovered in *ISP traffic* dataset.

---

[3] To further protect privacy of users from de-anonymization, the only human participants allowed to review the data was limited to the six authors of this paper.

PI type	Regular expression
Age Range	`/^[0-9]{1,3}-[0-9]{1,3}$/` (where the second number is larger than the first)
Email	`/^(\w|\-|\_|\.)+\@((\w|\-|\_)+\.)+[a-zA-Z]{2,}$/`
Geo	`/^[\+\-]{0,1}\d+\.\d{4}\d+$/` (where the value is within the range of the country)
Gender	`/^[mf]$/` or `/^(fe)?male$/` (or the corresponding words for male/female in local language)
Phone	`/^([+]code)?((38[{8,9}|0])|(34[{7-9}|0])|(36[6|8|0])|(33[{3-9}|0])|(32[{8,9}]))([\d]{7})$/`
Postal code	`/^\d{5}$/`

Table 3: Examples of regular expressions used for a subset of the seed rules. Some of the regular expressions require minor post-processing, such as a the "age range" PI category, where the second element of the range must be greater than the first.

of the domain-keys, but still retain the vast majority of the observed tuples in the trace.

5.2 Seed rules

We develop a list of constraints, or *seed rules*, based on the format of expected PI. For many of the different types of PI, seed rules can be expressed as simple *regular expressions*, and are sufficient to express the possible data formats. For example, in Table 3, regular expressions are sufficient to capture email addresses, genders, age ranges, geo-coordinates, postal codes, and phone numbers.[4] For some of these, some simple post-filtering is required (e.g., to express that an age range is from a lower number to a higher one).

However, other types of PI may not be as easily expressible as a regular expression. Examples of such PI include user's names, cities, and regions. To capture these, we also allow seed rules to be expressed as *dictionaries* containing lists of possible values. For example, for first names of users, we create a comprehensive list of names[5] by downloading a set of corresponding web pages with boys or girls' names from the given country. Similarly, we create a dictionary of different cities and regions in the country of interest in order to create a seed rule for the user's location.

Our dictionary-based rules do not need to be exhaustive to be effective. As we show in the next section, as long as our seed rules are sufficient to cover a significant fraction of the actual vales (in practice, we have found good performance with as low as 20% coverage), our Expansion step is able to discover the additional values as potential PI.

Lastly, we note that we limit our seed rules to the above eight PI instances simply for brevity, not because the expressiveness of the rules is limited to just these types of PI. We believe these exemplary rules are sufficient for demonstrating both the utility of our proposed method and the applicability to various other types of PI.

Of course, the seed rules that we have selected are unlikely to cover all the cases, formats, and languages; they can easily be improved and expanded, based on the input and results. Though the seed rule solution is not universally applicable, for example in the Table 3 "where the value is within the range of the country", we need to apply different things in the seed rules based on the input of dataset. However, once the seed rules are generated, they can help us in discovering domain-keys with different types of user PI in an efficient and automatic way.

5.3 Filtering domain-keys

Not all the domain-keys matching seed rules represent PI. To confirm that the domain-keys are indeed likely used as a container for transmitting PI, for each domain-key, we look

at all its values, and we compute a metric *ratio matched values* in relation to each seed rule. This metric is simply number of values that match the seed rule, divided by the total number of values. When the *ratio matched values* is above a given threshold as described below, we consider that this domain-key is likely to carry the type of PI with a confidence represented by the matching value ratio.

Again, choosing an appropriate *ratio matched values* is a tradeoff, where a small threshold *ratio matched values* increases the coverage, but results in higher false positive rates. To illustrate how we choose the threshold in practice, Figure 6 plots the distribution of *ratio matched values* across domain-keys in the *ISP traffic* dataset for each of the eight seed rules. For each rule, only those domain-keys that have *at least one* matching value are considered.

We make a number of interesting observations. First, we observe that while the distribution is different for each of the seed rules, all of the rules show a "knee" at some point in the curve. In the case of email addresses, for example, 21% of domain-keys have all their values matching the rule (i.e., the ratio is 1) and over half (58%) of the domain-keys have at least 20% of their values matching the seed rule. In contrast, the name domain-key shows that the vast majority (over 90%) of domain-keys that have at least one matching value have less than 10% of all their values match. This difference in performance is due to the nature of the seed rules; for email, the regular expression is unlikely to select values that are not actually email addresses, whereas the name seed rule is only a subset of the possible user names.

To choose a good tradeoff between false positives and coverage, for each rule, we choose a *ratio matched values* threshold to the knee points of the corresponding distribution. For example, we select a threshold to be 1 for postal codes, 0.9 for geo locations, and 0.2 for the rest.

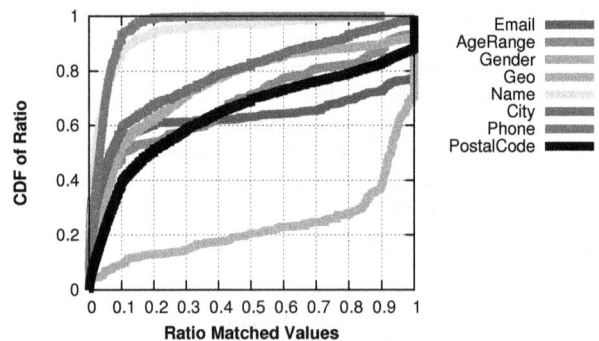

Figure 6: The cumulative distribution of *ratio matched values* for domain-keys in *ISP traffic* dataset for each of the eight different seed rules. For each rule, only those domain-keys that have *at least one* matching value are considered. Different rules show different properties, but most show a "knee" in the curve at some threshold.

---

[4]We note that our examples of phone numbers and postal codes use the local formats of the country where our dataset is from.

[5]http://www.babynamespedia.com/search/m/countryname

Domain	Key	Value
google-analytics.com	email	johnDoe@gmail.com
google-analytics.com	email	janeDoe@hotmail.com
google-analytics.com	email	johnDoe
google-analytics.com	email	janeDoe
facebook.com	gender	female
facebook.com	gender	m
facebook.com	gender	f
facebook.com	gender	1
facebook.com	gender	f-f
facebook.com	gender	f-m

Table 4: Examples of values that both match and do not match the seed rules. We observe that values that do not match the seed rules may still identify potential leaks, and may help to refine the seed rules.

5.4 Expanding candidate domain-keys

We understand our seed rules are not exhaustive, and it is challenging to develop perfect seed rules that can match all the possible formats of PI. To address this limitation, we expand the candidate values associated with selected domain-keys into our value pool, to compliment our findings. For example, if we pick 0.2 for the email case shown in Figure 5, we get a list of domain-keys with email, and each of them have at least 20% of their values matching the seed rule. When we consider the set of PI, we add the values that do not match the rule into our value pool as well. Though they do not match the exact regular expression, they may also contain user PI (e.g., the username without a domain, an email address with extra whitespace, etc).

A few examples of matching and non-matching values are presented in Table 4. The first four rows show values associated with domain-key (`google-analytics.com`, email). While the first two examples match the regular expression, next two rows with values "johnDoe" and "janeDoe" are truncated form of the first two email addresses used as usernames. The last six rows show values associated with the domain-key (`facebook.com`, gender). We observe that the first three match the seed rule, but the final three do not (although they likely contain some form of PI being conveyed by Facebook or a third-party application). In both cases, considering the values that do not match the seed rules can help to refine the seed rules, as well as present additional potential leaks to the administrator.

We note that there are a few reasons why a service would use different formats for the same key. First, the service may have different formats of values within different parts of HTTP header, such as url, referrer, and cookie. Second, some services provide APIs for the external developers, who may use formats that differ from the main service. For example, we notice that Facebook advertising API allows us to specify the key "gender" with value of 0 to target male users and value of 1 for female users. Instead, the main Facebook service uses a list of other values, such as male, female, m, and f to specify gender. Third, the values may be based on end user input, which is not always well-formatted.

6. EVALUATION

In this section, we apply our proposed approach to *ISP traffic* and evaluate its performance in comparison to a baseline approach. We then present interesting findings on user PI through an in-depth analysis on the discovered domain-keys.

PI Type	Dom.-keys selected	Ground truth	Coverage	Accuracy
Age Range	0	0	—	—
City	19	19	100%	100%
Email	22	22	100%	100%
Geo	34	7	0%	0%
Gender	38	14	100%	36.8%
Name	16	16	100%	100%
Phone	1	1	100%	100%
Post code	144	26	100%	18.1%
Total	274	105	100%	38.3%

Table 6: Comparison of domain-keys selected by the seeded method and ground truth in *Lab traffic* dataset.

6.1 Evaluation of seeded method

Having applied the seeded method to our datasets, we now analyze the performance of the method in terms of coverage and accuracy. To evaluate our proposed method in controlled environment with ground truth, in Section 6.1.1, we begin by analyzing results from small-scale *Lab traffic* dataset (§ 3.2). Then in § 6.1.2 through § 6.1.4, we evaluate the method on full-scale *ISP traffic* dataset (§ 3.3). Here, we first quantify *coverage* of our seeded method by comparing it to a baseline naïve method. We then further analyze the *accuracy* of our results by manually inspecting correctness on a sample of the discovered values.

6.1.1 *Verification on* Lab traffic *dataset*

Using the ground truth on PI we have in *Lab traffic* dataset, we measure the validity of domain-keys and their values obtained using the seeded method. Out of 20,810 tuples from 8,372 domain-keys available in the HTTP/S data, seeded rules extract 274 domain-keys as containing PI. A breakdown of domain-keys discovered by the rules, and those containing the ground truth PI leaks, is detailed in Table 6.

We make a number of interesting observations from our inspection of the results: overall, only 3.27% of all domain-keys are discovered as containing PI. Given the "needle in a haystack" observation we made in Section 4.1, it is reasonable that the selected domain-keys are only a small fraction of all domain-keys.

In a few particular cases, we find a single rule matching multiple instances (different values) of PI. For example, a domain-key (`cm.g.doubleclick.net`, ct) matching the City rule has a list of different values: Boston, Beijing, Seoul, Shanghai. While we consider Boston as the most "correct" answer (as it is the current residential city of the user), the rule found other cities that she visited in the past. At the same time, the existence of multiple PI instances supports the utility of the candidate value expansion in Section 5.4 as it accommodates broader range of the candidate values into user PI pool.

Occasionally, we found the expansion stage of the approach to introduce a few false negative values. For example, we find an extracted domain-key (`graph.facebook.com`, name) containing two application names, "Pinterest" and "iHeartRadio", along with the target user name "Yabing Liu" (one of the authors). The application names were found in the domain-key because the user was logging on to the applications through her Facebook account.

Overall, our evaluation on the *Lab traffic* dataset suggests that our approach is able to identify domain-keys that carry PI with high coverage. Moreover, we observed a significant

Type	Key semantics	True positive ex.	False positive ex.
Age Range	substring of age	age, age_range,	message, language, pagesize
City	substr. of city, citta, area, state, provincia, loc, region, where	city, location	client_state, locale
Email	substr. of email, user, account, login, logon, or equal to "e"	email, login_email	user_segment, login_password
Gender	substr. of gen, gnd, gdr, ycg, sex, or equal to "g"	gender, user_sex	pagename, useragent
Geo(Lat/Lon)	substr. of lat, lon, lng, geo	latitude, logitute	platform, relation
Name	substr. of name, nome, pers, author	name, person	app_name, slotname, listname
Phone	substr. of phone, pid, or equal to "p"	phone, pid	appid, sdkapid
Postal Code	substr. of zip, geo	zipcode, geo	gzip, gzipbyteencoding

Table 5: Examples of both true and false positives when using the key semantic method.

fraction of these (44%) were observed in unencrypted HTTP traffic, including the user's name, gender, city, and postal code. We now explore running our approach on the much larger *ISP traffic* dataset.

6.1.2 Improvement over a baseline approach

From this section on, we evaluate our method on a larger, realistic dataset of *ISP traffic*. To understand the improvement of our seeded method over baseline results, we begin this section by running a comparative study of our seeded method against a naïve, key-semantic based approach that analyzes *key names* (as opposed to *values* as in our seeded approach). Then we provide our reasoning on why seeded method constantly outperforms the baseline method without even considering the semantics of the keys.

Baseline key-semantics approach We create a strawman approach based on *key semantics* in which we leverage common intuition that keys that are suggestive of PI (e.g., keys named "email", etc) would carry the PI as their values. In other words, if the majority of keys containing PI have dictionary words such as "email", "gender", or "name", the baseline approach should be able to collect all such domain-keys with PI. We later compare the results of our seeded approach against that of the simple baseline approach, and quantify their gap in terms of coverage.

To create the baseline approach, we select a list of lexicons of each PI category. Table 5 presents the selected key terms for each of the eight PI categories we consider, along with some examples of true and false positives. Overall, we find 20,565 of our domain-keys match at least one of the rules (a breakdown is shown in Table 7, column six).

Performance comparison Table 7 presents a detailed comparison of the coverage of our seeded method to the coverage of the baseline method. In particular, comparing columns four and six shows the total number of domain-keys selected by the two methods in each category, respectively. We immediately observe that the baseline method finds many more potential domain-keys containing PI (in some cases, up to three orders-of-magnitude more). However, this result may be somewhat misleading, as these are only *potential* domain-keys that may or may not carry PI (e.g., the domain-key (`facebook.com`, function-name) would be selected by the baseline method, as it has `name` in the key name). Thus, to fairly compare the two methods, we need to estimate their false positive rate.

6.1.3 Accuracy analysis on samples of results

As we do not have the ground truth PI of the *ISP traffic* dataset users (*i.e.*, customers of the ISP), we instead rely on multiple human raters to identify potential PI. Due to the size of the dataset, we use sampling to make the evaluation tractable.

We first describe how we evaluate the accuracy of our seeded method. To evaluate the false positives, we began by choosing up to 170 random domain-keys from each of the eight PI category from the final output of the seeded method, hence choosing 873 flagged domain-keys in total (31.3% sampling rate out of the final 2,789 domain-keys). Similarly, to measure false negatives, we randomly sampled 1,000 domain-keys that the seeded method did not chose (0.032% sampling rate out of 3,110,907 non-flagged domain-keys). To measure the accuracy of the baseline key-semantic method, we take a similar approach. We select up to 25 random domain-keys from the domain-keys identified by the baseline method in each category of PI.

For each of the domain-keys tested, the six human raters either labeled positive (*i.e.*, the type of the PI), negative, and neutral (*i.e.*, don't know) for the question of whether the domain-keys contain PI or not. In all tests, for each domain-key, we then chose 10 values randomly to present to the human rater, alongside the domain and key name. Each domain-key was reviewed by three raters, allowing us to run majority voting when labels disagreed.

Seeded method Overall, we find that 221 out of the 873 domain-keys flagged by the seeded method to be false positives (*i.e.*, the human raters indicated not containing PI), resulting in a false positive rate of 25.3% (with the corresponding confidence interval from 22.4% to 28.2%). However, we notice that the false positive rate for the Postal Code rule is as high as 91.6%, which means our seeded rule does not work well in identifying only domain-keys that contain postal codes (instead, it captures many additional domain-keys as well). As detailed in Section 5.2, a seed rule generalizes particular patterns embedded in PI. In the case of postal codes, the seed rule of /^\d{5}$/ is not specific enough to separate the PI from random five digit numbers. For this reason, we filter out postal code from our ruleset, and obtain a resulting false positive rate of 13.6% (with the corresponding confidence interval from 11.3% to 15.9%).

We also find that 27 out of the 1,000 non-flagged domain-keys to be identified by the human raters as containing PI, thereby representing a false negative rate of 2.7% (with the corresponding confidence interval from 1.7% to 3.7%).

Baseline method For the baseline key-semantic method, we observe that the human raters found 179 of the 200 domain-keys flagged by the baseline to be false positives, resulting in an extremely high false positive rate of 89.5%.

Overall, the survey finds the false positive rate to be high for the seeded method, and unacceptably high for the baseline method. However, we believe that the 13.6% false positive rate of our seeded method is acceptable due to three reasons: First, PI is rare, and it is difficult to find the cor-

66

			Seeded		Baseline		Comparison		
PI Type	# DKs	Threshold	# DKs above threshold	False positives	# DKs	False positives	Common DKs	Unique to Seeded	Unique to Baseline
Age Range	199	0.2	17	0.0%	3,729	88.0%	0	17	3,729
City	1,402	0.2	465	8.8%	3,191	76.0%	241	224	2,948
Email	382	0.2	154	3.9%	3,253	76.0%	82	72	3,171
Gender	2,041	0.2	147	0.0%	1,358	100.0%	140	7	1,218
Geo (lat/lon)	341	0.9	214	10.0%	1,986	88.0%	110	104	1,876
Name	1,549	0.2	100	52.5%	2,142	92.0%	22	78	2,120
Phone	993	0.2	11	90.9%	3,864	100.0%	0	11	3,864
Postal Code	13,449	1	1,681	91.6%	1,044	92.3%	22	1,659	1,022
Total	20,356	—	2,789	13.6% (25.3%)	20,565	89.5%	617	2,172	19,948

Table 7: Comparison between our proposed seeded method and baseline key-semantic method. The seeded method has a dramatically lower false positive rate (13.6%, when disregarding postal code) than the baseline method.

rect PI from a huge dataset without any ground truth. Second, the false positive rate is tunable by selecting a different threshold; we opted for increased coverage in these experiments, and could easily lower our false positive rate at a cost of increased false negatives (currently 2.7%). Third, we observe that it is difficult even for humans to agree what is PI and what is not. For example, among the 873 labeled domain-keys from seeded method, only on 81% of them did the human raters agree: on 18% one rater disagreed, and 1%, all disagreed. The upshot is that our method is able to focus quickly on the small subset of domain-keys that potentially leak PI.

6.1.4 Exploring higher accuracy of seeded method

While the seeded method only focuses on the *syntax of values* (via regular expressions and dictionaries), it captures many more DKs with PI than the baseline approach focusing on the *semantics of keys*. To better understand the reason for the large difference, we take an in-depth look at the key semantics of the domain-keys found by the seeded method.

We first analyze domain-keys the baseline method selected but our seeded method did not. Column 8 of the Table 7 shows the number of domain-keys overlapping between the two methods. Compared to column 10 (*i.e.*, total number of domain-keys selected by the baseline method), we observe that only a small fraction (3.1%) of the domain-keys selected by the baseline method are indeed included in the final results of the seeded method, suggesting that the vast majority of services do not name their keys semantically accurately. For instance, a key term "name" does not always draw terms relevant to user names we target. Instead, as exemplified in Table 5, it erroneously includes mobile app names, names of data slot, and a binary representation of existence of a name.

We then analyze domain-keys the seeded method selected but the baseline method did not. As the small difference between column 4 and column 8 of Table 7 suggests, the majority of DKs seeded method selects are included in the selection of baseline method as well.

From the total of 20,356 domain-keys that match seed rules, the "ratio" thresholds we impose in Section 5.3 selects only 2,789 of them (13%) as the rest do not contain enough number of valid values. Figure 7 further explains this using the email category as an example. The curve shows the cumulative distribution of email domain-keys ordered by the fraction (ratio) of values matching our seed rule. Out of the total of 382 domain-keys that match seed rules, the seeded method selects 154 of them after imposing the pre-

set threshold ratio of 0.2. Upon our manual inspection on the 228 domain-keys that were left out, many of them contained values irrelevant to emails. For example, in domain-key (`static.ak.connect.facebook.com`, email), binary tags of 0 and 1 are used for its value, possibly encoding the existence of emails. In domain-key (`adserver.adtech.de`, city), indexes of cities are used, which we are unable to decipher without knowing its indexing mechanism.

In summary, we observed important shortcomings of the baseline key-semantic method to be applicable for automatic discovery of PI: sensitivity to selection of input domain-key categories and key terms, inability to discern domain-keys containing irrelevant values, and overly high false positives due to limited expressiveness of key terms. Our proposed seeded method, on the other hand, is deemed to be much more robust to the above issues.

6.2 Analysis on services leaking PI

Using the results of our seeded method, we now analyze the 2,789 domain-keys that contain user PI. In particular we aim to answer the following questions: (i) are there any specific types of user PI collected by particular kind of services and (ii) verify the existence of abusive domains that collect a broad range of user PI.

To this end, we focus on six types of PI: age range, city, email, gender, geo location, and name. For each root domain labeled as positive by our seeded method, we assign one of the following eleven service categories by manual inspection: Advertisement (*e.g.*, `ads.bluelithium.com`), Ad-

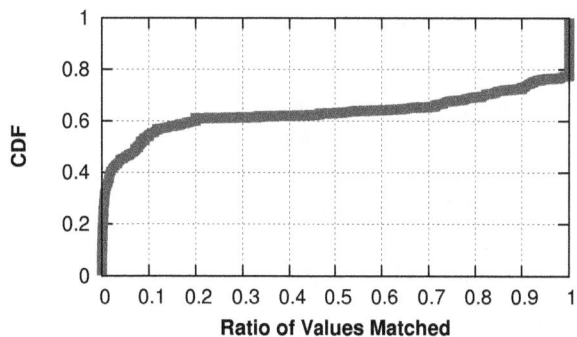

Figure 7: CDF of the ratio of values matched for email domain-keys discovered via seed rule.

67

ware[6] (`citibank.0009.ws`), Content Distribution Network (CDN) (`img-cdn.mediaplex.com`), User-tracking (`pixel.quantserve.com`), along with more familiar service categories of Game, OSN, Search-engines, Web-portals, and Adult. As an example of a domain with multiple services, we add Google in the category.

Figure 8 shows a heat map based on the probability density distribution of PI types by category. Comparing popularity of PI used across services, we notice that residential city turns out to be the most prevalently leaked PI (30.7%) followed by fine-grained geo-coordinates (15.2%) and gender information (10%).

PI leakage per service category With respect to question (i), we analyze the service categories that leak PI. CDNs highly benefit from spatial locality of cached data to users. Therefore, knowing user location is one of their primary interests. As shown in Figure 8, there is a high correlation between CDN and city. Similarly, for search engines, portals, and ad services, to which providing local information to users is also important, we observe high correlation to city and geo-location.

In contrary to the majority of the Internet service categories that exhibit high correlation to location information, OSNs show very low correlation to city and geo-location; they have comparatively high correlation with emails, gender, and age range. We speculate that this is due to the online-nature of the OSNs which weighs more on the knowledge of age and gender groups rather than physical locations.

In the case of adult services, knowledge on the age range and gender of users is deemed to be important as they may provide age-restricted, gender focused contents. From tracking category, we notice that some user-tracking web bugs, which are supposedly used for aggregated web analytics, can track and identify users by their email addresses.

PI leakage per service domain With respect to question (ii), we analyze the types of user PI leaked by different domains and identify domains more prone to leak user PI. Out of 588 different domains, we find 489 (83.1%) of them only have one type of PI leaked. 79 (13.4%) of them have two types of PI leaked, and overall, 20 (3.4%) of the domains have more than two types of PI. Interestingly, one domain in user-tracking category collects five types of PI. A cursory investigation reveals that this domain is identified by users as an invasive service and sometimes associated to spyware. From our traffic trace, we confirm similar suspicious behavior, as we observe the domain collecting email, name, gender, city, and location-related information, such as geographical coordinates. Among other examples of domains collecting above average amount of PI, we find large Internet service companies with ad services such as Google and Yahoo: `google.com` contains an average of 5 PI types per user, `google-analytics.com` with 4, `doubleclick.net` 6, and `yahoo.com` 5.

7. RELATED WORK

We now discuss the existing client-side privacy preserving tools, as well as related studies on measuring the personal information and privacy leakage.

---

[6]Different from advertisement services, we categorize adware as domains known to distribute undesired ads by means of phishing or malware.

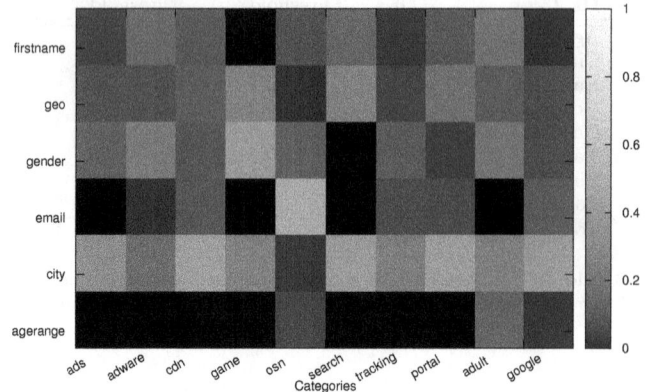

Figure 8: Heat map of PI leaked by categories of domains.

Measuring information leakage A number of projects [8–12] have examined privacy leaks by web sites, typically focusing on OSNs. By creating fake accounts on OSNs [8, 9, 11, 12] and on mobile services [10] and tracing all requests the browser makes, researchers were able to further examine how different information flows to third parties. In brief, these papers find that all OSNs exhibit some leakage of private information to third parties, typically via Request URIs and HTTP headers (e.g., `Host`, `User-Agent`, `Referrer`, and `Cookie`). These approaches are largely complimentary to the work presented in this paper, as we aim to develop a system that is able to detect leaks of (unknown) user data in a live network.

Client-side tools Researchers have developed client-side techniques such as browser extensions or add-ons, such as Adblock Plus [1, 2], RequestPolicy [19], NoScript [16], and NoTrace [17]. They have been widely used by many users, and also provide a way for researchers to measure the PI transmitted in the traffic. All the analyzed tools rely on standard blacklist/whitelist mechanisms of privacy protection. For example, AdBlock Plus is structured as a blacklist, blocking requests to a pre-defined list of advertisements and malware domains. Compared to our approach, these client-side tools offer users greater control over the process of blocking PI leaks, but face additional challenges obtaining large-scale deployment.

Recently, Ren et al. [18] have developed Recon, a client-side tool designed to capture mobile device traffic using a VPN and middlebox. Their system shares many of the same goals as ours, and the approach is largely complementary (the domain-keys that we identify as carrying PI can be leveraged by Recon as ones to flag, and their approach may offer visibility into HTTPS traffic if the user so chooses).

Static data flow analysis Static analysis aims to measure privacy leaks via the network between user applications and different web sites or mobile services. For example, PiOS [3] uses program slicing to detect privacy leaks in iOS apps. The use of static analysis enables exploring broad execution paths including infeasible ones. Similarly, Unsafe [7] focused on the advertising libraries the mobile apps contain. While static analysis has the potential to detect leaks before they occur, it often requires access to the application source code and can only feasibly be run on a small set of applications or web sites. In contrast, our approach only requires access to the network traffic, which can often be accomplished via a router tap.

Dynamic data flow analysis Different from the static analysis, dynamic analysis runs in real-time as a user executes applications. The major advantage of dynamic analysis is that, as users can provide relevance feedbacks to its false alerts, it can reduce false positives at runtime. For example, TaintDroid [4] used lightweight dynamic taint analysis built into modified Android middleware; the system alerts the user to the presence and nature of the leak in the whole apps. Similarly, Vision [6] directly instrumented the smartphone platform and tracked information flow at runtime. Leveraging unique Android execution model to reduce the search space, AppIntent [22] automatically presents a human analyst the UI manipulations that leads to the sensitive data transmission.

While these dynamic analyses can precisely pinpoint leaks from the devices they are installed, the intrinsic cost of their deployment (*e.g.*, having to install browser add-ons or custom Android builds) makes them difficult to deploy to a large userbase. Instead, integrating these data flow monitoring techniques to our approach which unobtrusively considers the network traffic at large, could lead to a more comprehensive solution to PI leakage detection (i.e., using static/dynamic analysis to identify additional potential keys of interest).

8. IMPACT AND LIMITATIONS

The method presented in this paper automatically locates personal information (PI) embedded in network traffic to Internet services. By detecting a limited number of instances of eight types of seed personal information the approach initially identifies a limited number of "containers" of personal information in terms of keys used by a specific service (or domain), hence domain-keys. Then, coverage is extended by inferring additional containers by analogy with the seeded ones. Our evaluation on a large-scale traffic trace collected on the network of a residential service provider shows that our proposed approach is able to locate the rare domain-keys that serve as containers for PI with low false negatives (2.7%) and acceptable false positives (13.6%).

Selecting thresholds The intervention of an analyst performing manual inspection on the PI identified by the methodology might be required in order to optimally set the thresholds at the basis of the operations of the proposed method. One of our future work directions will focus on automating threshold setting. For example, a "state space exploration" of the potential settings could be conducted to then pick the ones that perform best on a number of tests. This is not trivial as it might require a large amount of computation resources and carries the risk of overfitting. In the meantime, the need for having a human in the loop does not undermine the high value of the approach since it brings to the analyst attention only a small fraction of the large quantity of information flowing through the Internet. Without the support of this method, manually inspecting the full traffic has widely proven unfeasible.

Encrypted traffic Since the methodology here presented relies on inspection of data exchanged by Internet services its applicability can be limited when such data is encrypted or obfuscated. While the latter is a complexity that most service providers currently do not want to incur, in the last years the fraction of web traffic being encrypted (i.e., using HTTPS) has increased significantly. This does not undermine the relevance of the solution as it has several application areas of significant impact where the effectiveness of the methodology is not affected by the deployment of HTTPS.

PI leakage protection A service provider (being it an Internet, cloud, or cellular service provider) could offer to its customers a service to audit their traffic for PI that is potentially collected by third parties because it is being sent through the network in clear text form. This application does not require visibility into PI sent over encrypted connections as it does not represent a leakage in this context.

Enterprise protection against information leakage The proposed approach can be deployed by a company wanting to detect intentional and unintentional leakage of information critical to their business, which includes employees' PI. In this scenario the company will enforce all HTTP(S) traffic to go through a corporate (man-in-the-middle) proxy that terminates SSL sessions, thus acquiring visibility into encrypted traffic (in fact, there exist companies that use such proxies today). Such an approach requires applications (e.g., web browsers) to accept as legitimate the certificates that the proxy generates, signs with its own certificate, and presents in the initial SSL negotiation phase. This can be achieved by pre-loading the proxy certificate into corporate PCs as the certificate of a trusted certification authority. Employees that want to use their own devices to access the Internet through the corporate network are required to install the proxy certificate or manually accept the certificates offered when SSL sessions to new servers are negotiated.

PI disclosure assessment and control A provider could offer a service that identifies PI being embedded in the traffic of a user, both protected (i.e., through HTTPS) and unprotected. As it is common in many other contexts, such as online social networks, free e-mail services, etc., customers interested in the service are willing to grant the provider with visibility into their encrypted traffic. This can be achieved by the user either loading the certificate of a man-in-the-middle proxy operated by the service provider in the trusted certification authority repository, or installing a module (e.g., a browser plugin) that analyses the traffic before being encrypted [13]. Our technique can then be applied within the proxy or the plugin.

Future work As part of our future work we plan to extend the methodology to differentiate between PI the user has intentionally shared and other that was not, which is particularly valuable in the last application scenario listed above. One possible way to do this is by occasionally surveying users about observed leaks, learn of a few (in)voluntary ones, and extend the knowledge across users and web services. Eventually, we aim to build a system capable of informing users when personal information is being leaked without an explicit act on their side, so that they can decide whether the leak should be allowed or blocked (e.g., by substituting information with placeholders [18]).

Acknowledgements

We thank the anonymous reviewers and our shepherd, Ben Zhao, for their helpful comments. This research was supported in part by NSF grants CNS-1054233, CNS-1409191, CNS-1319019, and CNS-1421444. Any opinions, findings, and conclusions or recommendations expressed in this material are those of the authors and do not necessarily reflect the views of the NSF.

9. REFERENCES

[1] AdBlock Plus. https://adblockplus.org/.

[2] Adblock Plus : Statistics for Adblock Plus. http://bit.ly/10WEytx.

[3] M. Egele, C. Kruegel, E. Kirda, and G. Vigna. Pios: Detecting privacy leaks in ios applications. In *NDSS*, 2011.

[4] W. Enck, P. Gilbert, B.-G. Chun, L. P. Cox, J. Jung, P. McDaniel, and A. N. Sheth. Taintdroid: An information-flow tracking system for realtime privacy monitoring on smartphones. In *OSDI*, 2010.

[5] H. Falaki, D. Lymberopoulos, R. Mahajan, S. Kandula, and D. Estrin. A first look at traffic on smartphones. In *SIGCOMM IMC*, 2010.

[6] P. Gilbert, B.-G. Chun, L. P. Cox, and J. Jung. Vision: Automated security validation of mobile apps at app markets. In *MCS*, 2011.

[7] M. C. Grace, W. Zhou, X. Jiang, and A.-R. Sadeghi. Unsafe exposure analysis of mobile in-app advertisements. In *WISEC*, 2012.

[8] B. Krishnamurthy. Privacy and online social networks: Can colorless green ideas sleep furiously? In *IEEE Security and Privacy*, 2013.

[9] B. Krishnamurthy and C. Wills. Privacy diffusion on the web: a longitudinal perspective. In *WWW*, 2009.

[10] B. Krishnamurthy and C. E. Wills. On the Leakage of Personally Identifiable Information Via Online Social Networks. In *WOSN*, 2009.

[11] B. Krishnamurthy and C. E. Wills. Privacy leakage in mobile online social networks. In *WOSN*, 2010.

[12] D. Malandrino, A. Petta, V. Scarano, L. Serra, R. Spinelli, and B. Krishnamurthy. Privacy awareness about information leakage: Who knows what about me? In *WPES*, 2013.

[13] H. Metwalley, S. Traverso, M. Mellia, S. Miskovic, and M. Baldi. CrowdSurf: Empowering Informed Choices in the Web. *CCR*, 45(4), 2015.

[14] mitmproxy: a man-in-the-middle proxy. http://mitmproxy.org/.

[15] mitmproxy Installation. http://mitmproxy.org/doc/install.html.

[16] NoScript. http://noscript.net/.

[17] NoTrace. http://www.isislab.it/projects/NoTrace/.

[18] J. Ren, A. Rao, M. Lindorfer, A. Legout, and D. Choffnes. Recon: Revealing and controlling privacy leaks in mobile network traffic. http://arxiv.org/abs/1507.00255.

[19] RequestPolicy. https://www.requestpolicy.com/.

[20] A. Sapio, Y. Liao, M. Baldi, G. Ranjan, F. Risso, A. Tongaonkar, R. Torres, and A. Nucci. Per-user policy enforcement on mobile apps through network functions virtualization. In *MobiArch*, 2014.

[21] Q. Xu, J. Erman, A. Gerber, Z. Mao, J. Pang, and S. Venkataraman. Identifying diverse usage behaviors of smartphone apps. In *IMC*, 2011.

[22] Z. Yang, M. Yang, Y. Zhang, G. Gu, P. Ning, and X. S. Wang. Appintent: analyzing sensitive data transmission in android for privacy leakage detection. In *CCS*, 2013.

The City Privacy Attack: Combining Social Media and Public Records for Detailed Profiles of Adults and Children

Tehila Minkus
New York University
tehila@nyu.edu

Yuan Ding
New York University
dingyuan1987@gmail.com

Ratan Dey
New York University
ratan@nyu.edu

Keith W. Ross
NYU and NYU-Shanghai
keithwross@nyu.edu

ABSTRACT

Data brokers have traditionally collected data from businesses, government records, and other publicly available offline sources. While each data source may provide only a few elements about a person's activities, data brokers combine these elements to form a detailed, composite view of the consumer's life. The emergence of social media gives data brokers unprecedented opportunities to enhance their profiles. Data brokers are increasingly interested in combining the information collected from offline sources with information publicly available in social networks to profile not only adults but also children.

In this paper, we show how data brokers and other third parties can combine online and offline data sources – namely, public Facebook profiles and voter registration records – to create detailed profiles of adults, teens, and children in any target city in the US. We outline and execute an approach that leverages a Facebook user's social ties combined with the city's voter registration records to infer the Facebook users who reside in the city. These inferences enable a data broker to create detailed user profiles, which not only include information publicly available from Facebook but also the user's exact residential address, date and year of birth, and political affiliation. We further show how additional inferences can be made from the combined data. We then discuss how this city attack can be extended to create detailed profiles of minors and children. Finally, we make recommendations to Facebook, municipal authorities, and individuals to decrease the risk of this large-scale privacy breach.

1. INTRODUCTION

In a recent report, the Federal Trade Commission (FTC) alerted the public about the privacy risks of data brokers, calling for more transparency in the industry [2]. The primary business of data brokers is collecting personal information about individuals from a variety of sources in order to aggregate, analyze, and share that information and its derivatives for marketing products and performing credit checks. This information could also be sold to employers, dating sites, political parties, and college recruitment offices.

Data brokers have traditionally collected data from businesses, government records, and other offline sources. These include bankruptcy information, voting registration, consumer purchase data, warranty registrations, and other details of consumers' everyday interactions. While each data source may provide only a few elements about a consumer's activities, data brokers combine these elements to form a detailed composite of the consumer's life. Historically, data brokers have only offered lists about adults, rather than children or teenagers.

The emergence of social media gives data brokers unprecedented opportunities to enhance their profiles. Data brokers are increasingly interested in combining the information collected from offline sources with information publicly available online, such as social media and blogs [2]. Furthermore, because the children's market surpasses $200 billion in the US alone, it is not surprising that data brokers have recently also begun to compile dossiers on children as well [25] [26].

In this paper, we explore how profiles can be enriched by combining the public information available from a social network – namely, Facebook - with public records – namely, voter registration records. We consider not only the profiling of adults but also of minors, i.e. teens and children. We show that with just these two sources of information, data brokers can create alarmingly detailed profiles about adults, teens, and children. Data brokers with extensive financial resources and hundreds of employees can then build upon these profiles, creating a snowball effect.

1.1 Motivational Example

To motivate this study, let us consider an example of the potential outcomes from matching, say, an adult woman listed in a voter registration record and a specific Facebook account. Suppose that this woman has two children living at the same address, one son in high school and one daughter in elementary school. Further suppose the mother posts pictures of her children to Facebook, and her privacy settings make these photos publicly available [18]. Finally, we can also make the very reasonable assumption (as discussed in the body of this paper) that the voter record for this adult contains the woman's exact home address, birth date and year, and political affiliation. Then by combining this woman's Facebook profile with her voter registration record, the data

COSN'15, November 2–3, 2015, Palo Alto, California, USA.
ⓒ 2015 ACM. ISBN 978-1-4503-3951-3/15/11 ...$15.00.
DOI: http://dx.doi.org/10.1145/2817946.2817957.

broker immediately knows the woman's exact street address, birth day and year, political affiliation, profile picture, and all her public Facebook profile information, possibly including additional photos, her list of Facebook friends, education, workplace, likes, and so on. Beginning with this profile, the data broker can potentially further infer gender, religion, sexual orientation, economic level (as based on address of residence), ethnicity, and so on [16] [27] [6].

Continuing with the example, the data broker can also use Facebook to find all the high-school students living in the the adult woman's city [8]. For each of these students, the data broker can create profiles that include name, gender, profile photo, high school, graduation year, and friends. By matching the last name of the woman with the last names of the high-school students (or by making use of Facebook friend lists), the data broker can identify the Facebook account of the woman's high-school son. The data broker can then enhance the profiles of this high-school student by combining the high-school profiles in [8] with the information in the voter records, including exact home address, parents' full names, birth dates, and political affiliations.

Since the mother is also posting pictures of her children, the data broker can also compile dossiers on young children who may not even have Facebook accounts [18]. These profiles can include the child's name, birth date, and home address, as well as his parents' full names, birth dates and political affiliations.

1.2 Beyond Data Brokers

Up until this point, we have focused our discussion on profiles created by data brokers. But other parties are potentially interested in combining public records with social media to obtain combinations of social, personal and demographic datapoints. For example, as the political industry refines microtargeting techniques [15], there is increased demand for fine-grained information about individual voters. By matching a voter registration record to a specific Facebook profile, a political campaign would be able to send personalized messages to the voter in order to sway or influence his voting behaviors. However, a 2012 survey of American voters found that a majority of voters responded negatively to the idea of political data collection and microtargeting [28]. Moreover, creating a list of registered voters on Facebook would also identify which Facebook users are not registered to vote. This would allow political campaigns to target non-voters in voter registration drive for get-out-the-vote purposes.

The profiles could also be used to fuel a large-scale and highly personalized spear-phishing attacks. Messages could automatically be generated to include the target's address, birth date, Facebook friends and so on, with the goal of tricking the targets into installing malware or providing financial information to enable financial cybercrimes.

Finally, consider Facebook's own potential interest in public records. Because Facebook earns virtually all of its revenues from targeted advertising, there is a direct correlation between Facebook's stock price and the amount and quality of the information it has about its users. Facebook, as well as other social networks, is likely interested in obtaining offline information from public records (or indirectly from data brokers), and combining this information with the data it directly obtains and infers from user activity on Facebook. In fact, Facebook as already partnered with Acxiom, one of the largest data brokers [3].

1.3 Contribution

Combining information from Facebook and voter registration records hinges on *the ability to match a person in a voter registration list with a Facebook user with a high degree of certainty*. The problem is challenging because a name in a voter registration list can match with hundreds of Facebook accounts. In this paper, we show how a data broker can simplify the task by performing the voter-to-Facebook user matching on a *city-by-city basis*. Within a city, the number of possible name matches is substantially reduced, often to only one. When there are multiple matches, additional information in Facebook and the voter records can often reduce ambiguities. We refer to the *City Privacy Attack* as the problem of attempting to profile all the residents of a given city – including adults, teens, and children – by matching voter records with Facebook users.

In principle, for a given target city, matching the Facebook users residing in the city to the adults in the city's voter list should simplify the problem. But most Facebook users do not provide their current city information in their public profiles, making it difficult to match them to the voter records. In this paper, we develop a novel methodology for inferring the Facebook users who live in the target city. This methodology combines the information in the voter lists with the public Facebook friend lists. As a case study, we select a small city in the Northeast USA for analysis. After obtaining the voter list from municipal authorities, we propose and evaluate several methods to match each voter to a single Facebook account. We also discuss how the attack can be extended to profiling the minors and children in the city, show how the profiles can be enhanced by inference techniques, and finally make recommendations to Facebook and about voter data use.

The structure of this paper is as follows. In Section 2, we discuss voter registration records and their prevalence throughout the United States. We also detail how the characteristics of our dataset. In Section 3, we consider several naïve approaches to matching voter data with Facebook profiles. Since these approaches prove unsuccessful, we introduce a more sophisticated approach in Section 4 using social ties to match Facebook users to voters from the targeted city. In Section 5, we analyze the results and limitations of this approach. In Section 6, we show how this attack can be extended to teens and children in the targeted city. In Section 7, we show how the combination of voter and Facebook data allows an observer to infer new traits about the targeted voters. In Section 8, we present a survey of related work, and in Section 9 we discuss the implications of our findings. Finally, in Section 10, we conclude.

1.4 Ethical Considerations

Conducting privacy research on public data can be ethically sensitive. In this work, we took measures to ensure minimal risk of exposure for any individuals whose data was studied. For this reason, we do not mention identifying details about individuals in the course of this paper. Moreover, we believe that it is important to discuss the privacy risks that can attend public release of data, and that the benefits of public discourse on this subject outweigh the risks.

2. VOTER REGISTRATION RECORDS

According to a study by the California Voter Foundation in 2004 [4], all 50 states in the USA require voters to pro-

Data field	States Collecting
Name	50
Address	50
Signature	50
Date of birth	49
Phone number	46
Gender	34
All or part of SSN	30
Party affiliation	27
Place of birth	14
Driver's license number	11
Race	9
Special assistance requirements	4
Parent's name	3
Email address	2
Occupation	1

Table 1: Information that different states require voters to supply [4].

Data field	States Redacting	Sharing
Birthdates (some or all)	11	38
Phone numbers	5	41
Social Security numbers	29	1
Birthplace	2	12
Driver's license numbers	6	5

Table 2: Among the states who collect certain data fields, the number of states who redact the information or share it with third parties [4].

vide their name, address and signature prior to voting. In addition, many mandate that voters must additional information, such as phone number, gender, Social Security number, and additional demographic data. For a breakdown of state requirements, see Table 1.

These data are collected under the auspices of voter registration, yet their use is not strictly confined to usage by voting registrars and poll workers. The lists are put to use by government and judiciaries: in all 50 states, political parties and candidates are granted access to the voter rolls, and 43 states use voter lists as a source for jury duty service. 27 of the states allow certain voters (such as public figures or victims of domestic violence) the right to retract parts or all of their voter registration records before the lists are shared.

Beyond these political and judicial uses, voter data is shared with third parties in many states. 22 states grant unrestricted commercial access to their voter rolls. While some states redact certain fields (see Table 2), many data fields are left visible to anyone who can access the voter registration lists.

2.1 Obtaining Voter Data

For the analyses in this paper, we arbitrarily selected a small city in the Northeast USA. As per the 2010 United States Census, the target township has approximately 70,000 people, 27,000 households, and 19,000 families.[1] The city is

[1] A family consists of two or more people (one of whom is the householder) related by birth, marriage, or adoption residing in the same housing unit. A household consists of all people who occupy a housing unit regardless of relationship[1]

approximately 78% white and 22% minorities. The median annual income is about USD 90,000.

After contacting the municipality, we were able to purchase a CD of the voter registration records for USD 35.00. The records obtained include all adult citizens who have registered to vote in the specific county/municipality (check out terminology). Each voter registration record contains the following fields:

- **Name:** Every voter's first and last name was included. Additional fields, such as middle name, prefix, and suffix, were optional.

- **Gender:** 17.3% of the voters were male, 20.1% were female, and 62.5% chose not to identify their gender. (In Section 7.1 we discuss methods to infer genders for these voters.)

- **Address:** Each voter's complete street address and zip code was included.

- **Political affiliation:** Voters were allowed to choose between Democrat, Republican, and unaffiliated. 38.1% chose Democrat, 16.1% chose Republican, and 45.7% are not officially affiliated with any party.

- **Date of birth:** For all voters, the month, day, and year of birth were included.

- **Other dates:** The date on which each voter registered to vote is also included, as well as the date upon which they officially received their voting privileges. Additionally, when applicable, the date of the voter's party registration is also indicated.

Notably, the voter registration records do not specify the user's family members or marital status. In some cases, the voter's gender is also missing. In Section 7, we introduce methods to infer these characteristics as well.

3. TARGETED-INDIVIDUAL APPROACH

There are a variety of ways to attempt matching voter records to Facebook profiles. In this section, we discuss the category of approaches that focus on searching Facebook for specific voters, one by one.

3.1 Matching Voters by Name

Facebook uses a real name policy, requiring users to supply their actual names when they register with the social network. As such, it would seem easy to match a voter's name to a Facebook user's name. But this simple process is flawed due to the frequency of common names in Facebook. We illustrate with a small experiment, where we randomly choose 100 names from the voter registration list and search those for those names in the Facebook name directory.

For each user, we inserted their name into the custom search URL https://www.facebook.com/search/str/NAME/ users-named/intersect to search for matching profiles, replacing the string NAME with the user's first and last name. We then counted the number of profiles returned by the search.

In Figure 1, we show the distribution of how many people were matched to no profiles, one profile, or multiple profiles when using their names as keywords. As the figure shows,

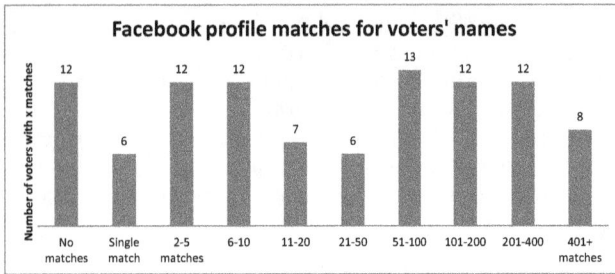

Figure 1: Matching voters by name across all of Facebook.

this results bears some strong limitations. A distinct, one-to-one Facebook profile match was found for only 6% of the randomly selected voters. More than half of the selected voters (58%) had more than 10 Facebook profiles that share their names. Therefore, it becomes apparent that this approach casts too wide a net. Since more than 1 billion people use Facebook[2], even relatively rare names can occur several times in the Facebook population. As such, using name as the single criterion is insufficient to match voter records to Facebook profiles.

3.2 Geo-targeted approach

What if one employs the location information from a Facebook user's profile to help narrow down the search space? Using location information can increase the matching precision, but many Facebook users do not include their current city in their public profile. For example, Dey et al. [9] found that only 36% people provided current city information publicly. As such, relying on the users' explicit location information will overlook many users who have not shared their location in their public profiles.

To illustrate this, we also searched for the 100 randomly selected voters on Facebook along with their city. We used the URL `https://www.facebook.com/search/str/NAME/users-named/intersect/str/CITY-ID/residents/intersect`, replacing `NAME` with the user's name and `CITY-ID` with the numerical ID of the targeted city. Of the 100 voters, 82 had no Facebook matches at all. 16 voters had exactly one match, while one voter had two matches and another voter had three matches.

As this experiment shows, searching for users' names and explicit location data has very low recall. Additionally, this class of approaches carries a high overhead, since an individual query is required for every user. In the next section, we explore a more efficient and effective approach towards matching voter records with Facebook profiles.

4. CITY ATTACK

In the previous section, we used the names from voter records as keywords to search for corresponding Facebook profiles with limited success. In this section, we develop a novel methodology for inferring the Facebook users who live in the target city. This methodology combines the information in the voter lists with the publicly available friend lists.

Figure 2 summarizes the approach. Using Facebook graph search, we first find some of the people who live in the

[2]https://newsroom.fb.com/company-info/

target city. Specifically, after logging into Facebook, we enter the URL `https://www.facebook.com/search/str/CITY-ID/residents/intersect` in the address bar of the browser, replacing `CITY-ID` with the numerical Facebook ID of the city. Facebook returns a list of some of the people who live or have lived in the target city; this list auto-populates as the user scrolls down. We automate this process, continuing to browse until we find "End of Results". This provides a partial list of people (including their Facebook names and IDs) who are currently living in the target city. We then add their IDs to a seed list as shown in Figure 2. For our target city example, we automated this process with four accounts, yielding a list of 10,200 people who currently live in the target city.

We then attempt to find corresponding matches in the voter registration records, using the first and last names from the Facebook profiles. We also enriched these lists using an auxiliary database of common nicknames. For each Facebook page, we checked if the first name was included in a list of common nicknames. If it was, then we also tried to find voter record matches for the full names corresponding to that nickname. We then put these matched IDs in the "match pool". Of the 10,200 seed Facebook accounts, we found corresponding voter records for 5,294. We then proceed as follows:

1. Repeat for all members of the match pool (until some threshold is reached):

   (a) Retrieve the user's friends list.

   (b) Check if a friend's name is found in the voter list. If so, add the friend to the potential match pool.

2. Output the match pool as the list of potential matches.

If a user self-identifies as a resident of the target city and also matches to a voter record, we consider the user to be a potential match. For Facebook users who have not identified their location, there is reasonable likelihood of being registered voters in the target city, since both *their names* and the name of *at least one respective friend* are found in the voter registration list.

5. RESULTS

Since there is no ground truth readily available for this dataset, we instead measuer the overall accuracy of the matches by employing a set of heuristics and filtering results. We report our results in this section.

Following the approach detailed in Section 4, we used Facebook's Graph Search to download a list of users in our target city. Beginning with these seeds, we iteratively crawled over 1 million users and identified 35,556 Facebook accounts whose name or nicknames correspond to an entry in the voter registration list.

For some of the voters, more than one match was found, since multiple Facebook accounts with the voter's name were discovered over the course of the crawling process. Thus, the set of candidate-match Facebook accounts corresponded to a smaller set of voter records. Specifically, 20,481 voter registration records had one or more matches in the Facebook set after two iterations. We stopped at this point since we had reached a significant coverage of the voting registration list (37 percent of records).

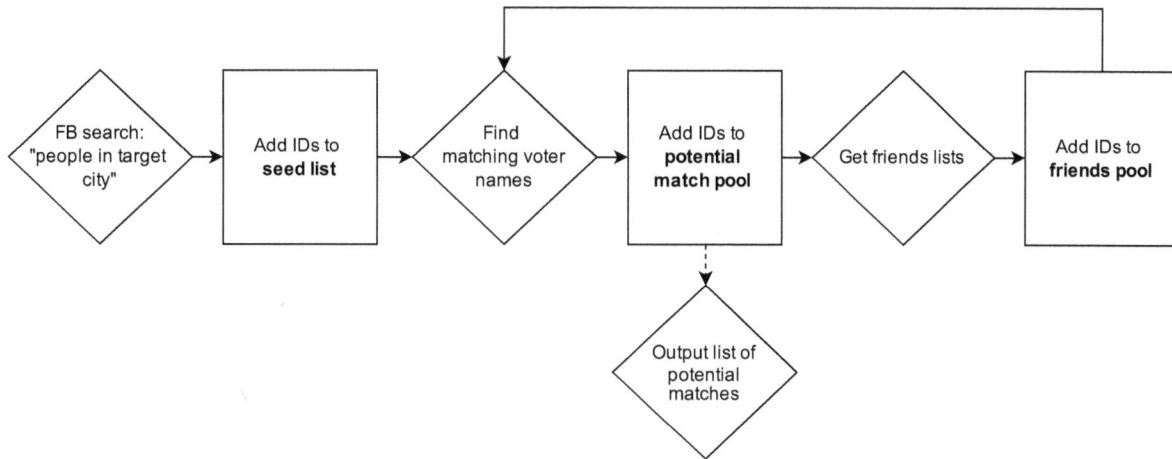

Figure 2: The process for crawling potential residents of the target city.

5.1 Filtering for Accuracy

In total, we had 20,481 records in the voter registration list matching to 35,556 users in Facebook. Among these Facebook users, we found that 15,501 of them had entered their current city and hometown as places other than the target city; therefore, we exclude them from further analysis. After this filtering step, we have a candidate set of 20,055 users in the set of candidate Facebook matches, corresponding to 16,457 voter records.

Among these users, 7,197 have shared on Facebook that their hometown or current location is the target city. The rest of the users have not specified where they live, but they have an average of approximately seven friends who have shared that they live in the target city. Considering the relatively small size of the target city, combined with the fact that many users don't share their location, this indicates that these users with unknown locations are likely to live in the target city.

5.2 Analysis of Social Ties for Location Inference

To ensure correct inference of the users' location, we conduct another filtering step based on the users' friends lists. Intuitively, we can expect that if a person has many friends from a given location, he is likely to be from that location as well.

For this purpose, we introduce a measure denoted f. For a user who has a public friends list, we can count how many friends he has among the other potential residents (in our case, 20,055 users); so for a Facebook user i, f_i is the number of friends in his list who are also in the potential match pool set.

5.2.1 Reverse Friends-List Lookup

Among the 20,055 Facebook candidate matches, 8,283 users hid their friends list from the public. This would make it difficult to measure the strength of their social ties within our dataset. However, the design of the Facebook friends list enables one to learn about a user's friendship ties based on the information that others have made public [8].

For example, imagine that John and Martha are both users of Facebook. John is privacy-conscious, so he hides his friends-list. Martha is more interested in a robust online social life, so she shares her friends list. Since Martha is friends with John, we are now able to learn of at least one of John's friendships even though he hid his friends list. If all of John's friends share their friends lists, then we will be able to learn all of his social ties despite his restrictive privacy settings.

We leverage this reverse look-up method to introduce an alternate measure for f for users who have hidden their friends lists: we count how many other users in the dataset have listed them as friends (i.e. for user i, $f_i = x$ if we can find this user in the friends lists of x other users in this dataset). In this way, we can indirectly infer how strongly they are socially tied to the other members of our dataset.

This method is not guaranteed to retrieve all friendships of the users with private friendlists; therefore, the inferred friend lists are usually shorter than the public friend lists. To correct for this disparity, we introduce a corrective weighting scheme. On average, the users with public friends lists had 189% as many friends in the dataset as those who did not share their friends lists. Therefore, we multiply the friend-count of the users who hid their friendslists by a factor of 1.89. This ensures that the f-measure of the more private users is on the same scale as the other users.

5.2.2 Parameter Selection

If user i has a high value for f_i, i.e. he has many friends who are in the dataset, then it is likely that he is indeed located in the target city. For lower values of f, more potential matches are allowed; higher values of f restrict the set of matches to users who have more social connections within the potential match pool. A natural heuristic is to assume that a Facebook user i is a resident of the target city if either (i) the user self-identifies as a resident of the city; (ii) or has an f_i value at least equal to some threshold f.

Let $N(f)$ be the number of Facebook users in the possible match pool who have f_i values of at least f or say they live in the target city. Thus $N(1) = 20,055$. Figure 3 plots N(f) as a function of the threshold F. For lower values of f, there are more matches allowed. As f is raised, the matching criteria become more restrictive and allow for fewer matches.

While choosing lower values of f allows for more matches, these matches are less precise and more prone to duplicate matches for a single voter. Raising the f-value results in

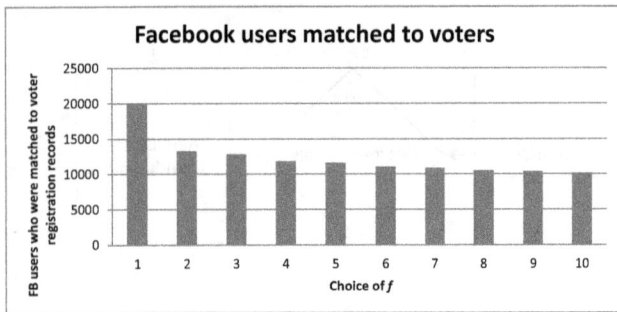

Figure 3: The number of Facebook users who were matched to a voter registration record, as a function of the choice of f.

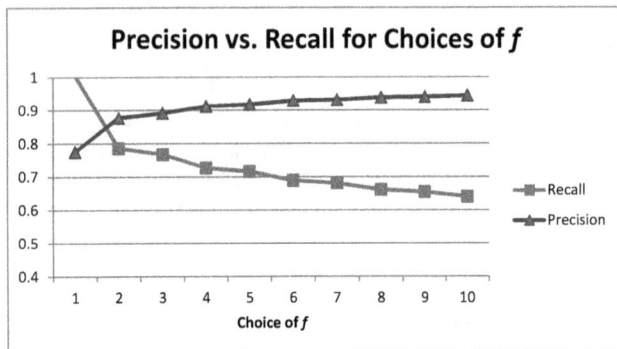

Figure 4: Precision and recall for each value of f. Precision measures the percentage of matches that were one-to-one. Recall measures the percentage of voters in our filtered set who were matched to at least one Facebook profile.

fewer duplicate matches. Thus, fewer voters are matched respectively to multiple Facebook pages, increasing precision. But raising the choice for this parameter also decreases the overall recall, by allowing fewer potential matches to be considered. As such, setting the f-value is a tradeoff between precision and recall. We quantify this tradeoff in Figure 4. Precision for a given value of f refers to the percentage of one-to-one matches among all users in $N(f)$. Recall for a given value of f refers to the percentage of the 16,457 voters in our dataset who had a match suggested from among $N(f)$.

5.3 Limitations

We point out several limitations which make it difficult or impossible to determine a precise match for each of the voters in the registration list. Firstly, it is likely that not all voters are registered users on Facebook. According to a Pew Research poll in September 2014, only 58% of American adults aged 18+ used Facebook [11]. For these voters, there are no corresponding Facebook accounts that can be correctly matched to their records.

Secondly, there are name-related ambiguities which can be difficult to solve. We explore possible reasons for finding multiple matching Facebook accounts for a single voter record. We randomly select 50 accounts from voting list who have double matches among the Facebook accounts, and discovered three patterns:

- **Multiple account creation**: Some people may retain multiple Facebook accounts. For example, two Facebook accounts matching to the same voter name shared a name, location, occupation, and some contacts, but one of the accounts has no new posts since 2012. It seems likely that this user abandoned the older Facebook account in favor of a new account but never deleted the older account. It would be of interest to attempt to filter out the duplicate inactive accounts, although it is not pursued here.

- **Multiple people with the same name**: There might be two or more people in the city with the same name, with only one of them registered to vote. For example, one voting record in our dataset was matched to two Facebook pages that seemed to belong to different people. As such, it is likely that for some names, there are multiple residents in the target city yet not all of them have registered to vote.

- **Low local-friendship threshold (f-measure)**: If a low threshold is set for the measure of local friendships, then incorrect matches might be suggested for voters. For example, in our dataset, one voter record matched to two Facebook accounts; one of these Facebook accounts had 26 local friends, but the other one has only 3 local friends. Thus the first match is more likely to be correct than the second.

Finally, when multiple voters share the same name, they may all be matched to the same set of Facebook accounts. For example, if several voters in the town are named Jane Doe, and there are also many women in the candidate Facebook set who are named Jane Doe, then there will be many potential matches between the two datasets. To disambiguate these cases, we may be able to use ages. Recall that the voter records typically give the ages of the voters. Although most Facebook users do not make their age publicly available, following the work of Dey et al. [10], it may be possible to estimate the ages of the Facebook users and thus employ age as a factor for more precise matching between voter records and Facebook. Additionally, by using face recognition and age estimation software, it may be possible to estimate a Facebook user's age based on his profile photo [13]. This estimated age could then be used as another data point in finding a correspondence to a distinct voter registration record. We leave this approach to future work.

We emphasize that the intention of this work is to provide a proof-of-concept for the idea of matching between offline databases and online social networking account. Since we did not have ground truth for this dataset, we have instead relied on reasonable assumptions to guide our algorithms towards likely matches. By demonstrating several matching techniques, we introduce a lower bound on matching accuracy and recall for real-life and online databases.

6. PROFILING TEENS AND CHILDREN

In the previous sections, we detailed how the combination of voter records and Facebook profiles enables an attacker to profile a large portion of the adults in a city. We now describe how it is possible to extend this profiling attack to high school students, who may have Facebook accounts but are too young to register to vote, as well as to children, who do not even have their own accounts on Facebook.

6.1 Profiling Teens

Facebook takes precautions to limit third parties from using its services to discover and profile minors. These precautions include banning young children from joining, excluding minors from search results, and displaying minimal public information for minors, no matter how they configure their privacy settings. Dey et al. recently showed, however, that an attacker, with modest crawling and computational resources, and employing data mining heuristics, can circumvent these precautions and create extensive profiles of *most* of the high school students in any targeted city [8]. Since some children lie about their ages when registering, this increases the exposure for themselves and also for their non-lying friends. In particular, using Facebook and for a given target high school, the attack described in [8] finds most of the students in the school, and for each discovered student infers a profile that includes significantly more information than their initial public profile. The information minimally includes the student's full name, profile picture, current high-school, graduation year, inferred birth year, and list of school friends.

We now outline how it is possible to significantly enhance these teen profiles by leveraging the techniques in this paper. Specifically, for each high-school student discovered and profiled using the techniques in [8], we can attempt to match the student to his/her parents in the voter registration list. There are two natural approaches to perform this matching. The first approach is to simply match the student's last name to the last names in the voter registration list. Given that most children inherit the last name of one or more of their parents, this simple approach should provide matches for almost all the high school students discovered in [8]. However, for students with common last names, there will likely be multiple matches, resulting in some ambiguity.

The second approach exploits the fact that some parents are Facebook friends with their children. In this approach, we examine the friend lists of all the high school students and also the friend lists of all of the adults profiled by the techniques in this paper, and look for common last names between adult and high-school student. As compared to the first approach, this last approach will give fewer duplicate matches but will also not provide as much coverage, as some children are not Facebook friends with their parents.

Once a high-school student is matched with a parent, then in addition to the profile information obtained in [8], the attacker now knows the teen's exact home address as well as the parent's full name, birthdate, marital status (see Section 7), and political affiliations. This additional information – and in particular the exact home address – is particular sensitive and can even put the teens at risk.

6.2 Profiling Children

Minkus et al. [18] showed that many parents post their children's photos along with their names and birthdates. This allows an outside observer, online service provider, or surveillant authority to learn facts about these young children. Using the techniques in this paper, a parent's Facebook account can also be matched to a voter registration record, allowing the attacker to develop detailed profiles of the parent. Thus, when a parent posts photos of her child, an attacker can generate a profile of the child that includes the child's address, name, birthdate and photos, as well as everything obtained about the child's parents using the methodology

described in the previous sections. This is troubling from a privacy perspective, particularly since these children are often too young to maintain their own Facebook accounts or consent to their information being shared.

7. ENHANCING THE COMBINED DATASET

In Section 4, we developed a methodology for matching Facebook users to voter registration records. The combination of these data sources allows a third party to construct profiles based on the voter records as well as social and personal traits gleaned from the public Facebook page. However, many important data fields are still sparse or unavailable in this dataset. Specifically, many of the voters and Facebook users have not specified their sex, marital status, or family units. These traits are of interest to third-party data aggregators, such as data brokers, political parties, and advertisers. Can they be inferred by using the combination of Facebook profiles, voter records, and some auxiliary information from the public domain?

7.1 Filling in Missing Genders

In the voter registration records that we acquired, many voters had not provided their gender; specifically, 62.5% of the registered voters had left the gender field blank. In this section, we detail an approach towards inferring a person's gender based on his or her name and some auxiliary data. Our approach enables us to assign a presumed gender to 91.9% of all the voters.

We collected a list of auxiliary name data. The United States Social Security Administration makes available a list of the top 1,000 names for boys and girls born in specific years or decades[3]. We collected and parsed the lists spanning the decades from 1910 through 1999, which encompassed the birth years of the voters in our targeted city. We created two name directories, one for boy names and one for girl names, with each name weighted by the number of times it had appeared in the top-thousand list for that gender.

We then used this auxiliary data source to predict a gender for voters who had not specified one. If a voter's name appeared only in the SSA list of boy names, we presume that voter to be male; likewise, if the name appears only the in the SSA female name list, then we consider that voter to be female.

However, in some cases, a name appeared in both the male and female lists of the SSA, thus leading to some ambiguity. For example, the name Linda was a top-thousand name for girls in all of the nine decades under consideration, but in three of the decades in question, it was also a top-thousand name for boys. In such cases, we apply a simple heuristic: since the name Linda appears more often in the top-thousand lists as a girl name, we assume that a voter named Linda is a woman. Using the SSA records with these heuristics allowed us to learn the genders of an additional 27,905 voters (83.9% of the voters who had not provided a gender).

Finally, some names were not included in the SSA lists due to their relative obscurity. To provide better coverage of these names, we utilized the voter registration lists to find other voters who had specified both such a name and the given gender. In cases where the name had been used for both men and women in the voter registration records, we resolved it by simple voting as explained in the previous

---

[3] Available at http://www.behindthename.com/top/

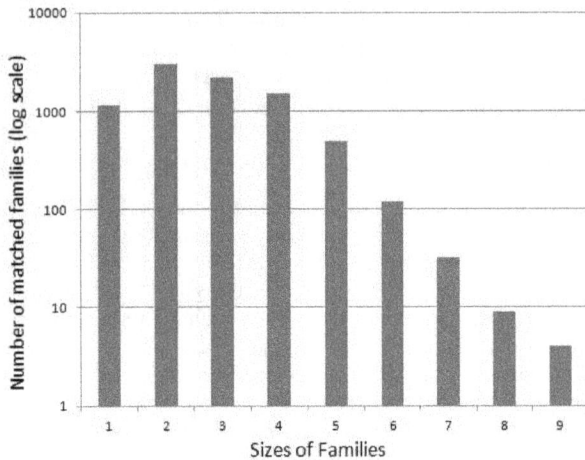

Figure 5: The number of families of each size, among families where at least one member who was matched to the voter records.

paragraph. This technique enabled us to learn the names of an additional 733 voters, or 14.5% of the voters who had not specified a gender and whose names did not appear on the SSA top-thousand lists.

After adding the 20,097 voters who initially provided their gender (37.5% overall) to the 29,178 voters for whom we inferred a gender (54.4% overall), we are left with gender data for 91.9% of voters.

7.2 Households and Family Units

We utilize the home address information of the 53,600 registered voters to infer households and family units. We predict household units using a simple heuristic: if people live in the same home or apartment, then we consider them to be a family or household. Specifically, if the house number, street name, and residential unit are identical for two or more residents, we consider them as a household. Using these approach, we group the voters into 25,007 households.

For each household, we check if any members have been precisely matched to a Facebook page. 8581 households have at least one member who was matched. Most of these households have only one member who has matched with the Facebook list; less than 10 households have six or more members who were matched to Facebook profiles.

In Figure 5, we show the distribution of family sizes for these 8,581 households. This family size is based on the voter registration list. Most of the households have 2-5 members, which is typical in the US.

7.3 Determining Marital Status

In this section, we examine the 25,007 presumed families to discover married couples. We use the following heuristics:

- Suppose there are only two people in a household, one male and one female, both of them are over 21 years old. Then we say they are married.

- Suppose there are three or more people in a household. Among those in the household, suppose there are a man and a woman, both of them are over 25, and the age difference between them is less than ten. Then we say they are married.

- All other people are presumed to be single.

After applying the above heuristics to our voter registration list augmented with gender predictions (as detailed in Section 7.1), we can detect 12,732 married couples among the 25,007 households.

Table 3 shows which traits can be learned about the voters by using each of the data sources individually, or in combination, or in combination with inference. Personal attributes like political affiliation, birth year, date and full home address are included in voter registration records. In Facebook, more than 95% of the people had hidden these fields from strangers, yet combining their profiles with voter registration data (when available) exposed this information.

7.4 Further Inferences

In this paper, we showed that the combination of voter records and Facebook profiles can be used to infer new facts about voters, such as gender, marital status, and family connections. In addition, it would be possible to infer additional facts based on the social connections and profile data of the users in question. For example, a third party could enrich these profiles with sexual orientation and race or ethnicity. This brings privacy concerns about big-data techniques into stronger relief.

Sexual Orientation.

Jernigan and Mistree [16] also showed that one can leverage a Facebook user's friends list to infer his or her sexual orientation. They found that the proportion of gay friends that a user had on Facebook held predictive power for classifying the user as straight or gay. This held even when a user had hidden or omitted his sexual orientation on his Facebook profile. Thus, the combination of these two data sources would also enable relatively accurate prediction of voters' sexual orientations, even though the majority of users did not specify their sexual orientations on their profiles.

Race and Ethnicity.

Elliott et al. [12] showed that by using U.S. Census records of popular last names, one can predict a given person's ethnicity with high accuracy given his last name and zip code. They implement a Bayesian approach using the prior probabilities of racial identity given a specific neighborhood, and they update this with the probability of the person's specific last name belonging to that ethnicity. Since our dataset includes each voter's last name as well as their address, one would be able to apply this method to our dataset to output predictions for each voter with regard to race and ethnicity.

8. RELATED WORK

8.1 Combining Online Profiles

A considerable body of research has explored methods for associating accounts from multiple online services to individual users. Notably, Narayanan and Shmatikov showed that the Netflix prize data, though anonymized, could be matched to the Internet Movies Database (IMDB) website to identify users [20]. Irani et al. [14] showed that by participating in larger numbers of online social networks, users exposed more private information. More recently, Perito et al. [21] showed that users could be linked across online services through their username choices. For example, Minkus and Ross [19] showed

Data field	Facebook	Voter registrations	Combined with inferences
Political affiliation	0.002%	100%	100%
Birth year (and age)	0.02%	100%	100%
Birth date	0.04%	100%	100%
Physical address	0%	100%	100%
Sex (M/F)	16.6%	33.2%	93.9%
Education	49%	0%	49%
Religion	0.003%	0%	0.003%
Sexual orientation	9%	0%	9%
Relationship status	21.1%	0%	56.6%
Friends list	21.2%	0%	96.3%

Table 3: For all users with a distinct match between a Facebook profile and a voter record, we show which data fields were available from the Facebook profile, from the voter record, and from the combined profile when enriched with inferences based on auxiliary data.

that eBay accounts could be matched to Facebook profiles, thus revealing a user's real name sand purchase history.

More generally, a large body of work has examined the problem entity matching in databases; see Köpcke and Rahm [17] for a survey of notable approaches. Entity matching deals with the problem of finding and resolving duplicate records across multiple databases. While this is similar to our problem, we find that our specialized approach is better able to leverage the unique properties of our datasets, thus vividly demonstrating the privacy risks of record linkage between social networking sites and public data.

8.2 Relating Online Data to Offline Data

In this paper we explored in some detail how to connect Facebook data with voter registration lists. Barbera [5] matched the voter registration records of Ohio voters to Twitter accounts, using their full names and counties and filtering out any duplicate matches. However, only users who explicitly provided their location were analyzed; no attempts were made to infer the location of users who had not included it in their profile. Chen et al. [7] used social media profiles to identify users' phone numbers and addresses based on online phonebook records, also removing any duplicate matches. However, their work fails to account for the many users who have unlisted phone numbers or cell phones that are not listed in phonebooks. Additionally, while phonebook records include address information, they do not include birthdates or political affiliation, which are contained in voter registration records. Finally, in both of these works, no methods were proposed to resolve ambiguous matches between multiple accounts. Our work is more rigorous in attempting to resolve ambiguous matches between multiple profiles and voter records. We utilize social relationships as side-channel clues that can hint at a user's undisclosed location, thus providing an additional datapoint that can narrow down the matching process.

Some work has also focused on learning the physical locations of users based on their social media activity [22] [23]. However, our approach does not rely on geo-tagged data or posts that are tied to specific locations. This extends the attack's coverage to users who do not have geo-tagged or location-specific data included in their posts.

9. DISCUSSION

In the previous sections, we introduced a technique for automatically matching large numbers of registered voters to Facebook profiles. We also leveraged the combined dataset to infer new descriptions of the targeted voters. In this section, we discuss what can be done to limit the privacy risks to individual voters who use Facebook.

9.1 Recommendations to Facebook

The attacks described in this paper were enabled primarily by two Facebook policies: the *real-name policy* and the *reverse-lookup friends lists capability*. We describe how changes to these two policies would allow users to exercise better control of their private information.

Abolish real names policy.

According to Facebook's Help Center[4], "Facebook is a community where people use their authentic identities. We require people to provide the name they use in real life; that way, you always know who you're connecting with. This helps keep our community safe... Pretending to be anything or anyone isn't allowed." While this policy is articulated in a manner that emphasizes trust, it also means that users may not use false names as a way to protect their privacy.

By abolishing the real-name policy, Facebook would allow users to create false identities to hide from advertisers, data brokers, mass surveillance, and unwelcome snooping by social acquaintances. The social network Google+ recently changed its real-name in order to be more inclusive, since they felt it "excluded a number of people who wanted to be part of it without using their real names". We recommend that Facebook do the same.

Implement symmetric privacy settings.

In the current implementation of the Facebook privacy settings, a good deal of information can be leaked by a private user's friends. Specifically, in this paper we leveraged the *reverse-lookup* capacities of the friendship list mechanism. Even if a user hides his own friends list, he can be found on the public friends list of any one of his acquaintances. Due to the social property of homophily, this often reveals a good deal about a user beyond his social ties; for example, gay people are more likely to have a higher proportion of gay friends [16], and a user's age can also be estimated by analyzing the ages of his social ties [10].

For these reasons, we recommend that Facebook institutes a *symmetric privacy policy* with regard to friendship ties.

---

[4] https://www.facebook.com/help/112146705538576

Namely, we believe that a user who hides his friends list should also be removed from the public friends lists of any other users. Alternatively, Facebook may consider making all friend lists invisible, even to friends. We note that WeChat, the hugely popular social network in China, has made this design choice, and is therefore not plagued like Facebook with inference attacks based on friend lists.

9.2 Voter Data Use Recommendations

As political campaigns increasingly digitize, the use of campaign and voter data in both political and commercial uses is gaining traction [15]. In a 2014 paper, Rubinstein [24] made several recommendations for better privacy practices governing the collection and use of voter data. We summarize them here:

- Increased transparency: when collecting data about voters, authorities should clearly state any uses for which the data may be used. Moreover, any secondary uses of the data should include a disclaimer about the origins of the voter data.

- Restricting commercial data practices: similar to the Fair Credit Reporting Act, individuals should be given the right to correct, remove, or access any of the information about them that is sold commercially.

10. CONCLUSION

In this paper, we empirically examined the problem of matching online and offline profiles. Specifically, we showed that matching voter records to Facebook profiles, though difficult, can be accomplished by leveraging both explicit and implicit features of the datasets. We then showed that the combination of these data sources allowed for new, richer inferences with negative privacy implications. Finally, we suggested policy changes to better protect the privacy of Facebook users and voters.

Acknowledgements

This work was supported in part by the NSF (under grants CNS-1318659 and DGE-0966187). The views and conclusions contained in this document are those of the authors and should not be interpreted as necessarily representing the official policies, either expressed or implied, of any of the sponsors.

11. REFERENCES

[1] Frequently asked questions. United States Census Bureau. Available: https://www.census.gov/hhes/www/income/about/faqs.html.

[2] Data brokers: a call for transparency and accountability. *Federal Trade Commission, Washington, DC*, 2014.

[3] Acxiom becomes an audience data provider in facebook marketing partner program. February 17, 2015.

[4] K. Alexander and K. Mills. Voter privacy in the digital age. *California Voter Foundation*, 2004.

[5] P. Barberá. Birds of the same feather tweet together: Bayesian ideal point estimation using twitter data. *Political Analysis*, 23(1):76–91, 2015.

[6] J. Chang, I. Rosenn, L. Backstrom, and C. Marlow. epluribus: Ethnicity on social networks. *ICWSM*, 10:18–25, 2010.

[7] T. Chen, M. A. Kaafar, A. Friedman, and R. Boreli. Is more always merrier?: a deep dive into online social footprints. In *Proceedings of the 2012 ACM workshop on Workshop on online social networks*, pages 67–72. ACM, 2012.

[8] R. Dey, Y. Ding, and K. Ross. The high-school profiling attack: How online privacy laws can actually increase minors' risk. In *Proc. of Internet Measurement Conference*, volume 13, 2013.

[9] R. Dey, Z. Jelveh, and K. W. Ross. Facebook users have become much more private: A large-scale study. In *PerCom Workshops*, pages 346–352. IEEE, 2012.

[10] R. Dey, C. Tang, K. Ross, and N. Saxena. Estimating age privacy leakage in online social networks. In *INFOCOM, 2012 Proceedings IEEE*, pages 2836–2840. IEEE, 2012.

[11] M. Duggan, N. B. Ellison, C. Lampe, A. Lenhart, and M. Madden. Social media update 2014. *Pew Research Center*, September 2014.

[12] M. N. Elliott, P. A. Morrison, A. Fremont, D. F. McCaffrey, P. Pantoja, and N. Lurie. Using the census bureau's surname list to improve estimates of race/ethnicity and associated disparities. *Health Services and Outcomes Research Methodology*, 9(2):69–83, 2009.

[13] Y. Fu, G. Guo, and T. S. Huang. Age synthesis and estimation via faces: A survey. *Pattern Analysis and Machine Intelligence, IEEE Transactions on*, 32(11):1955–1976, 2010.

[14] D. Irani, S. Webb, K. Li, and C. Pu. Large online social footprints–an emerging threat. In *International Conference on Computational Science and Engineering*, volume 3, pages 271–276. IEEE, 2009.

[15] S. Issenberg. *The victory lab: The secret science of winning campaigns*. Broadway Books, 2012.

[16] C. Jernigan and B. F. Mistree. Gaydar: Facebook friendships expose sexual orientation. *First Monday*, 14(10), 2009.

[17] H. Köpcke and E. Rahm. Frameworks for entity matching: A comparison. *Data & Knowledge Engineering*, 69(2):197–210, 2010.

[18] T. Minkus, K. Liu, and K. W. Ross. Children seen but not heard: When parents compromise children's online privacy. In *Proceedings of the 24th International Conference on World Wide Web*. IW3C2, 2015.

[19] T. Minkus and K. W. Ross. I know what you're buying: Privacy breaches on ebay. In *Privacy Enhancing Technologies*, pages 164–183. Springer, 2014.

[20] A. Narayanan and V. Shmatikov. Robust de-anonymization of large sparse datasets. In *IEEE Symposium on Security and Privacy, 2008*, pages 111–125. IEEE, 2008.

[21] D. Perito, C. Castelluccia, M. A. Kaafar, and P. Manils. How unique and traceable are usernames? In *Privacy Enhancing Technologies*, pages 1–17. Springer, 2011.

[22] T. Pontes, G. Magno, M. Vasconcelos, A. Gupta, J. Almeida, P. Kumaraguru, and V. Almeida. Beware of what you share: Inferring home location in social networks. In *IEEE 12th International Conference on Data Mining Workshops*, pages 571–578. IEEE, 2012.

[23] T. Pontes, M. Vasconcelos, J. Almeida, P. Kumaraguru, and V. Almeida. We know where you live: privacy characterization of foursquare behavior. In *Proceedings of the 2012 ACM Conference on Ubiquitous Computing*, pages 898–905. ACM, 2012.

[24] I. Rubinstein. Voter privacy in the age of big data. *Wisconsin Law Review*, 2014.

[25] S. Sengupta. Update urged on children's online privacy. *New York Times*, September 15, 2011.

[26] S. Stecklow. On the web, children face intensive tracking. *Wall Street Journal*, September 17, 2010.

[27] C. Tang, K. Ross, N. Saxena, and R. Chen. What's in a name: A study of names, gender inference, and gender behavior in facebook. In *Database Systems for Adanced Applications*, pages 344–356. Springer, 2011.

[28] J. Turow, M. X. D. Carpini, and N. Draper. Americans roundly reject tailored political advertising at a time when political campaigns are embracing it. 2012.

Impact of Clustering on the Performance of Network De-anonymization

Carla-Fabiana Chiasserini
Dipartimento di Elettronica e
Telecomunicazioni
Politecnico di Torino, Italy
chiasserini@polito.it

Michele Garetto
Dipartimento di Informatica
Universita' di Torino, Italy
michele.garetto@unito.it

Emilio Leonardi
Dipartimento di Elettronica e
Telecomunicazioni
Politecnico di Torino, Italy
leonardi@polito.it

ABSTRACT

Recently, graph matching algorithms have been successfully applied to the problem of network de-anonymization, in which nodes (users) participating in more than one social network are identified only by means of the structure of their links to other members. This procedure exploits an initial set of seed nodes large enough to trigger a percolation process which correctly matches almost all other nodes across the different social networks. Our main contribution is to show the crucial role played by clustering, which is a ubiquitous feature of realistic social network graphs (and many other systems). Clustering has both the effect of making matching algorithms more vulnerable to errors, and the potential to dramatically reduce the number of seeds needed to trigger percolation, thanks to a wave-like propagation effect. We demonstrate these facts by considering a fairly general class of random geometric graphs with variable clustering level, and showing how clever algorithms can achieve surprisingly good performance while containing matching errors.

Categories and Subject Descriptors

G.3 [**Mathematics of Computing**]: Probability and Statistics—*Probabilistic algorithms*; G.2.2 [**Discrete Mathematics**]: Graph Theory; H.1 [**Information Systems**]: Models and Principles

Keywords

Graph matching; bootstrap percolation; social networks; de-anonymization; privacy

1. INTRODUCTION

The advent of online social networks, and their massive worldwide penetration, can be well considered as one of the most influential changes brought by information and communication technologies into our lives during the last decade, with profound impact on all aspects of economy, society and culture. The extraordinary capitalization of the companies running these (typically free) online services can be explained by the huge amount of valuable information that can be extracted from the traces of activities performed by billions of users. Such information allows, for example, to build user profiles that can be effectively used for targeted advertisements, marketing and social surveys, and many other profitable business run by service providers and third parties. Privacy concerns raised by the collection, analysis and distribution of personal data, exposed more or less consciously by active users, have been recently hotly debated in the media. User privacy is especially threatened when data collected from different systems is combined together to construct richer and more accurate user profiles.

In this work we are specifically concerned with the problem of identifying users participating in different online social networks We emphasize that this problem can be perceived by people in totally different ways. Some users would prefer to hide any Personal Identifiable Information (PII) while using a service, and they see any attempt to correlate accounts created in different systems as a severe violation of their privacy. Other users instead are more than happy to merge or link together their various accounts, as this turns out to be convenient to the user itself. For example, the increasing practice of 'social logins' allow users to use existing accounts on social networks to directly sign into other services (different applications, websites, public Wi-Fi hotspots).

In our work, we are specifically interested in privacy issues, and consider the case of an 'attacker' trying to identify users belonging to two different social networks (without their consent). Recently, security experts have made the dramatic discovery that user privacy cannot be guaranteed when traces of communication activities are made available after applying the simple anonymization procedure which replaces real ID's by random labels [1].

A standard way to formalize the user identification problem is the following: each communication system (e.g., a given social network) generates (from the traces of user activities) a 'contact graph' in which nodes represent anonymized users, and edges denote who has come in contact with whom. The attacker then runs a *graph matching* algorithm on the contact graphs generated by different systems, which in the hardest case can make use only of the topologies of these graphs, without any additional side information [2]. The majority of algorithms proposed so far to achieve this goal are facilitated by an initial set of already matched nodes (called seeds). This is actually a realistic case, since, as explained above, some users explicitly link their accounts in different systems 'for free'. Many proposed matching strategies, based on heuristic algorithms, work by progressively expanding the set of already matched nodes, trying to identify all of the other nodes [1, 3, 4]. In particular, in their seminal paper Narayanan and Shmatikov [1] were able to identify a large fraction of users having account on both Twitter and Flickr (with only 12% error ratio).

COSN'15, November 2–3, 2015, Palo Alto, California, USA.
© 2015 ACM. ISBN 978-1-4503-3951-3/15/11 ...$15.00.
DOI: http://dx.doi.org/10.1145/2817946.2817953.

Significant progress has also been made towards theoretical understanding of the feasibility of network de-anonymization (in the first place), and of the asymptotic performance of graph matching algorithms applied to large systems. Recent analytical work has adopted the following convenient probabilistic generation model for two contact graphs G_1 and G_2: we consider the (inaccessible) 'ground-truth' graph G_T representing true social relationships among people, and then assume that G_1 is obtained by independently sampling each edge of G_T with probability s (similarly, and independently, G_2). Specifically, when the social network G_T is modeled as an Erdös–Rényi random graph, it has been shown in [5] that, under mild conditions, users participating in two different social networks can be successfully matched by an attacker with unlimited computation power, even without seeds. Still in the case of Erdös–Rényi random graphs, in [6] authors have proposed a practical identification algorithm based on bootstrap percolation, [7] showing an interesting phase transition phenomenon in the number of seeds that are required for network de-anonymization. The results in [6] have been recently extended to the more realistic case in which contact graphs are scale-free (power-law) random graphs. In particular, by modeling them as Chung-Lu graphs, [8] and [9] have independently shown that a much smaller set of seeds is sufficient to trigger the percolation-based matching process originally studied in Erdös–Rényi graphs.

While previous work has captured the impact of power-law degree distribution on percolation graph matching, another essential feature of real social networks, namely, clustering, has not been investigated so far. Interestingly, in [6] authors attempted to apply their basic algorithm also to highly clustered random geometric graphs, observing almost total failure (error rates above 50%). This preliminary finding has been the starting point of our work. In this paper we consider a fairly general model of random geometric graphs that allows us to incorporate various levels of clustering in the underlying social network, without concurrently generating a scale-free structure. By so doing, we separate the (unkown) impact of clustering from the (known) impact of power law degree, going back to the original case of Erdös–Rényi graphs and exploring a totally different, 'orthogonal' direction. Our main findings are as follows:

(i) Clustered networks can be indeed largely prone to matching errors when we naively apply the method proposed in [6]. Such errors can be mitigated and asymptotically eliminated by an improved matching algorithm still based on bootstrap percolation;

(ii) Once errors are eliminated, clustering turns out to have a surprising beneficial effect on the performance of graph matching, thanks to a wave-like propagation phenomenon that allows to progressively identify all nodes starting from a very small, *compact* set of seeds;

(iii) In contrast with previous results derived for Erdös–Rényi [6] and Chung-Lu graphs [8], we show that the minimum number of seeds required for network de-anonymization can increase with the average node degree of the graph.

Our results are qualitatively validated via experiments with synthetic and real social network graphs. We emphasize that, although we focus on network de-anonymization, the results derived in this work have much broader applicability, since graph matching problems are arising in many different domains, ranging from computer graphics to bioinformatics.

2. NOTATION AND PRELIMINARIES

Without loss of generality, we assume that $G_T(\mathcal{V}, \mathcal{E})$, $G_1(\mathcal{V}_1, \mathcal{E}_1)$ and $G_2(\mathcal{V}_2, \mathcal{E}_2)$ have the same set of nodes (or vertices)

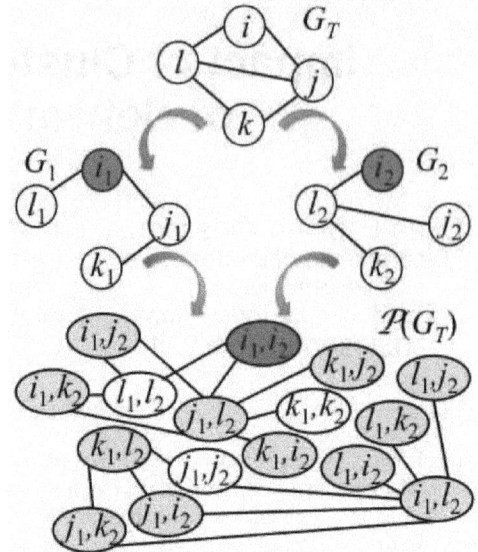

Figure 1: An example of G_1 and G_2 obtained from G_T by independent edge sampling, and of the pairs graph $\mathcal{P}(G_T)$. There is a single seed, highlighted in red. In $\mathcal{P}(G_T)$, good pairs are highlighted in white and bad pairs in grey.

with cardinality n, i.e., $\mathcal{V}_1 = \mathcal{V}_2 = \mathcal{V}$ [1]. Similarly to previous work [4, 5, 6, 8, 9] we assume that edges in G_1 and G_2 are obtained by independently sampling each edge of G_T with probability s. Specifically, each edge in G_T is assumed to be (independently) sampled twice, the first time to determine its presence in $\mathcal{E}_1$, the second time to determine its presence in $\mathcal{E}_2$. This model is a reasonable approximation of real systems which permits obtaining fundamental analytical insights.

To match G_1 and G_2, we build the pairs graph $\mathcal{P}(\mathcal{V}, \mathcal{E})$, with $\mathcal{V} \subseteq \mathcal{V}_1 \times \mathcal{V}_2$ and $\mathcal{E} \subseteq \mathcal{E}_1 \times \mathcal{E}_2$. In $\mathcal{P}(\mathcal{V}, \mathcal{E})$ there exists an edge between $[i_1, j_2]$ and $[k_1, l_2]$ iff edge $(i_1, k_1) \in \mathcal{E}_1$ and edge $(j_2, l_2) \in \mathcal{E}_2$. We will slightly abuse the notation and denote the pair graph associated to a generic ground-truth graph G_T simply as $\mathcal{P}(G_T)$. Fig. 1 shows the pairs graph built from a toy example.

We will refer to pairs $[i_1, i_2] \in \mathcal{P}(G_T)$, whose vertices correspond to the same vertex $i \in G_T$, as good pairs, and to all others (e.g., $[i_1, j_2]$) as bad pairs. Also, we will refer to two pairs such as $[i_1, j_2]$ and $[i_1, l_2]$, or $[i_1, j_2]$ and $[k_1, j_2]$, as conflicting. Finally, two adjacent pairs on $\mathcal{P}(G_T)$ will be referred to as neighbors. The seeds set will be denoted by $\mathcal{A}_0(n) \subset \mathcal{V}$, with cardinality a_0.

We now briefly describe the Percolation Graph Matching (PGM) algorithm originally proposed in [6]. The PGM algorithm maintains an integer counter (initialized to zero) for any pair of $\mathcal{P}(G_T)$ that may still be matched. It exploits a set $\mathcal{A}_t$, indexed by time step t, which is initialized (for $t = 0$) with the seed pairs. At any given time $t \geq 0$, the PGM algorithm extracts at random one pair from $\mathcal{A}_t$ matching the corresponding nodes, and increases by one the counter associated to each of its neighbor pair in $\mathcal{P}(G_T)$. Then the algorithm adds to $\mathcal{A}_{t+1}$ all pairs whose counter has reached r at time t with the exception of those pairs that are in conflict with either any of the already matched pairs or any of the pairs in $\mathcal{A}_t$. The algorithms stops when $\mathcal{A}_t = \emptyset$. It is straightforward to see that PGM takes at most n steps to terminate.

---

[1] This assumption can be easily removed by considering that only the intersection of vertices belonging to G_1 and G_2 has to be de-anonymized.

Table 1: Main system parameters

Symbol	Definition
$\mathcal{G}_T$	ground-truth graph
$\mathcal{G}_1$ and $\mathcal{G}_2$	contact graphs
$\mathcal{V}$, $\mathcal{V}_1$ and $\mathcal{V}_2$	set of vertices of $\mathcal{G}_T$, $\mathcal{G}_1$ and $\mathcal{G}_2$
$\mathcal{E}$, $\mathcal{E}_1$ and $\mathcal{E}_2$	set of edges of $\mathcal{G}_T$, $\mathcal{G}_1$ and $\mathcal{G}_2$
s	edge sampling probability
$\mathcal{P}(\mathcal{G}_T)$	pair graph
$\hat{\mathcal{P}}(\mathcal{G}_T)$	imperfect pair graph
$\mathcal{A}_0(n)$	seed set
$\mathcal{H}$	k-dimensional network domain
$p_{ij} = K(n)\min\left(1,\left(\frac{C(n)}{d_{ij}}\right)^{\beta}\right)$	edge (i,j) probability
$D(n)$	average degree of vertices

In the case where $\mathcal{G}_T$ is an Erdös–Rényi random graph, previous work [6] has established the following lower bound on the number of seeds that are needed to correctly match almost all nodes without errors. Table 1 summarizes the main parameters of the system.

Critical seed set size for Erdös-Rényi graphs [6]. *Let $\mathcal{G}_T$ be an Erdös-Rényi random graph $G(m,p)$. Let $r \geq 4$. Denote by a_c the critical seed set size:*

$$u_c = \left(1-\frac{1}{r}\right)\left(\frac{(r-1)!}{m(ps^2)^r}\right)^{\frac{1}{r-1}}. \tag{1}$$

For $m^{-1} \ll ps^2 \leq s^2 m^{-\frac{3.5}{r}}$, we have that, if $a_o/a_c \to a > 1$, the PGM algorithm matches w.h.p. a number of good pairs equal to $m - o(m)$ (i.e., all vertex pairs except for a negligible fraction) with no errors.

Critical seed set size for random graphs bounded by Erdös-Rényi graphs. *Let $\mathcal{H}(\mathcal{V},\mathcal{E}_H)$ and $\mathcal{K}(\mathcal{V},\mathcal{E}_K)$ be two random graphs insisting on the same set of vertices $\mathcal{V}$, where $\mathcal{E}_H \subseteq \mathcal{E}_K$. We define the following partial order relationship: $\mathcal{H}(\mathcal{V},\mathcal{E}_H) \leq_{st} \mathcal{K}(\mathcal{V},\mathcal{E}_K)$. Given that, we introduce the following extended results (in part borrowed from our previous work [8]):*

Theorem 1. *Consider $\mathcal{G}_T$ satisfying: $G(m,p_{\min}) \leq_{st} \mathcal{G}_T \leq_{st} G(m,p_{\max})$ with $p_{\min} \leq p_{\max}$. Applying the PGM algorithm to $\mathcal{P}(\mathcal{G}_T)$ guarantees that $m - o(m)$ good pairs are matched with no errors w.h.p., provided that:*

1. *$m \to \infty$;*

2. *$p_{\min} = \Theta(p_{\max})$ and $p_{\min} \gg m^{-1}$;*

3. *$p_{\max} \leq m^{-\frac{3.5}{r}}$;*

4. *$\liminf_{m \to \infty} a_o/a_c > 1$, with a_c computed from (1) by setting $p = p_{\min}$.*

Also, under conditions 1)-4), the PGM successfully matches w.h.p. $m - o(m)$ correct pairs (with no errors) also in any subgraph $\mathcal{G}'_T$ of $\mathcal{G}_T$ that comprises a finite fraction of vertices of $\mathcal{G}_T$ and all the edges between the selected vertices. The proof can be found in our technical report [10].

Corollary 1. *Under the same conditions as in Theorem 1, the PGM algorithm can be successfully applied to an imperfect pairs graph $\hat{\mathcal{P}}(\mathcal{G}_T) \subset \mathcal{P}(\mathcal{G}_T)$ comprising a finite fraction of the pairs in $\mathcal{P}(\mathcal{G}_T)$ and satisfying the following constraint: a bad pair $[i_1,j_2] \in \mathcal{P}(\mathcal{G}_T)$ is included in $\hat{\mathcal{P}}(\mathcal{G}_T)$ only if either $[i_1,i_2]$ or $[j_1,j_2]$ are also in $\hat{\mathcal{P}}(\mathcal{G}_T)$.*

The above results provide basic building blocks to perform the asymptotic analysis of the number of seeds that are sufficient to de-anonymize clustered networks described by the model presented next.

3. CLUSTERED NETWORK MODEL

To incorporate different degrees of clustering in the ground-truth social network $\mathcal{G}_T$, we have adopted the following geometric random graph model, which guarantees a large degree of flexibility, while inheriting the main features of the small-world graphs. We assume that nodes are located in a k-dimensional space corresponding to the hyper-cube[2] $\mathcal{H} = [0,1]^k \subset \mathbb{R}^k$, where the k dimensions could correspond to different attributes of the users. We consider n nodes independently and uniformly distributed over $\mathcal{H}$. Notice that the node density in the space is n. Given any two vertices $i,j \in \mathcal{V}$, with $i \neq j$, edge (i,j) exists in $\mathcal{G}_T$ with probability p_{ij} that depends only on the Euclidean distance d_{ij} between i and j (independently of everything else). We consider the following generic law for p_{ij}:

$$p_{ij} = K(n)f(d_{ij}). \tag{2}$$

In (2), f is a non-increasing function of the distance, and $K(n)$ is a normalization constant introduced to impose a desired average node degree $D(n)$, which is assumed to be the same for all nodes. It is customary in random graph models representing realistic systems to assume that the average node degree is not constant, but it increases with n due to network densification. Also, although a common choice is to assume $D(n) = \Theta(\log n)$, in our model we consider more in general $D(n) = \Omega(\log n)$.

Since we are interested in the order-sense asymptotic performance of network de-anonymization as n grows large, we further characterize the shape of function f as follows. We assume that $f(d)$ equals 1 for all distances $0 < d < C(n)$, where $C(n)$ is a parameter of the model (possibly scaling with n). Note that this implies that $K(n)$ must be less than or equal to 1 to obtain a proper probability function. For distances larger than $C(n)$, we assume that f decays according to a power-law with exponent β, with $\beta > 0$. In summary,

$$f(d_{ij}) = \min\left\{1,\left(\frac{C(n)}{d_{ij}}\right)^{\beta}\right\}. \tag{3}$$

The above characterization of the shape of $f(d)$ is fairly general and allows accounting for different levels of node clustering. In particular, our random-graph model degenerates into a standard Erdös–Rényi graph when $C(n)$ approaches 1, with arbitrary β. For $\beta \to \infty$, instead, edges can be established only between nodes whose distance is smaller than or equal to $C(n)$.

The average node degree is:

$$D(n) = \Theta\left(nK(n)\left(C^k(n) + C^{\beta}(n)\int_{C(n)}^{1}\rho^{k-1-\beta}\,d\rho\right)\right).$$

From the above equation it follows that for $\beta > k$ the dominant fraction of the neighbors of a given node lie at distance $\Theta(C(n))$ from it, while for $\beta < k$ only a marginal fraction of the neighbors of a node lie at distance $o(1)$ from it. Since we are interested in graphs with significant node clustering (so as to mimic real-world social networks), we restrict the analysis in this paper to the case $\beta > k$. In this case, the average node degree is:

$$D(n) = \Theta(nK(n)C^k(n)). \tag{4}$$

---

[2]To avoid border effects, we assume wrap-around conditions (i.e., a torus topology).

Since by construction $K(n) \le 1$, the average node degree is constrained to be $O(nC^k(n))$. Moreover, given that we assume $D(n) = \Omega(\log n)$, we have $C(n) = \Omega\left(\left(\frac{\log n}{n}\right)^{1/k}\right)$.

The clustering coefficient turns out to be $\Theta(K(n))$, as direct consequence of the fact that almost all neighbors of a node lie at distance $\Theta(C(n))$ from it. We remark that the clustering coefficient of the networks generated according to our model is always much larger than in an Erdös–Rényi graph having the same average node degree (recall that in $G(n, p)$ the clustering coefficient is p). To see this, we observe that in our model the ratio between the clustering coefficient $\Theta(K(n))$ and the graph density [3] is $\Theta(1/C^k(n))$. Since in general $C^k(n) = o(1)$, our graph model exhibits a high level of clustering. In the following, we will slightly abuse the language and refer to groups of vertices lying in sub-regions of side $\Theta(C(n))$ as *clusters* (not to be confused with the clustering coefficient).

In essence, in our model, which has been chosen in light of its flexibility, $K(n)$ and $C(n)$ provide the two knobs that allow us to directly control the clustering coefficient of the graph and the average node degree (or the graph density). We will see next that these are indeed the crucial parameters affecting the asymptotic performance of the proposed graph matching algorithms.

4. OVERVIEW AND MAIN RESULTS

In our analysis we have to distinguish two cases:
1) $K(n) = o((nC^k(n))^{-\gamma})$, for some $\gamma > 0$, which will be referred to as *sparse clusters* case;
2) $K(n) = \omega((nC^k(n)^{-\gamma}))$ for any $\gamma > 0$, which will be referred to as *dense clusters* case.
In the first case the clustering coefficient goes to zero "relatively" fast as the number of nodes within a cluster goes to infinity (i.e., when $nC^k(n) \to \infty$). In the second case, the clustering coefficient is either bounded away from zero or decreases very slowly. It comprises the particularly relevant sub-case in which $K(n) = \Theta(1)$.

In the *sparse clusters* case the density of edges within a cluster is sufficiently small that the PGM algorithm can be safely applied within it without incurring matching errors. We therefore apply the following de-anonymization procedure. We start from a set of seeds which are assumed to lie in a small sub-region of $\mathcal{H}$ of size $\Theta(C(n))$ (i.e., within a cluster). Then, using the PGM algorithm, we run a first 'trigger phase' in which we correctly match almost all nodes located sufficiently close (within a fixed distance) to the seeds. The identification procedure then goes on through a second phase in which nodes located in 'expanding rings' around the initial seeds are progressively identified through a sequence of steps (representing a discretized version of a wave-like expansion). Note that, in this second phase, we do not apply PGM any more, but a simpler direct strategy, matching at each step those pairs having a sufficiently large number of neighbor pairs matched at previous steps. Fig. 2 illustrates graphically this idea.

In the *dense clusters* case, de-anonymization is more complex, due to the high clustering coefficient (note that for large values of $K(n)$ the graph can have many cliques or quasi-cliques of nodes). In particular, if we tried to match the nodes using only the local structure of a cluster (as in the sparse clusters case) we would initially incur an intolerable amount of errors disrupting the entire identification process. It follows that, to guarantee that almost no errors are made, we have to ignore all edges whose length is too short

---

[3]Given a generic graph $\mathcal{G}(\mathcal{V}, \mathcal{E})$, the graph density is defined as $\frac{2|\mathcal{E}|}{|\mathcal{V}|(|\mathcal{V}|-1)}$. It can be interpreted as the probability that an edge exists between two randomly selected nodes of the graph.

Table 2: Minimum seed set size to achieve percolation

Scenario	Minimum seed set size
$K(n) = \omega((nC^k(n))^{-\gamma}), \forall \gamma > 0$	$O((nC^k(n))^{\varepsilon}), \forall \varepsilon > 0$
$K(n) = o((nC^k(n))^{-\gamma})$, with $\gamma > 0$	$\Theta\left(\frac{\log n C^k(n)}{K(n)}\right)$

(in particular, shorter than a properly defined threshold $\omega(C(n))$), and identify the nodes on the only basis of the 'fingerprint' provided by longer edges. More specifically, we devise a different 'trigger phase' which starts from two sub-regions of $\mathcal{H}$ of side $h(n) = \Theta(C(n))$, which are sufficiently far from each other (i.e., separated by a minimum distance $\omega(C(n))$, see Fig. 3). We assume that a suitable number of seeds are initially selected within each of these two sub-regions. To identify all of the other nodes in the sub-regions, we modify the PGM algorithm so that only the edges between nodes belonging to different sub-regions are used. After that, similarly to the *sparse clusters* case, we enter a second phase which progressively expands the set of matched nodes. This time we exploit the fact that, in the dense cluster regime, the distance between two nodes in $\mathcal{H}$ can be estimated quite precisely. Thus, given a sub-region where nodes have already been matched, we can select a set of compact nodes that are sufficiently far from the matched sub-region, and re-apply the modified PGM algorithm. This procedure can be iterated until almost all nodes throughout the network are correctly identified.

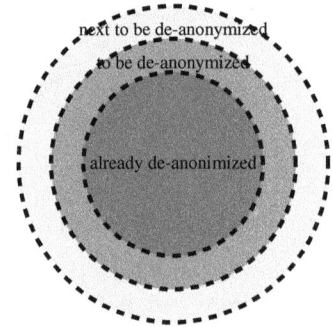

Figure 2: The de-anonymization procedure for $K(n) = o((nC^k(n))^{-\gamma})$.

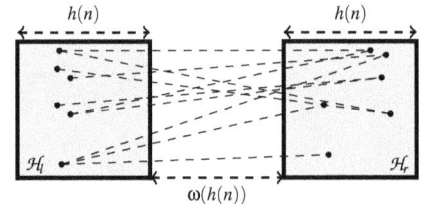

Figure 3: Bipartite graph construction for $K(n) = \omega((nC^k(n)^{-\gamma}))$.

In Table 2, we summarize our main results for the minimum seed set size that is required for successful network de-anonymization, assuming that seeds are selected within suitable clusters of $\mathcal{H}$. Observe that the minimum number of seeds depends on both $K(n)$ and $C(n)$, whereas it is independent of β. Specifically, in the *dense cluster* case (first raw of the table), the minimum number of seeds can be simply expressed in terms of the average number of nodes falling within a cluster ($nC^k(n)$). Indeed, a seed set whose size is equal to $(nC^k(n))^\varepsilon$, for any $\varepsilon > 0$, is enough to guarantee an almost complete successful network de-anonymization. In the relevant case in which $C(n) = \Theta(\frac{\log n}{n})^{1/k}$ (i.e., when the average degree of the graph $D(n) = \Theta(\log n)$), the above expression reduces to $(\log n)^\varepsilon$, with arbitrarily small $\varepsilon > 0$. This result readily reveals the strong beneficial impact of clustering on network de-anonymization. Somehow surprisingly, the minimum seed set size increases when we increase the average degree of the nodes (i.e., for increasing $C(n)$). This is in sharp contrast with previous results derived for Erdös–Rényi and Chung-Lu graphs [6, 8]. The intuition behind this result is that, by increasing $C(n)$, we increase the cluster size, making the problem of identifying nodes within a cluster intrinsically more challenging. In the *sparse clusters* case (second raw of the table), our de-anonymization techniques become less effective, and the minimum seed set size turns out to be roughly inversely proportional to $K(n)$.

5. SPARSE CLUSTERS

In this case, we assume $K(n) = o\left((nC^k(n))^{-\gamma}\right)$, for some $\gamma > 0$, and a set of seeds $\mathcal{A}_0$ ($|\mathcal{A}_0| = a_0$) whose maximum mutual distance is $d_s = O(C(n))$.

As first phase, we show how nodes in $\mathcal{H}$ lying sufficiently close to the seeds can be identified. To this end, we start by defining two sub-regions, $\mathcal{H}_{in} \subset \mathcal{H}$ and $\mathcal{H}_{out} \subset \mathcal{H}$. Intuitively, $\mathcal{H}_{in}$ ($\mathcal{H}_{out}$) can be seen as the set of points whose distance from any seed vertex is higher (lower) than a given threshold. More formally, denote by $\mathbf{x}$ a generic point in $\mathcal{H}$ and by $\mathbf{x}_\sigma$ the position in $\mathcal{H}$ of a generic seed vertex σ. Then, given two positive constants α and δ, s.t. $\delta \le 1$ and $\alpha(1+\delta) \le 1$, we define:

$$\mathcal{H}_{in}(\alpha, \delta) = \left\{ \mathbf{x} \text{ s.t. } \max_{\sigma \in \mathcal{A}_0} \|\mathbf{x} - \mathbf{x}_\sigma\| \le f^{-1}((1+\delta)\alpha) \right\}$$

$$\mathcal{H}_{out}(\alpha, \delta) = \left\{ \mathbf{x} \text{ s.t. } \min_{\sigma \in \mathcal{A}_0} \|\mathbf{x} - \mathbf{x}_\sigma\| > f^{-1}((1-\delta)\alpha) \right\}$$

where f is the non-increasing function defined in Section 3. The two sub-regions are depicted in Fig. 4. Note that, by construction, the area $|\mathcal{H}_{in}| = \Theta(C^k(n))$.

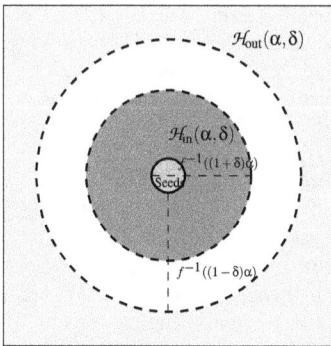

Figure 4: $\mathcal{H}_{in}(\alpha, \delta)$ and $\mathcal{H}_{out}(\alpha, \delta)$.

The theorem below proves that, given graph $\mathcal{G}_1$ ($\mathcal{G}_2$), it is possible to correctly distinguish nodes in $\mathcal{H}_{in}(\alpha, \delta)$ from nodes in $\mathcal{H}_{out}(\alpha, \delta)$ by counting the number of their neighboring seeds.

Theorem 2. *Given a node $i \in \mathcal{G}_1$ ($i \in \mathcal{G}_2$), let S_i be the number of seeds that are neighbors of i on $\mathcal{G}_1$ ($\mathcal{G}_2$). We say that node i is ac-*

cepted if $S_i > \alpha s K(n) a_0$. If $d_s = O(C(n))$ and $a_0 = \Omega\left(\frac{\log(nC^k(n))}{K(n)}\right)$, then for an arbitrary $\delta > 0$, the above procedure accepts all nodes located in $\mathcal{H}_{in}(\alpha, \delta)$, while it excludes all nodes located in $\mathcal{H}_{out}(\alpha, \delta)$.

PROOF. See Appendix A. □

Note that, in the above statement, $sK(n)$ is the probability that a node in $\mathcal{G}_1$ ($\mathcal{G}_2$) is connected with a seed node at distance $C(n)$ or less. Thus, $\alpha s K(n) a_0$ provides a suitable threshold on the number of connections between a node and the a_0 seed vertices.

Next, we denote by $\mathcal{N}^1(\alpha)$ and $\mathcal{N}^2(\alpha)$, respectively, the set of nodes from $\mathcal{G}_1$ and $\mathcal{G}_2$ that are classified as located in $\mathcal{H}_{in}(\alpha, \delta)$. By construction, we have $|\mathcal{N}^1(\alpha)| = \Theta(nC^k(n))$ and $|\mathcal{N}^2(\alpha)| = \Theta(nC^k(n))$. We build the pairs graph $\mathcal{P}(\mathcal{N})$ that is induced by the nodes of $\mathcal{G}_1$ and $\mathcal{G}_2$ that belong to, respectively, $\mathcal{N}^1(\alpha)$ and $\mathcal{N}^2(\alpha)$. While doing this, we can guarantee that a bad pair $[i_1, j_2]$ is included in $\mathcal{P}(\mathcal{N})$ only if either $[i_1, i_2]$ or $[j_1, j_2]$ are also included in $\mathcal{P}(\mathcal{N})$. This is accomplished as follows. We apply the previous classification procedure twice, using two different values α_1 and α_2, with $\alpha_1 > \alpha_2$, chosen in such a way that $\mathcal{H}_{out}(\alpha_1, \delta) \subseteq \mathcal{H}_{in}(\alpha_2, \delta)$. Then we insert in $\mathcal{P}(\mathcal{N})$ all pairs whose constituent nodes have been selected by at least one of the classification procedures, adding the constraint that at least one of the nodes must have been selected by both. Since, by construction, no good pair $[i_1, i_2]$ exists s.t. i_1 falls in $\mathcal{H}_{in}(\alpha_1, \delta)$ and i_2 in $\mathcal{H}_{out}(\alpha_2, \delta)$ (or vice versa), the above condition is ensured.

We then apply the PGM algorithm on $\mathcal{P}(\mathcal{N})$. Our goal is now to verify that the conditions in Theorem 1 hold so that, applying Corollary 1, we can claim that all good pairs in $\mathcal{P}(\mathcal{N})$ can be matched without errors. To this end, let us define $m = \Theta(nC^k(n))$, which in order sense equals the number of nodes in $\mathcal{N}^1(\alpha)$ and $\mathcal{N}^2(\alpha)$. Then note that $p_{min} = \Theta(p_{max})$, $p_{max} = K(n)$ and $K(n) = o(m^{-\gamma})$. Thus, for a sufficiently large r, $p_{max} \ll m^{-\frac{3.5}{r}}$. Furthermore, since by assumption $nC^k(n)K(n) = \Omega(\log n)$, it follows $p_{min} \gg m^{-1}$. At last, it is easy to see that $a_o/a_c \to \infty$. Indeed, from (1), $a_c = O(1/K(n))$ while, by assumption (see Theorem 2), $a_0 = \Omega\left(\frac{\log(nC^k(n))}{K(n)}\right)$. In conclusion, we have that all good pairs whose nodes fall in $\mathcal{H}_{in}(\alpha_1, \delta)$ can be correctly matched.

To further expand the set of identified pairs, we pursuit the following simple approach. Starting from the pairs already matched in the first phase, which act as seeds, we consider a larger region that includes the previous one. By properly setting a threshold r, we can match all pairs in this larger region having at least r neighbors among the seeds. So doing, we successfully match w.h.p. all good pairs in the region with no errors. More formally, the following theorem allows us to claim that our approach can be successfully employed.

Theorem 3. *Consider a circular region $\mathcal{D}(0, \rho)$ centered at 0, of radius ρ, with $\rho \ge C(n)$. Given that all (or almost all) nodes lying within $\mathcal{D}(0, \rho)$ have been correctly identified, it is possible to correctly identify (almost) all nodes in $\mathcal{D}(0, \rho_1) \setminus \mathcal{D}(0, \rho)$ with probability $1 - o(n^{-1})$, for $\rho_1 = \rho + C(n)/2$, when $K(n) = o((nC^k(n))^{-\gamma})$ for some $\gamma > 0$. In addition, none of the bad pairs formed by nodes in $\mathcal{H} - \mathcal{D}(0, \rho)$ will be identified, again with probability $1 - o(n^{-1})$.*
This is done by setting threshold $r = \frac{n}{2}|\mathcal{D}(0, \rho) \cap \mathcal{D}(\mathbf{x}, C(n))|\frac{K(n)}{2}$, with $|\mathbf{x}| = \rho_1$, and identifying as good pairs those in $\mathcal{H} \setminus \mathcal{D}(0, \rho)$ that have at least r neighbors among good pairs in $\mathcal{D}(0, \rho)$.

PROOF. The proof is based on the application of standard concentration results, namely, Chernoff bound and inequalities in [11, p. 16] (also reported in B for convenience). The detailed proof is given in [10]. □

Almost all good pairs can be matched w.h.p. by iterating the matching procedure of Theorem 3 a number of steps $\Theta(1/C(n))$. Indeed, each time the PGM algorithm successfully matches all good pairs whose constituent nodes lie within distance $C(n)/2$ from the set of previously matched pairs. Note that Theorem 3 also guarantees that, jointly over all steps, no bad pair is matched w.h.p.

6. DENSE CLUSTERS

The case $K(n) = \omega((nC^k(n)^{-\gamma}))$, for any $\gamma > 0$, is significantly different from the previous case since the de-anonymization algorithm must disregard all edges whose length is too short (shorter than a properly defined threshold $\omega(C(n))$) so as to avoid errors (i.e., matching bad pairs). The approach we propose to address this case relies on some results that we introduce next, in an more abstract sense, considering the case in which $\mathcal{G}_T$ is a bipartite graph. Then we apply such results to our clustered social network model, and derive the minimum seed set size that is required to trigger the identification process in this case.

6.1 Results on bipartite graphs

Let $\mathcal{G}_T$ be a $m_l \times m_r$ bipartite graph. Let $\mathcal{M}_l$ denote the set of vertices on the left hand side (LHS), with $|\mathcal{M}_l| = m_l$, and $\mathcal{M}_r$ the set of vertices on the right hand side (RHS), with $|\mathcal{M}_r| = m_r$. We assume that for any pair of vertices $i \in \mathcal{M}_l$ and $j \in \mathcal{M}_r$ an edge (i, j) exists in the graph with probability p_{ij}, with $p_{\min} \le p_{ij} \le p_{\max}$ and $p_{\max} = \eta p_{\min}$ for some constant $\eta > 1$. Our goal is to identify a minimum number of seeds a_0 located in either side of the graph, i.e., with $a_0 = |\mathcal{A}_0^l|$ in $\mathcal{M}_l$ and $a_0 = |\mathcal{A}_0^r|$ in $\mathcal{M}_r$, such that vertices in $\mathcal{M}_l$ and $\mathcal{M}_r$ can be correctly matched.

Let us first consider the case where $m_l = m_r = m$, for which the theorem below holds.

Theorem 4. *Assume that $\mathcal{G}_T$ is an $m \times m$ bipartite graph and that two sets of seeds, $\mathcal{A}_0^l$ and $\mathcal{A}_0^r$, both of cardinality a_0, are available on, respectively, the LHS and the RHS of the graph. Then the PGM algorithm with threshold $r \ge 4$ correctly identifies $m - o(m)$ good pairs w.h.p. on the RHS and the LHS of graph $\mathcal{P}(\mathcal{G}_T)$, with no errors, under the same 4 conditions listed in Theorem 1.*

PROOF. See Appendix C. □

Theorem 4 can be extended to the general case where $m_l \ne m_r$, as stated in the corollary below.

Corollary 2. *Assume that $\mathcal{G}_T$ is an $m_l \times m_r$ bipartite graph and define $m = \min(m_l, m_r)$. Under the same assumptions of Theorem 4, the PGM algorithm with threshold $r \ge 4$ successfully identifies w.h.p. $m - o(m)$ good pairs on both the LHS and the RHS of $\mathcal{P}(\mathcal{G}_T)$, with no errors. Furthermore, the PGM algorithm can be successfully applied to an imperfect pairs graph $\hat{\mathcal{P}}(\mathcal{G}_T) \subset \mathcal{P}(\mathcal{G}_T)$ comprising a finite fraction of pairs on both the LHS and the RHS of $\mathcal{P}(\mathcal{G}_T)$ and satisfying the following constraint: a bad pair $[i_1, j_2] \in \mathcal{P}(\mathcal{G}_T)$ is included in $\hat{\mathcal{P}}(\mathcal{G}_T)$ only if either $[i_1, i_2]$ or $[j_1, j_2]$ are also in $\hat{\mathcal{P}}(\mathcal{G}_T)$.*

PROOF. The assertion can be proved by following the same arguments as in Theorem 4 and applying Corollary 1. □

Finally, we prove the following result, which shows that all good pairs can be matched with no errors w.h.p.

Theorem 5. *Consider that $\mathcal{G}_T$ is an $m_l \times m_r$ bipartite graph with $m_l = \omega(\sqrt{m_r})$ and that a seed set $\mathcal{A}_0^l$ is available on the LHS of the graph, with $|A_0^l| = a_0 = \Theta(m_l)$. With probability larger than $1 - e^{-\frac{m_l}{\sqrt{m_r}}}$, all the m_r good pairs on the RHS can be successfully identified with no errors, provided that:*

1. $\frac{1}{\sqrt{m_r}} \ll p_{\min} \le p_{\max} \ll 1$

2. $p_{\min} = \Theta(p_{\max})$

3. *a matching algorithm is used on $\mathcal{P}(\mathcal{G}_T)$ that matches all pairs on the RHS that have at least r adjacent seeds on the LHS, with $r = a_0 \frac{p_{\min}}{2}$.*

The same result holds in case of imperfect pairs graph comprising a finite fraction of all possible pairs on the RHS.

PROOF. Without loss of generality, we assume $a_0 \ge cm_r$ for some $c > 0$. The proof is obtained by applying the inequalities reported in Appendix B and [11, p. 16]. First, observe that, given a good pair $[j_1, j_2]$ on the RHS of the pairs graph, the number of its adjacent seeds on the LHS is $E[N_g] \ge a_0 p_{\min} = 2r$. Thus, by applying inequality (8) and union bound, we have:

$$P(\text{all good pairs on the RHS have at least } r \text{ adjacent seeds})$$
$$\ge 1 - m_l e^{-cm_l p_{\min} H(\frac{1}{2})} \ge 1 - e^{-\frac{m_l}{\sqrt{m_r}}}$$

which imply that all good pairs on the RHS are successfully matched since $m_l = \omega(\sqrt{m_r})$. Similarly, considering a bad pair $[j_1, k_2]$ on the RHS, the number of its adjacent seeds on the LHS is $E[N_b] \le cm_r(p_{\max})^2 \ll r$. Thus, by applying inequality (10) and union bound, we have:

$$P(\text{all bad pairs on the RHS have less than } r \text{ adjacent seeds})$$
$$\ge 1 - m_r^2 e^{-cm_l \frac{p_{\min}}{4} \log\left(\frac{p_{\min}}{(p_{\max})^2}\right)} \ge 1 - e^{-\frac{m_l}{\sqrt{m_r}}}.$$

□

6.2 The de-anonymization procedure

We now outline how our proposed matching algorithm for the *dense clusters* case works. First, we consider two hyper-cubic regions, $\mathcal{H}_l \subset \mathcal{H}$ and $\mathcal{H}_r \subset \mathcal{H}$, whose side is $h(n) = \Omega(C(n))$ and whose distance is $g(n) = \omega(C(n))$ (see Fig. 3). Note that by construction, given two vertices $i \in \mathcal{H}_l$ and $j \in \mathcal{H}_r$, $p_{\min} = K(n)f(g(n) + \sqrt{k}h(n)) \le p_{ij} \le K(n)f(g(n)) = p_{\max}$. Let us assume $p_{\max} = \eta p_{\min}$ for some constant $\eta > 1$.

We then extract vertices in $\mathcal{H}_l$ and $\mathcal{H}_r$ from the rest of vertices so that we can focus on the bipartite graph induced by the nodes in the two sub-regions, along with the edges between them. To this end, we assume that two sufficiently large sets of seeds are available in $\mathcal{H}_l$ and $\mathcal{H}_r$ so that Theorem 2 can be applied. In this regard, observe that we can use the same procedure as in Section 5, to make sure that a bad pair $[i_1, j_2]$ is included in the pair graph only if either $[i_1, i_2]$ or $[j_1, j_2]$ are also included in it. We can then apply Corollary 2.

It follows that the execution of the PGM algorithm ensures that almost all of the good pairs in either the LHS or the RHS of the pairs graph are correctly de-anonymized. Without lack of generality, we assume that almost all pairs on LHS are de-anonymized, i.e., $m_l < m_r$, and that a non-negligible fraction of the good pairs on the RHS have still to be identified. Then the rest of good pairs on the RHS can be matched by applying Theorem 5.

To further expand the set of matched nodes, we first show how it is possible to estimate (at least in order sense) the length of the edges between two nodes, again by exploiting the dense structure of the clusters.

Proposition 1. *Given two nodes in region $\mathcal{H}$, it is possible to estimate with arbitrary precision their mutual distance d as far as $d \ll C(n)\left(nK^2(n)C^k(n)\right)^{\frac{1}{\beta}}.$*

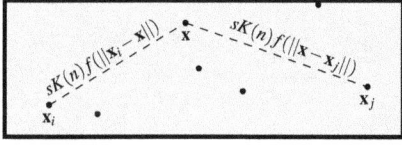

Figure 5: Computation of $\mathbb{E}[N_{ij}]$.

PROOF. Let us consider two nodes i and j on $\mathcal{G}_1$ ($\mathcal{G}_2$) whose mutual distance is d_{ij}. Let N_{ij} be the variable that represents the number of their common neighbors. By construction (see Fig. 5), we have:

$$\mathbb{E}[N_{ij}] = (n-2)s^2 K^2(n) \int_{\mathcal{H}} f(||\mathbf{x} - \mathbf{x}_i||) f(||\mathbf{x} - \mathbf{x}_j||) d\mathbf{x}$$
$$= \Theta(nC^k(n)K^2(n)f(d_{ij})).$$

Observe that $\mathbb{E}[N_{ij}]$ is continuous and strictly decreasing with d_{ij}, and thus invertible. Now, applying Chernoff bound we can show that for any $0 < \delta < 1$

$$\mathbb{P}\left(\frac{|N_{ij} - \mathbb{E}[N_{ij}]|}{\mathbb{E}[N_{ij}]} > \delta \right) \leq e^{-c(\delta)\mathbb{E}[N_{ij}]}$$

for a proper constant $c(\delta) > 0$. Since $\mathbb{E}[N_{ij}] \to \infty$ as long as $d \ll C(n)\left(nK^2(n)C^k(n)\right)^{\frac{1}{\beta}}$, the assertion follows. $\square$

We can therefore use the number of common neighbors between two given nodes as an estimator of their distance. We then set two thresholds, $d_L = \Theta(C(n)\log(n^{1/k}C(n)))$ and $d_H = \lambda d_L$ (with $\lambda > 1$), and we leverage the above result to correctly classify the edges going out of previously matched nodes into three categories: edges that are shorter than d_L, edges that are longer than d_H and edges of length comprised between d_L and d_H. In particular, we are interested in the latter, for which the following result holds.

Proposition 2. *Assume $K(n) = \omega((nC^k(n))^{-\gamma})$, $\forall \gamma > 0$. Consider a set comprising a finite fraction of the nodes in $\mathcal{G}_1$ ($\mathcal{G}_2$) lying in a region of side $\Theta(C(n))$, and the edges incident to them. For an arbitrarily selected $\delta > 0$, w.h.p (i.e., with a probability larger than $1 - [C(n)]^k$) we can select all edges whose length d is $(1+\delta)d_L \leq d \leq (1-\delta)d_H$. Furthermore, no edges whose length $d < (1-\delta)d_L$ and $d > (1+\delta)d_H$ are selected.*

The proof follows the same lines as in the proof in Appendix A (see [10] for further details).

At this point, we consider a bipartite graph whose LHS is still represented by $\mathcal{H}_l$, and whose RHS is given by the nodes that are connected with those in $\mathcal{H}_l$ through edges of length comprised between d_L and d_H. We can therefore apply Theorem 5 and match w.h.p. all good pairs on the RHS, with no errors. The procedure is then iterated so as to successfully de-anonymize the entire network. Note that, at every step we apply the following proposition to extract a group of matched nodes whose mutual distance is $\Theta(C(n))$.

Proposition 3. *Assume $K(n) = \omega((nC^k(n))^{-\gamma})$ $\forall \gamma > 0$. Given a node i, we can set a threshold $d_T = \Theta(C(n))$ and select all nodes in $\mathcal{G}_1$ ($\mathcal{G}_2$) whose estimated distance from i is less than d_T. So doing, for an arbitrarily selected $\delta > 0$, we successfully select with a probability larger than $1 - [C(n)]^k$ all nodes whose real distance is $d \leq (1-\delta)d_T$. Furthermore, no nodes whose distance from i is $d > (1+\delta)d_T$ are selected by our algorithm.*

The proof is similar to that of Proposition 2 (see also [10]).

6.3 Minimum seed set size

To explicitly derive the minimum seed set size, we need to further specify $h(n)$ and $g(n)$, which are to be carefully selected so as to minimize the resulting critical size a_c in Theorem 4 and Corollary 2.

Starting from the result provided by Theorem 4, a_c can be written as:

$$
\begin{aligned}
a_c &= \left(1 - \frac{1}{r}\right) \left(\frac{(r-1)!}{m(p_{\min}s^2)^r} \right)^{\frac{1}{r-1}} \\
&\leq \left(\frac{r-1}{(m(p_{\min}s^2)^{\frac{1}{r-1}}p_{\min}s^2} \right) \leq \frac{r-1}{p_{\min}s^2}.
\end{aligned}
\tag{5}
$$

The above expression can be minimized by maximizing $p_{\min}$, i.e., by minimizing $g(n)$ (recall that $p_{\min} = K(n)f(g(n) + \sqrt{kh(n)})$). However, $g(n)$ and $h(n)$ must also be selected in such a way that condition 1) of Theorem 4 is met. Additionally, as mentioned, it must be ensured that $h(n) = \Omega(C(n))$. At last, by standard concentration results, m_l and m_r turn out to be both $\Theta(nh^k(n))$ provided that $h(n) \geq (\log n/n)^{1/k}$.

Previous considerations suggest to fix $h(n) = \Theta(C(n)) \geq (\log n/n)^{1/k}$ (i.e., the minimum possible value in order sense), which corresponds to having $m = \Theta(nC^k(n))$ (recall that $m = \min(m_l, m_r)$). We then derive $g(n)$ by forcing $p_{max} \approx m^{-\frac{\alpha}{r}}$, with $3.5 < \alpha < 4$ and $r \geq 4$. Note that condition 1) of Theorem 4 is met since p_{max} and $p_{\min}$ are both $\Theta(m^{-\frac{\alpha}{r}})$. Hence, we have $p_{max} = \Theta((nC^k(n))^{-\frac{\alpha}{r}})$ and $g(n) = \Theta(n^{\frac{\alpha}{\beta r}}[C(n)]^{1+\frac{\alpha k}{\beta r}}[K(n)]^{\frac{1}{\beta}}))$.

Given the above expression for p_{max}, considering that $p_{max} = \eta p_{min}$ and using (5), the minimum seed set size can be made as small as $a_c = O([nC^k(n)]^\varepsilon)$, for any $\varepsilon > 0$, by choosing $r > \frac{4}{\varepsilon}$. Finally, we remark that the obtained a_c is in order sense greater than the minimum number of seeds needed to apply Theorem 2 while selecting nodes in regions $\mathcal{H}_l$ an $\mathcal{H}_r$, thus the whole construction is consistent.

7. EXPERIMENTAL VALIDATION

Although our results hold asymptotically as $n \to \infty$, we can expect to qualitatively observe the main effects predicted by the analysis also in finite-size graphs. We will first investigate the performance of graph matching algorithms in synthetic graphs generated according to our model of clustered networks, and then apply them to a real social network graph.

7.1 Synthetic graphs

In this section we consider bi-dimensional graphs having $n = 10,000$, the sampling probability $s = 0.8$ and, unless otherwise specified, the average node degree in the ground-truth graph $D(n) = 30$.

Fig. 6 reports the average number of correctly matched nodes across $1,000$ runs of the PGM algorithm (using $r = 5$) in various cases, as function of the number of seeds. In each run, seeds are either chosen uniformly at random among all nodes (label 'uniform seeds'), or as a compact set around one randomly chosen seed (label 'compact seeds'). In our model of clustered graphs, we have fixed $\beta = 3$ (the decay exponent of the edge probability beyond $C(n)$), and we consider either $K(n) = 0.05$ or $K(n) = 0.2$. As reference, in the plot we also show the phase transition occurring (at about 600 seeds) when $\mathcal{G}_T$ is a $G(n,p)$ graph having the same average node degree. The plot confirms the wave-like nature of the identification process as predicted by our analysis, namely: i) clustered networks (larger $K(n)$) can be matched starting from a much smaller seed set as compared to $G(n,p)$; ii) such huge reduction requires seeds to be selected within a small sub-region of $\mathcal{H}$.

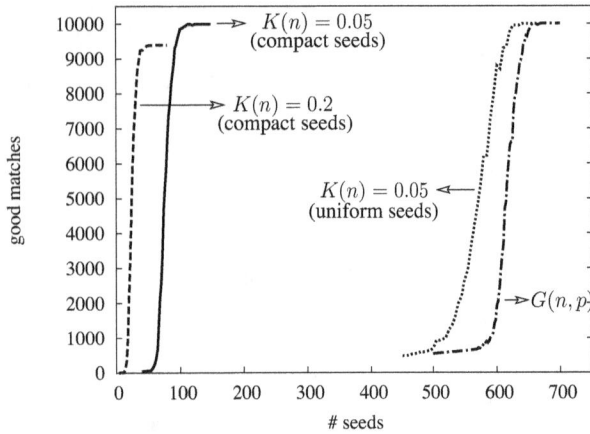

Figure 6: Comparison of PGM performance (with $r = 5$) in different networks with $n = 10,000$. Number of good matches (averaged over 1,000 runs) as a function of the number of seeds, chosen either uniform or compact.

What the plot in Fig. 6 does not clearly show (except for a rough estimate based on the maximum number of correctly matched nodes) is the error ratio incurred by the PGM algorithm, which is expected to become larger and larger as we increase the level of clustering in the network. This phenomenon is confirmed by Fig. 7, which reports the average error ratio (bad matches over all matches) incurred by PGM as a function of $K(n)$, starting from a compact set of seeds. In Fig. 7 we have considered also different values of β. The little circle denotes the operating point already considered for the left-most curve in Fig. 6 ($K(n) = 0.2$), having an error ratio of about 5%. The plot reveals that the error ratio increases dramatically when $K(n)$ tends to 1, confirming that PGM cannot be safely applied in highly clustered networks. The effect of β is more intriguing: smaller β's produce fewer errors since generated network graphs tend to become more similar to $G(n,p)$, where PGM is known to generate very few errors. As side-effect, smaller values of β tend to slightly increase the percolation threshold (not shown in the plot). For example, for $K(n) = 0.4$, the critical number of seeds (estimated from simulations) corresponding to $\beta = 2.2, 2.5, 3, 4$ are equal to $11, 15, 24, 45$, respectively.

Next, we focus on the 'hard' case corresponding to the little square shown in Fig. 7, i.e., $K(n) = 0.8$, $\beta = 3$. This case corresponds to networks having highly dense clusters, where the performance of the original PGM algorithm is rather poor (error ratio about 50%). Fig. 8 shows the average number of nodes matched by different algorithms as a function of the number of seeds: thick lines correspond to good matches, whereas thin lines (with the same line style) refer to bad matches produced by the same algorithm. For sake of simplicity, network de-anonymization is performed by applying a simplified version of the algorithm proposed and analysed in Section 6. This simple algorithm consists in adopting PGM after having removed all graph edges shorter than $x \cdot C(n)$. In the following, we will call this algorithm 'filtered PGM' and we will label the corresponding curves in the plots by '$f = <x>$'. We stress that filtered PGM approaches the performance that can be obtained by the algorithm in Section 6.

Looking at Fig. 8, it is important to remark that in this scenario the performance of the various algorithms is highly sensitive to the location of the set of seeds (in each run we uniformly select one

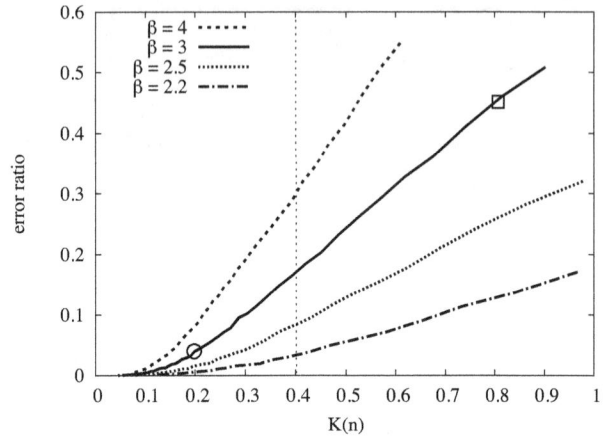

Figure 7: Error ratio of PGM as a function of $K(n)$ for different values of β, starting from compact seeds.

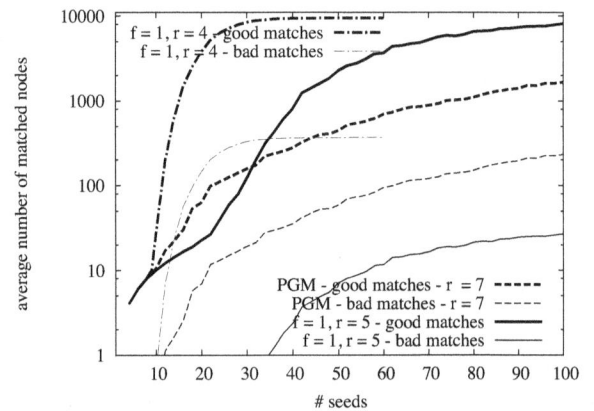

Figure 8: Average number of good and bad pairs matched by different Numbers close to the vertical line at $K(n) = 0.4$ denote corresponding estimates of the percolation thereshold derived via simulation.

seed among all nodes, and choose all of the other seeds among its neighbors). Since we average the results over 1,000 runs, this explains why all curves do not exhibit a sharp transition[4]. An average number of matched nodes equal to, say, 2,000, must be given the following probabilistic interpretation: about 1/5 of (uniformly chosen) initial locations allow us to match almost all nodes (10,000), while 4/5 of initial locations do not trigger the percolation effect.

Also, we note that the poor performance of standard PGM cannot be fixed by just increasing the threshold r: using $r = 7$, PGM still produces about 12% error ratio, while also requiring a disproportionally larger number of seeds (only about 2,000 nodes are matched on average starting from 100 seeds). Instead, filtered PGM, with $f = 1$ and $r = 4$, requires very few seeds to match almost all nodes, incurring about 3.7% error ratio. Using $f = 1, r = 5$, filtered PGM requires more seeds, but achieves as low as 0.3% error ratio.

Next, we fix r and increase the filtering factor f so as to diminish the number of errors while, however, reducing the average number of matched nodes (i.e., the probability to trigger percolation from a

---

[4]We verified that, if we instead fix the very first seed across all runs, a sharp transition appears. The transition threshold changes as we vary the initial seed (results not shown here).

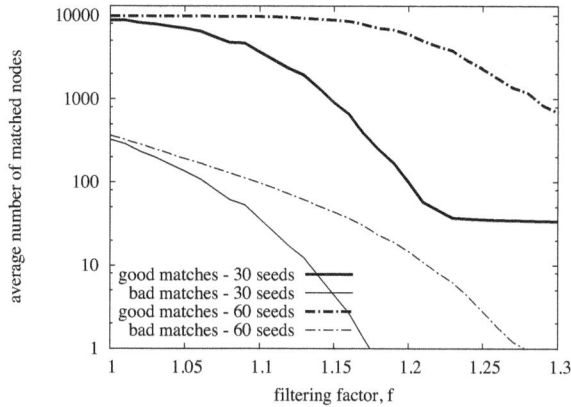

Figure 9: Effect of varying the filtering factor f for fixed $r = 4$ (scenario with $K(n) = 0.8$).

Table 3: Combinations of parameters achieving error ratio 3%, percolation probability 50%

average node degree	f	# seeds
36	1.1	22
45	1.2	24
53	1.3	28
64	1.4	32

given seed set). Fig. 9 illustrates this effect for $r = 4$, in the case of two different seed set sizes, 30 and 60. Having 60 seeds one could, for example, employ $f = 1.1$ obtaining very high chance of percolation (almost 100%) and small error ratio (around 1%).

Alternately, we can fix a desired error ratio and average number of matched nodes (i.e., the probability to trigger large-scale percolation), and look for the filtering factor and number of seeds that let us achieve the desired goals. Table 3 reports an example of this numerical exploration, in which we vary the average degree of the nodes in $\mathcal{G}_T$ corresponding to each examined scenario (the average degree can be increased, for fixed $K(n) = 0.8$, by increasing $C(n)$). The results in Table 3 validate, at least qualitatively, the counter-intuitive theoretical predictions in Table 2: as we increase $C(n)$ (and thus the average node degree), the seed set size necessary to achieve a desired matching performance increases as well.

7.2 Real social graph

We consider a real graph derived from the Slovak social network Pokec.The public data set, available at [12], is a directed graph with 1,632,803 vertices and 30,622,564 edges, where nodes are users of Pokec and directed edges represent friendships. Since the original graph contains too many vertices for our computational power, and since we would like to isolate the impact of clustering from the effect of long-tailed degree distributions, we considered only vertices having: i) in-degree larger than 20; ii) out-degree smaller than 200. We ended up with a reduced graph having $n = 133,573$ nodes, 5,449,236 edges, average (in or out) degree 40.8 and clustering coefficient 0.11. We use this graph as our ground-truth, and employ an edge sampling probability $s = 0.8$. Notice that we main-

tain the direct nature of the edges, since all considered algorithms immediately apply to direct networks as well [5].

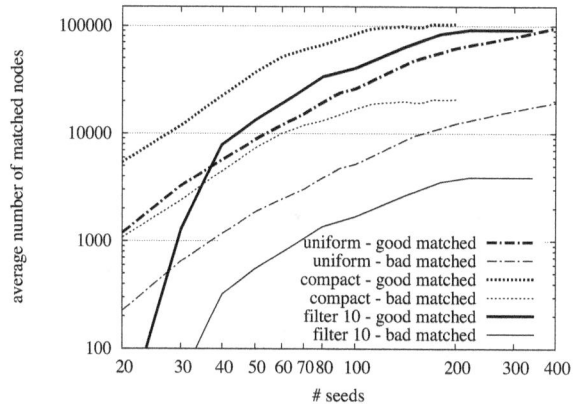

Figure 10: Performance of matching algorithms in a subset of the friendship graph of the social network Pokec.

Fig. 10 shows the performance of the different algorithms using threshold $r = 6$. As before, curves labelled 'uniform' refer to the PGM algorithm in which seeds are selected uniformly at random among the nodes. Curves labelled 'compact' refer to the PGM algorithm in which seeds are chosen among the closest neighbors of a uniformly selected node. Curves labelled 'filter 10' differ from the previous one in that the edges connecting each node to its nearest 10 neighbors are not used by the algorithm. We emphasize that a $G(n, p)$ having the same number of nodes and average degree would require $a_c = 5,783$ seeds, according to (1). In contrast, all considered algorithms require much fewer seeds to match almost all nodes, confirming that real social networks are much simpler to de-anonymize than $G(n, p)$. In particular, the uniform variant requires about 400 seeds to match on average 100,000 nodes, but incurs a quite large error ratio (about 17%). The compact variant reduces this number roughly by a factor 3, but produces the same error ratio. At last, the filtered variant requires a bit more seeds than the compact one, but it allows to lower down the error ratio to about 4%. The above results confirm the crucial performance improvement that can be obtained by jointly: i) starting from a compact set of seeds (to exploit the wave-propagation effect), ii) carefully discarding edges connecting nodes to their local clusters (to limit the errors).

8. CONCLUSIONS

We focused on the effect of node clustering on social network de-anonymization. We defined a flexible model of geometric random graphs that can incorporate different levels of clustering. Then we designed de-anonymization algorithms and analysed their performance by using bootstrap percolation. Our theoretical results highlight that clustering significantly helps to reduce the number of seeds required to trigger the identification process, and that our algorithms can correctly match almost all nodes while making errors negligible (asymptotically as the network grows large). Our findings were confirmed by numerical experiments on synthetic and real social graphs.

---

[5]In direct networks, counters of matchable pairs are incremented only by using outgoing edges from matched pairs.

APPENDIX

A. PROOF OF THEOREM 2

Without loss of generality, let us focus on $\mathcal{G}_1$ and let us consider a node $i \in \mathcal{H}_{\text{in}}(\alpha, \delta)$. By construction, the number of seeds that are neighbors of i on $\mathcal{G}_1$ is given by $S_i = \sum_{\sigma \in \mathcal{A}_0} X_{i\sigma} S_{i\sigma}^1 \geq_{st} Y_i \geq_{st} Y$ where

$$Y_i = \text{Bin}\left(a_0, sK(n)f\left(\max_{\sigma \in \mathcal{A}_0} ||\mathbf{x}_i - \mathbf{x}_\sigma||\right)\right)$$

and $Y = \text{Bin}(a_0, sK(n)(1+\delta)\alpha)$, with $\mathbb{E}[Y] = sK(n)(1+\delta)\alpha a_0$. Now, using the inequalities in Appendix B, we can bound:

$$P(Y_i < \alpha sK(n)a_0) \leq \exp\left(-\mathbb{E}[Y_i]H\left(\frac{\alpha sK(n)a_0}{\mathbb{E}[Y_i]}\right)\right)$$

$$\leq \exp\left(-(1+\delta)\alpha sK(n)a_0 H\left(\frac{1}{1+\delta}\right)\right) \quad (6)$$

with $H(b) = 1 - b + b\log b$.

If we consider jointly all nodes in $\mathcal{H}_{\text{in}}(\alpha, \delta)$ and we denote with N_{in} their number, we can bound the probability that every node in $\mathcal{H}_{\text{in}}(\alpha, \delta)$ is accepted with:

$$P(\text{all nodes in } \mathcal{H}_{\text{in}} \text{ are accepted} \mid N_{\text{in}})$$

$$\leq 1 - N_{\text{in}} \exp\left(-(1+\delta)\alpha sK(n)a_0 H\left(\frac{1}{1+\delta}\right)\right), \quad (7)$$

with (7) that tends to 1 if $\log N_{\text{in}} - (1+\delta)\alpha sH\left(\frac{1}{1+\delta}\right)K(n)a_0 \to -\infty$. This can be enforced by opportunely setting $a_0 = \Omega\left(\frac{\log N_{\text{in}}}{K(n)}\right)$. Since by construction $|\mathcal{H}_{\text{in}}| > C^k(n) \geq \frac{\log n}{n}$, we have w.h.p. $N_{\text{in}} \leq 2n|\mathcal{H}_{\text{in}}|$ by standard concentration results (see also [10, Lemma 2]). As consequence,

$$P(\text{all vertices in } \mathcal{H}_{\text{in}} \text{ are accepted}) \to 1$$

provided that $a_0 = \Omega\left(\frac{\log(nC^k(n))}{K(n)}\right)$. Then we focus on the nodes in $\mathcal{H}_{\text{out}}(\alpha, \delta)$ and we show that all those nodes are jointly rejected. Conceptually we repeat the same approach as before, however, the argument is made slightly more complex by the fact that, to achieve tight bounds on the probability that all nodes in $\mathcal{H}_{\text{out}}(\alpha, \delta)$ are jointly rejected, we need to partition $\mathcal{H}_{\text{out}}(\alpha, \delta)$ into smaller sub-regions containing nodes which lie at similar distance from the seeds.

Assuming $\delta < \frac{e^2 - 1}{e^2}$, we define $\mathcal{H}_{\text{out}}^1 = \mathcal{H}^1(\alpha, \frac{e^2-1}{e^2}) \subset \mathcal{H}_{\text{out}}(\alpha, \delta)$ and $\mathcal{H}_{\text{out}}^0(\alpha, \delta) = \mathcal{H}_{\text{out}}(\alpha, \delta) \setminus \mathcal{H}_{\text{out}}^1$. Furthermore, we partition $\mathcal{H}_{\text{out}}^1$ into disjoint sub-regions, i.e., $\mathcal{H}_{\text{out}}^1 = \cup_{h \geq 1} \mathcal{H}_{\text{out}}^{1,h}$, with

$$\mathcal{H}_{\text{out}}^{1,h} = \mathcal{H}_{\text{out}}\left(\frac{\alpha, h^\beta e^2 - 1}{h^\beta e^2}\right) \setminus \mathcal{H}_{\text{out}}\left(\alpha, \frac{(h+1)^\beta e^2 - 1}{(h+1)^\beta e^2}\right)$$

Now, given a vertex i in $\mathcal{H}_{\text{out}}^0$ ($\mathcal{H}_{\text{out}}^{1,h}$), the number of its neighbor seeds S_i on $\mathcal{G}_1$ can be bounded from above by a $\text{Bin}(a_0, sK(n)(1-\delta)\alpha)$ $\left(\text{Bin}(a_0, \frac{sK(n)}{h^\beta e^2}\alpha)\right)$. Furthermore, by elementary geometrical arguments, it can be shown that: i) $|\mathcal{H}_{\text{out}}^0| = \Theta(C^k(n))$, ii) $|\mathcal{H}_{\text{out}}^{1,1}| = \Theta(C^k(n))$ and iii) $\mathcal{H}_{\text{out}}^{1,h} = \Theta(h^{k-1}\mathcal{H}_{\text{out}}^{1,1})$.

Denoted with N_{out}^0 and $N_{\text{out}}^{1,h}$ the number of nodes in $\mathcal{H}_{\text{out}}^0$ and $\mathcal{H}_{\text{out}}^{1,h}$, respectively, by exploiting again the inequalities in [11, pag

16], w.h.p. we have:

$$P\left(\text{all nodes in } \mathcal{H}_{\text{out}}^0 \text{ are rejected}\right) \leq$$

$$1 - N_{\text{out}}^0 \exp\left(-(1-\delta)\alpha sK(n)a_0 H\left(1-\delta\right)\right) \to 1.$$

The above expression holds under the assumption that $a_0 = \Omega\left(\frac{\log(nC^k(n))}{K(n)}\right)$. Indeed, we remark that $N_{\text{out}}^0 \leq 2n|\mathcal{H}_{\text{out}}^0| = \Theta(nC^k(n))$ w.h.p. At last,

$$P\left(\text{all nodes in } \mathcal{H}_{\text{out}}^1 \text{ are rejected}\right)$$

$$\leq 1 - \sum_{h=1}^{\infty} N_{\text{out}}^{1,h} \exp\left(-\frac{\alpha sK(n)a_0}{2}(\beta \log h + 2)\right).$$

For every h, $N_{\text{out}}^{1,h} \leq 2n|\mathcal{H}^{1,h}| = \Theta(nh^{k-1}C^k(n))$; also, the number of sub-regions of $\mathcal{H}_{\text{out}}^1$ is $O(n/C^k(n))$. Thus, w.h.p. we have that jointly on all h's, the number of nodes in these sub-regions can be bounded by $2n|\mathcal{H}^{1,h}|$. Under the assumption that $a_0 = \Omega\left(\frac{\log(nC^k(n))}{K(n)}\right)$, it can be easily shown that

$$P\left(\text{all nodes in } \mathcal{H}_{\text{out}}^1 \text{ are rejected}\right) \to 1.$$

B. CONCENTRATION INEQUALITIES

For the reader's convenience, we report below the inequalities that can be found also in [11, p. 16].

Lemma 1. *Let* $H(b) = 1 - b + b\log b$ *for* $b > 0$. *Suppose* $n \in \mathbb{N}$ $p \in (0,1)$ *and* $0 \leq k \leq n$. *Let* $\mu = np$; *if* $k \leq \mu$, *then*:

$$P(\text{Bin}(n,p) \leq k) \leq \exp\left(-\mu H\left(\frac{k}{\mu}\right)\right) \quad (8)$$

if $k > \mu$, *then*:

$$P(\text{Bin}(n,p) \geq k) \leq \exp\left(-\mu H\left(\frac{k}{\mu}\right)\right) \quad (9)$$

if $k > e^2 \mu$, *then*

$$P(\text{Bin}(n,p) \geq k) \leq \exp\left(-\frac{k}{2}\log\frac{k}{\mu}\right). \quad (10)$$

Algorithm 1 The PGM algorithm

1: $\mathcal{A}_0 = \mathcal{B}_0 = \mathcal{A}_0(n)$, $\mathcal{Z}_0 = \emptyset$
2: **while** $\mathcal{A}_t \setminus \mathcal{Z}_t \neq \emptyset$ **do**
3:   $t = t + 1$
4:   Randomly select a pair $[*_1, *_2] \in \mathcal{A}_{t-1} \setminus \mathcal{Z}_{t-1}$ and add one mark to all neighboring pairs of $[*_1, *_2]$ in $\mathcal{M}(\mathcal{G}_T)$.
5:   Let $\Delta \mathcal{B}_t$ be the set of all neighboring pairs of $[*_1, *_2]$ in $\mathcal{M}(\mathcal{G}_T)$ whose mark counter has reached threshold r at time t.
6:   Construct set $\Delta \mathcal{A}_t \subseteq \Delta \mathcal{B}_t$ as follows. Order the pairs in $\Delta \mathcal{B}_t$ in an arbitrary way, select them sequentially and test them for inclusion in ΔA_t:
7:   **if** the selected pair in $\Delta \mathcal{B}_t$ has no conflicting pair in $\mathcal{A}_{t-1}$ or $\Delta \mathcal{A}_t$ **then**
8:     Insert the pair in $\Delta \mathcal{A}_t$
9:   **else**
10:     Discard it
11:   $\mathcal{Z}_t = \mathcal{Z}_{t-1} \cup [*_1, *_2]$, $\mathcal{B}_t = \mathcal{B}_{t-1} \cup \Delta \mathcal{B}_t$, $\mathcal{A}_t = \mathcal{A}_{t-1} \cup \Delta \mathcal{A}_t$
12: **return** $T = t$, $\mathcal{Z}_T = \mathcal{A}_T$

C. PROOF OF THEOREM 4

The following proof uses the PGM algorithm that has been introduced in [6] and here is reported for completeness in Alg. 1. The notation is briefly explained below; the reader may also refer to [10] for a detailed description of the PGM algorithm and associated notation.

With reference to PGM algorithm, we define:

- $\mathcal{B}_t(\mathcal{G}_T)$ as the set of pairs in $\mathcal{P}(\mathcal{G}_T)$ that at time step t have already collected a least r marks. It is composed of good pairs $\mathcal{B}_t'(\mathcal{G}_T)$ and bad pairs $\mathcal{B}_t''(\mathcal{G}_T)$;

- $\mathcal{A}_t(\mathcal{G}_T)$ as the set of matchable pairs at time t. Similarly to $\mathcal{B}_t(\mathcal{G}_T)$, it comprises good pairs $\mathcal{A}_t'(\mathcal{G}_T)$ and bad pairs $\mathcal{A}_t''(\mathcal{G}_T)$. In general, $\mathcal{A}_t(\mathcal{G}_T)$ and $\mathcal{B}_t(\mathcal{G}_T)$ do not coincide as $\mathcal{B}_t(\mathcal{G}_T)$ may include conflicting pairs that are not present in $\mathcal{A}_t(\mathcal{G}_T)$;

- $\mathcal{Z}_t(\mathcal{G}_T)$ as the set of pairs that have been matched up to time t. By construction, $|\mathcal{Z}_t(\mathcal{G}_T)| = t$, $\forall t$.

For the sake of readability, below we omit the dependency on the $\mathcal{G}_T$.

For any two vertices $i \in \mathcal{M}_l$ and $j \in \mathcal{M}_r$, let X_{ij} be the Bernoulli random variable that represents the presence of an edge $(i, j) \in \mathcal{E}$. By construction, $Ber(p_{\min}) \leq_{st} X_{ij} \leq_{st} Ber(p_{\max})$. I.e., two variables $\underline{X}_{ij}$ and $\overline{X}_{ij}$, with distribution, respectively, $Ber(p_{\min})$ and $Ber(p_{\max})$, can be defined on the same probability space as X_{ij} such that $\underline{X}_{ij} \leq X_{ij} \leq \overline{X}_{ij}$ point-wise.

We consider the corresponding pairs graph $\mathcal{P}(\mathcal{G}_T)$, which is, by construction, composed of all the pairs of vertices residing in $\mathcal{M}_l$ and $\mathcal{M}_r$ and of the edges connecting pairs of vertices in $\mathcal{M}_l$ with pairs of vertices in $\mathcal{M}_r$. We denote by $\mathcal{P}_l$ and $\mathcal{P}_r$, respectively, the set of pairs of $\mathcal{P}(\mathcal{G}_T)$, whose vertices lie in $\mathcal{M}_l$ and $\mathcal{M}_r$. Observe that, given two good pairs $[i_1, i_2] \in \mathcal{P}_l$ and $[j_1, j_2] \in \mathcal{P}_r$, the presence of an edge in $\mathcal{P}(\mathcal{G}_T)$ is associated with the random variable:

$$Y_{[i_1, i_2], [j_1, j_2]} = X_{ij} X_{ij} S_{ij}^1 S_{ij}^2 = X_{ij}^2 S_{ij}^1 S_{ij}^2$$

where S_{ij}^1 and S_{ij}^2 are mutually independent $Ber(s)$ random variables, which are in turn independent of X_{ij}. By construction,

$$p_{\min} s^2 \leq \mathbb{E}[Y_{[i_1, i_2], [j_1, j_2]}] \leq p_{\max} s^2.$$

Instead, given two bad pairs $[i_1, k_2] \in \mathcal{P}_l$ and $[j_1, l_2] \in \mathcal{P}_r$, we have $Y_{[i_1, k_2], [j_1, l_2]} = X_{ij} X_{kl} S_{ij}^1 S_{kl}^2$, with $p_{\min}^2 s^2 \leq \mathbb{E}[Y_{[i_1, k_2], [j_1, l_2]}] \leq p_{\max}^2 s^2$. Finally, if we consider one good pair and one bad pair (e.g., $[i_1, i_2] \in \mathcal{P}_l$ and $[j_1, k_2] \in \mathcal{P}_r$), we obtain $Y_{[i_1, i_2], [j_1, k_2]} = X_{ij} X_{ik} S_{ij}^1 S_{ik}^2$, with $p_{\min}^2 s^2 \leq \mathbb{E}[Y_{[i_1, i_2], [j_1, j_2]}] \leq p_{\max}^2 s^2$.

Recall that we assume that two seed sets, $\mathcal{A}_0^l \in \mathcal{P}_l$ and $\mathcal{A}_0^r \in \mathcal{P}_r$ (with $|\mathcal{A}_0^l| = |\mathcal{A}_0^r|$), are available. On $\mathcal{P}(\mathcal{G}_T)$ we run the PGM algorithm [6], opportunely modified, as follows. At every time step t, we extract uniformly at random one pair $\mathbf{z}^l(t) = [z_1^l, z_2^l]_t \in \mathcal{A}_{t-1}^l \setminus \mathcal{Z}_{t-1}^l$ and $\mathbf{z}^r(t) = [z_1^r, z_2^r]_t \in \mathcal{A}_{t-1}^r \setminus \mathcal{Z}_{t-1}^r$, adding a mark to all the neighbor pairs in $\mathcal{P}_r$ and $\mathcal{P}_l$, respectively. In other words, matched pairs in $\mathcal{P}_l$ contribute to the mark of pairs in $\mathcal{P}_r$ and vice versa. Thus, for a generic node pair $[i_1, j_2] \in \mathcal{P}_r \setminus \mathcal{Z}_t^r$, marks are updated according to the iteration: $M_{[i_1, j_2]}^r(t) = M_{[i_1, j_1]}^r(t-1) + Y_{\mathbf{z}^l(t), [i_1, j_2]}$. Similarly, for $[i_1, j_2] \in \mathcal{P}_l$ marks are updated according to $M_{[i_1, j_2]}^l(t) = M_{[i_1, j_2]}^l(t-1) + Y_{[i_1, j_2], \mathbf{z}^r(t)}$. For the rest, the algorithm proceeds exactly as described in Section 2.

Now, it is important to observe that marks of pairs on the RHS of the graph evolve exactly as the marks of a coupled PGM that operates over a pairs graph $\mathcal{P}_R$ defined as follows. Denote the

generic pair by $[*_1, *_2]$; then $\mathcal{P}_R$ is a graph insisting on the set of nodes $\mathcal{M}_r$ and in which the presence of edge $(\mathbf{z}^r(t), [*_1, *_2])$, for any $[*_1, *_2] \in \mathcal{P}_r \setminus \mathcal{Z}_t^r$, is dynamically unveiled at time t by observing variable $X_{z_1^l(t)*_1} X_{z_2^l(t)*_2} S_{z_1^l(t)*_1}^l S_{z_1^l(t)*_2}^r$. In other words, the edges originated from $\mathbf{z}^l(t)$ are replaced by the edges originated from $\mathbf{z}^r(t)$ and vice versa.

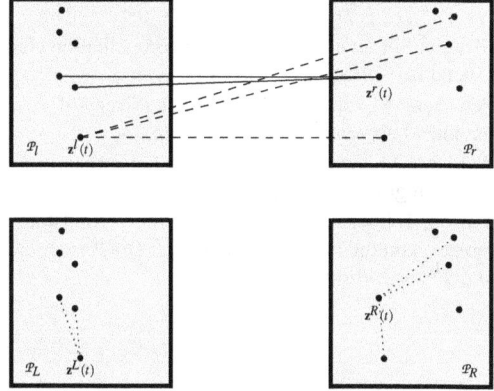

Figure 11: Graphical representation of the PGM evolution over coupled graphs.

Furthermore, we make the following observations.

(i) We assume that the sequence of matched pairs $\{\mathbf{z}_t^R\}_t \in \mathcal{P}^{(R)}$ exactly corresponds to the sequence of matched pairs $\{\mathbf{z}^r(t)\}_t \in \mathcal{P}_r$, i.e., $\mathbf{z}^r(t) = \mathbf{z}^R(t)$ at every t. This is made possible by the fact that given $\mathcal{Z}_{t-1}^r = \mathcal{Z}_{t-1}^R$, marks collected by every unmatched pair in the two graphs at time t exactly correspond.

(ii) Our construction is consistent since edges between pairs are unveiled only once, specifically at the time at which the first between the two edge endpoints in $\mathcal{P}_R$ is placed in $\mathcal{Z}_t^R = \mathcal{Z}_t^r$. Since then, the edge is replaced with an edge between two pairs that are both in $\mathcal{P}_R$, hence it will not be used again.

(iii) $\mathcal{P}_R$ is isomorphic to a pairs graph originated by a generalized Erdös–Rényi graph $\mathcal{G}_T^R$, in which the presence of every edge $(\mathbf{z}^r(t), *)$ can be represented by a Bernoulli r.v. and the probability that the edge is added to the graph takes values in the range $[p_{\min}, p_{\max}]$ and is independent of other edges. Indeed, observe that the presence of an edge in $\mathcal{P}_R$ deterministically corresponds to the presence of the corresponding edge in $\mathcal{P}(\mathcal{G}_T)$. Furthermore, by construction, different edges in $\mathcal{P}_R$ correspond to different edges in $\mathcal{P}(\mathcal{G}_T)$.

The same observations hold when we consider the evolution of the marks of the pairs on the left hand side and a pairs graph $\mathcal{P}_L$, which is originated from a coupled generalized Erdös–Rényi graph $\mathcal{G}_T^L$ with same properties as $\mathcal{G}_T^R$.

Now, clearly

$$G(m, p_{\min}) \leq_{st} \mathcal{G}_T^R \leq_{st} G(m, p_{\max})$$

and

$$G(m, p_{\min}) \leq_{st} \mathcal{G}_T^L \leq_{st} G(m, p_{\max}),$$

i.e., $\mathcal{G}_T^R$ ($\mathcal{G}_T^L$) can be obtained by opportunely thinning a graph $G(m, p_{\max})$, while a graph $G(m, p_{\min})$ can be obtained by opportunely thinning $\mathcal{G}_T^R$ ($\mathcal{G}_T^L$). Then we invoke Theorem 1 to conclude our proof and show that our algorithm correctly percolates over $\mathcal{G}_T^R$ and $\mathcal{G}_T^L$ and, thus, over the bipartite graph $\mathcal{G}_T$.

D. REFERENCES

[1] A. Narayanan, V. Shmatikov, "De-anonymizing social networks," *IEEE Symposium on Security and Privacy*, 2009.

[2] P. Pedarsani, D.-R. Figueiredo, M. Grossglauser, "A Bayesian method for matching two similar graphs without seeds," *IEEE Allerton* 2013.

[3] W. Peng, F. Li, X. Zou, J. Wu, "A two-stage deanonymization attack against anonymized social networks," *IEEE Trans. on Computers*, 63(2), 2014.

[4] N. Korula, S. Lattanzi, "An efficient reconciliation algorithm for social networks," *PVLDB*,2014.

[5] P. Pedarsani, M. Grossglauser, "On the privacy of anonymized networks," *SIGKDD*, 2011.

[6] L. Yartseva, M. Grossglauser, "On the performance of percolation graph matching," *COSN*, 2013.

[7] S. Janson, T. Luczak, T. Turova, T. Vallier, "Bootstrap percolation on the random graph $G_{n,p}$," *The Annals of Applied Probability*, 22(5), 2012.

[8] C.F. Chiasserini, M. Garetto, E.Leonardi, "De-anonymizing scale-free social networks by percolation graph matching," *INFOCOM*, 2015.

[9] K. Bringmann, T. Friedrich, A. Krohmer, "De-anonymization of heterogeneous random graphs in quasilinear time," *22nd Annual European Symposium on Algorithms, ESA'14.*

[10] C.F. Chiasserini, M. Garetto, E. Leonardi, "Impact of clustering on the performance of percolation-based graph matching," *Technical Report,* 2015, http://arxiv.org/abs/1508.02017.

[11] M. Penrose, *Random Geometric Graphs,* Oxford University Press, 2003.

[12] Pokec network dataset - KONECT, (website) http://konect.uni-koblenz.de/networks/soc-pokec-relationships

Overlap Between Google and Bing Web Search Results!
Twitter to the Rescue?

Rakesh Agrawal
Data Insights Laboratories
ragrawal@acm.org

Behzad Golshan
Boston University
behzad@bu.edu

Evangelos Papalexakis
Carnegie Mellon University
epapalex@cs.cmu.edu

Categories and Subject Descriptors

H.2.8 [**Database Applications**]: Data mining; H.3.3 [**Information Search and Retrieval**]: Search process

Keywords

Web search; social media search; search engine; search result comparison; Google; Bing; Twitter

1. EXTENDED ABSTRACT

Access to diverse perspectives nurtures an informed citizenry. Google and Bing have emerged as the duopoly that largely arbitrates which English language documents are seen by web searchers. We present our empirical study over the search results produced by Google and Bing that shows a large overlap. In order to measure search engine result overlap, in [1] we introduce two novel data mining tools. In a nutshell, the key ideas behind our tools are as follows:

1. TENSORCOMPARE: Using Tensor analysis, this tool produces a joint representation of different search engines (using their results for a set of queries over a period of time) into the same latent embedding space. By doing so, it enables visualization of search engines, clustering of their results and empirical inspection of overlap in search results.

2. CROSSLEARNCOMPARE: This tool is based on the following idea: Consider a feature representation of a search result. We can view the query that generated that result as a *class label* in a multi-class classification problem. Thus, suppose that we train a classifier that predicts the queries that generated the result of search engine **A**. If applying the model trained on **A** yields high classification accuracy on results obtained from search engine **B**, then **A**, **B** have high degree of search result overlap (in our chosen feature space). In the converse case, **A** and **B** have low overlap.

Given the aforementioned overlap between Google and Bing, citizens may not gain different perspectives by simultaneously probing them for the same query. Fortunately, our study [2] also shows that by mining Twitter data one can obtain search results that are quite distinct from those produced by Google and Bing.

Additionally, the users found those results to be quite informative. In particular, in Figure 1 we show the results of the Amazon Mechanical Turk study we conducted in [2] on results obtained using two query sets, 1) a set with popular, "head" queries, and 2) a set with "trunk" queries, spanning a wide range of the popularity spectrum. In our study, we asked users to label a Twitter search result as informative or not informative and we compute the "usefulness score" by taking the majority vote over all the users for every result of a given query, and counting the percentage of times the majority of the users deemed the results informative.

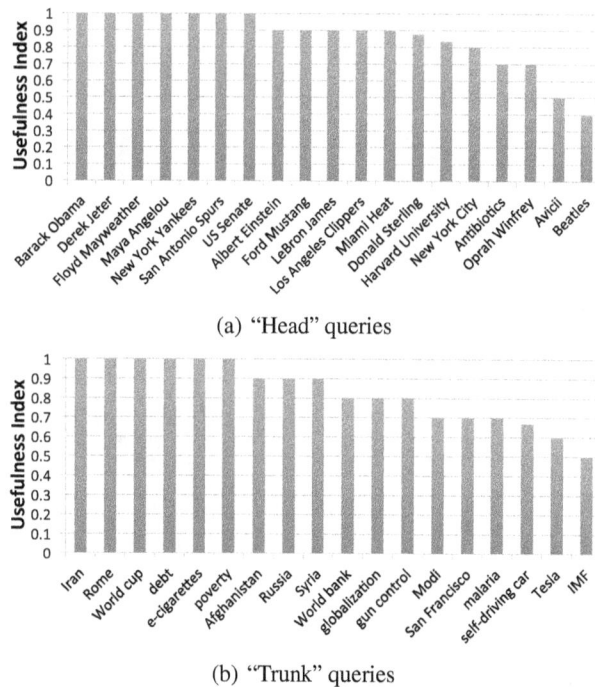

(a) "Head" queries

(b) "Trunk" queries

Figure 1: Usefulness index of search results mined from Twitter for various queries

Acknowledgements E. Papalexakis was partially supported by National Science Foundation Grant IIS-1247489.

2. REFERENCES

[1] R. Agrawal, B. Golshan, and E. Papalexakis. A study of distinctiveness in web results of two search engines. In *24th international conference on World Wide Web, Web Science Track*. ACM, May 2015.

[2] R. Agrawal, B. Golshan, and E. Papalexakis. Whither social networks for web search? In *21st ACM SIGKDD Conference on Knowledge Discovery and Data Mining*, Sydney, Australia, August 2015.

Discovering Opinion Spammer Groups by Network Footprints

Junting Ye   Leman Akoglu
Stony Brook University
Department of Computer Science
{juyye,leman}@cs.stonybrook.edu

ABSTRACT

Online reviews are an important source for consumers to evaluate products/services on the Internet (e.g. Amazon, Yelp, etc.). However, more and more fraudulent reviewers write fake reviews to mislead users. To maximize their impact and share effort, many spam attacks are organized as campaigns, by a *group* of spammers. In this paper, we propose a new two-step method to discover spammer groups and their targeted products. First, we introduce NFS (Network Footprint Score), a new measure that quantifies the likelihood of products being spam campaign targets. Second, we carefully devise *GroupStrainer* to cluster spammers on a 2-hop subgraph induced by top ranking products.

Our approach has four key advantages: (*i*) *unsupervised* detection; both steps require no labeled data, (*ii*) adversarial *robustness*; we quantify statistical distortions in the review network, of which spammers have only a partial view, and avoid any side information that spammers can easily evade, (*iii*) *sensemaking*; the output facilitates the exploration of the nested hierarchy (i.e., organization) among the spammers, and finally (*iv*) *scalability*; both steps have complexity linear in network size, moreover, *GroupStrainer* operates on a carefully induced subnetwork. We demonstrate the efficiency and effectiveness of our approach on both synthetic and real-world datasets from two different domains with millions of products and reviewers. Moreover, we discover interesting strategies that spammers employ through case studies of our detected groups.

COSN'15, November 2–3, 2015, Palo Alto, California, USA.
ACM 978-1-4503-3951-3/15/11.
DOI: http://dx.doi.org/10.1145/2817946.2820606.

You Can Yak But You Can't Hide

Carson L. Nemelka
Cameron L. Ballard
Kelvin Liu
NYU Shanghai

Minhui Xue
East China Normal University
NYU Shanghai

Keith W. Ross
New York University
NYU Shanghai

{cln261, clb478, kelvin.liu, minhuixue, keithwross}@nyu.edu

The recent growth of anonymous messaging services – such as 4chan, Whisper, and Yik Yak – has brought online anonymity into the spotlight. Ideally, anonymous posts allow users to say whatever they want, without having to fear people's reactions. This in principle allows for fully open discussion, and facilitates the sharing of controversial ideas. For these services to function properly, the integrity of user anonymity must be preserved.

With approximately two million active users, Yik Yak combines location-based services with anonymity to create a unique social-network experience. Yik Yak allows a user to post a short message, called a "yak", which can be seen by anyone else who has the app and is within a geometrical region centered around where the yak was posted. The Yik Yak site states that anyone within a 1.5 mile radius around the original post can see the yak. This location-based feature allows Yik Yak to foster anonymous discussions that are relevant to specific geographic communities, such as college campuses. Yik Yak enjoys enormous popularity on US college and university campuses.

In this research, we attempt to exploit the location-based feature of Yik Yak to determine the location from which a yak is posted. By knowing the location of a yak posting, the anonymity of the "yakker" (i.e., the person posting the yak) can potentially be compromised. For example, if we determine the post emanates from a specific off-campus residence, and we know the name of the student who lives at that residence, then we can predict with a fair amount of certainty who the yakker is. The basic idea of the attack is to use fake GPS to probe for the presence of the yak from multiple geographical locations (without physically moving), and then predict the location of the yakker by aggregating the probe results.

To do this, we use an android emulator, Genymotion, to simulate multiple android devices. Within each emulator we run the Yik Yak app. The emulator allows us to fake the phone's GPS coordinates, enabling us to use one device to probe from multiple locations. We probe at each location in a honeycomb layout consisting of 2,880 probes, each separated by 200 meters, and record the yaks at each of these locations. We use the task automation tool Sikuli to automate the data collection process and obtain the desktop images; we then process all the collected images through an optical character recognition (OCR) tool to extract the textual content corresponding to each probe.

We conducted our experiment across Missoula, home of the University of Montana. We first used our experimental setup to post five yaks scattered throughout the city. We then used six computers to probe from the 2,880 locations and record the yaks seen. At each location, the computer took screenshots of all the yaks seen. Each location took anywhere from 30 seconds to 2 minutes to record all the yaks.

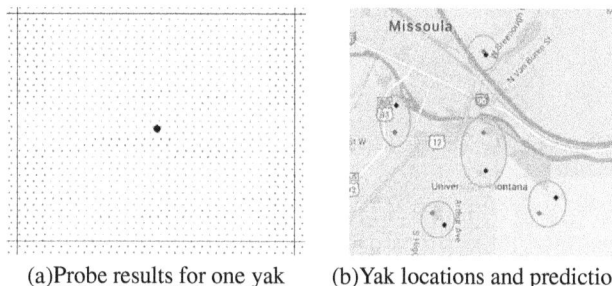

(a)Probe results for one yak   (b)Yak locations and predictions

Figure 1: Experimental Results

Figure 1(a) shows the results of all the probes in the honeycomb for one of our yaks. Green (resp. red) indicates presence (resp. no presence) of the yak at the probe. *Strikingly, for each of the messages, the shape of the set of green probes is square like.* Oddly, there are also small ears attached to the square, vaguely resembling the Yik Yak logo. (There are some points within the shape that are red, which are most likely due to small errors.). The other four yaks give rise to similar shapes. To predict the location of a yak based on the probe results, we can simply choose the center of this geometrical shape; specifically, we mark off the shape with a box as shown in Figure 1(a) and then choose the center of the box.

Figure 1(b) shows the actual and predicted locations for each of our five yaks. A black dot represents the true location while the corresponding red dot represents our prediction. As we can see, our predictions, although not perfect, are accurate within neighborhood regions and give strong clues as to the generally vicinity where a yak is located.

These preliminary results show that Yik Yak, and location-based services like it, potentially have a major privacy flaw. By knowing the general vicinity of the yak, other side information – such as the content of the yak along with the locations of college dorms, off-campus residences and local coffee shops – may allow one to further narrow down where the yak is coming from. The experimental results reported here are a proof of concept. A more in-depth experiment and analysis, possibly using a denser honeycomb and machine learning, may be able to predict yak locations with much greater accuracy.

COSN'15, November 2–3, 2015, Palo Alto, California, USA.
Copyright ACM 978-1-4503-3951-3/15/11.
DOI: http://dx.doi.org/10.1145/2817946.2820605.

Towards Graph Watermarks

Xiaohan Zhao, Qingyun Liu, Haitao Zheng and Ben Y. Zhao
Computer Science, UC Santa Barbara
{xiaohanzhao, qingyun_liu, htzheng, ravenben}@cs.ucsb.edu

ABSTRACT

From network topologies to online social networks, many of today's most sensitive datasets are captured in large graphs. A significant challenge facing the data owners is how to share sensitive graphs with collaborators or authorized users, *e.g.* ISP's network topology graphs with a third party networking equipment vendor. Current tools can provide limited node or edge privacy, but significantly modify the graph reducing its utility.

In this work, we propose a new alternative in the form of *graph watermarks*. Graph watermarks are small graphs tailor-made for a given graph dataset, a secure graph key, and a secure user key. To share a sensitive graph G with a collaborator C, the owner generates a watermark graph W using G, the graph key, and C's key as input, and embeds W into G to form G'. If G' is leaked by C, its owner can reliably determine if the watermark W generated for C does in fact reside inside G', thereby proving C is responsible for the leak. Graph watermarks serve both as a deterrent against data leakage and a method of recourse after a leak. We provide robust schemes for embedding and extracting watermarks, and use analysis and experiments on large real graphs to show that they are unique and difficult to forge. We study the robustness of graph watermarks against both single and powerful colluding attacker models, then propose and evaluate mechanisms to dramatically improve resilience.

1. INTRODUCTION

Many of today's most sensitive datasets are captured in large graphs. Such datasets can include maps of autonomous systems in the Internet, social networks representing billions of friendships, or connected records of patent citations. Controlling access to these datasets is a difficult challenge. More specifically, it is often the case that owners of large graph datasets would like to share access to them to a fixed set of entities without the data leaking into the public domain. For example, an ISP may be required to share detailed network topology graphs with a third party networking equipment vendor, with a strict agreement that access to these sensitive graphs must be limited to authorized personnel only. Similarly, a large social network like Facebook or LinkedIn may choose to share portions of its social graph data with trusted academic collaborators, but clearly want to prevent their leakage into the broader research community.

One option is to focus on building strong access control mechanisms to prevent data leakage beyond authorized parties. Yet in most scenarios, including both examples above, data owners cannot restrict physical access to the data, and have limited control once the data is shared with the trusted collaborator. It is also the case that no matter how well access control systems are designed, they are never foolproof, and often fall prey to attacks on the human element, *i.e.* social engineering. Another option is to modify portions of the data to reduce the impact of potential data leakages. This has the downside of making the data inherently noisy and inaccurate, and still can be overcome by data reconstruction or de-anonymization attacks using external input [27]. Finally, these schemes are hard to justify, in part because it is very difficult to quantify the level of protection they provide.

In this work, we propose a new alternative in the form of *graph watermarks*. Intuitively, watermarks are small, often imperceptible changes to data that are difficult to remove, and serve to associate some metadata to a particular dataset. They are used successfully today to limit data piracy by music vendors such as Apple and Wal-mart, who embed a user's personal information into a music file at the time of purchase/download [3]. Should the purchased music be leaked onto music sharing networks, it is easy for Apple to track down the user who was responsible for the leak. In our context, graph watermarks work in a similar way, by securely identifying a copy of a graph with its "authorized user." Should a shared graph dataset be leaked and discovered later in public domains (on Bit-Torrent perhaps), the data owner can extract watermark from the leaked copy and use it as proof to seek damages against the collaborator responsible for the leak. While not a panacea, graph watermarks can provide additional level of protection for data owners who want to or must share their data, and perhaps encourage risk-averse data owners to share potentially sensitive graph data, *e.g.* encourage LinkedIn to share social graphs with academic collaborators.

To be effective, a graph watermark system needs to provide several key properties. *First*, graph watermarks should be relatively small compared to the graph dataset itself. This has two direct consequences: the watermark will be difficult to detect (and remove) by potential attackers, and adding the watermark to the graph has minimal impact on the graph structure and its utility. *Second*, watermarks should be difficult to forge and should not occur naturally in graphs, ensuring that the presence of a valid watermark can be securely associated with some user, *i.e.* non-repudiation. *Third*, both the embedding and extraction of watermarks should be efficient, even for extremely large graph datasets with billions of nodes

COSN'15, November 2–3, 2015, Palo Alto, California, USA.
Copyright is held by the owner/author(s). Publication rights licensed to ACM.
ACM 978-1-4503-3951-3/15/11 ...$15.00.
DOI: http://dx.doi.org/10.1145/2817946.2817956.

and edges. *Finally,* our goal is to design a watermark system that works in any application context involving graphs. Therefore, we make no assumptions about the presence of metadata. Instead, our system must function for "barebones" graphs, *i.e.* symmetric, unweighted graphs with no node labels or edge weights.

In this paper, we present initial results of our efforts towards the design of a scalable and robust graph watermark system. Highlights of our work can be organized into the following key contributions.

- First, we identify the goals and requirements of a graph watermark system. We also describe an initial design of a graph watermark system that efficiently embeds watermarks into and extracts them out of large graphs. Graph watermarks are uniquely generated based on a user private key, a secure graph key, and the graph they are applied to. We describe constraints on its applicability, and identify examples of graphs where watermarks cannot achieve desirable levels of key properties such as uniqueness.

- Second, we provide a strict proof of uniqueness of graph watermarks, showing that it is extremely difficult for attackers to forge watermarks.

- Third, we evaluate our watermarks in term of distortion, uniqueness, and efficiency on several large graph datasets.

- Fourth, we identify two attack models, describe additional features to boost robustness, and evaluate them under realistic conditions.

To the best of our knowledge, our work is the first practical proposal for applying watermarks to graph data. We believe graph watermarks are a useful tool suitable for a wide range of applications from tracking data leaks to data authentication. Our work identifies the problem and defines an initial groundwork, setting the stage for follow-up work to improve robustness against a range of stronger attacks.

2. BACKGROUND AND RELATED WORK

In this section, we provide background and related work on graph privacy and watermark techniques in applications.

Graph Privacy. Graph privacy is a significant problem that has been magnified by the arrival of large graphs containing sensitive data, *e.g.* online social graphs or mobile call graphs. Recent studies [4, 27] show that deanonymization attacks can defeat most common anonymization techniques.

A variety of solutions have been proposed, ranging from anonymization tools that defend against specific structural attacks, or more attack-agnostic defenses. To protect node- or edge-privacy against specific, known attacks, techniques utilize variants of *k-anonymization* to produce structural redundancy at the granularity of subgraphs, neighborhoods or single nodes [23, 46, 12, 48]. Alternatively, randomization provides privacy protection by randomly adding, deleting, or switching edges [10, 44]. Others partition the nodes and then describe the graph at the level of partitions to avoid structural re-identification [11]. Finally, a different approach is taken by producing model-driven synthetic graphs that replicate key structural properties of the original graphs [35]. One extension of this work utilizes differential privacy techniques to provide a tunable accuracy vs. privacy tradeoff [36].

Our goals are quite different from prior work on graph anonymization, meant to protect data before its public release. We are concerned with scenarios where graph data is shared between its owner and groups of trusted collaborators, *e.g.* third party network vendors analyzing an ISP's network topology, or Facebook sharing a graph with a group of academic researchers. The ideal goal in these scenarios is to ensure the shared data does not leak into the wild. Once data is shared with collaborators, reliable tools that can track leaked data back to its source serve as an excellent deterrent. Watermarking techniques have addressed similar problems in other contexts, and we briefly describe them here.

Background on Digital Watermarks. Watermarking is the process of embedding specialized metadata into multimedia content [14]. The embedded *watermark* is later extracted from the file and used to identify the source or owner of the content. These systems include an embedding component and an extraction component. The embedding component takes three inputs: a watermark, the original data, and a key, aiming to embed the watermark with minimum impact on the data. The key is used as a parameter to generate a unique watermark for a specific user, and is kept confidential by the data owner. Extraction takes as input the watermarked data, the key, and possibly a copy of the original data. Extraction can directly produce the embedded watermark or a confidence measure of whether it is present.

Watermarking is widely used today to protect intellectual property. Significant work has been done in digital watermarking, particularly image watermarking [37, 24, 5, 34, 42]. Watermark techniques [29, 30] have been studied to protect the abuse of digital vector maps. Watermarks have also been used to protect software copyrights [47, 7], by adding spurious execution paths in the code that would not be triggered by normal inputs [39]. Moreover, watermark algorithms have been proposed for relational datasets [1, 22, 13]. Much of this has focused on modifying numeric attributes of relations, using the primary key attribute as an indicator of watermark locations, assuming that the primary key attribute does not change. Finally, watermarks, in the form of minute changes, have been applied to protect circuit designs in the semiconductor industry [31, 41].

3. GOALS AND ATTACK MODELS

To set the context for the design of our graph watermark system, we need to first clearly define the attack models we target, and use them to guide our design goals.

Graph watermarks at a glance. At a high level, we envision the graph watermark process to be simple and lightweight, as pictured in Figure 1. Embedding a watermark involves *overlaying* the original graph dataset (G) with a small subgraph (W) generated using the original graph and a secret random generator seed (Ω). Embedding the watermark simply means adding or deleting edges between existing nodes in the original graph G, based on the watermark subgraph W. Each authorized user i receives only a watermarked graph customized for her, generated using a random seed Ω_i securely associated with her. The seed is generated through cooperation of her private key and a key securely associated with the original graph.

If and when the owner detects a leaked version of the dataset, the owner takes the leaked graph, and "extracts the watermark," by iteratively producing all known watermark subgraphs W_i associated with G and each of the seeds Ω_i associated with an authorized user. The "extraction" process is actually a matching process where the data owner can conclusively identify the source of the leaked data, by locating the matching W_i in the leaked graph.

In our model of potential attackers and threats, we assume that attackers have access to the watermarked graph, but not the original G. Clearly, if an attacker is able to obtain the unaltered G, then watermarks are no longer necessary.

Attack Models. The attackers' goal is to destroy or remove graph watermarks while preserving the original graph. Watermarks are designed to protect the overall integrity of the graph data. Thus

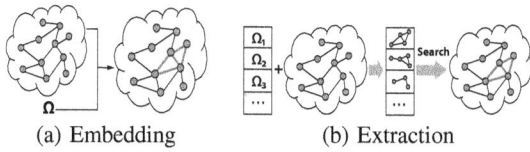

(a) Embedding   (b) Extraction

Figure 1: Embedding and extracting graph watermarks.

we do not consider scenarios where the attackers sample the graph or distort it significantly to remove the watermark. Under these constraints, we consider two practical attack models below.

- *Single Attacker Model.* For a single attacker with access to one watermarked graph, it will be extremely difficult to detect the embedded watermark. Without the key associated with another user, forging a watermark is also impractical. Instead, their best attack is to disrupt any potential watermarks by adding or deleting nodes or edges.

- *Collusion Attack Model.* If multiple attackers join their efforts, they can recover the original graph by comparing multiple watermarked graphs, identifying the differences (*i.e.* watermarks), and removing them.

Design Goals. The attack models help us define the key characteristics required for a graph watermarking system.

- *Low distortion.* The addition of watermarks should have a small impact on overall structure of the original graph. This preserves the utility of the graph datasets.

- *Robust to modifications.* Watermarks should be robust to modification attacks on watermarked graphs, *i.e.* watermarks should remain detectable and extractable with high probability, even after the graph has been modified.

- *Low false positives.* It is extremely unlikely for our system to successfully identify a valid watermark W_i in an unwatermarked graph or a graph watermarked by W_j where $i \neq j$. When we embed a single watermark (Section 4), we also refer to this property as *watermark uniqueness*.

Within the constraints defined above, designing a graph watermark system is quite challenging, for several reasons. First, the subgraph that represents the watermark must be relatively "unique," *i.e.* it is highly unlikely to occur naturally, or intentionally through forgery. A second, contrasting goal is that the watermark should not change the underlying graph significantly (low distortion), or be easily detected. Walking the fine line between this and properties of "uniqueness" likely means we have to restrict the set of graphs which can be watermarked, *i.e.* for some graphs, it will be impossible to find a hard to detect watermark that does not occur easily in graphs. Finally, since any leaked graph can have all metadata stripped or modified, watermark embedding and extraction algorithms must function without any labels or identifiers. Note that the problem of subgraph matching is known to be NP-complete [8].

4. BASIC WATERMARK DESIGN

We now describe the basic design of our graph watermarking system. The basic design seeks to embed and extract watermarks on graphs to achieve watermark uniqueness while minimizing distortion on graph structure. Our design has two key components:

- **Watermark embedding**: The data owner holds a graph key K^G associated with a graph G known only to her. Each user i generates its public-private cryptographic key pair $< K^i_{pub}, K^i_{priv} >$ through a standard public-key algorithm [25], where K^i_{pub} is user i's public key and K^i_{priv} is its corresponding private key. To share the graph G with user i, the system combines input from user i's

digital signature $K^i_{priv}(T)$ and graph key K^G to form a random generator seed Ω_i, and use Ω_i to generate a watermark graph W_i for graph G. The system embeds W_i into G by selecting and modifying a subgraph of G that contains the same number of nodes as W_i. The resulting graph G^{W_i} is given to user i as the watermarked graph.

- **Watermark extraction**: To identify the watermark in G', we use Ω_i to regenerate W_i and then search for the existence of W_i within G', for each user i.

In this section, we focus on describing the detailed procedure of these two components. We present detailed analysis on the two fundamental properties of graph watermarks, *i.e.* uniqueness and detectability in Section 5.

4.1 Watermark Embedding

The most straightforward way to embed a watermark is to directly attach the watermark graph to the original graph. That is, if W_i represents the watermark graph for user i, and G represents the original graph, the embedding treats W_i as an independent graph, and adds new edges to connect W_i to G. However, this approach has two disadvantages. *First*, direct graph attachment makes it easy for external attackers to identify and remove W_i from G without using graph key K^G and user i's signature $K^i_{priv}(T)$. New edges connecting W_i and G must be carefully chosen to reduce the chance of detection, which is very challenging. *Second*, attaching a (structurally different) subgraph W_i directly to a graph G introduces larger structural distortions.

Instead, we propose an alternative approach that embeds the watermark graph "in-band." That is, the embedding process first selects k nodes (k is the number of nodes in W_i) from G and identifies S, the corresponding subgraph of G induced by these k nodes. It then modifies S using W_i without affecting any other nodes in G. Because the watermark graph W_i is naturally connected with the rest of the graph, both the risk of detection and amount of distortion induced on the original graph G are significantly lower than those of the direct attachment approach.

We now describe the details of "in-band" watermark embedding, which consists of four steps: (1) generating a random generator seed Ω_i from user i's signature $K^i_{priv}(T)$ and graph key K^G; (2) generating the watermark graph W_i from the seed Ω_i; (3) selecting the placement of W_i on G by picking k nodes from G and identifying the corresponding subgraph S induced by these k nodes; and (4) embedding W_i into G by modifying S to match structure of W_i.

Step 1: Generating a random generator seed Ω_i. To generate an unforgettable watermarked graph, we form a random generator seed Ω_i [9] using user i's signature $K^i_{priv}(T)$ and graph key K^G.

Suppose the system intends to generate a watermarked version of graph G at time T to share with user i. We begin by first sending user i with the timestamp T. User i responds with its signature $K^i_{priv}(T)$, by encrypting the timestamp with its private key K^i_{priv}. Before proceeding further, we validate $K^i_{priv}(T)$ to ensure it is from user i, by decrypting it with user i's public key K^i_{pub}. If the timestamps match, we combine the signature $K^i_{priv}(T)$ and the graph key K^G to form the random generator seed Ω_i for user i. A mismatch may indicate that user i is a potential malicious user.

Note that Ω_i cannot be formed alone by the data owner who only holds the graph key K^G, or by user i who only owns its private key K^i_{priv}. Thus, results computed using Ω_i, including the random graph W_i generated (Step 2) and the choice of graph nodes to mark (Step 3), cannot be derived independently by the data owner or identified by user i.

103

Step 2: Generating the watermark graph W_i. We generate W_i as an Erdos-Renyi random graph with edge probability of p and node count k ($k \ll n$, where n is the number of nodes in G). The random edge generator uses Ω_i as the seed [9]. The k nodes of W_i are ordered as $\{v_1, v_2, ..., v_k\}$.

The key factor here is choosing the node count k and the edge probability p. To ensure watermark uniqueness, Section 5.1 shows that the two parameters must satisfy $k \geq (2 + \delta) \log_q n$, where $q = \frac{1}{\max(p, 1-p)}$ and δ is a constant > 0. Furthermore, it is easy to prove that $p = \frac{1}{2}$ minimizes the node count k and the average edge count $p \cdot \binom{k}{2}$ of the watermark graph W_i. Intuitively, using a compact watermark graph not only reduces the amount of distortion to G, but also improves its robustness against malicious attacks. Thus, we configure $p = \frac{1}{2}$ and therefore $k = (2 + \delta) \log_2 n$. This produces a reasonably sized watermark graph ($k < 100$) even for extremely large graphs, $e.g.$ the complete Facebook social graph ($\sim$1 billion nodes in 2014).

Step 3: Selecting the watermark placement on graph G. Next, we identify k nodes from G and its corresponding subgraph S to embed the watermark graph. To ensure reliable extraction, we must choose these k nodes carefully, meeting these two requirements. *First*, using Ω_i generated in Step 1, the k nodes must be chosen deterministically and remain distinguishable from the other nodes of G. *Second*, the set of the k nodes chosen for different watermarks (or different Ω_i values) must be easily distinguishable from each other to reinforce watermark uniqueness. Our biggest challenge in meeting these requirements is that we cannot use node IDs to distinguish nodes from each other. Node IDs or any type of metadata can be easily altered or stripped by attackers before or after leaking G', thereby making extraction impossible.

We address this challenge by using local graph structure around each node as its "label." Specifically, we define a *node structure description* (NSD) as a descriptive feature of each node. A node v's NSD is represented by an array of v's sorted neighbor degrees. For example, if node v has three neighbors with node degrees 2, 6, 4, respectively, then v's NSD label is "2-4-6." We then hash v's NSD label into a numerical value using a secure one-way hash $e.g.$ SHA-1 [33], and refer to the result as node v's *NSDhash*.

Next, we use Ω_i as the seed to randomly generate k hash values, and use each as an index ($e.g.$ using a mod function) to identify a node in G. It is possible that multiple nodes have the same NSD-hash, $i.e.$ a collision. If this happens, we resolve the collision by using Ω_i again as an index into a sorted list of these nodes with the same NSDhash. The nodes can be sorted by any deterministic order, $e.g.$ node IDs in the original graph. Note that this process is only required for embedding (and not extraction), so any deterministic order chosen by the graph owner will suffice.

At the end of this step, we obtain k ordered nodes from G, $X = \{x_1, x_2, ..., x_k\}$, and the corresponding subgraph $S = G[X]$ induced by the node set X on G.

Step 4: Embedding the watermark graph W_i into graph G. In this step, we embed the watermark graph W_i by modifying the subgraph $S = G[X]$ to match W_i. Specifically, we match each (ranked) node in W_i, $\{v_1, v_2, ..., v_k\}$ with the corresponding node in S (or X), $\{x_1, x_2, ..., x_k\}$, $i.e.$ $f : W \to S, f(v_i) = x_i$. And once the nodes are mapped, we then apply an XOR operation on each edge of the two graphs. That is, we consider the connection between (v_i, v_j) or (x_i, x_j) as one bit, $i.e.$ an edge between (v_i, v_j) or (x_i, x_j) means 1 and no edge between (v_i, v_j) or (x_i, x_j) means 0. If an edge (v_i, v_j) exists in W_i, we modify the corresponding edge value in S from (x_i, x_j) to $(x_i, x_j) \oplus 1$; and if no edge (v_i, v_j) exists in W_i, we modify the edge value (x_i, x_j) to $(x_i, x_j) \oplus 0$.

When the above edge modification process ends, we also explicitly create edges between nodes x_i and x_{i+1} to maintain a connected subgraph. As a result, we transfer the subgraph S into S^{W_i} with the watermark graph W_i embedded. The reason for choosing the XOR operation is that it allows the same watermark to be embedded in the graph multiple times (at multiple locations), thus reducing the risk of the watermark being detected and destroyed by attacks such as frequent subgraph mining. We will discuss this in more details in Section 6.

At the end of this step, we obtain a watermarked graph G^{W_i} for user i. Before we distribute it to user i, we anonymize G^{W_i} by completely (randomly) reassigning all node IDs. Such anonymization not only helps to protect user privacy, but also minimizes the opportunity for colluding attackers with multiple watermarked graphs to identify the embedded watermark (see Section 6).

4.2 Watermark Extraction

The watermark *extraction* process determines if a watermark graph W_i is embedded in a target graph G'. If so, then G' is a legitimate copy distributed to user i. The extraction process faces two key challenges. *First*, the target graph G' can easily be modified by users/attackers during the graph distribution process. In particular, all node IDs can be very different from that of the original G. Thus extraction cannot rely on node IDs in G'. *Second*, identifying whether a subgraph exists in a large graph is equivalent to a subgraph matching problem, known to be NP-complete. To handle large graphs, we need a computationally efficient algorithm.

Our design addresses these two challenges by leveraging knowledge on the structure of the subgraph where the watermark was embedded. This eliminates the dependency on node IDs while significantly reducing the search space during the subgraph matching process. We describe our proposed design in detail below.

Step 1: Regenerating the watermark. The owner performs the extraction, and has access to the original graph G, graph key K^G, and user's signature $K^i_{priv}(T)$. For each user i, we combine its signature $K^i_{priv}(T)$ and graph key K^G to form its random generator seed Ω_i. Then, we follow step $2 - 4$ described in Section 4.1 to regenerate the watermark graph W_i, identify the k ordered nodes from G and their NSD labels, and finally the modified subgraph S^{W_i} that was placed on a "clean" version of the watermarked graph G^{W_i}.

Step 2: Identifying candidate watermark nodes on G'. Given the k nodes $X = \{x_1, x_2, ..., x_k\}$ identified from the original graph G, in this step we need to identify for each x_j, a set of candidate nodes on the target graph G' that can potentially become x_j. We accomplish this by identifying all the nodes on G' whose NSD labels are the same of x_j in the "clean" version of the watermarked graph G^{W_i}. Since multiple nodes can have the same NSD label, this process will very likely produce multiple candidates. To shrink the candidate list, we examine the connectivity between candidate nodes of X on G' and compare it to that among X on G^{W_i}. If two nodes x_m and x_n are connected in G^{W_i}, we prune their candidate node lists by removing any candidate node of x_m that has no edge with any candidate node of x_n on G' and vice versa. This pruning process dramatically reduces the search space. After this step, we obtain for each x_i the candidate node list C_i on the target graph G'.

Step 3: Detecting watermark graph S^{W_i} on G'. Given the candidate node list of each node in X, we now search for the existence of S^{W_i} on the target graph G'. For this we apply a recursive algorithm to enumerate and prune the combinations of the candidate sets, until we identify S^{W_i} or exhaust all the node candidates. The detailed algorithm is listed in Algorithm 1. In this

Algorithm 1 Recursive Algorithm for Detecting S^{W_i} on G'.

1: **Function:** SubgraphDetection(G', S^{W_i}, $\{C_1, C_2, ..., C_k\}$, Y, m)
2: **Input:** Graph G', watermark graph S^{W_i}, candidate node list C_i for each node x_i in X, identified node list $Y = \{y_1, y_2, ..., y_m\}$ ($m < k$)
3: **Output:** Identified node list $Y = \{y_1, y_2, ..., y_{m+1}\}$
4: **for** each node $c \in C_{m+1}$ **do**
5:   **if** $c \notin Y$ and each edge (c, y_t) in G' ($t = 1..m$) is the same as the edge (x_{m+1}, x_t) in S^{W_i} ($t = 1..m$) **then**
6:     $Y = Y \cup c$
7:     $m = m + 1$
8:     **if** $m == k$ **then**
9:       Return Y
10:     **else**
11:       SubgraphDetection(G', S^{W_i}, $\{C_1, C_2, ..., C_k\}$, Y, m)
12:     **end if**
13:     $Y = Y \setminus c$
14:     $m = m - 1$
15:   **end if**
16: **end for**
17: Return Y

algorithm, we use a node list Y to record the nodes in G' which we have already finalized as the corresponding nodes in S^{W_i}, i.e. $Y = \{y_1, y_2, ..., y_m\}$ ($m \leq k$). When the process starts, $Y = \emptyset$, $m = 0$.

Discussion. The above design shows that our watermark extraction algorithm simplifies the subgraph search problem by restricting it to a small number of selected nodes from a graph, thus avoiding the NP-complete subgraph matching problem.

To illustrate the efficiency of our algorithm, we now show an estimation of the computational complexity. Assume that the number of candidates for each watermark node x_i is $|C_i|$, and the probability that an edge between node $c_{im} \in |C_i|$ and node $c_{jn} \in |C_j|$ is p_{ij}. Moreover, since we prove that the probability of an edge between node x_i and node x_j is $\frac{1}{2}$ in Section 5.1, the probability that the connectivity between (c_{im}, c_{jn}) matches the connectivity between (x_i, x_j) is $\frac{1}{2} \cdot p_{ij} + \frac{1}{2} \cdot (1 - p_{ij}) = \frac{1}{2}$. We can show that to identify a node list with m nodes in Algorithm 1, we need to match $\binom{m}{2}$ node pairs. Thus, the probability to identify a node list with m nodes is $\frac{1}{2}\binom{m}{2}$, and the expected number of node combinations is $\prod_{i=1}^{m} |C_i| \cdot \frac{1}{2}\binom{m}{2}$. Thus, the computational complexity of Algorithm 1 is proportional to the sum of node combinations at each step, i.e. $O(\sum_{m=2}^{k} \prod_{i=1}^{m} |C_i| \cdot \frac{1}{2}\binom{m}{2})$. Note that we do not consider the fixed $k - 1$ edges between (x_{i-1}, x_i) for simplicity.

This result shows that as more nodes are identified in Algorithm 1, fewer node combinations exists, which approximates to 0 (as shown in Section 5.1). This means the major computation cost of our algorithm comes from the initial few steps and is dominated by the size of their candidates. Note that we target real graphs with very high level of node heterogeneity, e.g. small-world, power-law or highly clustered graphs, which leads to small candidate size in most cases. In other words, the computational complexity of our algorithm is low in real graphs. In practice, our system can efficiently extract watermarks from real, million-node graphs, and do so in a few minutes on a single commodity server (Section 7.3).

5. FUNDAMENTAL PROPERTIES

Having described the basic watermark system, we now present detailed analysis on its two fundamental properties: *watermark uniqueness* where each watermark must be unique to the corresponding user, and *watermark detectability* where the presence of a watermark should not be easily detectable by external users without the knowledge of the seed Ω_i associated with user i.

5.1 Watermark Uniqueness

As a proof of ownership, each embedded watermark should be unique for its user. That is, given the original graph G and the seed Ω_i associated with user i, the embedded watermark graph S^{W_i} should not be isomorphic to any subgraph of G^{W_j} ($i \neq j$) where G^{W_j} is the watermarked graph for user j. Meanwhile, S^{W_i} should not be isomorphic to any subgraph of the original graph G. The following proof shows that with high probability, our proposed graph watermark system produces unique watermarks for any graph G.

THEOREM 1. *Given a graph G with n nodes, let $k \geq (2 + \delta) \log_2 n$ for a constant $\delta > 0$. We apply the following process to create a watermarked graph G^{W_i} for user i:*

- *We create k nodes, $V = \{v_1, v_2, ..., v_k\}$, and generate a random graph W_i on V with an edge probability of $\frac{1}{2}$.*

- *We randomly select k nodes, $X = \{x_1, x_2, ..., x_k\}$ from G, and identify the subgraph corresponding to these k nodes $S = G[X]$.*

- *Using W_i, we modify S as follows: we first map each node x_i in X to a node v_i in V. Let $e(u, v) = 1$ denote an edge exists between node u and v and $e(u, v) = 0$ denote otherwise. We modify each $e(x_i, x_j)$ in S to $e(x_i, x_j) \oplus e(v_i, v_j)$. We then explicitly connect nodes x_i and x_{i+1}, i.e. $e(x_i, x_{i+1}) = 1$. The resulting S now becomes S^{W_i}, and the resulting G becomes G^{W_i}.*

Let G^{W_l} denote a watermarked graph for user l ($l \neq i$), built using a different seed Ω_l. Then with low probability, any subgraph of G^{W_l} or G is isomorphic to S^{W_i}.

PROOF. We first show that with low probability, any subgraph of G^{W_l} is isomorphic to S^{W_i}. Let $Y = \{y_1, y_2, ...y_k\}$ be a set of ordered nodes in G^{W_l}, where each y_i maps to a node x_i in X. We define an event $\mathcal{E}_Y$ occurs if the subgraph $G^{W_l}[Y]$ is isomorphic to $G^{W_i}[X]$ or S^{W_i}. Then the event $\mathcal{E}$ representing the fact that there exists at least one subgraph on G^{W_l} that is isomorphic to S^{W_i} is the union of events $\mathcal{E}_Y$ on all possible Y, i.e. $\mathcal{E} = \cup_Y \mathcal{E}_Y$.

Next, we compute the probability of event $\mathcal{E}$ by those of individual event $\mathcal{E}_Y$. Specifically, we first show that the probability of an edge exists between node x_i and x_j ($j \neq i + 1$) in $S^{W_i} = G^{W_i}[X]$ is $\frac{1}{2}$. This is because each edge in the random graph W_i is independently generated with probability $\frac{1}{2}$. After performing the XOR operation between W_i and S, the probability of an edge exists between x_i and x_j ($j \neq i + 1$) on S^{w_i} is $\frac{1}{2} \cdot p_{ij} + (1 - p_{ij}) \cdot \frac{1}{2} = \frac{1}{2}$ where p_{ij} is the probability that an edge exists between x_i and x_j on S. Thus the result of XOR between W_i and S is also a random graph, and its edge generation is independent of that in G^{W_l}, $l \neq i$. Furthermore, it is easy to show that our design applies XOR operations on $\binom{k}{2} - (k - 1)$ node pairs on the k nodes, and each node pair has an edge with a probability of $\frac{1}{2}$. Thus, the probability of a subgraph $G^{W_l}[Y]$ being isomorphic to S^{W_i} is $P(\mathcal{E}_Y) = \frac{1}{2}\binom{k}{2}-(k-1) \cdot \beta$ where $\beta \leq 1$ is the probability that every (y_i, y_{i+1}) pair in $G^{W_l}[Y]$ is connected. Thus $P(\mathcal{E}_Y) \leq \frac{1}{2}\binom{k}{2}-(k-1)$.

Since $\mathcal{E} = \cup_Y \mathcal{E}_Y$ and there are less than n^k possible sets of k ordered nodes in G^{W_l}, we use the Union Bound to compute the probability of event $\mathcal{E}$ as follows:

$$P(\mathcal{E}) < n^k \cdot P(\mathcal{E}_Y) \leq n^k \cdot \frac{1}{2}\binom{k}{2}-(k-1)$$
$$= 2^{\frac{k^2}{2+\delta}} \cdot \frac{1}{2}^{\frac{k^2-3k}{2}+1} = \frac{1}{2}^{\frac{\delta k^2}{2(2+\delta)} - \frac{3k}{2}+1} \quad (1)$$

The above equation shows that the probability $P(\mathcal{E})$ reduces exponentially to 0 as k increases.

Graph Category	Graph	# of Nodes	# of Edges	Avg. Deg.	k	Node Degree Criterion $(k+1)/2$	$[N_{min}(G), N_{max}(G)]$	k-node Subgraph Density Criterion Watermark	$[D_{min}(k), D_{max}(k)]$	Suitability
Facebook	Russia	97,134	289,324	6.0	39	20	[1, 748]	390	[45, 701]	Yes
	L.A.	603,834	7,676,486	25.4	45	23	[1, 2141]	517	[44, 975]	Yes
	London	1,690,053	23,084,859	27.3	48	24	[1, 1483]	588	[47, 1128]	Yes
Other Social Networks	Epinions (1)	75,879	405,740	10.7	38	19	[1,3044]	370	[47,649]	Yes
	Slashdot (08/11/06)	77,360	507,833	13.1	38	19	[1, 2540]	370	[38, 668]	Yes
	Twitter	81,306	1,342,303	33.0	38	19	[1, 3383]	370	[44, 703]	Yes
	Slashdot (09/02/16)	81,867	497,672	12.2	38	19	[1, 2546]	370	[38, 669]	Yes
	Slashdot (09/02/21)	82,140	500,481	12.2	38	19	[1, 2548]	370	[38, 669]	Yes
	Slashdot (09/02/22)	82,168	543,381	13.2	38	19	[1, 2553]	370	[38, 673]	Yes
	GPlus	107,614	12,238,285	227.5	39	20	[1, 20127]	389.5	[53, 741]	Yes
	Epinions (2)	131,828	711,496	10.8	40	20	[1, 3558]	409.5	[51, 780]	Yes
	Youtube	1,134,890	2,987,624	5.3	47	24	[1, 28754]	563.5	[47, 815]	Yes
	Pokec	1,632,803	22,301,964	27.3	48	24	[1, 14854]	587.5	[47, 979]	Yes
	Flickr	1,715,255	15,555,041	18.1	48	24	[1, 27236]	588	[51, 1128]	Yes
	Livejournal	5,204,176	48,942,196	18.8	52	26	[1, 15017]	689	[51, 1326]	Yes
Citation Networks	Patents	23,133	93,468	8.1	34	17	[1, 280]	297	[37, 373]	Yes
	ArXiv (Theo. Cit.)	27,770	352,304	25.4	34	17	[1, 2468]	297	[36, 534]	Yes
	ArXiv (Phy. Cit.)	34,546	420,899	24.4	35	18	[1, 846]	314.5	[36, 544]	Yes
Collaboration Networks	ArXiv (Phy.)	12,008	118,505	19.7	32	16	[1, 491]	263.5	[45, 496]	Yes
	ArXiv (Astro)	18,772	198,080	21.1	33	17	[1, 504]	280	[37, 528]	Yes
	DBLP	317,080	1,049,866	6.6	43	22	[1,343]	472.5	[43,903]	Yes
	ArXiv (Condense)	3,774,768	16,518,947	8.8	51	26	[1, 793]	663	[50,1063]	Yes
Communication Networks	Email (Enron)	36,692	183,831	10.0	35	18	[1,383]	314.5	[43,515]	Yes
	Email (Europe)	265,214	365,025	2.8	42	21	[1,7636]	451	[74,683]	Yes
	Wiki	2,394,385	4,659,565	3.9	49	25	[1, 100029]	612	[65, 1066]	Yes
Web graphs	Stanford	281,903	1,992,636	14.1	42	21	[1,38625]	451	[66,861]	Yes
	NotreDame	325,729	1,103,835	6.8	43	22	[1,10721]	472.5	[60,903]	Yes
	BerkStan	685,230	6,649,470	19.4	45	23	[1,84230]	517	[79,990]	Yes
	Google	875,713	4,322,051	9.9	46	23	[1, 6332]	540	[72, 1033]	Yes
Location based OSNs	Brightkite	58,228	214,078	7.4	37	19	[1,1134]	351	[41,665]	Yes
	Gowalla	196,591	950,327	9.7	41	21	[1,14730]	430	[44,723]	Yes
AS Graphs	Oregon (1)	11,174	23,409	4.2	31	16	[1,2389]	247.5	[95,352]	Yes
	Oregon(2)	11,461	32,730	5.7	32	16	[1,2432]	263.5	[79,476]	Yes
	CAIDA	26,475	53,381	4.0	34	17	[1,2628]	297	[113,436]	Yes
	Skitter	1,696,415	11,095,298	13.1	48	24	[1, 35455]	588	[52, 1128]	Yes
P2P networks	Gnutella (02/08/04)	10,876	39,994	7.4	31	16	[1,103]	247.5	[30,80]	No
	Gnutella (02/08/25)	22,687	54,705	4.8	34	17	[1,66]	297	[0,0]	No
	Gnutella (02/08/24)	26,518	65,369	4.9	34	17	[1,355]	297	[0,44]	No
	Gnutella (02/08/30)	36,682	88,328	4.8	35	18	[1,55]	314.5	[35,70]	No
	Gnutella (02/08/31)	62,586	147,892	4.7	37	19	[1, 95]	351	[39,76]	No
Amazon Co-purchasing Networks	Amazon (03/03/02)	262,111	899,792	6.9	42	21	[1,420]	451	[88,132]	No
	Amazon (2012)	334,863	925,872	5.5	43	22	[1,549]	472.5	[0,0]	No
	Amazon (03/03/12)	400,727	2,349,869	11.7	43	22	[1,2747]	472.5	[52,285]	No
	Amazon (03/06/01)	403,394	2,443,408	12.1	43	22	[1, 2752]	473	[52, 333]	No
	Amazon (03/05/05)	410,236	2,439,437	11.9	43	22	[1,2760]	472.5	[50,333]	No
Road Networks	Pennsylvania	1,088,092	1,541,898	2.8	47	24	[1,9]	563.5	[0,0]	No
	Texas	1,379,917	1,921,660	2.8	47	24	[1,12]	563.5	[0,0]	No
	California	1,965,206	2,766,607	2.8	49	25	[1, 12]	612	[0, 0]	No

Table 1: Suitability of watermarking for 48 of today's network graphs, determined by comparing their node degree distribution $[N_{min}(G), N_{max}(G)]$ and k-node subgraph density $[D_{min}(k), D_{max}(k)]$ to those of the embedded watermark graphs. 35 out of these 48 graphs are suitable for watermarking.

Finally, we can apply the same method to show that with low probability, any subgraph of G is isomorphic to S^{W_i}. This is because the XOR operations between W_i and S produce a random graph that is independent of G. □

5.2 Watermark Detectability

In addition to providing uniqueness, a practical watermark design should also offer low detectability, *i.e.*, with low probability each watermark gets identified by external users/attackers. This means that without knowing the seed Ω_i associated with user i, the embedded watermark graph S^{W_i} should not be easily distinguishable from the rest of the graph G^{W_i}. Therefore, the detectability would depend heavily on the topology of the original graph G, *i.e.* a watermark graph can be well hidden inside a graph G^{W_i} if its structural property is not too different from that of G.

In the following, we examine the detectability of watermarks in terms of *a graph's suitability for watermarking*. This is because directly quantifying the detectability is not only highly computa-

tional expensive[1], but also lacks a proper metric. Instead, we cross-compare the key structural properties of S^{W_i} and G, and define G as being suitable for watermarking if its structure properties are similar to that of S^{W_i}, implying a low watermark detectability.

Suitability for Watermarking. To evaluate a graph's suitability for watermarks, we first study the key structural property of the embedded watermark graph S^{W_i}. To guarantee watermark uniqueness and minimize distortion, the watermark graph S^{W_i} needs to be a random graph with an edge probability of $\frac{1}{2}$ (except for the fixed edges between x_i, x_{i+1} node pairs), and include $k = (2+\delta) \log_2 n$ nodes. Thus its average node degree is at least $(k + 1)/2$ and its average graph density is $(\binom{k}{2} + k - 1)/2$.

---

[1] Each embedded watermark graph is similar to a random graph with $\frac{1}{2}$ edge probability. Thus the detectability is low if certain subgraphs of G are also random graphs with similar edge probabilities. Yet identifying these subgraphs (and the embedded watermark graph) on a large graph incurs significant computation overhead.

Graph	Subgraph		Watermark Graph		Suitability
	Node #	Avg. Deg.	k	Avg. Deg.	
Russia	4,794	22.2	39	20.0	**Yes**
L.A.	196,174	49.2	45	23.0	**Yes**
London	562,075	56.1	48	24.5	**Yes**
Epinions (1)	7,083	68.7	38	19.5	**Yes**
Slashdot (08/11/06)	9,908	53.4	38	19.5	**Yes**
Twitter	34,014	60.5	38	19.5	**Yes**
Slashdot (09/02/16)	10,065	53.0	38	19.5	**Yes**
Slashdot (09/02/21)	10,105	53.2	38	19.5	**Yes**
Slashdot (09/02/22)	10,605	53.4	38	19.5	**Yes**
GPlus	68,828	347.1	39	20.0	**Yes**
Epinions (2)	10,363	83.5	40	20.5	**Yes**
Youtube	31,720	45.1	47	24.0	**Yes**
Pokec	564,001	53.0	48	24.5	**Yes**
Flickr	136,202	174.5	48	24.5	**Yes**
Livejournal	945,567	57.5	52	26.5	**Yes**
Patents	2,370	15.6	34	17.5	**Yes**
ArXiv (Theo. Cit.)	12,054	43.4	34	17.5	**Yes**
ArXiv (Phy. Cit.)	14,785	37.9	35	18.0	**Yes**
ArXiv (Phy.)	2,860	62.5	32	16.5	**Yes**
ArXiv (Astro)	6,536	42.9	33	17.0	**Yes**
DBLP	15,004	17.3	43	22.0	**Yes**
ArXiv (Condense)	178,455	16.0	51	26.0	**Yes**
Email (Enron)	3,481	48.2	35	18.0	**Yes**
Email (Europe)	1,779	44.0	42	21.5	**Yes**
Wiki Talk	21,253	83.1	49	25.0	**Yes**
Stanford	35,600	42.1	42	21.5	**Yes**
NotreDame	16,831	38.7	43	22.0	**Yes**
BerkStan	110,202	57.0	45	23.0	**Yes**
Google	55,431	14.8	46	23.5	**Yes**
Brightkite	4,586	30.8	37	19.0	**Yes**
Gowalla	17,946	39.3	41	21.0	**Yes**
Oregon (1)	264	17.1	31	16.0	**Yes**
Oregon(2)	579	31.0	32	16.5	**Yes**
CAIDA	575	16.0	34	17.5	**Yes**
Skitter	146,601	50.0	48	24.5	**Yes**
Gnutella (02/08/04)	796	5.2	31	16.0	No
Gnutella (02/08/25)	499	2.0	34	17.5	No
Gnutella (02/08/24)	709	2.7	34	17.5	No
Gnutella (02/08/30)	1,001	3.8	35	18.0	No
Gnutella (02/08/31)	1,276	3.6	37	19.0	No
Amazon (03/03/02)	3,727	2.8	42	21.5	No
Amazon (2012)	5,318	2.5	43	22.0	No
Amazon (03/03/12)	25,717	6.7	43	22.0	No
Amazon (03/06/01)	28,081	7.3	43	22.0	No
Amazon (03/05/05)	28,044	7.5	43	22.0	No
Pennsylvania	0	0	47	24.0	No
Texas	0	0	47	24.0	No
California	0	0	49	25.0	No

Table 2: Size and density of subgraph on nodes with degree $> (k+1)/2$ in each graph. Size is the number of subgraph nodes, and density is quantified as average edges each node having inside the subgraph.

Given these properties of the embedded watermark, we note that watermark node degree and density can be higher than those of many real-world graphs, such as those listed in Table 1. Intuitively, to ensure low detectability of such a watermark graph, suitable graphs should include a set of nodes (D) that are difficult to distinguish from the watermark nodes in term of node degree and subgraph density. Specifically, a suitable graph dataset needs to contain a set of nodes D with degree comparable or higher than the watermark graph node degree; and the density of the subgraph on D is at least comparable to the watermark graph density. If these two properties hold, the embedded watermark graph cannot be easily distinguished from D in the graph, and therefore cannot be detected by attackers.

To capture the above intuition, we define that a graph G is suitable for watermarking if its node degree and graph density satisfy the following two criteria. First, the minimum and maximum node

degree of G, denoted as $N_{min}(G)$ and $N_{max}(G)$ respectively, need to satisfy $N_{min}(G) \leq (k+1)/2 \leq N_{max}(G)$. Second, across all k-node subgraphs of G whose node degree expectation is greater than $(k+1)/2$, the minimum and maximum graph density need to satisfy $D_{min}(k) \leq (\binom{k}{2} + k - 1)/2 \leq D_{max}(k)$ [2]. Together, these two criteria ensure that the embedded watermark graph can be "well hidden" inside G^{W_i}.

Suitability of Real Graph Datasets. We measure the suitability of watermarks in 48 real networks graphs. These graphs represent vastly different types of networks and a wide range of structural topologies with size ranging from $10K$ nodes and $39K$ edges to $5M$ nodes and $48M$ edges. These graphs represent vastly different types of networks and a wide range of structural topologies. They include 3 social graphs generated from Facebook regional networks matching Russia, L.A., and London [40]. They include 12 other graphs from online social networks, including Twitter [21], Youtube [43], Google+ [21], Slovakia Pokec [38], Flickr [26], Livejournal [26], 2 snapshots from Epinions [32], and 4 snapshots from Slashdot [20]. We also add 3 citation graphs from arXiv and U.S. Patents [18], 4 graphs capturing collaborations in arXiv [18] and DBLP [43], 3 communication graphs generated from 2 Email networks [19, 20] and Wiki Talk [17], 4 web graphs [16, 2], 2 location-based online social graphs from Brightkite and Gowalla [6], 5 snapshots of P2P file sharing graph from Gnutella [19], 4 Internet Autonomous System (AS) maps [18], 5 snapshots of Amazon co-purchasing networks [15, 43], and 3 U.S. road graphs [16]. The statistics of all graphs are listed in Table 1.

For all graphs, we use $\delta = 0.3$ to ensure a 99.999% watermark uniqueness, and list their watermark size k in Table 1. We also show the two above criteria: node degree and k-node subgraph density. If a graph satisfies both criteria, our results will hold for any watermarks embedded on it.

We can make two observations from Table 1. *First*, 35 out of our 48 total graphs are suitable for watermarking. Also note that graphs describing similar networks are consistent in their suitability. For example, all 15 graphs from various online social networks are suitable for watermarks! *Second*, all the 13 graphs unsuitable for watermarks come from only 3 kinds of networks, *i.e.* copurchasing networks, P2P networks, and Road networks. These results in each group are self consistent. These results support our assertion that our proposed watermarking mechanism is applicable to most of today's network graphs with low detection risk. In practice, the owner of a graph can apply the same mechanism to determine if her graph is suitable for our watermark scheme.

To understand key properties determining whether a graph is suitable for watermarking, we measure various graph structural properties, including average node degree, node degree distribution, clustering coefficient, average path length, and assortativity. We also consider the size and density of subgraphs on nodes with degree more than watermark minimum average degree $(k+1)/2$. Our measurement results show that the size and density of subgraphs on nodes with degree $> (k+1)/2$ are the most important properties to determine suitability. Here, the size of these subgraphs is the number of nodes in the subgraph, and the density of the subgraph is measured as the average edges each node has inside the subgraph, *i.e.* average degree inside the subgraph. As shown in Table 2, unsuitable graphs do not have subgraphs with density to comparable to watermarks, while subgraphs with the desired den-

---

[2]To avoid computationally prohibitive subgraph enumeration, we apply a sampling method to estimate them with full details in [45].

sity can be found in graphs deemed suitable. These results are consistent with our intuition on quantifying suitability of watermarks.

Summary. Since the average watermark subgraph has high node degree and density, a graph suitable for watermarking must include a set of nodes, whose degree and subgraph density are comparable or even higher than watermark subgraphs. We propose two criteria targeting at node degree and subgraph density respectively to quantify whether a graph is suitable for watermarking. We collect a large set of available graph datasets and find 35 out of 48 real graphs are suitable. We expect similar suitability results in other real network graphs.

6. MORE ROBUST WATERMARKS

Our basic design provides the fundamental building blocks of graph watermarking with little consideration of external attacks. In practice, malicious users can seek to detect or destroy watermarked graphs. Here, we first describe external attacks on watermarks, and then present advanced features that defend against the attacks. Note that these improvement techniques aim to increase the cost of attacks rather than disabling them completely. Finally, we re-evaluate the watermark uniqueness of the advanced design.

6.1 Attacks on Watermarks

As discussed earlier, our attack model includes attacks trying to destroy watermarks while preserving the topology of the original graph. Based on the number of attackers, attacks on watermarks fall under our two models: single attacker and colluding attackers. With access to only one watermarked graph, a single attacker can modify nodes and/or edges in the graph to destroy watermarks. With multiple watermarked graphs, colluding attackers can perform more sophisticated attacks by cross-comparing these graphs to detect or remove watermarks.

Single Attacker Model. The naive edge attack is easiest to launch, and tries to disrupt the watermark by randomly adding or removing edges on the watermarked graph. For the attacker, there is a clear tradeoff between the severity of the attack (number of edges or nodes modified), and the structural change or distortion applied to the graph structure.

At first glance, this attack seems weak and unlikely to be a real threat. The probability of the attacker modifying one edge or node in the embedded watermark graph W_i is extremely low, given the relatively small size of W_i compared to the graph. As shown later, however, this attack can be quite disruptive in practice. By modifying a node n_i or an edge connected to n_i, the attack impacts all of n_i's neighboring nodes, since their NSD labels will be modified. These NSD label changes, while small, are enough to make locating nodes in the watermark graph very difficult. This effect is exacerbated in social graphs that exhibit a small world structure, since any change to a supernode's degree will impact a disproportionately large portion of nodes in the graph.

Some versions of this attack would either release a partial subgraph of the watermarked graph, or merge multiple watermarked graphs. In both cases, this destroys the embedded watermarks, but also significantly distorts the graphs and reduces their usability. We do not consider these disruptive attacks in our study, and target them for future work.

Collusion Attacks. By obtaining multiple watermarked graphs, an attacker can compare these graphs to eliminate watermarks. Since we anonymize each watermarked graph by randomly reassigning node IDs (see Section 4.1), attackers cannot directly match individual nodes across graphs. To compare multiple graphs, we apply the deanonymization methods proposed in [27, 28]. Specifi-

cally, we first match 1000 highest degree nodes between two graphs based on their degree and neighborhood connectivity [28], and then start from these nodes to find new mappings with the network structure and the previously mapped nodes [27].

Using deanonymization techniques, attackers can then build a "clean" graph, where an edge exists if it exists in the majority of the watermarked graphs. Since embedded watermark graphs are likely embedded at different locations on each graph, a majority vote approach effectively removes the contributions from watermark subgraphs, leading to a graph that closely approximates the original G.

6.2 Improving Robustness against Attacks

The attacks discussed above can disrupt the watermark extraction process in two ways. First, adding or deleting nodes/edges in G' changes node degrees, and therefore nodes' NSD labels, thereby disrupting the identification of candidate nodes during the second step of the extraction process; second, adding or deleting nodes/edges inside the embedded watermark graph S^{W_i} can change the structure of the watermark graph, making it difficult to identify during the third step of the extraction process. To defend against these attacks, we propose five improvements over the basic extraction design to produce an improved watermark generation algorithm.

Improvements #1, #2: Addressing changes to node neighborhoods. Extracting a watermark involves searching through nodes in G' by their NSD labels. By adding or deleting nodes/edges, attackers can effectively change NSD labels across the graph. To address this, we propose two changes to the basic extraction design. *First*, we bucketize node degrees (with bucket size B) to reduce the sensitivity of a node's NSD label to its neighbors' node degrees. For example, with $B = 5$, a node with degree 9 will stay in the same bucket even if one of its edges has been removed (reducing its node degree to 8). *Second*, when selecting a watermark node's candidate node list, we replace the exact NSD label matching with the approximate NSD label matching. A match is found if the overlap between two bucketized NSD labels exceeds a threshold θ. For example, with $\theta = 50\%$, a node with bucketized NSD label "1-2-3-4" would match a node with label "1-2-3" since the overlap is $75\% > \theta$.

These changes clearly allow us to identify more candidates for each watermark node, thus improving robustness against small local modifications. On the other hand, more candidates lead to more computation during the subgraph matching step (step 3 in Section 4.2). Such expansion, however, does not affect watermark uniqueness and detectability, since they are unrelated to the size of candidate pools.

Improvement #3, #4: Addressing changes to subgraph structure. Random changes made to G' may directly impact a node or edge in the embedded watermark. To address this, we propose two techniques. *First*, we add redundancy to watermarks by embedding the same watermark graph W_i into m disjoint subgraphs $S_1, S_2, ... S_m$ from the original graph G. This greatly increases the probability of the owner locating at least one unmodified copy of W_i during extraction, even in the presence of attacks that make significant changes to nodes and edges in G'. Note that since we embed watermarks on disjoint subgraphs, this does not affect watermark uniqueness $1 - P(\mathcal{E})$. While embedding m watermarks will impact false positive, which is $1 - (1 - P(\mathcal{E}))^m$.

Second, it is still possible that all the watermark graphs are "destroyed" by the attacker and there are no matches in the extraction process. If this happens, we replace the exact subgraph matching in the step 3 of the extraction process with the approximate subgraph matching. That is, a subgraph matches the watermark graph if the amount of edge difference between the two is less than a threshold L. By relaxing the search criteria used in step 3 of the extraction process, this technique allows us to identify "partially" damaged watermarks, thus again improving robustness against attacks. However, it can also increase false positives in watermark extraction, reducing watermark uniqueness. We show in Section 6.3 that the impact on watermark uniqueness can be tightly bounded by controlling L.

Improvement #5: Addressing Collusion Attacks. Recall that for powerful attackers able to match graphs at an individual node level, they can leverage majority votes across multiple watermarked graphs to remove watermarks. To defend against this, our insight is to embed watermarks that have some portion of spatial overlap in the graph, such that those components will survive majority votes over graphs.

We propose a *hierarchical* watermark embedding process to defend against collusion attacks. To build watermarked graphs for M users, we uniform-randomly divide the M users into 2 groups (a_1 and a_2) and associate each group with a public-private key pair $< K_{pub}^{a_1}, K_{priv}^{a_1} >$ or $< K_{pub}^{a_2}, K_{priv}^{a_2} >$, which is generated and held by the data owner. We repeat this to randomly divide M users into another 2 groups (b_1 and b_2) associated with group key pairs $< K_{pub}^{b_1}, K_{priv}^{b_1} >$ and $< K_{pub}^{b_2}, K_{priv}^{b_2} >$ separately. After this step, each user is assigned to two groups [3]. For example, a user i is assigned to groups a_1 and b_2.

For user i, we then follow step 2-4 in Section 4.1 to embed the two *group watermarks* and its *individual watermark*. Specifically, by receiving user i's signature $K_{priv}^i(T)$, we first generate three seeds: Ω_i by combining $K_{priv}^i(T)$ and K^G, Ω_{a_1} by combining $K_{priv}^{a_1}$ and K^G, and Ω_{b_2} by combining $K_{priv}^{b_2}$ and K^G, where K^G is graph key for graph G. With the two group seeds Ω_{a_1} and Ω_{b_2}, we generate and embed two non-overlap group watermarks. Then we use user i's individual seed Ω_i to embed an individual watermark without overlapping with either of the embedded group watermarks. Note that because the group and individual watermarks are generated with different seeds, this hierarchical embedding process does not affect watermark uniqueness.

Under this design, a collusion attack can successfully destroy all the watermarks only if the attacker can perfectly match each individual node, and the majority of the graphs come from different groups. Otherwise, the majority vote on raw edges will preserve the *group watermark*. We can compute the upper bound of the attack success rate by Equation 2, *i.e.* the probability that the majority of the graphs obtained by the attacker come from different groups:

$$\lambda(M_a, J) = \left(1 - J \sum_{i=\lceil \frac{M_a+1}{2} \rceil}^{M_a} \binom{M_a}{i} \cdot (\frac{1}{J})^i \cdot (\frac{J-1}{J})^{M_a-i}\right)^2$$

(2)

where M_a is the number of watermarked graphs obtained by the attacker and J is the number of groups in each group partition. The above design chose $J = 2$ because it minimizes $\lambda(M_a, J), \forall M_a$. Furthermore, when M_a is odd, $\lambda(M_a, 2) = 0$; and when M_a is even, $\lambda(M_a, 2)$ is at most 0.25 when $M_a = 2$. Note that in equation (2) the operation $(.)^2$ is due to the fact that we group the users twice into two different group classes: a_1, a_2 and b_1, b_2. If we only perform the group partition once (*e.g.* dividing the users into a_1, a_2), then $\lambda(2, 2) = 0.5$. In practice we can further reduce λ by performing multiple rounds of group division (2 in the above design) and adding more group watermarks.

Note that group watermarks contain much less information than single user watermarks. In fact, the more robust a group watermark, the larger granularity (and less precision) it will provide. Our proposed solution is to extend the system by using additional "dimensions," *e.g.* go beyond the two dimensions of a and b mentioned above. Combining results from multiple dimensions will quickly narrow down the set of potential users responsible for the leak. However, since a colluding attack requires the involvement of multiple leakers, even identifying a single leaker is insufficient. Developing a scheme to reliably detect multiple (ideally all) colluding users is a topic for future work.

6.3 Impact on Watermark Uniqueness

To improve the robustness of our watermark system, we relax the subgraph matching criteria from exact matching to approximate matching with at most L edge difference. Such relaxation does not affect watermark detectability because it does not change the embedding process. However, it may affect watermark uniqueness, which we will analyze next.

Consider two watermarked graphs G^{W_i} and G^{W_j} that were independently generated for user i and j following the three steps defined in Theorem 1. Let S^{W_i} and S^{W_j} represent the embedded watermark graph in G^{W_i} and G^{W_j}, respectively. To examine the watermark uniqueness, we seek to compute the probability that a subgraph in G^{W_j} differs from S^{W_i} by at most L edges.

Our analysis is similar to Theorem 1's proof. Let $\mathcal{E}_Y$ denote the event where a subgraph of G^{W_j} built on k nodes $Y = \{y_1, y_2, ..., y_k\}$ only differs from S^{W_i} by $\leq L$ edges. Our goal is to calculate the probability of the event $\mathcal{E} = \cup_Y \mathcal{E}_Y$, which is the union on all combinations of k nodes.

We first compute the probability of individual $\mathcal{E}_Y$. Recall that the edges between $\binom{k}{2} - (k-1)$ node pairs in S^{W_i} are generated randomly with probability $\frac{1}{2}$ and are independent of G^{W_j}, while the rest $k-1$ edges ($< x_l, x_{l+1} >, l = 1...k-1$) are fixed. Thus we can show that the probability that a subgraph $G^{W_j}[Y]$ differs from S^{W_i} by h edges is upper bounded by $\frac{1}{2}^{e-k+1} \cdot \binom{e}{h}$ where $e = \binom{k}{2}$. Therefore, we can derive the probability of $\mathcal{E}_Y$ as $P(\mathcal{E}_Y) \leq \frac{1}{2}^{e-k+1} \cdot \sum_{h=0}^{L} \binom{e}{h}$. And consequently, we have $P(\mathcal{E}) \leq n^k \cdot \frac{1}{2}^{e-k+1} \cdot \sum_{h=0}^{L} \binom{e}{h}$, where $e = \binom{k}{2}$, $k = (2+\delta)log_2 n$, and n is the node count of G^{W_j}.

Next, given the probability of uniqueness $1 - P(\mathcal{E})$, we compute the upper bound on L to ensure $1 - P(\mathcal{E}) \geq 0.99999$ for all the graphs in Table 1 except Road graphs, Co-purchasing graphs, and P2P network graphs. Again we set $\delta = 0.3$. The result is listed in Table 3, where the maximum limit of L varies between 0 and 12. In general, the larger the graph, the higher the upper bound on L.

7. EXPERIMENTAL EVALUATION

We use real network graphs to evaluate the performance of the graph watermarking system in three key metrics: *false positives*, *graph distortion* and *watermark robustness*. Having analytically quantified watermark uniqueness in §5 and §6, we focus on examining graph distortion and watermark robustness while ensuring $\leq 0.001\%$ false positive rate. We also study the computational efficiency of the proposed watermark embedding and extraction schemes.

Experiment Setup. Given the large number of graph computations per data point, we focus our experiments on two larger network graphs in Table 1, *i.e.* the LA regional Facebook graph and the Flickr graph. The two graphs have very different sizes and graph structures. To guarantee $\leq 0.001\%$ false positives, we use $\delta = 0.3$, $k = 45$ for the LA graph, and $\delta = 0.3$, $k = 48$ for the

---
[3]More details about the group assignment are in [45].

Graph	Oregon (1)	Oregon (2)	CAIDA	Email (Enron)	arXiv (Theo. Cit.)
L Bound	0	1	1	1	1
Graph	arXiv (Phy. Cit.)	arXiv (Phy.)	arXiv (Astro)	Patent	Slashdot (08/11/06)
L Bound	1	1	1	2	3
Graph	Twitter	Slashdot (09/02/16)	Slashdot (09/02/21)	Slashdot (09/02/22)	Brightkite
L Bound	3	3	3	3	3
Graph	Russia	Epinions (1)	Google+	Epinions (2)	Standford
L Bound	4	4	4	5	5
Graph	Email (Europe)	Gowalla	BerkStand	DBLP	NorteDame
L Bound	5	5	6	7	7
Graph	L.A.	London	Flickr	Wiki	Google
L Bound	8	8	8	8	8
Graph	Skitter	Youtube	Pokec	arXiv (Condense)	Livejournal
L Bound	8	9	9	11	12

Table 3: Upper bound of L for the 35 network graphs.

Graph	Nodes (%)	Edges (%)	dK-2 Deviation
Watermarked LA	0.037%	0.033%	0.0008
Watermarked Flickr	0.014%	0.019%	0.0001

Table 4: Percentage of modified nodes/edges after embedding 5 **watermarks into a graph and dK-2 Deviation.**

Flickr graph. For our basic design, we generate 1 watermark per graph. For our advanced design, we set L to 8, the degree bucket size to 10, and the NSD similarity threshold to $\theta = 0.75$. For each user, we embed 5 watermarks in its graph, 3 individual watermarks and 2 group watermarks. We chose these settings because they work well in practice. We leave the optimization of these parameters to future work.

Next, we present experimental results on graph distortion, robustness against attacks, and computational efficiency.

7.1 Graph Distortion from Watermarks

We consider three metrics to measure graph distortion.

- *Modifications to the raw graph* – We count the number of nodes/ edges modified by embedding watermarks.

- *dK-2 Deviation* – dK-2 series, *i.e.* joint degree distributions, are an important graph structural metric [35]. We quantify graph distortion using the normalized Euclidean distance between the dK-2 series of the original and of the watermarked graphs [4].

- *Graph metrics w/ and w/o watermarks* – We measure the widely used graph metrics before and after the watermarking, including degree distribution, assortativity (AS) [35], clustering coefficient (CC) [35], average path length, and diameter. Large deviation in any of the metrics indicates large distortion.

We have examined the distortion introduced by both the basic and advanced designs. We only show the results of the advanced design because it adds more watermarks and thus leads to higher distortion. For LA and Flickr graphs, we generate 10 different watermarked graphs (using 10 different seeds) and present the average result across these graphs. Because computing shortest paths on the large graphs is highly computational intensive, we compute the average path length and diameter among 1000 random nodes [40].

Table 4 shows the percentage of modified nodes/edges by watermarking. Even after embedding 5 watermarks, the modification for both graphs is less than 0.04%, implying little distortion on the watermarked graphs. This is further confirmed by the average dK-2 distances. We also compare the original and watermarked graphs

---

[4]The Euclidean distance between dK-2 series is normalized by the number of tuples in the dK-2 series.

using 5 graph metrics: AS, CC, degree distribution, average path length, and diameter. Similarly, the metrics remain the same before and after watermarking, and we found no difference between the statistical distributions of each metric in the graphs.

Together, this indicates that embedding watermarks produces negligible impact on graph structure. Thus we believe watermarked graphs can replace the originals in graph applications and produce (near-)identical results.

7.2 Robustness against Attacks

Next, we study the robustness of the watermarking system under the attacks. For each of the two attacks discussed in §6.1, we vary the attack strength, repeat each experiment 10 times, and examine the following two metrics:

- *Robustness* – In the single attacker model, the robustness is the ratio of graphs from which we can successfully extract at least one of the 3 individual watermarks. In the collusion attack, in addition to this ratio, we also measure the ratio of graphs where we can extract at least one of the 5 watermarks (3 individual + 2 group watermarks).

- *Cost of the attack* – The normalized distortion on the attacked graphs. It represents the dK-2 deviation between the attacked graphs and the original graph, normalized by that between the "clean" watermarked graphs and the original graph. If the normalized distortion is > 1, the attack introduces more distortion than embedding watermarks.

Results on the Single Attacker Model. For the single attacker model, we quantify the attack strength by the number of modified edges. The robustness and the cost of the attack are measured as a function of the number of modified edges.

We first evaluate the robustness of the basic watermark. Figure 2 shows that randomly modifying a small number of edges disrupted the extraction process. For example, in LA, our basic design cannot recover the watermark with 100% probability when we only modify 20 edges. In each case, at least one of the nodes in the watermarks had a modified NSD label (one of its neighbors' degree changed), and it could not be located in the extraction process. We show the distortion on the attacked graphs in Figure 3. As expected, the small number of modifications causes small distortions in graph structures. Still in LA, when the robustness is 0, the distortion is around 3x more than that the watermarked graphs. Both results show that the basic watermark scheme is easily disrupted by small, single user attacks.

Figure 4 shows that robustness of the improved scheme decreases with attack strength, since more edges are modified to "destroy" watermarks. Like in Flickr, the system can handle attack strength up to 933K modified edges, which is > 400x stronger than the maximum attack strength in the basic design. On the other hand, Figure 5 shows that the cost of these attacks is large. For Flickr, with more than 1.4M modified edges, an attack leads to 800x more distortions over that caused by embedding 5 watermarks. Our improved watermark is highly robust against single user attacks.

Results on Collusion Attacks. To implement the collusion attack described in §6.1, we first generate 10 watermarked graphs and randomly pick M_a graphs from them as the graphs acquired by the attacker. We vary the number of graphs obtained by the attacker M_a between 2 to 5. For each M_a value we repeat the experiments 10 times and report the average value. Since basic watermarks are easily disrupted by the collusion attack, we focus on the robustness of the improved mechanisms.

Figure 6(a)-(b) shows the robustness of the watermarked LA and Flickr graphs against the collusion attack. Figure 6(a) shows that in

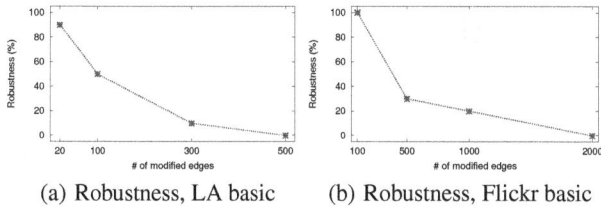

(a) Robustness, LA basic   (b) Robustness, Flickr basic

Figure 2: The robustness of the basic design against the single attacker model.

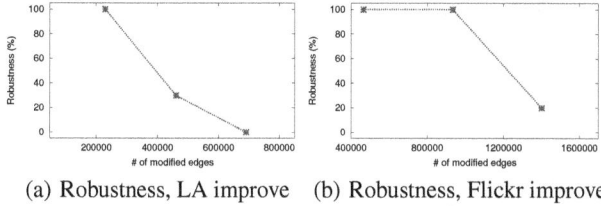

(a) Robustness, LA improve   (b) Robustness, Flickr improve

Figure 4: The robustness in the improved design against the single attacker model.

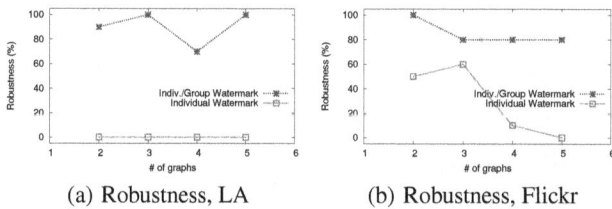

(a) Robustness, LA   (b) Robustness, Flickr

Figure 6: The robustness against the collusion attack.

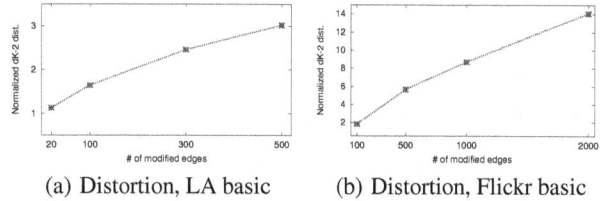

(a) Distortion, LA basic   (b) Distortion, Flickr basic

Figure 3: The distortion caused by the single attacker model in the basic design.

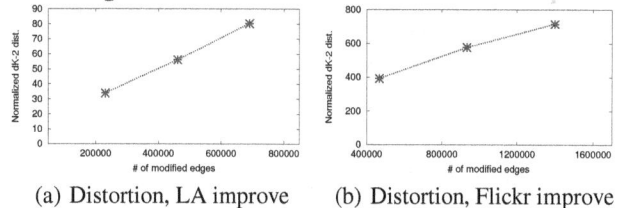

(a) Distortion, LA improve   (b) Distortion, Flickr improve

Figure 5: The distortion caused by the single attacker model in the improved design.

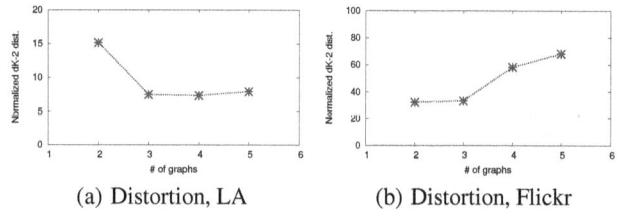

(a) Distortion, LA   (b) Distortion, Flickr

Figure 7: The distortion caused by the collusion attack.

Graph	Embedding (s)	Basic Extraction		Improved Extraction	
		Single(s)	Parallel (s)	Single (s)	Parallel (s)
LA	40	270	39	310	42
Flickr	80	767	195	776	197
Livejournal	695	2568	310	2605	317

Table 5: The efficiency of the watermarking system.

LA, by applying majority votes on raw edges, the collusion attack can effectively remove all 3 individual watermarks. However, the attack is ineffective in removing both group watermarks: we can extract at least one group watermark in more than 60% of the attacked graphs. Here the robustness values deviate slightly from that projected by Equation (2) because we limit the number of statistical sampling to 10 runs. Unlike LA, Figure 6(b) plots that the collusion attack cannot remove all the individual watermarks in Flickr when using 2 or 3 watermarked graphs. This is because the deanonymization method causes a large portion of nodes mismatched in Flickr (30% nodes). Finally, Figure 7 shows that the collusion attacks also introduce larger distortions in graph structure.

These results show that even a powerful collusion attack is ineffective in removing all embedded watermarks. Moreover, the potential inaccuracy of the deanonymization method makes the attack even weaker in removing individual watermarks. Of course, the attackers will eventually succeed in disrupting watermarks if they are willing to modify and sacrifice the utility of the graph. While we provide a robust defense against attackers with low level of tolerance for graph distortion, we hope follow-on work will develop more robust defenses against higher distortion attacks.

7.3 Computational Efficiency

We measure the efficiency of embedding and extracting watermarks, including the time to select candidates (step 2) and to identify watermarks (step 3). We accelerate the extraction process by parallelizing the key steps across servers. When a watermark is found or no more candidates are unchecked, the extraction process stops (for that user).

We perform measurements to quantify impact of parallelizing extraction over a cluster. All system parameters are the same as previous tests, except that we embed 1 watermark into a graph. We compare the improved watermark extraction method to the basic extraction method. In addition to Flickr and LA graphs, we also measure the efficiency on Livejournal graph [26], a larger graph with 5.2M nodes, 49M edges. We parallelize watermark extraction across 10 servers, each with 192GB RAM, and report the average times from 10 different watermarked graphs.

Table 5 shows that our system is efficient in embedding and extracting watermarks. Embedding one watermark into a graph is very fast, e.g. average embedding time for the largest graph, Livejournal, is around 12 minutes. Even using one server to extract watermarks, the computation time is small, e.g. 13 minutes in Flickr using both the basic and improved schemes. Time to identify the watermark graph on the candidate subgraphs (step 3) is much less than the time required to find candidates (step 2), which corresponds to 99% of total computation time. Since finding candidates takes $O(kn)$ computational complexity and $k = (2 + \delta) \log_2 n$, the complexity to extract a watermark from a real-world graph is $O(n \log_2 n)$. Here k is node number in the watermark graph and n is nodes in the total graph.

Second, we find that distributed extraction produces good speedup, 8 over 10 servers for Livejournal and 7 for LA (for both extraction methods). The speedup for Flickr is only around 4 using both methods, because one of the watermarked graphs takes much longer time than others in finding candidates, 4x longer. Without this outlier, the average parallel extraction time on Flickr is around 2.5 minutes for both methods, 5x faster than using single server.

111

Finally, there is no significant difference between computation time for the two extraction methods.

8. CONCLUSION

In this paper, we take a first step towards the design and implementation of a robust graph watermarking system. Graph watermarks have the potential to significantly impact the way graphs are shared and tracked. Our work identifies the critical requirements of such a system, and provides an initial design that targets the critical properties of uniqueness, robustness to attacks, and minimal distortion to the graph structure. We also identify key attacks against graph watermarks, and evaluate them against an improved design with additional features for improved robustness under attack. Finally, we show the watermarking system is efficient in both watermark embedding and watermark extraction.

Acknowledgments

The authors wish to thank the anonymous reviewers and our shepherd Daniel Figueiredo for their helpful comments. This work is supported in part by NSF grants IIS-1321083, CNS-1224100, CNS-1317153 and CNS-1527939.

9. REFERENCES

[1] AGRAWAL, R., AND KIERNAN, J. Watermarking relational databases. In *Proc. of VLDB* (2002).

[2] ALBERT, R., JEONG, H., AND BARABÁSI, A.-L. Internet: Diameter of the world-wide web. *Nature 401*, 6749 (1999), 130–131.

[3] ARRINGTON, M. How "dirty" mp3 files are a back door into cloud drm. TechCrunch, April 2010.

[4] BACKSTROM, L., DWORK, C., AND KLEINBERG, J. Wherefore art thou r3579x?: anonymized social networks, hidden patterns, and structural steganography. In *WWW* (2007).

[5] BENDER, W., GRUHL, D., MORIMOTO, N., AND LU, A. Techniques for data hiding. *IBM systems journal* (1996), 313–336.

[6] CHO, E., MYERS, S. A., AND LESKOVEC, J. Friendship and mobility: user movement in location-based social networks. In *KDD* (2011).

[7] COLLBERG, C. S., KOBOUROV, S. G., CARTER, E., AND THOMBORSON, C. D. Graph-based approaches to software watermarking. In *WG* (2003).

[8] COOK, S. A. The complexity of theorem-proving procedures. In *STOC* (1971).

[9] GILBERT, E. N. Random graphs. *The Annals of Mathematical Statistics* (1959), 1141–1144.

[10] HANHIJÄRVI, S., GARRIGA, G. C., AND PUOLAMÄKI, K. Randomization techniques for graphs. In *SDM* (2009).

[11] HAY, M., MIKLAU, G., JENSEN, D., TOWSLEY, D., AND WEIS, P. Resisting structural re-identification in anonymized social networks.

[12] HAY, M., MIKLAU, G., JENSEN, D., WEIS, P., AND SRIVASTAVA, S. Anonymizing social networks. Tech. Rep. 07-19, UMass, 2007.

[13] KAMRAN, M., ET AL. A robust, distortion minimizing technique for watermarking relational databases using once-for-all usability constraints. *IEEE TKDE* (2012).

[14] LEE, S.-J., AND JUNG, S.-H. A survey of watermarking techniques applied to multimedia. In *ISIE* (2001).

[15] LESKOVEC, J., ADAMIC, L. A., AND HUBERMAN, B. A. The dynamics of viral marketing. *TWEB* (2007).

[16] LESKOVEC, J., ET AL. Statistical properties of community structure in large social and information networks. In *WWW* (2008).

[17] LESKOVEC, J., HUTTENLOCHER, D., AND KLEINBERG, J. Predicting positive and negative links in online social networks. In *WWW* (2010).

[18] LESKOVEC, J., KLEINBERG, J., AND FALOUTSOS, C. Graphs over time: densification laws, shrinking diameters and possible explanations. In *KDD* (2005).

[19] LESKOVEC, J., KLEINBERG, J., AND FALOUTSOS, C. Graph evolution: Densification and shrinking diameters. *TKDD* (2007).

[20] LESKOVEC, J., LANG, K. J., DASGUPTA, A., AND MAHONEY, M. W. Community structure in large networks: Natural cluster sizes and the absence of large well-defined clusters. *Internet Mathematics 6*, 1 (2009), 29–123.

[21] LESKOVEC, J., AND MCAULEY, J. J. Learning to discover social circles in ego networks. In *Advances in neural information processing systems* (2012), pp. 539–547.

[22] LI, Y., SWARUP, V., AND JAJODIA. Fingerprinting relational databases: Schemes and specialties. *IEEE TDSC 2*, 1 (2005), 34–45.

[23] LIU, K., AND TERZI, E. Towards identity anonymization on graphs. In *SIGMOD* (2008).

[24] MACQ, B. M., AND QUISQUATER, J.-J. Cryptology for digital tv broadcasting. *Proceedings of the IEEE* (1995), 944–957.

[25] MENEZES, A. J., OORSCHOT, P. V., AND VANSTONE, S. *Handbook of Applied Cryptography*. CRC Press, Inc., 1996.

[26] MISLOVE, A., MARCON, M., GUMMADI, K., DRUSCHEL, P., AND BHATTACHARJEE, B. Measurement and analysis of online social networks. In *IMC* (2007).

[27] NARAYANAN, A., AND SHMATIKOV, V. De-anonymizing social networks. In *Proc. of IEEE S&P* (May 2009).

[28] NARAYANAN, A., AND SHMATIKOV, V. Link prediction by de-anonymization: How we won the kaggle social network challenge. In *IJCNN* (2011).

[29] OHBUCHI, R., UEDA, H., AND SHUH, E. Robust watermarking of vector digital maps. In *ICME* (2002).

[30] OHBUCHI, R., UEDA, H., AND SHUH, E. Watermarking 2d vector maps in the mesh-spectral domain. In *Shape Modeling International* (2003).

[31] QU, G., AND POTKONJAK, M. Analysis of watermarking techniques for graph coloring problem. In *ICCAD* (1998).

[32] RICHARDSON, M., AGRAWAL, R., AND DOMINGOS, P. Trust management for the semantic web. In *The Semantic Web-ISWC 2003*. Springer, 2003, pp. 351–368.

[33] ROBSHAW, M. J. B. MD2, MD4, MD5, SHA and other hash functions. Tech. Rep. TR-101, RSA Laboratories, 1995. v. 4.0.

[34] RUANAIDH, J. O., DOWLING, W., AND BOLAND, F. Phase watermarking of digital images. In *ICIP* (1996).

[35] SALA, A., CAO, L., WILSON, C., ZABLIT, R., ZHENG, H., AND ZHAO, B. Y. Measurement-calibrated graph models for social network experiments. In *Proc. of WWW* (2010).

[36] SALA, A., ZHAO, X., WILSON, C., ZHENG, H., AND ZHAO, B. Y. Sharing graphs using differentially private graph models. In *IMC* (2011).

[37] STEVE, W. Information authentication for a slippery new age. *Dr. Dobbs Journal* (1995), 18–26.

[38] TAKAC, L., AND ZABOVSKY, M. Data analysis in public social networks. In *International Scientific Conference AND International Workshop Present Day Trends of Innovations* (2012).

[39] VENKATESAN, R., VAZIRANI, V., AND SINHA, S. A graph theoretic approach to software watermarking. In *Information Hiding* (2001).

[40] WILSON, C., SALA, A., PUTTASWAMY, K. P. N., AND ZHAO, B. Y. Beyond social graphs: User interactions in online social networks and their implications. *ACM Trans. on the Web 6*, 4 (2012).

[41] WOLFE, G., WONG, J. L., AND POTKONJAK, M. Watermarking graph partitioning solutions. In *DAC* (2001).

[42] XIA, X.-G., BONCELET, C. G., AND ARCE, G. R. A multiresolution watermark for digital images. In *ICIP* (1997).

[43] YANG, J., AND LESKOVEC, J. Defining and evaluating network communities based on ground-truth. In *Proceedings of the ACM SIGKDD Workshop on Mining Data Semantics* (2012), ACM, p. 3.

[44] YING, X., AND WU, X. Randomizing social networks: a spectrum preserving approach. In *SDM* (2008).

[45] ZHAO, X., LIU, Q., ZHOU, L., ZHENG, H., AND ZHAO, B. Y. Graph watermarks. *Arxiv preprint arXiv:1506.00022* (2015).

[46] ZHOU, B., ET AL. Preserving privacy in social networks against neighborhood attacks. In *Proc. of ICDE* (2008).

[47] ZHU, W., THOMBORSON, C., AND WANG, F.-Y. A survey of software watermarking. In *ISI*. 2005.

[48] ZOU, L., CHEN, L., AND ÖZSU, M. T. K-automorphism: A general framework for privacy preserving network publication. In *VLDB* (2009).

Strength in Numbers:
Robust Tamper Detection in Crowd Computations

Bimal Viswanath
MPI-SWS
bviswana@mpi-sws.org

Muhammad Ahmad Bashir
Northeastern University
ahmad@ccs.neu.edu

Muhammad Bilal Zafar
MPI-SWS
mzafar@mpi-sws.org

Simon Bouget
IRISA/INRIA Rennes
simon.bouget@irisa.fr

Saikat Guha
Microsoft Research India
saikat@microsoft.com

Krishna P. Gummadi
MPI-SWS
gummadi@mpi-sws.org

Aniket Kate
Purdue University
aniket@purdue.edu

Alan Mislove
Northeastern University
amislove@ccs.neu.edu

ABSTRACT

Popular social and e-commerce sites increasingly rely on *crowd computing* to rate and rank content, users, products and businesses. Today, attackers who create fake (Sybil) identities can easily tamper with these computations. Existing defenses that largely focus on detecting individual Sybil identities have a fundamental limitation: Adaptive attackers can create hard-to-detect Sybil identities to tamper arbitrary crowd computations.

In this paper, we propose Stamper, an approach for detecting tampered crowd computations that significantly raises the bar for evasion by adaptive attackers. Stamper design is based on two key insights: First, Sybil attack detection gains *strength in numbers*: we propose statistical analysis techniques that can determine if a large crowd computation has been tampered by Sybils, even when it is fundamentally hard to infer *which* of the participating identities are Sybil. Second, Sybil identities *cannot forge the timestamps of their activities* as they are recorded by system operators; Stamper analyzes these unforgeable timestamps to foil adaptive attackers. We applied Stamper to detect tampered computations in Yelp and Twitter. We not only detected previously known tampered computations with high accuracy, but also uncovered tens of thousands of previously unknown tampered computations in these systems.

Categories and Subject Descriptors

J.4 [**Computer Applications**]: Social and Behavioral Sciences; K.6 [**Management of Computing and Information Systems**]: Security and Protection

General Terms

Security, Design, Algorithms, Measurement

Keywords

Sybil attacks; crowd computing; social networks; Twitter; Yelp

1. INTRODUCTION

Popular social networking and e-commerce sites are increasingly employing *crowd computing* to rate and rank content, users, products, and businesses. In such systems, crowd computations involve polling the "wisdom" or "opinions" of crowds—the users of the system—to provide a variety of recommendation services to their customers. For example, social networking and media sites like Facebook, Twitter, YouTube, and Reddit recommend content (be it business pages, news stories, videos, photos, or web pages) based on the number of users who posted, endorsed, or liked the content. Similarly, e-commerce sites like Amazon and eBay rely on their users to rate and review products and sellers. Some online sites like Yelp and TripAdvisor are dedicated to crowd-sourcing the rating of businesses.

In many crowd computation systems, users operate behind easy-to-create *weak* identities and consequently, they are vulnerable to Sybil attacks [18], where an attacker creates multiple fake identities with the goal of manipulating the aggregate opinion of the crowd. There are thriving underground markets for launching such tampering attacks on the crowd-sourcing sites mentioned above [27, 32, 35]; typically, the more popular a site, the greater the frequency and magnitude of such attacks. Existing Sybil defenses have mostly taken the approach of detecting individual Sybils [15, 36, 37, 41], enabling the operator to either suspend the Sybils or nullify their contribution to the crowd computation.

In this paper, we begin by highlighting a *fundamental limitation* of defenses based on detecting Sybil identities: when a weak identity has limited or no activity history (e.g., interactions with other identities or information they post), the defenses lack sufficient information to determine whether the identity is a Sybil or an inactive non-Sybil. This limitation allows adaptive attackers to create and stockpile large number of Sybil identities with limited prior activity and use them for tampering crowd computations. If the tampered computations involve legitimate content (e.g., promoting a real business on Yelp for a fee, as opposed to promoting malware links on Twitter), it can be hard to detect the tampering (because the act of recommending a real business is by itself not a sign of Sybil activity).

Given the basic limitation of existing defenses, in this paper, we propose to address Sybil attacks on crowd computations, by moving from *detecting individual Sybil identities* to directly *detecting crowd computations that have significant levels of Sybil identity participation*. Our approach, Stamper, is based on a realization that even when it is fundamentally hard to differentiate between individual Sybil and non-Sybil identities, large *groups* of Sybil and non-Sybil identities can be differentiated. Our approach is based on two key insights: *Key insight 1:* If an attacker tampers a computation using a large number of Sybil identities with limited activity, it would result in a *distributional anomaly* or a statistically significant deviation in the distribution of the activity-levels (e.g., number of reviews posted or number of friends formed) of the identities participating in the computation. By analyzing the statistical distributions of the activity-levels of all the identities participating in a crowd computation, we can easily detect such tampering. While there is prior work on detecting malicious activity in crowd computations on e-commerce sites [19,40] and peer-to-peer search networks [28] that looks for anomalies or specific abnormal patterns in feature distributions (where a feature can be some attribute associated with the user activity), our work stands out by providing improved resilience against adaptive attackers. *Key insight 2:* To evade detection by the above insight, a determined attacker would have to forge the activities of the Sybil identities under her control to match the distribution of the activity-levels of non-Sybil identities. To be robust against such adaptive attackers, we employ a novel method: we leverage the key observation that even as the attackers forge the activities of their identities, they *cannot forge the timestamps* of their activities (e.g., join date or friend link creation time). The timestamp information is typically recorded by operators for all activities of all identities in the system. By analyzing the statistical distributions of the times when the activity-levels of identities have changed, we can significantly raise the bar for evading detection by adaptive attackers (see Section 3.3).

Another distinguishing feature of Stamper's tamper detection is that it is agnostic to specific attacker strategies: Unlike existing Sybil detection approaches, Stamper does not make specific assumptions about attacker behaviors; instead it uses anomaly detection to detect tampering of any kind. As a result, Stamper can detect computations manipulated by a variety of different attacker strategies, and site operators can choose to further investigate the identities participating in computations flagged by Stamper to detect new and yet undiscovered Sybil identities and attack strategies.

We demonstrate the utility and practicality of Stamper approach by evaluating it over data gathered from two widely-used crowd computing systems: Yelp and Twitter. In the case of Yelp, we evaluate accuracy of Stamper in detecting known tampered computations (already identified by Yelp). We demonstrate that Stamper can detect businesses with highly tampered reviews, independently of the strategies attackers used to manipulate the reviews. Using the Twit-

ter dataset, we demonstrate how a site operator can apply Stamper to detect thousands of previously unknown tampered computations in which Sybil identities were used to boost user popularity. Finally, in section 6 we present a publicly accessible service designed using Stamper to detect tweet content in Twitter with tampered popularity.

2. RELATED WORK AND MOTIVATION

Weak identities and Sybil attacks   The systems that Stamper targets allow users to create identities, and require all interactions to be conducted via these identities. Many systems do not require that identities be certified by a trusted authority (to lower the sign-on overheads), and instead only require identities to be created with few credentials (typically, an email address and a solved CAPTCHA). Such identities, known as *weak identities*, are the vector for Sybil attacks, as the small amount of work required to create an additional identity makes it possible for an attacker to create many Sybils. Recent studies show that there are thriving underground "blackmarket" services, where human users or bots can be "hired" to create fake identities [27,39]. These Sybil identities are then profitably used to manipulate crowd-sourced information, such as followers in Twitter [4,33], reviews in Yelp [3], or content likes in Facebook [2,35].

Limitations with detecting individual Sybil identities   The traditional approach to detect if a computation is manipulated involves determining *which* of the participating identities are Sybils. Identities detected as Sybils are then suspended and their contributions to computations are nullified.

Significant recent research has focused on identifying Sybil identities in the system. A large body of work applied machine learning techniques to distinguish between behaviors (activities and profile characteristics) of Sybil and non-Sybil identities [12,26,37,38]. While most approaches in this space use supervised machine learning schemes, work by Wang et al. [37] and Viswanath et al. [35] proposed unsupervised learning schemes to detect Sybil identities. Another body of work has focused on detecting individual Sybil identities by leveraging the structure of the social network graphs formed by Sybils and non-Sybil connecting to one another [36].

However, all these approaches to detect Sybil identities suffer from a fundamental limitation: because weak identities are not backed by some external trusted authority, at their core, all Sybil detection schemes have to rely on analyzing an identity's activities (e.g., interactions with other identities or information they post) to determine if an identity is Sybil. As a result, if an identity has limited or no activity, the schemes lack sufficient evidence to determine if the identity is Sybil or non-Sybil. Studies have shown that many honest users create identities in online systems, but rarely use them [5].

Attackers can take advantage of the above limitations of Sybil detection schemes to create hard-to-detect Sybil identities with only legitimate or limited past activity. An attacker could stockpile a large number of accounts over a period of time, which can later be used to launch hard-to-detect attacks on computations.

Strength in numbers   Given the inherent difficulty in determining whether an *individual identity* is Sybil, we propose to shift the focus to detecting whether a *group of identities* participating in a computation are likely to have Sybil participants.

Few works have explored techniques for preventing Sybil-tampering of computations directly. Prominent among them are DSybil [42], SumUp [34], and Iolaus [23], which work by preventing or discounting votes based on trusted *guides* (DSybil) or the social network (SumUp and Iolaus). Unfortunately, these systems rely on assumptions that do not always hold in a generic crowd-sourcing system. For example, many crowd-sourcing systems do not have social network links interconnecting identities (as assumed by SumUp and Iolaus) and in many systems, a majority of users do not rate many items (preventing the assignment of guides in DSybil).

Prior work has also examined detecting product rating manipulation in e-commerce sites [19,40] and manipulation of authority scores in peer-to-peer Web search networks [28]. Among them, the most related piece of work is by Feng et al. [19] which explores detecting product rating manipulation in online market places by comparing the distribution of product rating scores of an item to known-good distributions. However, unlike Stamper, the approach by Feng et al. is vulnerable against adaptive attackers as it only considers distribution of product rating scores which can be easily forged to evade detection.

Two other works, SynchoTrap [16] and CopyCatch [13] also focused on analyzing behavior of a group of malicious identities. However, they have a similar limitation where they focus on detecting a specific attack behavior: *loosely synchronized actions*, where a group of malicious identities behave similarly at around the same time. For example, a group of Sybil identities liking a set of Facebook pages at around the same time can be potentially detected by such schemes. In contrast, Stamper does not make any assumptions about specific attacker strategies and thus, has the potential to detect computations tampered using diverse strategies.

3. Stamper: KEY INSIGHTS

3.1 System model and goal

We consider a crowd computing system (e.g., Twitter, Yelp, Facebook) that uses weak identities for its users. A crowd computation can be voting on a given business by a set of identities in Yelp, or promoting a tweet or following a certain identity by a set of identities in Twitter. A site operator is interested in defending against Sybil attacks on crowd computations within the system.

Goal For each computation, the goal of the system operator is to determine whether the set of identities participating in the computation included a *sizeable* fraction of Sybil identities. Stamper design focuses on the core challenge of *robustly detecting tampered computations*. The site-specific actions operators might take against the tampered computations are *not* integral to Stamper design. An operator might choose to suspend (remove) the computations detected as tampered or display the computations at the bottom in site-search results or attach warning labels to them.

Reputation scores We assume that each identity in the system is associated with one or more *reputation scores* that are computed by the operators based on the identity's past

activity. Reputation scores can take a variety of forms, and can be computed or obtained by the operators based on "certifications or endorsements", "proofs-of-work", "activity history", or a combination of these. For example, a reputation score could be the number of social network "friends" the identity has in the system, the number of messages it has posted, or the number of endorsements it received from its friends for its work. Given that weak identities are not backed by external trust, reputation scores reflect the system operators' estimation of trust they would place in the identities in the system, i.e., it is less likely (probable) that identities with higher reputation would misbehave (or be Sybils). Note that by definition all newly created identities (Sybils or non-Sybils) will have zero reputation as they have no prior activity.

Threat model We assume that an attacker can create arbitrary number of fake identities in the existing system. However, the attacker does not have unbounded economic resources to create and sustain Sybil identities on every newly created site on the Internet. We allow reputation scores to be *forged*, i.e., attackers may manipulate the different reputation scores of malicious identities they control with different amounts of effort. However, we assume that the site operator keeps detailed historical records of the reputation scores of identities over time.[1] The attacker can also obtain the complete historical records of identities' reputation scores; however, the attacker cannot go back in time and tamper with those records.

3.2 Detecting tampered computations

We describe how Stamper detects tampered computations in two steps below. We first tackle simple attackers and then consider stronger adaptive attackers.

Step 1 In practice, the distributions of the reputation scores of Sybil and non-Sybil identities tend to be quite different. In other words, some attackers today do not expend significant effort to make their Sybil identities similar to non-Sybil identities. Sybil identities as a group, particularly those with limited or no activity, tend to skew towards low reputation scores (as reputation scores are computed based on the identities' activities on the site), while the non-Sybil identities would naturally span a full spectrum of low to high reputation scores.

Insight 1 Due to the above observation, the participation of Sybil identities in a computation tends to distort the reputation score distributions of the nodes participating in the computation. Figure 1 illustrates this insight. It shows the reputation scores for untampered and tampered computations in the Twitter network.[2] The participation of Sybil identities tends to skew the reputation scores towards lower values and has the overall effect of decreasing the entropy in the distribution of scores. It is this difference in reputation score distributions that Stamper leverages to detect Sybil tampering.

We stress that the above insight allows us to determine that a computation has been tampered with even when we cannot determine which of the identities are Sybil. In Fig-

---

[1] Many site operators today including Facebook and Twitter are known to keep detailed historical records of identities.
[2] These are samples of real untampered and tampered computations in Twitter flagged by Stamper (See Section 5.2).

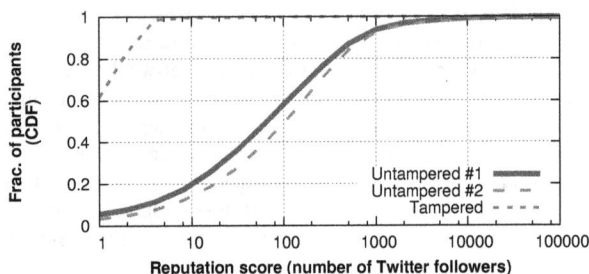

Figure 1: Reputation score (based on number of followers) distribution of tampered vs untampered computations. Most participants in the tampered computation have a low reputation score.

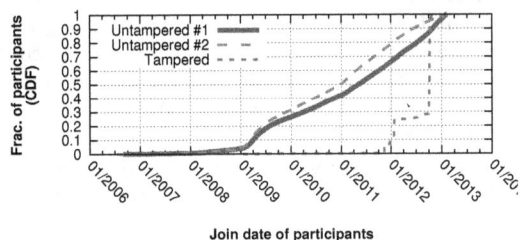

Figure 2: Join date distribution of participants of tampered and untampered computation.

ure 1, even as we infer that the skew towards lower reputation scores is due to Sybils, we cannot tell which of the identities with low reputation scores are Sybils as there *do* exist non-Sybil identities with such low reputation scores as well.

However, this insight alone would not allow us to design an approach that is robust against an adaptive attacker. For example, a determined attacker could expend additional effort to manipulate the reputation scores of her Sybil identities to match the distribution of reputation scores of non-Sybil identities.

Step 2   Even when an attacker can forge a malicious identity's reputation, she can only forge the *present and future* reputation scores of the identity, but she cannot go back in time and forge the past history (i.e., temporal evolution) of the identity's reputation as recorded by the operator. Thus, the distribution of temporal evolution of forged reputation scores of Sybils tend to exhibit distributions that are quite different than non-Sybils'.

Insight 2   To detect potential forging of reputations of Sybil identities by an adaptive attacker, we analyze the temporal evolution of reputation scores of the identities participating in the computation. Specifically, we examine the distributions of times (i.e., dates) when the identities have achieved a certain percentile (e.g., 0%, 10%, 25%, 50%) of their current reputation score.

Figure 2 illustrates this insight. It shows the times when the identities participating in untampered and tampered computations began to acquire reputation in the system (i.e., their join date).[2] The Sybil identities have acquired most of their reputation within the short period of time close to their participation date in the computation, while

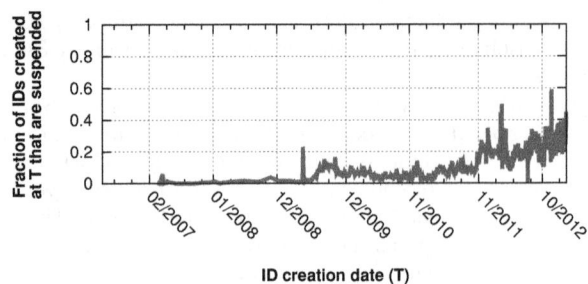

Figure 3: Growth in the fraction of identities in Twitter that are eventually suspended.

the non-Sybil identities have acquired their reputations over a much longer period of time. In fact, a significant fraction of untampered computations have identities with reputation histories dating back to the inception of the Twitter site (in 2006). It is this difference in the distributions of temporal evolution of reputation scores of identities that Stamper leverages to detect Sybil tampering of a computation.

3.3   Robustness and Limitations

In this section, we discuss how Stamper raises the bar for evasion by adaptive attackers and also point out limitations against adaptive attackers.

Robustness 1: Can an adaptive attacker create Sybil identities whose reputation histories match those of non-Sybils?   To tamper a computation without being caught by Stamper, an attacker would have to create new Sybil identities and groom their reputations from the inception of the system, i.e., when non-Sybils started being created.

In existing systems like Facebook, Twitter, or Yelp, the attacker is already too late to go back in time and forge identities whose reputation histories date back to the time when these sites came into existence. Figure 3 shows the growth in suspended identities in Twitter, since the time of its inception.[3] In the first two years, Twitter witnessed very few (0.036%) malicious identities. However, once Twitter reached a critical mass of users, it started attracting more attackers and the percentage of malicious identities sharply rises to as high as 40% of all identities created on a single day. So, it is hard for any attacker to gain control of Sybil identities with reputation histories dating back to the early years of these existing systems.

An attacker still has an opportunity to create and groom Sybil identities on newly (or yet to be) created online sites. However, the attacker cannot accurately predict which of the several new online sites are likely to succeed and acquire critical mass of users in the long run. So the attacker would have to create Sybil identities on *all* online sites from their inception to be prepared to launch an attack on any single site in the future. Considering the large number of new online sites that are created everyday, we argue that such attacks are not economically viable in practice.

Robustness 2:   Can an adaptive attacker create "sleeper cells" to launch an attack in the distant fu-

---

[3]We crawled 2.3M Twitter identities that joined Twitter at different points of time since its inception. Twitter API allows us to figure out which identities have been suspended.

ture? A determined attacker can start creating "sleeper" Sybil identities on popular sites like Facebook and Twitter today, with the goal of launching an attack several years down the road. While such attacks are not impossible, we argue that Stamper significantly raises the costs for the attacker making it economically non-viable. Since Stamper checks for temporal evolution of reputation scores, an attacker would need to actively groom the "sleeper" identities to evolve their reputation scores similar to how non-Sybils reputation scores evolve. As different reputation scores of user identities in different systems evolve in complex, unpredictable ways, an attacker would have to constantly track and mimic these changes. The difficulty of grooming such identities would be reflected in their cost for the attack.

To test our hypothesis about attacker costs for creating identities with high reputation histories, we collected pricing information for Sybil identities in Twitter and Facebook, by manually inspecting postings in 8 online black-market services (that we found via google search), where such identities are sold. A Facebook (Twitter) identity with no reputation costs $0.51 ($0.09), while those with 4 years of age cost $15 ($1) and those with 5000 (200) real and active friends (followers) costs $150 ($5). While the data we gathered does not constitute a rigorous proof, it indicates that identities with long running and high reputations could cost 10 to 100 times or more than newly created Sybil identities with no reputation.

Robustness 3: Can Stamper fundamentally alter the arms race between Sybil attackers and defenses? The root cause of arms race between Sybil attackers and defenses today is that every time a Sybil identity is detected and suspended, attackers can not only create a new Sybil identity and regain their lost attack power, but they can also derive knowledge about how to evade detection. With Stamper, every malicious identity suspended by the site operator would represent a loss in the power of the attacker because the attacker cannot replace the suspended identities with newly created identities. If used in an attack, Stamper would be able to detect the differences in how reputations of identities evolved over time for older and newer identities.

Most site operators today proactively deploy "spam filters" that over time detect Sybil identities and suspend them. While these spam filters are far from detecting all Sybil identities in a timely manner, Stamper fundamentally shifts the balance of the arms race in favor of these defenses because every suspended identity results in a near permanent reduction in attack power, which can be regained with a new Sybil identity only after waiting for the entire generation of existing identities to leave the system (see Robustness 2 above).

Limitation 1: Can Stamper detect attacks using non-Sybil identities that are incentivised to collude or whose login credentials are compromised? Stamper cannot provide the robustness guarantees discussed above for attacks involving non-Sybil identities that are compromised by an attacker or that have an incentive to collude with one another (e.g., to boost each other's popularity). However, there is still hope; Stamper would still be able to detect tampering as long as the colluding or compromised identities are not carefully chosen in such a way that the distribution of reputation scores and their temporal evolution match that of non-Sybil identities. In practice, it may not be easy for an attacker to selectively target and compromise

non-Sybil identities with varied levels of reputation scores. In fact, in our evaluation Section 5.2, we show that Stamper is able to detect identities colluding to follow one another in Twitter, because their collusion distorts the distribution of their reputation scores, which is easily flagged by Stamper.

Limitation 2: Can Stamper detect computations that involve only a few identities or that have been tampered using only a few Sybils? At its core, Stamper relies on identifying *statistically significant* deviations in distributions of reputation histories of identities participating in a crowd computation. So the robustness guarantees of Stamper do not hold when the number of participating identities is too small or when the degree of tampering is small. In practice, we show that Stamper can be used to detect tampering of computations with 100 or more participants (see Section 5.1). We also show that Stamper is very robust in detecting highly tampered computations (e.g., $> 50\%$ of identities are Sybil), but when the computations are tampered only to a small extent (e.g., $< 10\%$ of identities are Sybil), the detection accuracy suffers. While this is a fundamental limitation of Stamper's approach, it is worth noting that in practice, system operators would be more concerned about detecting heavily tampered computations than lightly tampered ones.

4. Stamper DESIGN

We design Stamper to satisfy the following requirements for a practical design: (i) *robustness:* any computation flagged as being tampered with should have been tampered with very high probability and any tampered computation has a good chance of being detected; (ii) *generality:* the system should be able to detect Sybil tampered computations independently of the attack method used.

Notation Let sets A, M, and H respectively represent all identities, all Sybil identities, and all non-Sybil (honest) identities in the crowd computing system (e.g., Twitter, Yelp, or Facebook) such that $A = H \cup M$. We assume that each identity is associated with a set of reputation scores $R = \{R_1, R_2, \ldots, R_\ell\}$, which are computed by the operators based on the identity's activity in the system to date. For a given set of identities that participated in a crowd computation c, we denote by $R_i(c)$ to be the probability distribution (or density) function (PDF) of the values of the reputation score R_i of the identities in computation c.

The system operator is interested in defending against Sybil attacks on a set of crowd computations $C = \{c_1, c_2, \ldots, c_n\}$ Let sets C_i, $M(C_i)$, $H(C_i)$ respectively represent all identities, Sybil identities, and non-Sybil identities that are involved in computation c_i.

4.1 Design overview

Our goal is to design a "detector" that can check if a given large crowd computation c_i was tampered with by Sybil identities, i.e., whether the (unknown) Sybil identities $M(C_i)$ constitute a significant fraction of all identities C_i participating in the computation c_i.

We compute the *relative entropy* or divergence between two distributions using a statistical measure called the Kullback—Leibler (KL) divergence [24]. The choice of KL-divergence as the statistical measure is not fundamental to the application of Stamper. We could have used other statistical distance measures [1], but as we show in our evaluation, KL-divergence is quite sufficient for our purposes. KL-divergence ranges from 0 (identical distributions) to ∞ (highly differing distributions); the (symmetric) divergence between two distributions P and Q is denoted by $\mathsf{KLD}(\mathsf{P}, \mathsf{Q})$, where

$$\mathsf{KLD}(\mathsf{P}, \mathsf{Q}) = \sum_{i=1}^{r} \left(\log(\frac{\mathsf{P}(i)}{\mathsf{Q}(i)}) \mathsf{P}(i) + \log(\frac{\mathsf{Q}(i)}{\mathsf{P}(i)}) \mathsf{Q}(i) \right)$$

Our insight suggests that in practice, the KL-divergence between distributions of untampered computations would be low, while those between untampered and tampered computations would be anomalously high.

4.1.1 Detecting anomalous distributions

We use *anomaly detection* [22, 25, 35] techniques to separate out the "outlier" or "anomalous" distributions of reputations scores (and their temporal evolution) observed for tampered computations. Specifically, we apply a variant of anomaly detection known as *semi-supervised* anomaly detection [30], where the site operator has *a priori* knowledge of a small subset of crowd computations, $\mathsf{UC} = \{uc_1, uc_2, \ldots, uc_k\}$ that are largely untampered with by Sybil identities.

We first analyze the KL-divergence in the distribution of a reputation score R_j between the known untampered computations. If we find that the distributions of most untampered computations lie within some small threshold divergence T_j from one another, then we could declare any other computation whose distribution lies far outside the threshold T_j as potentially tampered.

When identity participation is unbiased We can offer strong theoretical guarantees on the choice of the threshold T_j, if participants in any untampered crowd computation c_i are drawn uniformly at random (without any bias) from the set of all non-Sybil identities H in the system. Under the unbiased participation assumption, the probability distributions of the reputation scores of identities participating in all large untampered computations are guaranteed to converge to the same distribution. Specifically, as the size of a computation c_i grows, the distribution of reputation scores $R_j(c_i)$ quickly approximates the distribution of reputation scores for all non-Sybil identities $R_j(\mathsf{H})$. Formally, for all c_i such that $C_i = \mathsf{H}(C_i)$, and for some small ϵ,

$$\exists \, s \quad \text{s.t.} \quad \forall i, |C_i| > s \, \cap \, \mathsf{KLD}(R_j(\mathsf{H}), R_j(C_i)) < \epsilon.$$

We refer to s as the *size threshold* for the crowd computations. In fact, Roy [29] studied the thresholds theoretically as well as empirically and proved an upper bound of $1/|C_i|$ on KLD for a sampled distribution of size $|C_i|$. Thus, if an untampered computation involves over 100 or 1,000 identities, the KLD between the reputation score distributions of the computation participants and the non-Sybil identities will be lower than 0.01 or 0.001, respectively. As a result, a simple strategy for detecting whether a given large computation c_i (i.e., $|C_i| > s$) has been tampered with is as follows: First, select some *a priori* known untampered computation c_u of size greater than s. Then, compute the divergence in the distributions of reputation score R_j between the given computation and known untampered computation, i.e., compute $\mathsf{KLD}(R_j(c_u), R_j(c_i))$. If the divergence is greater than the divergence threshold $1/s$, declare the computation c_i as tampered (with high probability).

When identity participation is biased In practice, many crowd computations draw a biased population of identities: For example, in Yelp, many reviewers of businesses in San Francisco are likely to be drawn from San Francisco. Without the unbiased participation assumption, we cannot offer any *theoretical* guarantees on convergence of distributions of untampered computations. However, in practice we often observe that the *distributions for untampered computations are far closer to one another than they are to tampered computations*. We validate this claim using real-world data from Yelp and Twitter in the evaluation sections 5.1 and 5.2.

In the case of biased participation, we first derive a *reference* or expected distribution by "averaging" the distributions of known untampered computations and then select a KL-divergence threshold T_j that encompasses most, if not all, the untampered computations. To detect whether a given large computation c_i is tampered with, we compute its KL-divergence from the reference distribution. If it is larger than the threshold divergence T_j, we declare the computation c_i as tampered (with high probability).

While we defer the precise details of the threshold selection to Section 4.2, we make two observations on the choice of the divergence threshold. First, if for some reputation score R_j, the distributions of untampered computations do not converge in practice, then the observed threshold divergence T_j between the untampered computations would also naturally be quite large, and consequently there would be little risk of an untampered computation flagged as tampered. Thus, the risk of untampered computations being flagged as tampered is low, even when the distributions of untampered computations do not converge. Second, by raising and lowering the threshold T_j, an operator can trade-off between the precision and recall in detecting tampered computations. Depending on the application scenario, operators can either choose a more or less conservative threshold.

4.2 Detailed Design

The operator would deploy Stamper as follows:

1. Creating a pool of reputation scores The first step in deploying Stamper involves choosing a set of reputation scores $\{R_1, R_2, ..., R_l\}$ that can be computed for each identity in the system. Identities start with low (zero) reputation scores when they are created and can earn higher reputations over time. We do *not* assume that reputation scores are unforgeable: different reputation scores of an identity may be manipulated by the attacker with different amounts of effort.

2. Building a reference (expected) distribution To build a reference distribution for a given reputation score R_j, we first compute the distribution of the reputation score for each known-untampered computation (i.e., calculates $R_j(uc_i)$ for each $uc_i \in \mathsf{UC}$). Now, these distributions are aggregated into a single reference distribution $R_j(\mathsf{UC})$ using a *linear opinion pool* [17] model. We do so using a fair weighting scheme such that each crowd computation contributes a fair share towards building the final reference distribution. Formally, the reference distribution $R_j(\mathsf{UC})$ is defined as $Pr[v \leftarrow R_j(\mathsf{UC})] = \frac{1}{k} \sum_{i=1}^{k} Pr[v \leftarrow R_j(uc_i)]$

3. Selecting a threshold We now compute the KL-divergence of each of the crowd computations in set C from that of the reference distribution. We will obtain a range of KL-divergence values and will select a threshold T_j, such that KL-divergence values greater than T_j is anomalous with respect to the rest of KL-divergence values. To select this threshold, we use a simple statistical technique called the *box plot rule* [14] defined as follows: Let $Q1$ and $Q3$ be the lower and upper quartile respectively, for the KL-divergence values. A KL-divergence value is an outlier if it lies beyond the *upper outer fence*: $Q3 + 3 * (Q3 - Q1)$. We select the upper outer fence of the distribution as the threshold T_j.

4. Detecting anomalous computations With T_j and $R_j(UC)$, it is straightforward to detect anomalous computations. For a given computation c_i, the operator simply calculates the KL-divergence between $R_j(c_i)$ and $R_j(UC)$; if it is higher than T_j, the computation is flagged as anomalous. In fact, the higher divergence (above the threshold), the more anomalous the computation turns out when compared to the rest of the computations. The operator can experiment with the tradeoff of catching more tampered computations (when using a lower KL-divergence threshold) versus improving the efficiency of workers (when using a high KL-divergence threshold).

Operators typically use human workers to examine suspicious accounts or activities once they are flagged by their defense mechanisms [15]. Stamper can guide operators to focus the attention of their human verifiers on a set of flagged computations to verify if they are tampered with. More importantly, while Stamper has been designed to detect computation tampering, it can be used in practice for a broader range of Sybil defense tasks. The operator can manually investigate the anomalous computations—as they have a higher chance of containing Sybils—to further discover new Sybils and previously unknown attacker strategies. We demonstrate this in Section 5.2.2 where we investigate the identities that participate in tampered computations. However, it should be noted that an investigation phase is common in deployed defense schemes and it is not part of the core Stamper deployment workflow.

5. Stamper EVALUATION

This section presents two case studies of applying Stamper in two popular systems, namely Yelp and Twitter.

5.1 Case 1: Yelp review tampering

Goal: Find businesses with tampered reviews Yelp is a popular local directory service, where users can search for businesses in a given locality and retrieve crowd-sourced reviews and ratings for those businesses from other users. As Yelp is becoming popular, businesses (e.g., restaurants) have an incentive to manipulate their reviews and ratings in their favor. Today, there are plenty of black-market services [10], where one can easily buy Yelp reviews for a cheap price (e.g., three reviews cost $74.85 in one such service). The crowd computation that we are interested in is the set of identities that rate a given business in Yelp. Our goal is to evaluate how effectively Stamper can be leveraged to detect attacks that tamper the computation, i.e., detect businesses that have manipulated reviews.

For evaluating effectiveness of Stamper we leverage Yelp's *review filter* [8,9] feature to obtain "ground truth" for tampered reviews. Yelp filters suspicious reviews to defend against fake reviews. It should be noted that as is the case

with many online defense schemes deployed today, Yelp acknowledges that their review system is not perfect and may not be able to detect all types of tampered reviews and may even sometimes wrongly flag legitimate reviews. However, for the purpose of this analysis, we will consider a business to have tampered reviews if Yelp filters at least one review of the business. Note that we do not have any knowledge about specific strategies used by attackers of the filtered reviews (i.e., did the attacker create multiple fake accounts to tamper reviews or did she incentivize real users to write fake reviews in return for a monetary reward).

More precisely, we investigate the following three questions: (i) How easy or difficult is it to apply Stamper to detect review tampering in Yelp? (ii) Does the key requirement that distributions of reputation scores of large untampered computations converge (while those of large tampered computations diverge) hold in practice in Yelp? (iii) Can Stamper detect most of the *highly tampered* computations (businesses with a majority of reviews filtered) at a low false positive rate (fraction of businesses with no filtered reviews flagged)? Recall that Stamper is designed to detect *highly tampered* computations and cannot guarantee detection of computations tampered only to a small extent (see Section 3.3).

Data gathered We used Yelp data gathered by Kakhki et al. [23] in May 2012, which we updated with our own data gathering crawl in March 2013. This dataset consists of all businesses on Yelp in the city of San Francisco at that time. This includes 30,339 businesses with a total of 1,655,385 ratings from 340,671 reviewer identities. Each rating consists of a score from 1 to 5 stars. These ratings also include those *filtered* by Yelp's automated review filter. In total, Yelp filtered 195,825 (or 11.83%) ratings. As Stamper has been designed to infer tampering in large computations involving more than a certain number of identities, we threshold the size of the computation at 100 for Yelp. There are 3,579 businesses with more than 100 reviews. Out of these 3,579 businesses, there are 54 businesses which did not have a single review filtered by Yelp. We consider these 54 cases as untampered computations. Also, for each reviewer we collected information about a variety of reputation scores. (See the first column of Table 1.)

5.1.1 Ease of deploying Stamper

The four steps that constitute Stamper detection strategy (outlined in Section 4.2) can be applied in a straight-forward manner with very little overhead.

1. Creating a pool of reputation scores The first column in Table 1 lists all the 8 reputation scores used in our evaluation; e.g., the reputation score in the 8th row is a measure of the number of times reviews by an identity are marked useful by other identities in the service. To tamper a crowd computation by forging this reputation score, an attacker would have to put additional effort to boost the reputation for the malicious identities employed in the attack by obtaining a certain number of endorsements (by getting reviews marked useful) from other identities.

2. Building reference distributions We select businesses which had no (zero) review filtered as the set of untampered computations. There are 54 such businesses (with zero reviews filtered). Even though the number of untam-

Reputation score	# flagged	Percentage of computations flagged				
		0% filtered	(0,10]% filtered	(10,30]% filtered	(30,50]% filtered	> 50% filtered
# photos	158	**5.6 (3/54)**	0.2 (5/2280)	6.6 (72/1089)	32.9 (27/82)	**68.9 (51/74)**
# first badges	141	**0.0 (0/54)**	1.3 (30/2280)	4.4 (48/1089)	20.7 (17/82)	**62.2 (46/74)**
# fans	139	**0.0 (0/54)**	0.6 (14/2280)	5.0 (54/1089)	28.0 (23/82)	**64.9 (48/74)**
# compliments	173	**1.9 (1/54)**	0.7 (15/2280)	6.2 (67/1089)	35.4 (29/82)	**82.4 (61/74)**
# reviews marked funny	157	**0.0 (0/54)**	0.7 (15/2280)	5.0 (54/1089)	28.0 (23/82)	**87.8 (65/74)**
# reviews marked cool	174	**0.0 (0/54)**	1.0 (22/2280)	5.6 (61/1089)	35.4 (29/82)	**83.8 (62/74)**
# friends	227	**0.0 (0/54)**	0.2 (4/2280)	9.7 (106/1089)	56.1 (46/82)	**95.9 (71/74)**
# reviews marked useful	224	**3.7 (2/54)**	0.5 (11/2280)	9.2 (100/1089)	51.2 (42/82)	**93.2 (69/74)**
All scores combined	362	**5.6 (3/54)**	3.0 (68/2280)	14.8 (161/1089)	70.7 (58/82)	**97.3 (72/74)**

Table 1: Computations with varied levels of filtered reviews flagged by Stamper. Stamper flags most of the *highly tampered* (>50% filtered) computations while flagging very few (3/54) untampered computations.

pered computations might seem small, they have a large number of reviewers (14,223 reviewers) who wrote reviews for them.

3. Selecting a threshold We compute KL-divergence values for all 3,579 businesses from the reference distribution for each reputation score. Then, for each reputation score, using the box plot rule, we estimate a KL-divergence threshold for flagging anomalies; e.g., in the case of the reputation score, *#times review is marked useful* (we will call this as the number of review endorsements), we estimate a threshold of 1.2.

4. Detecting anomalous computations If the KL-divergence computed for a business is greater than the divergence threshold for any reputation score, the computation is marked as anomalous. The second column of Table 1 shows the number of businesses whose reviews have been flagged as tampered by Stamper.

The above discussion demonstrates how easily Stamper can be applied by operators of crowd computing systems today.

5.1.2 Detectability of tampered computations

We now investigate whether a key assumption behind Stamper design holds in practice. Specifically, we verify if the distributions of reputation scores of large untampered computations in Yelp tend to converge, while those of tampered computations diverge. Figure 4 shows the distribution of KL-divergence values using the endorsement count reputation score for untampered computations and computations with different levels of filtered reviews. Note that, computations with zero and with less than 10% reviews filtered show low KL-divergence values from the reference distribution, indicating a good convergence in the reputation score distributions. In fact, for 90% of untampered computations their divergence values are less than or equal to 0.36. While for tampered computations (computations with more than 20% and 50% reviews filtered), the KL-divergence values are higher and shows a diverging trend. We observe a similar trend for other reputation scores listed in Table 1.

5.1.3 Robustness of Stamper tamper detection

Next we investigate the robustness of Stamper detection. For the rest of the analysis, we divide businesses into five categories based on the level of filtering: 0% filtered (or untampered), 0 to 10%, 10 to 30%, 30 to 50%, and more than 50% filtered. We consider computations with more

than 50% reviews filtered to be highly tampered. Out of a total of 3,525 businesses with at least one filtered review, there are 74 businesses that are highly tampered.

1. Stamper can detect most of the highly tampered computations The last column in Table 1 shows the fraction of highly tampered computations that are flagged. By combining all 8 reputation scores (a computation is flagged if it is flagged by at least one reputation score), we detect more than 97% of highly tampered computations. It is interesting to note that combining multiple reputation scores can help to catch more tampered computations. Stamper also manages to catch a significantly high fraction (over 70%) of computations with 30 to 50% reviews filtered.

2. Stamper has low false positives The third column in Table 1 shows the fraction of untampered computations flagged. By combining all 8 reputation scores, we observe a false positive rate of only 5.6%. While interpreting this false positive rate, it is important to keep in mind that Yelp's review filter is not perfect and could have potentially missed flagging some fake reviews.

5.1.4 Discussion

Why is Stamper useful for a system like Yelp? Note that Stamper does not detect individual suspicious reviews. While this might sound like a limitation, Stamper can still be useful for Yelp in flagging businesses with highly tampered reviews. For example, Yelp is known to suspend businesses that were caught buying reviews [11], and display a warning when a user visits a business page suspected of tampering reviews [7]. Using Stamper, Yelp can do so even without detecting individual suspicious reviews as they might be very hard to detect for various reasons. For example, Yelp went

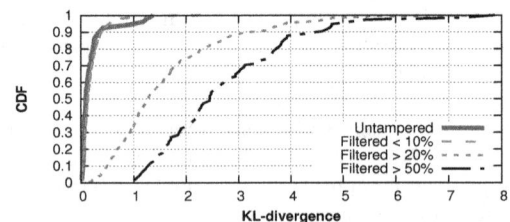

Figure 4: Distribution of KL-divergence values for untampered and tampered computations using number of review endorsements in Yelp.

to the extent of conducting sting operations to catch businesses trying to buy fake reviews [6] because we suspect that such type of tampering is very hard to detect by analyzing reviewer behavior or the content of their reviews. With Stamper, Yelp has the potential to catch highly tampered computations even with very minimum or no information about the behavior of the reviewers. Another huge advantage of our scheme is that compared to prior machine learning approaches, Stamper can detect highly tampered computations in Yelp without training on any pre-identified fake reviews.

Leveraging temporal evolution of reputation scores We tried to find anomalous computations by analyzing the temporal evolution of reputation scores. We used the timestamp at 0th percentile reputation, which is the join date of the user. Stamper flagged only 2 highly tampered computations (already caught by the other reputation scores) using join dates. We suspect that attackers on Yelp are not trying hard to forge their reputation scores today, and we are able to detect most of the highly tampered computations using simple reputation scores. In the next case study, we observe that temporal evolution of reputation scores are very helpful in catching adaptive attackers.

5.2 Case 2: Twitter follower tampering

Goal: Find Twitter users with fake followers In Twitter, to obtain real time information posted by specific users, users typically *follow* those users. Today, the influence of a user is often estimated by counting the number of followers. As a result, there are strong incentives for users to acquire more users to follow them and there have been numerous reports of follower count manipulations [31]. Thus, the crowd computation that we are interested in is the set of identities in Twitter that follow a given Twitter identity. Our goal is detect attacks that manipulate the computation, i.e., detect identities that have tampered follower counts.

We use this case study to showcase Stamper's capability of detecting yet unknown tampered computations. This provides an opportunity to evaluate how system operators (who in practice would not have a priori ground truth information about tampered computations) might use Stamper. More precisely, we investigate the following three questions: (i) How easy or difficult is it to apply Stamper to detect computation (follower count) tampering in Twitter? (ii) Can system operators analyze the computations flagged by Stamper further (potentially manually) to detect (potentially new) patterns of Sybil attacks? (iii) Can the newly discovered Sybil attack patterns be used to uncover more Sybil identities?

Data gathered We target detecting tampering of follower-counts only for popular Twitter user identities with more than 1,000 followers. We obtained the Twitter-UIDs (unique identifiers) of all users with more than 1,000 followers in all of Twitter (as of July 2012) from a research group which collected this data for a separate study [20]. This dataset contained 2,100,851 identities. We selected a random sample of 70,000 of these identities and gathered profile information of all their followers. Some of these accounts no longer existed on Twitter and their information could not be collected. In total, we discovered (in aggregate) over 176M followers for 69,409 of these users.

5.2.1 *Ease of deploying* Stamper

We briefly discuss the steps that constitute Stamper procedure for this case study.

1. Creating a pool of reputation scores We select *number of followers* as a reputation score to build our reference distribution (i.e., we consider the distribution of the number of followers *of the followers*). To account for the cases where an attacker forges this reputation score, we consider the temporal evolution of the reputation score (i.e., the distribution of times at which the identity acquired 0th, 25th, or 50th percentile of their reputation). Since it was easy for us to gather the timestamps at which the identities started building their reputation (i.e., the date at which the identities "joined" the service—corresponding to the 0th percentile of their reputation—we use the join dates of identities to build the reference distribution.

2. Building reference distributions In Twitter, we assume that the accounts verified by Twitter[4] do not knowingly tamper their follower counts. We use them as the set of known untampered computations. We randomly sample 30,000 verified accounts from the list of Twitter verified accounts with more than 1,000 followers, and crawled profiled information of their 266M followers to derive the reference distribution.

3. Selecting a threshold We compute KL-divergence values for all the 69,409 identities and estimate a KL-divergence threshold of 7.88 and 5.79 using the follower count reputation score, and join date, respectively.

4. Detecting tampered computations Among the 69,409 popular users, using follower counts, Stamper flags 620 users and using join dates, Stamper flags 1,129 users as having tampered follower counts. When we examine the overlap between computations flagged using follower count and join date (i.e., the 0th percentile of the follower count), it is very low, consisting of only 49 computations. Thus, using join dates, Stamper is able to flag 1,080 users (with potentially tampered follower counts) who were not flagged using the follower count reputation score. These 1,080 users were able to successfully hide or evade detection when using the follower count reputation score. This finding further shows the advantages of using unforgeable timestamps to detect tampering. Our discussion above once again demonstrates the ease of deploying Stamper.

5.2.2 *Investigating anomalies to detect new attacks*

For manual investigation, we randomly sample 50 computations out of each group of anomalous computations flagged using follower count and join dates, respectively. Three graduate students with prior experience in investigating suspicious identities in social networks spent roughly 15 to 20 minutes per computation for investigation.

First, we try to understand the characteristics of the distribution for each anomalous sample. Second, we attempt to localize our analysis to a subset of the identities within the tampered computation that are most likely to be Sybils. We can find such a subset by looking for regions within the anomalous distribution where it exhibits maximum diver-

---

[4]Twitter vouches for the authenticity of a small portion of all identities (43,901 identities as of April 2013) through an offline verification process.

gence from the reference distribution. To identify potential Sybil identities, for each candidate account, we analyze the Twitter profile picture, name, bio, content of tweets posted (including URLs posted), follower and following count, and profiles of followers of the account.

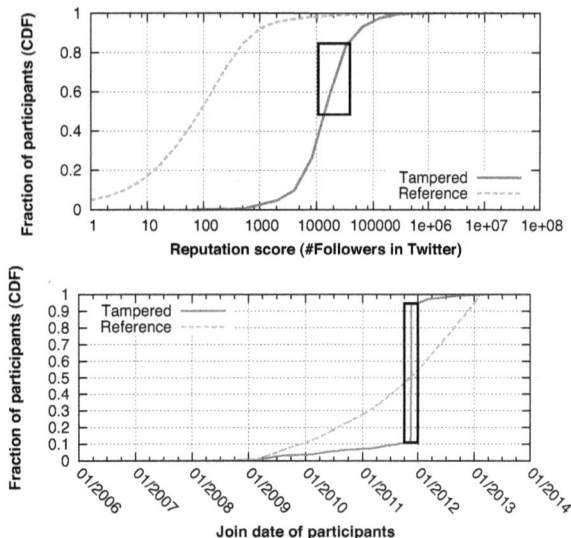

Figure 5: Detecting suspicious participants of a tampered computation. The highlighted region contains the identities suspected of tampering the computation.

Investigating anomalies in follower count distributions On investigating the distribution of follower counts we noticed two distinct patterns. In the first pattern, we found that most of the followers have very low reputation (e.g., almost all had less than 10 followers). 2 out of 50 computations exhibit this pattern. These followers look like fake accounts (fake looking profile, pictures and tweets talking about following activity) and some were already suspended by Twitter. While we would expect tampering to be carried out by unpopular Sybil identities, we were surprised to find only two such instances. The remaining 48/50 computations showed a different distribution pattern–an example is shown in Figure 5 (top figure). When analyzing these computations, we surprisingly discovered that these identities appear to be popular users (i.e., more than 1,000 followers) tampering their follower counts by *colluding* with one another and exchanging links with "you follow me, I follow you" deals. Such activity is referred to as "farming" links on the Twitter network. Link farming [21] is a well-studied problem in Twitter and their defining traits are as follows: they have a large number of followers (more than 1,000), a following per follower ratio in the range [0.9,1.1] and a majority of their followers satisfy these criteria as well. The identities we investigated match these link farmer traits. Using this definition we analyzed all the followers of each of the 48 computations, and found that all computations had at least 32% of their followers that matched the criteria for link farmers. In fact, for 44 out of 48 cases, a majority of their followers are link farmers.

Our analysis above reveals that even though Stamper has been designed to catch computations tampered by Sybil attacks, it is able to detect a broader category of attacks, including *colluding attacks* by non-Sybil identities. However, we do not claim that our robustness guarantees would extend to such non-Sybil attacks.

Investigating anomalies in join date distributions
We analyzed the distributions of the 50 random computations in this case and noticed that for a majority (33/50) of the computations, a significant fraction of the participating identities are tightly clustered in the time domain. Figure 5 (bottom figure) gives an example of such a tampered computation. More specifically, we check if at least 10% (12%) of the followers of the identity joined Twitter within a single day (or week).[5] In contrast, the join dates of identities in the reference (untampered) distribution are spread out over many years. The tight-clustering in the time domain suggests that these identities are possibly created by a Sybil attacker on a single day and then pressed into attack soon after.

To further test our hypothesis, we bought followers for 10 different Twitter identities under our control from 10 different online marketplaces. We discovered these services with a simple keyword search (e.g., "buy Twitter followers") on search engines like Google. In each case, we paid to receive 1,000 followers. When we analyzed the timestamp distribution of followers bought from the black-market for the 10 accounts, we observe that for 9 out of 10 accounts, a vast majority of followers were created on the same day or on a handful of days. This observation supports our hypothesis that identities discovered in anomalous distributions of join dates are Sybils from whom links have been bought.

We further analyzed the remaining 17 (out of 50) computations that did not exhibit tight clustering at a day or week granularity. On manual investigation of followers in the most divergent region, we found that 15/17 computations had very suspicious followers and are most likely tampered computations. Many followers look like fake profiles with no profile picture, names with specific patterns, meaningless tweet content, and some even had malware links in their tweets. An interested reader can browse through more details of the manual analysis of these 15 suspicious computations on this page: `http://trulyfollowing.app-ns.mpi-sws.org/local/stamper/tampered_fcounts.html`. Note that our manual investigation provides detailed information about why we think a computation looks suspicious along with a sample of suspicious participants of the computation.

5.2.3 Detecting new Sybil identities
We now show how an operator can leverage the newly discovered attacker strategies to detect new Sybil identities. We propose to identify cases of follower tampering by analyzing the join date distributions of followers of a given identity and checking if a non-trivial fraction of their followers joined Twitter within a small window of time (we use the same thresholds discussed in earlier section). We applied this technique to detect potential follower tampering activity in Twitter to over 2.1M identities in Twitter

---

[5]Note that we choose conservative thresholds where we found that over 95% of 69K computations did not exhibit this level of tight clustering in the time domain. To validate our thresholds of 10% followers in a day (and 12% in a week), we monitored accounts that exhibited tight clustering and those that did not, for 6 months. Identities forming clusters had a high Twitter suspension rate of 36% compared to a low suspension rate of 0.38% for the other accounts.

with more than 1000 followers. We detect 89,728 identities as having tampered follower counts. Interested readers can browse the data about these 89,728 identities at the site: `http://trulyfollowing.app-ns.mpi-sws.org/`. From these flagged computations, we identified over 23 million Sybil followers whose join dates fall within a small window of time.[5]

5.3 Ethics

All the data about user activity collected from Yelp and Twitter are publicly visible information. All money we paid to acquire followers from the black-market were exclusively for Twitter accounts under our control and set up for the sole purpose of conducting the experiments in the paper. Overall, we ensured that no user or page on Yelp and Twitter was abused or benefited as a result of our study.

6. Stamper DEPLOYMENT

Finally, to demonstrate the effectiveness of Stamper in the real world, we deployed a public online service at `http://trulytweeting.app-ns.mpi-sws.org/` which detects *tampered tweet promotions* in Twitter. Today, there are strong incentives for users to artificially boost popularity of their posts by hiring Sybil identities to promote their content. In this service, we are interested in three types of crowd computations involving a set of identities that: (1) tweet about a particular topic (described by a set of keywords) (2) tweet a URL, or (3) retweet a tweet. Our goal is to detect attacks that manipulate such computations, i.e., detect content (topic, URL or tweet) that is promoted by Sybil identities. Our service lists currently *trending topics*[6], popular URLs and tweets that are tampered and also provides a real time search interface to check arbitrary URL or topic computations for tampering in Twitter. We encourage interested readers to test the service to understand the potential and practicality of Stamper.

7. CONCLUSION

In this paper, we tackle the challenging problem of detecting when computations on crowdsourcing systems like Twitter or Yelp have been tampered by fake (Sybil) identities. We have advocated a fundamentally different approach called Stamper that can detect whether a computation has been tampered even when it is not feasible to detect which of the individual identities participating in the computation are Sybil. The key insight that enables our approach is that large statistical samples (groups) of Sybil and non-Sybil identities exhibit very different characteristics. We have leveraged this insight to design Stamper to (i) detect tampered computations and raise the bar for defense against adaptive attackers and (ii) detect computation tampering independent of the attacker strategy. We have demonstrated the robustness and practicality of Stamper by evaluating its performance using extensive data gathered from two widely used crowd computing systems, namely Yelp and Twitter.

Acknowledgements

We thank the anonymous reviewers and our shepherd, Jim Blomo, for their helpful comments. We also thank Arash Molavi Kakhki for his assistance with the Yelp dataset and Lisette Espín Noboa for her help with building the web user interface of the TrulyFollowing website. This research was supported in part by NSF grants CNS-1319019 and CNS-1421444. Any opinions, findings, and conclusions or recommendations expressed in this material are those of the authors and do not necessarily reflect the views of the NSF.

8. REFERENCES

[1] `http://en.wikipedia.org/wiki/Statistical_distance`.

[2] `http://tinyurl.com/guardian-cf-p`.

[3] `http://tinyurl.com/nyt-haggl`.

[4] `http://tinyurl.com/nyt-tw-sale`.

[5] `http://tinyurl.com/twitter-inactive`.

[6] `http://tinyurl.com/yelp-bought`.

[7] `http://tinyurl.com/yelp-consumer-alert`.

[8] `http://tinyurl.com/yelp-filter`.

[9] `http://tinyurl.com/yelp-filter-explained`.

[10] `http://tinyurl.com/yelp-halt`.

[11] `http://tinyurl.com/yelp-suspend`.

[12] F. Benevenuto, G. Magno, T. Rodrigues, and V. Almeida. Detecting spammers on twitter. In *Proceedings of the 7th Annual Collaboration, Electronic messaging, Anti-Abuse and Spam Conference (CEAS)*, 2010.

[13] A. Beutel, W. Xu, V. Guruswami, C. Palow, and C. Faloutsos. Copycatch: stopping group attacks by spotting lockstep behavior in social networks. In *Proceedings of the 22nd international conference on World Wide Web (WWW)*, 2013.

[14] NIST/SEMATECH e-Handbook of Statistical Methods. `http://www.itl.nist.gov/div898/handbook/`.

[15] Q. Cao, M. Sirivianos, X. Yang, and T. Pregueiro. Aiding the detection of fake accounts in large scale social online services. In *Proceedings of the 9th USENIX conference on Networked Systems Design and Implementation (NSDI)*, 2012.

[16] Q. Cao, X. Yang, J. Yu, and C. Palow. Uncovering large groups of active malicious accounts in online social networks. In *Proceedings of the 2014 ACM SIGSAC Conference on Computer and Communications Security (CCS)*, 2014.

[17] R. T. Clemen and R. L. Winkler. Combining probability distributions from experts in risk analysis. *Risk analysis*, 19(2):187–203, 1999.

[18] J. Douceur. The Sybil Attack. In *Proceedings of the 1st International Workshop on Peer-to-Peer Systems (IPTPS)*, 2002.

[19] S. Feng, L. Xing, A. Gogar, and Y. Choi. Distributional footprints of deceptive product reviews. In *Proceedings of the the 6th International AAAI Conference on Weblogs and Social Media (ICWSM)*, 2012.

[20] M. Gabielkov and A. Legout. The complete picture of the twitter social graph. In *Proceedings of the 2012 ACM conference on CoNEXT student workshop*, 2012.

[21] S. Ghosh, B. Viswanath, F. Kooti, N. K. Sharma, G. Korlam, F. Benevenuto, N. Ganguly, and K. P. Gummadi. Understanding and combating link farming

---

[6]Twitter periodically recommends a set of globally trending topics to users who are signed in to Twitter.

in the twitter social network. In *Proceedings of the 21st International Conference on World Wide Web (WWW)*, 2012.

[22] V. J. Hodge and J. Austin. A survey of outlier detection methodologies. *Artificial Intelligence Review*, 22(2):85–126, 2004.

[23] A. M. Kakhki, C. Kliman-Silver, and A. Mislove. Iolaus: Securing online content rating systems. In *Proceedings of the 22nd International World Wide Web Conference (WWW)*, 2013.

[24] S. Kullback and R. A. Leibler. On information and sufficiency. *The Annals of Mathematical Statistics*, 22(1):79–86, 1951.

[25] A. Lakhina, M. Crovella, and C. Diot. Diagnosing Network-wide Traffic Anomalies. In *Proceedings of the Annual Conference of the ACM Special Interest Group on Data Communication (SIGCOMM*, 2004.

[26] E.-P. Lim, V.-A. Nguyen, N. Jindal, B. Liu, and H. W. Lauw. Detecting product review spammers using rating behaviors. In *Proceedings of the 19th ACM international conference on Information and knowledge management (CIKM)*, 2010.

[27] M. Motoyama, D. McCoy, K. Levchenko, S. Savage, and G. M. Voelker. Dirty jobs: The role of freelance labor in web service abuse. In *Proceedings of the 20th USENIX conference on Security (Usenix Security)*, 2011.

[28] J. X. Parreira, D. Donato, C. Castillo, and G. Weikum. Computing trusted authority scores in peer-to-peer web search networks. In *Proceedings of the 3rd International workshop on Adversarial information retrieval on the web*, 2007.

[29] B. C. Roy. *The Birth of a Word*. PhD thesis, MIT Media Lab, Feb 2013. http://web.media.mit.edu/~bcroy/papers/bcroy-thesis_FINAL-sm.pdf.

[30] R. R. Sillito and R. B. Fisher. Semi-supervised learning for anomalous trajectory detection. In *Proceedings of the British Machine Vision Conference 2008 (BMVC)*, 2008.

[31] G. Stringhini, M. Egele, C. Kruegel, and G. Vigna. Poultry markets: on the underground economy of twitter followers. In *Proceedings of the 2012 ACM workshop on Workshop on Online Social Networks*, 2012.

[32] G. Stringhini, G. Wang, M. Egele, C. Kruegel, G. Vigna, H. Zheng, and B. Y. Zhao. Follow the green: growth and dynamics in twitter follower markets. In *Proceedings of the 2013 conference on Internet measurement conference (IMC)*, 2013.

[33] K. Thomas, D. McCoy, C. Grier, A. Kolcz, and V. Paxson. Trafficking fraudulent accounts: The role of the underground market in twitter spam and abuse. In *Proceedings of the 22nd USENIX Security Symposium (USENIX Security)*, 2013.

[34] N. Tran, B. Min, J. Li, and L. Subramanian. Sybil-resilient online content voting. In *Proceedings of the 6th Symposium on Networked Systems Design and Implementation (NSDI)*, 2009.

[35] B. Viswanath, M. A. Bashir, M. Crovella, S. Guha, K. P. Gummadi, B. Krishnamurthy, and A. Mislove. Towards Detecting Anomalous User Behavior in Online Social Networks. In *Proceedings of the 23rd USENIX Security Symposium (Usenix Security)*.

[36] B. Viswanath, M. Mondal, A. Clement, P. Druschel, K. P. Gummadi, A. Mislove, and A. Post. Exploring the design space of social network-based Sybil defense. In *Proceedings of the 4th International Conference on Communication Systems and Network (COMSNETS)*, 2012.

[37] G. Wang, T. Konolige, C. Wilson, X. Wang, H. Zheng, and B. Y. Zhao. You Are How You Click: Clickstream Analysis for Sybil Detection. In *Proceedings of the 22nd USENIX Security Symposium (Usenix Security)*, 2013.

[38] G. Wang, T. Wang, H. Zheng, and B. Y. Zhao. Man vs. machine: Practical adversarial detection of malicious crowdsourcing workers. In *Proceedings of the 23rd USENIX Security Symposium (Usenix Security)*, 2014.

[39] G. Wang, C. Wilson, X. Zhao, Y. Zhu, M. Mohanlal, H. Zheng, and B. Y. Zhao. Serf and turf: crowdturfing for fun and profit. In *Proceedings of the 21st International conference on World Wide Web (WWW)*, 2012.

[40] G. Wu, D. Greene, B. Smyth, and P. Cunningham. Distortion as a validation criterion in the identification of suspicious reviews. In *Proceedings of the First Workshop on Social Media Analytics*, 2010.

[41] Z. Yang, C. Wilson, X. Wang, T. Gao, B. Y. Zhao, and Y. Dai. Uncovering social network Sybils in the wild. In *Proceedings of the 11th ACM/USENIX Internet Measurement Conference (IMC)*, 2011.

[42] H. Yu, C. Shi, M. Kaminsky, P. B. Gibbons, and F. Xiao. DSybil: Optimal sybil-resistance for recommendation systems. In *Proceedings of the 2009 30th IEEE Symposium on Security and Privacy (IEEE S&P)*, 2009.

Diffusion Maximization in Evolving Social Networks

Nathalie T. H. Gayraud
Department of Computer
Science and Engineering
University of Ioannina
Ioannina, Greece
ngairo@cs.uoi.gr

Evaggelia Pitoura
Department of Computer
Science and Engineering
University of Ioannina
Ioannina, Greece
pitoura@cs.uoi.gr

Panayiotis Tsaparas
Department of Computer
Science and Engineering
University of Ioannina
Ioannina, Greece
tsap@cs.uoi.gr

ABSTRACT

Diffusion in social networks has been studied extensively in the past few years. Most previous work assumes that the underlying network is a static object that remains unchanged as the diffusion process progresses. However, there are several real-life networks that change dynamically over time. In this paper, we study diffusion on such evolving networks and extend the popular Independent Cascade and Linear Threshold models to account for network evolution. In particular, we introduce two natural variations, a *persistent* and a *transient* one, to capture diffusions of different types. We consider the problem of influence maximization where the goal is to select a few influential nodes to initiate a diffusion with maximum spread. We show that, surprisingly, when considering evolving networks the diffusion function is no longer submodular for the transient models, and not even monotone for the transient Independent Cascade model. We also show that, depending on the model, delaying the activation of the initiators may improve diffusion. Our experiments, using three real datasets, demonstrate the effect of network evolution on the diffusion process, and highlight the importance of timing in the selection process.

Categories and Subject Descriptors

J.4 [**Computer Applications**]: Social and behavioral sciences; H.2.8 [**Database Applications**]: Data Mining; H.4 [**Information Systems Applications**]: Miscellaneous

Keywords

Diffusion Maximization; Evolving Social Networks

1. INTRODUCTION

Information propagation and social influence have long been important topics for communication media and social sciences [10]. The growth of online social networks such as Facebook, Twitter, and Instagram, and the importance of influence and diffusion in viral marketing applications [8, 12],

COSN'15, November 2–3, 2015, Palo Alto, California, USA.
© 2015 ACM. ISBN 978-1-4503-3951-3/15/11 ...$15.00.
DOI: http://dx.doi.org/10.1145/2817946.2817965.

has intensified the research interest in the topic. A problem that has attracted considerable attention in this area is that of identifying "influencers": a small set of individuals that will initiate the diffusion of a trend and maximize its spread in the social network. This is a problem of great research interest, with immediate practical applications.

The problem of diffusion maximization was first defined in the seminal works of Domingos and Richardson [8] and Kempe et al. [15]. The work in [15] laid the theoretical and algorithmic foundations for understanding and addressing the problem. The paper introduced two basic diffusion models, the *Independent Cascade (IC)* model and the *Linear Threshold (LT)* model, and it formulated the influence maximization problem as a discrete optimization problem. They showed that the problem is NP-hard, but thanks to the submodularity property of the diffusion spread there exists a greedy algorithm with a constant approximation ratio.

The work in [15] was followed by an avalanche of work that proposed improvements or modifications to the basic models (e.g., [18, 4, 5, 19, 7]). Most of the follow-up work considers the network as a static object that remains unchanged as the diffusion process progresses. However, this assumption is often not true. There are many real-life networks that evolve dynamically, with nodes joining and leaving the network, and edges being formed and destroyed over time. Examples include mobile contact networks, location-based networks, collaboration networks and many more. Many of these networks evolve in predictable ways [6], enabling us to incorporate network evolution in the analysis and modeling of diffusion on the network.

To circumvent the evolving nature of the network, previous approaches aggregate the multiple instances over time into a single static graph. However, such approaches disregard the importance of *timing* in the diffusion process, that is, the importance of information being at the right place, *at the right time*, so that there is a path in the network on which to propagate. As we will see, network evolution has a significant effect on the process of information diffusion, and timing is critical in the correct selection of influencers.

In this work, we address the problem of diffusion maximization on evolving graphs, and we make the following contributions:

- We define the Independent Cascade and the Linear Threshold models on evolving networks. We introduce two variants for each model, a persistent and a transient one, to account for diffusions of different temporal nature.

- We consider the problem of diffusion maximization on evolving graphs and study theoretically its properties under the different models. We prove that, surprisingly, the optimization function is not submodular for the transient models, and for the transient Evolving Independent Cascade model it is not even monotone. We also show that, for some models, delayed activation of the seed nodes may improve the diffusion spread.

- We study experimentally the diffusion process on three real evolving datasets. Our experimental evaluation demonstrates the effect of network evolution on diffusion, as well as the importance of timing of node activations.

The rest of the paper is structured as follows. Section 2 reviews related work. In Section 3, we introduce preliminary definitions and in Section 4 we formulate our problem. In Sections 5, we define the Evolving Independent Cascade and the Evolving Linear Threshold models and study their properties. In Section 6, we report the results of our experimental evaluation. Section 7 concludes the paper.

2. RELATED WORK

The pioneering work of Domingos and Richardson [8] and Kempe et al. [15] generated significant amount of research [18, 4, 5, 7], focusing mostly on variations of the models, and efficient implementations of the algorithms. Surprisingly, there is little research on diffusion on evolving graphs.

Evolving networks: Most closely related to our work are the works of Zhuang et al., [26] and Aggarwal et al., [1] who, as in this paper, view an evolving graph as a sequence of graphs $\{G^t\}$ at different time instances. However, the work of Zhuang et al., [26] addresses a different problem. They apply diffusion maximization independently in each static graph G^t, and assuming that only the initial graph G^0 is fully known, they ask which b nodes to probe to get the edges incident on these nodes at time t, so as to approximate the diffusion on G^t. Our goal is maximizing diffusion over the sequence of graphs as a whole assuming that diffusion and evolution run in parallel.

The focus of the work of Aggarwal et al., [1] is on the efficient estimation of the influence spread by avoiding calculations among graph instances that are structurally similar. Our focus is not on algorithms, but instead on modeling evolution and understanding diffusion maximization in evolving networks under different models. In fact, we show that depending on the model, submodularity may not hold, thus raising the need for new algorithmic approaches.

Another work that considers diffusion on evolving graphs is that of Albano et al., [2]. They make a distinction between *extrinsic time* measured in seconds and *intrinsic time* where a time unit corresponds to a new edge appearing in the graph. Their goal is different from ours: they differentiate between diffusion and graph evolution, e.g., to understand whether an increase in diffusion is due to a sudden growth in the graph.

Time-varying and continuous networks: The notion of time has been introduced in the analysis of information diffusion, as a way of extending the basic diffusion model to capture the duration or latency of diffusion. The duration of diffusion is usually modeled by associating with

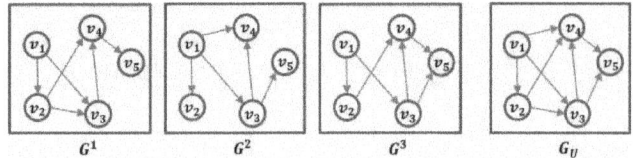

Figure 1: A sequence of three graph $\mathcal{G} = \{G_1, G_2, G_3\}$, and the union graph G_U.

each edge or node, in addition to its activation probability, a latency function that determines when the node reacts to an activation. The problem of influence maximization and estimation is studied for both discrete time (e.g., Liu et al., [19] and Chen et al., [3]) as well as for continuous time (e.g., Gomez-Rodriguez et al. [14] and Du et al., [9]) where the latency per edge entails a random spreading time drawn from a distribution over the time of activation. The recent work of Xie et al., [25] extends the continuous model to capture dynamic properties, but still the diffusion function remains submodular. An orthogonal line of research focuses on learning the influence graph by inferring the influence probabilities, as well as the latency functions of each edge, e.g., the work of Gomez-Rodriguez et al., [13].

The key difference of our work from previous work on time-varying or temporal graphs is that in time-varying graphs, the effect of time on the propagation probability is with respect to the activation time of each node. In our work, we assume that the network changes over time, independently of the diffusion process.

Epidemics: Another line of research focuses on virus propagation on dynamic networks using epidemics models. Such research addresses different problems such as determining the epidemic threshold [23]. Stattner et al., [24] studies the spread of infectious diseases by simulating the infection transmission using the SIR model (a model similar to Independent Cascade) on evolving networks. Their experimental results showed that changes of the underlying network greatly affect the spread of diseases.

3. PRELIMINARIES

In this section, we introduce the necessary concepts for describing the graph evolution and diffusion processes on evolving graphs.

Evolving graphs: We model an evolving graph as a sequence of n graphs $\mathcal{G} = \{G^1, G^2, ..., G^n\}$, defined over the same set of nodes V, where the set of edges differs between time-stamps. That is, $G^i = (V, E^i)$, where $E^i \subseteq V \times V$. Essentially, we can think of the graph sequence, as a sequence of sets of edges $E^1, E^2, ..., E^n$ over the same set of nodes V. Note that our model is general enough to allow for the addition and deletion of both edges and nodes in the graph over time. The set of nodes V contains all the nodes that appear in any snapshot. If a node is not present in a snapshot, there are no edges incident to it. Furthermore, our model can easily be extended to capture evolving probabilistic graphs, where at every time-step, an edge appears in the graph with some probability, that changes over time.

An example of a graph sequence $\mathcal{G} = \{G_1, G_2, G_3\}$ with three snapshots is shown in Figure 1. Given a sequence, we define the *union graph* $G_U = (V, E_U)$, where $E_U = \cup_{i=1}^{n} E^i$, to be the graph consisting of the union of all the graphs in the sequence. The union graph (which can also be defined as a multi-graph, or a weighted graph) is the aggregation of the sequence into a single graph. This is a common way to transform an evolving graph into a static one.

Diffusion and network evolution: In the following, we consider two commonly used models for diffusion: *Independent Cascade* (IC) and *Linear Threshold* (LT). We describe the models in detail in Sections 5.1 and 5.2 respectively. At a high level, both models assume that nodes are in two states: either *active* or *inactive*. Diffusion starts with a set of active nodes A^0 and then proceeds in discrete *steps*. At each diffusion step τ, given the already active nodes $A^{\tau-1}$, depending on the graph topology and the diffusion model, a new set of nodes S^τ is activated, resulting in a new set of active nodes $A^\tau = A^{\tau-1} \cup S^\tau$. The process continues until no more activations are possible.

Regardless of the diffusion model we consider, in order to define the diffusion process on an evolving graph, the first issue that we need to address is to define the notion of *time*. We have two distinct time-tracks that run in parallel: the *graph evolution time*, where a time-step is defined by a graph instance in the graph sequence, and the *diffusion time*, where a time-step is defined by one step in the diffusion process. We need to decide how to synchronize these two time-tracks. That is, we need to decide how many diffusion steps can happen on a graph instance G^t, or how many graph instances a diffusion step spans.

In this work, we make the decision to have the evolution time and the diffusion time run in lock-step. In our model, one time-step t corresponds to one graph instance G^t, on which a single diffusion step takes place. That is, entering time-step t there is a set of nodes $A^{t-1} \subseteq V$ that are active. Similar to the case of a static graph, a diffusion step happens on the graph G^t, and a new set of vertices S^t are activated, defining the set $A^t = A^{t-1} \cup S^t$. We then move on to time-step $t+1$ and graph G^{t+1}. Note that since the set of nodes is the same for all graph instances, the notion of a node u that is inactive at time $t-1$ and active at time t is well defined. Once a node becomes active, it remains active for all following steps. The diffusion process continues for as many steps as the graph sequences instances.

Our definition is general enough to include the possibility that the diffusion time runs faster than the evolution time. Assume for a example that s diffusion steps are executed on a graph instance G^i. We can simulate this process by adding s copies of the graph G^i in the sequence, and assume again that evolution and diffusion time are synchronized. Similarly, if diffusion time is slower than evolution time, we can aggregate the multiple graph instances that correspond to a single diffusion step, and assume again that diffusion and evolution time are synchronized.

Transient and persistent diffusion: Another issue that arises when considering diffusion on a time-evolving graph is to determine the temporal nature of diffusion. In all diffusion models, when a node u gets activated, the model makes a decision as to whether the neighbors of u will be affected. When the graph is static, this decision can be made at the time that u is activated. When the graph evolves over time, the neighbors of u also change over time. What is the time-span in which node u can affect its neighbors?

This question is not a simple technicality: the answer determines the *temporal nature* of the diffusion. In this work we consider two cases: (1) *Transient* diffusion processes, where the effect of a node activation is "local" in time. This models the case where the diffusion capability is short-lived and localized in time; (2) *Persistent* diffusion processes, where the activation of a node has an effect that lasts beyond a single time instance. This models the case where the diffusion capability can persist over time. We elaborate on these issues when we describe the specific models.

4. PROBLEM DEFINITION

We now define the diffusion maximization problem that we consider in this work. Similar to prior work on diffusion maximization, we assume that there is an *item* that we want to *spread* in the network. This may be a product, an idea, or a piece of information. Our goal is to select a small set of influential nodes in the network that will initiate the diffusion, such that the spread of the item is maximized. We will refer to this set of nodes as the *initiators*, or *influencers*, and denote it as $\mathcal{I}$.

In the following, we use A^n to denote the set of nodes that are active in graph G^n after the diffusion process has been completed. Given the sequence of graphs, and the diffusion model, the set A^n depends on the set of influencers $\mathcal{I}$ selected to be activated. We define $\sigma_\mathcal{D}(\mathcal{I}) = |A^n|$ to be the number of activated nodes under the diffusion model $\mathcal{D}$ for the set of initiators $\mathcal{I}$. We call $\sigma_\mathcal{D}(\mathcal{I})$ the *spread* of the diffusion for the set $\mathcal{I}$. Our goal is to select a set $\mathcal{I}$ of k nodes that maximizes $\sigma_\mathcal{D}(\mathcal{I})$.

Since we have an evolving graph, when selecting a node v to activate, we must also select the time t at which we want to activate it. Activating node v at time t means that the node v is added to the set of active nodes A^t, and it can influence its neighbors in future time-steps. It is also possible to activate node v at time $t = 0$ which means that v is active entering the graph evolution and diffusion process. We use v^t to denote the instance of node v in graph G^t at time t. The selection algorithm is thus required to select appropriate instances of k nodes from the set $V_T = \{v^t : v \in V, t = 0, ..., n-1\}$.

We can now define the following problem, which we call the *Spread Maximization on Evolving Graphs* problem (EVOLVEMAXSPREAD).

PROBLEM 1 (EVOLVEMAXSPREAD). *Given a sequence of graphs $\mathcal{G} = \{G^1, G^2, ..., G^n\}$ and an integer k, for a given diffusion model $\mathcal{D}$, find a set $\mathcal{I} = \{v_1^{t_1}, ..., v_k^{t_k}\}$, $v_i \neq v_j$, of k node instances to be activated, such that $\sigma_\mathcal{D}(\mathcal{I})$ is maximized.*

Our problem contains as a special case the problems defined in [15], since we can simulate the diffusion process in a static graph G, as the diffusion on a sequence of graphs, where all graph instances are copies of G, and the length of the sequence is sufficient for the diffusion to be completed. Therefore, we can conclude that the problem is NP-hard.

Following the work in [15], most works that consider variations of the diffusion maximization problem on a static graph are able to derive a constant factor approximation algorithm by making use of the fact that the spread function is *monotone* and *submodular*. Let $f : 2^V \to \mathbb{R}$ denote a set function that maps a subset $S \subseteq V$ of the nodes to a real number. We say that the function f is monotone if $f(S \cup \{v\}) - f(S) \geq 0$

for all $S \subseteq V$, $v \in V \setminus S$. We say that function f is submodular if $f(A \cup \{v\}) - f(A) \geq f(B \cup \{v\}) - f(B)$ for all $A \subseteq B$, $v \in V \setminus B$. The problem of finding a set S of size k that maximizes $f(S)$ is NP-hard for several submodular functions that arise in practice [16]. However, it is well known [21] that a greedy hill-climbing algorithm that builds a set incrementally by adding each time the element that yields the maximum increase in f, produces a solution that has approximation factor $(1 - 1/e)$ of the optimal, where e is the base of the natural logarithm. In the following, we show that, surprisingly, depending on the diffusion model, the spread function is not always submodular, and in some cases not even monotone.

As we have already discussed, when selecting the initiator set $\mathcal{I}$, we need to select not only the nodes to activate but also the time at which to activate them. For some of the diffusion models we consider, the best time to activate a node so as to maximize the spread is as early as possible, that is, at time $t = 0$. In this case we say that the model is *timing-insensitive*. Formally, a diffusion model $\mathcal{D}$ is timing-insensitive if for any graph sequence $\mathcal{G}$, and any initiator set $\mathcal{I} = \{v_1^{t_1}, \ldots, v_k^{t_k}\}$, for the initiator set $\mathcal{I}^0 = \{v_1^0, \ldots, v_k^0\}$ we have $\sigma_{\mathcal{D}}(\mathcal{I}) \leq \sigma_{\mathcal{D}}(\mathcal{I}^0)$. We will otherwise say that the diffusion model is *timing-sensitive*.

5. EVOLVING MODELS

In this section, we introduce our diffusion models that extend the Independent Cascade (IC) and the Linear Threshold (LT) models for evolving networks. We also study the properties of the diffusion spread function for each of the models, and the sensitivity to the timing of the activation of the initiators.

5.1 Evolving IC Model

In the case of a static graph, diffusion under the IC model proceeds in discrete steps, where at step t a new set of nodes S^t is activated. Entering time-step t, the nodes in the set S^{t-1} (where $S^{t-1} = A^0$ for $t = 1$, i.e., the set of active nodes at time zero) are said to be *infectious*. During time-step t, the nodes in S^{t-1} have a single chance to activate their inactive neighbors. Node $u \in S^{t-1}$ activates an inactive node v over the edge (u, v) with probability p_{uv}. If the activation is successful then v is added to the set S^t (and A^t). After step t, node u does not attempt to activate any of its neighbors.

We will now define two variants of the IC model for the case of evolving graphs. We will collectively refer to these models as the *Evolving Independent Cascade* model and denote it by EIC.

5.1.1 Transient EIC Model

In the first variant of the model, we assume that a node u can activate its neighbors only immediately after the time instance that it becomes active. In this case, the diffused item and the activation capability of the nodes in the network are *transient*. For example, consider an infectious disease that is transmitted through a human contact network. When a node becomes infected it has a probability of infecting its neighbors, and then it becomes inoculated. We refer to this model as the *Transient Evolving Independent Cascade* model, and denote it by tEIC.

Formally, similar to the static case, at step t the infectious nodes in S^{t-1} are given a single chance to activate their

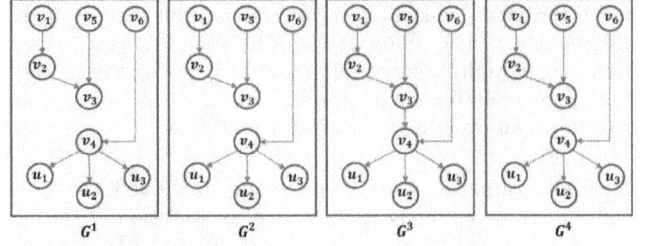

Figure 2: Counter-example graph sequence for EIC.

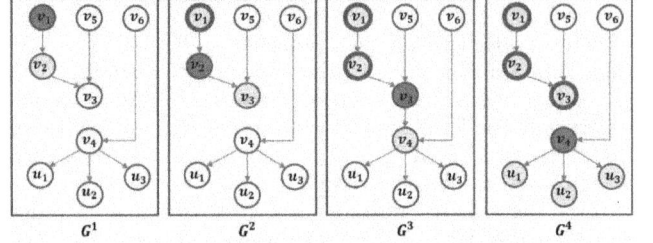

Figure 3: Diffusion with $\mathcal{I} = \{v_1^0\}$.

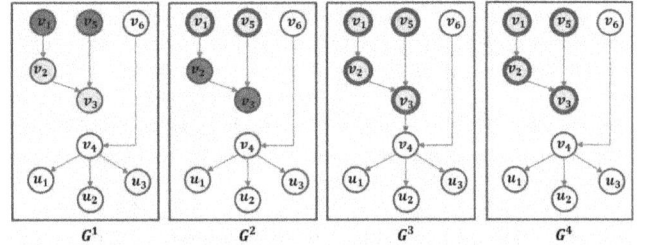

Figure 4: Diffusion with $\mathcal{I} = \{v_1^0, v_5^0\}$.

inactive neighbors, and node $u \in S^{t-1}$ activates the inactive node v over the edge $(u, v) \in E^t$ with probability p_{uv}^t. This yields a new set of recently activated and infectious nodes S^t. The difference in the evolving case is that at each time-step the graph is different, and the neighbors of node u are defined over the graph G^t.

This seemingly small variation makes a big difference in the properties of the model. We show that for the transient EIC model, the spread function is no longer monotone and submodular.

LEMMA 1. *The function σ_{tEIC} is neither monotone nor submodular.*

PROOF. For the proof we will construct a graph sequence $\mathcal{G}$ for which the function σ_{tEIC} is neither monotone nor submodular. For simplicity we will assume that all diffusion probabilities p_{uv}^t are 1, that is, if an edge (u, v) is present in the graph then it will cause the activation of a node. The set of nodes V consists of $N + 6$ nodes, $V = \{v_1, \ldots v_6, u_1, \cdots, u_N\}$, and we have a sequence of 4 graphs G^1, G^2, G^3, G^4 on these nodes. The sequence for $N = 3$ is shown in Figure 2. The four graphs are identical except for the fact that in G^3 there is also the edge (v_3, v_4). A key property of the sequence is that nodes $u_1, \ldots, u_N$ are connected only to node v_4.

Figure 3 shows the diffusion process for the initiator set $\mathcal{I} = \{v_1^0\}$. The dark (red) colored nodes are active nodes that are infectious when entering a given step. The light (cyan) colored nodes are the ones that are activated at that step, and will become infectious in the next step. The nodes with the heavy border are active nodes that are no longer infectious. The spread of the diffusion is equal to the number of colored nodes (any color) in graph G^4. Through the chain of activations of nodes v_1, v_2, v_3, v_4 at time-steps $t = 0, 1, 2, 3$ respectively, node v_4 is infectious at time $t = 4$, and it activates nodes $u_1, ..., u_N$. The resulting spread is $\sigma_{\text{tEIC}}(\{v_1^0\}) = N + 3$.

Consider now the addition of node v_5^0 to the set $\mathcal{I}$. Figure 4 shows the diffusion process in our example. The activation of v_5 at time $t = 0$ causes node v_3 to be activated at time $t = 1$. Node v_3 is infectious at time $t = 2$, but it has no neighbors. At time $t = 3$, node v_3 becomes connected to v_4, but it is no longer infectious, so it can not activate it. Furthermore, the diffusion that stared from node v_1 now stops at node v_2 and does not proceed any further. Intuitively, the activation of node v_5 at time $t = 0$ causes a premature activation of the node v_3 which then *blocks* the diffusion initiated at node v_1. Therefore, we have that $\sigma_{\text{tEIC}}(\{v_1^0, v_5^0\}) = 4 < \sigma_{tEIC}(\{v_1^0\})$ proving that σ_{tEIC} is not monotone.

The same sequence can be used to prove that σ_{tEIC} is not submodular. Consider the addition of node v_6^0 to the initiator set $\mathcal{I} = \{v_1^0\}$. The activation of node v_6 will cause the nodes v_4 and $u_1, ..., u_N$ to be activated earlier, however it has no effect on the overall spread since these nodes would have been activated anyway. Therefore, the increase in spread is $\sigma_{\text{tEIC}}(\{v_1^0, v_6^0\}) - \sigma_{\text{tEIC}}(\{v_1^0\}) = 1$, corresponding to the activation of v_6. However, adding v_6^0 to the initiator set $\mathcal{I} = \{v_1^0, v_5^0\}$ results in activating $N + 1$ additional nodes, whose activation was previously blocked. Thus, $\sigma_{\text{tEIC}}(\{v_1^0, v_5^0, v_6^0\}) - \sigma_{\text{tEIC}}(\{v_1^0, v_5^0\}) = N + 3$, meaning that σ_{tEIC} is not submodular. $\square$

The example demonstrates the importance of timing in the activation of nodes in an evolving graph. Node v_3 must become active at *exactly* time $t = 2$ in order to activate v_4 at $t = 3$, which in turn can activate nodes $u_1, ..., u_N$ at time $t = 4$. Diffusions originated from different nodes in the graph act competitively, and it is possible for one diffusion to block another, thus reducing the overall spread. Clearly, the tEIC model is *timing-sensitive*.

5.1.2 Persistent EIC Model

In the second variant of the model, we assume that the item to be diffused, and the interest of the nodes in the item are *persistent*. A node u that becomes active at time t is given a chance to activate another node v at the first time instance after t that u and v become connected. For example, in a social network, a user that adopts a product will show it to her friends the first time that they meet, affecting their decision process. We refer to this model as the *Persistent Evolving Independent Cascade* model, and we denote it by pEIC.

Formally, consider a node u that becomes active at time t. For a node v, let $t_{uv} \geq t$ denote the earliest time instance after time t where there is an edge between u and v (t_{uv} is not defined if there is no such edge). If v is not active at time t_{uv}, node u tries to activate v with probability $p_{uv}^{t_{uv}}$. If not successful it will not attempt to activate v again for any $t' > t_{uv}$.

For the persistent EIC model we can prove that the spread function is monotone and submodular when the activation probabilities per edge are constant over time, that is, $p_{uv}^t =$

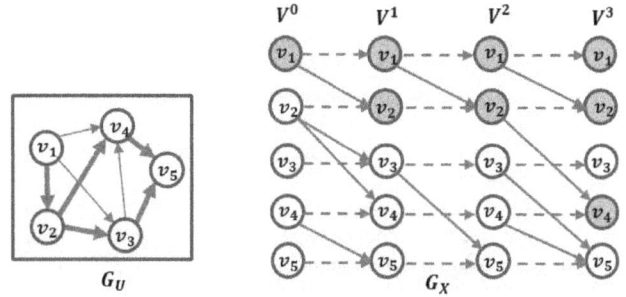

Figure 5: The union graph G_U, and the expanded graph G_X for the graph sequence in Figure 1.

p_{uv} for every edge (u, v), for all graph instances G^t, where $(u, v) \in E^t$. We say in this case that the graph sequence has *fixed probabilities*.

For the proof we make use of the union graph $G_U = (V, E_U)$ defined in Section 3, consisting of the union of all the graphs in the sequence. Similar to the work in [15], we assume that all random choices are made in advance. That is, for each edge $(u, v) \in E_U$, we make it "live" (active) with probability p_{uv}. Note that although an edge (u, v) may appear in multiple graph instances, it is used for the diffusion process exactly once, at time t_{uv}. Since, the probability p_{uv} is the same for all graph instances, we can assume that the decision to make the edge live is made in advance. We use $E_U^L \subseteq E_U$ to denote the set of live edges.

We will now create a graph that *unfolds* the graph sequence and the diffusion process into a single graph. A similar construction is described in [15]. We refer to this graph as the *expanded* graph $G_X = (V_X, E_X)$. The graph G_X consists of $n + 1$ layers of $|V|$ nodes, where the edges of graph G^i are placed between the nodes of layer $i - 1$ and i. Formally, let V^i denote the i-th layer of nodes, where $i = 0, 1, ..., n$. For each node $v \in V$ there is a corresponding node v^i in layer i. For every (directed) edge (u, v) in graph G^i we add an edge (u^{i-1}, v^i) to the set of edges E_X if it is also one of the live edges in E_U^L. Furthermore, we add a set of *transition* edges of the form (v^{i-1}, v^i) for all $v \in V$ and all layers $i = 0, 1, ..., n$.

An example of our construction for the sequence of three graphs in Figure 1 is shown in Figure 5. The bold edges in the union graph G_U correspond to the live edges E_U^L. The expanded graph G_X has four layers of nodes V^0, V^1, V^2, V^3. The dashed edges correspond to the transition edges of the graph G_X, and the solid edges correspond to the live edges in E_U^L. The shaded nodes show an example of the diffusion, when $\mathcal{I} = \{v_1^0\}$. As we will show below, the activated nodes are the ones reachable from node v_1^0 in graph G_X.

THEOREM 1. *For all instances of the persistent EIC model on a graph sequence with fixed probabilities, the spread function σ_{pEIC} is monotone and submodular.*

PROOF. Given a set of live edges, we will prove by induction that for a set of initiators $\mathcal{I}$, the set of active nodes at time-step A^t is the same as the set of nodes in V^t in graph G_X that are reachable from $\mathcal{I}$. The claim is trivially true for time-step $t = 0$. Assume that it is true at time $t - 1$. Consider now time-step t. First note that thanks to the transition edges, any node u that is reachable at $t - 1$ will remain reachable at t. If a node v becomes active at time t

then there must be an active node u in A^{t-1} that gets connected with v for the first time since u became active, and edge (u,v) is live. Since u is reachable, v will also become reachable. If v becomes reachable at time t then this means that at time t it became connected with a live edge with a reachable node u. Since u is active, this means that v will also become active.

Reachability defines a monotone and submodular function. Therefore, the expected spread σ_{pEIC} can be written as a linear combination of monotone and submodular functions, and thus it is also monotone and submodular. $\square$

In Figure 5 we can see the set of reachable nodes from the set $A^0 = \{v_1^0\}$, and the time-step at which each node is activated. Note that reachability in the graph G_X is different from reachability in the graph $G_U^L = (V, E_U^L)$ through live edges. In our example, in the G_U^L graph, all nodes are reachable from v_1 through live edges. However, in the graph G_X node v_3 never becomes reachable, since at the time that v_2 is activated the edge (v_2, v_3) no longer appears in the graph.

From the proof and the discussion above, it is clear that the best time to activate a node u in the pEIC model is at the beginning of the diffusion process, since this maximizes the chances of u to meet other nodes in the future. We can prove by induction that the pEIC model on a graph sequence with fixed probabilities is *timing-insensitive*.

However, monotonicity and submodularity properties do not hold if the activation probabilities vary over time.

LEMMA 2. *The function σ_{pEIC} is neither monotone nor submodular for arbitrary graph sequences.*

PROOF. The proof is similar to that for the tEIC model. We use the same graph sequence as in Figure 2 except for the fact that in graph G_2 we have an additional edge (v_3, v_4) with activation probability ε. All other activation probabilities are 1. As before, if we activate node v_1 at time $t = 0$, we have spread $\sigma_{pEIC}(\{v_1^0\}) = N+3$. If we add v_5 to the initiator set, the diffusion reaches node v_3 at time $t = 1$. As a result the first time that v_3 connects with v_4 is at time $t = 2$, where the activation probability of edge (v_3, v_4) is ε. The expected spread in this case is $\sigma_{pEIC}(\{v_1^0, v_3^0\}) = \varepsilon(N+1)+4$. It follows that σ_{pEIC} is not monotone. Using the same argument as in the previous proof we can show that it is also not submodular. $\square$

The intuition behind this counter-example is similar to that for the tEIC model in Section 5.1.1. Since the activation probability of (v_3, v_4) varies over time, it is important to time the activation of node v_3 appropriately, so that it gets activated when the edge activation probability is high. Otherwise, similar to before, the diffusion is blocked. The variation in the activation probabilities makes the pEIC model timing-sensitive.

5.2 Evolving LT Model

Given a static graph $G = (V, E)$, the LT model assumes that every edge (u,v) in E is associated with a weight b_{uv}, such that for any node $v \in V$, the weight of its incoming edges sums to a value less than 1. In diffusion under the LT model, each node has a threshold θ_v chosen uniformly at random in the interval $[0, 1]$. If (u, v) is an incoming edge to v, and u is active, we say that (u, v) is *live*. Node v is activated when the sum of weights over the live edges exceeds the threshold θ_v.

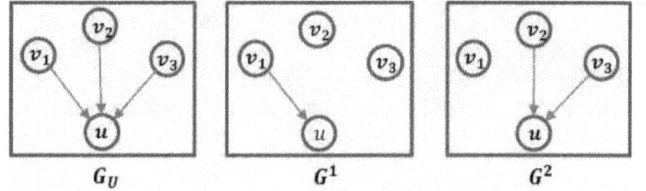

Figure 6: A counter-example for ELT submodularity.

In the case of an evolving graph, let $G_U = (V, E_U)$ denote the union graph defined in Section 3. Similar to the static case we assume that every edge (u, v) in E_U is associated with a weight b_{uv} independent of the time that the edge appears in the graph sequence. We also assume that for any node $v \in V$, we have that

$$\sum_{u:(u,v)\in E_U} b_{uv} \le 1$$

The threshold of a node is defined in the same way as for the static case.

Similar to the EIC model, we will consider two variations of the LT model for the case of evolving graphs that differ in the mechanism used for node activations. We will collectively refer to these models as the *Evolving Linear Threshold* model, and denote it by ELT.

5.2.1 Transient ELT Model

In this model, the diffusion process is similar to that in the static graph, but the total incoming weight of live edges is computed only over the live edges that are all present in a single graph instance. This model captures again a transient diffusion process, where a node is affected only by the neighbors present in a graph instance, and their influence dies off when not present. We refer to this model as the *Transient Evolving Linear Threshold* model, and denote it by tELT.

Formally, for a node v, let N_v^t denote the set of incoming neighbors of v at time t. Recall that A^t is the set of active nodes at time t, and let $\text{NA}_v^t = N_v^t \cap A^t$ denote the active neighbors of v at time t. Now, let W_v^t denote the total weight incoming to node v from live edges at time t. That is,

$$W_v^t = \sum_{u \in \text{NA}_v^t} b_{uv} \qquad (1)$$

A node v becomes active at time t if $W_v^t \ge \theta_v$.

We can prove by induction that σ_{tELT} is *monotone*, and *timing-insensitive* (i.e., the best time to activate a node is at time $t = 0$). We omit the proofs due to space constraints. Below we prove that σ_{tELT} is *not* submodular.

LEMMA 3. *The function σ_{tELT} is not submodular.*

PROOF. For the proof we use a simple example shown in Figure 6. There are two snapshots in the graph sequence G^1 and G^2, shown in the middle and right pane respectively. The left pane shows the union graph G_U. We assume that $b_{v_i,u} = 1/3$, for all edges (v_i, u). In this graph, it is clear that the only node that can be activated via the diffusion process is node u. Let $\Pr[u|\mathcal{I}]$ denote the probability that node u is active at the end of diffusion, given a set of initiator nodes $\mathcal{I} \subseteq \{v_1, v_2, v_3\}$. The expected diffusion spread is $\sigma_{tELT}(\mathcal{I}) = |\mathcal{I}| + \Pr[u|\mathcal{I}]$. Consider now the case that

130

$\mathcal{I} = \{v_1\}$. Clearly, u can only be activated in snapshot G^1, and this happens if $\theta_u \leq 1/3$. Therefore, $\Pr[u|\{v_1\}] = \Pr[\theta_u \leq 1/3] = 1/3$. Consider now the addition of node v_2 to the initiator set. Since the edges (v_1, u) and (v_2, u) do not appear in the same snapshot, we still need $\theta_u \leq 1/3$ in order for u to be activated. That is, $\Pr[u|\{v_1, v_2\}] = 1/3$. In a completely symmetric fashion, $\Pr[u|\{v_1, v_3\}] = 1/3$. Consider now the initiator set $\mathcal{I} = \{v_1, v_2, v_3\}$. In this case, node u is activated if $\theta_u \leq 2/3$, since the total weight of the live edges in G^2 is $2/3$, $\Pr[u|\{v_1, v_2, v_3\}] = 2/3$. Therefore, $\sigma_{\mathrm{tELT}}(\{v_1, v_3\}) - \sigma_{\mathrm{tELT}}(\{v_1\}) = 0$ while $\sigma_{\mathrm{tELT}}(\{v_1, v_2, v_3\}) - \sigma_{\mathrm{tELT}}(\{v_1, v_2\}) = 1/3$. That is, the addition of node v_3 to the set $\{v_1, v_2\}$ has a greater effect than the addition of v_3 to $\{v_1\}$. Hence, $\sigma_{\mathrm{tELT}}(\mathcal{I})$ is not submodular. $\quad\square$

5.2.2 Persistent ELT Model

In this model, we assume that influence *persists* over time. A node *accumulates* the influence of the active nodes it has met in the past. When the accumulated influence crosses the node's threshold it becomes activated. This is a reasonable model to capture the scenario where a user in a social network, who is interested in an item, collects opinions over time, and when the peer pressure exceeds her threshold, she makes the decision to adopt. We call this model *Persistent Evolving Linear Threshold* model, and denote it by pELT.

Formally, we define $\mathrm{CNA}_v^t = \cup_{\tau=1}^t \mathrm{NA}_v^\tau$ to be the set of active neighbors of v at any time up to t, and we use W_v^t to denote the total weight accumulated by the node v up to time t. That is,

$$W_v^t = \sum_{u \in \mathrm{CNA}_v^t} b_{uv} \qquad (2)$$

A node v becomes active at time t if $W_v^t \geq \theta_v$.

We will now show that for the persistent ELT model the spread function σ_{pELT} is monotone and submodular. The proof works by showing that the diffusion process is equivalent to reachability in the expanded graph G_X defined in Section 5.1.2. The set of live edges E_U^L in the case of the pELT model is defined in the same way as in [15]: Given the union graph G_U, for every node $v \in V$ we randomly select a *single* edge $(u, v) \in E_U$ with probability b_{uv}. With probability $1 - \sum_{(u,v) \in E_U} b_{uv}$ no edge is selected. This selection is performed for each of the nodes in V to define the set of live edges E_U^L. The diffusion then happens deterministically through the live edges on the graph G_X. A node connected with a live edge to an active node gets immediately activated.

Figure 7 shows the union graph for the example graph sequence in Figure 1, and the selected live edges. Note that, different from the EIC model, each node has exactly one incoming live edge. The expanded graph G_X is shown in the right part of the figure. The shaded nodes show the diffusion, when $\mathcal{I} = \{v_1^0\}$. We can show that the activated nodes are the ones reachable from node v_1^0 in graph G_X. Note again that reachability in the graph G_X is different from reachability in the graph $G_U^L = (V, E_U^L)$ through live edges.

THEOREM 2. *For all instances of the persistent ELT model the spread function σ_{pELT} is monotone and submodular.*

PROOF. The proof follows closely the one in [15], by showing by induction that the conditional distribution over the activated nodes at time $t = n$ given a set of initiators $\mathcal{I}$

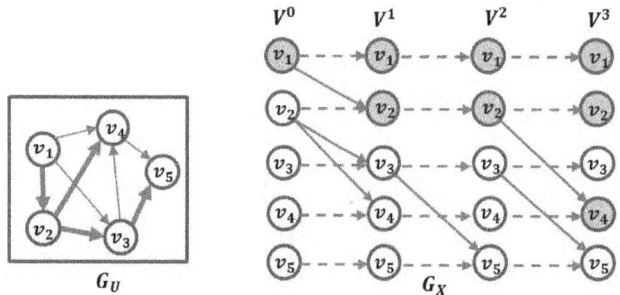

Figure 7: The union graph G_U, and the expanded graph G_X for the graph sequence in Figure 1.

is the same as the distribution over the reachable nodes at layer V^n from the set $\mathcal{I}$. We omit the details due to lack of space. Given that the reachability function is monotone and submodular, it follows that the function $\sigma_{\mathrm{pELT}}(\mathcal{I})$ can be expressed as a linear combination of monotone and submodular functions, and hence it is also monotone and submodular. $\quad\square$

It is also straightforward to see that the σ_{pELT} function is timing-insensitive, that is, the best time to activate the initiators is at time $t = 0$. This follows from the fact that nodes accumulate weight over time.

5.3 Summary of Model Properties

Table 1 summarizes our theoretical results regarding the properties of the diffusion spread function for the transient and persistent EIC and ELT models.

Table 1: Summary of the properties of the spread function for the evolving diffusion models.

	Timing	Monotone	Submodular
tEIC	sensitive	no	no
pEIC (fixed pr)	insensitive	yes	yes
pEIC (general)	sensitive	no	no
tELT	insensitive	yes	no
pELT	insensitive	yes	yes

6. EXPERIMENTAL EVALUATION

In this section, our goal is to evaluate experimentally how the diffusion spread is affected by network evolution using real datasets. We first describe the algorithms we use for the influence maximization problem, the datasets, and the experimental setup. We then present the evaluation results.

6.1 Algorithms

The algorithm most commonly used for diffusion maximization in static networks is Greedy. Greedy takes as input a candidate set of nodes C and a value k, and it selects a set $\mathcal{I}$ of k nodes to be activated. It proceeds iteratively, where at each iteration it computes for each candidate node the marginal increase in the expected spread that results by adding the node to $\mathcal{I}$. This is estimated by performing a large number of Monte-Carlo simulations of the diffusion process and taking the average spread. The node that causes the maximum marginal increase is added to $\mathcal{I}$ and removed

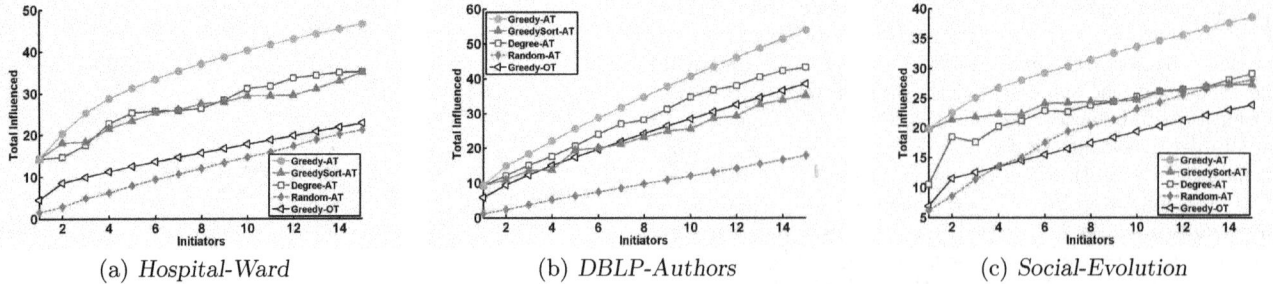

| (a) Hospital-Ward | (b) DBLP-Authors | (c) Social-Evolution |

Figure 8: Influence spread of the any-time algorithms for the Transient Evolving Independent Cascade model.

from the candidate set C. The process continues until k nodes are selected.

For submodular functions, the greedy algorithm provides a constant factor approximation guarantee. Despite the fact that, for evolving graphs, the spread function is not submodular for all models, the greedy algorithm is still a natural algorithm to consider.

To study the effect of timing of activation to the diffusion spread, we consider two variants of the Greedy algorithm by varying the set C of candidate initiators. The more general case is to have $C = V_T = \{v^t : v \in V, t = 0, ..., n-1\}$, that is, to be able to activate nodes at any graph instance. A node is activated once at the selected time instance. We will refer to this greedy algorithm as Greedy-AT (Greedy-Any-Time). The other variant corresponds to the typical setting in diffusion maximization which assumes that all initiators must be activated at a single time-step, namely at the beginning of the diffusion or evolution process. This is a reasonable setting in a viral marketing scenario, where an advertising budget is allocated to be used at a specific time-frame. In this case the set of candidates $C = \{v^0 : v \in V\}$ is the set of nodes V at time $t = 0$. We will refer to this greedy algorithm as Greedy-OT (Greedy-One-Time). We note that the comparison between Greedy-AT and Greedy-OT is of interest only for the EIC models that are time-sensitive. The ELT models are timing-insensitive, so the optimal activation time is at time $t = 0$.

For selecting each of the k initiators, Greedy runs for each of the $|C|$ candidates R simulations of the difussion process. Assuming that diffusion has complexity D, Greedy-AT runs in $O(kn|V|RD)$ and Greedy-OT in $O(k|V|RD)$ time, where n is the number of graphs in the sequence.

6.2 Datasets and Experimental Setup

We consider datasets from three real evolving networks. For each dataset, nodes correspond to users, and edges to interactions between them. All edges have time-stamps within a time period $\mathcal{T}$. We construct a graph sequence $\mathcal{G} = \{G^1, ..., G^n\}$ by breaking up the time period $\mathcal{T}$ into n intervals of equal length. The graph G^t captures all user interactions within the t-th time interval. If more than one interaction occurs between two users within interval t, multiple edges are created between the corresponding nodes in the graph. We provide next a short description of our datasets.

The Hospital-Ward dataset[1] [22] contains the network of contacts between 46 health-care workers and 20 patients of a

hospital ward for 4 days in December 2010. We construct a sequence of 16 graphs, where each graph represents a time-frame of 6 hours. The union graph G_U of this dataset is very dense and includes a central node adjacent to about 80% of the nodes. All graphs in the sequence are sparse with fluctuating degrees, following the day and night-time habits of the hospital residents.

The DBLP-Authors dataset corresponds to the co-authorship graph of authors that have published papers in a major data mining, database or theory conferences between 2004 and 2013 downloaded from DBLP[2]. We include only authors that have published in at least three distinct years during this period resulting in 1,249 authors. We construct a graph sequence of 10 graphs, where each graph represents collaborations within a single year. All graphs are sparse and highly fragmented.

The Social-Evolution dataset[3] [20] reports meetings between college students in an undergraduate dormitory based on mobile phones usage. The probability of two users meeting at a specific time instant is estimated using bluetooth information and proximity to WiFi access points. Thus each edge e is annotated with a time-stamp T and a probability q_e. We select all interactions in the first week of October 2008 and create a sequence of 7 graphs, where each graph corresponds to one day. There are 48 nodes. We view this graph sequence as a typical example of the weekly pattern of interactions of a group of users. All graphs in the sequence are connected and relatively dense except from the first one which contains few nodes and edges.

When simulating the diffusion process for the EIC model, we set $p = 0.01$ for the propagation probabilities of the edges, except for the DBLP-Authors network which is extremely sparse, for which we use $p = 0.1$. Note that due to the variation in the multiplicity of edges, the activation probabilities vary over time, making the persistent EIC model timing-sensitive. For the ELT model, the weight b_{uv} is set equal to the fraction of the edges incident on v in the union graph that are between u and v. Finally, R is equal to 10,000.

6.3 Results

We address two fundamental issues: (1) How does the timing of the activation of the influencers affect the diffusion spread? (2) Does the evolution of the network affect the estimation of the spread?

[1] http://www.sociopatterns.org

[2] http://dblp.uni-trier.de/xml/
[3] http://realitycommons.media.mit.edu/

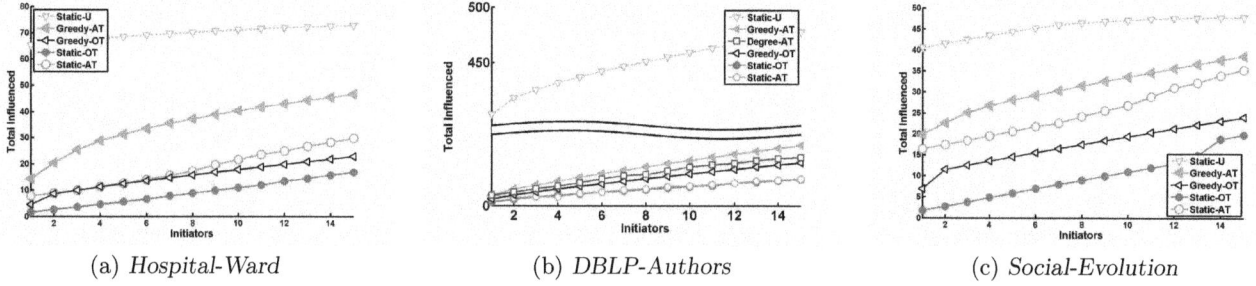

(a) *Hospital-Ward*   (b) *DBLP-Authors*   (c) *Social-Evolution*

Figure 9: Influence spread of static algorithms for the Transient Evolving Independent Cascade model.

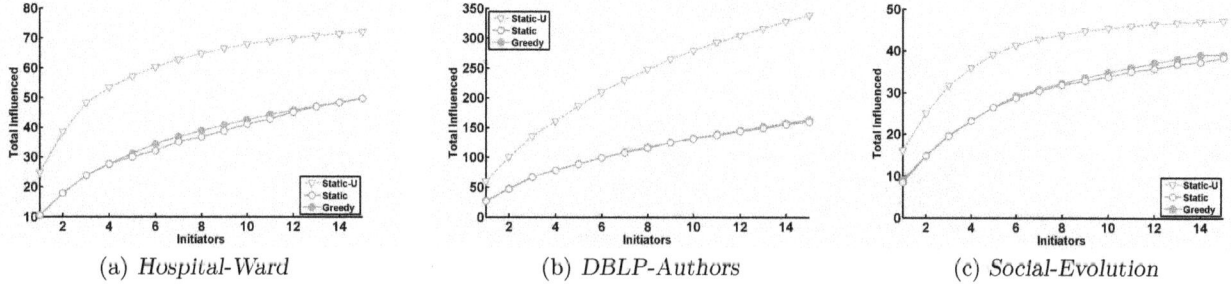

(a) *Hospital-Ward*   (b) *DBLP-Authors*   (c) *Social-Evolution*

Figure 10: Influence spread of the static algorithms for the Transient Evolving Linear Threshold model.

Timing of activations: We first look into the importance of timing in activating an initiator. For this experiment, we only consider the EIC model which is time-sensitive. Figure 8 shows the spread of the different algorithms as a function of the number of initiators for the transient EIC model. The first observation is that Greedy-AT significantly outperforms Greedy-OT. To stress the importance of timing we also consider two weaker any-time algorithms: the GreedySort-AT algorithm runs a single iteration of Greedy-AT and returns the k nodes with the highest spread; the Degree-AT algorithm selects as initiators the k nodes with the highest degree at any graph instance. We also consider Random that outputs a random selection of initiators at any graph snapshot.

We observe that all any-time algorithms, even the simple heuristics, outperform the Greedy-OT algorithm. In *Social-Evolution* and *Hospital-Ward*, Greedy-OT performs close or worse than random. It is competitive only on the *DBLP-Authors* dataset. The reason is that for both *Social-Evolution* and *Hospital-Ward*, the graphs become denser at later times, whereas, for *DBLP-Authors*, the graphs are so sparse that the timing of influence has a smaller effect. Even in this case though the Greedy-AT and Degree-AT algorithms perform noticeably better. It is interesting to point out that in the *Social-Evolution* the Degree-AT exhibits non-monotonic behavior. This is due to the effect of "blocking" that we described in Section 5.1. Our results clearly demonstrate the importance of the activation time of a node.

Our experiments with the the persistent EIC model show that the effect of timing is not noticeable for the specific datasets we consider (see Figure 11), most probably because the activation probabilities do not differ significantly over time.

Evolution-agnostic vs evolution-aware diffusion: Although most real-life networks evolve over time, most existing work on diffusion views the network as a static object and estimates the spread of influence and the set of initiators on a static graph, more specifically on the union graph G_U. We now compare such estimates with those obtained on the full graph sequence. In particular, we want to study (a) how accurate is the estimation of spread on the union graph compared to that obtained on the graph sequence, and (b) how good are the initiators computed for the static case when used on the dynamic graph.

For this experiment, we run the Greedy algorithm on the union graph G_U and select a set $\mathcal{I}$ of k initiators. We use Static-U to denote the spread obtained by using the selected set $\mathcal{I}$ on the *union graph G_U* (recall that the union graph is the graph with edge set the union of all edges in all snapshots). This is an optimistic estimation of the actual influence spread, assuming that all edges are present at all times. We then use the set $\mathcal{I}$ on the graph sequence $\mathcal{G}$ and compute the spread under the evolving diffusion model. For the EIC model, we use Static-OT to denote the algorithm that activates the nodes in $\mathcal{I}$ at time $t = 0$, and Static-AT to denote the algorithm that activates each node in $\mathcal{I}$ at the best time instant t, so that it (individually) achieves maximum spread. For the ELT model the best activation time is always $t = 0$, so we use Static to denote this algorithm.

Figures 9 and 10 show the results of the above algorithms for the transient EIC and ELT models respectively and Figures 11 and 12 for the persistent EIC and ELT models respectively. Note that in the pEIC case the curves for Static-OT and Static-AT, and Greedy-OT and Greedy-AT are almost identical. As we discussed before, the pEIC model is essentially timing-insensitive in our experiments.

133

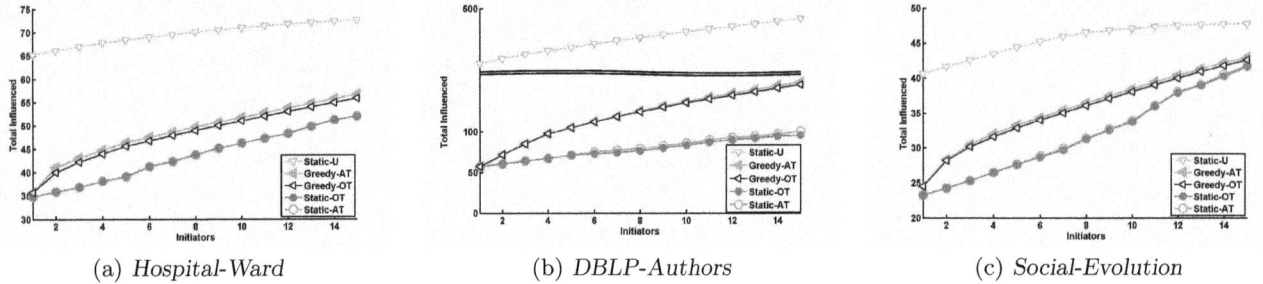

| (a) *Hospital-Ward* | (b) *DBLP-Authors* | (c) *Social-Evolution* |

Figure 11: Influence spread of static algorithms for the Persistent Evolving Independent Cascade model.

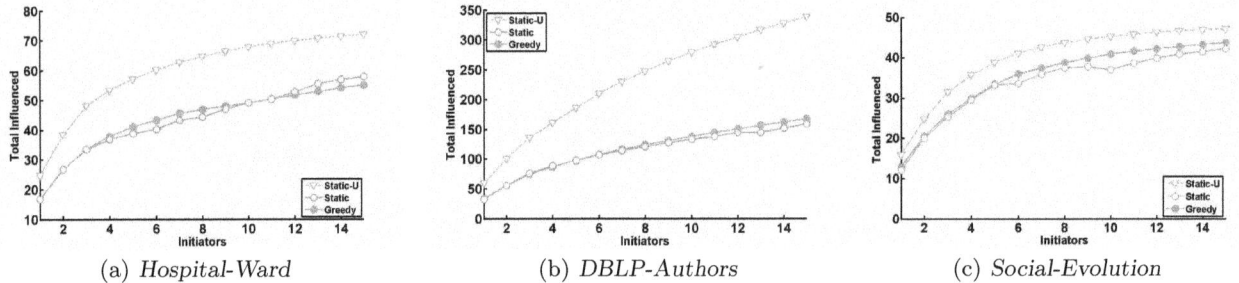

| (a) *Hospital-Ward* | (b) *DBLP-Authors* | (c) *Social-Evolution* |

Figure 12: Influence spread of the static algorithms for the Persistent Evolving Linear Threshold model.

A first observation is that the diffusion spread is severely over-estimated when using the union graph. Static-U achieves spread that is an order of magnitude higher than that of Greedy-AT. This is especially pronounced in the *DBLP-Authors* dataset which is highly fragmented. For any practical application that wants to make decisions based on the size of spread, using the static graph will yield a very poor estimate of the true diffusion on the evolving graph.

A second observation is that, when using the initiator set obtained for the static graph on the evolving graph, performance is poor, especially for the EIC model. Static-OT is clearly the worst algorithm indicating that the static union graph is a poor indicator of how the diffusion will progress on the evolving graph. Note though that the results can be significantly improved for the EIC model by adding some amount of time information. Static-AT achieves competitive performance, being the second best algorithm for the *Social-Evolution* dataset. Therefore, although the static graph provides some signal about which nodes are good initiators, it is important to time appropriately the activation of these initiators for the signal to be of any use. These differences are less evident in the ELT model. In this case, the initiators on the static graph perform well on the evolving graph sequence. This is reasonable given the activation mechanism of the model.

Another observation is with regards to the differences between persistent and transient diffusion models. In general, as expected, the actual spread of influence under the persistent models is larger than that of the corresponding transient variant, and slightly closer to the estimation obtained on the static graph.

7. DISCUSSION AND CONCLUSIONS

In this paper, we studied the problem of influence maximization on dynamic networks, where the network evolves while the diffusion process is in progress. We proposed the Evolving Independent Cascade (EIC) and the Evolving Linear Threshold (ELT) diffusion models, and studied them theoretically and experimentally. Our work reveals that there are key differences between diffusion in static and evolving graphs, both in theory and in practice, and that it is wrong to ignore the dynamic nature of the network. Our evolving models that incorporate the importance of timing in diffusion result in a fundamentally different diffusion process.

We note that in our problem definition we assume that the entire graph sequence is known in advance. It would be interesting to study diffusion on dynamic graphs that evolve following specific patterns, for example weekly ones [6]. Furthermore, instead of estimating the diffusion spread using the actual graph sequence, one could provide approximate estimations, e.g., based on studies of how real graphs evolve over time and corresponding graph generation models, such as those in [17]. Another approach would be to design algorithms that have only partial information about the future, e.g., only a subset of the future edges, or a window of the m next graphs. It would be interesting to understand and quantify the tradeoff between the amount of information available and the success of the initiator selection. Finally, it would be interesting to understand and analyze online algorithms for the problem.

Another possible direction for future work is to study in more detail the relationship between diffusion time and evolution time. Dynamic processes on dynamic graphs have been studied in the past (e.g., see [11] for random walks on dynamic graphs) and it would be interesting to investigate if such mathematical tools could be applied to the diffusion problem. Finally, we note that the greedy algorithm needs to run a large number of simulations for all candidate nodes to estimate the spread, making it computationally expensive. Recently, sketching algorithms have been proposed for the influence maximization problem in static graphs [7]. It would be interesting to consider such algorithms for the case of evolving graphs.

Acknowledgments

This work is supported by the Marie Curie Reintegration Grant project titled JMUGCS which has received research funding from the European Union.

8. REFERENCES

[1] C. C. Aggarwal, S. Lin, and P. S. Yu. On influential node discovery in dynamic social networks. In *SDM*, 2012.

[2] A. Albano, J.-L. Guillaume, S. Heymann, and B. L. Grand. A matter of time - intrinsic or extrinsic - for diffusion in evolving complex networks. In *ASONAM*, 2013.

[3] W. Chen, W. Lu, and N. Zhang. Time-critical influence maximization in social networks with time-delayed diffusion process. In *AAAI*, 2012.

[4] W. Chen, C. Wang, and Y. Wang. Scalable influence maximization for prevalent viral marketing in large-scale social networks. In *KDD*, 2010.

[5] W. Chen, Y. Yuan, and L. Zhang. Scalable influence maximization in social networks under the linear threshold model. In *ICDM*, 2010.

[6] E. Cho, S. A. Myers, and J. Leskovec. Friendship and mobility: user movement in location-based social networks. In *KDD*, 2011.

[7] E. Cohen, D. Delling, T. Pajor, and R. F. Werneck. Sketch-based influence maximization and computation: Scaling up with guarantees. In *CIKM*, 2014.

[8] P. Domingos and M. Richardson. Mining the network value of customers. In *KDD*, 2001.

[9] N. Du, L. Song, M. Gomez-Rodriguez, and H. Zha. Scalable influence estimation in continuous-time diffusion networks. In *NIPS*, 2013.

[10] D. Easley and J. Kleinberg. *Networks, Crowds, and Markets: Reasoning About a Highly Connected World*. Cambridge University Press, 2010.

[11] D. R. Figueiredo, P. Nain, B. F. Ribeiro, E. de Souza e Silva, and D. Towsley. Characterizing continuous time random walks on time varying graphs. In *SIGMETRICS/Performance*, 2012.

[12] J. Goldenberg, B. Libai, and E. Muller. Talk of the Network: A Complex Systems Look at the Underlying Process of Word-of-Mouth. *Marketing Letters*, pages 211–223, Aug. 2001.

[13] M. Gomez-Rodriguez, D. Balduzzi, and B. Schölkopf. Uncovering the temporal dynamics of diffusion networks. In *ICML*, 2011.

[14] M. Gomez-Rodriguez and B. Schölkopf. Influence maximization in continuous time diffusion networks. In *ICML*, 2012.

[15] D. Kempe, J. Kleinberg, and E. Tardos. Maximizing the spread of influence through a social network. In *KDD*, 2003.

[16] A. Krause and D. Golovin. Submodular function maximization. *Tractability: Practical Approaches to Hard Problems*, 3, 2012.

[17] J. Leskovec, J. M. Kleinberg, and C. Faloutsos. Graph evolution: Densification and shrinking diameters. *TKDD*, 1(1), 2007.

[18] J. Leskovec, A. Krause, C. Guestrin, C. Faloutsos, J. M. VanBriesen, and N. S. Glance. Cost-effective outbreak detection in networks. In *KDD*, 2007.

[19] B. Liu, G. Cong, D. Xu, and Y. Zeng. Time constrained influence maximization in social networks. In *ICDM*, 2012.

[20] A. Madan, M. Cebrián, S. T. Moturu, K. Farrahi, and A. Pentland. Sensing the "health state" of a community. *IEEE Pervasive Computing*, 11(4):36–45, 2012.

[21] G. Nemhauser, L. Wolsey, and M. Fisher. An analysis of the approximations for maximizing submodular set functions. *Mathematical Programming*, 1978.

[22] P. Vanhems et al. Estimating potential infection transmission routes in hospital wards using wearable proximity sensors. *PLoS ONE*, 8(9):e73970, 2013.

[23] B. A. Prakash, H. Tong, N. Valler, M. Faloutsos, and C. Faloutsos. Virus propagation on time-varying networks: Theory and immunization algorithms. In *ECML/PKDD*, 2010.

[24] E. Stattner, M. Collard, and N. Vidot. Diffusion in dynamic social networks: Application in epidemiology. In *DEXA (2)*, 2011.

[25] M. Xie, Q. Yang, Q. Wang, G. Cong, and G. de Melo. Dynadiffuse: A dynamic diffusion model for continuous time constrained influence maximization. In *AAAI*, 2015.

[26] H. Zhuang, Y. Sun, J. Tang, J. Zhang, and X. Sun. Influence maximization in dynamic social networks. In *ICDM*, 2013.

Process-driven Analysis of Dynamics in Online Social Interactions

Zhi Yang
Computer Science
Department
Peking University
Beijing, China
yangzhi@pku.edu.cn

Jilong Xue
Computer Science
Department
Peking University
Beijing, China
xjl@net.pku.edu.cn

Christo Wilson
College of Computer and
Information Science
Northeastern University
MA, USA
cbw@ccs.neu.edu

Ben Y. Zhao
Computer Science
Department
U. C. Santa Barbara
CA, USA
ravenben@cs.ucsb.edu

Yafei Dai
Computer Science
Department
Peking University
Beijing, China
dyf@pku.edu.cn

ABSTRACT

Measurement studies of online social networks show that all social links are not equal, and the strength of each link is best characterized by the frequency of interactions between the linked users. To date, few studies have been able to examine detailed interaction data over time, and studied the problem of modeling user interactions. A generative model can shed light on the fundamental processes that underlie user interactions.

In this paper, we analyze the first *complete* record of full interaction and network dynamics in a large online social network. Our dataset covers all wall posts, new user events, and new social link events during the first full year of Renren, the largest social network in China, including 623K new users, 8.2 million new links, and 29 million wall posts. Our analysis provides surprising insights into the evolution of user interactions over time. We find that users invite new friends to interact at a nearly constant rate, prefer to interact with friends with whom they share significant overlaps in social circles, and most social links drop in interaction frequency over time. We also validate our findings on Facebook, and show that they do generalize across OSNs.

We use our insights to derive a generative model of social interactions that accurately captures both our new results and previously observed network properties. Our model captures the inherently heterogeneous strengths of social links, and has broad implications on the design of social network algorithms such as friend recommendation, information diffusion and viral marketing.

1. INTRODUCTION

Without a doubt, online social networks (OSNs) have had an enormous impact on the lives of millions of people, and changed the way people communicate and interact online. For scientists in both engineering and social disciplines, OSNs offer a digital representation of human social behavior that is both overly-simplified and yet tantalizingly concrete, in the form of abstract social graphs that capture social network activity.

The last few years has seen the arrival of several measurement studies of user relationships and activities on popular OSNs, including Facebook [9, 25, 26], Twitter [7, 13], LinkedIn [18], Renren [15, 28] and others [5, 8, 22]. A common observation made across many platforms is that the presence of a social link connecting two users is a poor estimate of the "relationship strength" between them. Instead, many have proposed using the number or frequency of interactions on these networks to capture the strength of a social link [11, 27].

Despite this realization, we are still far from a real understanding of the processes that underlie user interactions. To capture strength of social links, recent studies proposed the use of weighted "interaction graphs" where each link is labeled with some measure of interaction frequency [8, 15, 26]. But these studies focus on a static view of interactions, and therefore only capture a small piece of the picture. Prior study [25] examined changing dynamics of user interactions on Facebook users, but was limited to a sample set of 60,000 users crawled from a single geographic network.

A deeper understanding of user interactions requires the formulation of a generative model, which can intuitively capture the processes that drive user interaction events. No generative graph model exists to explain properties observed in measured traces of user interactions, or to construct realistic arbitrary-sized user interaction traces. Not only would such a model advance our understanding of social networks, it would be immensely useful to a number of social network applications. For example, it can be used to make more accurate predictions in the link prediction problem [2], to reorder or filter user news feeds by accurately predicting the likelihood of specific user interactions, or improve resource planning by predicting about how data access patterns between users change over time.

In this paper, we seek to fill this void by building a model based on two large detailed traces of user interactions on *Renren* and *Facebook*. Our Renren trace covers over a year in length, and contains data on the creation of 600+K users, 8+Million new links, and 29+ Million interaction events. The Facebook dataset is a 1.6M node sample that includes 49M edges and 16M interactions. The

COSN'15, November 2–3, 2015, Palo Alto, California, USA.
ⓒ 2015 ACM. ISBN 978-1-4503-3951-3/15/11 ...$15.00.
DOI: http://dx.doi.org/10.1145/2817946.2817952.

core contribution of this paper is a new generative model that combines the growth of social links with the generation of user interaction events on those links. We use analysis of empirical data to understand and model the growth processes that lead to the observed network structure and link strength distributions.

We present detailed analysis of our growth data, and extract three processes that drive dynamics of social interaction during the network formation:

Forgetting process: A particular pair of users slowly decrease their interaction frequency over time. The potential reason is that users tend to forget each other as they cannot meet face to face on a regular basis, leading to the closeness between friends declined rapidly over time.

Reinforcement process: For each pair of users, the probability of continued interactions displays a memory reinforcement (inertia). In particular, the more two nodes interact with each other, the more it demonstrates a close relationship between them . Thus, the user are more likely to reinforce this relationship to counteract the forgetting process.

Exploration process: In order to replace existing ones which are no longer attractive, users continuously explore new interaction relationships at a nearly constant rate, irrespective of their age or degree. We find that users prefer to interact with friends with whom they share significant overlap in social circles (homophily). This reveals a positive correlation between social structure and interaction as complementary indicators of social closeness between individuals.

The above processes captures the fundamental fact that the interaction relationships require that we invest time to keep them alive, especially once it becomes physically difficult for friends to meet face to face on a regular basis.

Combining our new observations with previously studied processes of these networks, we propose a generative model for social and interaction networks. Our model is important for understanding how the pairwise user interaction and social network evolve together. It explains why the number of people a user communicate with does not scale linearly with the number of friends users declare, and also explains along which friendship links that interactions are more likely to occur. The model is directly useful in the future interaction prediction (*e.g.*, by taking a current existing network and further evolving it) and in the design of algorithms incorporating social influence and homophily effects (*e.g.*, by locating and highlighting stronger relationship).

In addition, our model can be used to construct interaction traces that can represent the full spectrum of relationship strengths (from weak to strong), which has not been captured by models before. This is an important application because real-world network datasets are often proprietary and hard to obtain. Controlling network parameters allows the generation of datasets with different properties which can be used for thorough exploration and evaluation of network analysis algorithms.

Our contributions include the following: First, we discover a number of new interrelated processes drive the evolution of social interactions. Second, we propose a co-evolution model that precisely captures both social link formation and user interactions afterwards. Finally, we provide a thorough evaluation of our model, showing that it produces realistic network evolution following the true evolution of network properties.

The remainder of this paper is organized as follows. Section 2 provides background and related work on the growth of social network and user interaction. Section 3 provides insights into the interaction evolution by observing Renren social network. Section 4

	Renren	Facebook
# of nodes	623,511	1,600,214
# of edges	8,266,149	48,949,304
Mean node degree	13.2	27.3
Mean path length	4.2	5.0
Mean clustering coefficient	0.18	0.19

Table 1: Properties of Renren and Facebook network

provides our evolution model that captures both social network and user interaction. Section 5 evaluates the accuracy of our model, and we finally conclude in Section 6.

2. PRELIMINARIES

In this section, we provide background on work related to the growth of OSNs, and then introduce our datasets.

2.1 Related Work

Previous studies on social network evolution mainly focus on friendship relations, and attempt to discover the underlying processes that produce properties observed in real networks. For example, the preferential attachment model [3] captures power-law degree distributions. The forest fire model [19] captures the densification and shrinking diameters over time. A recently proposed, microscopic evolution model [18] provides insights into the node and edge arrival processes, and confirms preferential attachment and triangle closure features. Similar conclusions were reached by studies on Flickr [20] and a social network aggregator [10]. Zhao et al. [31] study the early evolution of the Renren social network, and analyze its network dynamics at different granularities to determine their influence on individual users.

Another set of works begin to investigate the effect of node attributes on social network evolution. For example, Allamanis et al. [1] examine influence of spatial factors on the temporal evolution of online social ties. Gong et al. [12] study the influence of four attributes including school, major, employer and city. They found users share attributes are more likely to be connected, augmenting structure-based triangle closing.

However, these works on evolutionary process or growth models treat all friendship links as equal. In fact, a recent study [11] has demonstrated the strength of links varies widely, ranging from users' best friends to acquaintances. To differentiate links, interaction data has been utilized in predicting relationship strength [11,16,27].

While the recent studies [8, 21, 26] brought great insights into the structural difference between the interaction network the social network, little attention has been paid to the temporal evolution of pairwise user interactions. The study [25] examined user interactions dynamics on Facebook users, but no generative model has been developed to reveal the underlying processes driving user interaction dynamics. With respect to these results, our work provides a more systematic understanding of the evolution of user interaction behavior.

Prior works [4, 29] provide some models of traffic networks, whereas others [24,30] present a model for face-to-face interactions of users. Although these models generate interaction network, they are not suitable in the context of today's OSNs due to different underlying dynamics and network properties. Our work attempts to fill this void.

2.2 Social Dynamics and Interaction Data

To construct the interaction evolution model, the dataset should contain the information on both topology and interaction dynamics.

	Renren	Facebook
Period	2005.11~2006.12	2008.1~2009.6
# of wall posts along edges	23,000,141	16,313,273
# of interactions	7,697,270	3,233,780
# of users having interactions	420,978	324,430
# of edge having interactions	2,623,040	1,695,448

Table 2: Summary of Renren and Facebook interaction data

However, to our knowledge, there are no publicly available datasets satisfying this requirement. To fill this lack, this paper presents two datasets: [1]

Renren Dataset. With 120 million users, Renren is the largest and oldest online social network in China, and provides functionality and features similar to Facebook. Like Facebook, Renren first started in 2005 as a social network for college students in China, then saw its user population grow exponentially once it opened its doors to the non-student population. Like Facebook, Renren users maintain personal profiles and establish bidirectional friendship links with others. Below we use the term *edge* to mean a friendship link.

To study user interactions, Renren provides us two ground-truth datasets. The first dataset encompasses the timestamped creation events of all users and edges in the first year of Renren's growth. The dataset starts on Nov. 21, 2005 (when the first edge was created) and ends on Dec. 30, 2006. In all, it includes the creation times of 623,511 nodes and 8,266,149 edges. Table 1 shows the statistics of the social graph formed at the end of 2006.

The second dataset includes all 29,506,068 wall posts that occurred in our measurement period. To guarantee user privacy, we only get the anonymized IDs of sender and receiver for each wall post, without knowing the content. Since our goal is to characterize edge strength based on user interactions, we ignore the wall posts not along edges (e.g., greeting messages between strangers). As a result, we focus on the remaining 23,000,141 wall posts created along edge, representing the friendship maintenance effort of users (accounting for nearly 80% of the total wall posts).

Facebook Dataset. Our Facebook dataset comes from a complete crawl of a large regional network conducted in 2009 [26]. This crawl visited the 1.6M users in the region with default privacy settings (roughly half of the total population of the region). Each user's friend list and all interactions in the user's news feed between Jan. 1, 2008 and Jun. 30, 2009 were downloaded. These interactions cover a broad range of activities, with the most popular by far being wall posts and photo tags. Each interaction includes ther sender, receiver, and a timestamp. Table 1 lists the statistics of the dataset.

Unfortunately, the Facebook data is not as comprehensive as the Renren data. The Facebook data does not include creation timestamps of social links, thus we only focus on analyzing user interaction patterns on Facebook, not graph structural dynamics. Furthermore, the Facebook data includes social links and interactions with users outside the target regional network. Because these users were not crawled, our data on them is incomplete. Thus, in our analysis we focus exclusively on social links and interactions between users in the region.

Other Types of Interactions. Although our datasets focus on Wall posts and photo comments, modern OSNs may have many additional types of interactions, *e.g.* retweets, shares, *etc*. When our datasets were collected, Wall posts and photo comments were the most popular types of interactions on Renren and Facebook by a large margin, which is why we focus on them [26]. However, our model is general enough to incorporate other types of interactions.

2.3 Definitions and Dataset Cleaning

To better measure mutual relationship (tie strength) between users, we refer to a pair of reciprocal wall posts (or photo comments) as an *interaction*. For example, if node u sends m messages to v but receives n messages from v, the number of interactions between them is $\min(m, n)$. The wall posts that have not been replied are pruned. This definition means that u and v cannot be supposed to have strong mutual relationship if one sends many messages to the other but rarely receives replies (e.g., u trusts user v, but not necessarily vice versa). So we use the the number of interactions as a conservative estimate on the edge strength, instead of the total number of wall posts over the edge.

The interaction definition allows us to represent the interaction network evolution as a series of undirected, edge-weighted graphs $G_1, \ldots, G_T$, so that a snapshot G_t consists of the nodes, edges, and interactions that have arrived by time t. The term **interaction edge** represents the friendship edge along which at least one interaction is generated. We say a node u creates an interaction edge with a node v when u interacts with v for the first time, and we say v becomes one of u's interaction partners. We use the timestamp of an interaction as the creation time of the corresponding interaction edge.

Table 2 summarizes our Renren and Facebook interaction datasets. We see that Facebook users produce less than half as many interactions as Renren users, and fewer users and social edges are interactive. The reduced interactivity of Facebook users versus Renren users is very clear in our analysis in Section 3. However, as we will show, interactions on both OSNs still exhibit the same overall trends. Table 2 also shows that interaction edges only cover 32% and 3% of social edges on Renren and Facebook, respectively. This means that users only interact with a small subset of their friends.

3. ANALYSIS OF USER INTERACTIONS

In this section, we analyze the Renren and Facebook interaction data to uncover temporal patterns of user interactions. In particular, we want to answer three questions: First, at what rate do users choose new friends to interact with? Second, how do users choose which particular friend to begin interacting with? Finally, once a pair of users begin to interact, what are the temporal dynamics of the relationship? We shall leverage the answers to these questions to motivate the design of our generative model of user interactions.

3.1 Interaction Partners Addition

The first question we address is: what is the rate at which users add new interaction partners? Prior works [3, 18, 20] demonstrate that users accelerate the creation of social relations as their node degree (or age) increases, i.e., "rich-get-richer" type. Since users get friends more quickly, we want to examine whether they also ad-

---

[1] Available at http://net.pku.edu.cn\%7ezzh/data.

141

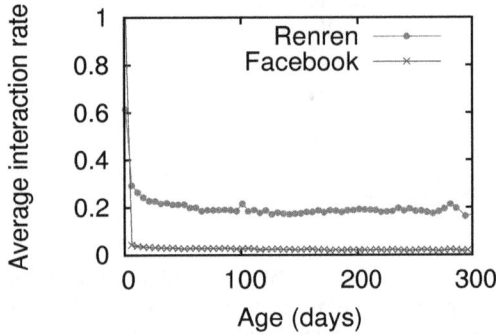

Figure 1: The average rate of adding new friends into interaction for nodes of different age.

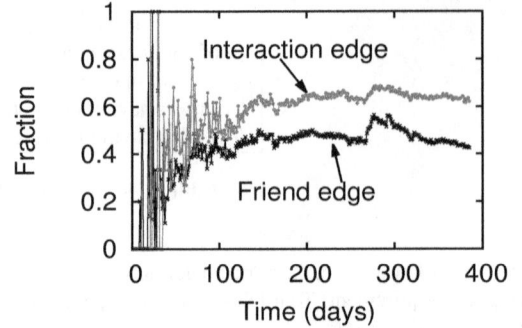

Figure 2: The fraction of friend and interaction edge creations targeting users with mutual friends in Renren.

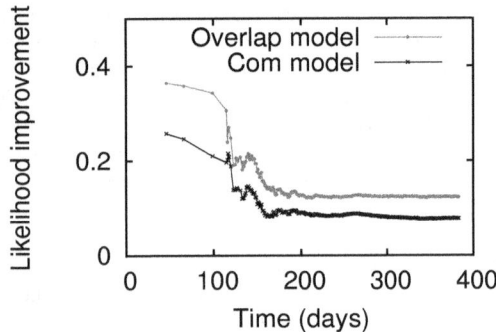

Figure 3: The likelihood improvement over the random selection in Renren.

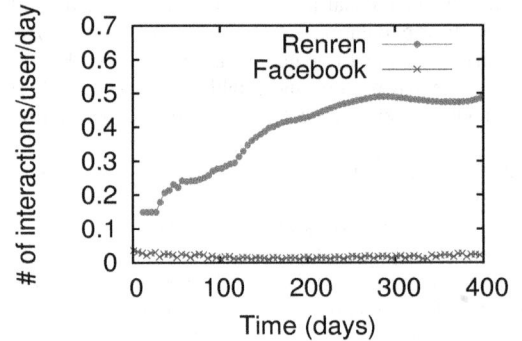

Figure 4: The average node-interaction frequency over time.

d interaction partners in an accelerate manner. Intuitively, making friends in an OSN is very easy, since the click of "add as friend" button does not need any energy cost. In contrast, interaction relationship requires more effort to create and maintain, e.g., a certain amount of time and energy used for reading and writing wall posts. Such energy cost will limit the rate at which users add new interaction partners, since they only have a finite amount of resources (e.g., time and energy).

To test this hypothesis, we examine the growth pattern of interaction edges. We define *node interaction rate* $\lambda_u(a)$ as the ratio of the number of interaction edges $n_u(a)$ that a node u has created to its current age a_u, i.e., $\lambda_u(a) = n_u(a)/a_u$. Interaction rate measures the speed at which users begin interacting with new friends. To examine the temporal pattern of interaction edge initiations, $\lambda(a)$, we calculate the average interaction rate of nodes achieving age a during our measurement period:

$$\lambda(a) = \frac{\sum_{t=1}^{T} \sum_{u \in S_t(a)} \lambda_u(a)/|S_t(a)|}{T} \quad (1)$$

where $S_t(a) = \{u|t - t_0 = a\}$ is the set of nodes achieving age a at time t. Here, t_0 is the arrival time of node.

As shown in Fig. 1, users in both Renren and Facebook are more interactive immediately after they join. However, the effect quickly wears off. For example, in Renren, the $\lambda(a)$ converges to a constant after only a week. The Pearson correlation coefficient between $\lambda(a)$ and node age is only -0.102, showing interaction rate is nearly independent of node age. This observation means that a node invites new interaction partners at a constant speed due to the interaction cost and limited time resource.

3.2 Interaction Partners Selection

The next question we address is: which friends do users select as interaction partners, given that only a small fraction of friends interact. Intuitively, strong relations are more likely to develop between socially similar people (*i.e.* homophily effects). We hypothesize that sharing common neighbors may have a strong impact on interaction partner selection.

To test this hypothesis, we unroll the evolution of the Renren network. Fig. 2 plots the fractions of friendship edge and interaction edge creation events occurring between users with mutual friends on each day. About 63% of interaction edge creation events occur between friends with mutual neighbors, as compared with 47% of friendship edge creation events. Thus, the common friend factor has a stronger influence on the creation of interaction relationship than on friendship.

After confirming the influence of common neighbors, we aim to understand the way that it affects how interaction targets are selected. Consider the case when a source node u initiates interaction with a friend v by sending the first wall post. We define *com* as the number of common neighbors and *overlap* as the Jaccard coefficient between u and v (i.e., $\frac{\Gamma_u \cap \Gamma_v}{\Gamma_u \cup \Gamma_v}$ where Γ_u and Γ_v are the sets of users connect to u and v, respectively). We examine the following alternatives for choosing node v: i) *com*: proportional to the number of common neighbors; ii) *overlap*: proportional to the Jaccard coefficient.

We apply the maximum likelihood principle to examine which model better explains the observed interaction data. Estimating the likelihood of a model M involves considering each interaction edge $s_t = (u, v)$ and computing the likelihood $P_M(s_t)$ that the

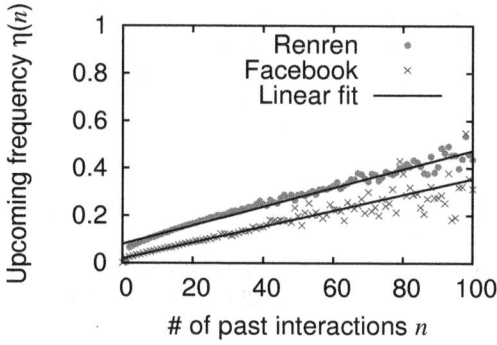

Figure 5: Upcoming interaction frequency $\eta(n)$ for an interaction edge that already has n interactions.

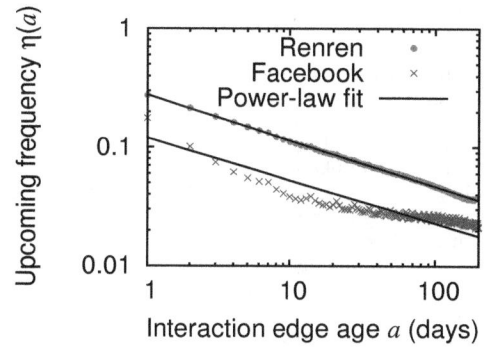

Figure 6: Upcoming interaction frequency $\eta(a)$ for an interaction edge of age a.

source u chooses v according to the model. In our case, $P_M(s_t) = c_v / \sum_{i=1}^{d} c_i$ where c_v (or c_i) is the numbers of common neighbors or neighborhood overlap between u and v (or ith friend of node u). The likelihood P_M that model M reproduces actual interaction edges across the graph is given by the product of the individual likelihoods: $P_M = \prod_t P_M(s_t)$. We use the log-likelihood $\log P_M$ for better numerical accuracy.

We compute the log-likelihood of `com` and `overlap` on each day. Fig. 3 shows the likelihood improvement of `com` and `overlap` over the random target selection, respectively. The `overlap` model shows improvement of 12.5%, compared to 8.5% for the `com` model. This result demonstrates that interactions are more likely to occur between friends with high neighborhood overlap, and that this effect is sustained over time, as the OSN matures.

Because the Facebook dataset does not include social link creation times, we cannot analyzing the correlation between social graph structure and user interaction over time. Instead, we analyze the neighborhood overlap between interactive (or non-interactive) friends on Facebook. We find that interactive friends have 0.085 neighborhood overlap on average, versus only 0.065 on average for non-interactive friends. The relatively low overlap numbers on Facebook are not surprising given that mean degree on Facebook is more than double mean degree on Renren (see Table 2). This result also demonstrates that users tend to initiate interactions with friends with high neighborhood overlap.

3.3 Interaction Generation and Distribution

The final question we ask is: how do users generate new interactions across existing interaction edges? We begin by analyzing the interaction creation process in absolute time, focusing on the speed that nodes generate interactions over their interaction edges.

We define the *node-interaction frequency*, as its total number of interactions averaged over time. Fig. 4 plots the average node-interaction frequency on each day of our dataset. In Renren, we see that the frequency increases early in its existence, but converges to a constant after day 230. Note that most users (and thus interactions) arrive after day 230 since Renren grows exponentially (as we shown later in Fig. 7). Our Facebook data was collected after the OSN had matured, and Fig. 4 shows that node interaction frequency is essentially constant. This result implies that an user spends a constant amount of time per day on interaction.

Next, we examine how users distribute new interactions over their existing interaction partners. We analyze the interaction distribution from two perspectives: first, what is the effect of *intensity*, *i.e.* is their correlation between the number of times friends have interacted in the past, and the number of times they will interact in the

future? Fig. 5 plots $\eta(n)$, the average number of new interactions between friends that already have n interactions:

$$\eta(n) = \frac{\sum_{t=0}^{T} \sum_{e \in S_n(t)} I_e(t) / |S_n(t)|}{T} \quad (2)$$

where $S_n(t) = \{e | \sum_{k=0}^{t-1} I_e(k) = n\}$ is the set of interaction edges that already have n interaction before time t. We observe that $\eta(n)$ is proportional to the number of past interactions across the edge in both networks. Intuitively, this means that the interactions between friends *reinforce* their relationship, leading to more future interactions.

Second, what is the effect of *time*, *i.e.* do friends tend to interact more or less over time? Fig. 6 plots $\eta(a)$, the average number of new interactions created along edges of age a:

$$\eta(a) = \frac{\sum_{t=0}^{T} \sum_{e \in S_a(t)} I_e(t) / |S_a(t)|}{T} \quad (3)$$

where $S_a(t) = \{e | t - t_0(e) = a\}$ is the set of interaction edges with age a at time t, and $I_e(t)$ is the number of new interactions generated along edge e at time t. We see that $\eta(a)$ is inversely proportional to edge age a in both networks. Intuitively, this means that a given pair of users tends to interact less over time. One possible explanation for this is users tend to forget each other as they cannot meet face to face on a regular basis, leading to the closeness between friends declined rapidly over time.

4. A SOCIAL CO-EVOLUTION MODEL

In this section, we introduce our *generative* model for creating interaction graphs that takes into account the coupled evolution in time of topology and user interaction. The model is based on the insights about user interactions derived in the previous section. Intuitively, a co-evolution model has two complementary processes: one concerned with forming social links (the *social graph model*), while the other generates interactions along the links (the *interaction model*). Although many social graph models exist [1, 3, 12, 18, 19], these models do not include an interaction model.

4.1 Social Link Generation

Before we introduce our interaction model, we need to first choose an underlying social graph model to build upon. Rather than attempting to invent and justify a new social graph model, we choose to use the microscopic evolution model [18] for social link generation, which is based on observing the temporal properties of large social networks.

Algorithm 1 Social Co-evolution model.

```
1: Node set V = ∅
2: for each time step t ∈ T do
3:     Node arrival. V = V ∪ V_{t,new}
4:     for each new node u ∈ V_{t,new} do
5:         Lifetime sampling
6:         First social linking
7:     end for
8:     for each living node u ∈ V_t do
9:         if u wakes up then
10:            Social linking
11:            Sleep time sampling
12:        end if
13:        if rand() ≤ γ_u then
14:            if rand() ≤ p then
15:                Requests a friend v it has not interacted with
16:            else
17:                for each its interaction partner v do
18:                    Update the weight w_{uv} ← n_{uv}/a_{uv}^τ
19:                end for
20:                Pick an existing partner v with prob. ∝ w_{uv}
21:                Generate an interaction with v
22:            end if
23:        end if
24:    end for
25: end for
```

The main ideas behind the microscopic evolution model are that nodes join the social network following a node arrival function, and each node has a lifetime l, during which it wakes up multiple times and creates new edges by closing triads two random steps away (*i.e.* befriending friends of friends). The key functions and parameters needed for the microscopic evolution model are:

Node arrival. New nodes $V_{t,new}$ arrive at time t according to a pre-defined arrival function $N(.)$.

Lifetime sampling. At arrival time t, node u samples lifetime a from $\lambda e^{-\lambda a}$, and becomes inactive after time $t + a$. Let V_t be the set of active nodes at time t.

First social linking: Node u declares its first friend v based on the preferential attachment model (*e.g.* connecting to v with probability proportional to v's degree).

Sleep time sampling: After creating an edge, node u goes to sleep for δ time steps, where δ is sampled from a power law with exponential cut-off distribution given by $p(\delta) = \frac{1}{Z}\delta^{-\alpha}e^{-\beta \cdot degree(u) \cdot \delta}$.

Social linking: When node u wakes up, it creates a new edge by befriending a two-hop neighbor (a friend of a friend).

These are the set of parameters needed for the microscopic evolution model: $N(.)$ is the node arrival function, λ is the parameter of the exponential distribution of the lifetime, and α, β are the parameters of the power law with exponential cut-off distribution for the node sleep time gap. Further details of the model can be found in the paper [18].

4.2 User Interaction Generation

Besides befriending with others, nodes also request a certain number of friends to interact with, and distribute interactions over their interaction friends. Based on the insights on user interaction behavior, we now introduce our interaction model. Algorithm 1 presents our co-evolution model. Its interaction evolution part mainly consists of the following processes:

Intuitively, not all the users are simultaneously present in system. Thus we assume that users can be in an active or an inactive state. If an user is active, she interacts with her friends; otherwise she simply rests without interacting. According to empirical observations (e.g., constant interaction frequency), we assume that, at each time step, one inactive user can become active with a probability r, while one active user can become inactive with probability $1 - r$. In practice this means that the user activity pattern, while stochastic, will display some regularity in time, interaction events following each other on average at $1/r$ steps, very long inter-event times are exponentially rare.

Once an user u is active, she would selects a target node v from her friends to make an interaction event, which increases the number of their interactions by one. The empirical observations show that an user invites new friends to interact at a constant rate, irrespective of node age or social degree. Therefore, we assume that, once a node is active, she selects the interaction target either from friends without any interaction with her yet or from existing interaction partners with probabilities p or $1 - p$, respectively. In other words, users are free to establish new interaction relationships with their social friends, and they are also responsible for maintaining existing interaction relationships with their partners, the degree of which is controlled by p.

In the case of selecting the target from its existing partners, interactions are biased by the interpersonal attraction built up over time. The more interest she raises in a partner, the more likely she will interact with this partner (inertia). Based on the empirical observations (e.g., effects of intensity and time), we measure the appeal η_{uv} of a partner v to an user u by $\eta_{uv} = n_{uv}/a_{uv}^\tau$, where n_{uv} is the current number of interactions between users u and v, a_{uv} is the current age of this interaction relationship and τ is the decay factor. Thus, if an user u chooses to interact with an existing partner, she will choose the partner v with a probability proportional to η_{uv}. In the other case, the probability to choose a friend as the target is proportional to their neighborhood overlap (homophily).[2] The new target node would be added into the set of existing interaction partners.

The interaction model captures the fundamental fact that the interaction relationships require that we invest time to keep them alive, especially once it becomes physically difficult for friends to meet face to face on a regular basis. In particular, each user has a *forgetting* behavior: the attraction between a pair of users declined rapidly when they lose contact (captured by the decay factor τ). Interestingly, our model on online relationships is consistent with the ecology model on real-life relationships. Prior work [6] investigated four annual surveys of colleague relationships for 345 bankers in a large financial organization, and found that the liveness of relationships decay over time and decay is also a power function of time. To counteract the effects of forgetting, each user exhibits a *reinforcing* behavior: she wants to keep the important relationships alive. Thus, with limited time to use, she biases towards relationships of more interactions. Also, each user has a *exploring* behavior: she continuously explores new interaction relationships (captured by the probability p), in order to replace existing ones which are no longer attractive.

4.3 Extension of the Model

The activation probability r represents user activeness in the social interaction. To this end, we have assumed that all users have the same tendency to be active, that is, the activation probability r does not depend on the user who is interacting. Real social systems display however additional complexity since the social behavior of individuals may vary significantly across the population. For example, individuals vary widely in the total time spent accessing OSNs [5], and may devote different amount of energy to interaction.

---

[2] One could further explore other social similarities, such as profile and geographic similarities, in choosing the new partner.

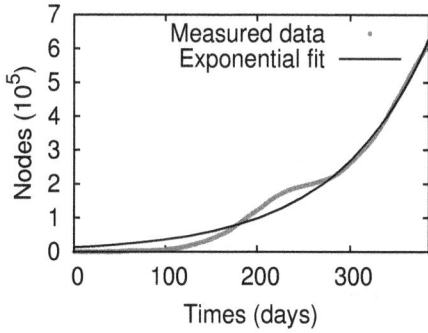

Figure 7: Nodes arrival over time, beginning Nov. 21, 2005.

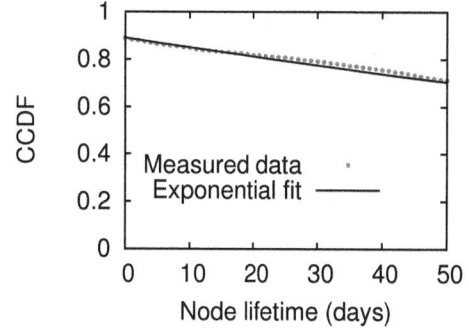

Figure 8: Complementary cumulative distribution of node lifetimes.

A natural extension of the model presented above consists therefore of making the probability r dependent on the user who is interacting. To this aim, we assign to each user u a parameter r_i that characterizes his/her propensity to form social interactions. In real networks this propensity will depend on the features of the users. In the model we assume that this propensity, that we call "sociability", is a quenched random variable randomly chosen from a prefixed distribution $\zeta(r)$ characterizing the system's heterogeneity, which is assigned to each agent at the start of the dynamical evolution and remains constant.

4.4 Desired Property

Before we evaluate our co-evolution model on real data, we first seek to demonstrate its theoretical soundness. To evaluate this, we focus on the relationship between social degree and interaction degree. Several studies of different social networks have all observed that the number of people a user communicates with (their interaction degree) *does not scale linearly* with social degree [14, 25, 26]. This means the social graph grows at a faster rate than the interaction graph. Given how universal this property is, the question becomes *does our model successfully capture this phenomenon*?

In on our co-evolution model, the growth of social degree and interaction degree are governed by different processes. Specifically, interaction edges are created at a constant rate, whereas the creation rate of friendship edges accelerates with social degree (*i.e.* the edge gap gets shorter). Thus, as the graph grows, the former quickly falls behind the latter, leading to a non-linear relationship.

We now formalize this relationship. Recall the friendship edge creation process: given the edge gap distribution $p(\delta|d;\alpha,\beta) = \frac{1}{Z}\delta^{-\alpha}e^{-\beta d\delta}$, a node creates the first edge and sleeps $\delta(1)$ time units sampled from $p(\delta|d = 1; \alpha, \beta)$, creates the second edge and sleeps for $\delta(2)$ time units sampled from $p(\delta|d = 2; \alpha, \beta)$, and so on. Thus, the time duration T needed by a user to achieve degree D is:

$$T = \sum_{d=1}^{D} \delta(d) \qquad (4)$$

To get the edge gap $\delta(d)$, we first compute the normalizing constant Z for the edge gap:

$$Z = \int_0^\infty \delta^{-\alpha}e^{-\beta d\delta}d\delta = \frac{\Gamma(1-\alpha)}{(\beta d)^{1-\alpha}} \qquad (5)$$

With the expression of constant Z, we obtain the expected time gap for a node to create its d_{th} edge:

$$E[\delta|d;\alpha,\beta] = \int_0^\infty \frac{1}{Z}\delta^{-\alpha}e^{-\beta d\delta}d\delta = \frac{\Gamma(2-\alpha)}{\Gamma(1-\alpha)}(\beta d)^{-1} \qquad (6)$$

Equation (6) shows that the gap gets shorter as the node's degree increases (*i.e.* $E(\delta) \propto 1/d$), manifesting the "rich-get-richer" phenomenon. On the other hand, the node creates interaction edges at a constant rate r. Hence, the average interaction degree K the node accumulates during T is:

$$K = r\sum_{d=1}^{D} E[\delta|d;\alpha,\beta] = r\sum_{d=1}^{D} \frac{\Gamma(2-\alpha)}{\Gamma(1-\alpha)}(\beta d)^{-1} = \Theta(lnD) \qquad (7)$$

Therefore, the co-evolution model produces a *logarithmic* relationship between average interaction degree K and social degree D.

5. MODEL EVALUATION

We now perform simulations based on our Renren dataset to validate the accuracy of our model. We focus on the Renren dataset because it is *complete*, unlike the Facebook data which is missing edge creation times. We fit the parameters of our interaction model to the interactions that occurred during the first 320 days of our Renren dataset. This time period corresponds to half of the overall nodes joining the social graph. Later, we evaluate the ability of the interaction models to generate synthetic data that captures the interaction characteristics of the full 385-day Renren graph. We observe that the co-evolution model accurately captures the characteristics of the 385-day Renren data, even when it is only trained on half the dataset.

5.1 Social Graph Parameter Fitting

We analyze the Renren network to get the values for model parameters. The *social* graph model [18] needs the following parameters to generate the underlying social graph:

Node arrival function $N(.)$: We start by modeling the node arrival process. Fig. 7 measures the number of nodes in the network $N(t)$ on each day t. We see that Renren gets a burst of growth around day 200 (June 4, 2006) due to launching a network campaign at some biggest universities in Beijing. And after that, the network maintains the stable growth from day 287 (the end of August, 2006). We focus on the stable growth stage since it captures the arrival of most nodes, and fit the node arrival process by exponent function $N(t) = a \exp(bt)$, where $a = 13,200$ and $b = 0.01$. Thus, Renren grows exponentially over much of our network. *The parameter λ for node lifetime distribution:* We define node arrival as the time when a node creates its first social edge, and departure if the node does not create an edge for 100 days. Node lifetime is the time between node arrival and departure. Fig. 8

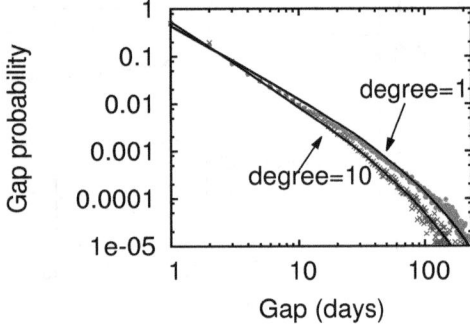

Figure 9: Edge gap distribution for a node to obtain the second edge.

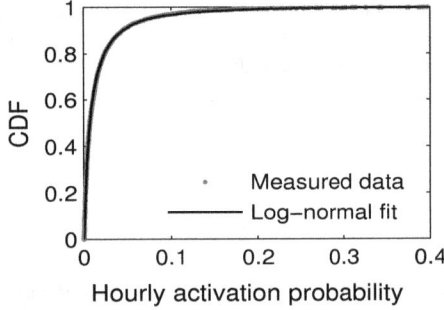

Figure 10: The distribution of user activation probability at an hourly time step.

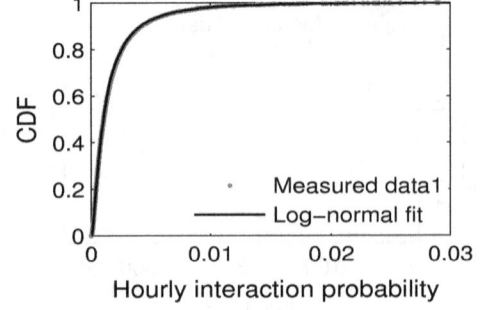

Figure 11: The distribution of edge interaction probability at an hourly time step.

Algorithm 2 Social Naïve model.
```
1: Node set V = ∅
2: for each time step t ∈ T do
3:     Node arrival. V = V ∪ V_{t,new}
4:     for each new node u ∈ V_{t,new} do
5:         Lifetime sampling
6:         First social linking
7:     end for
8:     for each living node u ∈ V_t do
9:         if u wakes up then
10:             Social linking (u, v)
11:             Sleep time sampling
12:             if rand() ≤ θ then
13:                 Adds v into interaction partner group
14:                 Samples probability η_{uv} from P(η)
15:             end if
16:         end if
17:         for each partner v do
18:             Generate a new interaction with η_{uv}
19:         end for
20:     end for
21: end for
```

---

shows the distribution of node lifetimes before day 230. Although about 10% nodes create an edge and never return, the lifetime of most nodes is fit by an exponential distribution with shape parameter $\lambda = 0.004$.

Parameters α, β of the sleep time gap distribution: The microscopic evolution model [18] defines edge gap δ as the time elapsing between the edge initiations from a node. In our case, we modify the model slightly since our dataset does not record which node initiates edge creation. Specifically, in our case, when edge (u, v) is created, both u and v perform sleep sampling according to their respective degrees. Although we modify the edge gap definition, we find that the edge gap distribution p_g can still be modeled by a power law with exponential cutoff: $p_g(\delta) \propto \delta^{-\alpha} \exp(-\beta d\delta)$. Fig. 9 confirms this model by showing the gap distributions and corresponding fittings ($\alpha = 1.735, \beta = 0.0008$) for nodes with different degree d.

5.2 Interaction Parameter Fitting

On the other hand, the *interaction* model needs the following parameters to generate interactions over the underlying social graph.

Decay factor τ: We compute $\eta(a)$, the interaction frequency for edges of age a, with equation (3) (note that T is limited to 320), and get the exponent $\tau = 0.4$.

Exploring probability p: We compute p by ratio of the existing interaction edges to the number of existing interactions by the end of training data (day 320), and get $p = 0.32$.

Activation probability r: In our evaluation, we use the heterogeneous model, which assumes that the activation probability r of an individual is randomly chosen from a prefixed distribution $\zeta(r)$. We compute the hourly activation probability r of an individual us-

er by the average number of her interactions per hour by the end of training data. Fig. 10 shows that $\zeta(r)$ is a log-normal distribution, *i.e.* $\zeta(r) = \frac{1}{r\sigma\sqrt{2\pi}} e^{-(\ln r - \mu)^2/2\sigma^2}$, with $\mu = -4.9$ and $\sigma = 1.5$.

5.3 Baseline Model

We propose a *naïve model*, which assumes the evolution of social network structure and user interaction are independent processes, and a stable interaction probability between a pair of users. This naïve model serves as a baseline for comparison.

At each time step, an node u creates social links using the microscopic evolution model (with the parameters outlined above). Once creating a new link, she selects this friend as interaction partner with a probability θ. At each time step, she interacts with each of her interaction partners with their own probability η_{uv} sampled from a given distribution $P(\eta)$ characterizing heterogeneous link strength. Algorithm 2 presents the naïve model in detail.

Using our training data, we get $\theta = 0.29$ as only about 29% of social edges have interactions. We quantify the hourly interaction probability of a pair of partners by their average number of interactions per hour by the end of training data. Fig. 11 shows that $P(\eta)$ is well-fit by a log-normal distribution, *e.g.* $P(\eta) = \frac{1}{\eta\sigma\sqrt{2\pi}} e^{-(\ln \eta - \mu)^2/2\sigma^2}$, with $\mu = -6.9$ and $\sigma = 1.1$.

5.4 Evaluation of Interaction Models

We now evaluate our interaction models. Using the parameter-

	Real Network	Co-evolution Model	Naïve Model
# of interactions	7,697K	7,979K	11,822K
# of users have interactions	421K	452K	470K
Mean # of interactions/user	18.3	17.7	25.1
# of edge have interactions	2,623K	2,654K	2,285K
Mean # of interactions/edge	2.9	3.0	5.2

Table 3: Statistics of a real network vs. synthetic ones

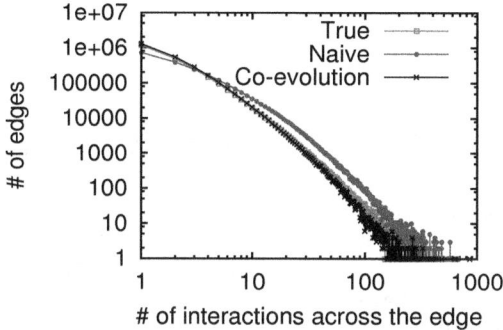

Figure 12: The number of interactions across interaction edges.

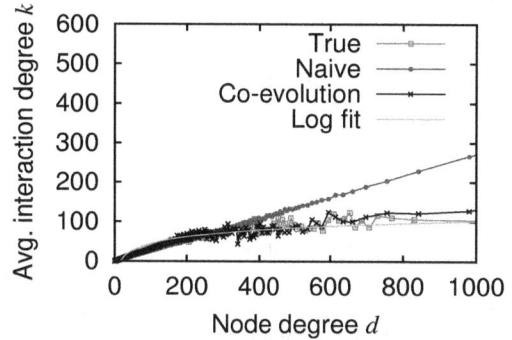

Figure 13: The correlation between node degree and interaction degree.

ization outlined above, we generate two social graphs with associated interactions (one from the naïve model, one from the co-evolution model). Each graph is evolved for 385 days, and then compared to the complete 385 days of ground-truth data from Renren. We focus on analyzing the interactions generated by the two models, rather than the social graph generated by the microscopic evolution model, because the microscopic model has already been thoroughly evaluated by prior work [18].

We analyze the generated interactions at two levels of granularity. First, we evaluate high-level interaction characteristics (*e.g.* total interactions, interactions per user/edge). Second, we examine the structural features of interaction graphs (*e.g.* degree distribution and clustering coefficient). In both cases, the output of the naïve model serves as a baseline for gauging the improvement of the co-evolution model.

We now present our evaluation results by comparing both the high-level characteristics (such as the total number of interaction edges and interactions) and microscopic structure features (e.g., clustering coefficient, degree distribution, and pairwise distance) of real and synthetic interaction graphs. The performance of the naïve model serves as a baseline that will help us to confirm the necessity of each process in the co-evolution model.

Interaction Analysis. Table 3 shows the overall interaction statistics of the real and synthetic graphs. The output of the co-evolution model is very close to the true data in every category. In contrast, the naïve model generates 54% too many interactions overall and 12% too many users become interactive. By capturing the fraction of interaction edges, the naïve model could roughly predict the total number of interaction edges, but severely overestimates the total number of interactions due to ignoring the recency effect in user interactions (i.e., the interaction frequency of user pairs tends to decrease markedly over time). As a comparison, the co-evolution model rightly captures the rates that users create both interaction edges and interactions, thus generating the very similar statistics to those of the real graph.

Next, we examine the number of interactions across interaction

edges (*i.e.* link strength) in Fig. 12. Since the naïve model does not take interaction recency into account (*i.e.* interactions along an edge tend to decrease over time), it overestimates link-strengths. In contrast, the co-evolution model takes interaction intensity and recency into account, and thus generates nearly the same link-strength distribution as the real graph.

Finally, we examine the correlation between social degree and interaction degree, since this non-linear correlation is an important observation in many social networks [14, 25, 26]. Fig. 13 shows the correlation for the Renren network, which exhibits the expected sub-linear relationship. The naïve model cannot generate this non-linear correlation. In contrast, the co-evolution model does generate the expected sub-linear relationship, and fits the ground-truth Renren data very closely. We further find that the logarithmic function fits true correlation curve well, validating empirically the derivation of a logarithmic correlation in Section 4.4.

Interaction Graph Analysis. To further evaluate our interaction models, we construct undirected *interaction networks*, where a link exists between a pair of users that interacts at least once (*i.e.* interaction edge). We then compare the structural properties of the 385-day Renren interaction network to the synthetic networks from the naïve and co-evolution models.

Fig. 14 shows the clustering coefficient distribution, degree distribution, and pairwise distance histogram for the Renren and synthetic interaction networks. We observe that both models produce accurate interaction degree distributions. However, the co-evolution model is much more accurate at reproducing accurate clustering and distance characteristics. The weakness of the naïve model in these two cases is due to the fact that it ignores the correlation between social structure and interactions. In contrast, the co-evolution model is designed to capture this correlation, and consequently generates interaction networks that closely match the true network.

We note that the true network has a slightly higher clustering coefficient than that generated by the co-evolution model. This indicates that the ground-truth interaction partners are more densely

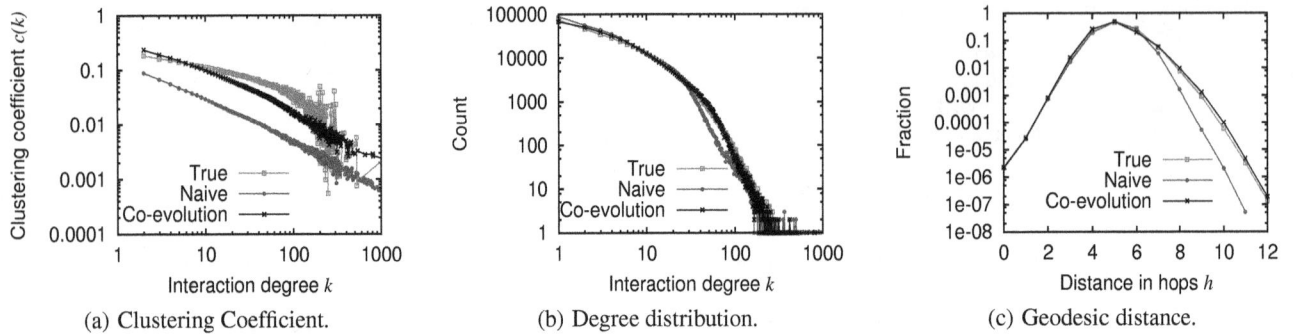

(a) Clustering Coefficient. (b) Degree distribution. (c) Geodesic distance.

Figure 14: Comparison between the real and synthetic Renren interaction graphs.

clustered than that predicted by the model (where the partner selection is proportional to the neighborhood overlap). To improve the accuracy of our model with respect to clustering coefficients, we could add an additional parameter to the model that increases its bias towards selecting interaction partners with high neighborhood overlap. However, this additional parameter adds complexity to the model, and we leave the study of how to tune this new parameter as future work.

6. CONCLUSION AND DISCUSSION

In this paper, we develop and evaluate a co-evolution model that generates interactions across social links. The insights behind our model are derived from large scale datasets from Renren and Facebook. This data reveals that users invite new friends to interact at a nearly constant rate, prefer to interact with friends with whom they share significant overlaps in social circles, and gradually lose interest in interacting with old friends. We believe that these observations not only affect the design of network interaction models but also have broader implications in other areas, such as friend recommendation, information diffusion, and news feed ranking.

Our co-evolution interaction model captures the important statistical properties of interaction networks, and provides new insights into the evolution of user interaction during network formation. To our knowledge, the co-evolution model is the first generative model for interactions on OSNs, and our evaluation shows that is it very accurate at capturing the observed properties of real OSN data. Although, we only evaluate our co-evolution interaction model when paired with the microscopic social graph evolution model, one of the strengths of our interaction model is that it can be paired with any underlying model for generating the social graph structure.

Another strength of the co-evolution model is that it is scalable, because individual nodes act locally (i.e., focusing on their neighbors) and independently (i.e., no coordination of one's own actions with those of others). Thus, the model can easily be parallelized, where each machine is responsible for performing the social linking and interaction processes of a subset of nodes.

Bursty Dynamics. In this paper, our interaction model mainly focuses on capturing user behavior in distributing interactions among friends as OSN structure evolves. However, our model simplifies reality by assuming that each interaction is immediately generated between a node and her target, so the fine-grained temporal features of interactions (such as bursty dynamics) are not captured by the model. One way to mitigate this issue would be to introduce response delay into the model, e.g., an user could respond only when she is active. This delay would control the speed at which

nodes respond to interactions; two nodes that both have low delay would thus generate fast bursts of interactions. Also, response delay could be various from the per edge perspective. Intuitively, this would capture cases where users quickly respond to interactions from strong friends, while delaying responses to acquaintances (or even ignoring these interactions entirely). We leave this extension of the model as future work.

Future Work. There are several directions to extend the current study. First, we can study the interaction graph evolution at the community level. Seshadhri et al. [17, 23] have proposed scalable models for reproducing social graphs with community structure. However, for interaction graphs, one needs to further study the correlation between link weight and community evolution, since links of various strength might play different roles on the community formation. Another direction is to accommodate more attributes of nodes to improve the accuracy of the model. Recent works [1, 12] begin to examine influence of spatial and profile attributes on the temporal evolution of friendship links, but how these factors affect interaction evolution remains unknown.

7. ACKNOWLEDGMENTS

We thank the anonymous reviewers for their comments, as well as our shepherd Cecilia Mascolo. This work was supported by the National Basic Research Program of China (Grant No. 2014CB340 400), the National Science Foundation for Young Scholars of China (Grant No.61202423), and the NSF under grant CNS-1319019, IIS-1321083 and CNS-1527939. Any opinions, findings, and conclusions or recommendations expressed in this material are those of the authors and do not necessarily reflect the views of the NSF.

8. REFERENCES

[1] ALLAMANIS, M., SCELLATO, S., AND MASCOLO, C. Evolution of a location-based online social network: Analysis and models. In *Proc. of IMC* (2012).

[2] BACKSTROM, L., AND LESKOVEC, J. Supervised random walks: Predicting and recommending links in social networks. In *Proc. of WSDM* (2011).

[3] BARABÁSI, A., AND ALBERT, R. Emergence of scaling in random networks. *Science 286*, 5439 (1999), 509–512.

[4] BARRAT, A., BARTHÉLEMY, M., AND VESPIGNANI, A. Modeling the evolution of weighted networks. *Physical review E* (2004).

[5] BENEVENUTO, F., RODRIGUES, T., CHA, M., AND ALMEIDA, V. Characterizing user behavior in online social networks. In *Proc. of IMC* (2009).

[6] BURT, R. S. Emergence of scaling in random networks. *Social Networks 1*, 22 (2000), 1–28.

[7] CHA, M., HADDADI, H., BENEVENUTO, F., AND GUMMADI, K. P. Measuring user influence in twitter: The million follower fallacy. In *Proc. of ICWSM* (May 2010).

[8] CHUN, H., KWAK, H., EOM, Y., AHN, Y., MOON, S., AND JEONG, H. Comparison of online social relations in volume vs interaction: a case study of Cyworld. In *Proc. of IMC* (2008).

[9] GAO, H., HU, J., WILSON, C., LI, Z., CHEN, Y., AND ZHAO, B. Y. Detecting and characterizing social spam campaigns. In *Proc. of IMC* (2010).

[10] GARG, S., GUPTA, T., CARLSSON, N., AND MAHANTI, A. Evolution of an online social aggregation network:an empirical study. In *Proc. of IMC* (2009).

[11] GILBERT, E., AND KARAHALIOS, K. Predicting tie strength with social media. In *Proc. of CHI* (2009).

[12] GONG, N. Z., XU, W., HUANG, L., MITTAL, P., STEFANOV, E., SEKAR, V., AND SONG, D. Evolution of social-attribute networks: Measurements, modeling, and implications using google+. In *Proc. of IMC* (2012).

[13] GRIER, C., THOMAS, K., PAXSON, V., AND ZHANG, M. @spam: the underground on 140 characters or less. In *Proc. of CCS* (2010).

[14] HUBERMAN, B. A., ROMERO, D. M., AND WU, F. Social networks that matter: Twitter under the microscope. *CoRR* (2008).

[15] JIANG, J., WILSON, C., WANG, X., HUANG, P., SHA, W., DAI, Y., AND ZHAO, B. Y. Understanding latent interactions in online social networks. In *Proc. of IMC* (2010).

[16] KAHANDA, I., AND NEVILLE, J. Using transactional information to predict link strength in online social networks. In *Proc. of ICWSM* (2009).

[17] KOLDA, T. G., PINAR, A., PLANTENGA, T., AND SESHADHRI:, C. A scalable generative graph model with community structure. arXiv:1302.6636, 2013.

[18] LESKOVEC, J., BACKSTROM, L., KUMAR, R., AND TOMKINS, A. Microscopic evolution of social networks. In *Proc. of KDD* (2008).

[19] LESKOVEC, J., KLEINBERG, J. M., AND FALOUTSOS, C. Graph evolution: Densification and shrinking diameters. *TKDD* (2007).

[20] MISLOVE, A., KOPPULA, H. S., GUMMADI, K. P., DRUSCHEL, P., AND BHATTACHARJEE, B. Growth of the flickr social network. In *Proc. of WOSN* (Seattle, WA, August 2008).

[21] NAZIR, A., WAAGEN, A., VIJAYARAGHAVAN, V. S., CHUAH, C.-N., D'SOUZA, R., AND KRISHNAMURTHY, B. Beyond friendship: Modeling user activity graphs on social network-based gifting applications. In *Proc. of IMC* (2012).

[22] SCHNEIDER, F., FELDMANN, A., KRISHNAMURTHY, B., AND WILLINGER, W. Understanding online social network usage from a network perspective. In *Proc. of IMC* (2009).

[23] SESHADHRI, C., KOLDA, T. G., AND PINAR, A. Community structure and scale-free collections of erdos-renyi graphs. *Physical Review E* (2012).

[24] STARNINI, M., BARONCHELLI, A., AND PASTOR-SATORRAS, R. Modeling human dynamics of face-to-face interaction networks. *Physics Review Letter* (2013).

[25] VISWANATH, B., MISLOVE, A., CHA, M., AND GUMMADI, K. P. On the evolution of user interaction in facebook. In *Proc. of WOSN* (2009).

[26] WILSON, C., BOE, B., SALA, A., PUTTASWAMY, K. P. N., AND ZHAO, B. Y. User interactions in social networks and their implications. In *Proc. of EuroSys* (2009).

[27] XIANG, R., NEVILLE, J., AND ROGATI, M. Modeling relationship strength in online social networks. In *Proc. of World Wide Web Conference* (2010).

[28] YANG, Z., WILSON, C., WANG, X., GAO, T., ZHAO, B. Y., AND DAI, Y. Uncovering social network sybils in the wild. In *Proc. of IMC* (2011).

[29] YOOK, S. H., JEONG, H., AND BARABÁSI, A.-L. Weighted evolving networks. *Physical review letters* (2001).

[30] ZHAO, K., STEHLÉ, J., BIANCONI, G., AND BARRAT, A. Social network dynamics of face-to-face interactions. *Physical review E* (2011).

[31] ZHAO, X., SALA, A., WILSON, C., WANG, X., GAITO, S., ZHENG, H., AND ZHAO, B. Y. Multi-scale dynamics in a massive online social network. In *Proc. of IMC* (2012).

Negative Messages Spread Rapidly and Widely on Social Media

Sho Tsugawa
Faculty of Engineering, Information and Systems
University of Tsukuba
Ibaraki 305–8573, Japan
s-tugawa@cs.tsukuba.ac.jp

Hiroyuki Ohsaki
School of Science and Technology
Kwansei Gakuin University
Hyogo 669-1337, Japan
ohsaki@kwansei.ac.jp

ABSTRACT

We investigate the relation between the sentiment of a message on social media and its virality, defined as the volume and the speed of message diffusion. We analyze 4.1 million messages (tweets) obtained from Twitter. Although factors affecting message diffusion on social media have been studied previously, we focus on message sentiment, and reveal how the polarity of message sentiment affects its virality. The virality of a message is measured by the number of message repostings (retweets) and the time elapsed from the original posting of a message to its Nth reposting (N-retweet time). Through extensive analyses, we find that negative messages are likely to be reposted more rapidly and frequently than positive and neutral messages. Specifically, the reposting volume of negative messages is 1.2–1.6-fold that of positive and neutral messages, and negative messages spread at 1.25 times the speed of positive and neutral messages when the diffusion volume is large.

Categories and Subject Descriptors

J.4 [**Computer Applications**]: Social and Behavioral Science

General Terms

Human Factors

Keywords

Social media, Twitter, Information diffusion, Retweet, Sentiment

1. INTRODUCTION

On social media, such as Twitter and Facebook, users post many messages including their opinions and feelings. One of the most successful social media, Twitter, allows users to post *tweets*, which are short messages with a limit of 140 characters. As of early 2014, 240 million users were posting over 500 million tweets on Twitter each day [33].

Some of the messages posted on social media are disseminated to many other users by word-of-mouth, which affects trends and public opinions in society. Social media users can disseminate

COSN'15, November 2–3, 2015, Palo Alto, California, USA.
ⓒ 2015 ACM. ISBN 978-1-4503-3951-3/15/11 ...$15.00.
DOI: http://dx.doi.org/10.1145/2817946.2817962.

messages to their friends via functionalities, such as *retweeting* in Twitter and *share* in Facebook. This word-of-mouth message diffusion on social media is an important mechanism that influences public opinion and can affect brand awareness and product market share [3]. Therefore, information diffusion in social media has attracted the attention of many researchers [4,14,17,18,22,26–28].

As we will discuss in Section 2, factors affecting word-of-mouth message diffusion in social media have been analyzed extensively [17, 22,28]. Researchers often focus on Twitter as one of the largest social media, and investigate the relation between features extracted from a tweet and its virality. For instance, it has been shown that tweets with features such as URLs, hashtags, and emotional words are more likely to be retweeted than those without these features [22]. It has also been shown that the tweet topic and the number of followers of the tweet publisher are major factors affecting tweet diffusion [17,28].

We focus on *sentiment* as a factor affecting message diffusion, and examine the effects of positive and negative sentiment in each tweet on its virality on Twitter. Behaviors of social media users are not necessarily objective and legitimate, and psychological and emotional factors are expected to affect the users' behaviors.

The relation between message sentiment and the virality of the message, defined as the volume and the speed of the message diffusion, has been studied [14,26,27]. However, different results have been reported for the volume of message diffusion. For instance, Gruzd *et al.* showed that positive tweets are retweeted more than negative tweets [14], whereas Stieglitz *et al.* showed the opposite [27]. Moreover, most studies focus on only the volume of diffusion and do not focus on the diffusion speed. Although Stieglitz *et al.* [27] performed pioneering work analyzing the relation between tweet sentiment and diffusion speed, their analyses used the time interval between the original tweet and only the first retweet as a measure of diffusion speed.

This paper aims to reveal how the sentiment of a tweet affects its virality in terms of both diffusion volume and speed on Twitter by using a large-scale dataset containing 4.1 million tweets. Our main contributions are as follows.

- We investigate 4.1 million non-domain-specific tweets to understand general effects of the sentiment of a tweet on its virality in social media. Previous studies used domain-specific tweets, such as tweets related to the Olympics [14] and political elections [26,27], and show different results. We used a dataset of mixed domain tweets, and examined the general relation between sentiment and virality in general situations.

- We reveal that negative messages are typically more viral in terms of diffusion volume than positive and neutral messages. Psychology studies suggest that negative things have a strong effect on people than positive things [6, 24, 31]. We provide empirical evidences of the existence of such bias on social media.

- We also reveal that negative messages spread faster than positive and neutral messages when the diffusion volume is large. We used the time interval between the original tweet and the Nth retweet (N-retweet time) to measure its diffusion speed. By collecting a large number of tweets, we obtained a dataset including tweets with a large retweet count. To the best of our knowledge, this is the first study to investigate the relation between the sentiment and diffusion speed of tweets with large diffusion volume.

The remainder of the paper is organized as follows. Section 2 introduces works related to analyses of message diffusion on social media. In Section 3, we introduce the theoretical background and research questions. Section 4 explains the methodology and dataset used for the analyses. Section 5 shows the results, and Section 6 discusses the implications of the results and the limitations of the work. Finally, Section 7 contains our conclusions.

2. RELATED WORK

Factors affecting retweetability of tweets (i.e., probability of retweet) have been analyzed in previous work [15, 22, 28]. Suh *et al.* analyzed 74 million tweets, and showed that the presence of hashtags and URLs significantly affects retweetability, whereas the number of past tweets does not [28]. Naveed *et al.* analyzed 60 million tweets, and showed that the presence of emotional words, hashtags, and URLs are major factors affecting retweetability [22].

Hansen *et al.* investigated the relation between emotions contained in a tweet and its retweetability [15]. Analysis of approximately 560,000 tweets showed that for tweets about news, negative tweets have higher retweetability than positive tweets, whereas the opposite is true for non-news tweets. These studies have focused on retweetability; however, in this work, we focused on the volume and speed of retweets.

Factors affecting the volume of retweets have been analyzed [14, 17, 27]. Hong *et al.* showed that tweet topics determined by topic modeling, which is a widely used natural language processing technique [9], and the number of followers of the tweet publisher are useful features for predicting the volume of retweets [17].

The relation between tweet sentiment and the volume of tweet diffusion has been examined [14, 26, 27]. Gruzd *et al.* analyzed 46,000 tweets related to the Winter Olympics in 2010, and found that positive tweets have a larger number of retweets than negative tweets [14]. In contrast, Stieglitz *et al.* analyzed approximately 170,000 tweets related to political elections in Germany [26, 27], and revealed that negative and positive tweets have a larger volume of retweets than neutral tweets [26, 27]. Moreover, in one dataset they showed that negative tweets had a larger volume of retweets than positive tweets, whereas in the other there was no significant difference in retweet volume between positive and negative tweets [27]. These studies used domain-specific tweets, where the tweets were related to specific social events, and reached different conclusions. Our study uses larger-scale non-domain-specific tweets, and investigates the relation between the sentiment of a tweet and its diffusion volume, eliminating the effects of the tweet domain.

Analyses of the relation between message sentiment and diffusion speed is limited. Stieglitz *et al.* investigated the relation between tweet sentiment and retweet speed [27]. They used the time interval between the original tweet and the first retweet (1-retweet time) as a measure of retweet speed, and showed that there was no significant difference between retweet speed of positive and negative tweets. Extending the methodology of their work, we used the time interval between the original tweet and the Nth retweet as a measure of diffusion speed, and investigate the effects of message sentiments on its diffusion speed.

Prediction of the volume of retweets is a related and active research topic [11, 20]. Cheng *et al.* predicted the volume of retweets with machine learning techniques [11]. Although these studies have constructed prediction models using several features, we examine the effects of the features (message sentiment in this study) on the retweet volume. Our results can be used to predict retweet volume and provide several suggestions for improving marketing and designing new functionality in social media, which is discussed in Section 6.

3. THEORY AND RESEARCH QUESTIONS

Psychology studies suggest that negative things have a stronger effect on people than positive things, which is called *negativity bias*, and this bias exists in many situations [6, 24, 31]. Moreover, positive and negative emotions affect virality [7, 8]. Psychological arousal increases virality, and news articles evoking positive and negative emotions often go viral [8]. Therefore, it is expected that negative tweets are retweeted more than positive and neutral tweets, and that positive tweets are retweeted more than neutral tweets.

However, empirical observations of the relation between tweet sentiment and retweet volume are limited; therefore, it is still unclear whether negativity bias exists in social media. As discussed in Section 2, tweets with different domains show different relations [14, 27]. Therefore, we tackle the following question using large-scale non-domain-specific tweets.

RQ 1 *How is tweet sentiment related to the retweet volume?*

As negativity bias theory suggests, negative emotion in a tweet may increase the reaction speed to the tweet. However, as discussed in Section 2, analyses of the relation between tweet sentiment and diffusion speed are also limited. Our second research question is as follows.

RQ 2 *How is tweet sentiment related to the retweet speed?*

In what follows, we tackle these two research questions by analyzing large-scale tweet data.

4. METHODOLOGY

In this section, we explain the dataset and methodology that we used to answer our research questions.

4.1 Overview

We collected tweets on Twitter, and investigated the relation between the sentiment of each tweet and its virality. To focus on users with the same culture and to eliminate the effects of different timezones, we used tweets from Japanese twitter users. Following the method in Ref. [27], we categorized the tweet sentiment as *positive*, *negative*, and *neutral*.

The tweet sentiment was determined by using two methods: objective classification using a dictionary of positive and negative words [29, 30]; and subjective classification by several people. For objective classification, we determined the sentiment of each tweet by counting the number of affective words used in the tweet. Since such objective classification could cause classification errors, we also used subjective classification of a subset of collected tweets.

Table 1: Distribution of the number of retweets in the dataset

Section	Number of retweets	Number of tweets
1	2–10	3,748,449
2	11–25	318,640
3	26–50	111,527
4	51–75	37,174
5	76–100	18,616
6	101–250	33,847
7	251–500	10,359
8	501–750	2,903
9	751–1000	1,227
10	1001 or more	2,295

Table 2: Statistics for the collected tweet dataset, D_A

	Mean	Median	Std. dev.
Number of retweets	9.70	3	70.80
Number of URLs	0.39	0	0.53
Number of hashtags	0.27	0	0.70
Number of followers	6237.30	515	36220.61

Table 3: Examples of positive and negative words. The English translation of the Japanese words listed in the dictionary are shown.

Positive	Negative
Happy, laugh, pretty, favorite good, comfortable, smile celebrate, beautiful, love	Sad, dislike, sick, fear bad, horrible, tired unlucky, anxiety, sorry

The two classification methods were used to check the robustness of the results. Details of these methods are explained in Section 4.3.

For each original tweet, we calculated the number of retweets and the time interval between the original tweet and the Nth retweet (N-retweet time). We investigated the relation between these measures and tweet sentiment.

4.2 Dataset

Using the Twitter application programming interface (API), we collected Japanese retweets posted during July 25-31 2013[1]. Retweets where the original tweet was posted before 25 July 2013 were discarded. For each original tweet, we counted the number of retweets and extracted original tweets that were retweeted multiple times, namely tweets with a retweet number of more than one. This was intended to focus on tweets with a certain amount of retweet volume. We obtained 4,285,037 original tweets, referred to hereafter as tweets. There were no special social events such as the Olympic and political elections during the period of data collection. The distribution of the number of retweets in the dataset is shown in Table 1. Table 1 shows that our dataset included tweets with a large diffusion volume. Because the distribution of the number of retweets is heavy-tailed [21] and a large retweet diffusion is a rare event, previous studies [14,27] use tweets with relatively small diffusion. In contrast, by collecting a large number of tweets, our dataset includes a sufficient number of tweets with a large diffusion volume, which allows us to analyze N-retweet time for a large retweet count, N.

From the 4,285,037 tweets, we chose 8,000 tweets for determining sentiment by manual evaluations. For obtaining 8,000 tweets, we used stratified sampling rather than random sampling to extract tweets with different diffusion volumes. We classified all tweets into 10 sections shown in Table 1, and we randomly chose 800 tweets for each section. We denote the dataset of all tweets as D_A, and the 8,000 sampled tweets as D_S. Statistics about collected tweet data, D_A, are shown in Table 2.

4.3 Methods for Inferring Tweet Sentiment

We inferred the sentiment of each tweet in dataset D_A by using a dictionary of affective words. The dictionary is compiled by manual evaluation of a dictionary of positive and negative words extracted according to a technique in Refs. [29,30]. The dictionary contains 2,871 positive words and 3,534 negative words. Examples of words are show in Tab. 3. We used MeCab [1] for morphological stemming of the Japanese tweet text, and obtained words used in each tweet. For each tweet, we counted the number of positive and negative words listed in the dictionary. We classified each tweet by the following rules: a tweet that had at least one positive word and no negative words was positive; a tweet that had at least one negative word and no positive words was negative; a tweet that had no positive and negative words was neutral; and other tweets were discarded. Following these rules, we obtained 863,830 positive tweets, 343,910 negative tweets, 2,929,324 neutral tweets, and 147,973 tweets were discarded. Previous research has [15, 22] used similar dictionary-based approaches to analyze the relation between tweet sentiment and virality. Therefore, this approach is reasonable for classifying large-scale tweet data.

Moreover, we inferred the sentiment of each tweet in dataset D_S by manual evaluation. We recruited 11 annotators from the undergraduate and graduate students in our laboratory. Annotators were instructed to read the tweets independently, and tag each tweet as *positive*, *negative*, *neutral*, or *uncertain*. For each tweet, three annotators independently gave a sentiment tag for the tweet. Following the method used in the sentiment analysis task in the SemEval workshop [23], we adopted *majority vote* for determining the sentiment label of each tweet. We discarded tweets that were given three different tags by the three annotators, and tweets that were given two or more uncertain tags. If two of the three annotators gave the tweet the same tag, the tweet was classified as having the sentiment corresponding to the tag. Using this method, we obtained 1,432 positive tweets, 976 negative tweets, and 4,737 neutral tweets (total of 7,145 tweets), and these tweets were used in the analyses. We discarded 855 tweets, of which 140 tweets were uncertain.

We examined the agreement between the objective classification using the dictionary of affective words, and subjective classification (Table 4). The overall agreement between objective and subjective classifications was approximately 60%. Evaluating the sentiment of short messages automatically is challenging [5], and the overall agreement is often low. However, the proportion of tweets classified as the opposite sentiment was only 2%, which suggests that objective classification can be used for our analysis, particularly for comparing negative and positive tweets.

4.4 Measures of Diffusion Volume and Speed

We obtained the number of retweets for each tweet and N-retweet time as measures of diffusion volume and speed, respectively. Each retweet has a timestamp and the ID of the original tweet. For each original tweet, T, we counted the number of retweets of tweet T. We obtained the N-retweet time of tweet T by calculating the in-

---

[1]We used the Search API in Twitter REST API v1.1, and collected Japanese tweets using the query q=RT, lang=ja.

Table 4: Tweet sentiment obtained by subjective and objective classifications

	Positive (subj.)	Negative (subj.)	Neutral (subj.)	Uncertain (subj.)	Discard (subj.)	
Positive (obj.)	559	95	870	5	134	1,662
Negative (obj.)	69	286	384	6	93	838
Neutral (obj.)	751	513	3,321	123	440	5,149
Discard (obj.)	57	82	158	5	49	351
	1,432	976	4,737	140	715	8,000

Table 5: Variables used in regression analysis

Variable	Description
RTnum	Number of retweets
NRTtime	Time interval between original tweet and Nth retweet
pos	Categorical variable that shows the tweet is positive
neg	Categorical variable that shows the tweet is positive
follower	Number of followers
URL	Categorical variable for whether the tweet includes a URL
hash	Categorical variable for whether the tweet includes a hashtag

terval between the time tweet T was posted and the time the Nth retweet was posted.

4.5 Methods for Statistical Analysis

Initially, we examined the mean and distribution of the measures of message virality for the message sentiments. We classified all tweets as positive, negative, or neutral. For each category, we obtained the mean and distribution of the number of retweets and N-retweet time. When analyzing dataset D_S, we estimated the mean of the number of retweets in the population because dataset D_S was obtained from dataset D_A by biased sampling. The method of estimating the mean number of retweets of positive tweets was as follows. Let μ_i^p be the sample mean of the number of retweets of positive tweets in section i (Table 1) and in dataset D_S, and let f_i^p be the number of positive tweets in section i and in dataset D_A divided by the number of positive tweets in dataset D_A. The mean number of retweets of positive tweets was estimated as $\sum_i f_i^p \mu_i^p$.

Next, we performed regression analysis to investigate the effects of message sentiment on its virality considering other factors related to retweet behavior. We used the variables shown in Table 5. Following the method in Ref. [27], we used the presence of URLs, hashtags, and the number of followers as control variables because these factors affect message diffusion [22,27,28]. Using these control variables, we examined the effects of message sentiment on its virality eliminating the effects of other factors. We did not include a variable for the activity of twitter users because this does not affect message diffusion [27]. We did not use dataset D_S for regression analysis because it was obtained from biased sampling.

Following the method in Ref. [27], we used a binomial regression model for regression of *RTnum* because the variance of the number of retweets is large (Tables 1 and 2). In the negative binomial regression model, the relation between dependent and independent variables is modeled as

$$\log(RTnum) = \beta_0 + \beta_1\, URL + \beta_2\, hash \\ + \beta_3 \log(follower) + \beta_4\, pos + \beta_5\, neg, \quad (1)$$

$$RTnum = e^{\beta_0} \times e^{\beta_1\, URL} \times e^{\beta_2\, hash} \\ \times follower^{\beta_3} \times e^{\beta_4\, pos} \times e^{\beta_5\, neg}, \quad (2)$$

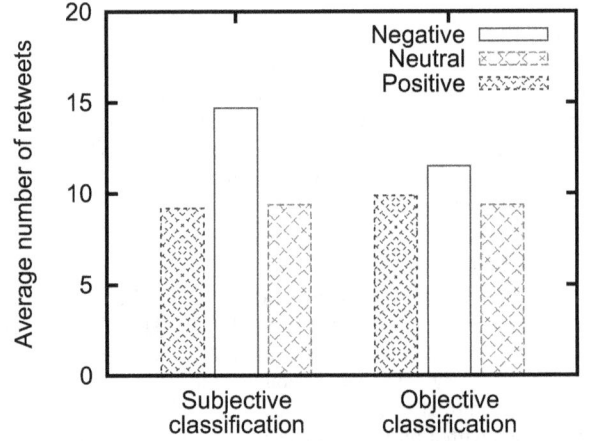

Figure 1: Relation between tweet sentiment and the mean number of retweets. Left-hand bars show the estimated mean values obtained from dataset D_S, and the right-hand bars show the simple mean values obtained from dataset D_A. The population is the tweets whose number of retweets is more than one. Retweet volume of negative tweets is larger than those of positive and neutral tweets.

where β_n is the regression coefficient. Note that *follower* is log transformed because the distribution of the number of followers is heavy-tailed. For the regression of *NRTtime*, we used a simple linear regression model.

5. RESULTS

5.1 Analysis of Descriptive Statistics

To address **RQ1**, we examined the mean number of retweets for each category based on tweet sentiment (Fig. 1). Bars on the left-hand side of the figure show the results obtained from dataset D_S, and bars on the right-hand side show the results obtained from dataset D_A. The results of dataset D_S show estimated mean values that are explained in Section 4.5.

(a) Subjective classification

(b) Objective classification

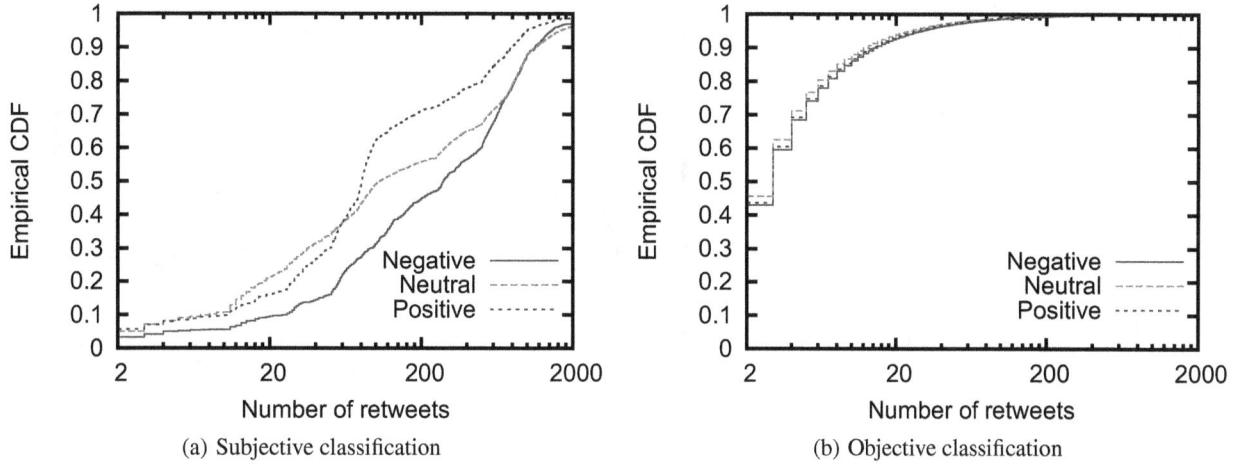

Figure 2: Cumulative distribution of the number of retweets for each category. Note that (a) shows the cumulative distributions of the retweet volume of the sampled tweets, not the total population. Negative tweets tend to have a larger retweet volume than positive and neutral tweets.

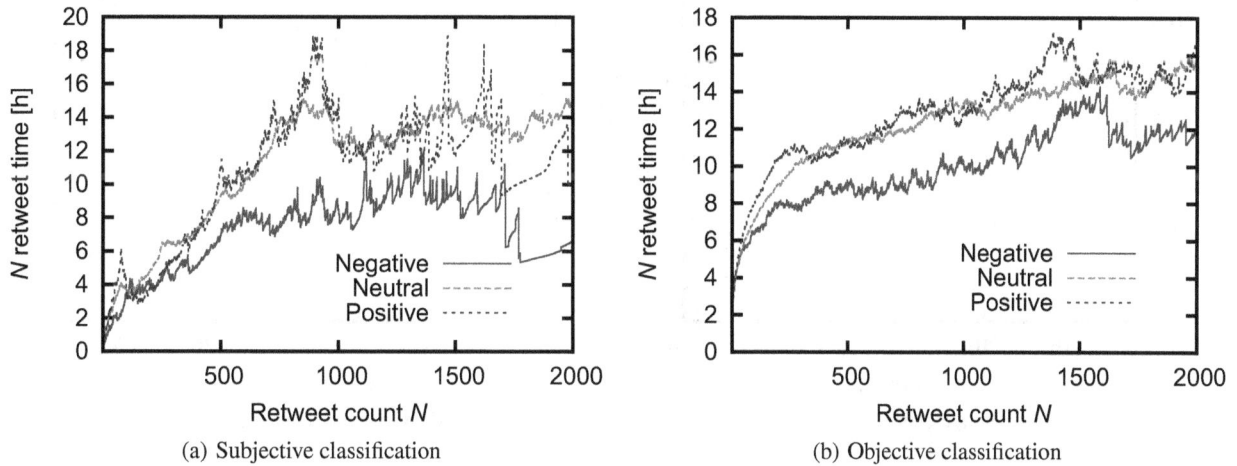

(a) Subjective classification

(b) Objective classification

Figure 3: Average N-retweet time for each category. Average N-retweet time of negative tweets is shorter than those of positive and neutral tweets.

Figure 1 shows that the retweet volume of negative tweets is approximately 1.2–1.6-fold that of neutral tweets, and the retweet volumes of positive and neutral tweets are similar to each other. We performed the pairwise test on the results of dataset D_A using the Steel-Dwass [12, 25] method, and found that there were significant differences in the number of retweets between any two categories based on sentiment ($p < 0.05$). These results suggest that the retweet volume of negative tweets is larger than that of neutral and positive tweets and the retweet volume of positive tweets is similar to neutral tweets. The differences of the mean values obtained with datasets D_S and D_A may be caused by the difference between objective and subjective classifications (Table 4).

Next, we investigated the distributions of the number of retweets for each category (Fig. 2). Figure 2 confirms that negative tweets tend to have a larger retweet volume than positive and neutral tweets. We can also find that positive tweets tend to have slightly larger retweet volume than neutral tweets (Fig. 2 (b)).

Next, we tackled retweet speed to answer **RQ2** by using average N retweet time. Figure 3 shows average N-retweet times for each

category. Average N-retweet time was obtained by calculating the average N-retweet time for tweets that were retweeted at least N times. Because the number of samples with a large retweet count, N, is limited, the average values fluctuate if N is large.

Figure 3 shows that average N-retweet time of negative tweets is shorter than those of positive and neutral tweets. In particular, when $N > 100$, the average N-retweet time of negative tweets is approximately 20% shorter than those of positive and neutral tweets. Note that the fraction of tweets retweeted more than 100 times is only 1% in the collected dataset. Namely, tweets with a retweet count of $N > 100$ have high virality in terms of diffusion volume. These results suggest that negative tweets spread faster than positive and neutral tweets, particularly for tweets with large diffusion volume. The diffusion time of negative tweets was approximately 20% shorter than that of positive and neutral tweets, namely the diffusion speed of negative tweets was about 1.25-fold that of positive and neutral tweets. In contrast, the N-retweet time of positive tweets was slightly longer than that of neutral tweets.

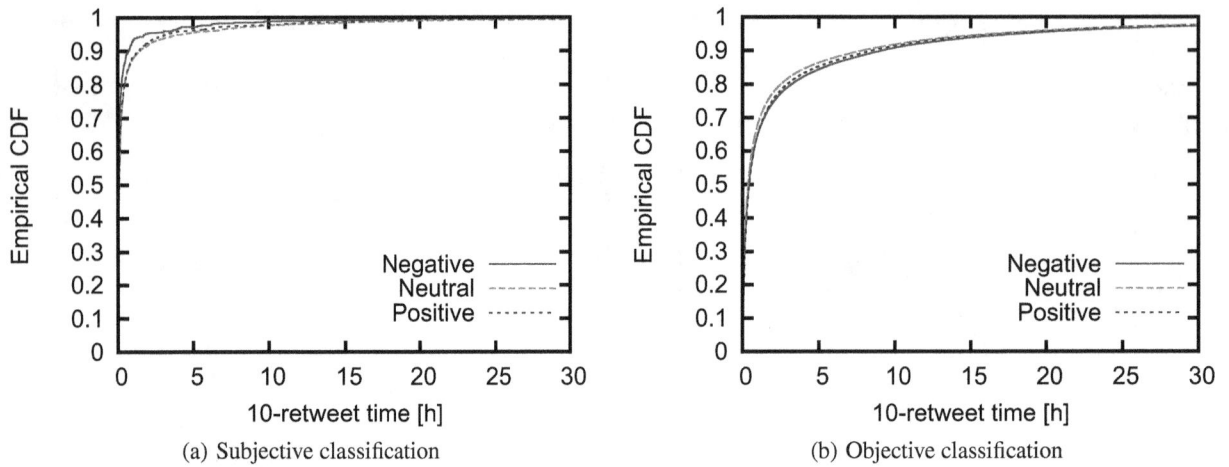

(a) Subjective classification   (b) Objective classification

Figure 4: Cumulative distribution of 10-retweet time for each category. 10-retweet time for negative tweets and tweets with other sentiment is similar.

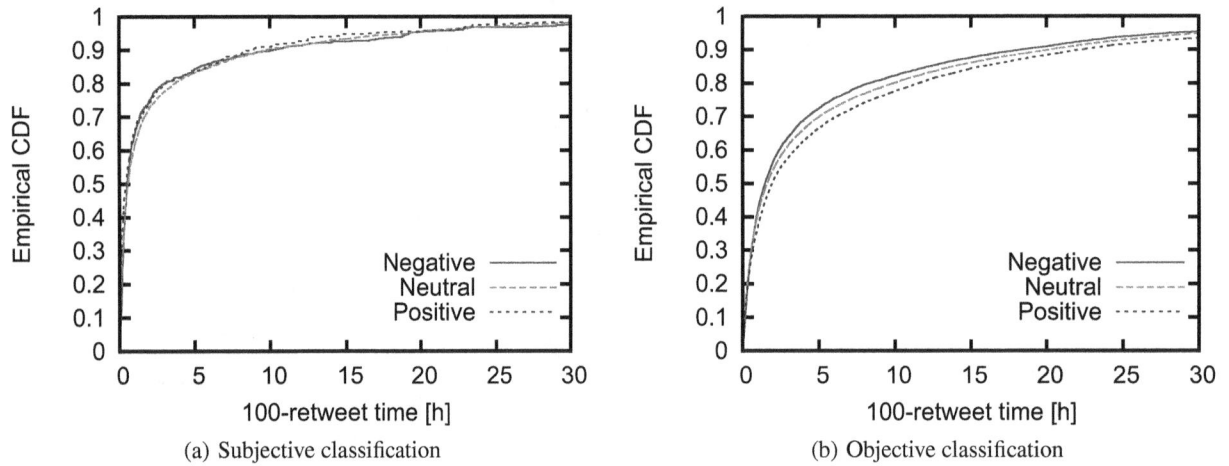

(a) Subjective classification   (b) Objective classification

Figure 5: Cumulative distribution of 100-retweet time for each category. 100-retweet time for negative tweets and tweets with other sentiment is similar.

We investigated the distribution of N-retweet time of tweets for each category. Figures 4, 5, and 6 show the cumulative distributions of N-retweet time for each category when $N = 10$, 100, and 1000, respectively.

These results confirm that negative tweets spread faster than neutral and positive tweets do if the retweet count, N, is large. Figure 6 shows that the diffusion speed of negative tweets is faster than tweets with other sentiment when $N = 1000$. In contrast, Figs. 4 and 5 show that N-retweet time for negative tweets and tweets with other sentiment is similar. The difference in N-retweet time between positive and neutral tweets was only observed in Fig. 5(b). The pairwise test with the Steel-Dwass method [12, 25] shows that there is a significant difference in 10-, 100-, and 1000-retweet time among tweet sentiment categories in dataset D_A ($p < 0.05$).

These analyses show similar results from datasets D_S and dataset D_A, which suggests that the results are robust. For **RQ1**, our results suggest that in terms of retweet volume, negative tweets were the most viral and the virality of positive tweets was similar to neutral tweets. For **RQ2**, negative tweets spread faster than neutral and

positive tweets, particularly when the retweet count was large, and positive and neutral tweets spread at similar speeds.

5.2 Regression Analysis

The results in the previous section show that the message sentiment and virality are closely related to each other. In this section, we perform regression analysis to investigate the relation between message sentiment and virality, eliminating the effects of other factors affecting message diffusion. We performed negative binomial regression analysis for investigating the effects of message sentiment on diffusion volume. The dependent variable was *RTnum*, and the independent variables were *pos*, *neg*, *follower*, *URL*, and *hash*. Table 6 shows the regression analysis results. The regression coefficient, β, and the values of e^{β} for each variable are shown in the table to demonstrate the effects of each independent variable on the dependent variable.

The result of the regression analysis shows that whether the sentiment of a tweet is negative or positive increases its number of retweets in the model. The strength of the effect of each variable can be estimated from the regression coefficient, e^{β} (Eq.(2)).

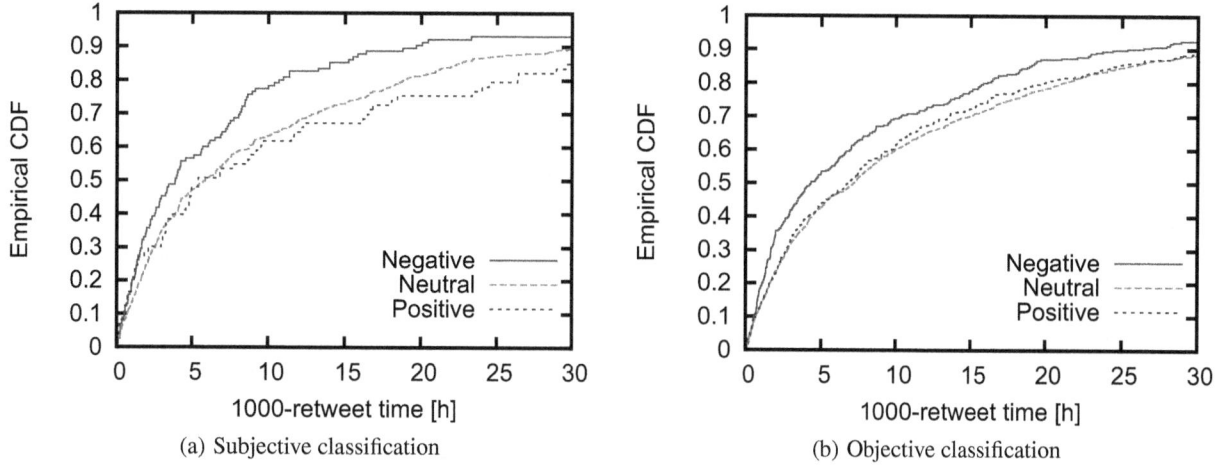

(a) Subjective classification   (b) Objective classification

Figure 6: Cumulative distribution of 1000-retweet time for each category. The diffusion speed of negative tweets is faster than tweets with other sentiment when $N = 1000$.

The regression coefficient of *neg* suggests that negative tweets are retweeted 36.5% more often than neutral tweets, which is consistent with the results in the previous subsection. This indicates that negative sentiment is a major driving factor of tweet diffusion, because the regression coefficient of *neg* is comparable with *hash*, which is a major driving factor for retweets [22, 28]. In addition, positive sentiment in a tweet increases retweet volume, although the effect is weaker than other factors. In summary, this result shows that negative sentiment is a strong driving factor for retweet diffusion and that positive sentiment is not a strong driving factor for retweet diffusion, although it slightly affects diffusion volume.

Note that pseudo R^2 of our model is low. Message diffusion on social media is often difficult to explain, and there are many other driving factors. In this analysis, we can conclude that the effects of negative and positive sentiment are statistically significant and the effect of negative sentiment is similar to that of hashtags. We do not claim that we can model the retweet volume only using these variables. We should also note that the value of pseudo R^2 of our model is lower than that obtained in [27]. This is because our dataset does not include tweets that are not retweeted. URLs or hashtags in tweets are strong factors affecting whether the tweets are retweeted or not [22,28]. Therefore, we can generally construct more accurate model explaining *RTNum* from these independent variables if the dataset includes tweets with no retweet than if the dataset only includes tweets with more than one retweet.

Finally, we examined the relation between message sentiment and its diffusion speed by regression analysis. We used 100-*RTtime*, and 1000-*RTtime* as dependent variables. In addition to the independent variables used in the diffusion volume regression analysis, we used *RTnum* as an independent variable. This is because tweets with a large diffusion volume are considered to spread fast. In the following analyses, a linear regression model was used. Tables 7 and 8 show the regression results for the dependent variables of 100-*RTtime*, and 1000-*RTtime*, respectively.

Table 8 indicates that the presence of negative sentiment in a message decreases the 1000-retweet time ($p < 0.1$). This result is consistent with the observation in the previous subsection that negative tweets spread fast when the number of retweets is large. Table 7 shows that the presence of negative sentiment in a message does not significantly affect 100-retweet time. This result suggests that negative sentiment does not have a significant effect on diffu-

Table 6: Negative binomial regression results for *RTnum*. ***: significant at the 1% level, **: significant at the 5% level, *: significant at the 10% level.

Dependent variable: *RTnum*		
Independent variables	Coeff. β	e^β
pos***	0.131	1.139
neg***	0.311	1.365
log(*follower*)***	0.203	
URL***	0.546	1.726
hash***	0.291	1.338
constant***	0.467	
Pseudo R^2		0.030
Num. of observations		4,137,064

sion speed when the diffusion volume is small. Looking at other control variables, as intuitively expected, we can find that *follower*, *URL*, and *RTnum* significantly affect diffusion speed.

These results do not show that positive sentiment increases diffusion speed. Positive sentiment in a tweet does not significantly affect 1000-retweet time and positively and significantly affect 100-retweet time.

Our findings are summarized in Table 9. We can conclude that negative tweets spread more widely than positive and neutral tweets, and it is suggested that negative tweets spread faster than tweets with other sentiments, particularly for tweets with a large diffusion volume,. The effect of positive sentiment is weaker than that of negative sentiment, although positive tweets are retweeted slightly more than neutral tweets. Moreover, the diffusion speed of positive tweets is similar to that of neutral tweets, although for tweets with a small diffusion volume, positive tweets sometimes spread slower than neutral tweets.

Table 7: Regression results for 100-*RTtime*[h]. ***: significant at the 1% level, **: significant at the 5% level, *:significant at the 10% level.

Dependent variable: 100-*RTtime* [h]	
Independent variables	Coeff. β
pos***	1.149
neg	0.052
log(*follower*)***	-0.632
URL***	1.889
hash***	1.992
RTnum***	-0.003
constant***	11.855
R^2	0.040
Num. of observations	48,814

Table 8: Regression results for 1000-*RTtime*[h]. ***: significant at the 1% level, **: significant at the 5% level, *: significant at the 10% level.

Dependent variable: 1000-*RTtime* [h]	
Independent variables	Coeff. β
pos	0.941
neg*	-1.922
log(*follower*)**	-0.331
URL***	5.055
hash	0.339
RTnum***	-0.002
constant***	17.365
R^2	0.080
Num. of observations	2,194

6. DISCUSSION

6.1 Findings and Implications

Our study shows that negative tweets are more viral than positive tweets in terms of retweet volume. This is a strong evidence of existence of negativity bias [6, 24, 31] on social media. As discussed in Section 2, prior work by Stieglitz *et al.* [27] only partly supported negativity bias, and Gruzd *et al.* [14] showed opposite results. These studies targeted domain-specific tweets, and as discussed in Ref. [27], the tweet domain alters how tweet sentiment affects the virality. However, our study investigates the effects of tweet sentiment after eliminating the effects of tweet domains. Consequently, our study shows that negative tweets are generally more viral than positive tweets, which indicates negativity bias on social media.

The results for retweet speed also partly support negativity bias. We investigated the relation between tweet sentiment and N-retweet time. For a large retweet count, N, negative tweets spread faster than positive and neutral tweets. Stieglitz *et al.* [27] only used 1-retweet time, and found that there was no significant difference in retweet speed between positive and negative tweets. Our study shows that negative tweets spread faster than positive tweets when the diffusion volume is large. To the best of our knowledge, ours is

the first study to show the effects of sentiment on diffusion speed of tweets with a large diffusion volume.

Our results also show that the effects of positive sentiment in a tweet on its virality are weak. This contradicts the results in Refs. [14, 22, 26, 27] suggesting that positive and negative sentiment in a message increase its virality. One possible cause of this difference between our study and previous studies might be the nationality. Ours is the first study to use Japanese tweets to investigate the relation between tweet sentiment and virality. The language and cultural difference may affect the results because usage patterns of Twitter users differ across languages [16]. However, more analyses are necessary to reveal the cause of this.

Our results have several implications. First, it is important for companies to address negative opinions about their products on social media. Even if there are the same number of users with positive as those with negative opinions, negative opinions may spread faster and further, and thus reach a larger number of people than the positive opinions. Second, it is important to track the sentiment of individual tweets to prevent unintentional tweet diffusion. Recently, negative rumors and misinformation spread on social media, known as *flaming*, have posed serious problems, and blocking rumor spread is of interest to researchers [10, 32]. Our results suggest that individual users should take care to avoid unnecessary negative terms to prevent the unintentional information spread. A mechanism to detect and alert users to tweet sentiment may be an effective approach.

6.2 Limitations

While we used a large-scale dataset including 4.1 million tweets, it was still a sample of messages on social media. We studied Twitter as a social media platform, and only analyzed Japanese tweets. We chose Twitter because of its availability of large-scale data; however, to generalize the results, it is necessary to analyze data from other platforms. Most previous studies used English tweets [14, 15, 22], some used German tweets [26, 27], whereas we used Japanese tweets. Our study shows that for Japanese tweets, tweet sentiment is a major driving factor for retweets. However, the research methodologies of this study are different from previous studies, particularly regarding tweet topics, and Twitter usage patterns are different across languages [16]. Therefore, the differences among different languages should be investigated. For examining the generalizability of our results, we are also interested in several tasks such as expanding the data collection period, and investigating messages during several social events (e.g., national festival holidays).

We used a simple approach for objective classification of large-scale tweets based on their sentiment [15, 22]. Although we obtained similar results from the datasets constructed by objective and subjective classifications, using a more sophisticated method to determine tweet sentiment should produce better results. Because tweets are short it is difficult to determine tweet sentiment and there several studies about determining tweet sentiment accurately [2, 5, 13, 19]. In future work, we intend to apply these techniques to our dataset, and validate the results in this paper.

7. CONCLUSION

We investigated the relation between the sentiment of a tweet and its virality in terms of diffusion volume and speed by analyzing 4.1 million tweets on Twitter. We used the number of retweets and N-retweet time as measures of tweet virality. We found that negative tweets spread more widely than positive and neutral tweets, and that negative tweets spread faster than positive and neutral tweets when the diffusion volume was large. We showed that the diffu-

Table 9: Summary of findings

RQ		Conclusion	Supporting results
1: Retweet volume	Negative vs. neutral	Negative is larger	Figs. 1, 2, and Tab. 6
	Negative vs. positive	Negative is larger	Figs. 1, 2, and Tab. 6
	Positive vs. neutral	Positive is slightly larger	Tab. 6
2: Retweet speed	Negative vs. neutral	Negative is faster for large diffusion volume	Figs. 3, 6, and Tab. 8[*]
	Negative vs. positive	Negative is faster for large diffusion volume	Figs. 3, 6, and Tab. 8[*]
	Positive vs. neutral	Neutral is slightly faster for small diffusion volume	Figs. 3(b), 5(b), and Tab. 7

[*] Tab. 8 is not so strong evidence, but supports this conclusion.

sion volume of negative tweets was 1.2–1.6-fold that of positive and neutral tweets, and that the diffusion speed of negative tweets was 1.25-fold that of positive and neutral tweets when the diffusion volume was large.

Acknowledgements

The authors would like to thank Dr. Mitsuo Yoshida of Toyohashi University of Technology for his support to the data collection, and Hisayuki Mori of Kwansei Gakuin University for helping the analyses. This work was partly supported by JSPS KAKENHI Grant Number 25280030 and 26870076.

8. REFERENCES

[1] Mecab: Yet Another Part-of-Speech and Morphological Analyzer. http://mecab.sourceforge.net.

[2] A. Agarwal, B. Xie, I. Vovsha, O. Rambow, and R. Passonneau. Sentiment analysis of Twitter data. In *Proceedings of the Workshop on Languages in Social Media (LSM'11)*, pages 30–38, June 2011.

[3] E. Bakshy, J. M. Hofman, W. A. Mason, and D. J. Watts. Everyone's an influencer: Quantifying influence on Twitter. In *Proceedings of the 4th ACM International Conference on Web Search and Data Mining (WSDM'11)*, pages 65–74, Feb. 2011.

[4] E. Bakshy, I. Rosenn, C. Marlow, and L. Adamic. The role of social networks in information diffusion. In *Proceedings of the 21st International Conference on World Wide Web (WWW'12)*, pages 519–528, Apr. 2012.

[5] L. Barbosa and J. Feng. Robust sentiment detection on Twitter from biased and noisy data. In *Proceedings of the 23rd International Conference on Computational Linguistics (COLING'10)*, pages 36–44, Aug. 2010.

[6] R. F. Baumeister and E. Bratslavsky. Bad is stronger than good. *Review of General Psychology*, 5(4):323–370, Dec. 2001.

[7] J. Berger. Arousal increases social transmission of information. *Psychological Science*, 22(7):891–893, July 2011.

[8] J. Berger and K. L. Milkman. What makes online content viral? *Journal of Marketing Research*, 49(2):192–205, Apr. 2012.

[9] D. Blei, A. Ng, and M. Jordan. Latent Dirichlet allocation. *Journal of Machine Learning Research*, 3:993l–1022, Jan. 2003.

[10] C. Budak, D. Agrawal, and A. El Abbadi. Limiting the spread of misinformation in social networks. In *Proceedings of the 20th International Conference on World Wide Web (WWW'11)*, pages 665–674, Mar. 2011.

[11] J. Cheng, L. Adamic, P. A. Dow, J. M. Kleinberg, and J. Leskovec. Can cascades be predicted? In *Proceedings of the 23rd International Conference on World Wide Web (WWW'14)*, pages 925–936, Apr. 2014.

[12] M. Dwass. Some k-sample rank-order tests. In *Contributions to Probability and Statistics*, pages 198–202. Stanford University Press, 1960.

[13] P. Gonçalves, M. Araújo, F. Benevenuto, and M. Cha. Comparing and combining sentiment analysis methods. In *Proceedings of the first ACM Conference on Online Social Networks (COSN'13)*, pages 27–38, Oct. 2013.

[14] A. Gruzd, S. Doiron, and P. Mai. Is happiness contagious online? A case of Twitter and the 2010 Winter Olympics. In *Proceedings of the 44th Hawaii International Conference on System Sciences (HICSS'11)*, pages 1–9, Jan. 2011.

[15] L. Hansen, A. Arvidsson, F. Nielsen, E. Colleoni, and M. Etter. Good friends, bad news - Affect and virality in Twitter. *Future Information Technology*, 185:34–43, Dec. 2011.

[16] L. Hong, G. Convertino, and E. H. Chi. Language matters in Twitter: A large scale study. In *Proceedings of the 5th International AAAI Conference on Weblogs and Social Media (ICWSM'11)*, pages 518–521, July 2011.

[17] L. Hong, O. Dan, and B. Davison. Predicting popular messages in Twitter. In *Proceedings of the 20th International Conference on World Wide Web (WWW'11)*, pages 57–58, Apr. 2011.

[18] D. Kempe, J. M. Kleinberg, and E. Tardos. Maximizing the spread of influence through a social network. In *Proceedings of the 9th ACM SIGKDD International Conference on Knowledge Discovery and Data Mining (KDD'03)*, pages 137–146, Aug. 2003.

[19] E. Kontopoulos, C. Berberidis, T. Dergiades, and N. Bassiliades. Ontology-based sentiment analysis of Twitter posts. *Expert Systems with Applications*, 40(10):4065–4074, Aug. 2013.

[20] A. Kupavskii, L. Ostroumova, A. Umnov, S. Usachev, P. Serdyukov, G. Gusev, and A. Kustarev. Prediction of retweet cascade size over time. In *Proceedings of the 21st ACM International Conference on Information and Knowledge Management (CIKM'12)*, pages 2335–2338, Oct. 2012.

[21] H. Kwak, C. Lee, H. Park, and S. Moon. What is Twitter, a social network or a news media? In *Proceedings of the 19th*

International Conference on World Wide Web (WWW'10), pages 591–600, Apr. 2010.

[22] N. Naveed, T. Gottron, J. Kunegis, and A. Alhadi. Bad news travel fast: A content-based analysis of interestingness on Twitter. In *Proceedings of the ACM Web Science Conference 2011 (WebSci'11)*, pages 1–7, June 2011.

[23] S. Rosenthal, P. Nakov, S. Kiritchenko, S. M. Mohammad, A. Ritter, and V. Stoyanov. SemEval-2015 task 10: Sentiment analysis in Twitter. In *Proceedings of the 9th International Workshop on Semantic Evaluation (SemEval'15)*, pages 451–463, June 2015.

[24] P. Rozin and E. B. Royzman. Negativity bias, negativity dominance, and contagion. *Personality and Social Psychology Review*, 5(4):296–320, Nov. 2001.

[25] R. G. D. Steel. A rank sum test for comparing all pairs of treatments. *Technometrics*, 2(2):197–207, May 1960.

[26] S. Stieglitz and L. Dang-Xuan. Political communication and influence through microblogging—an empirical analysis of sentiment in Twitter messages and retweet behavior. In *Proceedings of the 45th Hawaii International Conference on System Science (HICSS'12)*, pages 3500–3509, Jan. 2012.

[27] S. Stieglitz and L. Dang-Xuan. Emotions and information diffusion in social media—sentiment of microblogs and sharing behavior. *Journal of Management Information Systems*, 29(4):217–247, 2013.

[28] B. Suh, L. Hong, P. Pirolli, and E. Chi. Want to be retweeted? Large scale analytics on factors impacting retweet in Twitter network. In *Proceedings of the 2nd IEEE International Conference on Social Computing (SocialCom'10)*, pages 177–184, Aug. 2010.

[29] H. Takamura, T. Inui, and M. Okumura. Extracting semantic orientations of words using spin model. In *Proceedings of the 43rd Annual Meeting on Association for Computational Linguistics (ACL'05)*, pages 133–140, June 2005.

[30] H. Takamura, T. Inui, and M. Okumura. Extracting semantic orientations using spin model. *IPSJ Journal*, 47(2):627–637, Feb. 2006. (in Japanese).

[31] S. E. Taylor. Asymmetrical effects of positive and negative events: The mobilization-minimization hypothesis. *Psychological Bulletin*, 110(1):67–85, July 1991.

[32] S. Wen, J. Jiang, Y. Xiang, S. Yu, W. Zhou, and W. Jia. To shut them up or to clarify: Restraining the spread of rumors in online social networks. *IEEE Transactions on Parallel & Distributed Systems*, 25(12):3306–3316, Dec. 2014.

[33] S. Yang, A. Kolcz, A. Schlaikjer, and P. Gupta. Large-scale high-precision topic modeling on Twitter. In *Proceedings of the 20th ACM SIGKDD Conference on Knowledge Discovery and Data Mining (KDD'14)*, pages 1907–1916, Aug. 2014.

Location Prediction:
Communities Speak Louder than Friends

Jun Pang
University of Luxembourg
FSTC & SnT
jun.pang@uni.lu

Yang Zhang
University of Luxembourg
FSTC
yang.zhang@uni.lu

ABSTRACT

Humans are social animals, they interact with different communities of friends to conduct different activities. The literature shows that human mobility is constrained by their social relations. In this paper, we investigate the social impact of a person's communities on his mobility, instead of all friends from his online social networks. This study can be particularly useful, as certain social behaviors are influenced by specific communities but not all friends. To achieve our goal, we first develop a measure to characterize a person's social diversity, which we term 'community entropy'. Through analysis of two real-life datasets, we demonstrate that a person's mobility is influenced only by a small fraction of his communities and the influence depends on the social contexts of the communities. We then exploit machine learning techniques to predict users' future movement based on their communities' information. Extensive experiments demonstrate the prediction's effectiveness.

Categories and Subject Descriptors

H.2.8 [**Database Management**]: Database Applications—*Data mining*

General Terms

Algorithms, theory, experiments

Keywords

Human mobility, social networks, network communities

1. INTRODUCTION

Humans are social animals, everyone is a part of the society and gets influences from it. For example, our daily behaviors, such as what types of music we listen to, where we have lunch on weekdays and what activities we conduct on weekends, are largely dependent on our social relations. Normally, we categorize our social relations into different

COSN'15, November 2–3, 2015, Palo Alto, California, USA.
© 2015 ACM. ISBN 978-1-4503-3951-3/15/11 ...$15.00.
DOI: http://dx.doi.org/10.1145/2817946.2817954.

groups, i.e., social communities, using different criteria and considerations. By definition, *a community is a social unit of any size that shares common values.*[1] Typical communities include family, close friends, colleagues, etc. In daily life, humans are engaged in various social environments, and they interact with different communities depending on the environments. For our specific behaviors, social influences, in most of cases, are not from *all our friends* but from *certain communities*. For example, we listen to similar types of music as our close friends, but not as our parents; we have lunch together with our colleagues on weekdays, but not with our college friends living in another city; on weekends we spend more time with family, but not with our colleagues.

Location-based social network services (LBSNs) have been booming during the past five years. Nowadays, it is common for a user to attach his location when he publishes a photo or a status using his online social network account. Moreover, users may just share their locations, called *check-in*, to tell their friends where they are or to engage in social games as in Foursquare. Since these large amount of location and social relation data become available, studying human mobility and its connection with social relationships becomes quantitatively achievable (e.g., [16, 10, 9, 34, 15, 7, 8]). Understanding human mobility can lead to compelling applications including location recommendation [44, 41, 43, 14, 20], urban planning [42], immigration patterns [5], etc.

Previous works, including [1, 6, 10, 33], show that human mobility is influenced by social factors. However, there is one common shortcoming: they all treat friends of users equally. Similar to other social behaviors, in most cases mobility is influenced by specific communities but not all friends. For example, the aforementioned colleagues can influence the place a user goes for lunch but probably have nothing to do with his weekend plans. Meanwhile, where a user visits on weekends largely depends on his friends or family, but not his colleagues. Therefore, the impact on a user's mobility should be considered from the perspectives of communities instead of all friends. In a broader view, community is arguably the most useful resolution to study social networks [39].

Contributions. In this paper, we aim to study the impact from communities on a user's mobility and predict his locations based on his community information.

First, we partition each users' friends into communities and propose a notion namely community entropy to quantify a user's social diversity. Second, we analyze communities' influences on users' mobility and our main conclusions include:

---

[1] http://en.wikipedia.org/wiki/Community

(1) communities' influences on users' mobility are stronger than their friends'; (2) each user is only influenced by a small number of his communities; and (3) such influence is typically constrained by temporal and spatial contexts. Third, we predict users' locations using their community information. Experimental results on two real-life datasets with millions of location data show that the community-based predictor achieves a strong performance.

Organization. After the introduction, we present a few preliminaries and our datasets in Section 2. Then we describe the community detection process and propose the notion of community entropy in Section 3. The relationship between users and their communities on mobility is analyzed in Section 4. Based on our analysis, we propose a location predictor with features linked to community information and present experimental results in Section 5. We discuss related work in Section 6 and conclude our paper with some future work in Section 7.

2. PRELIMINARIES

We summarize the notations in Section 2.1 and describe the datasets that we use throughout the paper in Section 2.2.

2.1 Notations

All users are contained in the set $\mathcal{U}$ while a single user is denoted by u. We use the set $f(u)$ to represent u's friends. A community of a user u is a subset of his friends denoted by c and $c \subseteq f(u)$. Meanwhile, $C(u)$ represents all the communities of u, i.e., $C(u)$ is a set of sets of u's communities. Every friend of a user is assigned into one of the user's communities, the union of all his communities is the set of all his friends. In this work, we only consider non-overlapping communities, namely $c \cap c' = \emptyset$ for $c, c' \in C(u)$. However, this assumption is not crucial to our approach and our results can be extended for overlapping communities as well.

A check-in of u is denoted by a tuple $\langle u, t, \ell \rangle$, where t represents the time and ℓ is the location that corresponds to a pair of latitude and longitude. We use $CI(u)$ to represent all the check-ins of u. Without ambiguity, we use location and check-in interchangeably in the following discussion.

2.2 The datasets

We exploit two types of social network datasets for this work. The first one is collected by the authors of [10] from Gowalla – a popular LBSN service back in 2011. The dataset was collected from February 2009 to October 2010 and it contains 6,442,892 check-ins. Besides location information, the dataset also includes the corresponding social data which contains around 1.9 million users and 9.5 million edges. Due to the large data sparsity, we mainly focus on the check-in data in two cities in US, including New York (NY (G)) and San Francisco (SF (G)). They are among the areas with most check-ins in the dataset. In addition, when performing mobility analysis and location prediction, we only focus on users who have conducted at least 100 check-ins in each city and we term these users as *active users*.

The second dataset is collected from Twitter from December 2014 to April 2015 by the authors of this paper. Again, we focus on the data in New York (NY (T)) and San Francisco (SF (T)) and treat all the geo-tagged tweets (tweets labeled with geographical coordinates) as users' check-ins.

We exploit Twitter's Streaming API[2] to collect all the geo-tagged tweets. Each check-in is organized as a 4-tuple.

$$\langle uid, time, latitude, longitude \rangle$$

Figure 1 depicts a sample of check-ins in New York. To collect the social relationships among users, we adopt Twitter's REST API[3] to query each user's followers and followees. Two users are considered friends if they follow each other mutually.

Similar to the Gowalla dataset, we only focus on active users (users with more than 100 check-ins) in the Twitter dataset. Moreover, we also filter out the users who have more than 2,000 check-ins since most of them are public accounts such as @NewYorkCP which publishes 16,681 check-ins at the exact same location. Table 1 summarizes the two datasets. The Twitter dataset is available upon request.

3. COMMUNITIES

We first show how to detect communities in social networks in Section 3.1 and then propose a new notion to characterize users' social diversity in Section 3.2.

3.1 Community detection in social networks

Community detection in networks (or graphs) has been extensively studied for the past decade (e.g., see [25, 31, 2, 18, 32, 22, 38, 37, 21, 39, 23]). It has important applications in many fields, including physics, biology, sociology as well as computer science. The principle behind community detection is to partition nodes of a large graph into groups following certain metrics on the graph structure [18]. In the context of social networks, besides the social graph, each user is also affiliated with attributes. These information can also be used to detect communities (e.g., see [22, 38, 23]). For example, people who graduate from the same university can be considered as a community. Since the datasets we use only contain social graphs and no personal information are provided, we apply the algorithms that are based on information encoded in graph structure to detect communities.

According to the comparative analysis [18], among all the community detection algorithms, Infomap [31] has the best performance on undirected and unweighted graphs and has been widely used in many systems [26, 29]. Therefore, we apply it in this work. Next we give a brief overview of Infomap and describe how we use it to detect communities. The main idea of Infomap can be summarized as follows: information flow in a network can characterize the behavior of the whole network, which consequently reflects the structure of the network. A group of nodes among which information flows relatively fast can be considered as one community. Therefore, Infomap intends to use information flow to detect communities in a network. In the beginning, Infomap simulates information flow in a network with random walks. Then the algorithm partitions the network into communities and exploits Huffman coding to encode the network at two levels. At the community level, the algorithm assigns a unique code for each community based on the information flow among different communities; at the node level, the algorithm assigns a code for each node based on the information flow within the community. Infomap allows the Huffman codes in different communities (node level) being

---

[2] https://dev.twitter.com/streaming/overview
[3] https://dev.twitter.com/rest/public

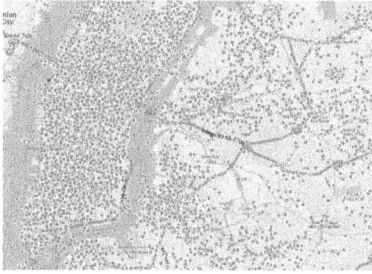

Figure 1: Check-ins in New York.

	NY (G)	SF (G)	NY (T)	SF (T)
# of users	7,786	6,617	207,805	113,383
# of check-ins	176,324	177,357	2,325,907	2,163,959
Avg.# of check-ins	21.6	26.8	11.2	19.1
# of active users	175	236	1,636	1,626
Avg.# of friends (active user)	79.4	69.7	376.9	289.0

Table 1: Summary of the datasets.

duplicated which results in a more efficient encoding (less description length). In the end, finding a Huffman code to concisely describe the information flow while minimizing the description length is thus equivalent to discovering the network's community structure. In other words, the objective of Infomap is to find a partition of a network such that the code length for representing information flow among communities and within each community is minimized. Since it is infeasible to search all possible community partitions, Infomap further exploits a deterministic greedy search algorithm [11, 36] to find partitions.

In our work, to detect communities of u, we first find all his friends as well as the links among them. Then, we delete u and all edges linked to him and apply Infomap algorithm to the remaining part of the graph. Figure 2 presents the detected communities of two users in the Gowalla dataset. Each community is marked with a different color.

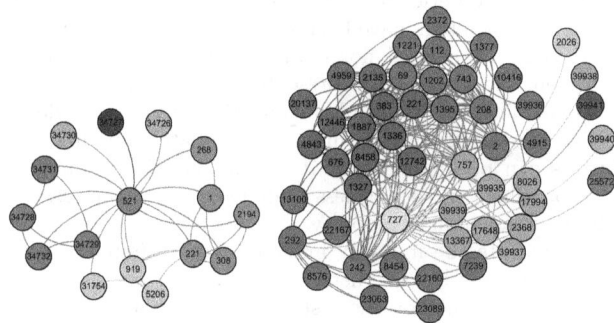

(a) User 521 (15 friends) (b) User 727 (50 friends)

Figure 2: Communities of users 521 and 727.

	Gowalla	Twitter
Avg.# of communities	4.5	5.3
Avg. community size	13.2	20.8

Table 2: Community summary of active users.

Table 2 lists the summary of community information of all active users in the two datasets. Each active user in Gowalla has on average 4.5 communities while the value is 5.3 for the Twitter users. In addition, the average community size of Twitter users is bigger than Gowalla users (20.8 vs. 13.2). This is because active users in the Twitter dataset have more friends than those in the Gowalla dataset

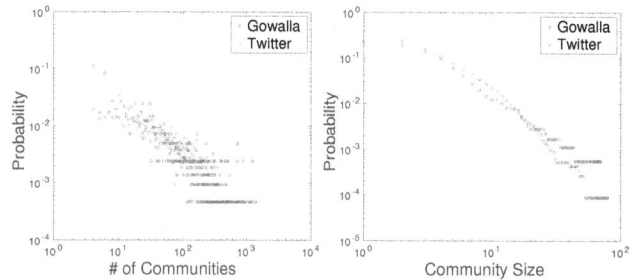

Figure 3: Distribution of users w.r.t the number of communities and distribution of communities w.r.t their size.

(see Table 1), which indicates general social network services, such as Twitter, contain more users' social relationships than LBSN services, such as Gowalla. In spite of the differences on the average value in Table 2, community number and community size in the two datasets follow a similar distribution. As we can see from Figure 3, both community number and size follow the power law: most of the users have small number of communities and most of the detected communities are small as well.

3.2 Community entropy

After detecting communities, we are given a new domain of attributes on users. We are particularly interested in how diverse a user's communities are. We motivate this *social diversity* through an example. Suppose that a user is engaged in many communities, such as colleagues at work, family members, college friends, chess club, basketball team, etc, then he is considered an active society member. Users of this kind are always involving in different social scenarios or environments, and his daily behaviors are largely dependent on his social relations.

Although we do not have the semantics of each of our detected communities, such as the aforementioned colleagues at work or chess club, we can still use the information encoded in the graph to define a user's social diversity. For instance, for a user with several communities whose sizes are more or less the same, his social diversity is for sure higher than those with only one community.

To quantify the social diversity of a user, we introduce the notion of *community entropy*.

Definition 1. For a user u, his *community entropy* is defined as

$$coment(u) = \frac{1}{1-\alpha} \ln \sum_{c \in C(u)} (\frac{|c|}{|f(u)|})^{\alpha}.$$

Our community entropy follows the definition of Rényi entropy [30]. Here, α is called the order of diversity, it can control the impact of community size on the value which gives more flexibility to distinguish users when focusing on the sizes of their communities. In simple terms, our community entropy,

- when $\alpha > 1$, values more on larger communities;

- when $\alpha < 1$, values more on smaller communities.

The limit of $coment(u)$ with $\alpha \to 1$ is the Shannon entropy.[4] In general, if a user has many communities with sizes equally distributed, then his community entropy is high and this indicates that his social relations are highly diverse.

We set $\alpha > 1$ in the following discussion to limit the impact of small communities since a user may randomly add strangers as his friends in online social networks and these strangers normally form small communities (such as a one-user community[5]), which have less impact on the user's mobility. For example, if a user u has three communities with sizes equal to 1, 1 and 10, then his communities are not that diverse following the above intuition. When we set α less than 1, such as 0.5, we have $coment(u) = 0.79$ which is a high value indicating u's social circles are diverse. On the other hand, if we set α bigger than 1, such as 10, $coment(u)$ drops to 0.20 which captures our intuition. In the following experiments, we set $\alpha = 10$ when calculating users' community entropies. Note that we have also set α to other numbers bigger than one and observed similar results. Figure 4 shows the histogram of community entropies of all active users in two datasets.

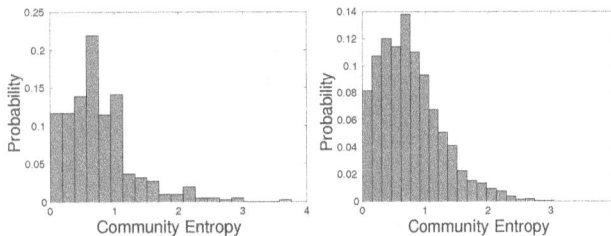

Figure 4: Distribution of community entropies of active users in Gowalla (left) and Twitter (right).

4. COMMUNITIES AND MOBILITY

It has been proved that social factors play an important role on users' mobility, e.g., see [10]. For instance, one may go to lunch with his friends or go to a bar to hangout with his friends. Meanwhile, for a user, friends of his social networks (as well as in real life) are not all equal. Instead friends normally belong to certain communities. When considering a user's mobility, intuitively different communities can impose different influence within certain contexts or social environments. Continuing with the above example, the people the user has lunch with are normally his colleagues while the people he meets at night are his close friends. Therefore, in order to analyze the impact from a user's social relations on

---

[4]https://en.wikipedia.org/wiki/Renyi_entropy
[5]In our community detection algorithm, if u' himself forms a community of u, then it indicates that u' does not know any other friends of u.

his mobility, it is reasonable to focus on social influence at the community level.

In this section, we first study communities' influence on users' mobility. After that, we study the characteristics of the influential communities with the following two intuitions in mind: (1) a user's daily activities are constrained, and the number of communities he interacts with is limited; (2) communities influence a user's social behavior under different contexts.

4.1 Influential communities

Figure 5a depicts a user's two communities' check-ins in Manhattan of the New York City. We can observe a quite clear separation between these two communities' check-ins: members of community 1 mainly visit Uptown and Midtown Manhattan while community 2 focuses more on Midtown. This indicates that different communities have their social activities at different areas. In a broader view, this shows that partitioning users' check-ins at the social network level (through community detection) can result in meaningful spatial clusters as well.

A single community also has several favorite places. For example, community 1 in Figure 5a visits Times Square and Broadway quite often while members of community 2 like to stay close to Madison square park. A user may socialize with different communities at different places, for example, he may go to watch a basketball game with his family at the stadium and have lunch with his colleagues near his office. Therefore, to study influences on mobility from communities to a user, we need to summarize each community's *frequent movement areas*. To discover a community's frequent movement areas, we perform clustering on all locations that the community members have been to. Each cluster is then represented by its central point and a community's frequent movement areas are thus represented by the centroids of all clusters. The clustering algorithm we use is the agglomerative hierarchical clustering. We regulate that any two clusters can be aligned only if the distance between their corresponding centroids is less than 500m which is a reasonable range for human mobility.

To illustrate the mobility influence from communities to users, we choose to use 'distances'. More precisely, we represent the influence by the distances between a user's locations and the frequent movement areas of his communities. Shorter distances imply stronger influences. For each location a user has visited, we calculate the distances between the location and all his communities' frequent movement areas. Then, for each community of the user, we choose the shortest distance between the location and the community's frequent movement areas as the *distance* between the location and the community. The community which has the smallest distance to the location is considered as the *influential community* of the user at this location. The distance between the influential community and the user's location is further defined as the distance between the user's location and his communities. Note that a user can have multiple influential communities and an influential community can influence a user on multiple locations.

Figure 5b depicts the distribution of distances between users' locations and their communities in New York and San Francisco in the two datasets. As we can see, most of the distances are short which indicates the communities are quite close to users' locations. To illustrate that these

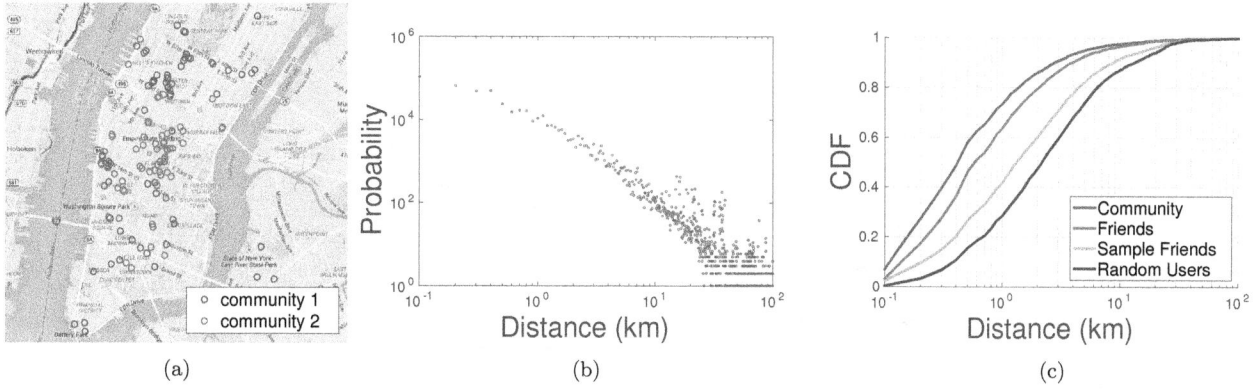

Figure 5: (a) A user's two communities' check-ins in Manhattan; (b) distribution of distances between users and their communities; (c) cumulative distribution function of distances between users and their communities, friends, sample friends and random users.

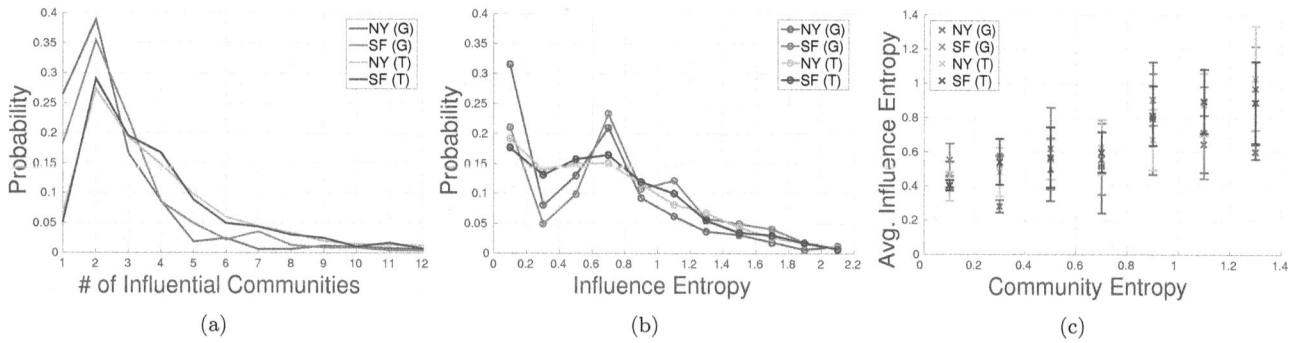

Figure 6: (a) Distribution of the number of influential communities; (b) distribution of influence entropies (bucketed by 0.2) (c) influence entropy vs. community entropy.

short distances are not due to the limits of the city areas, for each location of a user, we pick some random users in the city, summarize their frequent movement areas through clustering and find the minimal distance between their frequent movement areas and the location. In Figure 5c[6], the curve of cumulative distribution function (CDF) for these random users (purple) is much lower than the one for communities (blue). This means that these random users are farther away from the users than communities. To show that community is a meaningful level to study mobility, we also calculate distances between a user and all his friends. The curve for friends (red) in Figure 5c is lower than the one for communities as well, meaning that a user is closer to his communities than to all his friends in general. As a user's community is a subset of his friends, to illustrate that the shorter distances for communities than friends are not caused by frequent movement areas clustered from a small number of friends' check-ins, for each community of a user, we randomly sample the same number of his friends to build a "virtual" community and calculate the distances between the user and his virtual communities. The CDF curve in Figure 5c (yellow) shows that these virtual communities are even farther away from users than all friends.

From the above analysis, we conclude that (1) communities have strong influences on users' mobility and (2) community is a meaningful resolution to study users' mobility.

4.2 Number of influential communities

Research shows that a user's mobility is constrained geographically (see [9, 10]), e.g., a user normally travels in or around the city where he lives. Meanwhile, social relations are not restricted by geographic constrains. For instance, a user's college friends as a community can spread all over the world. Now we focus on how many communities actually influence a user's mobility i.e., how many influential communities a user has. Intuitively, this number should be small as each user only interacts with a limited number of communities in his daily life such as colleagues and family.

We plot the distribution of the number of user's influential communities in Figure 6a. From two datasets, we can observe a similar result. Most of the users are influenced only by a small number of communities and there are more users who have two influential communities than others. For example, almost 30% of users in New York have two influential communities in the Twitter dataset.

Each location corresponds to an influential community. We proceed with studying how a user's influential communities are distributed over his check-ins. We first propose a

---

[6]The results in Figure 5c are based on the data from two cities in both datasets.

notion named *influence entropy*, it is defined as

$$infent(u) = - \sum_{c \in C(u)} \frac{|CI(u,c)|}{|CI(u)|} \ln \frac{|CI(u,c)|}{|CI(u)|}$$

where $CI(u,c)$ represents u's check-ins that are closest to the community c. The influence entropy is defined in the form of Shannon entropy: higher influence entropy indicates that the user's locations are close to his different communities more uniformly. Figure 6b depicts the distribution of users' influence entropies. As we can see, in New York (NY (T)), around 20% of users' influence entropies are between 0 and 0.2 which means they have one dominating influential community that is close to most of their locations. We also notice that there is a peak around 0.6 in all the cities. For example, if a user u's 50% check-ins corresponds to one influential community and the other 50% corresponds to another one, then $infent(u) = 0.69$ which falls into this range. This shows that around 20% of users are influenced by their two major communities at a similar level.

Community entropy introduced in Section 3 is a notion for capturing a user's social diversity. We further study the relationship between community entropy and influence entropy. As shown in Figure 6c, more diverse a user's social relationship is, more probably his locations are distributed uniformly over his influential communities.

From the above analysis, we conclude that only a small number of communities have influences on users' mobility.

4.3 Communities under contexts

Influential communities are constrained by contexts. For instance, a user has lunch with his colleagues and spends time with his family near where he lives. Here, the lunch hour and the home location can be considered as social contexts, and the two communities (colleague and family) have impact on the user's behavior under each of the context, respectively. Thus it is interesting to study whether this hypothesis holds generally.

Temporal contexts. First, we focus on temporal contexts. The pair of contexts we choose are *Lunch* (11am–1pm) and *Dinner* (7pm–9pm) hours on Wednesday. For each user, we extract his check-ins during lunch and dinner time and find his influential communities w.r.t. these two contexts. We randomly choose four users and plot the distributions of their check-ins over their influential communities under these two contexts in Figure 7. As we can see, a user's communities behave quite differently on influencing his check-ins during lunch and dinner time. For example, the first user in New York in the Twitter dataset is only influenced by his community 3 during lunch time while communities 1 and 2 give him similar influences during dinner time. This simply reflects the fact that the people who users have lunch and dinner with are different. In addition, users' average influence entropies drop as well under different temporal contexts compared with the general case (see Table 3), this suggests that the influential communities tend to become more unique.

For each user during lunch (dinner) time, we create a vector where the i-th component counts the number of locations that are the closest to community i. We then exploit the cosine similarity between a user's lunch and dinner vectors as his *influence similarity*. The results are listed in Table 4. Note that, we also choose other pairs of temporal contexts

for analysis, such as working hours (9am–6pm) and nightlife (10pm–6am) and have similar observations.

Spatial contexts. Next we study the influence of spatial contexts. In each city, we pick two disjoint regions (called *Region 1* and *Region 2*, respectively) including Uptown and Downtown Manhattan in New York and Golden Gate Park and Berkeley in San Francisco. Then, we extract users' check-ins in these areas. By performing the same analysis as the one for temporal contexts, we observe similar results (see Figure 8, Table 3 and Table 4). Note that we choose the areas without special semantics in mind, e.g., business areas or residential areas.

Influence entropy	NY (G)	SF (G)	NY (T)	SF (T)
General	0.56	0.73	0.69	0.70
Temporal (*Lunch*)	0.35	0.39	0.22	0.25
Temporal (*Dinner*)	0.27	0.43	0.30	0.31
Spatial (*Region 1*)	0.45	0.20	0.52	0.23
Spatial (*Region 2*)	0.42	0.21	0.61	0.26

Table 3: Influence entropy under different social contexts.

Influence similarity	NY (G)	SF (G)	NY (T)	SF (T)
Temporal	0.80	0.74	0.67	0.66
Spatial	0.77	0.56	0.48	0.41

Table 4: Influence similarity w.r.t. social contexts.

From the above analysis, we can conclude that community impact is constrained under spatial and temporal contexts.

5. LOCATION PREDICTION

Location prediction can drive compelling applications including location recommendation and targeted advertising. On the other hand, it may also threat users' privacy [35]. Following the previous analysis, we continue to investigate whether it is possible to use community information to effectively predict users' locations, using machine learning techniques. More precisely, the question we want to answer is: given a user's community information, whether he will check in at a given place at a given time. Note that the time here is a certain hour on a certain day (Monday to Sunday).

We first list all the features in the community-based location prediction model. Then, we present the baseline predictors. Experimental results are described in the end.

5.1 Community-based location predictor

To predict whether a user will visit a certain location, we use one of his communities' information to establish the feature vector, i.e., the influential community of the location (see Section 4).

Community related features. Having chosen the community, we extract its following features for prediction.

- Distance between the community and the location. This is the distance between the location and the community's nearest frequent movement area.

- Community size. Number of users in the community.

(a) NY (G) (b) SF (G) (c) NY (T) (d) SF (T)

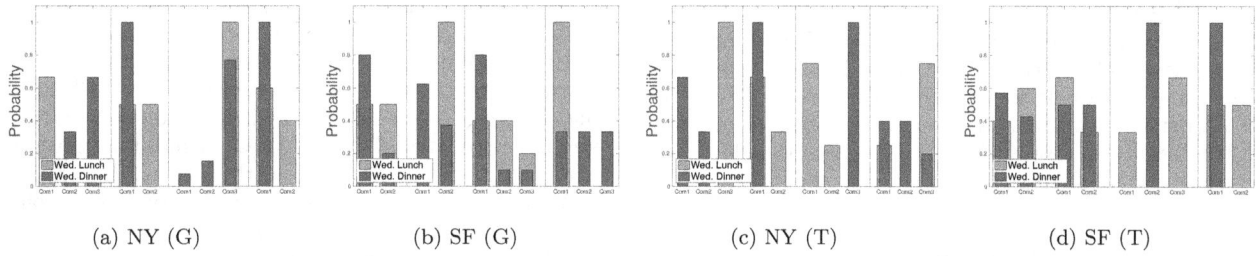

Figure 7: Distribution of influential communities on users' check-ins (temporal contexts).

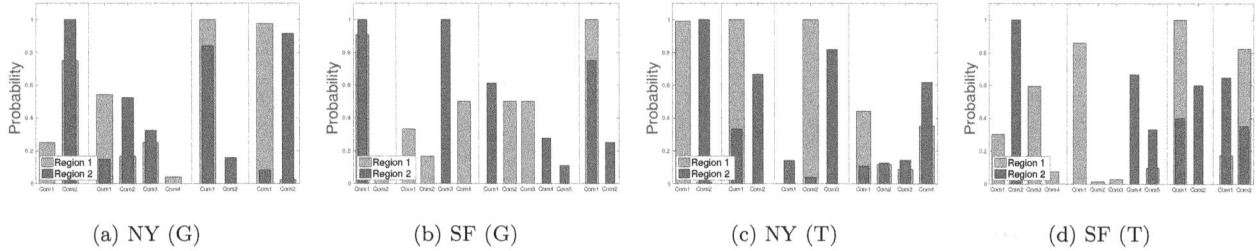

(a) NY (G) (b) SF (G) (c) NY (T) (d) SF (T)

Figure 8: Distribution of influential communities on users' check-ins (spatial contexts).

- Number of the community's frequent movement areas.

- Community's total number of check-ins.

- Community connectivity. This is the ratio between the number of edges in the community and the maximal number of possible edges.

Time. Check-ins are related to time as well. Figure 9a (Figure 9b) plots the total number of check-ins in New York and San Francisco in a daily (weekly) scale. Since we aim to predict whether a user will check in at a place at a certain time, the time-related features we consider are the total number of check-ins at the time[7] and the day (i.e., Monday to Sunday) from all users.

5.2 Baseline models

Sample friends. In our community-based predictor, each location corresponds to the user's nearest community. To illustrate the effectiveness of communities on predicting a user's mobility, in the first baseline model, for each location, we randomly sample the same number of friends as the community and use these friends to build a "virtual community" (as in Section 4). We then replace the community related features with this virtual community's corresponding ones. The time-related features of this model are exactly the same as the ones for the community-based model.

Friends. In the second baseline model, we consider a user's all friends instead of his communities. The features include the shortest distance from his friends to the location and the time-related features.

User. It has been shown in [10, 6] that a user's past mobility can predict his future mobility effectively. Therefore, we also extract features from a user himself to perform prediction. The features include the following.

(a) Daily

(b) Weekly

Figure 9: Check-in time in the datasets.

- The shortest distance from a user's frequent movement areas (through hierarchical clustering with cut-off distance equal to 500m) to the location.[8]

- The total number of check-ins during the day.

- The total number of check-ins during the hour.

User and community. In the last baseline model, we combine the features from the user's model and our community-based predictor.

---

[7]We consider time at a per hour unit, thus the feature is the number of check-ins of all the users at that hour.

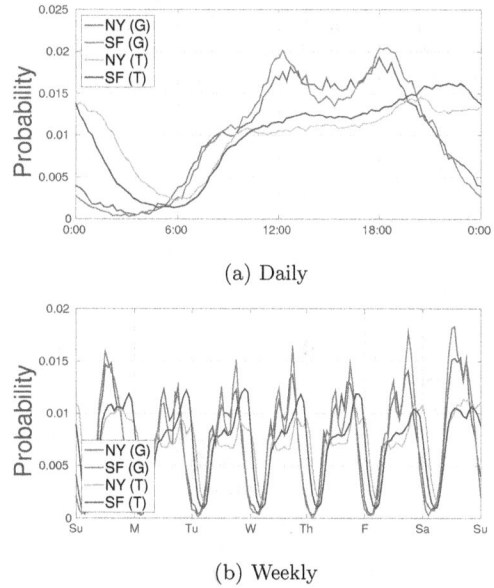

[8]To avoid overfitting, we use half of each user's check-ins to discover his frequent movement areas and the other half are used for training and testing the model.

5.3 Metrics

We partition the cities into 0.001×0.001 degree latitude and longitude cells, a user is said to be in a cell if he has been to any place belonging to the cell. Let TP, FP, FN and TN denote true positives, false positives, false negatives and true negatives, respectively. The metrics we adopt for evaluation include (1) Accuracy,

$$Accuracy = \frac{|TP| + |TN|}{|TP| + |FP| + |FN| + |TN|};$$

(2) F1 score,

$$F1 = 2 \cdot \frac{Precision \times Recall}{Precision + Recall}, \text{ with}$$

$$Precision = \frac{|TP|}{|TP| + |FP|}, \ Recall = \frac{|TP|}{|TP| + |FN|};$$

and (3) AUC (area under the ROC curve).

5.4 Experiment setup

We build a classifier for each user. A classifier needs both positive and negative examples. So far we only have the positive ones, i.e., a user visits a location. To construct the negative examples, for each location a user visits, we randomly sample a different location (within the city) as the place that he does not visit at that moment. In this way, a balanced dataset for each user is naturally formed. As in the data analysis, we only focus on active users who have at least 100 check-ins in the city. For each user, we sort his check-ins chronologically and put his first 80% check-ins for training the model and the rest 20% for testing. The machine learning classifier we exploit here is logistic regression. In all sets, we perform 10-fold cross validation.

5.5 Results

Performance in general. As depicted in Figure 10, our community-based predictor's performance is promising and it outperforms two baseline models that exploit friends' information. Especially for the sample friends model, the community-based model is almost 20% better among all three metrics in the Twitter dataset. By studying logistic model's coefficients, the most important feature is the distance between the community and the location, followed by the community connectivity and size.

On the other hand, two predictions that are based on user's own information perform better than our community-based predictor. Also, the predictor combining user and community information does not improve the performance. This indicates that a user's past check-ins are the most useful information for predicting where he will be in the future which also validates the results proposed in [10, 6].

Prediction vs. community entropy. In Figure 11, we bucket community entropy by intervals of 0.2 and plot its relationship with the prediction results (AUC). As we can see, with the increase of community entropy, the AUC grows for the community-based model which means the predictor works better for users with high community entropies. For example, the AUC value increases more than 5% in San Francisco in the Gowalla dataset (community entropy from $[0, 0.2)$ to $[1.2, 1.4)$).

We further calculate the Pearson's correlation coefficient[9] between community entropy and our prediction results. In the Twitter dataset, the correlation coefficient for New York and San Francisco is 0.88 and 0.97 respectively,[10] indicating that community entropy and the prediction results are strongly correlated. This validates our intuition that a user with high social diversity is clearly influenced by his communities. We can conclude that community information can be explored to achieve promising location predictions, especially for those users with high community entropies.

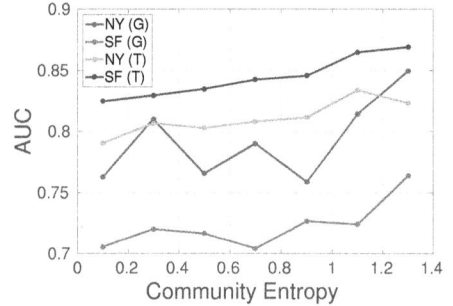

Figure 11: AUC as a function of community entropy, values of the Pearson's correlation: 0.60 (NY (G)), 0.75 (SF (G)), 0.88 (NY (T)), 0.97(SF (T)).

Difference between cities. In Figure 10 and Figure 11, we observe that the prediction results are different between two cities. New York has the better performance than San Francisco in the Gowalla dataset. On the other hand, the prediction results are similar in the Twitter dataset. The reason for different performances in different cities could be due to the density of the cities (e.g., New York's population density is higher than San Francisco), or the adoption of LBSN services by users in different cities. We leave the investigation as a future work.

5.6 Other strategies to choose communities

So far, we have shown that exploring community information can lead to effective location prediction. The community we choose is the one that has the closest frequent movement area to the target location. We would like to know if other strategies to choose community can achieve similar results. We consider three strategies including choosing the community with most users (max-size), the community with highest connectivity (max-con) and random community (random). Table 5 summarizes the prediction performances in New York in the Twitter dataset. As we can see, our original strategy outperforms these three. Among these three strategies, max-con performs slightly better than the other two, but it is still relatively worse than our original strategy to choose community. This again validates our observation in Section 4 that influential communities are constrained by contexts (spatially or temporally), in other words one community cannot influence every location of the user.

---

[9]Pearson's correlation coefficient is the covariance of two variables divided by the product of their standard deviations.

[10]The two values are slightly smaller for the Gowalla dataset, which is probably due to the fact that the Twitter dataset contains more information on social relations than the Gowalla dataset (see discussions in Section 3).

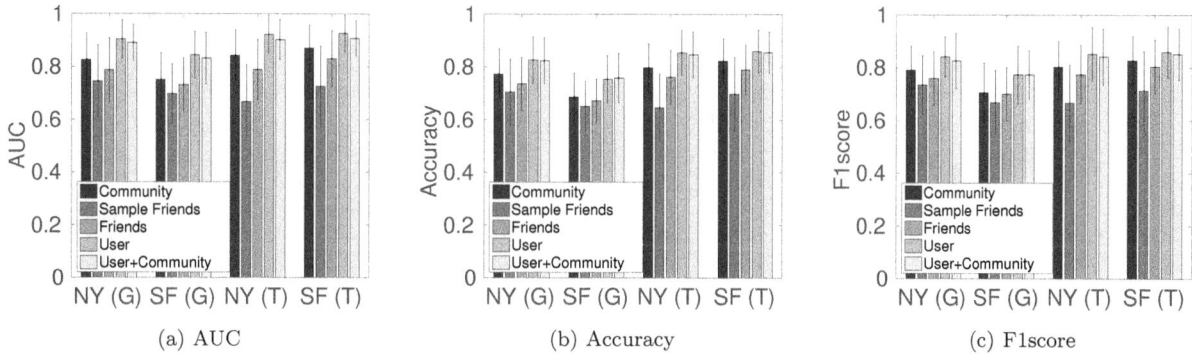

(a) AUC (b) Accuracy (c) F1score

Figure 10: Prediction results.

	AUC	Accuracy	F1score
Community	0.83	0.78	0.79
max-size	0.73	0.72	0.74
max-con	0.74	0.73	0.74
random	0.71	0.71	0.72

Table 5: Performance of community-choosing strategies.

5.7 Comparison with the PSMM model

In [10], the authors establish a mobility model (PSMM) for each user based on his past check-ins. The assumption behind this model is that a user's mobility is mainly centered around two states such as home and work. Each state is modeled as a bivariate Gaussian distribution and the total mobility is then formalized into a dynamic Gaussian mixture model with time as an independent factor. The check-ins that do not fit well with the two states are considered as social check-ins and are modeled through another friends-based distribution. We implement the PSMM model and compare its performance with our community-based predictor. Each user's first 80% check-ins are used for training his PSMM model. For testing, besides the rest 20% check-ins, we also construct the same number of locations that the user does not go at the moment (as our classification setup). As the PSMM model's output is the exact location of the user, we consider the prediction is correct when the output location is within 1km of the real location. Table 6 shows the accuracy between our model and PSMM. In all the datasets, our community-based predictor significantly outperforms PSMM. As suggested in [33], this is probably because two states are not enough to capture a user's mobility in a city. Moreover, a user's check-in data is also too sparse to train a good PSMM model. We leave the further investigation as a future work.

	NY (G)	LA (G)	NY (T)	SF (T)
Community	0.76	0.67	0.78	0.81
PSMM	0.55	0.60	0.67	0.65

Table 6: Comparison with PSMM on prediction accuracy.

6. RELATED WORK

Thanks to the emerging of LBSNs, mobility as well as its connection with social relations have been intensively stud-

ied [9, 34, 15]. There are mainly two directions of research going on in the area. One direction is to use the location information from LBSNs to predict friendships (see e.g. [19, 13, 12, 6, 33, 28, 40]), the other studies the impact from friendships on locations [1, 6, 10, 33, 24] which is what we focus on in the current work.

Backstrom, Sun and Marlow [1] study the friendship and location using the Facebook data with user-specified home addresses. They find out that the friendship probability as a function of home distances follows a power law, i.e., most of friends tend to live closely. They also build a model to predict users' home location based on their friends' home. Their model outperforms the predictor based on IP addresses. The authors of [6] use the Facebook place data to study check-in behaviors and friendships. They train a logistic model to predict users' locations. Besides that, they also investigate how users respond to their friends' check-in and use the location data to predict friendships. Cho, Myers and Leskovec [10] investigate the mobility patterns based on the location data from Gowalla, Brightkite as well as data from a cellphone company. Based on their observation, they build a dynamic Gaussian mixture model for human mobility involving temporal, spatial and social relations features. Sadilek, Kautz and Bigham [33] propose a system for both location and friendship prediction. For location prediction, they use dynamic Bayesian networks to model friends' locations (unsupervised case) and predict a sequence of locations of users over a given period of time. McGee, Caverlee and Cheng [24] introduce the notion of social strength based on their observation from the geo-tagged Twitter data and incorporate it into the model to predict users' home locations. Experimental results show that their model outperforms the one of [1]. Jurgens in [17] proposes a spatial label propagation algorithm to infer a user's location based on a small number initial friends' locations. Techniques such as exploiting information from multiple social network platforms are integrated into the algorithm to further improve the prediction accuracy.

The main difference between previous works and ours is the way of treating friends. We consider users' friends at a community level while most of them treat them the same (except for the paper [24] which introduce 'social strength', which is based on common features but not on communities). Moreover, our location predictor doesn't need any user's own information but his friends' to achieve a promising result, especially for users' with high community entropies. Other minor differences include the prediction target: we want to predict users' certain locations in the future not their home [1, 24, 17] or a dynamic sequences of locations [33].

We focus on understanding users' mobility behavior from social network communities. The authors of [4] tackle the inverse problem, i.e., they exploit users' mobility information to detect communities. They first attach weights to the edges in a social network based on the check-in information, then the social network is modified by removing all edges with small weights. In the end, a community detection algorithm (louvain method[2]) is used on the modified social graph to discover communities. The experimental results show that their method is able to discover more meaningful communities, such as place-focused communities, compared to the standard community detection algorithm.

More recently, Brown et al. [3] analyze mobility behaviors of pairs of friends and groups of friends (communities). They focus on comparing the difference between individual mobility and group mobility. For example, they discover that a user is more likely to meet a friend at a place where they have not visited before; while he will choose a familiar place when meeting a group of friends.

7. CONCLUSION AND FUTURE WORK

In this paper, we have studied the community impact on user's mobility. Analysis leads us to several important conclusions: (1) communities have a stronger impact on users' mobility; (2) each user is only influenced by a small number of communities; and (3) different communities have influences on mobility under different spatial and temporal contexts. Based on these, we use machine learning techniques to predict users' future locations focusing on community information. The experimental results on two types of real-life social network datasets are consistent with our analysis and show that our prediction model is very effective. The scripts for conducting the analysis and experiments as well as the Twitter dataset are available upon request.[11]

In the future, we plan to extend our work in several directions. First, we have shown in this paper that communities can be exploited to achieve a promising location prediction. We are also interested in extending our work to other applications such as location recommendation. It is possible to redesign the cost function in matrix factorization based methods for location recommendation by taking into account community information. Second, we would like to conduct the analysis of community impact on other social behaviors such as information sharing or interests adoption. Third, in a broader point of view, our current work is actually a demonstration of the communities' effect on human behaviors. As pointed by [39], community is the most meaningful resolution to study social network. Therefore, we also plan to investigate a user's role in his social network based on the structure of his communities.

8. REFERENCES

[1] L. Backstrom, E. Sun, and C. Marlow. Find me if you can: improving geographical prediction with social and spatial proximity. In *Proc. 19th International Conference on World Wide Web (WWW)*, pages 61–70. ACM, 2010.

[2] V. D. Blondel, J.-L. Guillaume, R. Lambiotte, and E. Lefebvre. Fast unfolding of communities in large networks. *Journal of Statistical Mechanics: Theory and Experiment*, 2008(10):P10008, 2008.

[3] C. Brown, N. Lathia, C. Mascolo, A. Noulas, and V. Blondel. Group colocation behavior in technological social networks. *PLoS ONE*, 9(8):e105816, 2014.

[4] C. Brown, V. Nicosia, S. Scellato, A. Noulas, and C. Mascolo. The importance of being placefriends: discovering location-focused online communities. In *Proc. ACM Workshop on Online Social Networks (WOSN)*, pages 31–36. ACM, 2012.

[5] S. Castles, M. J. Miller, and G. Ammendola. *The Age of Migration: International Population Movements in the Modern World*. Taylor & Francis, 2005.

[6] J. Chang and E. Sun. Location³: How users share and respond to location-based data on social networking sites. In *Proc. 5th AAAI Conference on Weblogs and Social Media (ICWSM)*, pages 74–80. The AAAI Press, 2011.

[7] X. Chen, J. Pang, and R. Xue. Constructing and comparing user mobility profiles for location-based services. In *Proc. 28th ACM Symposium on Applied Computing (SAC)*, pages 261–266. ACM, 2013.

[8] X. Chen, J. Pang, and R. Xue. Constructing and comparing user mobility profiles. *ACM Transactions on the Web*, 8(4):article 21, 2014.

[9] Z. Cheng, J. Caverlee, K. Lee, and D. Z. Sui. Exploring millions of footprints in location sharing services. In *Proc. 5th AAAI Conference on Weblogs and Social Media (ICWSM)*, pages 81–88. The AAAI Press, 2011.

[10] E. Cho, S. A. Myers, and J. Leskovec. Friendship and mobility: user movement in location-based social networks. In *Proc. 17th ACM Conference on Knowledge Discovery and Data Mining (KDD)*, pages 1082–1090. ACM, 2011.

[11] A. Clauset, M. E. Newman, and C. Moore. Finding community structure in very large networks. *Physical Review E*, 70(6):066111, 2004.

[12] D. J. Crandalla, L. Backstrom, D. Cosley, S. Suri, D. Huttenlocher, and J. Kleinberg. Inferring social ties from geographic coincidences. *Proceedings of the National Academy of Sciences*, 107(52):22436–22441, 2010.

[13] J. Cranshaw, E. Toch, J. Hone, A. Kittur, and N. Sadeh. Bridging the gap between physical location and online social networks. In *Proc. 12th ACM International Conference on Ubiquitous Computing (UbiComp)*, pages 119–128. ACM, 2010.

[14] H. Gao, J. Tang, X. Hu, and H. Liu. Exploring temporal effects for location recommendation on location-based social networks. In *Proc. 7th ACM Conference on Recommender Systems (RecSys)*, pages 93–100. ACM, 2013.

[15] H. Gao, J. Tang, and H. Liu. Exploring social-historical ties on location-based social networks. In *Proc. 6th AAAI Conference on Weblogs and Social Media (ICWSM)*, pages 114–121. The AAAI Press, 2012.

---

[11] Preliminary results of this work are reported as a poster [27].

[16] M. C. Gonzalez, C. A. Hidalgo, and A.-L. Barabasi. Understanding individual human mobility patterns. *Nature*, 453(7196):779–782, 2008.

[17] D. Jurgens. That's what friends are for: Inferring location in online social media platforms based on social relationships. In *Proc. 7th AAAI Conference on Weblogs and Social Media (ICWSM)*. The AAAI Press, 2013.

[18] A. Lancichinetti and S. Fortunato. Community detection algorithms: a comparative analysis. *CoRR*, abs/0908.1062, 2010.

[19] Q. Li, Y. Zheng, X. Xie, Y. Chen, W. Liu, and W.-Y. Ma. Mining user similarity based on location history. In *Proc. 16th ACM SIGSPATIAL International Conference on Advances in Geographic Information Systems (GIS)*, page 34. ACM, 2008.

[20] B. Liu and H. Xiong. Point-of-interest recommendation in location based social networks with topic and location awareness. In *Proc. 13th SIAM International Conference on Data Mining (SDM)*, pages 396–404. SIAM, 2013.

[21] E. L. Martelot and C. Hankin. Fast multi-scale detection of relevant communities in large-scale networks. *The Computer Journal*, 56(9):1136–1150, 2013.

[22] J. J. McAuley and J. Leskovec. Learning to discover social circles in ego networks. In *Proc. 26th Annual Conference on Neural Information Processing Systems (NIPS)*, pages 548–556. NIPS, 2012.

[23] J. J. McAuley and J. Leskovec. Discovering social circles in ego networks. *ACM Transactions on Knowledge Discovery from Data*, 8(1):article 4, 2014.

[24] J. McGee, J. Caverlee, and Z. Cheng. Location prediction in social media based on tie strength. In *Proc. 22nd ACM International Conference on Information & Knowledge Management (CIKM)*, pages 459–468. ACM, 2013.

[25] M. E. Newman. Modularity and community structure in networks. *Proceedings of the National Academy of Sciences*, 103(23):8577–8582, 2006.

[26] S. Nilizadeh, A. Kapadia, and Y.-Y. Ahn. Community-enhanced de-anonymization of online social networks. In *Proc. 21st ACM Conference on Computer and Communications Security (CCS)*, pages 537–548. ACM, 2014.

[27] J. Pang and Y. Zhang. Exploring communities for effective location prediction (poster paper). In *Proc. 24th World Wide Web Conference (Companion Volume) (WWW)*, pages 87–88. ACM, 2015.

[28] H. Pham, C. Shahabi, and Y. Liu. EBM: an entropy-based model to infer social strength from spatiotemporal data. In *Proc. 2013 ACM International Conference on Management of Data (SIGMOD)*, pages 265–276. ACM, 2013.

[29] D. Quercia, R. Schifanella, L. M. Aiello, and K. McLean. Smelly maps: the digital life of urban smellscapes. In *Proc. 9th AAAI Conference on Weblogs and Social Media (ICWSM)*, pages 237–236. The AAAI Press, 2015.

[30] A. Rény. On measures of information and entropy. In *Proc. 4th Berkeley Symposium on Mathematics, Statistics and Probability*, pages 547–561, 1960.

[31] M. Rosvall and C. T. Bergstrom. Maps of information flow reveal community structure in complex networks. *Proceedings of the National Academy of Sciences*, 105(4):1118–1123, 2008.

[32] M. Rosvall and C. T. Bergstrom. Multilevel compression of random walks on networks reveals hierarchical organization in large integrated systems. *PLoS ONE*, 6(4):e18209, 2011.

[33] A. Sadilek, H. Kautz, and J. P. Bigham. Finding your friends and following them to where you are. In *Proc. 5th ACM International Conference on Web Search and Data Mining (WSDM)*, pages 459–468. ACM, 2012.

[34] S. Scellato, A. Noulas, R. Lambiotte, and C. Mascolo. Socio-spatial properties of online location-based social networks. In *Proc. 5th AAAI Conference on Weblogs and Social Media (ICWSM)*, pages 329–336. The AAAI Press, 2011.

[35] R. Shokri, G. Theodorakopoulos, J.-Y. L. Boudec, and J.-P. Hubaux. Quantifying location privacy. In *Proc. 32nd IEEE Symposium on Security and Privacy (S&P)*. IEEE CS, 2011.

[36] K. Wakita and T. Tsurumi. Finding community structure in mega-scale social networks (extended abstract). In *Proc. 16th International Conference on World Wide Web (WWW)*, pages 1275–1276. ACM, 2007.

[37] J. Yang and J. Leskovec. Overlapping community detection at scale: a nonnegative matrix factorization approach. In *Proc. 6th ACM International Conference on Web Search and Data Mining (WSDM)*, pages 587–596. ACM, 2013.

[38] J. Yang, J. J. McAuley, and J. Leskovec. Community detection in networks with node attributes. In *Proc. 13th IEEE International Conference on Data Mining (ICDM)*, pages 1151–1156. IEEE CS, 2013.

[39] J. Yang, J. J. McAuley, and J. Leskovec. Detecting cohesive and 2-mode communities indirected and undirected networks. In *Proc. 7th ACM International Conference on Web Search and Data Mining (WSDM)*, pages 323–332. ACM, 2014.

[40] Y. Zhang and J. Pang. Distance and friendship: A distance-based model for link prediction in social networks. In *Proc. 17th Asia-Pacific Web Conference (APWeb)*, LNCS. Springer, 2015. To appear.

[41] V. W. Zheng, Y. Zheng, X. Xie, and Q. Yang. Collaborative location and activity recommendations with GPS history data. In *Proc. 19th International Conference on World Wide Web (WWW)*, pages 1029–1038. ACM, 2010.

[42] Y. Zheng, F. Liu, and H.-P. Hsieh. U-air: when urban air quality inference meets big data. In *Proc. 19th ACM Conference on Knowledge Discovery and Data Mining (KDD)*, pages 1436–1444. ACM, 2013.

[43] Y. Zheng, L. Zhang, Z. Ma, X. Xie, and W.-Y. Ma. Recommending friends and locations based on individual location history. *ACM Transactions on the Web*, 5(1), 2011.

[44] Y. Zheng, L. Zhang, X. Xie, and W.-Y. Ma. Mining interesting locations and travel sequences from GPS trajectories. In *Proc. 18th International Conference on World Wide Web (WWW)*, pages 791–800. ACM, 2009.

Not All Trips are Equal: Analyzing Foursquare Check-ins of Trips and City Visitors

Wen-Haw Chong, Bing Tian Dai, and Ee-Peng Lim
Dept. of Information Systems, Singapore Management University
80 Stamford Road, Singapore 178902
whchong.2013@phdis.smu.edu.sg, btdai@smu.edu.sg, eplim@smu.edu.sg

ABSTRACT

Location-Based Social Networks (LBSN) such as Foursquare allow users to indicate venue visits via check-ins. This results in much fine grained context-rich data, useful for studying user mobility. In this work, we use check-ins to characterize trips and visitors to two cities, where visitors are defined as having their home cities elsewhere. First, we divide trips into two duration types: long and short. We then show that trip types differ in check-in distributions over venue categories, time slots, as well as check-in intensity. Based on the trip types, we then divide visitors into long-term and short-term visitors. We compare visitor types in terms of popularities of check-in venues and proximities to friends' check-ins. Our findings indicate that short-term visitors are more biased towards popular venues. As for proximity to friends' check-ins, the effect is more consistently observed for long-term visitors. These findings also illustrate that locations of incoming visitors can effectively be analyzed using LBSN data in addition to conducting user surveys which are relatively costlier.

Lastly, we investigate the importance of visitor type information in models for venue prediction. We apply models including a state of the art kernel density estimation technique and ranking based on venue popularity. For each model, we consider two settings where visitor type information is absent/present. For long-term visitors, we observed little differences in accuracies. However, for short-term visitors, predictions are significantly more accurate by using type information. These findings suggest that venue prediction or recommender systems should consider visitor type to improve accuracy.

Categories and Subject Descriptors

H.4 [**Information Systems Applications**]: Miscellaneous;
H.2.8 [**Database Applications**]: Data Mining

COSN '15 November 02-03, 2015, Palo Alto, CA, USA
©2015 ACM. ISBN 978-1-4503-3951-3/15/11 ...$15.00.
DOI: http://dx.doi.org/10.1145/2817946.2817958.

Keywords

check-in; visitors; Foursquare; long-term; short-term

1. INTRODUCTION

In recent years, Location-Based social Social Networks (LBSN) such as Foursquare and Yelp have grown rapidly in popularity. In particular, users can *check-in* with their mobile devices to various venues, thus providing researchers with a wealth of fine-grained data about visitation behavior.

In our current work, we are interested in the check-in behavior of travelers visiting a city away from their indicated home city. We simply term them as *visitors*. Visitors differ in their purpose, e.g. not all visitors are tourists or behave similarly. For better planning of city resources and promotion of tourism, some host countries/cities had conducted surveys on incoming visitors to determine their travel patterns and needs. One example is the survey on inbound visitors conducted by the Office of Travel and Tourism Industries (OTTI) of US Department of Commerce [1]. Such surveys are costly and do not always capture more fine grained mobility patterns of the visitors. In addition, they do not consider the social dimension of visits.

On the other hand, in the context of venue prediction for LBSNs, there has been little work that specifically studies the behavior of visitors considering their types and type-specific visit patterns [7, 14, 20, 9, 12, 18]. In particular, we note that for visitors who broadcast their check-ins while traveling, Foursquare provide sufficient data to estimate conservatively the trip duration or the lower bound. With the observed trip durations, one can now categorize trips into long or short and consequently, categorize visitors into long/short-term types. This leads to several research questions which we study via detailed empirical analysis on the Foursquare data collected for two major Asian Cities, Singapore and Jakarta. The **research questions** and our corresponding **contributions** are listed as follows:

1. *What are the differences between long and short trips?*

    (a) We showed that there are significant differences between long and short trips in their distributions over check-in venue categories.

    (b) Short trips have higher check-in intensity than long trips.

2. *What are the differences between long-term and short-term visitors?*

    (a) Short-term visitors tend to check-in at more popular venues, compared to long-term visitors.

(b) Check-ins for long-term visitors are slightly nearer those of his friends, compared to non-friends. For short-term visitors, this was only observed for one city.

3. *Does knowing the visitor type help to improve the accuracy of venue prediction?*

   (a) We can improve accuracy for short-term visitors if a prediction model is aware of their type.

   (b) For long-term visitors, we do not observe gain in prediction accuracy.

The outline of the paper follows the sequence of analysis steps that we have taken:

1. *Datasets construction*: We extract Foursquare check-ins and user profile data for the two cities being studied. See Section 2.1

2. *Trip categorization*: In Section 2.2, we extract trips from check-ins and categorize each trip as long/short.

3. *Visitor categorization*: Section 2.3 categorizes each visitor to a city as long/short-term based on his trip duration.

4. *Trip analysis*: Section 3 conducts empirical analysis on trips to contrast the differences between long and short trips.

5. *Visitor analysis*: Section 4 discusses our empirical analysis on visitors to contrast the differences between long-term and short-term visitors.

6. *Prediction experiment*: Lastly in Section 5, we apply models to predict check-in venues for visitors. For each model, we consider settings which include/exclude visitor type information. This ascertains the impact of visitor type on prediction tasks.

2. DATA AND CATEGORIZATION

2.1 Datasets

We study Foursquare check-in data collected for users visiting/residing in two Asian cities: Singapore and Jakarta, where Foursquare users are known to be highly active. We recognize that more cities can be studied to enhance this study. At the moment, we are limited to the two cities which we are collecting data on.

Besides check-ins, we also collect user profile information in Foursquare. Each user profile includes the *user-indicated* home city which we used to differentiate visitors from locals, as well as a list of friends. The friendship information is subsequently used when we analyze visitors' proximity to friends in terms of their check-in venues.

For Jakarta, we define a polygon based on the city boundaries and exclude the suburbs. This allows us to collect public check-in data that fall within Jakarta city. This step is not required for the island-state of Singapore, which is surrounded by the sea with limited entry points. Also note that Singapore is both a city and a country, hence visitors to Singapore are necessarily foreigners. In contrast, visitors to Jakarta comprise both foreigners and domestic travelers.

We apply a widely used method [8, 14] to collect check-in data, i.e. via crawling Twitter. As check-ins are publicly available only if the user broadcast them via Twitter, our data sets are gathered from related tweets. Each user is tracked throughout the study period, hence any of his check-ins outside the cities of interest are collected as well. This is necessary for us to estimate trip duration. In addition, for greater reliability in analysis, we only consider active users, which we define as having at least 10 public check-ins over the study period. Note that this is different from requiring a visitor to have at least 10 check-ins at his visited city.

For Singapore, the study period spans June 2013 to Nov 2014, comprising of 1,769,000+ check-ins, prior to filtering for active users. For Jakarta, 100,000+ check-ins are collected over a period of July 2014 to Feb 2015. Further statistics are listed in Sections 2.2 and 2.3 which discuss how we categorize trips and visitors.

2.2 Trip Categorization

To analyze the differences between long and short trips, we first need to extract and then categorize trips. The first step is straightforward. By tracking a user's check-ins over time, one can extract segment(s) where he check-ins at some given city of interest, say A, i.e. hence indicating trip(s) to A. Also recap that we define a user as a visitor to city A only if his listed home location is not in A.

For the second step, we need to categorize trips as long/short based on the trip duration. The simplest estimate is to use the time difference between the first and last check-in for a segment in A. However this requires the first and last check-in at A to be extremal: user check-ins at the moment of arrival and just before he departs from A. Otherwise the trip duration is underestimated. Obviously, it is also tricky to determine whether each user fits such a scenario.

To circumvent the described issues, we adopt a more general approach to estimate trip durations. Given two consecutive check-ins in two different cities, the crossing time is the time where the user crosses from one city to the other. This can be estimated as the mid-point of the two check-in times. It can be seen that a trip to a host city is necessarily bounded by two crossing times, the first being the arrival time at the host city and the second being the departure time from the host city. With the estimated arrival and departure time, the trip duration can then be estimated as the difference. This is a conservative estimate, not biased towards overestimating/underestimating the trip duration. Furthermore, it can be applied even if the trip contains only one check-in.

Formally, let the tuple $< t_j, C_j >$ represent a user's j-th check-in, occurring at time t_j at city C_j. As an example, assume the following sequence of check-ins involving cities A and B: $\{< t_j, B >, < t_{j+1}, A >,...,< t_{j+m}, A >, < t_{j+m+1}, B >\}$. The trip duration for A is estimated as

$$(t_{j+m} + t_{j+m+1})/2 - (t_j + t_{j+1})/2 \qquad (1)$$

Figure 1 presents a conceptual illustration.

Note that trip durations can be estimated only for uncensored trips, i.e. bounded by two crossings corresponding to the estimated arrival and departure times at the host city. After estimating the durations for all such trips, we apply two-mode Gaussian Mixture Modeling (GMM) to cluster trips into long and short trips. We also use GMM to derive a duration threshold[1], whereby out of sample trips with

---

[1] The threshold is an equiprobable point between the two modes using standard GMM formulation.

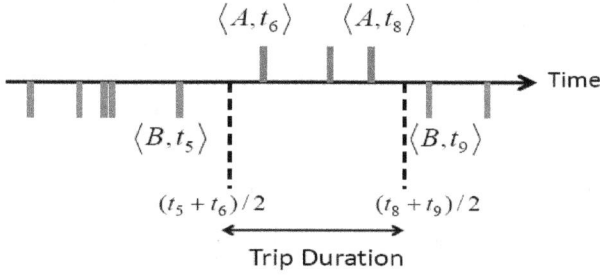

Figure 1: Estimating duration for a trip to city A. Red/blue tick marks are check-ins at city A/B.

Table 1: Statistics from trips by visitors. Thresholds and durations are in days. Last row list the check-in count from locals.

	Singapore	Jakarta
Threshold (days)	9.9	8.34
Long trip mean duration	45.4	22.81
Short trip mean duration	2.8	2.24
No. of long trips (check-ins involved)	1,490 (37,124)	1,768 (6,708)
No. of short trips (check-ins involved)	2,976 (9,114)	5,350 (11,704)
Check-ins from locals	918,786	43,808

longer/shorter duration than the threshold are categorized as long/short.

Table 1 displays statistics derived for both Singapore and Jakarta, including check-ins generated by locals, i.e. from users listing their home locations as Singapore/Jakarta. In Section 3, we shall analyze the trips and local check-ins summarized in Table 1.

Reassuringly, the mean duration for short trips to Singapore is only slightly lower than the official statistics for average length of stay (3.5 days) for tourists [4]. The latter statistic excludes visitors from neighboring Malaysia, where short cross-border trips will have the effect of lowering the mean duration. For Jakarta, the city limits do not constitute a border between countries, hence the equivalent visitor statistics are not captured.

Instead of just long and short trips, one can also differentiate trips into more fine-grained duration categories. This will bring out larger differences when comparing extremal categories, e.g. very long versus very short trips. In the current work, we have used only two categories for brevity and to simplify our analysis. As will be evident in subsequent sections, this is already adequate for us to observe significant differences between long and short trips.

2.3 Visitor Categorization

Given a city A, we consider users to be locals if they indicate their home city in Foursquare as A, otherwise they are considered visitors if they check-in at A at least once. For locals, we only include those with at least half of their check-ins in A, thus excluding cases where locals are mostly staying elsewhere. For the visitors, we categorize them as long-term or short-term based on the following criterion:

- Short-term: The visitor has only short trips to A.

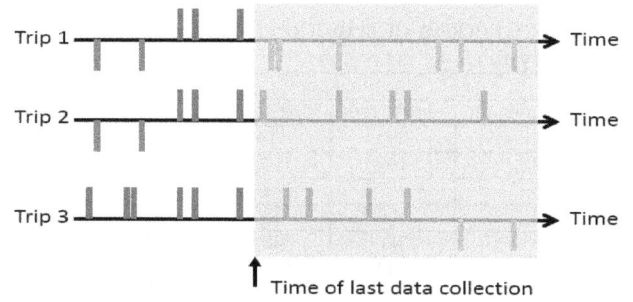

Figure 2: Red tick marks are check-ins during a trip. The shaded block is unobserved data. Trip 1 is short while trip 2 is long, but they are undifferentiable by their observed trip durations. Trip 3 is unambiguously a long trip as the observed trip duration is already long enough.

Table 2: Count of visitors and locals. Ambiguous visitors have censored trips which appear to be short and no long trips, hence it is uncertain if they are short-term or long-term.

	Singapore	Jakarta
Long-term visitors	2,282	1,337
Short-term visitors	835	948
Ambiguous visitors	782	316
Locals	8,597	1,466

- Long-term: The visitor has at least one long trip to A.

whereby trips are categorized as described in Section 2.2. Furthermore, short trips are required to be uncensored and long trips can be censored. This is because if a trip is censored, the estimated duration is only a lower bound. It is then possible for a short trip to become a long trip as more data is collected. However if a trip is already of long duration, more data will not change the fact that it is a long trip. Figure 2 illustrates the concept.

It is possible to refine the criterion above to account for other factors, e.g. thresholding the number of trips such that visitors with too many short trips are treated as a separate category. We defer this to future work. For ease of analysis and brevity here, we categorize visitors into just long/short-term, showing that significant differences already exist.

Table 2 displays the visitors/locals statistics for Singapore and Jakarta as gathered from Foursquare. We shall analyze these users in Section 4. We exclude visitors who are ambiguous, i.e. having censored trips which appear to be short and no long trips. With more data, their censored trips may well become long trips. Table 3 gives a breakdown of the number of check-ins per visitor type per city. For example, 388 short-term visitors to Singapore only made 1 check-in during their trip. As will be elaborated in Section 5.1, such sparse data impacts how we design personalized prediction models.

3. TRIP ANALYSIS

In this section, we study the differences between long and short trips by a number of measures including check-in distributions over venue categories/subcategories, check-in distributions over time and check-in intensity.

Table 3: Check-in distribution at the visited city per visitor type

Check-in count	Singapore		Jakarta	
	short-term	long-term	short-term	long-term
1	388	114	323	137
2	141	57	155	112
3	85	54	137	107
4	44	43	81	91
5	33	42	61	76
> 5	144	1972	191	814

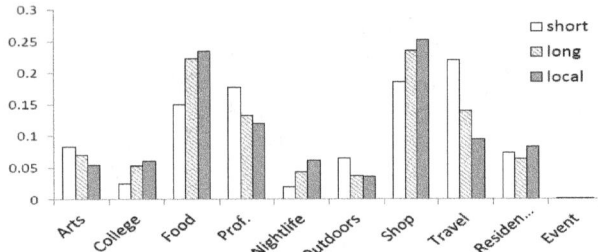

(a) Singapore

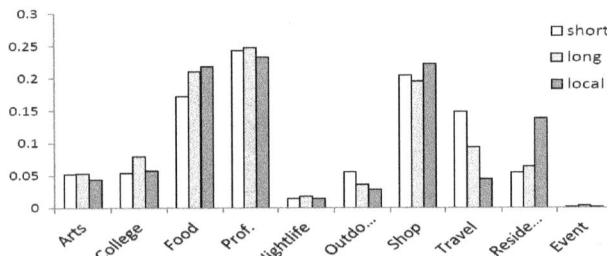

(b) Jakarta

Figure 3: Check-in distributions over main categories for long trips (long), short trips (short) and from locals (local).

3.1 Venue Categories

Trips to a city are made for various purposes, affecting both the trip duration and the categories of venues visited. In this section, we examine the distribution over venue categories to understand trip purposes. Our task is facilitated by the fact that Foursquare already categorizes venues into 10 top-level categories which indicates their functions. These are: Arts & Entertainment (Arts), College & University (College), Food, Professional & Other Places (Prof.), Nightlife Spot (Nightlife), Outdoors & Recreation (Outdoors), Shop & Service (Shop), Travel & Transport (Travel), Residence and Events.

Figures 3(a) and 3(b) show the check-in distribution over venue categories for Singapore and Jakarta respectively. For example in Singapore, the probability of having a check-in from a long trip at a shopping venue (the 'Shop' category) is 0.24. The same probability is lower at 0.19 when the check-in comes from a short trip. For comparison, we also include the probability if the check-in is from a local.

From Figure 3, our key observation is: **long trips have check-in distributions more similar to that of local check-ins, when compared to short trips**. To quantify these differences, we compute the Jenson-Shannon di-

vergence (JS) of distribution pairs as shown in Table 4. Note that the divergence values are small, but statistically significant, indicating that the differences are not due to chance. (We describe a test for significance in Appendix A.) In particular, divergence values between distributions from long trips and local check-ins are smaller for both Singapore and Jakarta, consistent with our key observation.

Table 4: Jenson-Shannon divergence values between pairs of category distributions. All values are statistically significant (p-value < 0.05)

JS divergence	Singapore	Jakarta
(long, local)	0.0047	0.0137
(short, local)	0.0363	0.0281
(long, short)	0.0185	0.0067

The key observation is intuitive since long-term visitors may have different focuses from short-term visitors or be assimilated to some extent in terms of check-in patterns. For example, if one stays for a long duration, shopping and dining needs tend to take on greater importance as compared to sightseeing or attraction hopping. There may also be a higher likelihood to visit places frequented by locals [27], instead of the usual tourist hangouts.

Besides the key observation, Singapore and Jakarta share other similarities:

- For 'Travel', short trips have much higher probabilities than long trips, which in turn have higher probabilities than local. This is intuitive since under this category, the various venue sub-categories are generally interesting to travelers, e.g. hotels, resorts, airports etc. (In Section 3.2, we shall examine the subcategories in more detail.)

- For both cities, long trips and local are also more similar in probabilities for 'Food'. This suggests that food places are more popular in long trips and among locals.

For observations specific to Singapore, long trips are closer in probabilities to local than short trips for 'Shop', 'Nightlife', 'College', 'Arts' and 'Prof'.

Lastly we note that the differences between long/short trips and local are more pronounced for Singapore than Jakarta. One contributing factor is the following: Singapore is both a city and a country, hence visitors are foreigners by definition. For Jakarta, visitors may be foreigners or fellow Indonesians residing elsewhere. We can expect the latter group to have somewhat similar visitation patterns/preferences to Indonesians residing in Jakarta. This brings down differences when we compare visitors and locals. For example, Indonesia is a Muslim majority country. One will expect most domestic visitors and locals to not visit nightlife venues where alcohol may be served. Consistent with this, Figure 3(b) shows little differences in 'Nightlife' probabilities between check-ins from trips and local. In contrast, Figure 3(a) shows that for Singapore, local check-ins have the highest probability for 'Nightlife', followed by long trips and with short trips last in place. As a side note, since visitors' ethnic composition affect their travel patterns, one can conduct interesting analysis of a city's ethnic composition or to quantify how cosmopolitan or mixed a population is. This may be useful as metrics for expat livability index for different cities [2].

3.2 Venue Subcategories

Earlier, we have seen that for check-in distributions over main venue categories, long trips are more similar to local check-ins, than short trips. As main categories are coarse and each can comprise many subcategories, we further analyze check-in distributions over subcategories as well. However it is not informative to display the complete distributions here due to the large number of subcategories (>700). Instead, we examine most probable travel-related subcategories where differences are more discernible.

Our procedure is as follows. First, for all trip types and local check-ins, we sort subcategories by probability. From the most probable 30 subcategories for short trips, we then manually select those that are travel-related and examine how their probabilities vary with trip types. The selected subcategories are either places of interest or provide transport and accommodation services required by typical travelers. Note that it suffices to select from short trips since we do not observe any travel-related subcategories that are probable for long trips / local but not among the top probable in short trips. We also observe the travel-related subcategories to be specific to cities, e.g. casinos have zero probabilities in our Jakarta data, but not in our Singapore data.

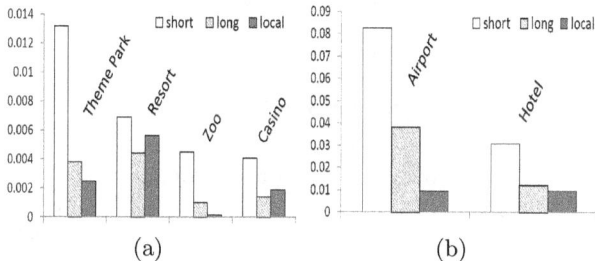

Figure 4: Travel-related subcategories (Singapore)

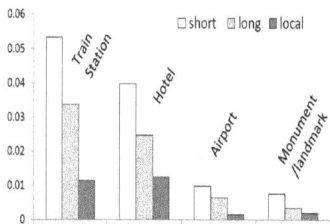

Figure 5: Travel-related subcategories (Jakarta)

Figure 4 displays the travel-related subcategories for Singapore. The subcategories are divided into the two figures 4(a) and 4(b) for better visibility due to differences in probability range. Figure 5 depicts similar information for Jakarta. From both figures, it is evident that short trips have higher probabilities in travel-related subcategories in both cities. Also consistent with the earlier observation for main categories, long trips have distributions that are closer to that of local check-ins, when we consider travel-related subcategories. Thus our key observation follows: **short trips have higher check-in probabilities for travel-related subcategories than long trips and local check-ins.**

For example short trips to Singapore has a check-in probability of 0.013 to theme parks[2], much higher than the probabilities of 0.004 for long trips and 0.002 for local check-ins. Interestingly, among the six subcategories displayed for Singapore, locals have the lowest probability for casinos. This is expected since the Singapore government imposes a levy of $100 [3] on local residents to enter casinos. The levy is exempted for foreigners.

From the most probable 30 subcategories for short trips, Jakarta has fewer travel-related subcategories (than Singapore). The inclusion of 'Train Station' warrants explanation since it was also probable for short trips in Singapore, but excluded. We include train stations as travel-related for Jakarta since visitors may arrive by train from other parts of Indonesia. This is rather different from train stations in Singapore, which we manually found to be referring to the local intra-city subway stations in many cases.

For Jakarta, Figure 5 shows the most probable subcategories i.e. 'Train Station', 'Hotel', 'Airport' and 'Monument/landmark'. For each subcategory, short trips have highest probability, followed by long trips and lastly, local. Thus short trips are again more biased towards travel-related subcategories.

Lastly, we observe that for both cities, locals do have some non-zero check-in probabilities at hotels, which is counter intuitive. We attribute this to the trend of *staycations*, a form of in-country get-away, where one spends some nights at a local hotel for rest and relaxation. In fact, online searches of 'staycation' for both cities return a long list of hotels offering staycation packages to attract locals.

3.3 Check-in Probabilities over Time

We now compare the check-in probability distribution over hour of the day. Recap that we have observed long trips and local check-ins being more similar in category/subcategory distribution. For consistency, we now expect the mentioned pair to be more similar in temporal distribution as well (than short trips versus local check-ins).

Firstly, we compute the Jenson-Shannon divergence values between distributions in each city. This does not contradict what we expect, however the divergence values are not statistically significant. For example in Singapore, between short trips and local, we have divergence of 0.006 while between long trips and local, we obtain 0.0032. Nonetheless the divergence values are computed over all hours, which may obscure certain local differences. In the next paragraph, we describe differences that we observed by zooming in on certain hours.

Figure 6 presents the check-in probabilities over hour of the day for Singapore. It is clear that all distributions slightly peaked around lunch and dinner time. This is expected as we have earlier seen that the category 'Food' is very popular. On closer analysis, long trips and local check-ins appears more similar, especially around dinner time, i.e. 1800 to 2000 hours. This suggests a pick up in activities after office/school hours, leading to more check-ins. For short trips, one observes relatively more check-ins between lunch and dinner timings. Certainly, some of these check-ins would have been contributed by tourists who are not constrained by office hours, being free to spend the day visiting attractions, sight-seeing or shopping.

---

[2]Many check-ins are at the Universal Studios theme park, a popular attraction for tourists [5]

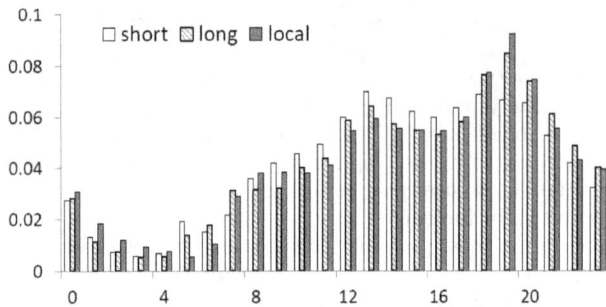

Figure 6: Check-in probability (Y-axis) over hour of day (X-axis) for Singapore.

For brevity, we omit the plot for Jakarta, which is rather similar, except that check-in probabilities are lower than those of Singapore during the early hours (hours 0 to 5), probably due to less nightlife activities. For the check-in distributions over day of the week, the differences between trip types and local check-ins are small for both cities and we omit them from further discussion here.

3.4 Check-in Intensity

How frequent are check-ins made at city A when a visitor makes long/short trips to A? Our key observation is the following: **Short trips have higher check-in intensity than long trips at the destination, with smaller time gap between consecutive check-ins.**

Using trips with more than one check-in, we compute the time gap between consecutive check-ins and tabulate for different trip types. For short/long trips to Singapore, the time gaps are computed using 7,530/36,811 check-ins from 1,392/1,177 short/long trips. For short/long trips to Jakarta, time gaps are computed using 8,931/6,143 check-ins from 2,577/1,203 short/long trips.

Figure 7 plots the Cumulative Distribution Function (CDF) for time gaps. For both cities, it is clear that short trips have smaller time gaps, or equivalently higher check-in intensity. For example in Figure 7(a) for Singapore, around 93% of time gaps from long trips have duration less than 100 hours, whereas the corresponding figure for short trips is close to 100%. In Figure 7(b) for Jakarta, we have 78% of time gaps from long trips and 99% of time gaps from short trips to be under 100 hours.

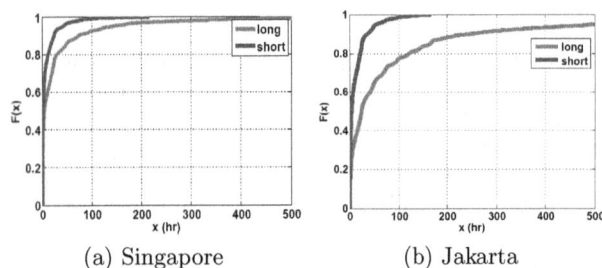

(a) Singapore   (b) Jakarta

Figure 7: CDF for time gap (hours) between consecutive trip check-ins. (Red:long trips, blue:short trips)

Time gap measurement requires more than one check-in in the trip segment, thus excluding a number of trips from analysis. However this does not affect our key observation. As a robustness check, we have computed another statistic: average time covered per check-in. For each trip, we simply divide the estimated trip duration by the check-in count, e.g. if a trip contains two check-ins over two days, each check-in covers one day on average. In this manner, all trips with at least one check-ins are also included. Results show that each check-in in short trips covers a shorter time duration on average, thus reaffirming our key observation. For Singapore, each check-in from short/long trips covers 1.7/11.1 days on average. For Jakarta, values for short/long trips are 1.6/12.5 days. The CDFs are similar in form as Figure 7 and omitted for brevity.

To understand the reasons behind the intensity differences, it is desired to conduct field studies or surveys of the visitors. We leave this to future work. Currently, we offer some intuitive reasons: short trips are more likely to be undertaken by tourists, who may visit more venues over a shorter period of time. Thus higher check-in intensity simply reflects more intense visitation activities. Another potential reason is that for short trips, one may tend to focus on key venues that are main draws since there is a need to maximize utility over limited time. Visiting such venues then increases one's propensity to check-in for the 'cool' factor or to enhance self-presentation [10]. Indeed, we shall see in Section 4.1 that short-term visitors (who make only short trips) tend to visit more popular venues.

4. VISITOR ANALYSIS

In this section, we conduct analysis on a visitor level. Since trip characteristics should carry over to visitors, we examine characteristics that are orthogonal to what we have studied previously in trips. For example, given that check-ins from short and long trips have different probabilities over categories, the resulting visitor types will naturally differ in this aspect as well.

Recap that we categorize visitors as long/short-term in Section 2.3. Based on this categorization, we now examine the differences between different types of visitors in terms of the popularity of check-in venues and their proximity to friends' check-ins. In summary, we observe:

- Short-term visitors are more biased towards popular venues than long-term visitors.

- For Singapore, both long and short-term visitors tend to check-in at venues closer to that of their friends than non-friends. For Jakarta, this proximity effect is only observed for long-term visitors.

4.1 Venue Popularities

For each venue, we quantify its popularity using two measures: *check-in count* and *no. of unique visitors*. The two measures differ since each visitor can check-in multiple times at one venue. For each check-in instance from long/short-term visitors, we compute venue popularities. Figures 8 and 9 plot the Complementary Cumulative Distribution function (CCDF) for Singapore and Jakarta respectively.

Our key observation is the following: **short-term visitors tend to check-in at more popular venues than long-term visitors.** This is consistent across both cities and both popularity measures.

In both Figures 8 and 9, the CCDF curves for short-term visitors (blue) are above that for long-term visitors (red) over a wide interval of popularity values (X-axis) thus supporting our key observation. For example, in Figure 8(b) for Singapore, 20% of check-ins by short-term visitors are to venues with at least 2000 unique visitors. For long-term visitors, the same proportion is only 8%. When we consider popularity in terms of check-in count, Figure 8(a) shows that 20% of check-ins by short-term visitors are to venues with at least 3000 check-ins. The corresponding proportion for long-term visitors is only 13%.

Venues are popular for various reasons, e.g. main attractions, must-try restaurants, key shopping areas etc. Given the limited time short-term visitors have, it is natural to focus on more popular venues where one is assured of a minimal level of utility or satisfaction. In contrast, long-term visitors will have more time and can afford to go off the well beaten track [27]. Such visitor behavior is well supported by the results here.

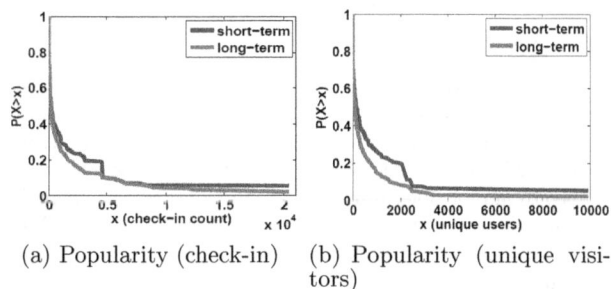

(a) Popularity (check-in)   (b) Popularity (unique visitors)

Figure 8: CCDF for venue popularities for long-term (red) and short-term visitors (blue) to Singapore

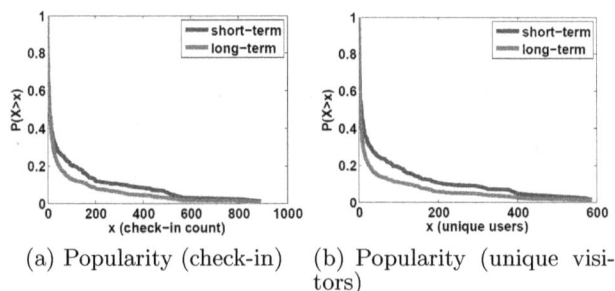

(a) Popularity (check-in)   (b) Popularity (unique visitors)

Figure 9: CCDF for venue popularities for long-term (red) and short-term visitors (blue) to Jakarta

4.2 Proximity to Friends' Check-ins

It has been established [7, 16, 12] that a user's friendships and his check-in venues are weakly related. Here, we investigate to what extent this is true for visitors. Our focus is different, since we specifically study visitors, who may not have deep social connections at the cities they are visiting. Our research question is: to what extent are check-ins and friendships related for short/long-term visitors.

Recap that we are using the friendship information that visitors have declared in their Foursquare profile (Section 2.1). We consider the case where visitor u to city A have friend(s) who also check-in at A. We do not differentiate between friends who are locals residing in A or other visitors. For u and each of his friend, we then compute the average

distance between their sets of venues. This is repeated over all of u's friends, following which we take the mean to obtain a 'friend' statistic value for u. We compare this value with one from a 'non-friend' null model, where we replace u's friends with the same number of non-friends which are randomly sampled. Larger differences between the two values indicate that a visitor's check-ins and his friends' check-ins are more strongly related.

For a more rigorous approach that does not over-amplify the distance of non-friends, we restrict the null model sampling to nodes from the social network that u belongs to, based on visitor type. For example, if u is a short-term visitor, we sample from a social network comprising of all short-term visitors and their friends. Note that some users may be friends of both short and long-term visitors, thus existing in both short/long-term social networks. To collect more comprehensive 'non-friend' statistics, we sample for 10 trials such that each visitor has 10 non-friend values. Figures 10 and 11 compare the CDF for the 'friend'/'non-friend' values for Singapore and Jakarta respectively.

Figure 10 shows that for both visitor types in Singapore, visitors check-in at venues closer to that of their friends, when compared to randomly sampled non-friends. This is indicated by the CDF for 'friend' values (red) being consistently above that of 'non-friend' (blue). The effect of friends are rather similar for both visitor types in Singapore. Comparing the CDF median at $F(x) = 0.5$, the 'friend'/'non-friend' statistics are around 13/14 km in Figure 10(a) . For long-term visitors in Figure 10(a), at the median, 'friend'/'non-friend' statistics are around 9.6/10.5 km. Thus at the median, the distance reduction due to friends is around 1 km. It is also evident that the distance reduction is fairly constant for a wide band around the median.

Figure 11(a) shows that the distance reduction due to friends are barely discernible for short-term visitors to Jakarta. This contrasts with long-term visitors in Figure 11(b) where some reduction is observable. Thus, not all observations from Singapore carry over to Jakarta and city characteristics do affect whether visitors check-in close to that of their friends.

Following the analysis, we can now summarize our key observations as: **For long-term visitors, his check-in venues and friendships are weakly related. For short-term visitors, this was only observed for Singapore.**

Lastly, we point out that proximity to friends' check-ins is related to the homohily phenemenon which is driven by two processes: [15]: social influence and selection. Under social influence, visitors' check-in behavior are influenced by their friends. For selection, visitors with similar preference visit similar or nearby venues and bond with each other, thus becoming friends, e.g. nightclubbers connecting at clubbing sessions.

5. PREDICTION EXPERIMENTS

Based on each visitors' indicated home cities and trip duration, we have extracted and categorized visitors to Singapore and Jakarta into long/short-term. We have also shown that both visitor types have different characteristics. We now examine if the visitor type information can improve venue prediction accuracy for different models.

For each visitor, our task is to *predict the set of venues in the last 10% of his check-ins during the trip*. For example, if a visitor makes 20 check-ins during his trip to Singapore,

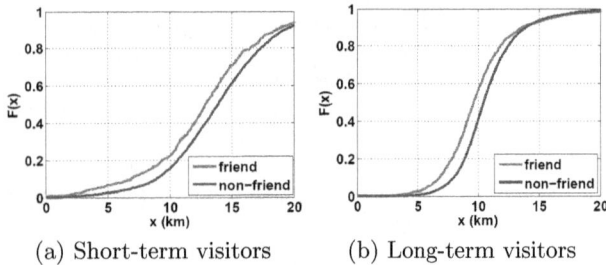

(a) Short-term visitors	(b) Long-term visitors

Figure 10: CDF of average distance to venues of friends(red) /non-friends(blue) for Singapore

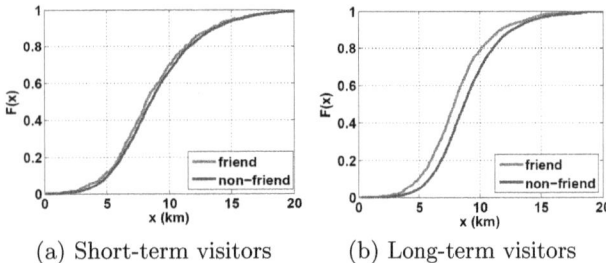

(a) Short-term visitors	(b) Long-term visitors

Figure 11: CDF of average distance to venues of friends(red) /non-friends(blue) for Jakarta

we predict the venues involved in the last 2 check-ins. If a visitor has less than 10 check-ins for his trip, we simply predict for the last 1 check-in. Our results show that:

- **We can improve prediction accuracy for short-term visitors if a model is aware of their type.**

- For long-term visitors, it is not necessary to differentiate them from short-term visitors and we do not observe accuracy gains.

The reason for the second point depends on the prediction model employed, but for personalized models, the amount of personal data plays a part. As shown in Table 3, long-term visitors generally have more check-ins during their trips than short-term visitors. Hence if the model is able to exploit personal check-in history to make good predictions, then visitor type information is immaterial.

Inclusion/exclusion of visitor type information. To predict for each visitor, we use two experiment settings. In the first setting, the prediction models are aware of the visitor type and use only check-ins from the correct type for training or ranking. This can be seemed as a form of stratification in the hope of achieving better accuracies. In the second setting, the visitor type is unknown and the models simply utilized all visitor check-ins. For each setting, we use different models to rank venues per visitor such that high ranking venues are regarded as more likely to be check-in to. Henceforth we compare the results across settings per model and ascertain if the first setting gives better accuracy. Our prediction models include a sophisticated *Kernel-Density Estimation (KDE)* model adapted from a recent work [18] and simpler popularity-based ranking techniques.

In summary, for **Setting A**, our visitor-type aware prediction models are as follows:

- KDE model that includes a background component comprising check-ins from the specific visitor type

- Ranking of venues based on number of check-ins from the specific visitor type

- Ranking of venues based on number of unique visitors from the specific visitor type

In **Setting B**, the models are unaware of the visitor type:

- KDE model that includes a background component comprising check-ins from all visitors

- Ranking of venues based on number of check-ins from all visitors

- Ranking of venues based on overall number of unique visitors

Ranking venues based on check-ins/unique visitors are straightforward and self-explanatory. In the next section, we briefly explain the KDE model and the notion of the background component.

5.1 KDE Model

For each visitor in his city of visit, we fit a continuous two dimensional KDE model that estimates his check-in probability density at any city location. Compared to traditional spatial modeling techniques with Gaussian mixtures, the KDE model does not assume any parametric form for the spatial distribution and is better able to handle sharp transitions in spatial densities due to man-made or natural terrain.

We compute the probability of a visitor's check-in at a venue by predicting the density at the venue's spatial location: $e = <x, y>$. The density conditional on the training data $E = \{e_1, ..., e_n\}$, can be written as:

$$f(e|E) = \frac{1}{n} \sum_i^n \frac{exp[-\frac{1}{2}(e - e_i)^t C_{h(e_i)}^{-1}(e - e_i)]}{2\pi h(e_i)} \quad (2)$$

where we have used the Gaussian kernel with a diagonal covariance matrix, $C = \mathbf{I}h(e_i)$, and $h(e_i)$ is the local bandwidth for training point e_i, estimated by taking the distance to the k-th neighbor of e_i. Compared to using a global bandwidth, locally estimated bandwidths vary the degree of smoothing to better handle regions with sparse or high density of training points [18, 6].

5.1.1 KDE Models in Setting A

For a long-term visitor u, we can use solely his personal check-in history E_u for modeling. However to include additional information, we use a mixture of KDE components instead, (each component is equivalent to a KDE model on its own). Our choice of components differs from that of [18]. We include a component from the history of friends' check-ins $E_f(u)$, due to our analysis in Section 4.2. We also include a background component. In Setting A, the background component is estimated from the check-in history of other long-term visitors E_{L-term}. Formally, the KDE model contains 3 components:

Long-term, Setting A: $f(e|E) = \alpha_u f(e|E_u) +$
$\alpha_f f(e|E_{f(u)}) + (1 - \alpha_u - \alpha_{f(u)})f(e|E_{L-term})$ $\quad (3)$

where 'α's are the mixture weights.

For short-term visitors, we again utilize a mixture of KDE components. However such visitors usually have very few check-ins at the visited city. For example Table 3 shows that

82.75%/79.85% of short-term visitors to Singapore/Jakarta have 5 or less check-ins at the visited city. This makes it difficult to build a KDE component from personal history. Hence, our KDE mixture uses only 2 components: friend's check-in history and a background component. As friends are specific to each visitor, there is still some personalization, although at much lower degree than long-term visitors. In Setting A, the background component is estimated from the history E_{S-term} of other short-term visitors. The mixture model is as follows:

$$\text{Short-term, Setting A: } f(e|E) = \alpha_f f(e|E_{f(u)}) + \\ (1 - \alpha_{f(u)}) f(e|E_{S-term}) \quad (4)$$

5.1.2 KDE Models in Setting B

The KDE models in Setting B differs from that of Setting A only in terms of how the background component is constructed. For both short and long-term visitors, the background component utilizes the check-ins of *all* visitors E_{All}, without any differentiation of visitor type. Other components in the respective mixture models are retained.

For long-term visitors, the KDE model is now:

$$\text{Long-term, Setting B: } f(e|E) = \alpha_u f(e|E_u) + \\ \alpha_f f(e|E_{f(u)}) + (1 - \alpha_u - \alpha_{f(u)}) f(e|E_{All}) \quad (5)$$

For short-term visitors, the model is written as:

$$\text{Short-term, Setting B: } f(e|E) = \alpha_f f(e|E_{f(u)}) + \\ (1 - \alpha_{f(u)}) f(e|E_{All}) \quad (6)$$

5.2 Experiment Design and Metrics

For each visitor, we hide check-in venues from the last 10% of his trips (by check-in count). We then build the KDE and popularity-based models to rank all candidate venues and assess ranking accuracies. Note that for model building, we only include friend and background check-ins that occur earlier than the last 10% of the trip. For long-term visitors, we only consider visitors with > 6 check-ins at the visited city such that the personal KDE component can be reasonably constructed. KDE mixture parameters, i.e. the 'α's are inferred using a grid search in step size of 0.05.

We refer to each visitor and his hidden venues as a test case. For Singapore, we obtained 1,498 test cases for long-term visitors and 582 test cases for short-term visitors. There are 65,701 candidate venues for ranking. For Jakarta, we have 461 test cases for long-term visitors and 382 test cases for short-term visitors. It is required to rank 30,254 venues in Jakarta. Note that due to the large number of venues per city, randomly ranking the venues will produce accuracies much lower than the KDE model or popularity ranking.

To measure ranking accuracy, each hidden venue is considered only once for the visitor even if he check-ins multiple times. We use the following accuracy metrics:

- **Mean Precision.** Given the p highest ranked venues for a visitor, precision at p, $Prec(p)$ is the proportion of hidden venues, i.e. venues that he actually check-in to. We then average precision over all test cases to obtain the mean precision at position p, **MP**(p).

- **Mean Recall.** Given the p highest ranked venues for a visitor, recall at p, $r(p)$ is the number of hidden venues retrieved at position p, divided by the total number of hidden venues. We then average recall over all test cases to obtain mean recall **MR**(p).

- **Mean Average Precision (MAP).** This is based on Average Precision (AP), commonly used in document retrieval tasks. For a test case, AP attains a perfect accuracy of 1 if all hidden venues are ranked higher than all other candidate venues. AP is computed as:

$$AP = \sum_p Prec(p)\Delta r(p) \quad (7)$$

where $\Delta r(p)$ is the change in recall from position $p-1$ to p. We average AP over all test cases to obtain MAP. Also note that for each test case, we evaluate AP over all ranked venues (instead of just the top p).

5.3 Results

Tables 5 and 6 display the best prediction results in terms of MAP obtained for long-term and short-term visitors to Singapore. The corresponding KDE parameters are shown in Table 7.

5.3.1 Singapore

For each model, we compare the accuracies across settings A and B. For long-term visitors to Singapore, the relative differences are extremely small and negligible for both KDE and popularity ranking. In contrast for short-term visitors, all models perform much better in Setting A. For such visitors, the MAP gain of Setting A over B ranges around 100% for popularity ranking to 56% for KDE. Large gains are also observed for the other metrics of recall and precision. Hence for short-term visitors, it is beneficial to identify them as such, and use only check-ins from the correct visitor type. If one simply uses all visitor check-ins, there is too much noise from long-term visitors.

Evidently, check-ins from short-term visitors do not impose a problem of noise if included in the model for long-term visitors. There are several possible reasons, one of which is many check-in venues of short-term visitors are popular and also frequented by long-term visitors. For example, Singapore's main shopping belt is Orchard Road which attracts both short and long-term visitors (and locals). On the other hand, long-term visitors may frequent less accessible suburban malls, which draw fewer short-term visitors.

For personalized models such as KDE, the length of check-in history also plays a part. Short-term visitors spend much shorter duration at the visited city and many have insufficient check-ins for estimating the personal component (refer Table 3). On the other hand, long-term visitors have richer check-in history and the personal component plays an important role, i.e. weighted by α_u in Table 7. There is then less sensitivity to the background component, and in turn, to whether the background uses all visitor check-ins or not.

Table 7 displays the optimal KDE parameters. Interestingly for long-term visitors, the component for friends are not important, i.e. $\alpha_{f(u)} = 0$, which on the surface, seems contradictory to our earlier empirical analysis (Section 4.2). This can be explained by the fact that the visitor's personal check-in history has already captured the same information provided by his friends' check-ins. For example, if a visitor u and his friends frequent a shopping mall, u's check-ins alone may suffice for the KDE model to infer a high density value for that shopping mall.

5.3.2 Jakarta

Tables 8 and 9 display the results for long-term and short-term visitors to Jakarta, with corresponding KDE parame-

Table 5: Results for long-term test cases (Singapore)

Models					
Setting	MP(10)	MP(30)	MR(10)	MR(30)	MAP
KDE model					
A	0.0796	0.0346	0.172	0.201	0.1523
B	0.0798	0.0347	0.174	0.201	0.1524
Ranking venues by check-in count					
A	0.0496	0.0276	0.127	0.180	0.1118
B	0.0503	0.0277	0.132	0.181	0.1121
Ranking venues by unique visitor count					
A	0.0515	0.0282	0.134	0.197	0.1129
B	0.0482	0.0280	0.132	0.196	0.1130

Table 6: Results for short-term test cases (Singapore)

Models					
Setting	MP(10)	MP(30)	MR(10)	MR(30)	MAP
KDE model					
A	0.0320	0.0132	0.309	0.380	0.1748
B	0.0182	0.0072	0.174	0.206	0.1124
Ranking venues by check-in count					
A	0.0328	0.0143	0.316	0.411	0.1794
B	0.0155	0.0080	0.144	0.227	0.0823
Ranking venues by unique visitor count					
A	0.0332	0.0144	0.319	0.413	0.1836
B	0.0211	0.0087	0.200	0.247	0.0958

ters displayed in Table 10. Again, for each prediction model, we compare the results between settings A and B. Table 8 shows that for long-term test cases, Setting A does not consistently provide accuracy improvement across all models and metrics, when compared to Setting B. On the other hand, accuracies for short-term test cases (Table 9) are consistently higher for Setting A across all metrics and models. This agrees with our earlier observation for Singapore.

We note that for short-term test cases in Jakarta, Setting A provides a smaller magnitude of improvement over Setting B, as compared to Singapore. For example, MAP for KDE model increases by 10.39%, from 0.0635 to 0.0701, much less than the corresponding increase for Singapore (55.6%). One explanation is that both short and long-term visitors to Jakarta include fellow Indonesians residing outside the city. Such domestic visitors may have check-in behaviors that are more similar to each other, although trip durations may differ. Thus the differences between short and long-term visitors are reduced.

5.3.3 Comparisons

Comparing the optimal KDE parameters for Singapore (Table 7) and Jakarta (Table 10), the background component $1 - \alpha_u - \alpha_{f(u)}$ for long-term Jakarta visitors has much smaller weights than the case for Singapore. Concurrently, long-term Jakarta visitors also have larger weights α_u for their personal history component than long-term Singapore visitors. Both observations suggest that long-term Jakarta visitors are relatively more personalized in their behavior.

To investigate further, we compute the normalized entropy of the distributions over venues for long-term visitor groups. We obtain 0.795 for long-term Jakarta visitors versus 0.74 for long-term Singapore visitors. Thus the former visitor group contains more uncertainty, which supports the notion of each visitor being more personalized. Various

Table 7: Optimal KDE parameters for visitors to Singapore

KDE model (long-term)			
Setting	α_u	$\alpha_{f(u)}$	$1 - \alpha_u - \alpha_{f(u)}$
A	0.40	0.00	0.60
B	0.45	0.00	0.55
KDE model (short-term)			
Setting	-	$\alpha_{f(u)}$	$1 - \alpha_{f(u)}$
A	-	0.15	0.85
B	-	0.20	0.80

factors may contribute to this, including city planning, car ownership and the availability of public transport etc. For example, the subway[3] is a popular transport mode in Singapore while Jakarta does not currently have a subway system. In the trivial extreme case, if all visitors only take the subway and check-in at venues near subway stations, then personalization is low.

Lastly, our results show that sophisticated models do not always outperform simpler techniques. While the KDE model easily outperforms ranking by popularity for long-term visitors (Tables 5 and 8), it fails to do so for short-term visitors (Tables 6 and 9). As mentioned earlier in the discussion of Singapore results and also shown in Table 3, such visitors have very few check-ins in their trip history for modeling, thus the KDE loses its advantage of being more personalized.

Table 8: Results for long-term test cases (Jakarta)

Models					
Setting	MP(10)	MP(30)	MR(10)	MR(30)	MAP
KDE model					
A	0.0245	0.0101	0.117	0.128	0.0928
B	0.0262	0.0106	0.131	0.138	0.0964
Ranking venues by check-in count					
A	0.0102	0.0062	0.0690	0.107	0.0352
B	0.0093	0.0066	0.0601	0.105	0.0318
Ranking venues by unique visitor count					
A	0.0102	0.0061	0.0671	0.109	0.0303
B	0.0111	0.0060	0.0724	0.109	0.0315

Table 9: Results for short-term test cases (Jakarta)

Models					
Setting	MP(10)	MP(30)	MR(10)	MR(30)	MAP
KDE model					
A	0.0128	0.0055	0.122	0.158	0.0701
B	0.0120	0.0041	0.114	0.116	0.0635
Ranking venues by check-in count					
A	0.0139	0.0072	0.132	0.203	0.0788
B	0.0126	0.0060	0.119	0.174	0.0703
Ranking venues by unique visitor count					
A	0.0136	0.0066	0.130	0.192	0.0769
B	0.0131	0.0067	0.124	0.195	0.0684

Remarks. We have shown that predictions are more accurate if we know a visitor is a short-term one, based on his trip duration, i.e. trip has ended. However, real applications require knowing the visitor type as early as possible, such

[3]www.lta.gov.sg/content/ltaweb/en/public-transport/mrt-and-lrt-trains.html

Table 10: Optimal KDE parameters for visitors to Jakarta

KDE model (long-term)			
Setting	α_u	$\alpha_{f(u)}$	$1 - \alpha_u - \alpha_{f(u)}$
A	0.75	0.15	0.10
B	0.80	0.15	0.05
KDE model (short-term)			
Setting	-	$\alpha_{f(u)}$	$1 - \alpha_{f(u)}$
A	-	0.05	0.95
B	-	0.00	1.00

that predictions can be made *during* the trip. For this, other data sources will be useful, e.g. content from tweets before or during the trip, immigration declarations etc. In other scenarios, we can motivate the visitors themselves to directly provide their trip duration to the prediction model. This is especially true for venue recommendation apps (related to venue prediction) in mobile phones, where the durations can be used to improve recommendations [25].

6. RELATED WORK

Users of location-based social networks have been well studied in prior work [13, 26, 7, 17, 16, 7, 14, 20, 9]. Gao and Liu [11] had provided a good survey in this area. However much focus has been on locally active users [16, 7, 14, 20, 9], which by excluding users with too few check-ins, may ignore most short-term visitors. In our case, we do not exclude short-term visitors even if they have only one check-in at their visited city. Some other works [17, 27, 19] studied inter-city visitation behavior, but do not differentiate between visitor types. In contrast, we study the differences between long/short trips and long/short-term visitors.

Liu et al. [19] define trips as city visits, which resembles our work. However trips are used differently to derive city-level interaction models as well as group cities into spatial communities. Wu et al. [24] define trips differently as each user's transition between different activity types, whereby activity types are derived from venue categories. They proposed a model for the transition probabilities of users.

Zhao et al. [27] matched interest communities (e.g. foodies) across regions, to recommend venues that are locally interesting for tourists, but omitted by dominant tourist resources. All city visitors are regarded as tourists, regardless of trip duration. As we have shown, short/long-term visitors have different check-in characteristics. Hence it will be interesting to compare recommendation accuracies across visitor types. We also envisage that numerous other recommendation/prediction models [7, 21, 17] are applicable and likely to perform differently on different visitor types. For example, topic models [14, 20, 13, 9] that model each user as a document and venues as words will encounter challenges for short-term visitors. Such users usually have little check-in history at the visited city and are analogous to extremely short documents.

Our analysis can be easily repeated on other forms of trajectory data, e.g. cell phone tower logs or GPS data, where trip durations can be estimated even more precisely. For GPS data, some related work includes [28, 29, 25], where the common goal is to make venue recommendations. In particular, Yoon et al [25] utilizes trip duration, input by users on their mobile devices, to make more useful recom-

mendations. This supports our finding that visiting behavior is dependent on visitor type as determined by trip duration.

7. CONCLUSION

We have categorized trips and visitors to two cities and showed that significant differences exist between short and long trips and subsequently between short-term and long-term visitors. Our empirical analysis has been extensive and covers multiple aspects of check-in behavior. Many of the differences are intuitive and can be reasonably explained. For example, short-term visitors are biased towards more popular check-in venues as there may be a need to maximize utility over limited trip duration.

We follow up on the analysis by a venue prediction experiment. The results indicate that it is beneficial to identify short-term visitors properly and include that information in prediction models. Doing so increases prediction accuracy significantly. Equivalently, this indicates that trip duration and check-in behavior are highly related and that to make good predictions (or recommendations), one should factor in the trip duration. In certain scenarios, e.g. mobile apps, the app user himself can be easily motivated to input his intended trip duration to obtain better recommendations.

For further work, an interesting direction is to explore dynamic predictions as a trip progresses. In the context of a trip, the predictions may not only depend on the observed trip history to-date, but also on the estimated *remaining* trip duration. In fact estimating the latter is akin to the problem of *Survival Analysis*[23]. In survival analysis, one predicts the failure time of equipment or time of death of patients. In our problem domain, the failure time is analogous to the end of the trip. Check-ins and other data features are analogous to emitted symptoms which can help to refine the estimated trip end time. To our knowledge, it is still unexplored how one can estimate the trip end time and exploit this in a prediction model to achieve better prediction accuracies. At the moment, this seems to be a highly challenging problem, especially for short-term visitors. In fact the trade-off of latency versus accuracy in predictions arises [22].

8. ACKNOWLEDGEMENTS

This research is partially supported by DSO National Laboratories, Singapore; and the Singapore National Research Foundation under its International Research Centre@Singapore Funding Initiative and administered by the IDM Programme Office, Media Development Authority (MDA).

9. REFERENCES

[1] http://travel.trade.gov/research/programs/ifs/index.html.

[2] http://www.labourmobility.com/2011-top-cities-to-live-and-work-in-the-middle-east/.html.

[3] www.ifaq.gov.sg/cra/apps/fcd_faqmain.aspx.

[4] www.singstat.gov.sg/publications/publications-and-papers/reference/mdscontent#tourism.

[5] www.yoursingapore.com/content/traveller/en/experience.html.

[6] L. Breiman, W. Meisel, and E. Purcell. Variable kernel estimates of multivariate densities. *Technometrics*, 19(2), 1977.

[7] C. Cheng, H. Yang, I. King, and M. R. Lyu. Fused matrix factorization with geographical and social influence in location-based social networks. *AAAI*, 2012.

[8] Z. Cheng, J. Caverlee, K. Lee, and D. Z. Sui. Exploring millions of footprints in location sharing services. *ICWSM*, 2011.

[9] W.-H. Chong, B. T. Dai, and E.-P. Lim. Prediction of venues in Foursquare using flipped topic models. *ECIR*, 2015.

[10] H. Cramer, M. Rost, and L. E. Holmquist. Performing a check-in: emerging practices, norms and 'conflicts' in location-sharing using Foursquare. *MobileHCI*, 2011.

[11] H. Gao and H. Liu. Data analysis on location-based social netwoks. *Mobile Social Networking: An Innovative Approach, Springer*, 2014.

[12] H. Gao, J. Tang, and H. Liu. Exploring social-historical ties on location-based social networks. *ICWSM*, 2012.

[13] B. Hu and M. Ester. Spatial topic modeling in online social media for location recommendation. *Recsys*, 2013.

[14] K. Joseph, C. H. Tan, and K. M. Carley. Beyond âĂIJlocalâĂİ, âĂIJcategoriesâĂİ and âĂIJfriendsâĂİ: clustering Foursquare users with latent âĂIJtopicsâĂİ. *UbiComp*, 2012.

[15] D. B. Kandel. Homophily, selection, and socialization in adolescent friendships. *The American Journal of Sociology*, 84(2), 1978.

[16] A. S. H. Kautz and J. Bigham. Finding your friends and following them to where you are. *WSDM*, 2012.

[17] T. Kurashima, T. Iwata, T. Hoshide, N. Takaya, and K. Fujimura. Geo topic model: joint modeling of user's activity area and interests for location recommendation. *WSDM*, 2013.

[18] M. Lichman and P. Smyth. Modeling human location data with mixtures of kernel densities. *KDD*, 2014.

[19] Y. Liu, Z. Sui, C. Kang, and Y. Gao. Uncovering patterns of inter-urban trip and spatial interaction from social media check-in data. *PLoS ONE*, 9(1):e86026, 2014.

[20] X. Long, L. Jin, and J. Joshi. Exploring trajectory -driven local geographic topics in Foursquare. *UbiComp*, 2012.

[21] A. Noulas, S. Scellato, N. Lathia, and C. Mascolo. Mining user mobility features for next place prediction in location-based services. *ICDM*, 2012.

[22] R. Sen, Y. Lee, K. Jayarajah, A. Misra, and R. K. Balan. Grumon: fast and accurate group monitoring for heterogeneous urban spaces. *SenSys*, 2014.

[23] T. M. Therneau and P. M. Grambsch. Modeling survival data: extending the Cox model. *Springer-Verlag*, 2011.

[24] L. Wu, Y. Zhi, Z. Sui, and Y. Liu. Intra-urban human mobility and activity transition: Evidence from social media check-in data. *PLoS ONE*, 9(5):e97010, 2014.

[25] H. Yoon, Y. Zheng, X. Xie, and W. Woo. Smart itinerary recommendation based on user-generated gps trajectories. *UIC*, 2010.

[26] Q. Yuan, G. Cong, Z. Ma, A. Sun, and N. Magnenat-Thalmann. Who, where, when and what: discover spatio-temporal topics for Twitter users. *KDD*, 2013.

[27] Y.-L. Zhao, L. Nie, XiangyuWang, and T.-S. Chua. Personalized recommendations of locally interesting venues to tourists via cross-region community matching. *TIST*, 5(3):50:1-26, 2014.

[28] Y. Zheng and X. Xie. Learning travel recommendations from user-generated gps traces. *TIST*, 2(1):2, 2011.

[29] Y. Zheng, L. Zhang, X. Xie, and W.-Y. Ma. Mining interesting locations and travel sequences from gps trajectories. *WWW*, 2009.

APPENDIX

A. SIGNIFICANCE TEST

We design a significance test for Jensen–Shannon (JS) divergence based on sampling. Given two probability distributions X and Y, JS divergence is defined as

$$JS(X||Y) = [KL(X||M) + KL(Y||M)]/2 \qquad (8)$$

where $M = (X+Y)/2$ and KL(.) is the Kullback-âĂŞLeibler divergence.

If X and Y are not significantly different, both will be close to M. Thus we regard M as a form of null model and use this in our significance test. Each time, we draw 2 sets of samples from M and estimate the distribution per sample set. This gives a pair of distributions, from which we compute the JS divergence. Since both distributions are in fact generated from M, the divergence value can be interpreted as what is expected by chance given an identical distribution pair. We do this over multiple pairs and count the number of pairs with higher divergence values than $JS(X||Y)$. Such occurrences should be very low if X and Y are very different.

Formally, let X, Y be 2 empirical distributions estimated from samples of size S_x and S_y respectively, we test if they are significantly different via the following steps:

1. Compute $M = (X + Y)/2$, $d = JS(X||Y)$. Initialize counter $c := 0$.

2. For $i = 1$ to P

   (a) From M, draw 2 sets of samples, of sizes S_x and S_y.

   (b) For each sample set, estimate the multinomial distribution by proportions. Hence from 2 sample sets, obtain a pair of distributions: $M_{i,x}$, $M_{i,y}$.

   (c) Compute $d_i = JS(M_{i,x}||M_{i,y})$. if $d_i \geq d$, update counter $c := c + 1$.

3. Compute c/P. If this is less than α, then $JS(X||Y)$ is significant at p-value=α.

In all our significance tests, we have used $P = 1000$.

"I don't have a photograph, but you can have my footprints."[*]
– Revealing the Demographics of Location Data

Chris Riederer, Sebastian Zimmeck, Coralie Phanord, Augustin Chaintreau, Steven M. Bellovin
Computer Science Department, Columbia University, New York, NY
{mani,sebastian,augustin,smb}@cs.columbia.edu, Coralie.S.Phanord.16@dartmouth.edu

ABSTRACT

Location data are routinely available to a plethora of mobile apps and third party web services. The resulting datasets are increasingly available to advertisers for targeting and also requested by governmental agencies for law enforcement purposes. While the re-identification risk of such data has been widely reported, the *discriminative* power of mobility has received much less attention. In this study we fill this void with an open and reproducible method. We explore how the growing number of geotagged footprints left behind by social network users in photosharing services can give rise to inferring demographic information from mobility patterns. Chiefly among those, we provide the first detailed analysis of *ethnic* mobility patterns in two metropolitan areas. This analysis allows us to examine questions pertaining to spatial segregation and the extent to which ethnicity can be inferred using *only* location data. Our results reveal that even a few location records at a coarse grain can be sufficient for simple algorithms to draw an accurate inference. Our method generalizes to other features, such as gender, offering for the first time a general approach to evaluate discriminative risks associated with location-enabled personalization.

Categories and Subject Descriptors

K.4.1 [**COMPUTERS AND SOCIETY**]: Public Policy Issues—*Privacy*

Keywords

Location Data; Machine Learning; Privacy; Segregation; Social Networks

1. INTRODUCTION

Human mobility is intimately intertwined with highly personal behaviors and characteristics. As Justice Sotomayor of the United States Supreme Court stated, "disclosed in [GPS] data ... [are] trips the indisputably private nature of which takes little imagination to conjure: trips to the psychiatrist, the plastic surgeon, the abortion clinic, the AIDS treatment center, the strip club, the criminal defense attorney, the by-the-hour motel, the union meeting, the mosque, synagogue or church, the gay bar and on and on [47]." For that reason, previous studies of mobility centered on the risk of either re-identification in sensitive anonymized location datasets or on protecting visits to private locations [9, 16].

However, the re-identification risk based on individual locations is not the only threat. Many users are producing a series of footprints, which might be innocuous individually, however, taken together can create a sparse yet informative view allowing inferences from their whereabouts. The benefits of revealing locations are obvious: location data can be used for personalizing recommendations [39] and displaying more relevant advertising [28] in order to finance free online services. However, the downsides are more difficult to assess. While an individual data point may create no privacy risk, an aggregated dataset might enable inferences beyond a user's expectation.

In this paper we explore the discriminative power of location data. Solely based on mobility patterns, which we extracted from photosharing network profiles, we infer users' ethnicities and gender both on a demographic and an individual level. As we discuss in §2, this exploration stands in contrast to limitations of previous studies as our paper brings together the following contributions:

- We show how photosharing network data can be leveraged to extract mobility patterns using a new method for creating location datasets from publicly available resources. Our method combines the use of online social networks and crowdsourcing platforms. It has the advantage that it generally enables *anyone* to study human mobility and does not mandate access to Call Detail Records (CDRs) or other proprietary datasets. (§3).

- To assess the quality of the created datasets we show that mobility patterns extracted from photosharing networks are comparable in terms of their essential characteristics to those previously observed and reported for CDRs. For the first time, we extend the analysis of mobility patterns to *ethnic groups*. We show how comparisons lead to statistically significant differences that are meaningful for assessing residential and peripatetic segregation. (§4).

- Finally, we demonstrate the discriminative power of location data on an *individual* level. Our analysis confirms for the first time that location data alone suffices to predict an individual's ethnicity, even with relatively simple frequency-based algorithms. Moreover, this inference is robust: a small amount of location records at a coarse grain allows for an inference competitive with more sophisticated methods despite of data sparsity and noise. (§5).

---

[*]Groucho Marx, *A Night at the Opera*

2. RELATED WORK

Our study complements works on human mobility patterns and attribute inference in multiple ways.

First, the use of location data relates our study to previous inquiries into human mobility [7, 14, 36]. In particular, we aggregate location data into mobility patterns and compare our patterns to those published in earlier studies [3, 20, 21] for validation, but furthermore we analyze those patterns both at an individual level and aggregated in multiple demographic groups, including, for the first time, from the perspective of ethnicity. This analysis complements previous studies which have shown that mobility is correlated to social status [6] and community well-being [25] measured at city and neighborhood levels. While some studies already demonstrated that mobility traces can uniquely identify individuals [9, 44], the inference of individuals' demographic attributes from location data, that is, the *discriminative* power of location data, remained unexplored. We make inferences beyond trip purpose identification [11], activity type prediction [27, 29], and identification of location types [19].

Previous studies aimed to infer the ethnicities, gender, and other attributes of online users. Often they leveraged linguistic features, such as Facebook or Twitter user names, stated first and last names [5, 35], or Tweet content [39, 40]. Those studies demonstrated an underrepresentation of females and minorities online [35]; a finding which we extend and confirm using photosharing services. Mobility data from mobile phones were used to predict personality traits [10], age [4], and gender [43], but, in addition to relying on proprietary data, all of these studies solely analyzed call patterns or social network properties as opposed to locations. In contrast, we attempt to infer attributes using *only* location data, making our work more broadly applicable to any technology that can collect mobility information, such as GPS, Wi-Fi, or mobile apps. We additionally examine whether predictions become more accurate with more data, similar to [1], and how the granularity of data impacts prediction accuracy.

More generally, our analysis fits into the category of works on extracting information from social networks, such as [8]. Probably, the closest work is [50], which also aims to infer meaning from locations, however, is not concerned with ethnicity. We obtain our data from profiles of the photosharing service Instagram, and our analysis is enhanced with auxiliary information from the geo-social search service Foursquare and the United States Census 2010 [46] (Census). To our knowledge this is the first study demonstrating that it is possible to extract from social networks mobility patterns that are enriched with ethnic or gender information at an individual level. It should be noted in particular that all aforementioned studies of mobile data rely on proprietary data, primarily CDRs, that are only available with the consent of the data owner (e.g., [9, 25]). In contrast, our methodology is principally reproducible by anyone at a small cost, and our data will be made available shortly after publication. Our study provides a contribution to overcome the lack of publicly available mobility datasets and serves as a validator for their patterns.

3. METHODOLOGY AND APPLICATION

User profiles on photosharing networks often contain a significant amount of photos tagged with latitude-longitude GPS locations. Over time the accumulated location data can build up to comprehensive mobility profiles. Based on this insight and given that many user profiles on photosharing networks are publicly accessible we now introduce a methodology and its application to construct mobility datasets from readily available data. An overview of our methodology is shown in Figure 1.

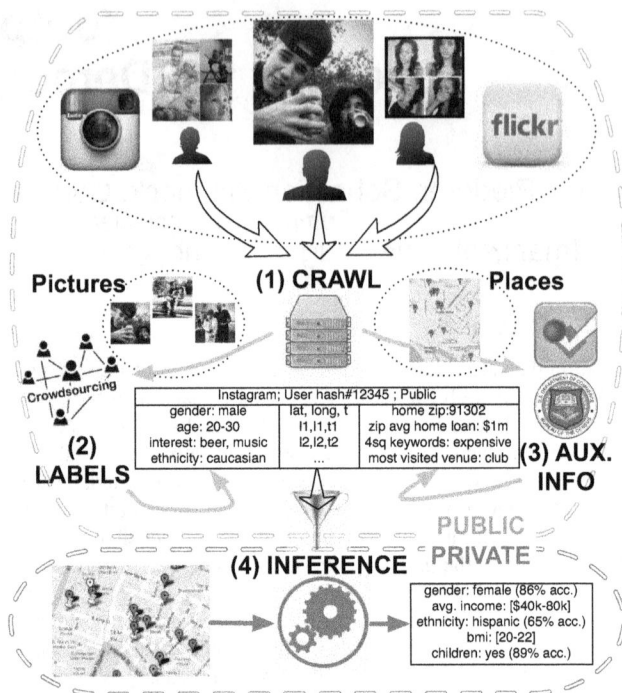

Figure 1: Methodology overview. A mobility dataset can be built in the following steps: (1) Public user profiles of a photosharing service are crawled and photo metadata are extracted into a database (Data Collection). (2) Corresponding photos are labeled (with labels for ethnicity, gender, etc.) by crowd workers in an online labor marketplace (User Labeling). (3) The dataset is further enhanced with auxiliary data, e.g., with the information that a certain location is close to a restaurant (Adding Auxiliary Information). (4) The dataset can then be used to analyze attributes on various demographic levels or train and test classifiers for individual inferences.

Data Collection.

Applying this methodology, we collected publicly available photo metadata from Instagram covering data for the years from 2011 through 2013. This data collection and use was exempt from user informed consent under our institution's IRB rules since (1) we only collected publicly available online metadata, (2) after we used the metadata and the users were labeled, any identifying information, such as usernames, were removed, and (3) we only kept track of users' identities separately and for one single purpose (ensuring that the data we collected still belongs to a public Instagram profile). We started our crawl from a root user (the founder of Instagram, on whose feed a large and diverse group of users comment) and followed further users subsequently through comments and likes. We skipped users with no geotagged photo in their first 45 photos. Our crawl retrieved a total of 35,307,441 photo location points belonging to 118,374 unique users.

User Labeling.

To match previous studies [19, 20, 21] that leveraged ZIP codes of CDR billing addresses from the Los Angeles (LA) and New York City (NY) metropolitan areas we randomly chose users from those areas as well. A user's home is the ZIP code where he or she had the most checkins (that is, photos taken). Note that this mitigates the content produced by tourists and other occasional visitors to LA and NY unless those have no other Instagram activity. A combination of workers on Amazon Mechanical Turk (MTurk) and undergraduate students were asked to annotate users' ethnicities and gender based on the users' photos. However, in order to ensure that user pictures on Instagram profiles are sufficient to make a conclusive determination of users' ethnicities and genders we ran a preliminary experiment by selecting 200 profiles at random (excluding celebrities and business accounts) and having each labeled independently by two undergraduate students. We observed a strong agreement on gender (98%). The errors corresponded to a family profile belonging to multiple people and profiles with one picture.

For ethnicity labeling we leveraged Census categories. We asked the student annotators to categorize each user either as Hispanic or Latino (Hispanic), White alone (Caucasian), Black or African American alone (African American), or Other (combining all remaining Census categories, including Asian). Merging all remaining Census fields in the last category limits our detail view, although we would otherwise have some annotations being quite rare. Just as in the Census, our Hispanic category includes Hispanics and Latinos of any race, while the remaining categories do not include any Hispanics or Latinos. We found that our profiles are diverse: 45% Caucasian, 21% Hispanic, 15% African American, and 19% Other. The students' labels matched 87% of the time and when evaluated as a binary classification task (Caucasian vs. all other categories) the agreement reached 94%. It should be noted that the two labeling students were of different gender and ethnicity themselves. In conclusion, despite sparse data and ethnicity spanning a continuous spectrum, we found that labels are surprisingly predictable and consistent across annotators. As studies confirmed that 91% of teens post a photo of themselves on social networks [31] and that 46.6% of photos are either selfies or show the user posing with other friends [17] there is also evidence in many cases that it is actually the account owner who is shown in the pictures.

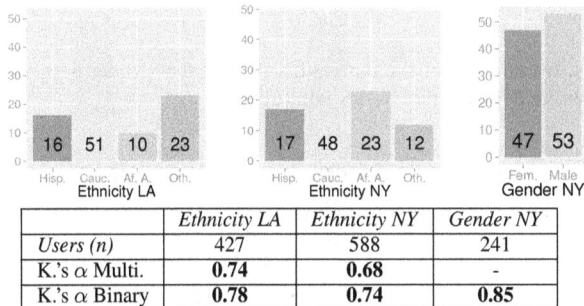

	Ethnicity LA	Ethnicity NY	Gender NY
Users (n)	427	588	241
K.'s α Multi.	**0.74**	**0.68**	-
K.'s α Binary	**0.78**	**0.74**	**0.85**

Figure 2: Annotations for LA and NY. Top: percentages of user labels for the different categories. Bottom: absolute numbers of labeled users and annotation agreement results.

To scale our annotation, we asked MTurk annotators to label a larger number of profiles for the same metropolitan areas using the same label categories. For consistency, we did not reuse the profiles used for the preliminary experiment described above. Each profile was labeled by two MTurk annotators. In cases of disagreement between the MTurk annotators we asked one of our undergraduate annotators for an additional label to break the tie or assign a label from a different third category. We decided to use a tiered annotation mechanism with the undergraduate annotator making the final decision in case of disagreements as unsupervised crowd workers on MTurk or similar platforms tend to be less attentive than physically available workers [37], who also have the possibility to ask clarifying questions. We were also careful to not drop any labels to avoid the introduction of a systematic annotation bias. Over two days 117 MTurk annotators participated in our task resulting in 1,015 properly labeled users with the labels shown in Figure 2.

On the first day the annotators were compensated \$0.10 per annotation and on the second day \$0.05. The undergraduate annotator was compensated the regular stipend at our institution.

In order to measure the quality of agreement among the annotators we made use of Krippendorff's α [23]. Generally, values above 0.8 are considered as good agreement, values between 0.67 and 0.8 as fair agreement, and values below 0.67 as dubious [32]. Figure 2 shows that we obtained fair and good agreement and, thus, reliable ground truth for both our ethnicity and gender classifications.

Adding Auxiliary Information.

We collected auxiliary information from two sources. First, for the comparative analysis of demographic patterns with our data in §4.2 we used data from the Census [46] to associate geographic regions with gender and ethnicity distributions. Throughout the study we use Census-defined geographic granularities, ranging from block groups of 600-3k people to neighborhood tabulation areas (NTAs; 15k people), public use microdata areas (PUMAs; 100k people), and counties with populations of up to 2.6 million. We adjusted the distributions by ethnicity- and gender-specific Internet [13, 30] and Instagram [12] usage numbers. As explained in §4.2 we also took into account that Caucasian Hispanics are often perceived as Caucasian alone [34]. Second, for each checkin we obtained Foursquare information on the ten closest venues. We then used Foursquare's average venue popularities and venue categories as features for our inference algorithms (§5) since those features could provide an estimate of the types of places a user would visit.

4. MOBILITY-DEMOGRAPHICS

We now present a mobility pattern analysis for various population levels. Our dataset reveals mobility trends similar to those of CDRs (§4.1) and generally represents the adjusted Census population well (§4.2). In many cases we are able to detect differences in mobility patterns between ethnic groups and genders that can be plausibly explained by previous sociological findings (§4.3), and we are also able to detect segregation among ethnic groups (§4.4).

4.1 Mobility Patterns

In order to compare the mobility patterns of our dataset to those in the CDR dataset of [20, 21] we only consider checkins for the years 2011 through 2013 each for the Spring months from March 15 to May 15 and for the Winter months from November 15 to January 31 (the LA and NY Spring and Winter subsets, respectively). Table 1 shows the distribution of the data in our subsets compared to those in the CDR dataset [20]. The mobility traces from our subsets are much more sparse. Most notably, while the CDR dataset has at least eight location points from call activity per day for the median user in LA and NY—and even 12 if text messages are added—the data in all of our subsets account for only one location point for the median user per day.

Another insightful metric for comparing mobility patterns is the *daily range*, defined as the maximum straight line distance a phone has traveled in a single day [21]. Daily ranges are characteristic for mobility because, for example, median daily ranges on weekdays represent a lower bound for a commute between home and work locations [21]. Figure 3 shows a subset of our results. Our ranges are generally smaller than those reported by [20, 21]. However, the general trends in both datasets are similar. Most importantly, people in LA have generally greater ranges than people in NY. Also, in both areas people tend to travel longer during the day than at night. However, there are also differences: according to our data New Yorkers in the 98th percentiles travel farther than Angelinos.

Statistic	Spring		Winter	
	LA	NY	LA	NY
Total Checkins	135,503	109,506	118,446	98,286
(Total CDRs)	(74M)	(62M)	(247M)	(161M)
Min. Loc./Day	1	1	1	1
1st Qu. Loc./Day	1	1	1	1
Med. Loc./Day	**1**	**1**	**1**	**1**
(Med. Calls/Day)	**(9)**	**(10)**	**(8)**	**(9)**
(Med. Texts/Day)	-	-	**(4)**	**(3)**
Mean Loc./Day	1.97	2.12	1.96	2.1
3rd Qu. Loc./Day	2	2	2	2
Max Loc./Day	73	62	98	69

Table 1: Statistics of our LA and NY subsets compared to the CDR dataset in [20] (where available, in parentheses). Our calculations do not consider any day where a user had no checkins.

4.2 Demographic Patterns

As our LA and NY subsets are annotated with ethnicity and gender labels (§3) we are able to compare the resulting demographic distributions to the respective Census distributions. However, initial comparisons reveal substantial differences. For example, according to the Census there are more females than males (53% vs. 47%) living in Kings County [46] while our observed label frequencies suggest that there should be substantially fewer (43% vs. 57%). This result is even more surprising as the gender-specific usage rates of Internet (70% vs. 69%) [13] and Instagram (16% vs. 10%) [12] should further increase the percentage of females beyond the Census. However, while 86% of female social network account owners set their profile to private, only 74% of males do so [30]. Adjusting the Census distribution for this difference (as well as for gender-specific Internet and Instagram usage rates) leads to a distribution of females and males (49% vs. 51%) much closer to the distribution we observed for our labels.

Similarly to gender, we make adjustments to the Census distributions for the varying percentages of Internet and Instagram usage rates among different ethnicities as well. However, even then we still observed a substantial Hispanic underrepresentation, which was also observed for the southwest of the United States by [35]. We found this phenomenon difficult to assess, specifically, as ethnicity is not significant for setting a profile private [26], activity levels (posting pictures, etc.) are not lower for Hispanics [45], and our annotation disagreements are not higher when the Hispanic label is involved. However, we believe that the reason for the underrepresentation is the perception of Caucasian Hispanics as Caucasian alone. In a study, six of seven Caucasian Hispanics reported that others see them as Caucasian alone [34]. Therefore, we believe that most Caucasian Hispanics were actually labeled as Caucasian (i.e., our annotators agreed on an incorrect classification). Thus, we adjusted the observed label frequencies by adding to the Hispanic labels a number of labels corresponding to the Census percentage of Caucasian Hispanics and subtracting the same number from the Caucasian labels.

We perform chi square tests for goodness of fit comparing the gender and ethnicity distributions of our labels to the corresponding Census distributions for different levels of granularity. In most cases we obtain a value of $p > 0.05$ and find no evidence to reject the null hypothesis that the observed gender and ethnicity distributions follow the corresponding Census distributions. For example, as shown in Figure 4, for eight out of 11 counties in the NY area our tests resulted in $p > 0.05$ providing no evidence that our multi-category ethnicity distributions deviate significantly from the Census distributions. However, there are also cases with differences. It is no surprise that this is true for the state level as our distributions only cover users from the LA and NY metropolitan areas. How-

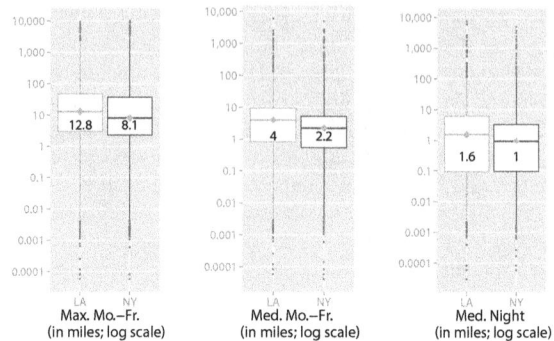

%	Max. Mo.–Fr.		Med. Mo.–Fr.		Med. Night	
	LA	NY	LA	NY	LA	NY
98	2,471.7	3,625.6	133	209.9	117.4	129.9
	(2,467)	(2,455)	(32)	(29)	(23.1)	(19.4)
75	47.5	37	9.3	5.3	6.1	3.3
	(130)	(111)	(10)	(8.2)	(8)	(5.6)
50	**12.8**	**8.1**	**4**	**2.2**	**1.6**	**1**
	(36)	(27)	(5)	(3.8)	(4)	(2.6)
25	3	2.3	0.8	0.5	0.1	0.1
	(17)	(12)	(2)	(1.3)	(1.4)	(0.7)
02	ϵ	ϵ	ϵ	ϵ	ϵ	ϵ
	(1.6)	(1.3)	(0)	(0)	(0)	(0)

Figure 3: Daily ranges in miles. Top: boxes show the 25th, 50th, and 75th percentiles; whiskers the 2nd and 98th percentiles. Bottom: table with the percentiles represented in the boxplots. The maximum range (Max. Mo.–Fr.) is a user's longest distance and the median range (Med. Mo.–Fr.) a user's median distance, each taken on a single day for the entire Spring subset on a weekday [21]. The median range at night (Med. Night) represents the median distance a user has traveled on a day for the entire combined Spring and Fall subset from 7pm–7am [20]. Previous results [20, 21] are shown in parentheses. Our calculations do not consider any day where a user had a zero range, that is, had multiple checkins at the same location or a single checkin only. We define $\epsilon < 0.005$ miles.

ever, overall we believe our results suggest that geotag data often replicate demographic trends faithfully.

4.3 Mobility Patterns by Demographic

By combining our methodologies from the previous two subsections we now show the differences in mobility patterns between ethnic groups and between males and females, respectively. In particular, we examine differences in daily ranges, home ranges, and temporal checkin characteristics.

Daily Ranges.

Figure 5 shows some of our daily range results for ethnic groups and genders based on our sets of labeled users for LA and NY. We obtained the same types of daily ranges as described earlier in Figure 3, however, this time for all days of the year. It is striking that Caucasians generally have a higher maximum daily range than the other ethnic groups. Indeed, a two sample Kolmogorov-Smirnov test reveals that the Caucasian range distribution differs significantly ($p < 0.05$) from the African American and Hispanic distribution. This result illustrates a more general finding: daily ranges of Caucasians often differ significantly from those of minorities. For 44% (8/18) of the comparisons of a Caucasian distribution to a minority distribution (three comparisons for maximum weekday, three for median weekday, three for median at night—each for LA and NY) the difference is significant at the 0.05 level. However, for the comparisons among minority distributions we only find 6% (1/18) to be significantly different from each other.

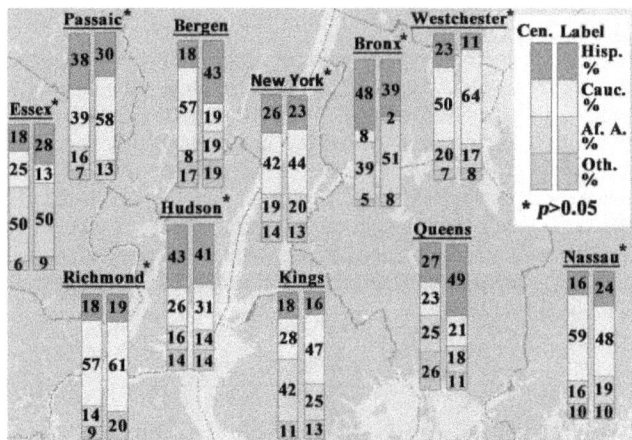

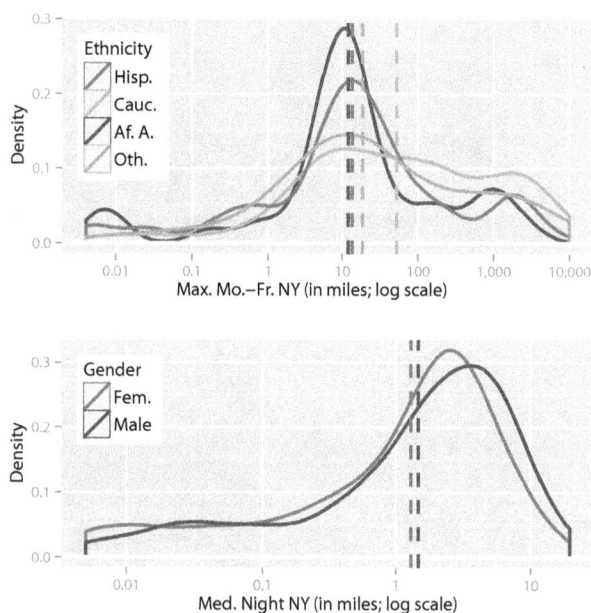

	Ethnicity Multi-Cat.		Ethnicity Binary		Gender
Gran.	LA	NY	LA	NY	NY
State	0/1 (0%)	0/1 (0%)	1/1 (100%)	0/1 (0%)	1/1 (100%)
County	1/2 (50%)	**8/11 (73%)**	2/2 (100%)	6/8 (75%)	4/4 (100%)
PUMA	12/16 (75%)	11/17 (65%)	2/2 (100%)	5/6 (83%)	1/1 (100%)
NTA	- -	9/16 (56%)	- -	7/7 (100%)	2/2 (100%)
ZIP	3/3 (100%)	8/14 (57%)	1/1 (100%)	3/3 (100%)	-

Figure 4: Chi square goodness of fit test results for ethnicity and gender at various levels of Census-defined granularity. Top: detailed view of the multi-category ethnicity distributions for the NY county level. Left bars show the Census distributions (Cen.) and right bars the label distributions (Label). Bottom: complete results of the chi square tests. NTAs are specific to NY and not available for LA. Below the ZIP code and NTA levels we did not have enough data to perform chi square tests. We follow [42] and require the average expected frequency for a chi square test with more than one degree of freedom to be at least two and for a test with one degree of freedom to be at least 7.5. To prevent skewing due to small sample sizes we also use a Monte Carlo simulation with 2,000 replicates.

	Max. Mo.-Fr. NY				Med. Night NY	
%	Hisp.	Cauc.	Af. A.	Oth.	Fem.	Male
98	2,480.8	6,509.4	2,270.9	6,788.1	9.8	11.5
75	50.8	592.3	44	187	3.2	4.7
50	**13.5**	**52.1**	**11.9**	**18.4**	**1.8**	**1.9**
25	4.9	7	5.5	3.7	0.4	0.6
02	ϵ	ϵ	ϵ	ϵ	ϵ	ϵ

Figure 5: Daily ranges in miles. Top: density plot of the maximum daily ranges by ethnicity. Middle: density plot of the median daily ranges at night by gender. Bottom: table with the percentiles of the daily ranges represented in the plots. We rounded extremely small daily ranges up to 0.005 miles. Our calculations do not consider any day where a user had a zero range, that is, had multiple checkins at the same location or a single checkin only. We define $\epsilon < 0.005$ miles.

The differences in ranges by ethnicity can be most prominently observed in the comparisons of Caucasians to African Americans and to Hispanics. However, it should be noted that at night all ethnicities exhibit very similar ranges. This finding stands in contrast to the difference in daily ranges between males and females. In fact, the only statistically significant difference ($p < 0.05$) that we observed between male and female ranges occurs for the median daily ranges at night. As shown in Figure 5, females tend to travel smaller distances at night than males. There are many possible explanations for this phenomenon. One reason could be that women travel fewer times at night due to safety concerns [2] and, consequently, also avoid longer trips. In general, for both males and females—as well as for all ethnicities—we find that our observed daily ranges follow a (skewed) log normal distribution.

Home Ranges.

In order to evaluate differences in mobility with respect to an individual's home location we complement the analysis of daily ranges with the evaluation of *home ranges*. A home range is a straight line distance between someone's home and another place to which the person travels. Different from daily ranges we calculate the home ranges not on a daily basis, but instead consider all home ranges—whether they were the maximum travel distance for a day or not. Based on a user's home location, as specified in §3, we calculate the distance between the home and each checkin for the

different ethnic groups and genders. Figure 6 shows the resulting CCDFs for the home ranges of the NY users.

Both graphs show a noticeable decrease around the 2,500 mile mark, which is the distance from NY to major hubs on the West Coast of the United States (most notably LA (2,475 miles), San Francisco (2,563 mi), and Seattle (2,405 miles)). Males and females have very similar home ranges at the edges of the graph. However, females travel farther in the medium home ranges. This finding could be based on the fact that women generally take more often vacations [22] and travel longer distances to work when they are employed full-time [24]. It should be noted that the larger home ranges are not inconsistent with the previous observation of shorter ranges for females at night as that result does obviously not consider ranges during the day. The plot for ethnicity is in line with our previous observation that Caucasians travel farther from home than minorities.

Temporal Checkin Characteristics.

Beyond spatial differences we explore differences in temporal activity as well. Figure 7 shows histograms for checkins by hour of day. As might be expected, we observe periodic behaviors with low checkin levels between 4–6am and peak levels from 3–8pm. On weekends the lows occur at later times than on weekdays suggesting that users wake up later on weekends. We also see a dramatic increase in activity after 5pm on weekdays, which could correspond

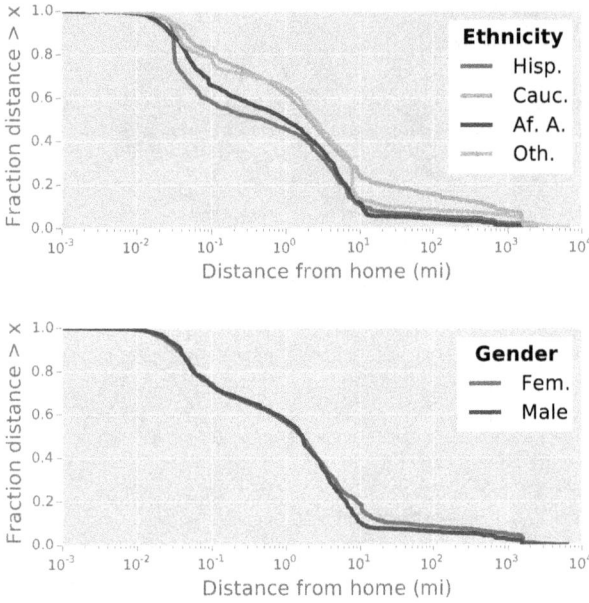

Figure 6: CCDFs of home ranges for NY. Top: CCDFs for different ethnic groups. Bottom: CCDFs for males and females.

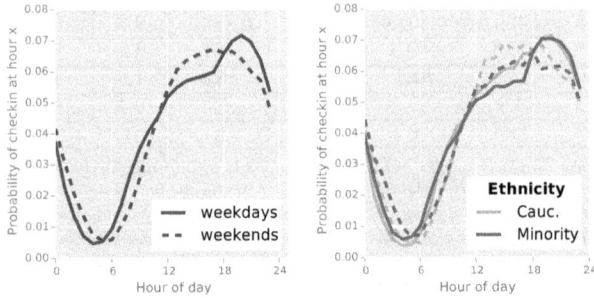

Figure 7: Histograms of checkin times for NY. Left: Comparison of weekends and weekdays for all user groups. Right: Comparison of Caucasian and minority user groups for weekends and weekdays. Dashed lines correspond to weekends, solid lines to weekdays.

to the time at which many users get off of work. When broken up into Caucasians and minorities, we see fairly similar curves, except with a more pronounced weekday after-work increase for minorities. It could be the case that Caucasians work more often in flexible environments. We observe no substantial differences between genders or NY and LA.

4.4 Ethnic Segregation

Location data are the basis for measuring residential segregation, that is, the degree to which two or more groups live separately from one another in different parts of the urban environment [33]. Trends in residential segregation characterize a group's proximity to community resources (e.g., health clinics) and its exposure to environmental and social hazards (e.g., poor water quality and crimes) [41]. In addition to *residential* segregation we also introduce and evaluate *mobility* segregation, which we understand as the degree to which two or more groups *move* to and from different parts of an area. Mobility segregation allows for a dynamic view of segregation, for example, in order to determine a group's ease of access to community resources away from home.

Methodology.

Various intersecting dimensions of segregation can be distinguished [33]. We explore two standard measures, each for a different dimension: the interaction index measures the dimension of exposure (the extent to which minority group members are exposed to majority group members in an area [33]) and the entropy index measures the dimension of evenness (the extent to which minority group members are over- or underrepresented in an area [33]). The interaction index, B, can be understood as the probability of a minority group member interacting with a majority group member and is defined [48] by

$$B_{kl} = \sum \left(\frac{n_{ik}}{N_k}\right)\left(\frac{n_{il}}{n_i}\right), \qquad (1)$$

where n_{ik} is the population of ethnic minority group k in area i (e.g., in a ZIP code area), N_k is the number of persons in group k in the total population of all areas, n_{il} is the population of ethnic majority group l in area i, and n_i is the area population.

The entropy index was used in social network research before [8] and has the advantage over other indices that it can be used to measure segregation for more than two groups. We define the entropy index [48], H, as

$$H = \frac{H^* - \bar{H}}{H^*}, \qquad (2)$$

where H^* is the population-wide entropy defined by

$$H^* = -\sum_{k=1}^{K} P_k ln(P_k), \qquad (3)$$

and $\bar{H}$ is the weighted average of the individual areas' entropies defined by

$$\bar{H} = -\sum_{i=1}^{I} \frac{n_i}{N} \sum_{k=1}^{K} P_{ik} ln(P_{ik}), \qquad (4)$$

where K is the number of different ethnic groups, P_k is the proportion of ethnicity k in the total population, I is the number of different areas, n_i is the population in an area, N is the sum of the population from all areas, and P_{ik} is the proportion of the population of ethnicity k in area i (while it is defined that $P_{ik}ln(P_{ik}) = 0$ for $P_{ik} = 0$).

For both interaction and entropy indices we make use of our sets of labeled users for LA and NY, however, exclude all areas for which the label distribution deviated significantly from the Census distribution as indicated by $p \le 0.05$. Thus, for example, as shown in Figure 4, on the county level we do not include Queens, Kings, and Bergen. These exclusions are necessary as otherwise the accuracy of our results decreases substantially. Recall that we define a user's home as the ZIP code where he or she had the most checkins (§3) and that we adjust label and Census distributions (§4.2).

Residential Segregation.

Tables 2 and 3 show our results for the interaction and entropy indices, respectively. For the most part the interaction between Caucasian and minority group members can be considered fairly high [18]. All three minorities in LA and NY have similar probabilities of interacting with Caucasians. The measurement errors of 5% (Hisp./Cauc. and Oth./Cauc.) and 6% (Af. A./Cauc.) between our labeled data and the Census suggest that our results are overall reliable. The inaccurate results for LA on the ZIP code level appear

	Hisp./Cauc.		Af. A./Cauc.		Oth./Cauc.	
Gran.	LA	NY	LA	NY	LA	NY
County	0.29 (-2%)	0.34 (+2%)	0.27 (+1%)	0.3 (-2%)	0.3 (-3%)	0.4 (0%)
PUMA	0.32 (-6%)	**0.39** (**+3%**)	0.43 (+4%)	0.42 (+7%)	0.31 (-10%)	0.49 (+5%)
NTA	- -	0.54 (+6%)	- -	0.43 (+3%)	- -	0.55 (+7%)
ZIP	0.36 (-19%)	0.56 (0%)	0.33 (-23%)	0.55 (+1%)	0.58 (-1%)	0.5 (-7%)
∅ % Diff.	5%		6%		5%	

Table 2: *Interaction index (B) for different granularities based on labeled Instagram data. Differences to the interaction index calculated from Census data are shown in percentage points in parenthesis. For example, the probability of a Hispanic person to interact with a Caucasian person on the PUMA granularity level for NY is 39%. However, as shown in parenthesis, this result is an overestimation by three percentage points over the Census distribution probability of 36%. The last row of the table shows the mean difference between our labels and the Census for the three different ethnicities in absolute percentage points for both LA and NY together. Note that NTAs are not available for LA and that we also did not analyze the state level as the label and Census distributions differ significantly (Figure 4).*

	Entropy				
Metro	County	PUMA	NTA	ZIP	∅ % Diff.
LA	0.01 (-2%)	0.15 (+8%)	- -	0.15 (+9%)	3%
NY	0.08 (0%)	0.14 (+1%)	0.08 (0%)	0.09 (+4%)	

Table 3: *Entropy index (H) for different granularities based on labeled Instagram data. Differences to the entropy index calculated from Census data are shown in percentage points in parenthesis. As explained in Table 2, the last column shows the measurement error. As further explained in Table 2, we did not consider NTA (LA) and state granularities (LA and NY).*

to have been caused by the smaller number of data points. While the level of interaction seems to increase when areas become more fine-grained, this phenomenon seems to be caused by the different area coverage for the various granularities. For example, it is not present when considering all NY city areas, where the Census distributions for the interaction of African Americans and Caucasians are: 0.41 (County), 0.25 (PUMA), 0.2 (NTA), and 0.22 (ZIP).

With entropy index scores ranging from 0.01 to 0.15, as shown in Table 3, we find another indicator for low segregation [18]. However, it should be noted that this low level of segregation is a characteristic of the particular areas we investigated. For example, for all NY city areas at the NTA level we calculated an entropy of 0.31 indicating higher segregation. However, with mean differences of 5% (Hisp./Cauc.) and 6% (Af. A./Cauc. and Hisp./Oth.) between the results for our labeled data and the Census-based calculation our findings are generally reliable. As in the case of interaction, we believe that any existing inaccuracies could be due to small numbers of data points.

Mobility Segregation.
We evaluate mobility segregation based on the same measures as residential segregation—interaction and entropy indices. However, instead of using home locations we leverage checkin data. More specifically, for each user we calculate the percentage that he or she spent at a certain area and sum the resulting values for all users of a certain ethnicity. This method aims to avoid overcounting of active users. Our results are shown in Table 4 and indicate that segregation levels in terms of where people go are similar to levels of where people live. Indeed, it would have been surprising to see higher segregation levels as members of minority groups may work in predominantly Caucasian areas. Furthermore, it would also have

been a surprise to see lower levels of segregation as residential segregation is already relatively low.

	Interaction			Entropy
Metro	Hisp./Cauc.	Af. A./Cauc.	Oth./Cauc.	All Eth.
LA	0.55 (+1%)	0.57 (0%)	0.58 (-1%)	0.06 (+1%)
NY	0.54 (-2%)	0.53 (-1%)	0.53 (-5%)	0.06 (+2%)
∅ % Diff.	1%	1%	3%	1%

Table 4: *Mobility interaction and entropy indices for ZIP code granularity based on labeled Instagram checkin data. Differences to the residential interaction and entropy indices calculated from Census data are shown in percentage points in parenthesis. The last row of the table shows the mean difference between our labels and the Census in absolute percentage points for both LA and NY together.*

5. INFERENCES FROM MOBILITY DATA

We now show how location data by itself allows to infer ethnicity and gender of individual Internet users. We introduce a simple frequentist approach (§5.1), describe considerations informing our methodology (§5.2), and present the results of its application (§5.3).

5.1 A Simple Inference Algorithm

Our approach yields two advantages: (1) it provides a formulation of the problem that is intuitive and (2) it remains generic so as to be easily applicable to any sparse location dataset. We use the following assumptions: each user, i, belongs to one of two classes, C_1 or C_2. Class C_1 (respectively C_2) is associated with a probability distribution μ_1 (respectively μ_2) over a discrete set of locations, representing the fraction of time spent by users of that class in that location. Our main assumption is that a user i makes n checkins, denoted $X^{(i)} = (X_1^{(i)}, \dots, X_n^{(i)})$ at locations that are drawn independently from this user's class probability distribution. The prior probability that a user is in class C_1 or C_2 is denoted π_1 and π_2, respectively.

Note that this model does not use notions of times of the day, geographies, or auxiliary information. It applies to most location datasets as it is agnostic to how they were generated, anonymized, or in which granularity they are available. Such model serves as a starting point to approximate human mobility [15]. However, in practice humans show periodicity [14] or even social bias [7] in their movements, and users in a class may not be identically distributed, which is why it is important to test our technique using real data (§5.3). Under our assumptions, the problem of classifying users in their respective class reduces to a simple hypothesis testing. If i is in class C_1 then for any location l, we have

$$\forall j,\ P(X_j^{(i)} = l | i \in C_1) = \mu^{(1)}(l), \qquad (5)$$

so that

$$P(X^{(i)} = (l_1, \dots, l_n) | i \in C_1) = \mu^{(1)}(l_1) \dots \mu^{(1)}(l_n), \qquad (6)$$

by independence, and applying Bayes' rule

$$P(i \in C_1 | X^{(i)} = (l_1, \dots, l_n)) = \frac{1}{1 + \frac{\pi_2 \mu^{(2)}(l_1) \dots \mu^{(2)}(l_n)}{\pi_1 \mu^{(1)}(l_1) \dots \mu^{(1)}(l_n)}}. \qquad (7)$$

The Neyman-Pearson lemma states under the assumptions above that the most powerful statistical test to determine which class a user belongs to from its checkins is the likelihood ratio test. A maximum likelihood rule classifies a user in class 1 iff

$$\pi_2 \mu^{(2)}(l_1) \dots \mu^{(2)}(l_n) < \pi_1 \mu^{(1)}(l_1) \dots \mu^{(1)}(l_n) \qquad (8)$$

Task	Best Algorithm	Parameters	Important Features	Baseline Accuracy	Accuracy	AUC	F1
Ethnicity NY	Logistic Regression	L1, $C = 0.01$	Avg. ZIP ethnicities	0.52	**0.72**	**0.76**	**0.74**
Ethnicity LA	Logistic Regression	L1, $C = 1$	Avg. ZIP ethnicities	0.50	**0.63**	**0.66**	**0.64**
Gender NY	Logistic Regression	L2, $C = 0.1$	Men's Store	0.53	**0.58**	**0.59**	**0.55**

Table 5: Results for the binary classifications of ethnicity and gender in NY and LA. The algorithms ran on all available features, such as counts of visits to different neighborhoods, the ethnicity of the most visited block, and the categories of nearby Foursquare venues. The baseline was obtained by predicting the class of a user based on the label distribution.

or, equivalently, if we have

$$\sum_{k=1}^{n} \ln \frac{\mu^{(1)}(l_k)}{\mu^{(2)}(l_k)} > \ln \frac{\pi_2}{\pi_1} . \tag{9}$$

We expect that our predictions are more accurate on users with more checkins. One can show under these assumptions that this classifier's error probability for a user decreases *exponentially* as the number of checkins n grows, that is,

$$P(\text{error}|n \text{ checkins}) \approx_{n \to \infty} 2^{-n\mathcal{C}(\mu_1, \mu_2)}, \tag{10}$$

where μ_1 and μ_2 are the probability distributions associated with C_1 and C_2, and $\mathcal{C}$ denotes the *Chernoff information*, defined as $\mathcal{C}(\mu_1, \mu_2) = -\min_{0 \leq \lambda \leq 1} \ln \sum_l \mu_1(l)^{1-\lambda} \mu_2(l)^{\lambda}$.

Based on this analysis, a simple algorithm to infer ethnicity or gender can first estimate μ_1, μ_2 and π_1, π_2 using the training data and then classify according to this likelihood rule.

5.2 Methodology

Our purpose is to explore generally what might be inferred about users from their location data only. This affected our methodology in a few key ways. First, we utilized well-understood, commonly-applied techniques that could easily be employed by anyone with access to mobility data. We also used publicly available data-sources. Second, to make our results applicable to other sources of location data beyond Instagram, we did not use features specific to Instagram, such as the social network graph or user-generated descriptions. Thus, our work should be viewed as a lower-bound on the accuracy of what can be inferred using location data. Adversaries with access to more detailed auxiliary information, more data about each user (such as a contact list or recent purchases), or more advanced machine learning techniques might achieve better results.

We considered two questions: (1) Can minorities be distinguished from Caucasians? (2) Can women be distinguished from men? We represented users as feature vectors, using three classes of features: **geographic** features, such as counts or percentages of visits to locations; **semantic** features derived from Foursquare, such as the popularity of visited venues or counts of visits to venues with certain categories like "Restaurant" or "Park" (the collection of which we explained in §3); and **Census** derived features, such as the average ethnic makeup of all visited locations or the ethnic makeup of a user's most-visited location.

We performed all our experiments using the scikit-learn library [38] and tested the algorithms logistic regression, decision trees, naive Bayes, and support vector machines (SVMs). As a baseline, we predicted ethnicity or gender based on the class distribution, giving us baseline accuracies of 52% for ethnicity in NY, 50% for ethnicity in LA, and 53% for gender in NY.

Auxiliary Data.

Auxiliary information about a location derived from Foursquare or the Census may not always be available, e.g., in countries without publicly available census data or when locations are anonymized. Furthermore, a labeled training set of user data may not always be available either. To understand the performance of an algorithm that does not have access to any data beyond counts of visits to locations, we applied our **Bayesian** algorithm to our data. To test if labeled data was necessary to guess ethnicity, we developed a simple decision rule that used no labels. Based on Census data we calculated the average percentage of Caucasians living in all locations that a user visited. If this percentage was over the metropolitan area's average, we predicted that the user was Caucasian. If it was below, we predicted that the user was of a minority ethnicity. We called this the **Unsupervised Threshold** algorithm. We compared this algorithm to an algorithm with access to labeled data, which learned an optimal threshold rather than using one derived from publicly available Census data and which we dubbed the **Supervised Threshold** algorithm. Finally, we compared these algorithms against our best performing algorithm, run with all features at the lowest granularity. We call this the **Full** algorithm.

Data Granularity.

The granularity of location data can vary greatly depending on how it is created. Previous research has investigated the impact of location granularity on anonymity [9, 49]. To investigate the impact of granularity on inferences, we represented our location data at several different granularities defined by the Census ranging from block groups to states. The ethnic makeup of a large granularity area, such as a county, will typically be more similar to the overall metropolitan area's ethnic makeup than a small granularity area like a city block. Thus, increasing the granularity should make inferences more difficult.

Data Quantity.

Finally, with four different analyses, we studied the impact of data quantity on prediction accuracy. First, to explore the impact of user activity on inference accuracy, we grouped users according to their number of geolocated Instagram photos. Next, we investigated the impact of location diversity by grouping users according to the number of distinct ZIP codes they visited. Both of these are impacted by choices made by users—users who post more might be inherently easier to identify or predict. We thus did two more analyses where we sampled locations from a user's full set of checkins. In the first, we ran the Supervised Threshold algorithm on a user's k most visited locations. In the second, we ran the Supervised Threshold algorithm on n randomly sampled checkins.

5.3 Results

The results of our best-performing algorithms are displayed in Table 5, and a detailed comparison of accuracy as a function of granularity can be seen in Figure 8. Our results suggest that geotag data can be used to infer an individual's ethnicity and gender. The accuracy for predicting ethnicity falls squarely within what has been reported for other types of datasets. On the lower bound, in their work of predicting individual Twitter users as African American or not based on linguistic features of Tweets [39] report as best performance an F-1 score of 0.66. On the upper bound, for predicting whether the ethnic origin of a phone user is inside or outside the United States based on a rich feature set containing Internet

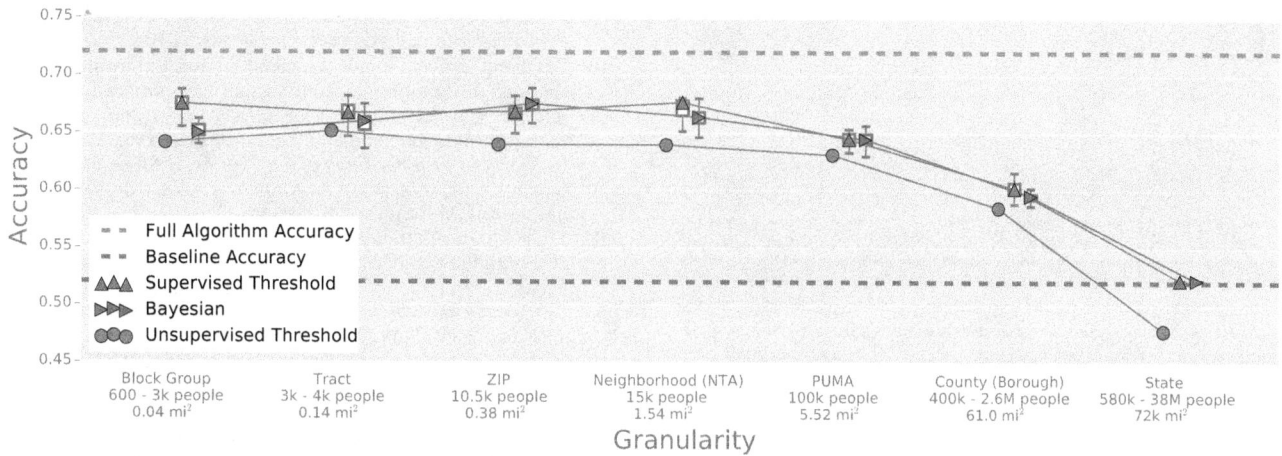

Figure 8: Accuracy of ethnicity prediction versus granularity for our NY population using several different inference techniques. Accuracy increases slightly at the ZIP code and neighborhood granularities and then decreases. Interestingly, the Bayesian algorithm, which uses only counts of visits to locations, performs comparably to the Supervised Threshold algorithm, which uses data on the ethnicity of visited locations.

usage, call, text message, and location features [1] achieved an F-measure of 0.81 and for gender an F-measure of 0.61. For gender [50] achieved an F-measure of 0.81 for social network users in Beijing and 0.82 for Shanghai based on spatial, temporal, and location context knowledge. Given that our dataset contains far fewer features our results demonstrate that geotags are surprisingly powerful in predicting gender and ethnicity.

Auxiliary Data.

It can be observed in Figure 8 that the Supervised Threshold algorithm performs much better than the Unsupervised Threshold algorithm suggesting that labeled data improves the algorithmic accuracy across the board by roughly 5%. Interestingly, the Bayesian algorithm performs comparably to the Supervised Threshold algorithm. Thus, an algorithm with no semantic information about visited locations performs just as well as one that knows the ethnic makeup of all visited locations. This suggests that an adversary with enough location data labeled with demographic data could obtain reasonable levels of accuracy with no knowledge of what locations were visited. Even if locations are "anonymized," that is, GPS coordinates or venue names were obscured, they can still be used to infer demographic information about the user.

Data Granularity.

The Full algorithm (that is, our best performing algorithm, with access to all features at all levels of granularity) achieves the best performance; no algorithm with access to restricted, coarser-grained features is as accurate.

The performance of all algorithms decreases at the most coarse granularities. This is most likely because the ethnicity distributions of larger regions are closer to the overall distribution of the metropolitan area and provide less information. Several algorithms improve in performance at medium granularities, such as ZIP and neighborhood. This is most likely caused by the sparsity of our dataset at the most detailed granularity as many blocks are only visited by a few users.

Data Quantity.

It appears that the accuracy of ethnicity prediction improves with the total number of checkins a user has made as shown in Figure 9. The distinct number of ZIP checkins of a user provides a separate measure of user activity as a user could have a large fraction of

checkins in few ZIP codes. We can observe a substantial boost in accuracy after a user checked in at 12 distinct ZIP codes.

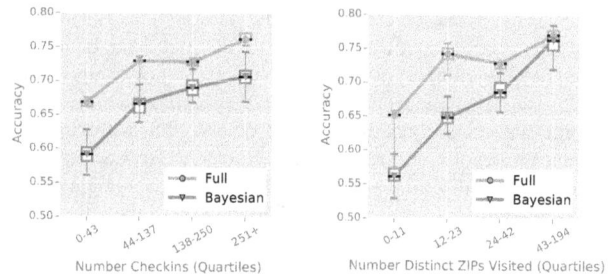

Figure 9: Checkin user activity. Left: accuracy as a function of total number of checkins at ZIP code locations. Right: accuracy as a function of number of checkins at distinct ZIP code locations.

We also found that when a user is only observed in a limited set of locations, the inference accuracy increases fast with a relatively small increase in the number of locations. Moreover, it is not even required to focus on the most significant locations of a user to get good inference accuracy. Observations of a user in a few random locations at the tract or neighborhood level might be enough for predicting ethnicity, and those locations may be even selected randomly and must not be necessarily related to the user's most significant places. These results, which are displayed in Figure 10, suggest that inference for the purpose of ethnicity identification is quite robust to data sparseness and obfuscation methods.

6. CONCLUSION

This study highlights the risks and opportunities of discriminative big data analysis by demonstrating that it is possible to infer Internet users' ethnicities and genders based on location data *alone*. It also shows that mobility patterns can be studied using publicly available data. Internet users may often be unaware that releasing such data could also disclose possibly sensitive personal information. Simply reducing granularity proved to be insufficient to prevent such privacy leakage as mobility remains discriminative. However, the trove of geotagged pictures available through individual online profiles also yields important insights for beneficial uses, for example, by city planners and social scientists.

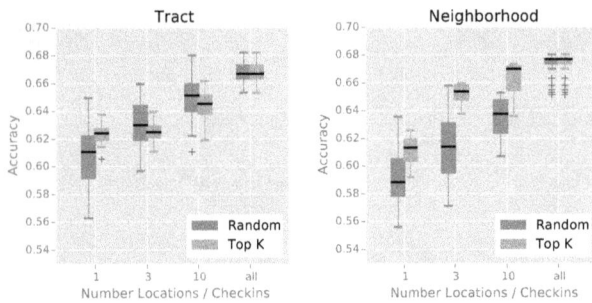

Figure 10: Accuracy of predicting a user's ethnicity from a small number of locations chosen either as most frequently visited locations or randomly. The algorithm used is the Supervised Threshold algorithm. Left: tract granularity. Right: neighborhood granularity.

As our dataset is similar, both demographically and mobility-wise, to other datasets as shown in §4, we believe that our results are generalizable and applicable to other unlabeled datasets. Although it could be claimed that our data is biased by the fact that the users in our study have willingly disclosed their gender and ethnicity by publicly using Instagram, we want to stress that it would be difficult and possibly unethical to create a labeled dataset of users who *do not* want to disclose their gender and ethnicity.

This work motivates multiple avenues of further research: First, it enables the extension of demographic mobility analysis to many researchers using shareable public datasets and reproducible results. Beyond ethnicity and gender, attributes such as age, occupation, and other lifestyle features may be extracted from users' pictures, and naturally there are many other mobility properties to account for beyond, for example, daily ranges. Second, better understanding the discriminative power of location data might inform the design of tools for raising user awareness about the information they reveal. This insight motivates revisiting mobility modeling and the inferences it renders possible to empower users to make at will their locations as clear as a photograph or as opaque as footprints in the mud.

7. ACKNOWLEDGMENTS

We would like to thank Danny Echikson and Stephanie Huang for their help labeling, Mathias Lécuyer for valuable discussion, and the anonymous reviewers for their useful suggestions.

8. REFERENCES

[1] Y. Altshuler, N. Aharony, M. Fire, Y. Elovici, and A. Pentland. Incremental learning with accuracy prediction of social and individual properties from mobile-phone data. In *SocialCom/PASSAT*, pages 969–974. IEEE, 2012.

[2] E. Badger. This is how women feel about walking alone at night in their own neighborhoods. http://www.washingtonpost.com/blogs/wonkblog/wp/2014-/05/28/this-is-how-women-feel-about-walking-alone-at-night-in-their-own-neighborhoods/, May 2014.

[3] R. Becker, R. Cáceres, K. Hanson, S. Isaacman, J. M. Loh, M. Martonosi, J. Rowland, S. Urbanek, A. Varshavsky, and C. Volinsky. Human mobility characterization from cellular network data. *Communications of the ACM*, 56(1), Jan. 2013.

[4] J. Brea, J. Burroni, M. Minnoni, and C. Sarraute. Harnessing Mobile Phone Social Network Topology to Infer Users Demographic Attributes. In *SNAKDD'14: Proceedings of the 8th Workshop on Social Network Mining and Analysis*. ACM Request Permissions, Aug. 2014.

[5] J. Chang, I. Rosenn, L. Backstrom, and C. Marlow. epluribus: Ethnicity on social networks, 2010.

[6] Z. Cheng, J. Caverlee, K. Lee, and D. Sui. Exploring millions of footprints in location sharing services, 2011.

[7] E. Cho, S. A. Myers, and J. Leskovec. Friendship and mobility: user movement in location-based social networks. In *KDD '11: Proceedings of the 17th ACM SIGKDD international conference on Knowledge discovery and data mining*. ACM Request Permissions, Aug. 2011.

[8] J. Cranshaw, E. Toch, J. Hong, A. Kittur, and N. Sadeh. Bridging the gap between physical location and online social networks. In *Proceedings of the 12th ACM International Conference on Ubiquitous Computing*, UbiComp '10, pages 119–128, New York, NY, USA, 2010. ACM.

[9] Y.-A. de Montjoye et al. Unique in the crowd: The privacy bounds of human mobility. *Sci. Rep.*, 3, 2013.

[10] Y.-A. de Montjoye, J. Quoidbach, F. Robic, and A. S. Pentland. Predicting personality using novel mobile phone-based metrics. In *Proceedings of the 6th International Conference on Social Computing, Behavioral-Cultural Modeling and Prediction*, SBP'13, pages 48–55, Berlin, Heidelberg, 2013. Springer-Verlag.

[11] Z. Deng and M. Ji. *Deriving Rules for Trip Purpose Identification from GPS Travel Survey Data and Land Use Data: A Machine Learning Approach*, chapter 72, pages 768–777. 2010.

[12] M. Duggan and J. Brenner. The demographics of social media users - 2012. *Pew Research Center*, 2013.

[13] T. File. Computer and internet use in the united states. http://www.census.gov/prod/2013pubs/p20-569.pdf, May 2013.

[14] M. González, C. Hidalgo, and A.-L. Barabasi. Understanding individual human mobility patterns. *Nature*, 2008.

[15] M. Grossglauser and D. Tse. Mobility increases the capacity of ad hoc wireless networks. *Networking, IEEE/ACM Transactions on*, 10(4):477–486, 2002.

[16] S. Guha, M. Jain, and V. N. Padmanabhan. Koi: a location-privacy platform for smartphone apps. In *NSDI'12: Proceedings of the 9th USENIX conference on Networked Systems Design and Implementation*. USENIX Association, Apr. 2012.

[17] Y. Hu, L. Manikonda, and S. Kambhampati. What we instagram: A first analysis of instagram photo content and user types, 2014.

[18] J. Iceland, D. Weinberg, and L. Hughes. The residential segregation of detailed Hispanic and Asian groups in the United States: 1980-2010. *Demographic Research*, 3:593–624, 2014.

[19] S. Isaacman, R. Becker, R. Cáceres, S. Kobourov, M. Martonosi, J. Rowland, and A. Varshavsky. Identifying important places in people's lives from cellular network data. *Pervasive Computing*, pages 133–151, 2011.

[20] S. Isaacman, R. Becker, R. Cáceres, S. Kobourov, M. Martonosi, J. Rowland, and A. Varshavsky. Ranges of human mobility in Los Angeles and New York. In *Pervasive Computing and Communications Workshops (PERCOM Workshops), 2011 IEEE International Conference on*, pages 88–93, 2011.

[21] S. Isaacman, R. Becker, R. Cáceres, S. Kobourov, J. Rowland, and A. Varshavsky. A tale of two cities. In *HotMobile '10: Proceedings of the Eleventh Workshop on Mobile Computing Systems & Applications*. ACM Request Permissions, Feb. 2010.

[22] Kelton. 4th annual springhill suites annual travel survey. http://news.marriott.com/springhill-suites-annual-travel-survey.html, April 2013.

[23] K. Krippendorff. *Content analysis: An introduction to its methodology*. SAGE, Beverly Hills, CA, USA, 1980.

[24] M.-P. Kwan. Gender, the home-work link, and space-time patterns of nonemployment activities. *Economic Geography*, 75(4):pp–370, 1999.

[25] N. Lathia, D. Quercia, and J. Crowcroft. The hidden image of the city: Sensing community well-being from urban mobility. In J. Kay, P. Lukowicz, H. Tokuda, P. Olivier, and A. Krüger, editors, *Pervasive*, volume 7319 of *Lecture Notes in Computer Science*, pages 91–98. Springer, 2012.

[26] K. Lewis, J. Kaufman, and N. Christakis. The taste for privacy: An analysis of college student privacy settings in an online social network. *J. Computer-Mediated Communication*, 14(1):79–100, 2008.

[27] L. Liao, D. Fox, and H. Kautz. Extracting places and activities from GPS traces using hierarchical conditional random fields. *Int. J. Rob. Res.*, 26(1):119–134, Jan. 2007.

[28] J. Lindamood, R. Heatherly, M. Kantarcioglu, and B. Thuraisingham. Inferring private information using social network data. In *Proceedings of the 18th International Conference on World Wide Web*, WWW '09, pages 1145–1146, New York, NY, USA, 2009. ACM.

[29] F. Liu, D. Janssens, G. Wets, and M. Cools. Annotating mobile phone location data with activity purposes using machine learning algorithms. *Expert Syst. Appl.*, 40(8):3299–3311, June 2013.

[30] M. Madden. Privacy management on social media sites. *Pew Research Center*, 2012.

[31] M. Madden, A. Lenhart, S. Cortesi, U. Grasser, M. Duggan, A. Smith, and M. Beaton. Teens, social media, and privacy. *Pew Research Center*, 2013.

[32] C. D. Manning, P. Raghavan, and H. Schütze. *Introduction to Information Retrieval*. Cambridge University Press, New York, NY, USA, 2008.

[33] D. S. Massey and N. A. Denton. The dimensions of residential segregation. *Social Forces*, 67(2):281–315, 1988.

[34] S. McDonough and D. L. Brunsma. Navigating the color complex: How multiracial individuals narrate the elements of appearance and dynamics of color in twenty-first-century america. In R. E. Hall, editor, *The Melanin Millennium*. Springer, Dordrecht, 2013.

[35] A. Mislove, S. Lehmann, Y.-Y. Ahn, J.-P. Onnela, and J. N. Rosenquist. Understanding the Demographics of Twitter Users. In *Proceedings of the 5th International AAAI Conference on Weblogs and Social Media (ICWSM'11)*, Barcelona, Spain, July 2011.

[36] A. Noulas, S. Scellato, C. Mascolo, and M. Pontil. An empirical study of geographic user activity patterns in foursquare, 2011.

[37] G. Paolacci, J. Chandler, and P. G. Ipeirotis. Running experiments on amazon mechanical turk. *Judgment and Decision Making*, 5(5):411–419, 2010.

[38] F. Pedregosa et al. Scikit-learn: Machine learning in Python. *Journal of Machine Learning Research*, 12:2825–2830, 2011.

[39] M. Pennacchiotti and A.-M. Popescu. A machine learning approach to twitter user classification, 2011.

[40] D. Rao, D. Yarowsky, A. Shreevats, and M. Gupta. Classifying latent user attributes in twitter. In *Proceedings of the 2Nd International Workshop on Search and Mining User-generated Contents*, SMUC '10, pages 37–44, New York, NY, USA, 2010. ACM.

[41] S. F. Reardon. *A Conceptual Framework for Measuring Segregation and its Association with Population Outcomes*, chapter 7, pages 169–192. John Wiley Sons, San Francisco, CA, USA, 2006.

[42] J. T. Roscoe and J. A. Byars. An Investigation of the Restraints with Respect to Sample Size Commonly Imposed on the Use of the Chi-Square Statistic. *Journal of the American Statistical Association*, 66(336):755–759, Dec. 1971.

[43] C. Sarraute, P. Blanc, and J. Burroni. A study of age and gender seen through mobile phone usage patterns in Mexico. In *Advances in Social Networks Analysis and Mining (ASONAM), 2014 IEEE/ACM International Conference on*, pages 836–843, 2014.

[44] C. Song, Z. Qu, N. Blumm, and A.-L. Barabási. Limits of predictability in human mobility. *Science*, 327(5968):1018–1021, 2010.

[45] Statista. Social networking time per user in the united states in july 2012, by ethnicity (in hours and minutes). http://www.statista.com/statistics/248158/social-networking-time-per-us-user-by-ethnicity/, 2012.

[46] United States Census Bureau. 2010 census. http://factfinder2.census.gov/faces/nav/jsf/pages/index.xhtml, 2010.

[47] United States v. Jones. 2012. 132 S. Ct. 945, 955 (Sotomayor, J., concurring) (quoting People v. Weaver, 12 N.Y.3d 433, 441-42 (2009)).

[48] M. J. White. Segregation and diversity measures in population distribution. *Population Index*, 52(2):198–221, 1986.

[49] H. Zang and J. Bolot. Anonymization of location data does not work: a large-scale measurement study. In *MobiCom '11: Proceedings of the 17th annual international conference on Mobile computing and networking*. ACM Request Permissions, Sept. 2011.

[50] Y. Zhong, N. J. Yuan, W. Zhong, F. Zhang, and X. Xie. You are where you go: Inferring demographic attributes from location check-ins. In *Proceedings of the Eighth ACM International Conference on Web Search and Data Mining*, WSDM '15, pages 295–304, New York, NY, USA, 2015. ACM.

Information Seeking and Responding Networks in Physical Gatherings: A Case Study of Academic Conferences in Twitter

Xidao Wen
University of Pittsburgh
135 Bellefield Ave.
Pittsburgh, USA
xiw55@pitt.edu

Yu-Ru Lin
University of Pittsburgh
135 Bellefield Ave.
Pittsburgh, USA
yurulin@pitt.edu

ABSTRACT

With the allure of immediacy, social media like Twitter have been widely used in physical gatherings as a "backchannel" to facilitate the conversations among participants. Studies have been centered around identifying the characteristics of such collective activities in different event settings. It has remained largely unexplored though, how event participants seek information in those situations. On the other hand, studies that examine information seeking in social media have not addressed the information needs in a particular social context. This study takes the first initiative to characterize the information seeking and responding networks in a concrete context—academic conferences—as one example of physical gatherings. By studying over 190 thousand tweets posted by 66 academic communities over five years, we unveil the landscape of information-seeking activities and the associated social and temporal contexts during the conferences. We leverage crowdsourcing and machine learning techniques to identify distinct types of information-seeking tweets in academic communities. We show that the information needs can be differentiated by their posted time and content, as well as how they were responded to. Interestingly, users' tendencies of posting certain types of information needs can be inferred by prior tweeting activities and network positions. Moreover, our results suggest it is also possible to predict the potential respondents to different types of information needs. Our study has implications for understanding the design of social search engines that facilitate the information seeking and responding in physical gatherings.

Categories and Subject Descriptors

H.2.8 [**Database Management**]: Database Applications— *Data mining*; J.4 [**Computer Applications**]: Social and Behavioral Sciences

COSN'15, November 2–3, 2015, Palo Alto, California, USA.
ⓒ 2015 ACM. ISBN 978-1-4503-3951-3/15/11 ...$15.00.
DOI: http://dx.doi.org/10.1145/2817946.2817960.

Keywords

Information Seeking; Informational and Social Needs; Social Search; Physical Gatherings; Social Media Analysis; Community Dynamics;

1. INTRODUCTION

Social media, Twitter in particular, have been playing an increasingly important role in hosting and fostering the concurrent communications surrounding breaking news events (e.g., earthquakes in Japan [32], bombings [18]), large-scale planned events (e.g., presidential debates [17, 19], conferences [37], musical concerts [12], and sports events [22]). Researchers unveiled the collective patterns of user behaviors [17] and built applications to enhance users' experience in these microblogging live events (e.g., by enriching information sources across social media sites [1], real-time summarizing the events [4, 26], and visualizing the tweets [6, 3, 39]).

This paper aims at understanding online information-seeking behaviors surrounding the primary activity occurring at the physical gatherings or venues – such as conferences, art exhibitions, music concerts, and sports events. Such situation brings unique opportunity and challenges to potential information applications. First, participants of these venues often find themselves exposed to new places, new people, and new topics, and the need for social search [20] surges in the vicinity of new experience. Second, the participants may seek and disseminate information, ideas and opinions online while they rush over talks, meetings and other activities. The miscellaneous informational and social needs can easily be overlooked in the flood of social media messages. Thus, how to properly identify and quickly address different needs is crucial to facilitate meaningful interactions in these situation.

In this study, we aim to characterize the networks pertaining to information-seeking behaviors in academic conferences. We select academic conferences as examples of physical gatherings because 1) Twitter has become widely adopted at conferences to maintain conversations among and beyond conference participants [31] (users post messages with conference specific hashtag as a convention, such as "#www" for WWW conference), and 2) academic conferences are usually held regularly (mostly annually) and people tend to participate in the same conferences repeatedly, which provides a unique opportunity to examine users' information needs in a concrete context.

Hence, we collect 190,158 tweets posted in 66 academic conferences over five years (2009 to 2013). We develop a new categorization scheme through *crowdsourcing* and machine classifiers. To explore the social and temporal contexts associated with these information-seeking tweets, we apply statistical analyses and machine learning frameworks on these categorized tweets, and characterize users' tendencies of posting and responding certain types of information needs in relating to their prior tweeting patterns and social network positions. Our key contributions include:

- We develop a new taxonomy suitable for characterizing users' information-seeking behaviors during the academic conferences, and acquire and evaluate a large set of human labels with pilot studies and *crowdsourcing*.
- By leveraging machine classifiers, we are able to discern the types of information needs and their associated social and temporal contexts in the entire set of information-seeking tweets. In particular, we find different types of information-seeking behaviors can also be differentiated by when and what users raised in these tweets and how the needs were responded to.
- Using a set of logistic regression models, we discover a significant relationship between users' past tweeting activities, network positions and their future tendencies to express certain types of information needs.
- We observe that utilizing our proposed feature sets and using a Bagging model allow us to predict the replying action to the information needs with 0.859 AUC.

These findings have implications in understanding the design aspects of social search engines to better satisfy the informational and social needs, and improve the event participation experience.

2. BACKGROUND

This work is related to studies on information seeking in social media and the use of social media (Twitter in particular) in academic conferences.

2.1 Information Seeking and Responding in Social Media

With the rise of social media, several studies have made tremendous contributions in understanding the social interactions in the information seeking process.

Information-seeking behaviors in social media have been studied through the identifications of different types of information needs. Studies strive to characterize the overall information-seeking patterns from the general audience [7, 11, 20, 27, 40], or from a particular group of users [9, 24, 33]. Morris et al. illustrated the types of information needs asked in social media [24], which have been used in several subsequent studies (e.g., on information-seeking in an enterprise microblogging platform [33], on searching on Twitter [27], and on cultural differences in information-seeking behaviors on social media [38]). Another related work is that of Lampe et al. [14], in which authors associated the mobilization requests with the characteristics of Facebook users, and found users who posted mobilization requests have more Facebook friends and visited Facebook less frequently.

Another line of work studies the responses to the requests in social media. Research in this direction primarily focus on routing the questions to the relevant expert or the right *person* [41, 13, 30] who can meet the information needs. The latest work in this field is that of Ranganath et al. [28],

in which authors presented a novel framework to infer the shared social context between the asker and the potential answerers, drawing from the social foci theory.

In light of the literature reviewed above, the study of information-seeking dynamics during microblogging live events faces two new challenges: 1) the content of the questions become more event- and time-specific, and 2) the information-seeking dynamics between the users that are involved in these events become more sensitive, or subjective to the individuals' specific characteristics with respect to the events. As the first step to address these challenges, we empirically take academic conferences as a case study to understand the information seeking and responding behaviors in physical gatherings.

2.2 Twitter Use in Academic Conferences

Academic conferences usually take place in physical settings, but users who participate in the related conversations through Twitter may or may not physically attend the conferences. Letierce et al. found in their study that Twitter users tag their tweets with the official hashtag of the conference during the event and follow the hashtag stream to keep up with the discussions [15]. By adding the hashtag to their tweets, participants show their strong interest to be part of the ongoing conferences.

As Twitter has been raised as the back-channel of the academic conferences [31], there is an increasing amount of attentions from researchers to understand scholars' Twitter usage during academic conferences. Wen et al. provided an analysis on the trend of Twitter usage in a large set of academic conferences over years and how the individuals' usage relates to their future conference participation [37]. Researchers also provided insights on why scholars tweet [29] and what they tweet [31] based on case studies for a few conference. However, to the best of our knowledge, most research in this field contribute to the understanding of users' participation and engagement in the conference community. There is relatively less attention given to how researchers seek information during conferences and how this relates to their participation patterns in the past.

3. RESEARCH QUESTIONS

In this study, we focus on a particular social context—the conference gatherings. To address the issues in prior studies and to establish a concrete understanding about users' information-seeking behaviors in such contexts, we ask:

- How do we *meaningfully* capture the distinctive information needs on Twitter during academic conferences?
- Are different information-seeking behaviors pertaining to users' different activities in conferences? This question can be further described as:
  - Are different information needs associated with different activity contexts? Specifically (a) when the users are posting the information needs in the conferences and what are they about? and (b) do different information needs receive different forms of responses?
  - Can communications of information needs be inferred from users' prior tweeting patterns and network positions? Specifically (a) who are the users that tend to post certain types of information needs, and (b) can we identify potential responders to answer these information needs?

4. DATA COLLECTION

In this work, we seek to explore the information-seeking behaviors on Twitter during academic conferences in the domain of Computer Science. There were three steps to obtain the dataset: 1) manually identify the list of computer science conferences and the corresponding date for each conference; 2) automatically crawl conference related tweets; and 3) filter the potential information-seeking tweets.

We followed CORE[1], which contains the list of the Computer Science Conferences, and obtained the acronym of each conference from this list. The convention that is widely used in many academic conferences is to post conference-messages on Twitter through the official hashtag, which is typically composed by combining its acronym and the year, e.g., *#WWW2012* or *#WWW12*. For each conference in each year when the conference took place, we used the TOPSY API[2] to collect the conference tweets by searching for the conference hashtag as the keyword and limiting the period to be between two weeks before the conference and two weeks after that. We then manually examined the tweets retrieved to ensure that they were actually posted within the conferences of interest. After removing the noisy conference tweets (tweets that shared the same hashtag with the conference that were clearly not related to the conference), we obtained 190,158 tweets from 66 conferences between 2009 and 2013.

To identify the information-seeking tweets, we used the heuristics from [27] and extracted the tweets in our collection that contained at least one "?". We focused on English tweets and excluded the retweets as well because they were often regarded with information broadcasting [37], which is not of interest for this study. Finally, our data collection contains 11,940 information-seeking tweets.

5. CATEGORIZING INFORMATION SEEKING IN ACADEMIC CONFERENCES

In order to discover the types of information needs during conferences via Twitter, we conducted a semi-open coding process to develop a suitable categorization schema to cope with the social context in our study.

5.1 Information Seeking Categorizations

With various types of information-seeking categorizations available, it is non-trivial to determine the one most suitable to this study. Researchers [11] developed a taxonomy to distinguish *informational* needs from *conversational* needs, but it is based on social Q&A sites, where the context differs from the search in social media and the categorization is also too general for our study. Another two studies drew the categories from queries in social media (Twitter), and aimed to capture users' subtle intentions in their respective categorizations [7, 24]. However, their categories are based on a relatively small-scale dataset on general Twitter use and are too imprecise for our needs. We therefore decided it was necessary to develop our categories using them as a reference instead.

We report the process in which we developed our own categories. We sampled 400 information-needs-bearing tweets from our corpus and performed a semi-open coding to label

the type of each information-seeking tweet with the categorization by Efron and Winget and the one from Morris et al.'s study. We found that i) the categorization of Morris et al. misses the promotional type of information-seeking tweets that frequently appeared in our dataset; ii) although Efron and Winget's categorization recognizes this promotional type of information needs, it seems ambiguous or unnecessary in certain categories from the perspective of our dataset. For instance, one of their categories is the type of promotional questions, for which we observed many tweets that promote information not for the sake of socialization, yet are still from users' *bona-fide* friends. Besides, the categories "invite an action" and "coordinate action" are themselves very close in the settings of the conferences. For example, "invite for a drink" and "coordinate a meet-up" would be hard to separate based on their definitions. Considering these ambiguities would harden humans' judgement, we decided to merge the categorizations from the original taxonomy in Efron and Winget's paper. Our final categories for studying information-seeking behaviors on Twitter in the conferences are shown in Table 1.

We investigated the feasibility of this coding schema through pilot studies. We recruited five subjects (included the first author of this paper) to label 60 information-seeking tweets randomly drawn from our dataset. Each subject was required to match each of the 60 tweets to one of the five categories. Therefore, for one single tweet, we collected five independent votes. We revised the code book where subjects reported ambiguities and conflicts in the definitions. After two rounds of pilot studies, we computed the *fleiss kappa* to be 0.58 (close to substantial agreement). This suggests human coders are able to distinguish the categories based on our coding schema with a fairly acceptable agreement, although we acknowledge that the coding schema may not work comparably well for all case (e.g., several of our coders reported that the identification of "Express Opinions" was more difficult, as it was rather a subjective perception).

5.2 Crowdsourcing Annotations

Our pilot studies suggest the proposed categorization meaningful to human judgements and feasible to harness the power of *crowdsourcing* to acquire a large volume of human annotations for the information-seeking behaviors.

We designed a human-intelligence task (HIT) on Amazon Mechanical Turk (AMT) to label the type of information needs by crowd workers (turkers). Each HIT consisted of 60 tweets, and each tweet was labeled by seven turkers. To ensure the quality of the task, turkers were required to take a qualification test before the HIT. The qualification test consisted of 20 questions from the pilot study, of which turkers needed to answer more than 15 of them correctly in order to qualify for our HITs. Each turker was paid $1.2 for one accepted HIT.

Finally, 2,160 tweets were labeled by 61 turkers. We employed the majority voting to determine the category for each information-seeking tweet and obtained 1,908 "Golden Labels" from the tweets where a majority vote exists (at least half of the votes for the question tweet agreed on the majority vote). We computed the *fleiss kappa* for the annotators' agreement in the "Golden Labels" as 0.52 (moderate agreement). Table 1 lists the percentage of each category in set of "Golden Labels" and "Predicted Labels" respectively.

---

[1]http://www.core.edu.au/
[2]http://topsy.com

Category	Description	Example	Golden Labels (1,908)	Predicted Labels (10,032)
(C) Coordinate events or ask favors	The intent of the user is to coordinate a face-to-face or virtual interaction, or to ask for a favor that is actionable for the audience, e.g., the user intended to announce an event, to invite people to participate in an event, or to encourage their audience to respond to an action, etc.	*"Getting set to head to LA for #siggraph2012 with a stable of #makerbot replicators. Anyone wanna join me there?"*	8.5%	3.2%
(E) Express opinions	The intent of the user is to express his or her opinion or to report the user's current status, which does not directly expect any informational answers from the audience.	*"Is there a way to grab the URL for a #CHI2013 talk in the iOS app to make tweeting about talks easier? Otherwise, what the hell #CHI?"*	23%	19.7%
(P) Promote information	The intent of the user is to promote some information by asking a question with an answer provided (e.g., providing a link to an external website).	*"Can't make it to #FAST13 this week? Consider attending via live stream instead: https://t.co/mNyA4IGe"*	32.8%	32.7%
(R) Request Information	The intent of the user is to look for some information that can be objective (e.g., factual knowledge, clarification) or subjective (e.g. recommendation, opinions).	*"I wish I was at #CHI2010. I wish I got to listen to Genevieve Bell. Does anyone know if I can listen to the keynote online?"*	35.2%	44.4%
(N) Not clear	The intent of the user is not clear or does not belong to any of the categories above.	*"@XXX wait, what? why? #cscw2013"*	0.5%	–

Table 1: **Categories of question tweets in conferences.** The categories are derived from a semi-open coding process and have been tested by pilot studies and crowdsourcing annotations. "Golden Labels" are tweet categories given by crowdsourcing annotation where a category was agreed by at least 4 of the 7 human coders. "Predicted Labels" are the predicted tweet categories given by our best machine classifier.

5.3 Machine Classifiers

With the "Golden Labels", we trained a machine classifier to automatically categorize the information-seeking tweets in the entire corpus.

Text Preprocessing. We first standardized the content of the tweets by replacing certain commonly occurring components to the corresponding uniform representations. The transformation rules were inherited from Wei et al [36] with modifications for the identification of information needs as follows: @username → "_ATMENTION_", #hashtag → "_HASHTAG_", URLs → '_HTTPURL_", punctuation → "_PUN_", digits → "_NUM_", question mark → "_QUESTION_", exclamation mark → "_EXCLAMATION_". Then, we applied *Snowball Stemmer* for word stemming.

Feature Engineering. We used *N*-grams as our features. *N*-gram is a sequence of terms in the text and has been proved to be useful features in text classification tasks [21, 25, 40]. We extracted the *N*-gram features of each tweet, including *unigrams*, *bigrams*, and *trigrams*.

Features Selection. The initially extracted *N*-grams resulted in a high-dimensional set of features (52,807 in total). To reduce the computation complexity and also to remove the noisy features, we first dropped the features with low appearances (we set it to be 1 in this study), and we applied the state-of-art feature evaluation methods to extract the most highly discriminative features. A variety of feature evaluation techniques have been used for reducing dimensions in text classification. Forman [8] compared different feature evaluation metrics and showed that "Bi-Normal Separation" (BNS) outperformed other commonly used metrics,

such as "Information Gain" (IG), "Chi-Squared", and "Term frequency" by a substantial margin. Thus, we adopt BNS as the candidate for the feature evaluation metric, with modification for a multi-class setting. We also selected a native feature evaluation metric for multi-class classification, "Multi-class Odds Ratio" (MOR) [5].

Evaluation of the Classifiers. We excluded the class "Not Clear" as it only takes a negligible proportion of all tweets (0.5%) in the "Golden Labels." We trained SVM-OVO [10] classifiers and evaluated the features with a set of 1,898 remaining tweets using 10-fold cross validation. The resultant best classifier was built based on the top 1,500 *N*-gram features selected by MOR ($Accuracy = .721$, $F1\ score = .70$, $AUC = .76$). We then applied the classifier to the remaining corpus (10,032 in total, as "Predicted Labels"). Table 1 lists the percentage of each category. We noticed that the distribution of predicted labels closely resembled the one from golden labels except a noticeably lower proportion of tweets were classified as information needs that coordinate events (C). This is not surprising since "C" is the minority class in the dataset, and our classifier indeed performed fairly poor in predicting for this type given the limited number of training tweets. In fact, when we examined the performance of the pairwise classifiers, the one that distinguishes between class (C) and class (R) was not one of the best classifiers (tweets that coordinate events tend to be classified as requests). Future investigation would be needed in devising more sophisticated classifiers to tackle this problem.

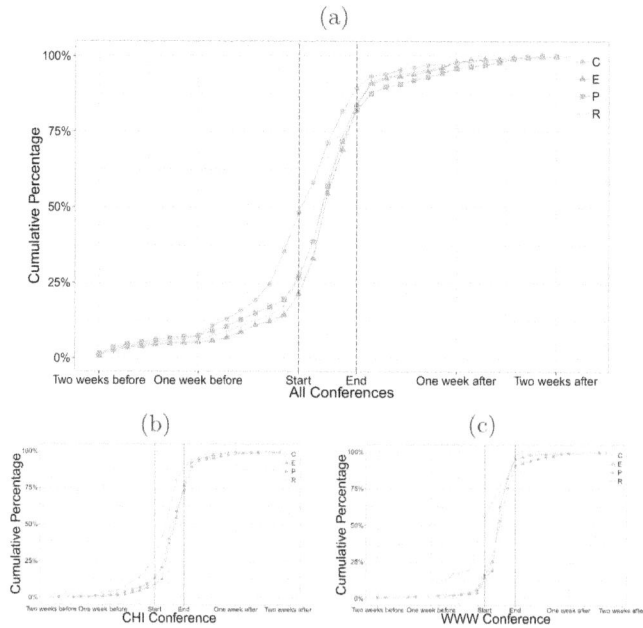

Figure 1: **Cumulative percentages of different types of information-seeking behaviors with respect to the conference duration.** We show (a) the aggregated timeline as in *All* (all conferences between 2009 and 2013), and the aggregated timeline over five years for (b) *CHI* conference and (c) *WWW* conference. The start and end of the conference are indicated by dashed lines. The detailed description for each type of information needs refers to Table 1.

C		E		P		R	
anyone	0.035	people	0.009	can	0.009	can	0.012
dinner	0.022	can	0.008	want	0.008	anyone	0.009
want	0.018	like	0.007	data	0.008	will	0.007
tonight	0.012	just	0.007	see	0.006	people	0.005
going	0.010	question	0.006	will	0.005	know	0.005
join	0.008	talk	0.006	booth	0.005	get	0.005
meet	0.008	dont	0.005	come	0.005	talk	0.004
lunch	0.008	good	0.005	talk	0.005	whats	0.004
will	0.008	will	0.005	check	0.004	session	0.004
see	0.007	web	0.005	web	0.004	going	0.004

Table 2: **Keyword distribution for each type of information-seeking tweets during the conference from conference day 0 to day 4.** The header in this table refers to the types of information seeking from Table 1. We list the top 10 most frequent keywords appearing in each type of information needs, with the their probabilities.

6. INFORMATION NEEDS AND ACTIVITY CONTEXTS

With the rich collection of information needs on Twitter during the conferences, combined from "Golden Labels" and "Predicted Labels", we are able to provide a comprehensive understanding of information-seeking behaviors on Twitter in terms of the corresponding activity contexts: *when are the information needs raised, what are they about,* and *how they are responded to.*

6.1 When are the information needs raised and What are they about

As our corpus contains the tweets posted within the month of the conference, this presents us a unique opportunity to study how users' information needs evolve over the course of the conferences. In particular, we are interested in when researchers in the conferences raised each type of information needs, and what were they about.

To answer the first question, we encoded an aggregated timeline of the conferences, ranging from two weeks before the conference started to two weeks after the conference ended. Then by subtracting the conference starting time from the posted time of the each information-seeking tweet, we placed the tweets to a single conference timeline.

Fig 1 shows the cumulative percentage of information seeking in each type over the conference timeline. We plotted the aggregated distribution in comparison with two individual conferences, one major conference in Human Computer Interaction, *CHI*, and one Web Science conference, *WWW*. From the aggregated distribution (Fig 1(a)), it seems that information needs that coordinate events followed a quite distinct distribution, as opposed to the rest. We performed a *Kolmogorov-Smirnov* two sample test to compare the needs of "coordinate events" to each of the three remaining types and examined if each pair of them came from the same distribution over the time. The results show that information-seeking behaviors that coordinate events came from a significantly different distribution from the rest ($D_{CE} = 0.27$ and the approximate $p < .001$; $D_{CP} = 0.21$ and the approximate $p < .001$; $D_{CR} = 0.21$ and the approximate $p < .001$).

We also examined the different focuses of information seeking on Twitter in three periods: before, during and after the conferences. We noticed that information needs that coordinate events were the ones increased rapidly early on, starting from about a week before the conference. These tweets were usually about their travel logistics. For example, in "*#cscw2010 Anyone flying through Brunswick on Sat., 02/06? Share a car to Savannah?*," the poster inquired that if any of his peers happened to arrive at the same time. Almost half of information-seeking tweets that coordinate events were posted before the conferences started, in contrast to the proportions of the other three types (about only a quarter for each). However, more than half of the information needs that contribute to "Express opinions", "Promote Information", and "Request Information" were raised during the conferences. This is expected because the main purpose of attending conferences is to share, discuss, and comment on the research progress, and we guess that information seeking in "Twittersphere" would reflect a similar view. After the conferences, the information needs continued to grow, at a much slower pace until about two weeks after.

We observed the similar pattern across two popular conferences, where the information needs that coordinate events tend to grow quickly early on prior to the conferences, compared to the rest. It is worth mentioning that for *CHI* conference, although information needs that coordinate events were raised as early as two weeks prior to the conference, it only accumulated to about one fourth before the conference started, while the majority of them were posted during the

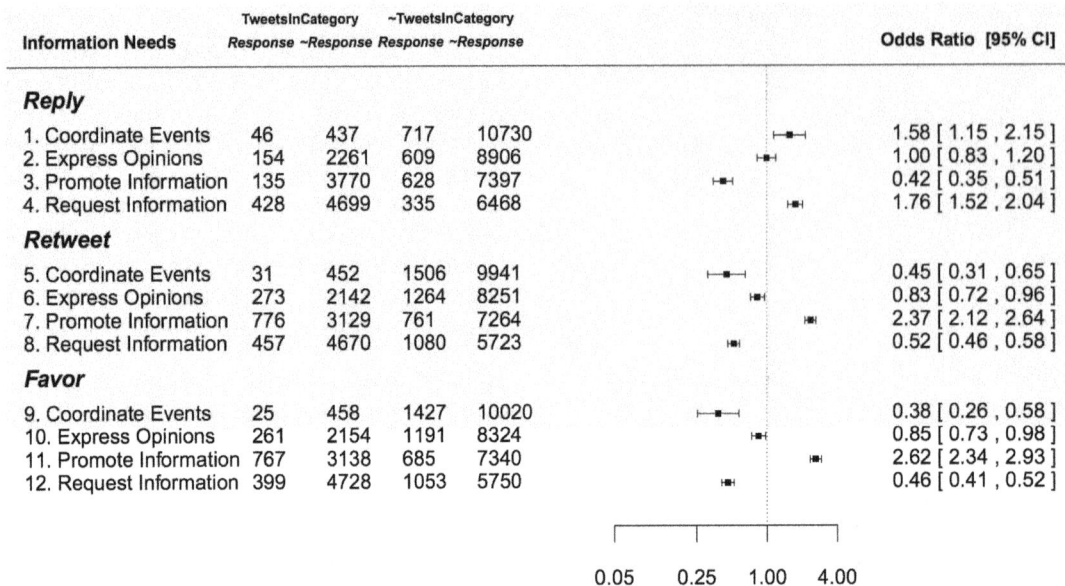

Information Needs	TweetsInCategory		~TweetsInCategory			Odds Ratio [95% CI]
	Response	~Response	Response	~Response		
Reply						
1. Coordinate Events	46	437	717	10730		1.58 [1.15 , 2.15]
2. Express Opinions	154	2261	609	8906		1.00 [0.83 , 1.20]
3. Promote Information	135	3770	628	7397		0.42 [0.35 , 0.51]
4. Request Information	428	4699	335	6468		1.76 [1.52 , 2.04]
Retweet						
5. Coordinate Events	31	452	1506	9941		0.45 [0.31 , 0.65]
6. Express Opinions	273	2142	1264	8251		0.83 [0.72 , 0.96]
7. Promote Information	776	3129	761	7264		2.37 [2.12 , 2.64]
8. Request Information	457	4670	1080	5723		0.52 [0.46 , 0.58]
Favor						
9. Coordinate Events	25	458	1427	10020		0.38 [0.26 , 0.58]
10. Express Opinions	261	2154	1191	8324		0.85 [0.73 , 0.98]
11. Promote Information	767	3138	685	7340		2.62 [2.34 , 2.93]
12. Request Information	399	4728	1053	5750		0.46 [0.41 , 0.52]

Figure 2: **Results from Odds Ratio tests**. Each row (1-12) presents an odds ratio test for one type of information needs to receive one certain type of response. Each line with a black-box represents the odds ratio and its confidence interval. "TweetsInCategory" indicates the number of information-seeking tweets that belong to one type and "~TweetsInCategory" indicates the number of information-seeking tweets that are not in that category; "Response" indicates the number of tweets that received at least one response and "~Response" indicates the number of tweets with no response.

conference. We also notice that for *WWW* conference, it seems that users started coordinating events relatively late (about one week prior to the conference). Further research is needed to investigate why different conferences present different temporal patterns of information-seeking behaviors.

To understand what are the information needs about during the conferences, we computed the keyword distribution for each type of information-seeking tweets. Table 2 shows the top 10 keywords that frequently appeared in each type. We observe that some interesting keywords emerged for each type. Keywords, such as *"dinner"*, *"lunch"*, *"join"* frequently appeared in the tweets that coordinate events. For instance, *"Waiting for XXX and XXX at the sheraton lobby. Who else wants to join us for lunch? #www2010."* Tweets like this often imply the users' needs for socialization. Interestingly, a dining table seems to be one of the most popular places to do so, considering the conference sessions are usually held at a fast pace. For information needs that express opinions, frequently appearing keywords such as *"people"*, *"question"*, *"talk"* reveal the main concerns of what speakers commented about. For the information-seeking tweets that promote information, we thought the information concerned were primarily associated with external materials linked to their research. However, the frequently occurring words, such as *"booth"* and *"come"* suggest that while the main intention of the tweets was to promote their work, it could be realized through the way of mobilization requests. For instance, *"Want to know about IGaaS(tm)? This page has info and helpful links http://t.co/WQCzojajE3 OR stop by booth 9 at #AIIM13. #infogov #cloud"*. In the information-seeking tweets that requested information, words with the most appearances, such as *"talk"*, *"session"*, reveal the information of interest was very related to the conferences.

6.2 How the information needs are responded to

We seek to examine whether the responses of the conference communities vary on the types of information needs, that is whether, an information-seeking tweet that has a certain type of purpose would be more likely to receive attentions than one does not.

In Twitter, there are three types of responses that one tweet could receive: replies, retweets, and favorites. We leveraged the Twitter API to retrieve the meta information about all the information-seeking tweets. Then we tagged each tweet if it was retweeted, favored, or replied. To each type of information-seeking tweets, we counted the number of them that were responded to and the number of them that were not. We also counted the number of information-seeking tweets that do not belong to this type, of which the number of them were responded to, and the number of them that not. We then used Odds Ratio (OR) to study the association between an exposure and an outcome. In this study, it was computed as the ratio of: (i) the probability of information-seeking tweets that belong to one category that were responded to, divided by the probability of information-seeking tweets that belong to that category but were not, and (ii) the probability of information-seeking tweets that do not belong to one category that were responded to, divided by the probability of information-seeking tweets that do not belong to that category and were not responded to.

Fig 2 presents OR of different responses (Reply, Retweet, Favor) to each type of information needs. It is not surprising that those needs that coordinate events or request information are less likely to be retweeted ($OR = .45$, $p < .001$, .52, $p < .001$, respectively), or favored ($OR = .38$, $p < .001$, .46, $p < .001$, respectively), while being more likely to be replied to ($OR = 1.58$, $p = .004$, 1.76, $p < .001$, respectively).

7. INFORMATION NEEDS IN COMMUNICATION NETWORKS

In this section, we further examine how communications about different information needs are carried in the networks, in terms of *who would raise the information needs* and *who would respond to them*.

7.1 Who would raise the information needs

We are interested in who were posting the information needs. In particular, what attributes are associated with the users who have a higher tendency to post certain kind of information-seeking tweets. We speculate that users' information-seeking behaviors may relate to what they usually do on Twitter. According to the *Nature* article [35], the focus of Twitter usage for each individual scholar can vary based on their purposes, e.g., "discover peers", "follow discussions", "comment on research", "share links to authored content", or "contact peers". We computed the "URL Ratio", "Mention Ratio", "Retweet Ratio" to capture the purpose of users' activities on Twitter. For example, if the user has a large proportion of tweets contain URLs, it suggests that this user perceives Twitter primarily as a platform to "share links to authored content". Besides, in the paper of Budak and Agrawal's, the authors found several other individual characteristics as well as group characteristics are of significant importance in predicting users' retention, e.g., tweets count, perceived receptivity (e.g., whether the user has been mentioned, whether the use has been retweeted) [2]. We guess that these traits of one user in one conference may also shed light in predicting his or her information-seeking behavior when attending future conferences. For instance, Budak and Agrawal recognized the total number of tweets one posted in the group as a measurement for the *extroversion* dimension of the big five theory [23]. Extrovert users tend to be more visible, more sociable, more talkative in the group. We presume with these characteristics, they may be more likely to express their information needs. Nevertheless, one's network positions in the conference may also contribute to his or her information-seeking behaviors. For example, if the user is peripheral in the network, he would be kept out of the information flow about the information related to the conference and therefore the chance of seeking information would be higher.

To understand if there exists a tendency for a group of people with certain attributes to seek a particular type of information during conferences on Twitter, we first constructed a set of user-conference pairs by identifying if a user ($N = 1,668$) appeared in one particular conference in the past (from 2009 to 2012) and also posted at least one information-seeking tweet in 2013 in the same conference. We then built simultaneous logistic regression models to analyze if there exists significant predictors to signal their future information-seeking behaviors. The dependent variables are whether the user was more likely to post information-seeking tweets in each of the four types in 2013 and three sets of predictors are *Individual Characteristics*, *Network Positions*, and *Conference Characteristics*. As the number of information-seeking tweets each user posted in each type in the year of 2013 was very skewed, we selected the median number of information-seeking tweets users posted as the cutoff to indicate the positive and negative set of users. Thus, for coordinating-events type of information needs ($N = 1,668, M = .094, Mdn = 0, SD = .326$), we

identified the positive set of users who posted at least one of this type and negative set of users who had nothing. For expressing-opinion type of information needs ($N = 1,668, M = .44, Mdn = 0, SD = 1.17$), we selected the positive set of users who posted at least one of this type. For the information-seeking tweets that promote information ($N = 1,668, M = .9, Mdn = 1, SD = 2.44$), we treated the users who posted at least two of this type as positive set of users. For the information-seeking tweets that request information ($N = 1,668, M = .81, Mdn = 0, SD = 1.72$), we defined the positive set of users as users who posted at least one of this type and negative set of users those who had nothing.

We computed the following sets of variables regarding users' Twitter usage in the conference, network positions, and conference overall Twitter usage, as listed in Table 3:

Individual Characteristics: *usertweetcount* measures the amount of tweets that the user posted on Twitter with the conference hashtag. The three ratios capture the proportion of URL tweets, mentions, and retweets respectively. We used the median times of being mentioned and being retweeted as the cutoff to indicate the users who were more often being mentioned in the conference and the users who were more often being retweeted in the conference.

Network Positions: This set includes three centrality measures of one user in the conversation network and in the retweet network respectively. The construction of both network followed the approach described in the study of Wen et al. [37]. Conversation network is the directed network of Twitter users in one conference and a link from A to B indicates A replied or mentioned B at least once. In the retweet network of the conference, a link from C to D denotes C has retweeted at least one of D's tweets. The reason to choose the three above metrics instead of other metrics, like "betweenness centrality" or "eigenvector centrality", was because these metrics are found to be highly correlated [34].

Conference Characteristics: For whom the prediction would be made, *conferencetweetcount* measures the number of tweets in the conference, in which this user participated in the past. The three ratios capture the proportion of URL tweets, mentions, and retweets in the conference respectively.

The full regression results were shown in Table 3 and we summarizes the regression results as follows:

Coordinate Events / Ask favors (Model 1 in Table 3): There is a significant prediction by all the predictors, $\chi^2(16, N = 1668) = 41.2, p < .001$, Negelkerke $R^2 = .06$. Users' URL ratio is negatively correlated with the occurrence of posting a coordination in the future. The closeness centrality in the retweet network is positively correlated with the likelihood of posting a coordination.

Express Opinions (Model 2 in Table 3): There is a significant prediction by all the predictors, $\chi^2(16, N = 1668) = 221, p < .001$, Negelkerke $R^2 = .18$. One thing to note, is that we predict whether a user would express opinions in a rhetorical manner while not inferring if they would do it in a declarative way. The variables *userrtoutdegree*, *userurlratio*, and *userretweetratio* are all negatively correlated with the chance of expressing opinions on Twitter. However, the users who have been mentioned more often

	Dependent variable:			
Predictors	C	E	P	R
	Model 1	Model 2	Model 3	Model 4
Individual Characteristics				
usertweetcount	0.003*** (0.001)	0.01*** (0.001)	0.02*** (0.002)	0.01*** (0.002)
userurlratio	−1.37*** (0.40)	−1.96*** (0.26)	1.54*** (0.31)	−2.21*** (0.21)
usermentionratio	0.02 (0.39)	−0.25 (0.25)	0.39 (0.35)	−0.71*** (0.22)
userretweetratio	−0.31 (0.49)	−1.06*** (0.33)	−0.74 (0.51)	−0.51* (0.28)
userismentioned	0.27 (0.25)	0.33** (0.16)	0.91*** (0.25)	0.44*** (0.14)
userisretweeted	−0.21 (0.25)	0.18 (0.16)	1.03*** (0.30)	0.09 (0.14)
Network Positions				
userrtindegree	−1.84 (1.16)	−0.44 (0.73)	0.33 (0.86)	−0.09 (0.68)
userrtoutdegree	−1.11 (0.95)	−1.49** (0.71)	−2.25** (0.98)	−0.26 (0.65)
userrtcloseness	0.95*** (0.34)	−0.08 (0.25)	0.10 (0.32)	−0.69*** (0.22)
userconvindegree	0.25 (1.00)	−0.22 (0.70)	−0.20 (0.84)	0.49 (0.64)
userconvoutdegree	1.64 (1.04)	−0.07 (0.83)	−2.83** (1.25)	−0.46 (0.77)
userconvcloseness	−0.46 (0.36)	0.26 (0.25)	0.45 (0.32)	0.09 (0.22)
Conf. Characteristics				
conferencetweetcount	0.00 (0.00)	0.00 (0.00)	0.00 (0.00)	0.00 (0.00)
conferenceurlratio	3.40** (1.60)	−1.48 (1.06)	1.75 (1.37)	−0.48 (0.93)
conferencementionratio	−0.67 (2.70)	−2.16 (1.56)	1.91 (2.05)	−1.93 (1.43)
conferenceretweetratio	−0.38 (1.08)	−3.02*** (0.68)	−0.63 (0.94)	−0.05 (0.60)

Note: $^*p<0.1$; $^{**}p<0.05$; $^{***}p<0.01$

Table 3: **Results for "who are raising the information needs."** Model 1 to 4 are logistic regression models for each type of information-seeking behaviors. In each model, the dependent variable is whether the user has a higher tendency to pose information needs of certain kind through their participation in the conference in year 2013; the three sets of independent variables are the user's individual characteristics and network positions (based on his or her past participation), and the conference characteristics. The regression coefficient for each variable in the four models are listed with standard errors in the parenthesis.

in the past are more likely to express opinions in the future than those who have been less mentioned.

Promote Information (Model 3 in Table 3): There is a significant prediction by all the predictors, $\chi^2(16, N = 1668) = 268$, $p < .001$, Negelkerke $R^2 = .27$. Users who have less out degree in retweet network and in conversation network are found to be more likely to promote information. The variable *userurlratio* is positively correlated with the chance of posting a promotion in the future, and so as to the variables *userismentioned* and *userisretweeted*.

Request Information (Model 4 in Table 3): There is a significant prediction by all the predictors, $\chi^2(16, N = 1668) = 272$, $p < .001$, Negelkerke $R^2 = .20$. Variables *userurlratio*, *usermentionratio*, *userretweetratio*, and *userrtcloseness* are negatively correlated with the chance of requesting information on Twitter, while *userismentioned*

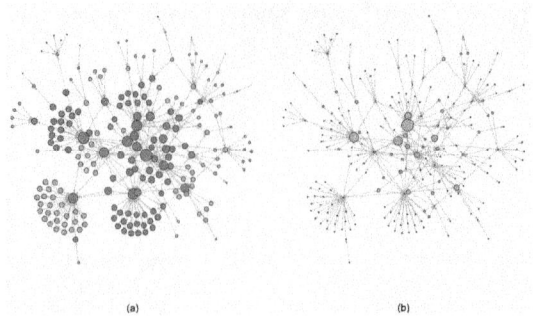

Figure 3: **Retweet Network of the *SIGKDD* conference as an illustration of the relationship between the users' network metrics and their future information-seeking behaviors.** The size of nodes in (a) are proportional to the closeness centrality, and red nodes users are more likely to coordinate events while being less likely to request information; The size of nodes in (b) represents the outdegrees, and green nodes users are less likely to promote information.

is positively correlated the likelihood of requesting information in the future.

The models presented in Table 3 suggest there exists four prototypical users corresponding to different information needs, with distinctive prior tweeting patterns and network positions. We illustrate their network positions in Fig. 3 using the example of the SIGKDD conference. The size of the nodes reflects the respective network centrality measure and the node colors indicate the prototypical users who tend to post certain information needs. The prototypical users are summarized as follows:

Coordinators are users who are more likely to coordinate events or ask favors in the networks. They are more likely to be central in the networks (higher closeness centrality, see Fig 3(a)) but less likely to give information pointers (via posting URLs).

Opinionators are users who are more likely to express opinions. They tend to not echo others (lower retweet outdegree) or give information pointers, but are more likely to be mentioned before.

Promoters are users who are more likely to promote information. Not surprisingly, they are more likely to give information pointers, be retweeted and mentioned before. However, they tend to have less communication partners (lower retweet and conversation outdegrees, see Fig 3(b)).

Requestors are users who are more likely to request information. They are more likely to be periphery in the networks (lower closeness centrality, see Fig 3(a)). They are also less likely to give information pointers and mention others before. However, they are more likely to be mentioned, which might suggest that their requests are responded by the communities.

7.2 Who would respond to the information needs

Up to this point of the paper, we studied what the information needs were about, when were they posted, and who were raising the information needs. As our aim is to facilitate the creation of the question-answer pairs, our next step is to ask if we can identify the users who were responding to the information needs.

Feature Sets	RF	ADA	Bagging	SVM
Baseline	0.73	**0.774**	0.77	0.669
Baseline+Network	0.824	0.774	**0.834**	0.689
Baseline+Content	0.784	0.783	**0.81**	0.688
Combined	0.843	0.783	**0.859**	0.714

Table 4: **Area under the ROC curve (AUC) for predicting continuing participation in the coming year with different feature sets and learning algorithms.** The best algorithm for each feature set is highlighted. Methods used are Random Forest (RF), Adaptive Boosting (ADA), Bagging, and support vector machines (SVM).

We formulated the problem as a link prediction task by using a feature-based classification, to predict whether one user would reply to the information needs. We first took 1,602 *user-reply-to-question* relationships in 2013, and regarded them as the positive instances of this link prediction problem. For each information-seeking tweet in this set, we randomly selected one user from the same conference, in which the tweet was posted, as *user-not-reply-to-question* relationships, the negative instances. It is crucial to define and extract a set of features that are appropriate and meaningful for this task. We defined our baseline feature as the last check-in time of the users on Twitter (*lastCheckIn-Time*), as we conjecture that users who are active on Twitter at the moment when the information-seeking tweet is posted are more likely to respond to it. In addition, we induced two sets of features from our dataset: network- and context-based feature sets. Network-based features consist of five popular link prediction measures, including Common Neighbors (CN), Katz Index (KI), Jaccard Index (JI), Preferential Attachment (PA), and rooted PageRank (RP) from the conversation network and from the retweet network respectively (A brief introduction of these measures can be found in [16]). Our content-based feature sets consist of three similarity measures, including the text similarity between the information-seeking tweet and the potential respondent's past conference tweets (*textSimilarity*), the user similarity between the asker and the potential respondent's past conference tweets (*userSimilarity*), and the LIWC similarity between the asker and the potential respondent's past conference tweets (*liwcSimilarity*).

To evaluate the binary classification model, we deployed different supervised learning algorithms and used the area under ROC curve (AUC) as our main evaluation metric to determine the performance of our feature sets. The evaluation was performed using 10-fold cross validation, and the results of the prediction model are shown in Table 4. The Bagging model achieved the highest performance across almost all the feature sets (except in the baseline). Furthermore, we observe that the baseline feature achieved best performance when they are accompanied with network-based features. Finally, the combination of all the features reached the best performance.

As from our previous analysis, there are four types of information needs, we are interested in how this model works for each of them. We employed our combined feature sets and built Bagging models for each type of them. Among the four models, we found that the model for "Coordinate Events" presented relatively inferior performance ($AUC_C = 0.785$, $\#instances = 208$), while the performance of the rest were rather similar to the one for the whole dataset ($AUC_R = 0.853$, $\#instances = 1534$; $AUC_E = 0.862$, $\#instances = 666$; $AUC_P = 0.842$, $\#instances = 796$). We suspect the difference might be due to the size of the dataset available to the model for information-seeking tweets that coordinate events. However, we could not exclude the possibility that our feature sets have not captured the more influential factors that can contribute to the prediction for the response to this type of information needs. In our next step, we would like to expand our dataset as well as to investigate more features for this prediction task.

We further examined the feature importance in the combined set based on their information gain measures. Fig 4 shows the relative importance of different features, with respect to predicting the reply behavior to each type of information needs. As expected, user's last check-in time on Twitter pertains the highest predictive power across all tasks. In Zhou's work that finds experts for questions in CQ&A [41], authors chose to model the profile of the askers over the content of the asker's question due to the fact that the questions are usually short. However, we found that in event situations, the content of the questions are particularly important. In Fig 4, *textSimilarity* holds higher ranks than *userSimilarity* in three out of the four categories. This suggests that users' interests of questions might be somewhat deviated from their main topical profiles, under the event situation, where they are exposed to new places, new people, and new topics. Besides, we also noticed that content- and network-based features poss different importance in predicting different types of questions. For example, *conv_JI* plays a relatively more important role in predicting the reply behavior to the information-seeking tweets that coordinate events, while in Fig 4(c) and Fig 4(d), *textSimilarity* top the rest. In the recent paper by Ranganath et al. [28], the proposed framework has shown to perform differently on different categories of questions. Our results suggest that the framework can be potentially optimized based on the type of questions.

8. IMPLICATIONS AND DISCUSSIONS

Summary of findings. In this paper, we studied the information seeking and responding networks in physical gatherings and used Twitter adoption in academic conferences as a case study. We found that the needs of coordinating events usually were raised prior to the conference, and most of them related to the users' socialization purpose. This type of information-seeking tweets, joined by the tweets that request information were more likely to be replied to, while less likely to be favored or retweeted. Users' posed information needs on Twitter during the conference for various reasons. We found that their information-seeking behaviors in the future could be predicted by their past tweeting characteristics and their positions in the conference networks. On the other hand, we also found that users' replying intention to these information needs could also be explained by a variety of similarity measures with respect to what they tweeted about in the past and how similar the users were in the conference networks.

We discovered a significant relationship between the characteristics of users' past tweeting activities and network po-

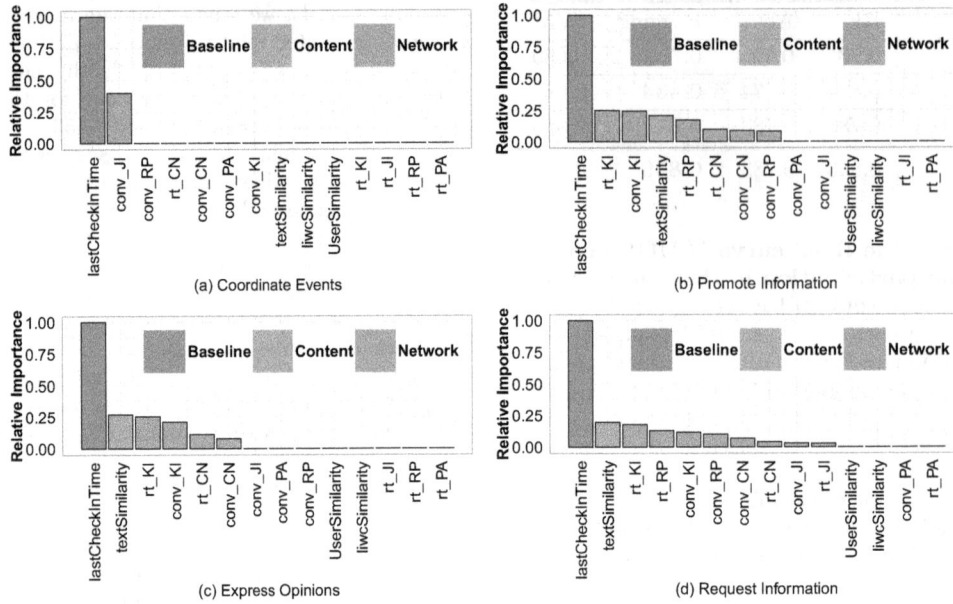

Figure 4: **Relative Importance of the features in predicting the reply action to different types of information-seeking tweets.** Not surprisingly, questions should be directed to the people who are active at the moment when the questions are asked (high ranks for *lastCheckInTime* across four types); Unlike the Q&A in general social media context, in event situations, the similarity between the asker's and the respondent's profile (*UserSimilarity*) does not contribute as much as the similarity between the asker's particular question and the respondent's profile (*textSimilarity*); Network-based and content-based metrics possess different importance in predicting the replying action to different types of information needs.

sitions, and their future tendencies to ask certain types of questions. For example, users' URL ratio is negatively correlated with the occurrence of coordinating events, expressing opinions, and requesting information in the future. This may correspond to the subset of visitors to Twitter who use it primarily as a platform to "share links to authored content" [35], for professional use during the conferences. Users' retweet ratio is negatively correlated with the likelihood of expressing opinions, or requesting information in the future. By having a large proportion of tweets attributing to retweets, it emphasizes the users' role of disseminating information during the conferences. Being mentioned in the past increases the chance of posting questions significantly in all kinds except for the type of coordinate events (for which we suspect would also be significant with a larger size of dataset). A possible explanation is that being mentioned in the past might due to the person's tendency of actively requesting or promoting information, or expressing opinions. People who have such tendency continue to actively post those information-seeking tweets in future events. Further investigations are needed to verify such hypothesis or seek for alternative explanations.

As our ultimately goal is to connect the information need with its potential respondents in a timely manner during the events, it is crucial to identify the information needs and those people who are likely to ask. We approached the second problem through a link prediction task in Section 7.2. We constructed network- and content-based feature sets, in addition to the baseline feature, and found the proposed features achieved compelling performance in predicting the reply behavior to the information needs. As the baseline

feature suggests, information needs should be directed to the users who have been actively tweeting about the conference at the very moment. Furthermore, upon the type of the information needs, the feature sets reveal different levels of discriminative power. Text similarity between the potential respondents' past tweets and the information-seeking tweet in predicting the replying to tweets that coordinate events is not as important as it is in predicting the replying to the rest. However, the ratio of their shared contacts to their overall contacts is particularly helpful in determining the replying action to this type of information-seeking tweets.

Our findings suggest that users' information-seeking behavior are predictable based on their past tweeting activities, there network positions in the conference. We also show that the replying behavior can be predicted based on our model. The design of social search engines for physical gatherings could utilize this fact to address the potential information needs from those users, so that their information needs would not be missed by the flood of data. Taking a conference like *SIGKDD* for example, it would be nice that the event organizers composite a list of information-seeking leaders from the audience for each category (e.g., coordinators, opinionators), so that people with various interests can selectively joined the discussions more quickly. At the meantime, we can apply our prediction model to route the less noted questions to the *right* person. We believe this would be especially helpful to newcomers in the conference community who do not usually possess the attentions at the beginning. By these means, we hope that the efficient matching of questions and respondents can stimulate the conversations and interactions around the events.

Limitations. There are several limitations in the current work. First, although our multi-class classifier reaches a fairly modest accuracy (0.72), the classifier is less accurate in distinguishing between "Request Information" and "Coordinate Events", and between "Request Information" and "Express Opinions". Second, we presented the aggregated patterns of information-seeking behaviors from all Computer Science conferences in our dataset; however, as we have shown in Section 6.1, different conferences are likely to show different patterns and it would be interesting to further examine these differences. Last but not the least, our findings would not necessarily be generalizable to information-seeking behaviors in other event settings. As this research was a first step in this direction, we hope that our work could spark further research in examining the phenomenon in more varied set of events.

This paper has used Computer Science conferences as a case study of online information seeking in academic conferences. CS communities have a very different tradition of participating in conferences – compared with other research fields, CS scholars consider attending academic conferences as part of the publication process. They are also the most tech-savvy users who are likely to embrace social and mobile technology when attending conference events. The focus of CS communities in this work may limit its generalizability to the broader academic communities. However, we believe the networking and information seeking patterns we discovered from CS conference tweets can shed lights on understanding the increasingly popular use of social and mobile media in broader communities in the near future. We also believe the methodology used in this work is applicable to studying online information seeking behaviors in more general physical gatherings.

9. CONCLUSION & FUTURE WORK

There is a growing interest from the research community to understand the information-seeking paradigm. However, there is relatively less understanding in the information-seeking behavior from the perspective of a particular group under certain social context. This research has a unique contribution via providing a case study of the information seeking and responding networks in physical gatherings. We crawled a large-scale dataset of tweets that consists of 66 computer science conferences over five years. Based on this rich dataset, we developed an effective categorization schema for information-seeking behaviors in the conference settings and obtained a sufficient amount of "Golden Labels" for training the machine classifiers. We then provided a comprehensive analysis of the information needs and activity contexts in academic conferences on Twitter, who would seek information and who would respond, and how this relates to their network properties.

We would like to employ our findings to develop an application that runs in the conferences and evaluate if the application fulfils its mission. We are also interested in investigating the characteristics of information-seeking in different types of events with social media "backchannels", e.g., presidential debates, shows, sports events. These events pertains different nature of interactions, and this brings us interesting questions with respect to how the information-seeking behavior differs in different occasions, and how we can support the information needs in these settings.

10. REFERENCES

[1] H. Becker, D. Iter, M. Naaman, and L. Gravano. Identifying content for planned events across social media sites. In *WSDM*, pages 533–542. ACM, 2012.

[2] C. Budak and R. Agrawal. On participation in group chats on twitter. In *WWW*, pages 165–176, 2013.

[3] N. Cao, Y.-R. Lin, X. Sun, D. Lazer, S. Liu, and H. Qu. Whisper: Tracing the spatiotemporal process of information diffusion in real time. *IEEE TVCG*, 18(12):2649–2658, 2012.

[4] D. Chakrabarti and K. Punera. Event summarization using tweets. In *ICWSM*, volume 11, pages 66–73. Citeseer, 2011.

[5] J. Chen, H. Huang, S. Tian, and Y. Qu. Feature selection for text classification with naïve bayes. *Expert Systems with Applications*, 36(3):5432–5435, 2009.

[6] M. Dork, D. Gruen, C. Williamson, and S. Carpendale. A visual backchannel for large-scale events. *IEEE TVCG*, 16(6):1129–1138, 2010.

[7] M. Efron and M. Winget. Questions are content: a taxonomy of questions in a microblogging environment. *ASIST*, 47(1):1–10, 2010.

[8] G. Forman. An extensive empirical study of feature selection metrics for text classification. *JMLR*, 3:1289–1305, 2003.

[9] A. Forte, M. Dickard, R. Magee, and D. E. Agosto. What do teens ask their online social networks?: social search practices among high school students. In *CSCW*, pages 28–37. ACM, 2014.

[10] M. Galar, A. Fernández, E. Barrenechea, H. Bustince, and F. Herrera. An overview of ensemble methods for binary classifiers in multi-class problems: Experimental study on one-vs-one and one-vs-all schemes. *Pattern Recognition*, 44(8):1761–1776, 2011.

[11] F. M. Harper, D. Moy, and J. A. Konstan. Facts or friends?: distinguishing informational and conversational questions in social q&a sites. In *SIGCHI*, pages 759–768. ACM, 2009.

[12] T. Highfield, S. Harrington, and A. Bruns. Twitter as a technology for audiencing and fandom: The# eurovision phenomenon. *ICS*, 16(3):315–339, 2013.

[13] D. Horowitz and S. D. Kamvar. The anatomy of a large-scale social search engine. In *WWW*, pages 431–440. ACM, 2010.

[14] C. Lampe, R. Gray, A. T. Fiore, and N. Ellison. Help is on the way: Patterns of responses to resource requests on facebook. In *CSCW*, pages 3–15. ACM, 2014.

[15] J. Letierce, A. Passant, J. Breslin, and S. Decker. Understanding how twitter is used to spread scientific messages. 2010.

[16] D. Liben-Nowell and J. Kleinberg. The link-prediction problem for social networks. *JASIST*, 58(7):1019–1031, 2007.

[17] Y.-R. Lin, B. Keegan, D. Margolin, and D. Lazer. Rising tides or rising stars?: Dynamics of shared attention on twitter during media events. *PloS one*, 9(5):e94093, 2014.

[18] Y.-R. Lin and D. Margolin. The ripple of fear, sympathy and solidarity during the boston bombings. *EPJ Data Science*, 3(1):31, 2014.

[19] Y.-R. Lin, D. Margolin, B. Keegan, and D. Lazer. Voices of victory: A computational focus group framework for tracking opinion shift in real time. In *WWW*, pages 737–748, 2013.

[20] Z. Liu and B. J. Jansen. Almighty twitter, what are people asking for? *ASIST*, 49(1):1–10, 2012.

[21] H. Lodhi, C. Saunders, J. Shawe-Taylor, N. Cristianini, and C. Watkins. Text classification using string kernels. *JMLR*, 2002.

[22] D. Margolin, D. Liao, and Y.-R. Lin. Conversing in reflective glory: A systematic study using national football league games. In *ICWSM 2015*, 2015.

[23] R. R. McCrae and P. T. Costa. Validation of the five-factor model of personality across instruments and observers. *JPSP*, 52(1):81, 1987.

[24] M. R. Morris, J. Teevan, and K. Panovich. What do people ask their social networks, and why?: a survey study of status message q&a behavior. In *SIGCHI*, pages 1739–1748. ACM, 2010.

[25] P. Náther. N-gram based text categorization. *Lomonosov Moscow State Univ*, 2005.

[26] J. Nichols, J. Mahmud, and C. Drews. Summarizing sporting events using twitter. In *IUI*, pages 189–198. ACM, 2012.

[27] S. A. Paul, L. Hong, and E. H. Chi. Is twitter a good place for asking questions? a characterization study. In *ICWSM*, 2011.

[28] S. Ranganath, J. Tang, X. Hu, H. Sundaram, and H. Liu. Leveraging social foci for information seeking in social media. *arXiv preprint arXiv:1502.06583*, 2015.

[29] W. Reinhardt, G. Beham, and C. Costa. How people are using twitter during conferences.

[30] F. Riahi, Z. Zolaktaf, M. Shafiei, and E. Milios. Finding expert users in community question answering. In *WWW*, pages 791–798. ACM, 2012.

[31] C. Ross, M. Terras, C. Warwick, and A. Welsh. Enabled backchannel: Conference twitter use by digital humanists. *Journal of Documentation*, 67(2):214–237, 2011.

[32] T. Sakaki, M. Okazaki, and Y. Matsuo. Earthquake shakes twitter users: real-time event detection by social sensors. In *WWW*, 2010.

[33] C. Seebach. Searching for answers–knowledge exchange through social media in organizations. In *HICSS*, pages 3908–3917. IEEE, 2012.

[34] T. W. Valente, K. Coronges, C. Lakon, and E. Costenbader. How correlated are network centrality measures? *Connections (Toronto, Ont.)*, 28(1):16, 2008.

[35] R. Van Noorden. Online collaboration: Scientists and the social network. *Nature*, 512(7513):126–129, 2014.

[36] Z. Wei, L. Zhou, B. Li, K.-F. Wong, W. Gao, and K.-F. Wong. Exploring tweets normalization and query time sensitivity for twitter search. In *TREC*, 2011.

[37] X. Wen, Y.-R. Lin, C. Trattner, and D. Parra. Twitter in academic conferences: Usage, networking and participation over time. In *Hypertext*, HT '14, New York, NY, USA, 2014. ACM.

[38] J. Yang, M. R. Morris, J. Teevan, L. A. Adamic, and M. S. Ackerman. Culture matters: A survey study of social q&a behavior. In *ICWSM*, volume 11, pages 409–416, 2011.

[39] J. Zhao, N. Cao, Z. Wen, Y. Song, Y.-R. Lin, and C. Collins. #fluxflow: Visual analysis of anomalous information spreading on social media. *IEEE TVCG*, 20:1773–1782, Dec. 2014.

[40] Z. Zhao and Q. Mei. Questions about questions: An empirical analysis of information needs on twitter. In *WWW*, pages 1545–1556, 2013.

[41] G. Zhou, S. Lai, K. Liu, and J. Zhao. Topic-sensitive probabilistic model for expert finding in question answer communities. In *CIKM*, pages 1662–1666. ACM, 2012.

Mining User Deliberation and Bias in Online Newsgroups: A Dynamic View

Teng Wang
Department of Computer
Science
University of California, Davis
tewang@ucdavis.edu

Fredrik Erlandsson
Department of Computer
Science
Blekinge Institute of
Technology
fredrik.erlandsson@bth.se

S. Felix Wu
Department of Computer
Science
University of California, Davis
sfwu@ucdavis.edu

ABSTRACT

Social media is changing many different aspects of our lives. By participating in online discussions, people exchange opinions on various topics, shape their stances, and gradually form their own characteristics. In this paper, we propose a framework for identifying online user characteristics and understanding the formation of user deliberation and bias in online newsgroups.

In the first section of the paper, we propose a dynamic user-like graph model for recognizing user deliberation and bias automatically in online newsgroups. In addition, we evaluate our identification results with linguistic features and implement this model in our SINCERE system as a real-time service. In the second section, after applying this model to two large online newsgroups, we analyze the influence of early discussion context on the formation of user characteristics. Our conclusion is that user deliberation and bias are a product of situations, not simply dispositions: confronting disagreement in unfamiliar circumstances promotes more consideration of different opinions, while recurring conflict in familiar circumstances evokes close-minded behavior and bias. Based on this observation, we also build a supervised learning model to predict user deliberation and bias at an early online life-stage. Our results show that having only the first three months of users' interaction data generates an F1 accuracy level of around 70% in predicting user deliberation and bias in online newsgroups. This work has practical significance for people who design and maintain online newsgroups. It yields new insights into opinion diffusion and has wide potential applications in politics, education, and online social media.

Categories and Subject Descriptors

H.2.8 [**Database Applications**]: Data mining; J.4 [**Social and Behavioral Science**]: Sociology

COSN'15, November 02-03, 2015, Palo Alto, California, USA.
ⓒ 2015 ACM. ISBN 978-1-4503-3951-3/15/11 ...$15.00.
DOI: http://dx.doi.org/10.1145/2817946.2817951.

General Terms

Measurement, Algorithms, Human Factors

Keywords

Social Media; Opinion Diffusion; Dynamic Graph

1. INTRODUCTION

As one of the most popular uses of social media, online newsgroups have generated torrents of opinion-based data on a wide variety of topics. During online discussion, people exchange ideas, influence group interactional norms [10], and change opinion dynamics [27, 33] over time. On the other hand, users are also influenced by the content of others. In online newsgroups, people shape their stances and build their own characteristics during interactions [14, 6].

In general, people usually show the following two characteristics in online environments: deliberation and bias. Deliberation is a process of thoughtfully weighing options, a concept mainly studied in political science and sociology. In political science, deliberation is a practice in citizenship that allows people with differing political goals to listen to alternative viewpoints and seek common ground [21]. In sociology, deliberative skill involves the ability to listen actively without being tempted to respond to statements in a rash or disruptive manner [24]. All of these explanations emphasize open-mindedness and matter-of-factness during interaction. In contrast, bias is an inclination to hold on to a partial perspective and refuse to even consider the possible merits of alternative points of view [35]. Bias can be found in almost any scenario where opinions are expressed. In politics, for example, biased views are considered *partisan*, a label placed on people who practice selective attention toward the views of their political party and show closed-mindedness about alternatives [21]. Understanding the formation of deliberation and bias has profound implications for many application areas:

- *Education:* Deliberation is regarded as a cognitively oriented collaborative skill [36]. Many previous studies in learning science have focused on developing educational software in a collaborative environment to support development in self-regulated learning skills and reflective reasoning skills [34, 20]. With the formation model of deliberation and bias, teachers can adjust their methods to effectively teach these skills at an early stage.

- *Politics:* All campaigns confront three distinct populations: supporters, opponents, and spectators. To get elected, candidates not only need to activate the enthusiasm of their supporters and guard against the attacks of their opponents, but also require new supporters. In light of this, spectators become very important targets. By gaining insights into the formation of deliberation and bias, campaigners are able to not only detect open-minded people more accurately, but also target those people at an earlier stage to make their ads campaign more effective.

- *Social media:* Maintaining active discussion groups for a long time is the most important job for website developers. Previous research [22, 1] on group formation indicates that a healthy group should consist of different roles of participants at different stages. By detecting and predicting deliberation and bias in online groups effectively, social website designers can add more functions to promote group activity, such as inviting users with differing characteristics into certain discussion groups to balance member composition.

However, it is not an easy task to study deliberation and bias. Both are composite characteristics that are deeply involved in the evolutionary process of user opinions. In general, there are two main challenges. The first is to figure out an effective and efficient method to detect user deliberation and bias from online activities. The second is to identify the factors that influence the formation of user deliberation and bias. In this paper, we consider the definition of the deliberation and bias from the perspective of user dynamic behavior. In summary, our main contributions are listed as follows:

- We design a dynamic model of user-like graph and use the evolutionary path of user opinions to identify user characteristics. In order to analyze the big dataset in online social networks, we develop an unsupervised learning algorithm to automatically process user behavior data without any model training step. In addition, we leverage linguistic analysis tools to evaluate our identification results and implement the model in our SINCERE[1] system as a real-time service. Considering the diversity and huge amount of our dataset, it is impossible for us to obtain enough ground truth by employing human workers to rate user interaction records manually. The linguistic evaluation step, which is discussed in Section 3, offers an alternative way of validating behavior analysis results from a different perspective.

- We analyze the influence of different interaction contexts on user characteristics in large online datasets. We perform a large-scale study of user interaction on two online newsgroups: the official Occupy Wall Street Facebook page[2] and Occupy Together Facebook page[3]. These two newsgroups include a total of 101,553 unique users, 311,302 comments, 175,088 posts, and 1,914,718 likes. Our conclusion is that user deliberation and bias

are a product of situations, not simply feedback content or dispositions. To be specific, confronting disagreement in unfamiliar circumstances promotes more consideration of different opinions, while recurring conflict in familiar circumstances evokes close-minded behavior and bias. Furthermore, we also develop a framework to predict user deliberation and bias from their behavior information at an early stage. Our results show that having only the first three months of users' interaction data generates an F1 accuracy level of around 70%.

The rest of the paper is organized as follows. In Section 2, we talk about related work on the identification and formation of user deliberation and bias in online newsgroups. Then, in Section 3, we discuss our main contribution of identifying user online characteristics by user-like graph and its diffusion model. Based on this method, in Section 4, we analyze the influence of context on user characteristic formation in online newsgroups. Conclusions are in Section 5.

2. RELATED WORK

In this section, we review previous research on user deliberation and bias in online newsgroups.

Identification of Deliberation and Bias. In the past few decades, deliberation and bias have been widely discussed in political science and sociology. Among previous work, most researchers design their experiments using questionnaires or volunteer surveys [21, 2]. However, these methods severely limit the scale of experimental datasets. In order to deal with the huge amount of data in online social networks, it is necessary to use an automated method to identify user characteristics from their online activities. In recent years, researchers in Natural Language Processing have proposed linguistic models to identify user deliberation and bias in online discussion forums: Xiaoxi et al. [36] build the L_1 Regularized Logistic Regression model to identify social deliberative behavior using lexical, discourse, and gender demographic features. Zhao et al. [38] study confirmation bias on controversial topics and identify biased user groups through the use of social context analysis. Tae et al. [37] propose a model using Amazon Mechanical Turk judgements and show that lexical indicators strongly associate with bias. All of these machine learning methods require a complex training process, and every model is only valuable for its source corpus. In online newsgroups, textual features of user-generated content are highly dynamic, and it is very difficult to find ground-truth or labeled data to help us do model training. Therefore, in this paper, we leverage user behavior features to capture contextual information. The most similar work to our method is the transfer learning framework proposed by Pedro et al. [6]. They exploit user endorsement information to do real-time sentiment analysis, but their static model only deals with biased opinions with high degrees of opinion polarization. In online newsgroups, users often have many different perspectives that fall outside of the binary of *agree* and *disagree*. This paper, to the best of our knowledge, is the first work to propose a dynamic user behavior model that identifies both user deliberation and bias at the same time.

Formation of Deliberation and Bias. In general, the formation of deliberation and bias is influenced by user dispositions and the content of interaction. Disposition is the

[1]http://sincere.se
[2]http://www.facebook.com/OccupyWallSt
[3]http://www.facebook.com/OccupyTogether

natural tendency of each individual to take a certain position in any field [4]. Previous research [11] shows that people often use their prior opinions to make an evaluation. Instead of using all available information, people usually reply based on their heuristics or cognitive shortcuts [26]. As to the content of interaction, framing is the most common effect. It refers to alternative conceptualizations of an issue or event. A number of studies over the past quarter-century show that framing effects can substantially shape opinions and stance [12, 8]. Furthermore, in recent years, researchers have shown that the time effect of interaction content also influences the formation of different opinions and stances. In this paper, we claim that information processing is also context specific: confronting disagreement in unfamiliar circumstances promotes more consideration of different opinions, while recurring conflict in familiar circumstances evokes close-minded behavior and bias. Our result matches the conclusion of the civic engagement research by Michael et al [21] in political science. However, their work emphasizes emotional effects on citizenship under different circumstances, and their experiment is limited to political content with only 215 participants. Our work gives a large-scale analysis of the influence of context on user deliberation and bias. Additionally, we propose a prediction model from behavior information taken at an early stage.

3. IDENTIFICATION OF DELIBERATION AND BIAS

The interactions of individuals in online newsgroups are temporal and dynamic in essence. Examining their evolutionary pattern and network structures provides deep insights into user activities online. Dynamic graph models have been proposed to do outliers detection [18, 31] and topic extraction [28]. In this chapter, we focus on identifying user characteristics in online newsgroups.

3.1 Data Collection

Our data is crawled from public pages on Facebook [13]. These pages are open to the public, and anyone can leave comments on existing posts. We collect all the user interaction information from these public newsgroups, including the content of comments, *user-like* information, and their time-stamps. *User-like* information includes all the clickstream data when people press the *Like* button on others' Facebook comments. In this paper, we select two Facebook public pages as our dataset: Occupy Wall Street and Occupy Together. These two news pages are excellent datasets for studying user deliberation and bias: Both of them have been active since the beginning of the Occupy movement in September 2011. Occupy Wall Street is the largest newsgroup in the Occupy movement, and Occupy Together is a comprehensive public page where people share information and opinions on any Occupy movements. Moreover, in both of these two public newsgroups, users share their opinions on various topics that include not only political events, but also local daily news. Unlike online debate forums, where user opinions are extremely polarized, our dataset includes user comments from many different perspectives, which is an ideal resource for analyzing user characteristics. In summary, we collect a total of 311,302 comments on 175,088

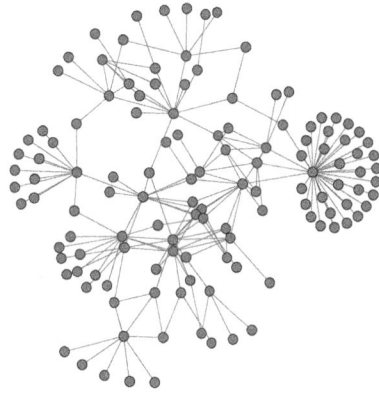

Figure 1: One Snapshot of User-Like Graph

posts from September 2011 to July 2012. Statistics of the two datasets are given in Table 1.

	OccupyTogether	OccupyWallSt
Duration (Days)	299	247
Posts	79,931	95,157
Comments	74,835	236,457
Likes	509,665	1,405,053

Table 1: Statistics of the Occupy Together and the Occupy Wall Street Newsgroups.

3.2 Dynamic User-like Graph Model

The general idea of our dynamic user-like graph model is as follows: first, we use a graph partition algorithm to classify user opinions into different subgroups at each snapshot of the user-like graph. Then, we connect those opinion subgroups together to build opinion diffusion paths. Finally, we identify deliberation and bias by analyzing user's stability and transition among the detected paths.

User-like Graph. For all the comments data in one Facebook public newsgroup, we divide them into a sequence of consecutive static graph snapshots $\{G_1, G_2, ..., G_n\}$. At each time stamp t_k, the graph G_{t_k} aggregates all the *user-like* information [32] within the interval $[t_{k-1}, t_k]$. In the graph $G_{t_k} = (V_{t_k}, E_{t_k})$, nodes V_{t_k} stand for the users who liked a comment or whose comments were liked by others during the time slot $[t_{k-1}, t_k]$. Edges E_{t_k} stand for the like connections between those users. Figure 1 shows an example of *user-like* graph. In our experiment, considering the dynamic features of online newsgroups, we set the interval time $\Delta T = [t_{k-1}, t_k]$ as one hour for each time slot. In summary, we build an undirected weighted user-like graph for each hour since the beginning of data collection.

Opinion Classification. In previous work [32], Teng et al. showed that the user-like graph is a powerful tool to do opinion classification: people who have strong like-connections with each other show similar opinions in online newsgroups. However, their method can only classify user comments into one or two opinions. In this paper, we use the fast greedy modularity optimization algorithm [9] to classify user opinions into more than two subgroups.

In 2004, Newman and Girvan proposed a modularity func-

18:00 | 19:00 | 20:00 | 21:00 | 22:00 | 23:00 | 0:00 | 1:00 | 2:00 | 3:00 | 4:00 | 5:00 | 6:00 | 7:00 | 8:00 | 9:00 | 10:00 | 11:00 | 12:00 | 13:00 | 14:00 | 15:00 | 16:00 | 17:00 | 18:00

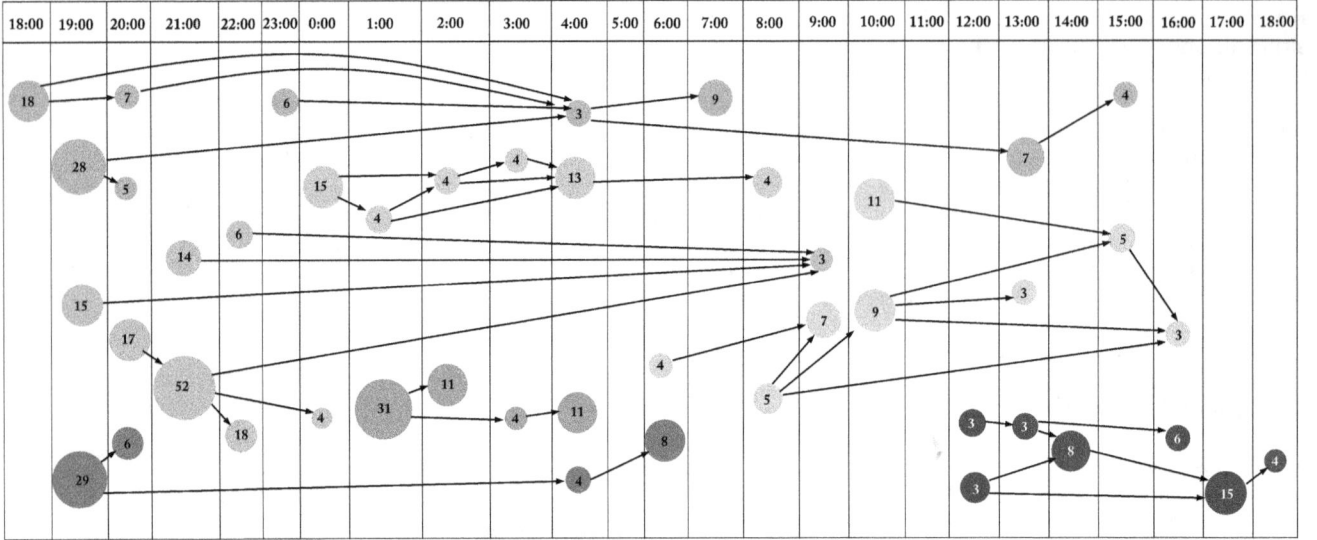

Figure 2: Examples of Opinion Diffusion Paths Detected in the Occupy Together Newsgroup.

tion to measure the quality of a particular clustering of nodes in a graph [15]. Vertices are divided into communities such that vertex v belongs to community c_v and vertex w belongs to community c_w. We use A_{vw} to record the connection within the network: $A_{vw} = 1$ if vertices v and w are connected. Otherwise, $A_{vw} = 0$. Based on the work by Clauset and Newman [9], the modularity Q can be written as

$$Q = \frac{1}{2m} \sum_{vw} [A_{vw} - \frac{d_v d_w}{2m}] \delta(c_v, c_w) \qquad (1)$$

where $d_v = \sum_w A_{vw}$ is the degree of a vertex v and $m = \frac{1}{2} \sum_{vw} A_{vw}$ is the number of edges in the graph. At each step of the algorithm operation, we go through the amalgamations of each pair of communities in the user-like graph and perform the amalgamation which can improve modularity Q the most. Although this fast greedy algorithm can only give us a locally optimal partition of the user-like graph, it is a very efficient algorithm that runs in essentially linear time on some real-world networks [9]. Considering the huge amount of user interaction data and the requirement of real-time analysis, the fast greedy algorithm is the most suitable algorithm for our framework.

Opinion Diffusion Paths. Using the modularity optimization algorithm, we classify users into many different opinion subgroups at each static graph snapshot. In order to build opinion diffusion paths for the whole newsgroup, we need to connect the subgroups with the same opinion together over different time stamps. At this step, we regard subgroups detected at adjacent time stamps as communities sharing the same opinion if the number of common members is above a certain threshold. Suppose we find a set of l opinion subgroups $\mathbb{C}_{t_k} = \{C_{t_k 1}, C_{t_k 2}, ..., C_{t_k l}\}$ at time stamp t_k in graph G_{t_k} and their predecessors $\mathbb{C}_{t_{k-1}} = \{C_{t_{k-1} 1}, C_{t_{k-1} 2}, ..., C_{t_{k-1} l'}\}$ at time stamp t_{k-1} in graph $G_{t_{k-1}}$. To match adjacent subgroups together between $\mathbb{C}_{t_k}$ and its predecessors $\mathbb{C}_{t_{k-1}}$, the most widely-adopted method is to use Jaccard coefficient [19]. Given a current subgroup

$C_{t_k a}$ and a predecessor $C_{t_{k-1} i}$, the Jaccard coefficient between the pair is calculated as:

$$Jaccard(C_{t_k a}, C_{t_{k-1} i}) = \frac{|C_{t_k a} \cap C_{t_{k-1} i}|}{|C_{t_k a} \cup C_{t_{k-1} i}|} \qquad (2)$$

However, this classic definition can only be used for identifying state transition of two communities of similar size. During the evolution of opinion subgroups, we still need to consider other dynamic events where community size changes significantly, such as forming, dissolving, expanding, contracting, splitting and merging. Although the subgroups involved in those events should be regarded as well-connected in our framework, the Jaccard coefficient may often report them to be low similarity communities. In order to deal with this problem, researchers [7, 29] have developed many definitions to handle these events separately. In our framework, we propose another definition to evaluate community similarity in all possible events:

$$sim(C_{t_k a}, C_{t_{k-1} i}) = \frac{|C_{t_k a} \cap C_{t_{k-1} i}|}{min(|C_{t_k a}|, |C_{t_{k-1} i}|)} \qquad (3)$$

If the similarity value exceeds the threshold $\theta \in [0, 1]$, this pair of communities will be matched. With this definition, we can effectively evaluate community similarity for all the state transition events with only one threshold parameter: When the size of two adjacent communities does not vary much, this definition keeps the property of the Jaccard coefficient; When dynamic evolution events occur where the community size changes significantly, this definition can match the communities together because of the high proportion of common nodes in the smaller community. Many previous works [3, 16] show that a reasonable similarity threshold in synthetic dynamic networks is between 0.3 and 0.4. In order to give a general model of user behavior in online newsgroups, we set the threshold θ to be 0.35, which can provide a reasonable compromise between community matching accuracy and identifying the optimal number of diffusion paths.

Furthermore, we also add the concept of *gap interval* [16] into our model when building the opinion diffusion paths.

(a) Deliberative Users

(b) Biased Users

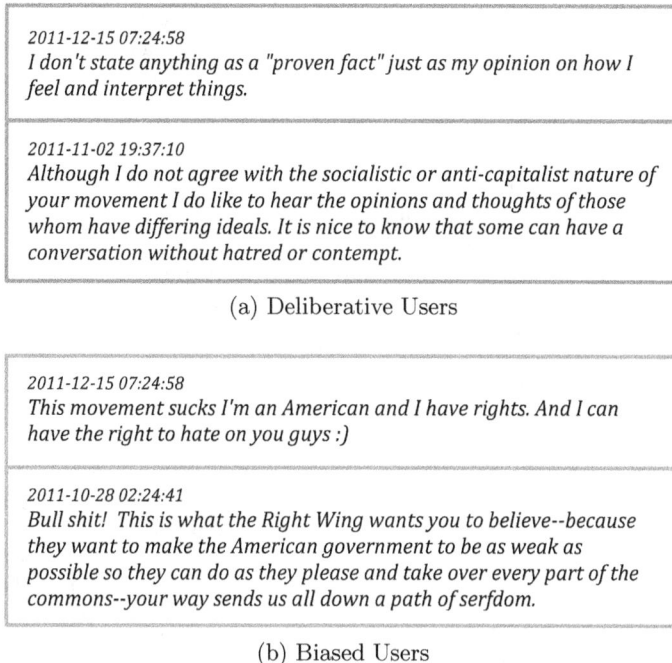

Figure 3: Example Comments of Deliberative Users and Biased Users.

For a subgroup $C_{t_k a}$, we not only consider the subgroups $\mathbb{C}_{t_{k-1}}$ detected at the prior time stamp t_{k-1}, but also include all the subgroups $\{\mathbb{C}_{t_{k-1}}, \mathbb{C}_{t_{k-2}}, \mathbb{C}_{t_{k-P}}\}$ detected within the last P steps into consideration. In online newsgroups, user attention and behavior are highly dynamic. Allowing a reasonable number of gap intervals helps us to detect more opinion diffusion paths. Considering the periodicity of online user behavior, we set *gap interval* as one day in our model, i.e. we allow possible connections between detected subgroups within 24 hours.

After connecting those opinion subgroups at different timestamps together, we get a new graph showing the evolution of user opinions along the whole timeline. In this graph, each node represents a detected opinion subgroup. As the last step, we find all the connected components in this graph and define them as the opinion diffusion paths in this newsgroup. Figure 2 shows some examples of the opinion diffusion paths detected in Occupy Together newsgroup from Oct. 15, 2011 to Oct. 16, 2011. The number inside each node represents the size of the detected opinion subgroup, i.e. the number of people in that opinion subgroup. Each connected component in this graph represents a detected opinion diffusion path, which are shown in different colors.

Identifying User Characteristics. In our dynamic user-like graph model, a subgroup detected at one snapshot represents a group of users who share the same opinion during that time slot. And an opinion diffusion path aggregates all the users who share that specific opinion within the whole newsgroup. As we discussed in the introduction section, there are many different definitions of deliberation and bias in various domains. In this paper, we consider their definitions from the perspective of people's dynamic behavior. To be specific, our hypothesis is: If a person appears in many different opinion diffusion paths, he may show deliberation in this newsgroup. On the other hand, if a very

active user is found in only one opinion diffusion path, he may show bias towards that specific opinion in the newsgroup. To be specific, if a user appears in three or more different opinion diffusion paths, we will consider him to be a deliberative member. If a very active user who has made more than 30 comments in this newsgroup only shows up in one opinion diffusion path, we will consider him to be a biased member.

For the Occupy Wall Street newsgroup and the Occupy Together newsgroup, we run our dynamic graph model to identify user deliberation and bias. To get enough interaction content for each target user, we only collect information from people who have made more than 10 comments in the newsgroup. We find that, in the Occupy Together Facebook newsgroup, there are 787 people who made more than 10 comments. Based on our model, 201 of them are identified to be deliberative members and 26 of them are flagged as biased members. In the Occupy Wall Street newsgroup, we find a total of 2928 people with more than 10 comments. Among them, 916 people are found to be deliberative and 151 people are biased. Figure 3 shows some example comments of users who are identified to be deliberative or biased members in our dataset.

3.3 Evaluation with Linguistic Features

Considering the huge size of our dataset, it is impossible for us to obtain the ground truth of online user characteristics by employing human workers to rate user interaction records manually. In this paper, we evaluate the effectiveness of our dynamic user-like graph model by comparing the linguistic features of user comments, which is a totally different view from the dynamic structure of a user-like graph.

We use the Linguistic Inquiry and Word Count (LIWC) tool [30] to study the linguistic features of user comments.

LIWC is a popular natural language processing tool that calculates the matching frequency of words within each of 68 categories including linguistic dimensions and psychological aspects. The LIWC features we use in this evaluation process are based on previous work on Natural Language Processing. In [36, 23], researchers claim that deliberative behavior contains different lexical characteristics in the following five LIWC features: total word counts (WC), number of dictionary words (Dic), number of big words (Sixltr), words per sentence (WPS), and cognitive processes words (cogmech). In [37], Tae et al. use Amazon Mechanical Turk judgments to study biased sentences on American political blogs. Their result shows that the following LIWC features are indicators of bias: negative emotion (negemo), positive emotion (posemo), causation (cause), and anger (anger). In addition, they also include a list of 11 *kill verbs* [4] as indicators of bias based on the study of Green and Resnik [17]. Based on their results, we use five of these LIWC features (WC, Dic, Six|tr, WPS, cogmech) to evaluate user deliberation and six features (negemo, posemo, cause, anger, anx, kill verbs) to evaluate user bias. Table 2 shows some selected LIWC features we use in the evaluation process.

Categories	Abbrev	Selected Examples
Cognitive processes	cogmech	cause, know, ought
Positive emotion	posemo	Love, nice, sweet
Negative emotion	negemo	Hurt, ugly, nasty
Anxiety	anx	Worried, fearful
Anger	anger	Hate, annoyed

Table 2: Selected Linguistic Categories in LIWC.

Newsgroup	Population	Graph	Linguistic
OccupyTogether	787	201	135 (67.2%)
OccupyWallSt	2928	916	662 (72.3%)

Table 3: Evaluation of User Deliberation Identification.

Newsgroup	Population	Graph	Linguistic
OccupyTogether	787	26	15 (57.7%)
OccupyWallSt	2928	151	83 (55.0%)

Table 4: Evaluation of User Bias Identification.

For each of the detected deliberative users and biased users, we want to check if their linguistic features are significantly different ($p \leq 0.05$) from the average level of the whole population. This is a classic Z-test problem. Taking the evaluation of deliberative users as an example, we use WC, Dic, Sixltr, WPS and cogmech as linguistic features. For each of these five LIWC features, we calculate the mean and standard deviation of the comments made by the whole population in the target newsgroup. Denote their mean values as $[\mu_{01}, \mu_{02}, ..., \mu_{05}]$ and their standard deviation as $[\sigma_{01}, \sigma_{02}, ..., \sigma_{05}]$. Then for each of the detected

[4]Those verbs are: kill, slaughter, assassinate, shoot, poison, strangle, smother, choke, drown, suffocate, and starve.

deliberative users, we denote the mean of his comments as $[\bar{\mu}_1, \bar{\mu}_2, ..., \bar{\mu}_5]$ and the number of his comments as n. Furthermore, we calculate the Z-score which represents the distance from the sample mean to the population mean in units of the standard error:

$$Z_k = \frac{\sqrt{n}(\bar{\mu}_k - \mu_{0k})}{\sigma_{0k}} \qquad k = [1, 2, ..., 5] \qquad (4)$$

Now we have a list of Z-scores $[Z_1, Z_2, ..., Z_5]$ for each of the detected deliberative users. As the last step, if the absolute value of any of these five Z-scores is larger than the predetermined significance threshold ($|Z| \geq 1.96$), we conclude that the comments made by this user show significant difference ($p \leq 0.05$) on deliberative features in this newsgroup.

Table 3 and 4 show our evaluation results for user characteristics in the Occupy Together newsgroup and the Occupy Wall Street newsgroup. The item *Population* denotes the number of users who made more than 10 comments in the target newsgroup. The item *Graph* denotes the number of users who are detected to be deliberative/biased based on our dynamic graph model. The item *Linguistic* denotes the number and the percentage of the detected users who also show significant difference in our linguistic evaluation. From the results, we find that our dynamic graph model does a good job identifying user characteristics in the two online newsgroups. Furthermore, we notice that biased user identification does not perform as well as deliberative user identification. A possible reason is that biased users show different behavior patterns in various discussion topics. In topics where discussion is always intense, e.g., elections and religious issues, biased users are very likely to leave a large amount of comments. But in topics where discussion is less active, biased users may leave fewer comments in one opinion path. By defining a constant threshold for the number of comments in biased user identification, we may lose some accuracy. In summary, around 71.4% of identified deliberative users and 55.4% of identified biased users show linguistic features significantly different from the average level of the whole population. Additionally, because our dynamic graph model does not require any training process or manually labeled ground truth, it is an efficient algorithm for user characteristics analysis in online social networks.

3.4 System Development

In order to evaluate the effectiveness of our dynamic graph model on social media, we also implement this algorithm in our SINCERE system as a real-time service. SINCERE stands for Social Interactive Networking and Conversation Entropy Ranking Engine. It is a diversified search engine based on user social informatics, which stores all the user interaction data of more than 1,800 Facebook public pages.

Figure 4(a) shows a screenshot of our user characteristics identification algorithm in SINCERE. By choosing a Facebook newsgroup from the drop-down menu, people can get real-time analysis results of the list of representative deliberative and biased users in that newsgroup. Both of their comments and Facebook links are also shown on that page. This function can help commercial institutions target people for political or entertainment advertisements.

Furthermore, we also use our algorithm to improve information presentation under each post of an online newsgroup. In Figure 4(b), we show comments made by deliberative (Blue) and biased (Green) users highlighted in different col-

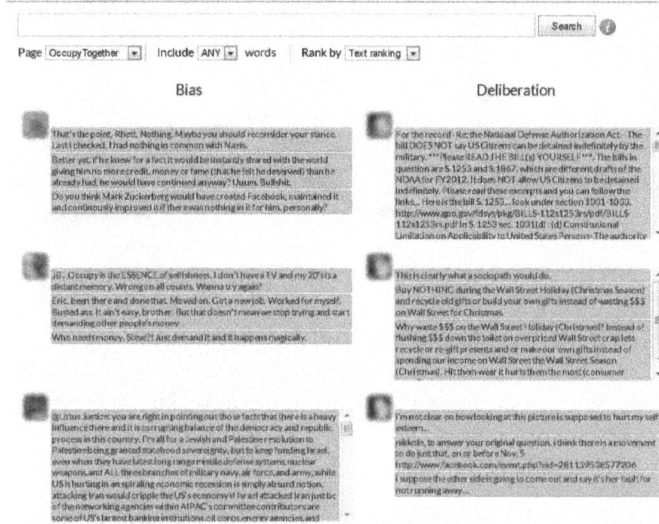

(a) User Characteristics Identification Service on SINCERE System.

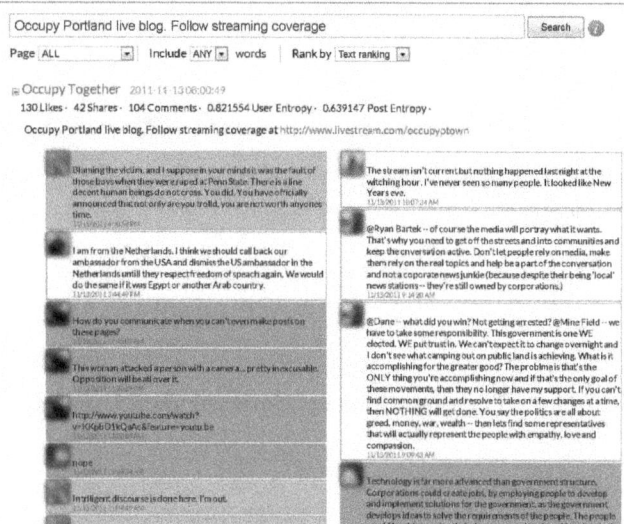

(b) Information Highlighting on SINCERE System.

Figure 4: Screenshots of SINCERE System.

ors. This function is very useful for online users to obtain quick knowledge of different opinions and stances under a post.

4. PREDICT USER DELIBERATION AND BIAS

The dynamic user-like graph model gives us a powerful tool to analyze the online characteristics of users. However, we must first collect all of the user interaction information before we can identify characteristics. Now we proceed to ask a deeper question: how can we predict deliberation and bias from user activities at early stages of interaction? In this section, we answer this question in two steps. First, we analyze the influence of different discussion circumstances at early stages on the formation of user online characteristics. Then, based on the analysis, we propose a supervised learning model to predict user deliberation and bias using content gathered at the early stages of user interaction.

4.1 The Influence of Early Discussion Context on the Formation of User Characteristics

Our hypothesis is as follows: if people confront disagreements in unfamiliar circumstances at an early stage, they may tend to show deliberation in later interactions. On the other hand, if users receive disapproval under familiar discussion circumstances, they are likely to become biased later. To verify this hypothesis using our online social network dataset, we first need to define some sociology concepts quantitatively:

- *User online lifetime.* We use the timestamps of feedback comments to define a user's online lifetime. To be specific, we consider the timestamp of the user's first received feedback comment as the starting point of his

experience in the target newsgroup, and we consider him to have left the newsgroup after he has received the last feedback comment. In addition, we define the *life-stage* of a user as the percentage of time he has spent, out of his total lifetime, in the newsgroup. Obviously, a life-stage of 0% represents *birth*, which is the moment the user joins the discussion in the newsgroup, and a life-stage of 100% represents *death*, which is the moment the user leaves the newsgroup.

- *Different feedback opinions.* In Facebook public newsgroups, there is no exact *reply* function during user interactions: people just make comments one after another in the time-line under each post. Therefore, we define the comments given within three hours after an individual makes a comment as his feedback replies. To classify these feedback comments into different opinions, we follow the same method used in our dynamic user-like graph model: we use the fast greedy modularity optimization algorithm to split the hourly graph snapshot into different opinion subgroups. Each user may get three kinds of feedback: the same opinion, different opinions, and opinion undetermined.

- *Stranger and Acquaintance.* We classify the people who give feedback into three types: stranger, acquaintance, and undetermined. We define a stranger as a person who has never given feedback to the target user before and an acquaintance as a person who has given at least three feedback comments to the target user before the current timestamp. Obviously, based on our definition, when a user first joins a newsgroup, every member there is a stranger to him. As the user starts to be involved in the discussion of the newsgroup, he will *accumulate* more and more acquaintances. One common concern about this definition is

215

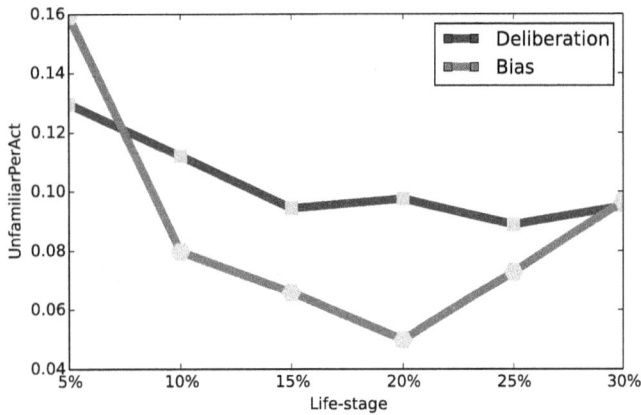

(a) Conflicting with Strangers

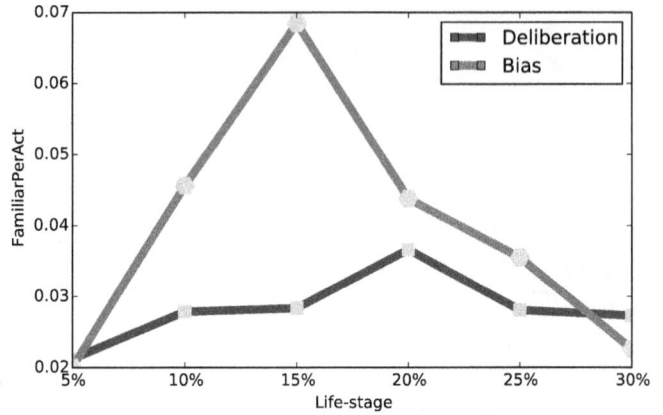

(b) Conflicting with Acquaintances

Figure 5: The Relationship Between Different Discussion Circumstances and User Characteristics at Early Life-stages.

pre-existing friendships between users in online social networks. However, the dataset we use in this experiment is crawled from online newsgroups where group interaction is very different from that of private friendship groups. Members in online newsgroups have little social connection in real life since most interaction happens in an online environment [32]. Therefore, pre-existing friendships are a small concern for our definition of stranger and acquaintance.

In online environments, we assume that the discussion circumstances are mainly determined by the people who give feedback comments. Therefore, we define two context parameters to represent the extent of familiarity of the circumstances:

- *UnfamiliarPerAct* measures the percentage of feedback comments of different opinions received from strangers out of all the feedback comments this person received during the current life-stage.

- *FamiliarPerAct* measures the percentage of feedback comments of different opinions received from acquaintances out of all the feedback comments this person received during the current life-stage.

According to the identification results of our dynamic user-like graph model, we have 1117 deliberative users, 177 biased users and 2421 users with uncertain characteristics. Based on the definitions above, we plot the average context parameters for each category of users at different life-stages. Figure 5(a) shows the relationship between UnfamiliarPerAct and user characteristics at different life-stages. Figure 5(b) shows the relationship between FamiliarPerAct and user characteristics at different life-stages. Because we are only interested in the relationship at an early user life-stage, we only consider life stages before 30%. Comparing the two curves in each of the two figures, we find that the result supports our hypothesis pretty well: The users who are identified as deliberative experienced more conflicts in unfamiliar circumstances in their early stages and the users who are identified as biased experienced more conflicts in familiar circumstances at their early stages. Note that at

the very first life-stage (5%) in both Figure 5(a) and Figure 5(b), the correlative relationship of the two curves does not fit our hypothesis well. The reason is that when a user joins a newsgroup, almost everybody is a stranger to him, which makes the effect of familiar circumstances quite weak. Considering this *slow-start* factor, we need to dismiss the effect of discussion circumstances at the very first stage in our following prediction model.

4.2 Supervised Prediction Model of User Deliberation and Bias

In this section, we leverage early discussion context factors to predict user deliberation and bias in online social networks.

Features used for learning. We define the following three features in our prediction model:

- *CommentsPerAct*: It measures the average number of received feedback replies after a user makes a comment.

- *EarlyUnfamiliarPerAct*: This features is similar to the definition of *UnfamiliarPerAct*. It measures the percentage of feedback comments in different opinions given by strangers out of all the feedback comments this person received during the *early stage*. Considering the *slow-start* factor we mentioned in the previous section, we define the *early stage* as the time duration from the second week to the third month of the user's lifetime in this newsgroup.

- *EarlyFamiliarPerAct*: This measures the percentage of feedback comments in different opinions given by acquaintances out of all the feedback comments this person received during the *early stage*.

Experimental setup. We use two supervised learning models to design our experiments: the binary logistic classifier (BLR) and the support vector machine (SVM). The ground-truth data in these models comes from the characteristics identification results of our dynamic graph model. Although binary logistic classifiers can only use linear predictor functions to build learning models, we can get explicit

Model	Deliberation			Bias		
	Precision	Recall	F1	Precision	Recall	F1
Binary Logistic Classifiers	65.2	67.2	66.2	56.4	71.0	62.9
Support Vector Machines	63.4	85.6	72.8	60.0	82.3	69.4

Table 5: User Deliberation and Bias Prediction Results.

Features	Deliberation	Bias
CommentsPerAct	2.30**	−3.43
EarlyUnfamiliarPerAct	2.09***	−2.29*
EarlyFamiliarPerAct	5.07***	2.57

*: $p < 0.05$, **: $p < 0.01$, ***: $p < 0.001$

Table 6: Coefficient Analysis of the Learned BLC model.

results about the regression coefficients in logistic classifiers, which can help us evaluate the effectiveness of each feature. In each of our experiments, we split 60% of the data for training and 40% for testing. Because our data is seriously imbalanced, especially for the sample of biased users, we downsample both experiments for deliberative and biased users.

Experimental results. AUC (Area Under the Curve) of the predicted user deliberation is 0.72, and AUC of the predicted user bias is 0.64. Table 5 also summarizes our prediction results for user deliberation and bias. We find that our framework does a good job of predicting both user deliberation and bias. Both supervised learning techniques, Binary Logistic Classifier (BLC) and Support Vector Machine (SVM), perform well. The SVM model gives an additional 6% absolute (10% relative) improvement in F1 scores for user deliberation and user bias.

To get a deeper insight into the effect of the discussion context features on our prediction results, we also examine the coefficients of the learned Binary Logistic Classifiers in Table 6. We find that the feature *EarlyUnfamiliarPerAct* shows statistical significance ($p < 0.05$) in the experiments of both user deliberation and bias. Furthermore, the sign of its coefficient in both experiments fit our conclusion in the previous section perfectly: the more conflicting comments people receive in unfamiliar circumstances at their early stage, the more likely he will become deliberative in the future; meanwhile, the conflicting experiences people have in unfamiliar circumstances at their early stage will also reduce the probability of him becoming a biased user in the newsgroup. However, we did not see a clear effect of *EarlyFamiliarPerAct* on the BLC model. There may be many possible reasons: First, in contrast to the classification of *strangers*, everybody has their own understanding of what makes familiar discussion circumstances. Some people may regard a person who has talked with him more than two times online as an acquaintance, while others may require ten times. By simply defining the acquaintance threshold as three, we may fail to evaluate some users' discussion experiences. Second, the feeling of familiar discussion circumstances may decay as time goes on. Instead of keeping a static table of acquaintances for each user, it may be better to set a sliding window of acquaintances, so that we can recognize familiar circumstances dynamically.

5. CONCLUSION AND DISCUSSION

In this work, we propose a framework for identifying characteristics of online users and understanding the formation of user deliberation and bias in online newsgroups. First, we propose a dynamic user-like graph model for recognizing user deliberation and bias automatically. Then, after applying this model to two large online newsgroups, we analyze the influence of early discussion context on the formation of user characteristics. Our conclusion is that user deliberation and bias are a product of situations, not simply their dispositions: Confronting disagreement in unfamiliar circumstances promotes more consideration of different opinions, while recurring conflict in familiar circumstances evoke close-minded behavior and bias. Furthermore, based on this observation, we also build a supervised learning model to predict user deliberation and bias using information from the early life-stages of newsgroup participation. Our results show that having only the first three months of users' interaction data generates an F1 accuracy level of around 70% in predicting user deliberation and bias in online newsgroups.

In politics, the influence of contextual factors on people's behavior is widely discussed. Researchers find that people pursue two different kinds of citizenship, deliberative and partisan, under different circumstances and they explain that this is a result of emotion [25, 5]. Michael et al. [21] claims that it is emotion that conveys information about the environment and guides the kind of citizen behavior people pursue. When people are in novel circumstances, they may feel anxiety, making them more likely to engage in deliberative mechanisms in order to handle uncertainty. When people find themselves involved in conflicts under familiar circumstances, they may feel aversion, which pushes them to rely on previously learned solutions and become close-minded to alternatives. Although emotions of anxiety and aversion can explain the formation of deliberation and bias more directly, they can hardly be applied to large-scale data analysis in online social networks, because it is very challenging to differentiate user anxiety and aversion accurately by natural language processing methods. By leveraging user behavior information, our framework shows good performance for both identification and prediction of user deliberation and bias.

For future work, we plan to incorporate the interaction of different newsgroups into our analysis framework. In this paper, we only consider the influence of user interaction within the same newsgroup. However, it is highly likely that online users participate in many different online newsgroups at the same time. Because of the dynamics of online user membership, an opinion that seems to disappear in one newsgroup may actually begin to dominate the discussion in another newsgroup. By incorporating cross-group interactions, we can get a clearer picture about opinion diffusion and user characteristic formation in social media.

6. ACKNOWLEDGMENTS

We would like to thank Shijia Che, Haifeng Zhao and Ran Cao for their insightful comments and suggestions on this paper. This work is partially supported by the Cyber Security Research Alliance of United State Army Research Laboratory.

7. REFERENCES

[1] H. Arrow, M. S. Poole, K. B. Henry, S. Wheelan, and R. Moreland. Time, change, and development the temporal perspective on groups. *Small group research*, 35(1):73–105, 2004.

[2] J. Barabas. How deliberation affects policy opinions. *American Political Science Review*, 98(04):687–701, 2004.

[3] S. P. Borgatti. 2-mode concepts in social network analysis. *Encyclopedia of Complexity and System Science*, pages 8279–8291, 2009.

[4] P. Bourdieu. The specificity of the scientific field and the social conditions of the progress of reason. *Social Science Information Sur Les Sciences Sociales*, 14:19–47, 1975.

[5] T. Brader. *Campaigning for hearts and minds: How emotional appeals in political ads work*. University of Chicago Press, 2006.

[6] P. H. Calais Guerra, A. Veloso, W. Meira Jr, and V. Almeida. From bias to opinion: a transfer-learning approach to real-time sentiment analysis. In *Proceedings of the 17th ACM SIGKDD international conference on Knowledge discovery and data mining*, pages 150–158. ACM, 2011.

[7] Z. Chen, W. Hendrix, and N. F. Samatova. Community-based anomaly detection in evolutionary networks. *Journal of Intelligent Information Systems*, 39(1):59–85, 2012.

[8] D. Chong and J. N. Druckman. Dynamic public opinion: Communication effects over time. *American Political Science Review*, 104(04):663–680, 2010.

[9] A. Clauset, M. E. Newman, and C. Moore. Finding community structure in very large networks. *Physical review E*, 70(6):066111, 2004.

[10] C. Danescu-Niculescu-Mizil, R. West, D. Jurafsky, J. Leskovec, and C. Potts. No country for old members: User lifecycle and linguistic change in online communities. In *Proceedings of the 22nd international conference on World Wide Web*, pages 307–318, 2013.

[11] J. N. Druckman and T. Bolsen. Framing, motivated reasoning, and opinions about emergent technologies. *Journal of Communication*, 61(4):659–688, 2011.

[12] J. N. Druckman, E. Peterson, and R. Slothuus. How elite partisan polarization affects public opinion

formation. *American Political Science Review*, 107(01):57–79, 2013.

[13] F. Erlandsson, R. Nia, H. Johnson, and F. S. Wu. Making social interactions accessible in online social networks. *Information Services and Use*, 33(2):113–117, 2013.

[14] M. Gamon, S. Basu, D. Belenko, D. Fisher, M. Hurst, and A. C. König. Blews: Using blogs to provide context for news articles. In *2nd AAAI Conference on Weblogs and Social Media (ICWSM 2008)*. American Association for Artificial Intelligence, 2008.

[15] M. Girvan and M. E. Newman. Community structure in social and biological networks. *Proceedings of the National Academy of Sciences*, 99(12):7821–7826, 2002.

[16] D. Greene, D. Doyle, and P. Cunningham. Tracking the evolution of communities in dynamic social networks. In *Advances in social networks analysis and mining (ASONAM), 2010 international conference on*, pages 176–183. IEEE, 2010.

[17] S. Greene and P. Resnik. More than words: Syntactic packaging and implicit sentiment. In *Proceedings of human language technologies: The 2009 annual conference of the north american chapter of the association for computational linguistics*, pages 503–511. Association for Computational Linguistics, 2009.

[18] M. Gupta, J. Gao, Y. Sun, and J. Han. Community trend outlier detection using soft temporal pattern mining. In *Machine Learning and Knowledge Discovery in Databases*, pages 692–708. Springer, 2012.

[19] P. Jaccard. The distribution of the flora in the alpine zone. 1. *New phytologist*, 11(2):37–50, 1912.

[20] M. C. Linn. Designing the knowledge integration environment. *International Journal of Science Education*, 22(8):781–796, 2000.

[21] M. MacKuen, J. Wolak, L. Keele, and G. E. Marcus. Civic engagements: Resolute partisanship or reflective deliberation. *American Journal of Political Science*, 54(2):440–458, 2010.

[22] L. Meeussen, E. Delvaux, and K. Phalet. Becoming a group: Value convergence and emergent work group identities. *British Journal of Social Psychology*, 2013.

[23] T. Murray, X. Xu, and B. P. Woolf. An exploration of text analysis methods to identify social deliberative skill. In *Artificial Intelligence in Education*, pages 811–814. Springer, 2013.

[24] W. Reich. Deliberative democracy in the classroom: A sociological view. *Educational Theory*, 57(2):187–197, 2007.

[25] I. J. Roseman, C. Wiest, and T. S. Swartz. Phenomenology, behaviors, and goals differentiate discrete emotions. *Journal of Personality and Social Psychology*, 67(2):206, 1994.

[26] D. A. Scheufele and B. V. Lewenstein. The public and nanotechnology: How citizens make sense of emerging technologies. *Journal of Nanoparticle Research*, 7(6):659–667, 2005.

[27] K. Sznajd-Weron and J. Sznajd. Opinion evolution in closed community. *International Journal of Modern Physics C*, 11(06):1157–1165, 2000.

[28] M. Takaffoli, J. Fagnan, F. Sangi, and O. R. Zaïane. Tracking changes in dynamic information networks. In *Computational Aspects of Social Networks (CASoN), 2011 International Conference on*, pages 94–101. IEEE, 2011.

[29] M. Takaffoli, F. Sangi, J. Fagnan, and O. R. Zaïane. A framework for analyzing dynamic social networks. *Applications of Social network Analysis (ASNA)*, 2010.

[30] Y. R. Tausczik and J. W. Pennebaker. The psychological meaning of words: Liwc and computerized text analysis methods. *Journal of Language and Social Psychology*, 29(1):24–54, 2010.

[31] T. Wang, C. V. Fang, D. Lin, and S. F. Wu. Localizing temporal anomalies in large evolving graphs. In *Proceedings of the 2015 SIAM International Conference on Data Mining*, pages 927–935. SIAM, 2015.

[32] T. Wang, K. C. Wang, F. Erlandsson, S. F. Wu, and R. Faris. The influence of feedback with different opinions on continued user participation in online newsgroups. In *Advances in Social Networks Analysis and Mining (ASONAM), 2013 IEEE/ACM International Conference on*, pages 388–395. ACM, 2013.

[33] D. J. Watts and P. S. Dodds. Influentials, networks, and public opinion formation. *Journal of consumer research*, 34(4):441–458, 2007.

[34] B. Y. White, T. A. Shimoda, J. R. Frederiksen, et al. Enabling students to construct theories of collaborative inquiry and reflective learning: Computer support for metacognitive development. *International Journal of Artificial Intelligence in Education (IJAIED)*, 10:151–182, 1999.

[35] Wikipedia. Bias — Wikipedia, the free encyclopedia, 2014. [Online; accessed 16-February-2014].

[36] X. Xu, T. Murray, B. P. Woolf, and D. A. Smith. Mining social deliberation in online communication: If you were me and i were you. In *Educational Data Mining 2013*, 2013.

[37] T. Yano, P. Resnik, and N. A. Smith. Shedding (a thousand points of) light on biased language. In *Proceedings of the NAACL HLT 2010 Workshop on Creating Speech and Language Data with Amazon's Mechanical Turk*, pages 152–158, 2010.

[38] H. Zhao, W. Kallander, H. Johnson, and S. F. Wu. Smartwiki: A reliable and conflict-refrained wiki model based on reader differentiation and social context analysis. *Knowl.-Based Syst.*, 47:53–64, 2013.

Dawn of the Selfie Era: The Whos, Wheres, and Hows of Selfies on Instagram

Flávio Souza[†]   Diego de Las Casas[†]   Vinícius Flores[†]   SunBum Youn[*]
Meeyoung Cha[*]   Daniele Quercia[*]   Virgílio Almeida[†]
[†]Computer Science Department, UFMG, Belo Horizonte, Brazil
[*]Graduate School of Culture Technology, KAIST, South Korea

ABSTRACT

Online interactions are increasingly involving images, especially those containing human faces, which are naturally attention grabbing and more effective at conveying feelings than text. To understand this new convention of digital culture, we study the collective behavior of sharing *selfies* on Instagram and present how people appear in selfies and which patterns emerge from such interactions. Analysis of millions of photos shows that the amount of selfies has increased by 900 times from 2012 to 2014. Selfies are an effective medium to grab attention; they generate on average 1.1–3.2 times more likes and comments than other types of content on Instagram. Compared to other content, interactions involving selfies exhibit variations in homophily scores (in terms of age and gender) that suggest they are becoming more widespread. Their style also varies by cultural boundaries in that the average age and majority gender seen in selfies differ from one country to another. We provide explanations of such country-wise variations based on cultural and socioeconomic contexts.

Categories and Subject Descriptors

J.4 [**Computer Applications**]: Social and Behavioral Sciences; H.3.5 [**Information Storage and Retrieval**]: Online Information Services—*Web-based services*

General Terms

Human Factors; Measurement

Keywords

Instagram; Selfies; Cultural Boundaries

1. INTRODUCTION

The amount of rich media is increasing exponentially on the Internet. Online conversations and interactions now involve more images, which are naturally attention grabbing and effective at conveying feelings [21, 39]. Social media in particular has seen a rapid uptake of pictures containing human faces. One notable example is the *selfie* or digital self-portrait, which have become a phenomenal ubiquitous convention of online culture.

Numerous research studies proposed the psychological and sociological framing behind posting selfies, broadly based on narcissism [36], self-exploration [32], self-embellishment [25], and a new genre of art [39]. Other studies approached with the Human Computer Interaction framing to understand pictures with faces and demonstrated their engaging effects [2]. In addition, a project called Selfiecity examined the image traits of single-person self-portraits in five cities across the world [34]. Until now, little effort has been made to quantitatively defining and examining selfies based on a large amount of data.

This paper presents a measurement study of a popular media sharing website, Instagram (www.instagram.com), and characterizes how people appear on Instagram selfies and which patterns emerge from their attention grabbing behaviors. Since selfies are pictures of people, they represent a structured (i.e., social-by-design) form of interaction in social networks. We hence seek to understand whether this new content type can uncover patterns of social interactions. We ask the following two specific questions.

1. **The whos and wheres of selfies:** Can we characterize selfies in terms of age, gender, geography, country, and other cultural variables?

2. **The hows of selfies:** How much attention do selfies receive in terms of likes and comments and to what extent their interactions depend on cultural boundaries?

The first question provides a holistic understanding of what selfies represent in social media. We utilize a subset of photos with hashtags containing the word 'selfie' to determine what kinds of photos are explicitly called as selfies by Instagram users (e.g., how many persons appear in a photo and what kinds of moods these photos contain). Several critical hypotheses related to gender empowerment, group membership, and perceived privacy are tested to better understand the contexts through which users post selfies in a given culture.

Through the second research question, we try to understand how selfie users interact with their audience. Selfies and pictures with faces are more than mere self-expressions; they are phenomenal in grabbing attention and have settled as a popular online practice. By studying the dyadic relationships between selfie users and their audience, we aim to understand what principles rule in pair-wise interactions that involve rich media content. This study tests whether conventional theories such as homophily become strengthened or weakened under the new form of interaction among users.

COSN'15, November 2–3, 2015, Palo Alto, California, USA.
© 2015 ACM. ISBN 978-1-4503-3951-3/15/11 ...$15.00.
DOI: http://dx.doi.org/10.1145/2817946.2817948.

This paper utilizes a large amount of data gathered from Instagram and carefully selected data about selfies[1] based on three different approaches: (i) pictures containing the word 'selfie' or its immediate variations in hashtags (e.g., #selfie, #myselfie), (ii) pictures containing hashtags related to selfie, but composed only of indirect variations of the word (e.g., #selfcamera, #me), and (iii) pictures containing one or more faces, irrelevant to the choice of hashtags. In this manner, findings in this paper are not dependent on a particular definition of selfies but can provide a holistic view of what people consider selfies. We make the following observations, which are explained throughout the paper.

1. The amount of selfies increased by 900 times over 3 years from 2012 to 2014, which indicates the phenomenon has become a truly ubiquitous convention.

2. Selfies are effective in grabbing attention in social media; they receive 1.1–3.2 times more likes and comments from audience than general posts on Instagram.

3. Young females are the most prominent group who appear in selfies around the world, except for certain countries such as Nigeria and Egypt that show male dominance.

4. There is a complex relationship between taking selfies and a country's culture. The chance of using selfie-related hashtags was higher for cultures with stronger local community membership as well as weaker perception of privacy.

5. Beyond cultural boundaries, selfie-based interactions present homophily variations over time in terms of both age and gender, suggesting that selfies are becoming more mundane.

This work contributes towards better understanding selfies as a popular online phenomenon that have evolved beyond fads, becoming an effective medium of interaction that is attention grabbing and increasing in demand. Our findings demonstrate that selfies are a new window to study collective user behaviors, providing important insights into subjects like perception of privacy, digital cultural norms, and designs of social-networking platforms.

2. BACKGROUND

The rise of selfies is a key trend in the visual Web, assisted by new technological tools and services like Flickr, Pinterest, and Instagram that allow people to better express themselves visually. This section describes several findings from research on self-portrait images, selfies, and Instagram.

2.1 The Meaning of Selfies

Selfies are a ubiquitous phenomenon of modern digital culture. The term was added to the Oxford Dictionaries[2] in 2013, with description: a photograph that one has taken of oneself, typically one taken with a smartphone or webcam and shared via social media.

Different theories emerged to explain why people take selfies. Some state selfies are a mean of self-exploration. As one takes multiple selfies and combine them with different filters, one can re-see herself [9]. A slightly different view is self-embellishment from psychology that states when exposed to slightly modified pictures of themselves, people tend to identify a more attractive version as the original picture [22]. With the ability to control aesthetics of a

picture, selfies are a perfect tool for showing the world one's subjective self-image.

A sociological framing recognizes technological possibility to be a necessary condition and also highlights other behavioral factors to be important for selfies [8]. One is a culture of sharing and belonging fostered by the online environment and transmitted through memes. Another is the constant work of shaping and reaffirming self-identity through social actions. In this perspective, selfies could symbolize a convention that is governed by culture and society.

2.2 Advocates and Opponents of Selfies

Selfies are a prominent online culture that have been both criticized and advocated by different parties. Critics say selfies are vain, narcissistic, and attention-seeking; some argue a wide adoption of selfies by female users exacerbates sexual objectification and male gaze [6]. One research demonstrated that adults with the Dark Triad personality trait (e.g., narcissism, psychopathy, and machiavellianism) have a higher chance of posting selfies and editing images on social media [13]. Self-objectification is also known to correlate with increasing photo sharing activities on Facebook among young women [28]. This leads to a worry about the loss of control over one's self-image in an increasingly sharing and hackable culture, where the notion of privacy becomes dependent on the types of interactions that are allowed [31]. The mere presence of an individual's face in a public photo stream can reveal a great detail of information about that person [10].

Defenders of the selfie culture not only deny the above claims but argue selfies are the pinnacle of control and self-expression; selfies allow people to take control over how they and their peers are represented in public, which mobilizes the power dynamics of representations and promotes empowerment [7]. One study interviewed 20 participants who had posted sexual self-portraits and showed how the exchange of such self-portraits can be a transformative experience, increasing their critical self-awareness in a positive manner [35].

2.3 Selfies by Numbers

In contrast to the rich body of work on sociological interpretation of selfies, relatively little attention has been given to data-driven analysis of selfies. A report by eBay Deals states that selfie activity is platform dependent and is well distributed in particular media, for instance Instagram than Twitter [11]. A research conduced by TIME looked at how many "selfies per capita" each city produced by dividing the amount of users posting selfies by the population of each city. They noticed that it was difficult to find a proper local translation for the hashtag 'selfie', as different variations were used everywhere [38].

The largest scale analysis of selfies to date, however, probably was a data visualization project called Selfiecity that aimed at describing features of single selfies (i.e., photos containing a single person's face) in five cities across the world [34]. They investigated demographics, poses, face features, and the moods of 3,200 selfies on Instagram using both automatic and manual methods. Nonetheless, many of the considerations and theories behind selfies (e.g., the contexts, interactions) have not yet been studied under the perspective of data analysis, which is the goal of this paper.

2.4 Studies on Instagram

When it comes to general user behaviors, a number of research utilized the logs gathered from Instagram. For example, researchers examined how color patterns varies between photos posted in two cities [17], how the behaviors of teens and adults on the network differ [20], how users can be grouped based on the types of

[1] Data used in this study are available for research purposes at http://instagram.camps.dcc.ufmg.br/selfies/

[2] http://www.oxforddictionaries.com

content they share [19], and even how Instagram photos shared on Twitter can be used as sensors to study user characteristics in different cultures [33]. Therefore, the present research can be seen yet as an additional contribution for Instagram characterization efforts, complementing previous works in this direction.

3. INSTAGRAM DATA

We started data collection by inferring ranges of user IDs. This step involved forward sampling batches of 10,000 numeric IDs for every range of 10 million, starting from zero. None of the inspected IDs were valid after the count of 1.6 billion. Through this process, we could identify which specific ranges are valid ID space. Based on these ranges, we next randomly sampled 1% or 16 million IDs to build an initial seed set and found 42% of them to be in use; the remaining IDs were either deleted or not in use. Not all of these in-use accounts could be viewed publicly due to privacy settings; 78% of them were public accounts and the remaining 22% were private accounts, whose profile and feed information could be viewed only by confirmed friends on Instagram.

We gathered profile information of all public users (5,170,062 in total) as well as all of their publications (known as "feeds" on Instagram) for a three-year period between December 2011 and December 2014. There were 153,979,348 data objects called "media", which include a picture or a video along with some metadata such as hashtags, caption, timestamp, and URLs. This paper only focuses on pictures, which takes up a large majority (97%) of all media on Instagram. Figure 1 shows an example profile and feed, where profile includes user-level counts (e.g., posts, followers and following) and feed includes images and picture-level metadata (e.g., likes, caption, hashtags, comments and geolocation, if any). All of these pieces of information can be accessed through Instagram's Application Programming Interface (API).

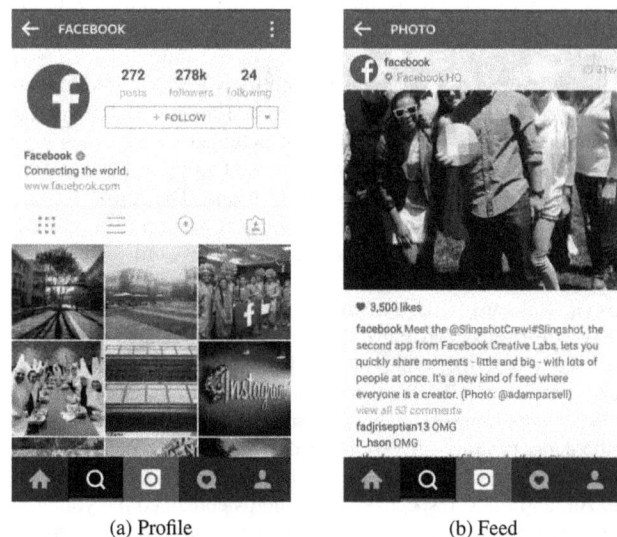

(a) Profile   (b) Feed

Figure 1: Instagram mobile application interface.

One important aspect considered in this paper is geography of selfie users, which were inferred by mapping geolocation tags in the photo content. Instagram is known to have high rates of photos that contain geotags. Among all media gathered, 35,030,356 pictures published by 770,095 users contained any geolocation information. The Global Administrative Areas database [16] was used to map location coordinates to corresponding country and city names.

Another aspect considered is user demographics, which we inferred from photos of users by the Face++ tool [27]. Face++ is an online API that detects faces in a given photo and predicts information about each person in the photo such as age and gender. Its accuracy is known to be over 90% [2]. Age is given in years along with a confidence range; gender is given as 'male' or 'female' with a confidence value between 0 and 100; and smile is given as a score between 0 and 100. We ran Face++ for a random subset of photos and gained demographic information for 2,286,401 pictures posted by 738,901 distinct users.

3.1 Data Validation

To understand potential bias in data, we compare statistics obtained from our data with those of other reports on Instagram. The service reached 300 million active users in 2014 with more than 30 billion photos shared on the network.[3] A research conducted by Pew showed that Instagram is not only increasing its overall user base, but also is seeing a significant growth in almost every demographic group in the United States. Most notably, 53% of young adults between age 18 and 29 used the service in 2014, compared to 37% a year before. The service is also known to have more female users than males [30].

Given its massive scale, findings in this study are bound to insights from a small subset of data. Nonetheless, data we observed had similar properties to what was reported on Instagram. We examined the age and gender distribution of users in our data. We selected a random sample of 100,000 users with at least 10 pictures and examined the profile pictures of such users. The resulting age and gender distribution is shown in Figure 2, where 62% of the sample users are inferred as female and the median ages are 18 and 23 for females and males, respectively. The proportions of different age groups are similar to other reports, like the Pew research and the Selfiecity project [34].

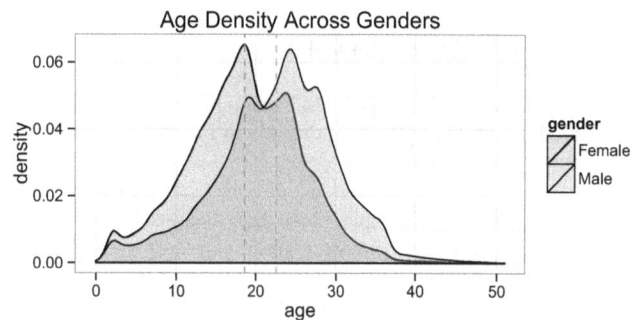

Figure 2: Density plot of users ages, separated by gender.

3.2 Extracting Selfies

We devised three methods to extract selfie posts. Photos with selfie-related tags indicate what Instagram users identify explicitly as selfies. In addition to two datasets found in this manner, we also examine pictures with faces in general. Note that not all photos belonging to this category are selfies (i.e., photos taken of oneself), yet the third dataset will help us understand the engaging effects of faces. Lastly we utilized a random set of photos for comparison. The summary of the four datasets used in the remainder of the paper follows:

---

[3]http://instagram.com/press/

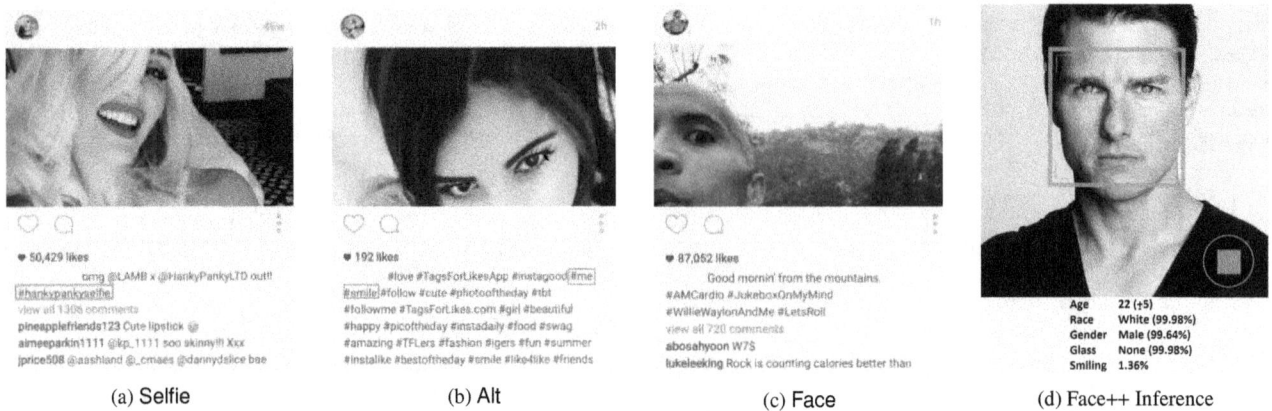

(a) Selfie   (b) Alt   (c) Face   (d) Face++ Inference

Figure 3: Example pictures of Selfie, Alt, and Face datasets as well as features predicted by Face++.

Dataset	Description	# Pictures	# Users
Selfie	Pictures with hashtags containing 'selfie' (e.g., #selfie, #selfietoday)	1,196,080	214,656
Alt	Pictures with alternative hashtags for 'selfie' (e.g., #selca, #selstagram)	2,453,749	242,650
Face	Pictures with face(s) detected using the Face++ tool	1,921,207	315,751
All	Randomly chosen set of pictures	10,000,019	184,615

Table 1: Number of media and users in each of the four datasets used in this paper.

1. **Selfie**: a collection of pictures that contain the word 'selfie' in hashtags. Examples include #selfie, #selfietime, and #selfiesunday, which are an explicit indicator.

2. **Alt**: a collection of pictures that include hashtags related to selfie but use variations of the word. For instance, 'selca' can be used instead of 'selfie' in some contexts.

3. **Face**: a collection of pictures containing one or more faces detected using the Face++ tool.

4. **All**: a random collection of 10M Instagram pictures. We compared it with the other three datasets to identify the distinct characteristic of selfies.

Photos in Figure 3 are examples of the three datasets, which were all posted by popular users on Instagram. Figure 3(a) is classified as Selfie due to its hashtag #hankypankyselfie, whereas Figure 3(b) is classified as Alt for its hashtag #me and #smile. The face photo in Figure 3(c) did not contain any selfie-related hashtags, hence it was classified as Face by the Face++ tool. Note that all three types of photos are valid selfie content, which we consider in this paper. Figure 3(d) shows features detected by Face++ on a celebrity photo of Tom Cruise. Table 1 summarizes the description and quantity (the number of pictures and distinct users) of three selfie datasets as well as that of All.

Now we describe our heuristic method to identify Alt photos. For this we first need to examine what users call as selfies on Instagram. The Selfie dataset involved a total of 43,874 distinct hashtags containing the word 'selfie'. To find alternative hashtags for 'selfie', we calculated a similarity score for each hashtag in a way akin to Pointwise Mutual Information [5]. First, we separated all pictures into two sets: one set containing pictures that either have a single-person face or the hashtag #selfie (called True or T) and another set containing pictures that neither have a face nor the hashtag #selfie (called Unknown or U). The similarity score was then designed in an approximate manner to give higher scores to hashtags in the first set, T, as follows:

$$S_h = \frac{f_{h,T} \times u_{h,T}}{f_{h,U} \times u_{h,U}} \quad (1)$$

where S_h is the similarity score for a hashtag h in relation to selfie posts. $f_{h,[T,U]}$ is the frequency of the hashtag h in the set T or the set U and $u_{h,[T,U]}$ is the number of users who use the hashtag h in T or U.

In this manner, we were able to identify words that describe selfies in various languages such as Turkish, Russian, Malaysian, Indonesian, Filipino, etc. Note that the obtained hashtags had high potential to appear with other selfie-related terms, yet they do not cover a complete set of selfie-related terms. The top-10 variant hashtags found with this method were: #shamelessselfie, #gaybeard, #butfirst, #özçekim (the word representing selfie in Turkish), #ethanymotagiveaway, #gaysian, #лиф-толук (Russian), #dolledup, #ozcekim (Turkish), as well as #pacute (Malaysian and Filipino). We also included words that are used to describe selfies such as #me and #self in the Alt dataset. The final Alt dataset contained a total of 81 variant hashtags.

When we examined the photo content through Face++, the three selfie datasets varied slightly in terms of user demographics. First, the median age of the users in photos were 22, 20, and 21 for Selfie, Alt, and Face respectively. Alt photos contained the youngest users. The proportion of females to males varied from 64%, 69%, and 59% for the three datasets (in same order as above). Photos in Alt were more likely to contain faces of female users, while Face had a better balance of male and female users. Finally, we compared how many faces appear in a given photo, as sometimes multiple faces may appear in a photo (i.e., groupie). The three datasets contained on average 1.12, 0.76, and 1.75 number of faces for the three datasets (in the same order as above). Some photos in Alt were selfies of pets or body parts, in which case they contained zero human face. These variations, although not prominent, may indicate the differences in base demographics.

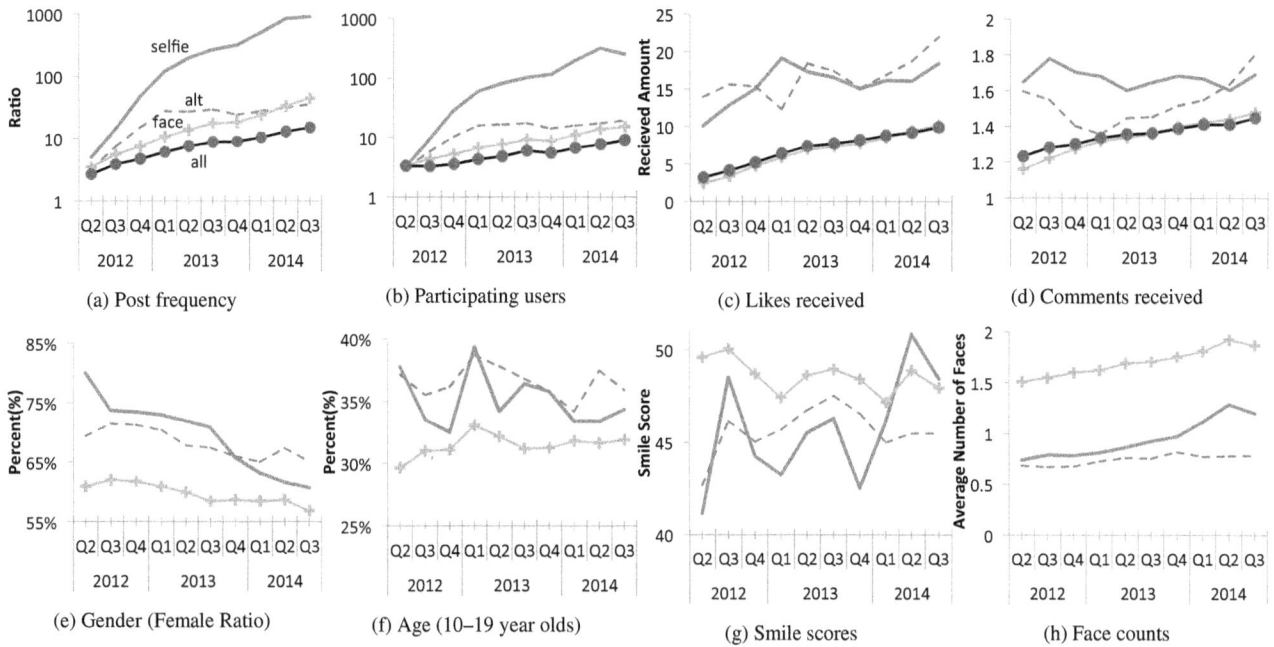

Figure 4: Longitudinal trend of selfie posts across the datasets.

The subfigure captions read:

(a) Post frequency (b) Participating users (c) Likes received (d) Comments received

(e) Gender (Female Ratio) (f) Age (10–19 year olds) (g) Smile scores (h) Face counts

4. TEMPORAL DYNAMICS

The longitudinal data provides a unique opportunity to examine post and interaction trends from 2012 to 2014.

4.1 Patterns of Selfies Over Time

We first study how a wide range of features changed over time. We examine post frequency, attention (likes and comments), demographics (gender and age), and image (smile score and number of faces in a given photo) for different definitions of selfies. Demographics and image features depend on Face++ data, thus the All dataset was excluded from these analyses.

4.1.1 Post Frequency

Post frequency measures how popular a given photo type is over time. Figure 4(a) shows the post frequency trends over time, where the x-axis represents time in quarters (i.e., three-month periods) and the y-axis represents the relative increment or decrement compared to the initial quarter (i.e., the first quarter of 2012). Therefore, a value of 1.0 in this figure means the post volume is identical to what was measured in the initial quarter and a value of 10.0 means an increment by 10 times.

While the frequency of All increased 15 times (from 103,520 in the first quarter of 2012 to 1,560,697 in the third quarter of 2014), the post frequency of Selfie increased rapidly by 900 times (from 297 to 269,454) over the same time period. Alt and Face also became popular compared to All, yet not at the same degree as Selfie. When we compare the speed, All and Face show a relatively steady growth in volume, whereas the growth of Selfie and Alt is rapid at first and becomes stagnant towards the end of 2014. A similar trend is seen in the graph of participating users who post selfies in Figure 4(b). Selfie again shows orders of magnitude larger growth than any other content type. Selfie and Alt show a stagnant growth towards the end of 2014 as opposed to All and Face. These growth trends capture well the rapid rise of selfies on Instagram, which seemed to have peaked between 2012 and 2013.

4.1.2 Content Popularity

The amount of attention a photo gained can be inferred by examining the number of likes and comments. Figure 4(c) shows the absolute geometric mean of likes per picture, which demonstrates that Selfie and Alt receive nearly 2-3 times more likes than the other content types. This means pictures with an explicit marker about 'selfie' grab more attention from audience than merely containing a face in a photo. Examining closely, however, the relative gap between Selfie and All decreases over time from nearly 3.2 times during the thriving initial spread to 1.3 times in 2014.

The geometric mean of comments received in Figure 4(d) shows a similar trend. Again Selfie and Alt receive 1.1–1.5 times more comments than the other content types, although this gap is decreasing over time. This observation indicates that pictures owning a selfie-related hashtag are effective in grabbing attention, yet their engaging effect becomes less pronounced over the years (perhaps as selfies become widespread and become mundane).

When compared to the recent literature on the effect of containing faces in pictures, the work in [2] demonstrated pictures with faces tend to get 38% more likes and 32% more comments compared to other content on Instagram. While we cannot make a direct comparison, our results further highlights that attributing particular hashtags (such as #selfie) could incur even a higher level of attention than merely posting photo with faces.

4.1.3 Demographics

We next investigate what kinds of users post selfies, by employing the Face++ tool to infer their age and gender based on profile pictures. Figure 4(e) shows the proportion of female users over time. The high female-gender ratio indicates that selfies were initially posted primarily by female users than male users for all three datasets. These rates are high even when we consider the high female prevalence on Instagram. During the 3 year period, however, this difference diminished until the ratio almost reached the base gender ratio of the network, as seen by Face.

225

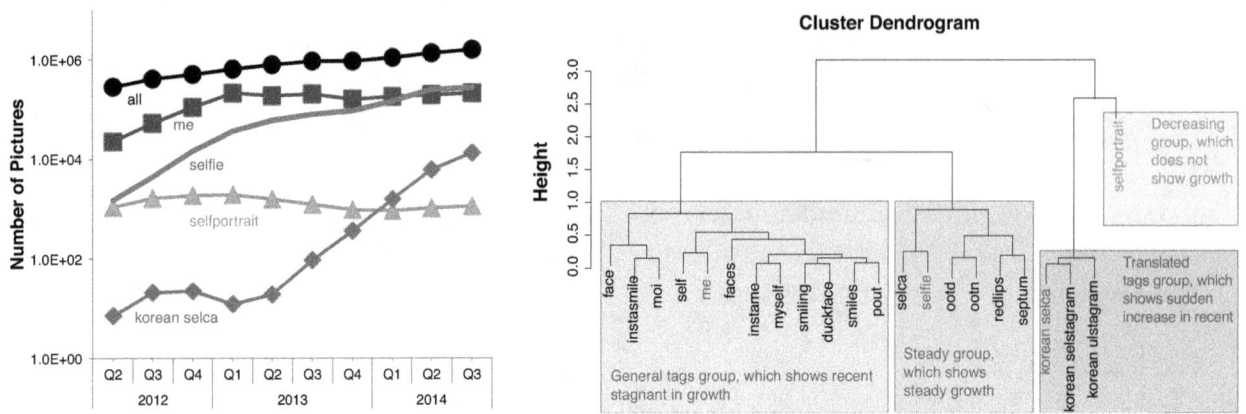

Figure 5: Evolution of tags in Alt and hierarchical clustering based on Pearson correlation.

Figure 4(f) shows the demographic makeup for 10–19 year olds. The age distribution of Face confirms the general perception that young people are the most active users who post photos with faces on Instagram, constituting nearly 32% of all participating users. Nonetheless, this ratio is even larger for Selfie and Alt, meaning that young people are more likely to tag their pictures with selfie-related hashtags. The gender and age analysis together indicates that young female users on Instagram drove the selfie momentum during the initial stage in 2012, which is indeed confirmed by the plot of percentage of young females over time for each dataset (not included here due to space limitations).

4.1.4 Smiles and Face Counts

Would face pictures that are tagged as selfies present more joyful atmosphere? The smile score, detected by Face++, indicates the degree of smile in a face, with a score of 100 indicating the highest level of smile. Comparing the average smile scores in Figure 4(g), faces in Selfie and Alt are not more joyful than Face. Overall, the scores of all three datasets are ranged between 40 and 52, which do not necessarily represent a big pleasant smile. We do not see any particular correlation between the smile score and the type of data.

Another question we had was to measure how many faces appear in selfie photos. Would people associate single-person photos as selfies? Figure 4(h) shows the average number of faces per picture for the three datasets. At a glance, Face contains the highest number of faces (1.5–2.0 faces per picture) than Selfie and Alt. The latter types sometimes included zero faces thereby pushing the average below 1.0, where pictures were on parts of body, pets, or other animals. From mid 2013 and onward, there is a gradual increase in face counts for Selfie dataset, which implies that Instagram users increasingly recognize pictures containing multiple faces as selfies.

4.2 Trajectory of Selfie Hashtags

We have so far found similarity between Selfie and Alt, both of which contain hashtags about selfies. It is natural to observe *multiple* variants of the hashtag as they could indicate cultural traits and contexts. In order to observe how different hashtags gained popularity over time, we looked at their adoption trajectory over time. We identified all hashtags in Alt that appeared more than 10,000 times (21 variants) along with #selfie, then calculated the Pearson's correlation coefficient for growth trajectories of all of these variations. A hierarchical clustering approach was applied to identify hashtags that showed similar growth patterns.

Figure 5 shows the result, where hashtags are divided into four groups. The first group, which is the largest in size, contains gene-

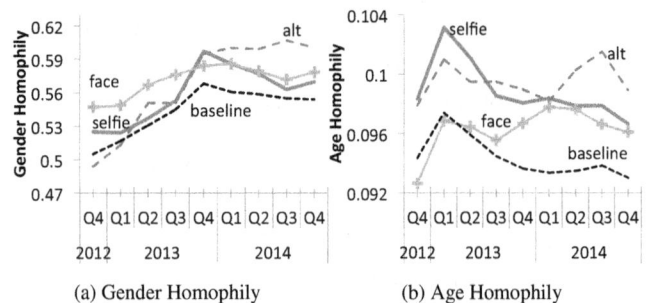

(a) Gender Homophily (b) Age Homophily

Figure 6: Homophily scores for likes. The *baseline* gives the expected scores for random interactions considering the three datasets.

ral description of selfies such as #me and #face. Hashtags in this group initially showed high popularity and then became stagnant over time. The second group, which includes social media specific terms such as #selfie, #selca and #ootd (outfit of the day), shows steady growth over time. The third group, containing hashtags in languages other than English, shows a rapid uptake later in time, indicating that the selfie convention has become widely adopted at different times around the world. The last group contains a single hashtag, #selfportrait, whose growth does not change much over the years. These differences in popularity trajectory of hashtags suggest that underlying mechanisms (i.e., culture, platform) played important roles in how the selfie phenomenon settled.

4.3 Selfies as an Interaction Medium

Since selfies are pictures of people, they represent a structured form of interaction. As shown in the previous subsection, they are an effective medium of communication that incur more likes and comments than other types of content on Instagram. Next, several questions motivate us to examine interaction patterns involving selfies; for instance, how likely males will respond to selfies of other males or other females? Do people tend to interact more frequently with others of the same age? Would these patterns change for pictures explicitly marked as selfies?

One method to examine these questions is homophily, which describes the tendency of individuals to associate and relate with similar others. Homophily is a central hypothesis that can explain user behaviors in various offline and online social networks [26]. This study tested homophily by studying the dyadic relationship between selfie owners and their audience based on likes and com-

226

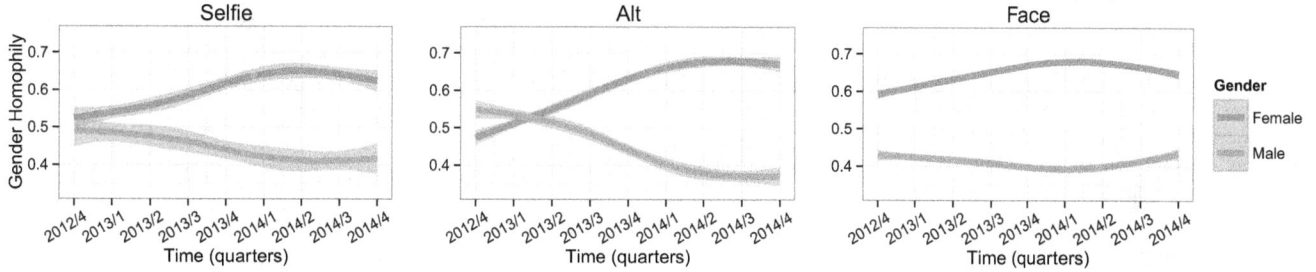

Figure 7: Intra-gender homophily evolution for likes interactions across three datasets: Selfie, Alt, and Face.

ments. In particular, we designed the following experiment: first we built three samples, each containing 200,000 randomly chosen pictures from Selfie, Alt, and Face datasets. We then fetched a random set of likes and comments for each of the pictures and determined the age and gender of such interacting users based on Face++. Next, two measures were defined, following the literature on homophily: Gender Homophily (*H_Gender*) and Age Homophily (*H_Age*). *H_Gender* was calculated as follows:

$$H\_Gender = \frac{F_{mm} + F_{ff}}{F_{interactions}} \quad (2)$$

where $F_{interactions}$ is the total number of interactions of any kind, F_{mm} is the number of male-male interactions, and F_{ff} is the number of female-female interactions. Hence, *H_Gender* measures the rate of same-sex interactions out of all combinations seen in data. Its values range from 0 to 1, where 1 represents the highest level of homophily.

Similarly, *H_Age* was calculated in the following way:

$$H\_Age = \text{RMSE}(A_i, A_j)^{-1} \quad (3)$$

where A_i and A_j are lists containing the ages of interacting users and RMSE is the Root Mean Squared Error of two lists, which represents how close they are related. For example, if *H_Age* = 0.1, then $1/\text{RMSE}(A_i, A_j) = 0.1$, that is, $\text{RMSE}(A_i, A_j) = 10$, which indicates the mean difference in age between interacting users is roughly 10 years. The smaller the differences in age, the higher *H_Age* will be, indicating greater homophily. We have chosen RMSE instead of mean absolute difference in order to increase the penalty for higher age differences.

Gender and age homophily scores for likes are shown in Figure 6 for each dataset, along with the expected scores for random interactions (labeled as *baseline*) considering the three datasets together. The baseline was built using bootstrap sample in order to get both source and destination users in each quarter, and then calculating the homophily scores for these random pairs of users.

It is possible to observe that Alt and Selfie present more variation in gender homophily scores over the course of three years than Face. To further investigate this finding, we calculated intra-gender homophily scores for likes as follows:

$$H\_Male = \frac{F_{mm}}{F_{m\_all}} \qquad H\_Female = \frac{F_{ff}}{F_{f\_all}} \quad (4)$$

where F_{mm} and F_{ff} are defined as previously, F_{m_all} is the total number of interactions of any kind with males, and F_{f_all} is the total number of interactions of any kind with females. Thus, *H_Male* and *H_Female* are proportions of same-sex interactions calculated for each gender separately. The values of each one range from 0 to 1, where 1 represents the highest level of homophily.

The intra-gender homophily scores of males and females are plotted together for each dataset in Figure 7. Two main facts arise from the graphs. First, there is a clear female bias in likes interactions, which goes in line with female prevalence in the network. Second, both Selfie and Alt present a unique gender homophily evolution. In the beginning, males tend to engage in like interactions more than females, as the scores are close to 0.5 and there are more females in the network. Then over time, their behavior converges to Face's, suggesting that selfies are becoming more mundane. No significant pattern of gender-level homophily emerged for comments in the datasets.

In the case of age homophily in likes interactions, the scores for Selfie follow the pattern of Alt's until the beginning of 2014. After that, Selfie follows the same trend as Face, with decreasing homophily scores, while Alt scores peak and then also decrease. This finding suggests once more that selfies are becoming more widespread. Again, homophily for comments does not present a clear distinction among datasets, although its values are in the same range (0.092 to 0.104) as homophily for likes. The pattern is more pronounced for likes than comments possibly because likes are larger in volume than comments – likes are a lightweight communication form that happen more often on Instagram than comments.

5. CULTURAL INTERPRETATION

Having examined the longitudinal trends, we now provide explanations for the selfie patterns and examine cultural aspects. We investigate whether the new selfie convention portrays any cultural and socioeconomic contexts (i.e., country-wise variations). This is an important question because other online behaviors have been shown to depend on culture [14]. To group selfies by cultural boundaries, we aggregated all geotagged pictures by countries and considered only those countries with at least 20 pictures for analysis. The total number of countries analyzed in each dataset is shown in Table 2 for all indicators used.

Ind.	Selfie	Alt	Face
GGI	111	115	117
PV	54	55	56
IDV	67	68	68
LCS	53	54	55
WCS	53	54	55
Choice	54	55	56
Trust	54	55	56
UAI	67	68	68

Table 2: Number of countries per dataset for each indicator.

As one might expect, selfie patterns differed from one country to another. For instance, the mean age and female-to-male ratio varied as shown in Table 3, which shows the top-5 and bottom-5 countries based on female prevalence of selfies. South Korea is ranked the top with its 71% of selfies shared by female users. Even though there is a general bias towards female users that we have demonstrated in the previous section, several countries such as Nigeria and Egypt present a heavy male bias.

	Top 5			Bottom 5	
Country	M.age	F.prev	Country	M.age	F.prev
KOR	16.9	0.71	NGA	23.5	0.31
KAZ	19.3	0.68	EGY	22.7	0.28
PHL	17.9	0.68	SAU	20.4	0.28
CHN	16.6	0.67	KWT	22.0	0.28
UKR	20.9	0.66	IND	23.9	0.20

Table 3: Top and bottom countries by female prevalence.

In order to test whether these country-wise variations can be explained by cultural contexts, we utilized popular international socioeconomic indicators as well as indicators from two important sources: (i) World Values Survey (WVS) that is an individual-level survey probing cultural values of citizens in 59 countries between 2010 and 2014 [1] and (ii) Hofstede's Cultural Dimensions (HCD) that is a five-dimensional model of cultural differences studied since 1971 by Geert Hofstede [18].

5.1 Hypotheses

We set up three hypotheses that could enrich our understanding of country-wise variations in selfie trends:

1. **Gender Empowerment (H_1).** There is no consensus on whether selfies enhance male oppression or allows for a way of asserting agency, although the answer is probably more nuanced [23]. Nevertheless, it is reasonable to expect that differentiation in gender roles within a country will be reflected in the proportion of women or men taking selfies. We hence hypothesize that women in countries with higher gender equality are more comfortable in sharing selfies publicly than in less equal countries.

2. **Self Embellishment & Membership (H_2).** If selfies are indeed a manifestation of self embellishment, it is expected that they will be more prevalent in individualistic societies than in collectivist countries [12]. If, on the contrary, selfies are more widely used as means of belonging and a norm, then they will be more prevalent where citizens feel a strong tie with their local community or with a global connected community.

3. **Intimacy & Privacy (H_3).** If selfies represent one's sense of intimacy and privacy in an online world, then trust in people and the perception of control over one's own life should mediate the behavior. Among relevant socioeconomic indicators, one may consider the level of perceived uncertainty and loss of control. We hypothesize that countries where people are aversive to uncertainty will post comparatively fewer selfies than otherwise.

5.2 Independent and Control Variables

To test the first hypothesis, we compared the proportion of females detected by Face++ in each country with several measures

of gender equality. Since the proportion of women in each country varies, we calculated the relative increase or decrease of female prevalence against the observed proportion of women in the World Bank data.[4] We define *GenderBias* as follows:

$$GenderBias = \mathrm{P}_{\text{selfies}} - \mathrm{P}_{\text{census}} \qquad (5)$$

where $\mathrm{P}_{\text{census}}$ is the proportion of females observed in a country.

We used two relevant socioeconomic measures: (i) the Gender Gap Index (GGI) and (ii) Patriarchal Values (PV). The former is published yearly by the World Economic Forum and measures the relative gaps between women and men across four key areas: health, education, economy, and politics [3]. The score represents how much the gaps has been closed, so a high score means a more equal society. The latter is a scale of four questions from the WVS in which the respondents state whether they agree with values tied to stereo-typical gender roles [24]. A high score here means a less equal society in that cultural values are strongly associated with gender inequality.

To test the second hypothesis, we compared the rate of selfie posts at each country, *Prevalence*, as follows:

$$Prevalence = \log \frac{F_T}{F_{All}} \qquad (6)$$

where F_T is the frequency of posts in dataset T and F_{All} is the set of posts in the All dataset. We used a logarithmic value since the trend is heavy tailed across countries.

We used three relevant socioeconomic measures: (i) the Individualism score (IDV), (ii) Local Community Score (LCS), and (iii) World Citizen Score (WCS). The first indicator is from Hofstede's Cultural Dimensions and describes how separated is an individual from larger social groups in a country. The second and third are from a recent work [37] and represent the average value of the response to the following propositions: "I see myself as a part of my local community" and "I see myself as a world citizen". A high score indicates a strong community membership. These scores are proxies for how strongly tied citizens of a country are to their local community as well as to the international community at large.

To test the third hypothesis, we resorted to the part of WVS that is used as an indicator of *generalized trust*, i.e., the trust in people outside one's social circle [4]. This question is: "Generally speaking, would you say that most people can be trusted or that you need to be very careful in dealing with people?" We used the proportion of citizens who agree with the "Most people can be trusted" answer as our *Trust* indicator. We selected the following question to probe for the perception of choice and control: "How much freedom of choice and control do you feel you have over the way your life turns out?" Responses are situated in a scale from 1 (*no choice at all*) to 10 (*a great deal of choice*), which we averaged per country and used as our *Choice* indicator.

We also selected the dimension *Uncertainty Avoidance* (UAI) from HCD, which indicates a society's tolerance for uncertainty and ambiguity and to what extent the members of a culture feel either uncomfortable or comfortable in unstructured (novel, unknown, unusual) situations. Our hypothesis was that Trust and Choice would be positively correlated and UAI would be negatively correlated to the prevalence of selfies in a country.

Finally, we also considered the following sets of *control* variables to take into account that Instagram is not used evenly across countries. Although the measures reported in the *Hypotheses* subsection make intuitive sense, they are strongly related to confounding factors that varies either in Instagram or between countries.

---

[4]http://data.worldbank.org/

We chose three variables to control and calculated the *partial correlations* between the variables of interest. Partial correlations allow us to estimate the relationship of two variables X and Y after partialling out the effect of the control variable Z. They are equivalent to constructing two linear models using X and Y as dependent variables and Z as independent variable, then correlating the residuals of each linear model.

The control variables we chose were *log GDP per capita* as an indicator of economic development, *Internet penetration* as a proxy for technology diffusion, and the *average age* of Instagram users (estimated with Face++ data) to account for the different age profiles between countries. Thus, all correlations we report are between the residuals of the variables after their covariance with the control variables has been partialled out. The correlations between measures/indicators and the control variables are not shown here due to space limitations, but are available in our shared repository.

5.3 Results

Results are displayed in Table 4. The positive relationship between GenderBias and gender equality indicators is clear in all datasets, thus confirming H_1. This is true both for the equality measured by the country's socioeconomic structure—parity of gender in social living and access to public institutions—as for the cultural values in which the citizens of a country believe. The presence of an effect in all datasets show that this relationship holds for many definitions of selfies. However, if one is not to consider the Face dataset as representing actual selfies, one can argue that this is the consequence of a broader effect of the presence of women in the network. It is interesting to note, however, that the strongest correlations in each of the indicators was not with the Face dataset, but with the Alt dataset.

We could not detect a meaningful relationship between Individualism Score (IDV) and Prevalence for either direction, and Local Community Score (LCS) and World Citizen Score (WCS) show significant correlations in opposite directions. LCS is moderately correlated to selfies tagged as such, which goes in line with the idea that selfies are tied to a sense of belonging to a community, namely the local community. However, this effect seems exclusively related to the Selfie dataset, as the coefficients are negative (although non-significant) in the other datasets. Moreover, WCS is negatively correlated with the Alt dataset and not meaningfully correlated with the other datasets.

This finding demonstrates a complex relationship between taking selfies and a country's culture of individuation and connectedness. The effect of a country's individualism, if exists, is much smaller than other factors related to belonging to a community, and could not be detected by us. But even these other factors are not easily interpretable and may be related to different conceptions of selfies. The positive relationship between the Selfie dataset and LCS advocate for the idea that taking selfies—and tagging them as such—is related to the importance a culture gives to belonging to a community. However, we expected that the relationship with WCS would follow the same path, which did not. A possible explanation is that, since the Alt dataset includes many hashtags that represent similar concepts of a selfie in a given country, its negative relationship with WCS spans from the attitude of citizens of the country to adapt and transform foreign "memes" into their cultural reality. Thus, a country with citizens that do not strongly identify themselves as world citizens will still have selfies, but adopt different tags. It is worth mentioning that the correlation between the Prevalences of these two datasets (Selfie and Alt) is only moderate ($r = 0.60, p < 0.0001$).

Hypotesis: Measure	Ind.	Selfie	Alt	Face
H_1 : GenderBias	GGI	0.34^{***}	0.41^{***}	0.32^{***}
	PV	-0.20°	-0.38^{***}	-0.19°
H_2 : Prevalence	IDV	0.09	0.06	-0.04
	LCS	0.22^{*}	-0.13	-0.07
	WCS	0.08	-0.17°	-0.03
H_3 : Prevalence	Choice	-0.04	-0.19°	0.13
	Trust	-0.19°	-0.17	-0.29^{**}
	UAI	0.14	0.21^{*}	0.31^{***}

Stars represent significance values: $p < 0.0001(^{***})$, $p < 0.001(^{**})$, $p < 0.01(^{*})$ and $p < 0.05(^{\circ})$.

Table 4: Correlations between selfie-related measures and sociocultural measures. There is a complex relationship between taking selfies and a country's culture. The chance of using selfie-related hashtags was higher for cultures with stronger local community membership as well as weaker perception of privacy.

As for H_3, Choice, Trust and Uncertainty Avoidance (UAI) are related to Prevalence, but in the opposite direction that we expected. In countries where the citizens trust each other and feel they have more control over their lives or are not as aversive to uncertain outcomes, people take *fewer* selfies relative to other kinds of pictures. The analysis shows that selfies are not inhibited by a sense of lack of control and certainty but somewhat stimulated by it. We may speculate two (non-excluding) scenarios that could explain our finding: 1) selfies are an assertion of control over one's identity, so they are more important in places where citizens feel they need this; 2) part of what drives selfies is an attitude or set of values that also promotes lack of trust, a sense of lack of control, and aversion to uncertainty. Unfortunately, we cannot distinguish these two scenarios from our results.

6. DISCUSSION AND CONCLUSION

6.1 Implications

Selfies are ever more present in today's online culture. This work presented a measurement study based on a large amount of data gathered from Instagram, and defined selfies through three different ways to understand the whos, wheres, and hows of its patterns. We investigated the distributions of post frequency, likes, comments, age, gender, smile scores, and face counts over the course of three years. These patterns collectively show that selfies have become extremely popular (i.e., spreading to a wider set of users in terms of number, age, and gender bias). We examined how different variants of the selfie hashtag gained popularity over time. The longitudinal study also explored the role of homophily in terms of age and gender in selfie-oriented lightweight interactions.

These temporal patterns showed country-wise variations, some of which could be explained by cultural contexts and others need further investigation. This paper showed that gender equality indicators are tightly related to the proportion of women that appear in different definitions of Instagram's selfies, which goes in line with views that selfies mobilize the power dynamics of representations and promotes empowerment (in this case for women) [7]. This paper also showed that there is a complex relationship between taking selfies and a country's culture of individuation and connectedness. Finally, in contrast to our expectation, selfies were less prevalent in more trustful and not risk averse cultures. These findings show general tendency and we do not claim that there is any causal relationship with culture and selfies.

In a recent interview, Instragram founder Kevin Systrom said that "the selfie is something that didn't really exist in the same way before Instagram."[5] Indeed, selfies take center stage on Instagram, and this work shows that they do so in very specific ways. In quantitatively capturing those ways, we offer two main insights to designers of social-networking platforms. First, the adoption of selfies show a high variability across countries. In countries lacking considerable adoption (because of, e.g., gender issues), designers should think about new ways of encouraging specific segments of the population. Second, it is well known that individuals tend to interact with like-minded others. For selfies on Instagram, however, this tendency is further emphasized. As a result, a filter bubble might well emerge [29]: users become separated from other dissimilar users, effectively isolating them in their own cultural and self-portrait bubbles. In a way similar to what researchers in recommender systems have done [40], designers should build and integrate new algorithmic solutions that partly counter the ominous consequences of self-portrait bubbles.

6.2 Limitations

One limitation of this work is that selfies have different meanings to social media users. Face count varied in that some considered single-person photos as selfies, while others allowed multiple faces to be included. Some explicitly identified photos containing human faces, while others tagged pictures of their pets, animals, personal belongings, as well as body parts as selfies. These examples illustrate the paradigm shift in how people define selfies. The current study tried to capture these diverse meanings by borrowing three different definitions. Nonetheless, our methodology is limited by the use of hashtags and images, as not all selfies will contain such explicit markers.

Another limitation is in the scope of cultural interpretation. Understanding cultural contexts is immensely important, but also very challenging because it is difficult to separate out the complex interplay among socioeconomic factors. This work employed a handful of popular indicators and attempted to provide better explanations for country-wise variations. This, although preliminary, is a meaningful first step towards understanding how a new online phenomenon spread across the world.

6.3 Future Directions

Many questions addressed by this work could be investigated in greater detail to highlight possible nuances not captured by the experiments done. For example, an evaluation of how exactly Face++ accuracy is impacted by the particularities of selfies (close-up, distorted or partial views of a face, etc.) could help to know if there are adjustments to be made in this respect; a detailed analysis of usage patterns and spread of Instagram across countries could reveal how local differences affect the overall temporal dynamics found.

Another possible direction would be to dig further into user-level analyses. For instance, a deeper investigation of general differences in users activities in the network could allow to identify how to appropriately take these differences into account when studying interactions among users. A diverse approach could be to verify how selfie-related behaviors vary from user to user or even across different classes of users (e.g., celebrities and occasional users). This could also bring information about the effect of users characteristics on the engagement associated with the selfies they publish.

Given its multifaceted character, selfies present yet many dimensions not explored in this research. The attachment of selfies with emotions, for example, could be investigated combining different

sentiment analysis methods [15] based on comments, captions and hashtags related to selfies.

Acknowledgments

We thank the reviewers and our shepherd, Emre Kiciman, for providing valuable comments that helped us improve the paper.

This work was partially supported by CAPES, CNPq, FAPEMIG, and the Brazilian National Institute of Science and Technology for the Web – InWeb. This work was also supported by the IT R&D program of MSIP/KEIT (R0184-15-1037) and the BK21 Plus Postgraduate Organization for Content Science of Korea.

7. REFERENCES

[1] W. V. S. Association. World values survey wave 6 2010-2014. http://www.worldvaluessurvey.org/, Apr 2015.

[2] S. Bakhshi, D. A. Shamma, and E. Gilbert. Faces engage us: Photos with faces attract more likes and comments on instagram. In *ACM Conference on Human Factors in Computing Systems*, 2014.

[3] Y. Bekhouche, R. Hausmann, S. Zahidi, and L. D. Tyson. The global gender gap report 2014. Technical report, World Economic Forum, 2014.

[4] C. Bjørnskov. Determinants of generalized trust: A cross-country comparison. *Public Choice*, 130(1-2):1–21, 2007.

[5] K. W. Church and P. Hanks. Word association norms, mutual information, and lexicography. *Computational Linguistics*, 16(1):22–29, Mar. 1990.

[6] N. L. Cole. The Selfie Debates, Part I. http://sociology.about.com/od/Ask-a-Sociologist/fl/The-Selfie-Debates-Part-I.htm.

[7] N. L. Cole. The Selfie Debates, Part II. http://sociology.about.com/od/Current-Events-in-Sociological-Context/fl/The-Selfie-Debates-Part-II.htm.

[8] N. L. Cole. Why we selfie. http://sociology.about.com/od/Ask-a-Sociologist/fl/Why-We-Selfie.htm.

[9] J. Crook. Know thy selfie. http://techcrunch.com/2014/02/24/know-thy-selfie/, Feb 2014.

[10] R. Dey, M. Nangia, K. W. Ross, and Y. Liu. Estimating heights from photo collections: A data-driven approach. In *ACM Conference on Online Social Networks*, 2014.

[11] Ebay. Digital Vanity. http://deals.ebay.com/blog/the-selfie-revolution/, Oct 2013.

[12] J. D. Foster, W. K. Campbell, and J. M. Twenge. Individual differences in narcissism: Inflated self-views across the lifespan and around the world. *Journal of Research in Personality*, 37(6):469 – 486, 2003.

[13] J. Fox and M. C. Rooney. The dark triad and trait self-objectification as predictors of men's use and self-presentation behaviors on social networking sites. *Personality and Individual Differences*, 76(0):161 – 165, 2015.

[14] R. Garcia-Gavilanes, D. Quercia, and A. Jaimes. Cultural dimensions in twitter: Time, individualism and power. In *International AAAI Conference on Weblogs and Social Media*, 2013.

---

[5]http://goo.gl/cpqhhE

[15] P. Gonçalves, M. Araújo, F. Benevenuto, and M. Cha. Comparing and combining sentiment analysis methods. In *ACM Conference on Online Social Networks*, 2013.

[16] R. Hijmans. GADM database of Global Administrative Areas, version 2.0. http://www.gadm.org/, Jan 2012.

[17] N. Hochman and R. Schwartz. Visualizing instagram: Tracing cultural visual rhythms. In *International AAAI Conference on Weblogs and Social Media*, pages 6–9, 2012.

[18] G. Hofstede. Cultural dimensions in management and planning. *Asia Pacific Journal of Management*, 1(2):81–99, 1984.

[19] Y. Hu, L. Manikonda, and S. Kambhampati. What we instagram: A first analysis of instagram photo content and user types. In *International AAAI Conference on Weblogs and Social Media*, 2014.

[20] J. Y. Jang, K. Han, P. C. Shih, and D. Lee. Generation like: Comparative characteristics in instagram. In *ACM Conference on Human Factors in Computing Systems*, 2015.

[21] J. Joo, W. Li, F. Steen, and S.-C. Zhu. Visual persuasion: Inferring communicative intents of images. In *IEEE Conference on Computer Vision and Pattern Recognition*, 2014.

[22] J. Kilner. The science behind why we take selfies. http://www.bbc.com/news/blogs-magazine-monitor-25763704, Jan 2014.

[23] E. Losh. Beyond biometrics: Feminist media theory looks at selfiecity. Technical report, Softtware Studies Initiative, 2014.

[24] K. S. Lyness and M. K. Judiesch. Gender egalitarianism and work–life balance for managers: Multisource perspectives in 36 countries. *Applied Psychology*, 63(1):96–129, 2014.

[25] A. E. Marwick. Instafame: Luxury selfies in the attention economy. *Public Culture*, 27(1 75):137–160, 2015.

[26] M. McPherson, L. Smith-Lovin, and J. M. Cook. Birds of a feather: Homophily in social networks. *Annual Review of Sociology*, 27(1):415–444, 2001.

[27] Megvii Inc. Face++ research toolkit. http://www.faceplusplus.com/, Dec 2013.

[28] E. P. Meier and J. Gray. Facebook photo activity associated with body image disturbance in adolescent girls. *Cyberpsychology, Behavior, and Social Networking*, 17(4):199–206, 2014.

[29] E. Pariser. *The Filter Bubble: What the Internet Is Hiding from You*. The Penguin Group, 2011.

[30] Pew Research Center. Social media update 2014. http://www.pewinternet.org/2015/01/09/social-media-update-2014/, Jan 2015.

[31] E. Sarigol, D. Garcia, and F. Schweitzer. Online privacy as a collective phenomenon. In *ACM Conference on Online Social Networks*, 2014.

[32] O. Schwarz. On friendship, boobs and the logic of the catalogue: Online self-portraits as a means for the exchange of capital. *Convergence: The International Journal of Research into New Media Technologies*, 16(2):163–183, 2010.

[33] T. H. Silva, P. O. S. V. de Melo, J. M. Almeida, J. Salles, and A. A. F. Loureiro. A picture of Instagram is worth more than a thousand words: Workload characterization and application. In *IEEE International Conference on Distributed Computing in Sensor Systems*, 2013.

[34] A. Tifentale and L. Manovich. Selfiecity: Exploring photography and self-fashioning in social media. Technical report, Softtware Studies Initiative, 2014.

[35] K. Tiidenberg. Bringing sexy back: Reclaiming the body aesthetic via self-shooting. *Cyberpsychology: Journal of Psychosocial Research on Cyberspace*, 8(1), 2014.

[36] J. M. Twenge and W. K. Campbell. *The Narcissism Epidemic: Living in the Age of Entitlement*. Free Press, April 2010.

[37] T. Vinson and M. Ericson. The social dimensions of happiness and life satisfaction of australians: Evidence from the world values survey. *International Journal of Social Welfare*, 23(3):240–253, 2014.

[38] C. Wilson. The selfiest cities in the world: Time's definitive ranking. http://time.com/selfies-cities-world-rankings/, Mar 2014.

[39] J. Winston. Photography in the age of facebook. *Intersect: The Stanford Journal of Science, Technology and Society*, 6(2), 2013.

[40] Y. C. Zhang, D. Ó. Séaghdha, D. Quercia, and T. Jambor. Auralist: Introducing serendipity into music recommendation. In *ACM International Conference on Web Search and Data Mining*, pages 13–22, 2012.

Characterizing Conversation Patterns in Reddit: From the Perspectives of Content Properties and User Participation Behaviors

Daejin Choi
Seoul National University
djchoi@mmlab.snu.ac.kr

Jinyoung Han
University of California, Davis
rghan@ucdavis.edu

Taejoong Chung
Seoul National University
tjchung@mmlab.snu.ac.kr

Yong-Yeol Ahn
Indiana University
yyahn@indiana.edu

Byung-Gon Chun
Seoul National University
bgchun@snu.ac.kr

Ted "Taekyoung" Kwon
Seoul National University
tkkwon@snu.ac.kr

ABSTRACT

It becomes the norm for people to communicate with one another through various online social channels, where different conversation structures are formed depending on platforms. One of the common online communication patterns is a threaded conversation where a user brings up a conversation topic, and then other people respond to the initiator or other participants by commenting, which can be modeled as a tree structure. This paper seeks to investigate (i) the characteristics of online threaded conversations in terms of volume, responsiveness, and virality and (ii) what and how content properties and user participation behaviors are associated with such characteristics. To this end, we collect 700 K threaded conversations from 1.5 M users in Reddit, one of the most popular online communities allowing people to communicate with others in the form of threaded conversations. Using the collected dataset, we find that 'social' words, difficulties of texts, and document relevancy are associated with the volume, responsiveness, and virality of conversations. We also discover that large, viral conversations are mostly formed by a small portion of users who are reciprocally communicate with others by analyzing user interactions. Our analysis on discovering user roles in conversations reveal that users who are interested in multiple topics play important roles in large and viral conversations, whereas heavy posting users play important roles in responsive conversations. We expand our analysis to topical communities (i.e., subreddits) and find that news-related, image-based, and discussion-related communities are more likely to have large, responsive, and viral conversations, respectively.

Categories and Subject Descriptors

H.3.5 [**Online Information Services**]: Web-based services; H.4.3 [**Communications Applications**]: Bulletin

boards; J.4 [**Computer Applications**]: Social and Behavioral Sciences

Keywords

Reddit; Online Communication; Threaded Conversation; Comment; Subreddits; User Behavior; Virality;

1. INTRODUCTION

The advances in information technology over a couple of decades have been revolutionizing how people communicate with one another. *Online* communication channels, such as messengers, online social networks (OSNs), or social media, have become important in everyday life. These online digital channels of communications are not only facilitating the communications among people, but also producing a deluge of social data. Such data in turn enables computational data-driven studies on human behaviors and communication patterns, often dubbed as "Computational Social Science" [20].

From the old message boards such as USENET or BBS to the recent OSNs like Twitter and Facebook, there have been many computational data-driven studies that provide valuable insights into communication patterns on various online spaces [14, 18, 22–24, 26]. One of the common communication patterns is a *threaded conversation* that can effectively capture how people communicate with each other for a given particular topic in a structural fashion. In a threaded conversation, a person (or an initiator) brings up a conversation topic (by uploading a write-up or posting her opinion), and then other people (or participants) respond to the initiator or other participants recursively, which can be modeled as a tree structure.

This paper first seeks to model and characterize a threaded (online) conversation from three perspectives: (i) **volume** — how big the conversation is, (ii) **responsiveness** — how fast conversation participants react to the conversation initiator or other participants, and (iii) **virality** — how many participants elicit others to join the conversation. Note that the virality mostly refers to how content (or information) is spread by word-of-mouth mechanisms, or more specifically, how many nodes in a cascade are responsible for attracting other nodes. In this sense, we explore *the virality of a threaded conversation* that can quantify how participants' comments elicit others' responses, which signifies a multi-

COSN'15, November 2–3, 2015, Palo Alto, California, USA.
© 2015 ACM. ISBN 978-1-4503-3951-3/15/11 ...$15.00.
DOI: http://dx.doi.org/10.1145/2817946.2817959.

generative property of the threaded conversation. We also investigate what factors (e.g., participant or content properties) are associated with the volume, responsiveness, and virality of a threaded conversation, which might be the key to modeling online conversation patterns. Such a model has a great utility in predicting future online conversation patterns, which can provide valuable implication on content providers, opinion leaders, or marketers.

To this end, we collect and analyze posts and comments on `Reddit`, one of the most popular online communities where users can communicate with one another in a threaded conversation for sharing their topical interests. In Reddit, there are various topical communities, so-called *"subreddits"*, each of which provides an independent space for users who are interested in any particular topic, e.g., game, politics, or sports. According to *Reddit*[1], as of May 2015, more than 169 M unique users (from 209 countries) have visited more than 7.5 B pages in Reddit. As of May 2015, Reddit is the 25th and 11st most popular web site in the world and the United States, respectively [1]. A user in Reddit can (i) visit a topical community (subreddit) to browse content, (ii) submit either self-writing or URL link content, (iii) write a comment on such content, and (iv) write a comment to another comment.

Using the collected dataset, we seek answers to the following questions by investigating the patterns of threaded conversations observed in Reddit: How can we characterize an online threaded conversation in terms of volume, responsiveness, and virality? What are the main drivers (e.g., user participation behaviors or content properties) that determine large, responsive, or viral conversations? How do conversations in different topical communities (or subreddits) show similar or different patterns?

To answer such questions, we analyze a large dataset (700 K posts and 18 M associated comments generated by 1.5 M users) that we collected from March 13 to April 18, 2014 from Reddit. By keeping track of all the newly-uploaded posts and their follow-up comments, we extract 700 K threaded conversations, each of which is represented as a *comment tree* model. That is, since users can leave comment(s) for all posts and comments, each post or comment can have follow-up comments in a nested fashion, forming a tree structure for a conversation[2]. Based on the comment tree model, we investigate the volume, responsiveness, and virality of each online conversation, and explore how the content properties and user participation behaviors are associated with them.

We highlight the main contributions of our work as follows:

- **Measurement:** To our knowledge, this is the first large-scale, extensive measurement study that characterizes the online conversation patterns in Reddit in terms of volume, responsiveness, and virality, based on 700 K comment trees shared by 1.5 M users. We make our anonymized dataset online at: `http://mmlab.snu.ac.kr/traces/reddit`.

- **Content Properties of Conversations:** We explore whether content properties, e.g., sentiment or difficulty, are associated with the volume, responsiveness,

---

[1] http://www.reddit.com/about

[2] In this paper, we consider a (threaded) conversation as a set of communications among participants associated to a post (i.e., the root).

and virality of conversations. We find that large, responsive, and viral conversations tend to have (i) social words and (ii) high document relevancy between parent and child comments. Interestingly, the difficulty of content texts is an important indicator that can differentiate large/viral and responsive conversations; a large/viral conversation is likely to have difficult texts, whereas a responsive conversation tends to have plain texts.

- **Users' Participation in Conversations:** We investigate how characteristics of users' participation behaviors in a conversation (i.e., a comment tree) are associated with the volume, responsiveness, and virality of the comment tree. We find that a large and viral comment tree is often generated from a small portion of users who reciprocally communicate to each other in the tree. Interestingly, users who are interested in multiple topics play important roles in large and viral conversations, whereas heavy posting users play more roles in responsive conversations.

- **Conversations in Different Topical Communities (Subreddits):** We explore the conversation patterns in different topical communities (i.e., subreddits) in Reddit. We find that the news-related and image-based subreddits are more likely to have large and responsive conversations, respectively. On the other hand, we observe that the conversations in discussion-related subreddits tend to be viral, implying that discussions are likely to elicit many other users to join the conversations.

The rest of this paper is organized as follows. We present the background of Reddit and review the related work in Section 2. We explain our measurement and analysis methodology in Section 3. We start our analysis by investigating characteristics of comment trees in Section 4. We then analyze how the comment trees show different patterns across topical communities in Section 5, followed by concluding remarks in Section 6.

2. BACKGROUND

2.1 Reddit

Reddit allows users to share news, articles, and opinions with each other on the areas of interests. The areas of topical interests in Reddit are called "subreddits", each of which serves as an independent community. A subreddit can be created by any user who is interested in any particular topic, e.g., game, politics, or sports. Each subreddit is managed by several "moderators" who are responsible for moderating and policing conversations among members. In each subreddit, users can (i) submit content (i.e., write a post), (ii) write a comment to a post, or (iii) write a comment to another comment. Figure 1 shows an illustration of a post and its associated comments in "Today I Learned (TIL)" subreddit. Note that we collectively refer to both a post and a comment as a "message".

2.2 Related Work

Online conversation: Online communications with diverse forms (e.g., messengers, social media) have begun to dominate everyday social interactions. This has spurred

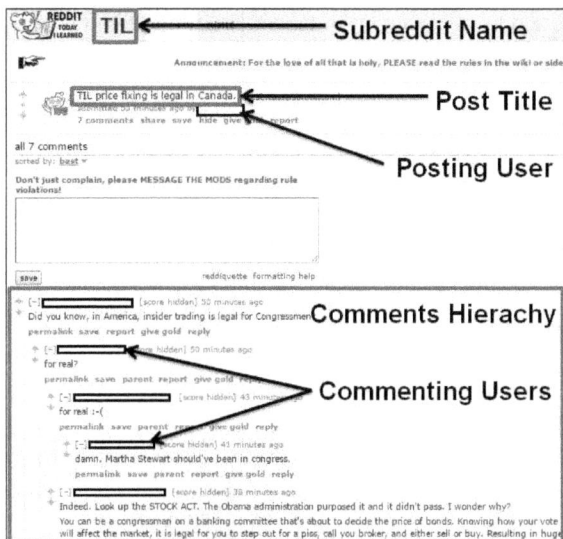

Figure 1: A post with its associated comments in the subreddit "Today I Learned (TIL)" is illustrated.

studies on online communication behavior across different systems such as online chatting [23], online communities [14, 18, 22], and OSNs [24, 26]. Mayfield *et al.* investigated a way to disentangle the conversation threads from multipart chatting [23]. With Yahoo!, USENET, and Twitter datasets, Kumar *et al.* investigated (i) the volume, depth, and degree of posts, and (ii) the number of users in each conversation thread, and proposed a conversation growth model based on the properties [18]. Marcoccia investigated conversation threads in USENET newsgroups [22], similar to subreddits in Reddit, and found that their sizes tend to be small and sometimes messages are misplaced. Gomez *et al.* explored discussion patterns on Slashdot [14], which is a technology-related news website where users can post and comment, and found that the degree distribution of conversations follows a log-normal distribution, and conversation threads show the strong heterogeneity and self-similarity. Rossi *et al.* analyzed conversations generated from specific hashtags in Twitter, and found that a choice of hashtags could make a conversation between users with non-reciprocal friendship [24]. Wang *et al.* proposed a model to predict the volume of conversations in Digg.com, and also applied the model to different platforms such as Twitter and Reddit [26]. We focus on analyzing what factors (e.g., participant or content properties) are associated with the volume, responsiveness, and virality of a threaded conversation in Reddit, which can provide important implications on modeling and understanding online conversation patterns.

Reddit – popular online communities: Reddit has recently received a great attention as it becomes one of the largest online communities where people can communicate with one another sharing a variety of interests [11, 25]. Recently, many researchers have investigated user behaviors [9, 17], commenting patterns [10, 27], and content popularity [11, 19, 21, 25] on Reddit. Singer *et al.* investigated the user preferences for different topics shared among Reddit users [25]. The two case studies on "Hurricane Sandy" [21] and "duplicated image submissions" [19] some distinct factors that affect content popularity in Reddit. Gilbert showed

popular images attract more attention and newly-uploaded images are under-provisioned in Reddit [11]. Weninger *et al.* analyzed top-scoring posts and their comments in Reddit, and showed that comments in closer positions in a comment tree are topically more similar than the ones in farther positions [27]. Choudhury *et al.* investigated texts of the posts and comments that contain self-discourse about mental health in Reddit, and found that posts with higher emotional intensity tend to receive more comments [10]. In this paper, we characterize conversations in terms of volume, responsiveness, and virality, and explore what and how characteristics of content and user participation are associated with such criteria.

Information/Content cascade in OSNs: As OSNs have become popular platforms in sharing information or content, there have been great efforts in investigating the patterns of information (or content) cascades in OSNs [4, 6, 7, 13, 16]. Cha *et al.* analyzed photo propagation patterns in Flickr and showed that photos do not spread widely and quickly in Flickr [6]. Goel *et al.* [13] analyzed the cascades of URLs in Yahoo! and Twitter, and found that the majority of the diffusions occur within one hop from a seed node. Han *et al.* analyzed the cascades of pins (i.e., images) in Pinterest, and showed that pin propagation in Pinterest is mostly driven by pin's properties such as its topic, not by user's characteristics like the number of followers [16]. Cheng *et al.* showed that temporal and structural features are key factors to predict the size of a photo cascade generated by resharing in Facebook [7]. These studies have analyzed how information (or content) such as images or URLs is reshared, thereby generating a cascade, and what factors drive such information/content cascades in OSNs. On the other hand, we consider a threaded conversation cascade among participants associated to a post (i.e., the root). We further explore how user participation or content properties issued by a post lead to large, responsive, and viral conversation cascades on Reddit.

3. METHODOLOGY

In this section, we detail our measurement methodology for data collection, and describe the dataset used in this paper. We then characterize a conversation in terms of volume, responsiveness, and virality, with *a comment tree* model.

3.1 Data Collection

We first analyze the patterns of posting/commenting activities in Reddit and then derive user interactions from the activities. To retrieve posts and associated comments, we developed our measurement system for data collection and analysis as shown in Figure 2. The measurement system consists of three parts: (i) Reddit interface module, (ii) core module, and (iii) DB module. The Reddit interface module communicates with Reddit.com through the APIs[3] provided by Reddit. We utilize 'Python Reddit API Wrapper (PRAW)[4]' package.

To monitor all the posts and their follow-up comments, we developed two key submodules in the core module: the post observer and comment observer. Once in every minute, the post observer monitors and fetches all new posts in

---

[3]Reddit provides public APIs, through which third party applications such as crawlers and readers are supported.
[4]http://praw.readthedocs.org/en/v2.1.16/

235

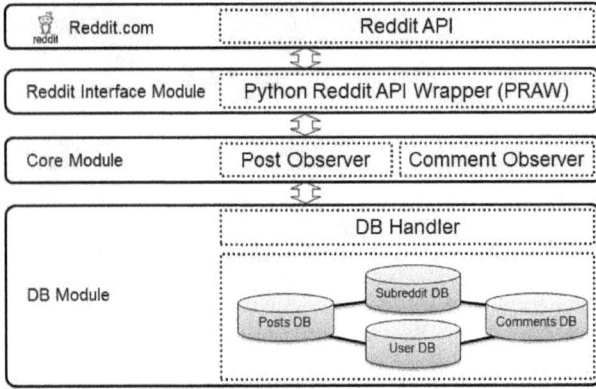

Figure 2: The architecture of the Reddit measurement system is depicted.

each subreddit. At the time of our data collection, Reddit APIs provided up to $1,000$ recent posts in each subreddit in the chronological order; hence our crawler fetches up to $1,000$ posts every minute not to miss newly-uploaded posts. Whenever the post observer identifies a new post, the comment observer begins to keep track of all the comments relevant to the post. Similarly, the comment observer monitors and collect every comment associated with the posts that we have fetched. We collected every single post and comment during our measurement period since the observed maximum number of messages per minute was 722, which did not exceed the collected message limit of the Reddit API. The collected dataset is stored in the DB module.

Our measurement focuses on the top 100 subreddits in terms of the number of subscribers, which are responsible a large portion of Reddic conversations. Note that the top 100 subreddits account for more than 60% of all subscribers (out of $378,293$ subreddits, as of Oct. 22, 2014) in Reddit. We collected the dataset for 35 days from March 13 to April 18, 2014, which contains $1,016,342$ posts and $18,626,530$ comments, shared by $1,531,247$ users. We then extracted $695,857$ (68.5%) posts that each have at least one comment, and their $18,093,422$ comments; posts and comments are written by $1,455,293$ users. Each post contains the `author id`, `title`, `subreddit id`, and `timestamp`, while each comment contains the `original post id`, `user id`, `comment text`, and `parent id` from which the comment is generated.

3.2 Comment Tree

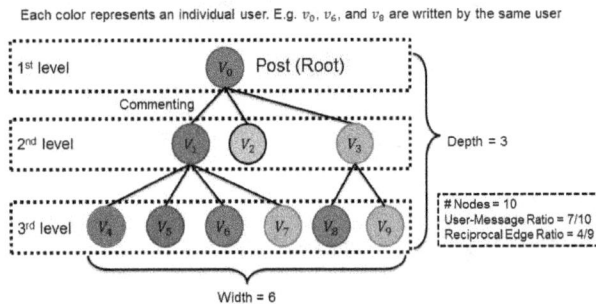

Figure 3: A comment tree is illustrated for a post that has 9 comments.

To model a conversation thread from a given post and its follow-up comments, we define a *comment tree* as an undirected tree, $T = (V, E)$, where V is the set of all messages, which includes the original post (root) and all the follow-up comments in the thread, and E is the set of edges, each of which connects two messages that are linked by commenting. Figure 3 illustrates a comment tree that has one post and nine comments.

We characterize comment tree T based on the following three metrics:

- **Volume** (N_T): The volume of tree T is the number of nodes, $|V|$, in the tree. For instance, N_T of the tree in Figure 3 is 10.

- **Responsiveness** (R_T): To capture how quickly users participate in (or respond to) a conversation, we first calculate the time differences between a comment and its parent node (the post or comment). We only consider the time differences within the range of $[\mu - 2\sigma, \mu + 2\sigma]$ to exclude outliers, where the μ is the average time difference of parent-child edges of the given tree. We then calculate the average of the inverses of time differences, *responsiveness* R_T, which indicates the average number of messages generated in a comment tree (during a minute). Hence, the higher responsiveness a tree has, the faster users add comments to the tree.

- **Virality** (V_T): The *(structural) virality* of a cascade, also known as Wiener Index (WI) [7,12], seeks to quantify the average range of a node's effect on the conversation in terms of connectivity. That is, given the same number of nodes, the WI becomes the minimum when all comments are directly added to the root, and the maximum when the tree becomes a chain (the depth of a tree is the number of nodes in the tree). The former indicates that no subsequent spreading has occurred except at the first generation and the latter indicates that every comment (except the last one) is followed by another comment as shown in Figure 4 (the leftmost and rightmost ones, respectively). Formally, the WI of a tree is defined by the average hop count over all node pairs in the tree. The WIs are calculated for the four 10-node comment trees in Figure 4 for illustration purposes.

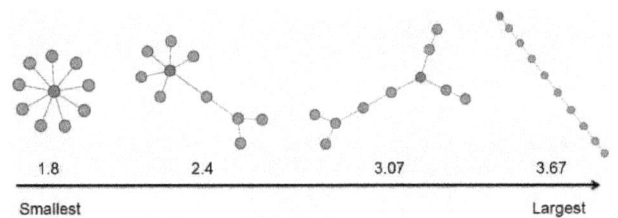

Figure 4: Virality values are calculated for 10-node comment trees ($N_T = 10$).

Figure 5 shows the distributions of the volume, responsiveness, and virality values of the comment trees. The volume distribution exhibits a heavy tail that spans several orders of magnitudes. For instance, as shown in Figure 5(a), while

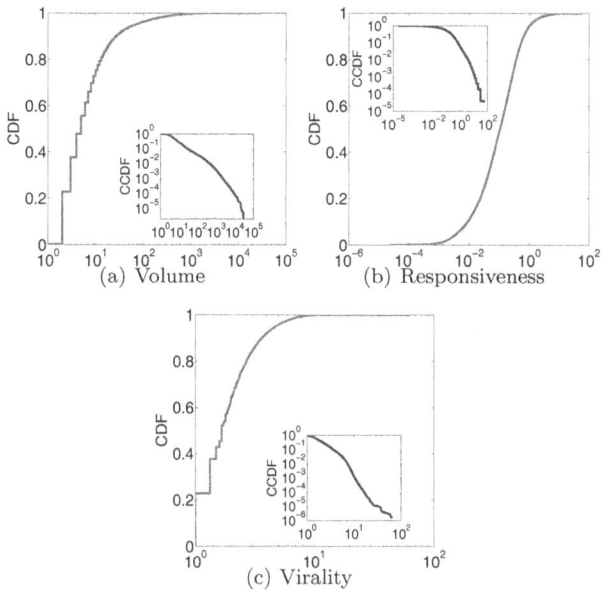

Figure 5: Distributions of volume, responsiveness, and virality of comment trees are plotted for all the comment trees.

72.8% of trees consist of less than 10 nodes, top 0.1% of the trees attracted more than 2, 211 messages, indicating a large deviation among threads. The virality distribution also exhibits a heavy-tailed distribution although the range of virality values only spans two orders of magnitudes. As shown in Figure 5(c), around 99.8% of the virality values are smaller than 10, and top 0.1% of the virality values greater than 50 (the maximum is 63.44). The average virality values of the comment trees is 2.09, which implies a comment in a tree are likely to span around 2 levels on average. On the other hand, the responsiveness distribution follows a Gaussian-like distribution. The average of responsiveness values is 0.32, which implies that an average inter-comment time is around 3 minutes. In addition, the responsiveness values of the top 5% of trees are more than one (i.e., more than one comment every minute), meaning that those trees are highly responsive, while the comments of the bottom 15% of trees are generated once per hour on average.

4. COMMENT TREE ANALYSIS

In this section, we analyze the conversations (i.e., comment trees) in terms of content and user participation properties. To this end, we first divide comment trees into five intervals in terms of volume, responsiveness, and virality, respectively, and then explore the characteristics of the comment trees in each interval. Note that we perform one-way ANOVA tests for our analyses, and we find that all the p-values are smaller than 0.05.

4.1 Content Perspectives

We first perform the text analysis for every comment tree by measuring its semantics and other properties to characterize the content of the tree. We then investigate how these characteristics are related to the volume, responsiveness, and virality of the comment trees.

4.1.1 Semantic Characteristics

We first perform a semantic analysis by using LIWC (Linguistic Inquiry and Word Count), which is text analysis software that counts words that belong to psychologically meaningful categories. For a given text, the LIWC tool provides various sentimental scores, each of which is calculated as the relative frequency of the words in the given sentiment category on a percentile scale, out of all the words in the text. We use the three categories: social, positive and negative emotions. For example, the words "family" and "friends" belong to the social category, and "love" and "sweet" are in the positive emotion category, while "hurt" and "nasty" belong to the negative emotion category. Note that we compute the LIWC scores for (i) titles of posts (since there are some posts containing only multimedia content without any text), and (ii) all the texts written in comments.

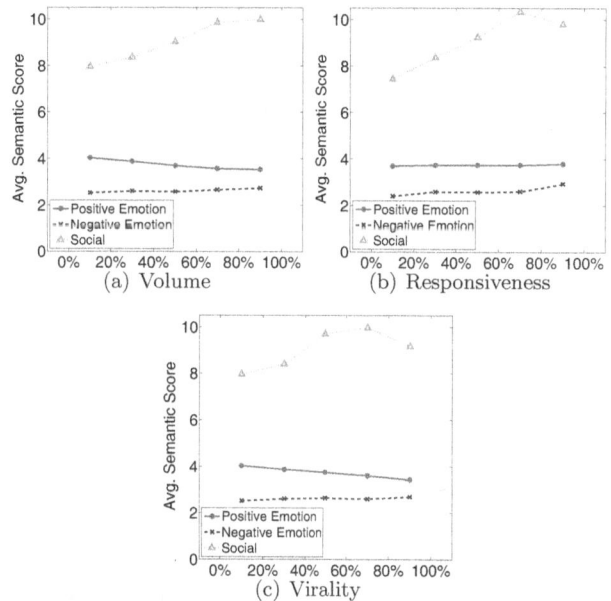

Figure 6: The distributions of emotional scores of posts are plotted.

Figures 6 and 7 indicate that social words are more frequently used than words of positive emotions, which in turn are more frequently used than words of negative emotions. We notice that this trend is also in line with the sentiment analysis on blogs, emotional writing, and talking [2]. There are no significant differences in the two emotional scores as the volume, responsiveness, and virality increase. On the other hand, the social scores of the titles tend to be high in larger, more responsive, and viral trees. The plotting of social scores of titles implies that a post whose title contains more social words is likely to be able to generate large, responsive, and viral trees to a certain degree.

4.1.2 Document Difficulty

We next measure whether the (readability) difficulties of titles and texts of trees are related to their volume, responsiveness, and virality. To this end, we compute Gunning-Fog Index, a popular readability score to estimate what grade of students is suitable to read the text [15]. That is, if the index of a text is 12, the text requires the 12th grade ability (around 18 years old). The Gunning-Fog index of a comment

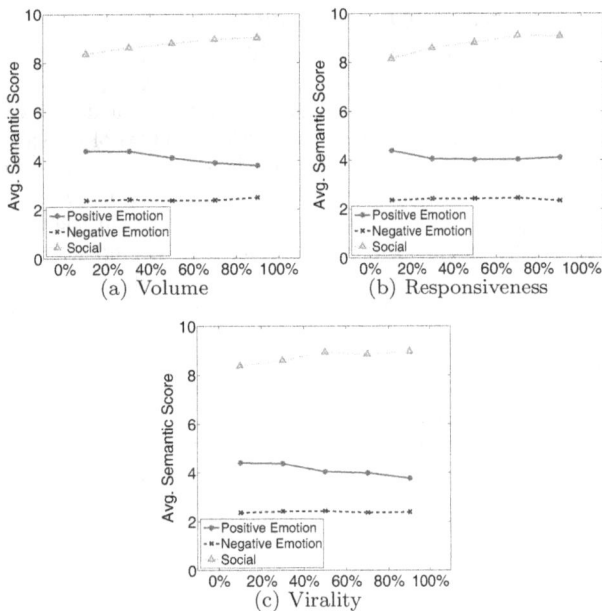

Figure 7: Semantic scores of texts in conversation trees are plotted.

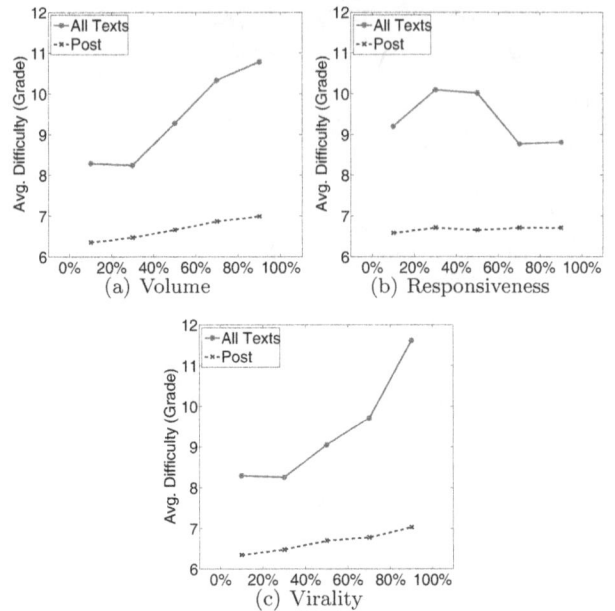

Figure 8: The average difficulties of trees and posts are plotted as the volume, responsiveness, and virality increase.

tree T is defined by:

$$G_T = 0.4[(\frac{N_{words}^T}{N_{sentences}^T}) + 100(\frac{N_{complex}^T}{N_{words}^T})] \qquad (1)$$

where N_{words}^T, $N_{sentences}^T$, and $N_{complex}^T$, are the numbers of words, sentences and complex words in texts, respectively. A complex word is defined as the word that contains three or more syllables excluding proper nouns, familiar jargon, compound words, and words with common suffixes such as -es, -ed. As similar to the semantic analysis, we finally calculate the difficulties of comment trees for (i) title of a post and (ii) all texts of a comment tree (including its title).

Figure 8 plots the text difficulties of the title and the texts of the comment trees. As shown in Figure 8, the average difficulty of the texts of a tree ranges mostly from 8 to 12, and is generally larger than that of its title (around 6 to 7) since a title is usually short and consists of a few keywords. Interestingly, the difficulties of both the titles of posts and the texts of comment trees increase notably as the volume increases, and more rapidly as the virality increases. This implies that a larger and more viral tree tends to consist of comments with more difficult words on average. On the other hand, the difficulties of the texts of the top 40% responsive trees are lower than less responsive trees, which implies using less and more plain words is positively related to the quick responsiveness.

4.1.3 Document Relevancy

We finally observe whether the relevance between two messages are related to volume, responsiveness, and virality. To this end, we compute the message relevance by using the Term Frequency-Inverse Document Frequency (TF-IDF) similarity, one of the popular metrics to measure the similarity between two documents in information retrieval area [3]. For each word, its TF-IDF is defined as the product of TF and IDF, each of which quantifies how frequently the word is used in a document, and whether the word is common or

rare between two documents, respectively. Thus, a TF-IDF similarity score (of a given word) is high (i) if the word is used in the document frequently and/or (ii) if the word is rarely used in the two documents, and vice versa. Before calculating the TF-IDF similarity, we remove stop-words (e.g., at, which), and perform Porter stemming by using *Natural Language Toolkit*. After measuring the TF-IDF score for each word, we then compute the cosine similarity of two score vectors between two documents. (The vector dimension is the number of distinct words in the two documents.) The cosine similarity being 1 means the two documents are almost identical, while 0 indicates no words are shared.

Figure 9 shows the document similarity (1) between a post and its child comments, or (2) between a parent and its child comments. As a reference, we measure the cosine similarity between any pair of messages in a tree (even if there is no parent-child link), labeled as baseline. As shown in Figure 9, the average document similarity in the first case decreases as the volume and virality increase, while the one in the second case increases. This result reveals that topics may somewhat digress in large and viral conversations although the parent-child comments become increasingly relevant as the volume and virality grow from their medians. Furthermore, highly responsive trees exhibit high similarity in both cases, which implies quickly-generated comments are more relevant to their parent messages.

4.2 User Participation in Comment Trees

We seek to understand how (user) participation behaviors are associated with volume, responsiveness, and virality of comment trees. To quantify participation behaviors, we compute Gini coefficients, reciprocal edge ratio, and user-message ratio across the five intervals. We then investigate how different roles of users are related to generating large, responsive, and viral comment trees.

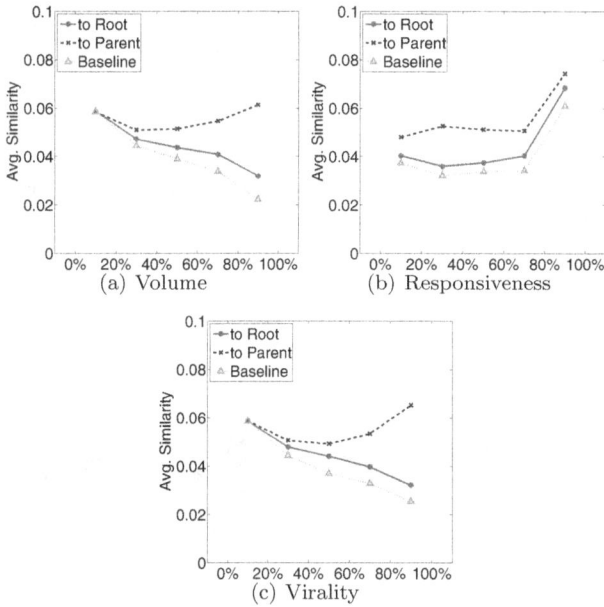

Figure 9: The relevance among messages of a comment tree is plotted.

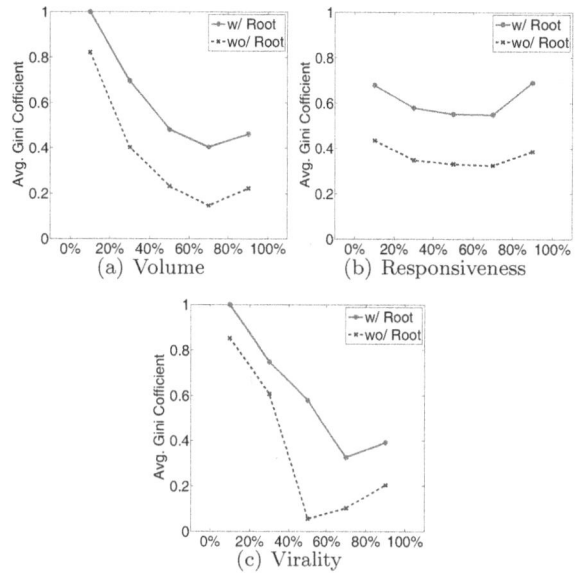

Figure 10: Average of Gini coefficients of comment trees are plotted as the volume, responsiveness, and virality increase.

4.2.1 Participation Behaviors of Users

We first quantify the skewness (variability) of comment generation in a tree by computing the *Gini Coefficient*, a metric that is most commonly used to capture inequality of income distribution in Economics [8]. The Gini coefficient, represented in the range of [0, 1], increases as the distribution of incomes is increasingly skewed. Thus, in our case the coefficient becomes 0 if every node in a tree has the same number of child nodes, and the coefficient is 1 in the opposite case (i.e., only one node (i.e., post) has all the child nodes). Note that we calculate two kinds of Gini coefficients for a tree: with or without a root (i.e., a post).

Figure 10 plots the average Gini coefficients for each interval in terms of volume, responsiveness and virality. Overall, the Gini coefficient with roots is higher than the one without roots, which implies users are more likely to reply to posts in general. For both cases, the values sharply decrease as the volume and virality increase, except for the rightmost interval. This indicates that comments in large and viral trees uniformly attract other comments to a certain degree, but extremely large and viral trees have comments that elicit many more follow-up comments than others.

On the other hand, as the responsiveness increases, the Gini coefficients of trees with and without roots do not decrease as much as in the case of volume and virality, and show more symmetric convex patterns. Note that moderately viral trees show low Gini coefficients, which means that messages with the relatively uniform distribution of follow-up comments take somewhat longer inter-message time.

We next investigate how many users are likely to make comments and how reciprocally users communicate in a tree by computing the user-message ratio and reciprocal edge ratio, respectively. The user-message ratio for tree T is defined as the ratio of the number of users participating in T to the volume of T. If every user in a tree submits only one message, its user-message ratio is 1, meaning that every participating user generates exactly one message for the

tree. The reciprocal edge ratio is the ratio of the number of edges generated by reciprocal user pairs (i.e., they exchange comments) to the number of all the edges in the given tree.

Figure 11 shows the reciprocal edge ratio and user-message ratio as the volume, responsiveness, and virality increase. Obviously, the user-message ratio drops in larger and more viral trees, whereas the reciprocal edge ratio increases. This result implies that comments of a large and viral tree are usually generated by a small portion of users who reciprocally communicate to one another. Note that the tendency is more noticeable as the virality increases, which means that extremely viral trees tend to result from intensively reciprocal communications.

Figure 11(b) reveals that the top 20% responsive trees have the smaller reciprocal edge ratio and the higher user-message ratio. This result is in line with Figure 10 in the sense that the portion of reciprocal communications in a comment tree is low since users are more likely to respond to a post in moderately responsive trees.

4.2.2 Roles of Users

To investigate users' special roles in large, responsive, and viral comment trees, we first identify users based on behavioral types as follows:

- U_{post} (or **initiators**) are the top 1% of users in terms of the number of uploaded posts. We call them *initiators* as they initiate conversations by writing many posts.

- U_{cmt} (or **commentators**) are the top 1% users in terms of the number of comments. They participate in conversations by actively commenting to other messages.

- U_{rcvcmt} (or **attractors**) are the top 1% users identified by the number of received comments from others. These users attract many comments from others, and

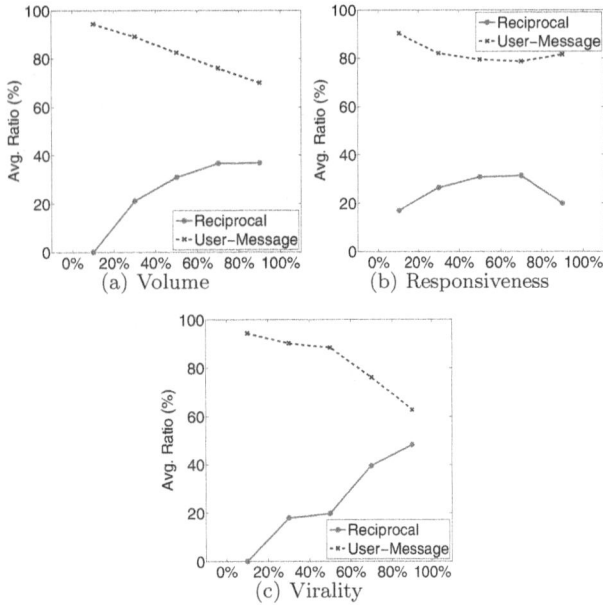

Figure 11: Reciprocal edge ratio and User-Message Ratio are plotted.

	U_{post}	U_{cmt}	U_{rcvcmt}	U_{uni}
U_{post}	1.0	0.14	0.29	0.07
U_{cmt}	0.14	1.0	0.53	0.18
U_{rcvcmt}	0.29	**0.53**	1.0	0.12
U_{uni}	0.07	0.18	0.12	1.0

Table 1: Conditional probabilities among role types are described.

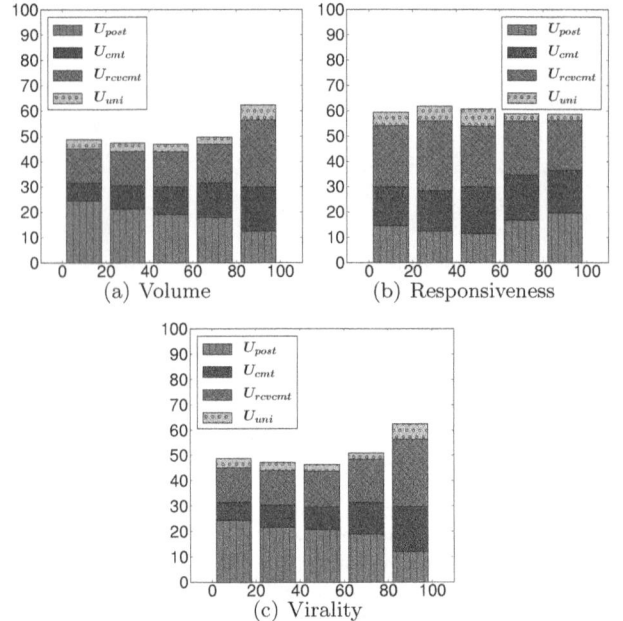

Figure 12: Contribution ratios of four user role types are plotted.

may play a major role in developing large, responsive, or viral conversations.

- U_{uni} **(or translators)** are the users who participate in a number of subreddits. These users are often known as *translators* [5] or *generalists*, who are translating or cross-pollinating content/ideas across multiple communities. To identify such translators, we count the number of messages (i.e., posts and comments) a user has submitted for each subreddit, and then calculate the *subreddit entropy* for each user, U, as follows:

$$Entropy_u = - \sum_{m=1}^{N_{sub}^u} p_m^u \log p_m^u \qquad (2)$$

where N_{sub}^i is the number of subreddits where the user u uploaded messages and p_m^u is the relative message portion of the mth subreddit. We finally choose the top 1% of users based on the subreddit entropy. Since we do not normalize the subreddit entropy with the number of subreddits, the identified translators tend to be those who participate in many subreddits.

Note that the identified users can have multiple role types, and user types can be correlated in principle.

We first measure how (identified) role types are overlapped by calculating the conditional probabilities of each pair of role types in Table 1. As shown in Table 1, 14% of users in U_{post} and U_{cmt} are overlapped, indicating that a small portion of users play important roles both in posting and commenting on Reddit. Note that the probability $p(U_{cmt}|U_{rcvcmt})$ is larger than 0.5, meaning that the users who comment a lot also tend to receive many comments, probably as a result of their active commenting behaviors. Interestingly, the probability of U_{uni} and other role types are mostly low, which implies that users who are interested in multiple topics are distinctive from the users in other activity-related roles.

We now investigate how each role type contribute in large, responsive, and viral conversations, respectively. Figure 12

shows the portions of comments received by the users in each role type. As shown in Figure 12, around 50% of comments are elicited by the four role types, and this portion increases up to about 60% in the top 20% of large and viral conversations. The portion of comments elicited by U_{post} decreases as the conversations are larger and more viral, whereas the ones elicited by others increase, which indicates the users in the U_{post} play diminishing roles in large and viral conversations. Interestingly, U_{uni} attract more comments in the top 20% intervals both by the volume and virality, implying that translators who have broad interests are likely to more attract comments in a large or viral conversation. The responsive conversations show distinctive patterns; the portion of comments elicited by U_{post} increases as the conversations become more responsive, meaning that heavy-posting users play more roles in attracting others' comments in responsive conversations where many of comments are just quick responses to a post content.

5. CONVERSATIONS IN DIFFERENT COMMUNITIES

In this section, we compare subreddits based on conversation patterns captured in volume, responsiveness, and virality of comment trees. Based on these patterns, we also extract the top 10 subreddits in terms of each of the three criteria and further analyze the content properties and users' participation behaviors in each subreddit.

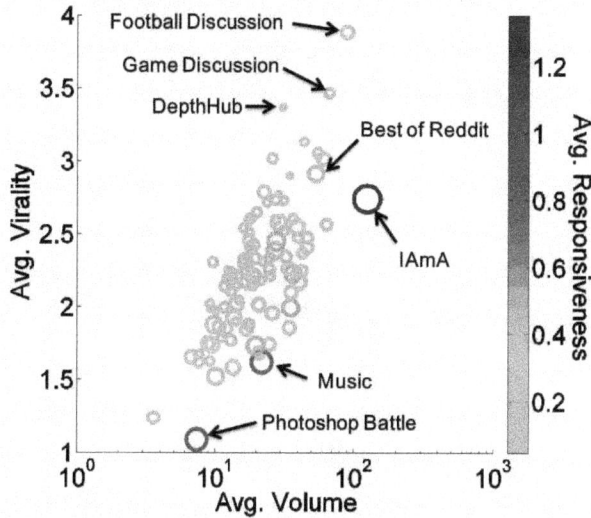

Figure 13: We map subreddits by calculating the average values of their trees in terms of the volume, responsiveness, and virality.

Rank	Volume (S_{vol})	Responsiveness (S_{rsp})	Virality (S_{vrl})
1	IAmA	IAmA	Football Discussion
2	Football Discussion	Photoshop Battle	Game Discussion
3	Game Discussion	Music	DepthHub
4	Technology	Reddit Gold Mine	Android
5	Soccer	Mystery of the soda	You Should Know
6	You Should Know	AskReddit	The Dismal Science
7	Best of Reddit	Science	Soccer
8	World News	Game of Thrones	Best of Reddit
9	TIL	FoodPorn	Frugal Living
10	Android	EarthPorn	Game Deals

Table 2: Top 10 subreddits in terms of volume, responsiveness, and virality are described.

5.1 Conversations in Subreddits

We investigate how conversations in different communities (or subreddits) show different patterns in terms of the volume, responsiveness, and virality. To this end, we first calculate the averages of the three quantities in each subreddit. We then plot *a subreddit map* in Figure 13 where each circle represents a subreddit. The position of a subreddit displays the average volume and virality, while the responsiveness is shown with colors. Note that a larger circle a subreddit is, its conversations tend to have higher responsiveness. For instance, the conversations in subreddit IAmA tend to have the highest volume (i.e., 100) and highest responsiveness (i.e., 1.4), but their virality lies in the middle (i.e., 2.7) among subreddits.

Overall, Figure 13 shows that the average volume and virality of most subreddits exhibit a strong correlation, while there are some outliers. For instance, the conversations in Music or IAmA show large volumes but their viralities tend to be low, while the conversations in DepthHub tend to be viral but their volumes are relatively small. Some subreddits (e.g., Photoshop Battle or Music) show interesting patterns; while their conversations show small volume and low virality, their responsiveness is relatively high, meaning that participants of the conversations in those subreddits are likely to be responsive.

To further analyze conversation patterns in different subreddits in detail, we select the top 10 subreddits ranked by the volume, responsiveness, and virality, respectively, which are listed in Table 2. We refer to the three lists for the volume, responsiveness, and virality as S_{vol}, S_{rsp}, and S_{vrl}, respectively. As shown in Table 2, the three lists, S_{vol}, S_{rsp}, and S_{vrl}, are substantially different. In particular, the 9 subreddits in the S_{rsp} exist in neither S_{vol} nor S_{vrl}, which again indicates that the responsiveness is not so correlated to volume and virality of conversations.

The two lists, S_{vol} and S_{vrl}, are relatively similar; they share six subreddits. The common subreddits between S_{vol} and S_{vrl} are mostly discussion-related subreddits such as Football Discussion, Game Discussion, or Soccer. Yet, subreddits such as Technology, World News, and Today I

Learned (TIL) that are focused on sharing news and useful information tend to appear in S_{vol}, whereas discussion-oriented subreddits such as DepthHub[5] and The Dismal Science are found in S_{vrl}.

On the other hand, S_{rsp} contains many subreddits associated with multimedia content; users are allowed to only upload photos in Photoshop Battle, Reddit Gold Mine, Mystery of the soda, FoodPorn, and EarthPorn, and to link music streaming in Music. This implies that multimedia content usually leads users' quick responses, while quick responses may not lead to large and viral conversations.

Interestingly, IAmA, where people introduce themselves or find some other people to ask something, shows a unique pattern; it ranks the first in terms of both volume and responsiveness, both of which are two disparate lists. Since the conversations in IAmA are often driven by celebrities and imply real-time interactions where an initiator answers questions from commenters, it often draws huge attention (large volume) and is highly responsive (real-time Q&A).

5.2 Content and User Characteristics

We now analyze how content properties and users' participation behaviors are different across the top 10 topical communities in Table 2. For the content properties, we report the three representative metrics, which turn out to be relevant ones with the large, responsive, and viral conversations in Section 4.1: (i) the semantic (social) score of a post, (ii) the document difficulty of a conversation by Gunning-Fog indexes, and (iii) the document relevancy to a post in a conversation.

Figure 14(a) first shows the distributions of the social scores of posts across different topical communities. Note that we exclude outliers to present ones ranging from 25% to 75% of the distribution (as a box plot) to focus on the normal user behavior. For brevity, we refer to n^{th} subreddits in S_{vol}, S_{rsp}, and S_{vrl} as $S_{vol}(n)$, $S_{rsp}(n)$, and $S_{vrl}(n)$, respectively. Overall the distributions of the social scores are different across different topical communities. As shown in Figure 14(a), the medians of the social scores of both IAmA ($S_{vol}(1)$ or $S_{rsp}(1)$) and AskReddit($S_{vol}(6)$) are higher than 10.0, which means that posts in those subreddits tend to use more social words than other subreddits. On the other hand, the social scores of FoodPorn ($S_{rsp}(9)$) and EarthPorn ($S_{rsp}(10)$) are mostly zero, meaning that the posts in those subreddits tend to have few social words.

When we look at the distributions of the document difficulties of comment trees in Figure 14(b), we find that some subreddits in S_{vrl} have higher difficulties than oth-

---

[5]DepthHub gathers the best in-depth submissions and discussions on Reddit.

(a) Semantic (social) Scores of a Post

(b) Document Difficulty of Tree

(c) Document Relevancy to a Post

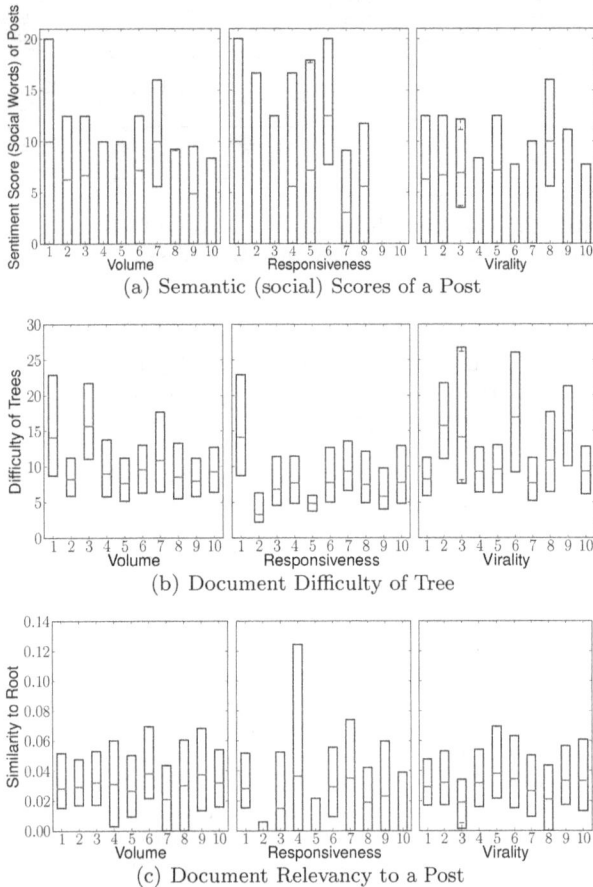

Figure 14: Three content properties across different subreddits are plotted in terms of semantic scores of a post, document difficulty of a tree, and document relevancy to a post.

(a) User-Message Ratio

(b) Reciprocal Edge Ratio

Figure 15: User-message and reciprocal edge ratio values are plotted across subreddits.

ers. For example, the difficulty values of comment trees of Game Discussion $(S_{vrl}(2))$, DepthHub $(S_{vrl}(3))$, The Dismal Science $(S_{vrl}(6))$, and Frugal Living $(S_{vrl}(9))$ are higher than those of other subreddits, most of which are associated with discussion-related subreddits. Note that the conversations in Photoshop Battle $(S_{rsp}(2))$ and Mystery of the soda $(S_{rsp}(5))$ are likely to be easy, which results in responsive conversations. The average document difficulty of IAmA $(S_{vol}(1)$ or $S_{rsp}(1))$ are also high, even though it does not belong to the list S_{vrl}, which suggests that the post of a conversation in IAmA tends to contain social words but its generated comments (including itself) are likely to be difficult.

Figure 14(c) next shows the document relevancy to a post across different subreddits. We find that the document relevancy values of subreddits in S_{vol} and S_{vrl} are almost similar. However, we observe that subreddits in S_{rsp} show different patterns of the document relevancy. The comments in Photoshop Battle and Mystery of the soda are rarely relevant to their posts, whereas the comments in Reddit Gold Mine $(S_{rsp}(4))$ are closely relevant to their posts, which implies that posts in Reddit Gold Mine $(S_{rsp}(4))$ tend to drive users to make their comments on themselves (not on comments, but on posts).

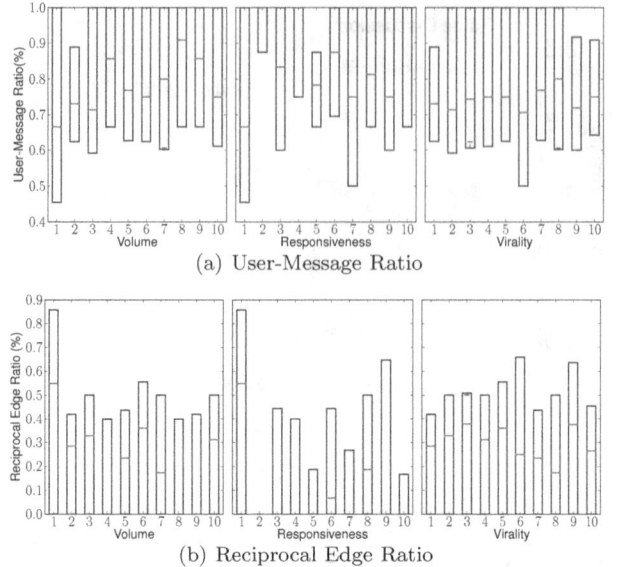

We next investigate users' participation behaviors across the top 10 topical communities in Table 2 with two user metrics plotted in Figure 15: (i) user-message ratio and (ii) reciprocal edge ratio. We find that the user-message ratio values of the most subreddits in S_{vol} and S_{vrl} are relatively lower than the ones in S_{rsp}; the reciprocal edge ratio values of the most subreddits in S_{vol} and S_{vrl} are substantially higher than the ones in S_{rsp}. This result is in line with Section 4.2 that revealed large and viral conversations are likely to have low user-message ratio and high reciprocal edge ratio. However, Technology $(S_{vol}(4))$, World News $(S_{vol}(8))$, and TIL $(S_{vol}(9))$ show an opposite tendency; their user-message ratio values are high but their reciprocal edge ratio values are low, which implies that participants in those subreddits for news-related topics tend to submit a small number of comments and not to reciprocally communicate with others. Note that IAmA $(S_{vol}(1))$ shows a noticeable pattern; its user-message ratio is much lower and reciprocal edge ratio is much higher than the other subreddits.

The responsive subreddits (in S_{rsp}) tend to have high user-message ratio and low reciprocal edge ratio in general. However, the user-message and reciprocal edge ratio values of AskReddit $(S_{rsp}(6))$ and Game of Thrones $(S_{vol}(8))$ show somewhat inconsistent tendency, meaning that participants in those subreddits tend to be not only responsive but also reciprocal with other people. Note that both user-message and reciprocal edge ratio values of Science $(S_{rsp}(7))$ are relatively lower than those of other subreddits, which implies that participants in the science-related subreddit are likely to submit more comments, but they do not actively interact with others.

6. CONCLUSIONS

We have conducted a large-scale and comprehensive measurement study on online conversation patterns in Reddit. Using the collected dataset, we characterized online conversation patterns in terms of volume, responsiveness, and virality, and explored what and how content properties and user participation behaviors are associated with the three metrics. We found that large, responsive, and viral conversations tend to have high document relevancy between parent and child comments. In addition, a large/viral conversation is likely to have difficult texts whereas a responsive conversation tends to have plain texts. We also discovered that large/viral conversations are built by reciprocal communications from relatively a small portion of users. As to user types in Reddit, we found users with wide interests play important roles of eliciting others' comments, which leads to large/viral trees, while heavy posting users tend to attract comments in responsive trees. We then expand our analysis to subreddits (topical communities), and learned that each community shows different characteristics; news-related, image-based, and discussion-related communities are more likely to have large, responsive, and viral conversations, respectively. We believe our analyses provide valuable insights to understand online conversations, e.g., content providers who want people to talk about their contents, or opinion leaders who want to obtain fast responses.

7. ACKNOWLEDGEMENTS

This work was supported in part by Basic Science Research Program through the "National Research Foundation of Korea(NRF)" funded by the Ministry of Science, ICT & future Planning (2013R1A2A2A01016562), Seoul National University Big Data Institute through the Data Science Research Project 2015, and Institute for Information & communications Technology Promotion(IITP) grant funded by the Korea government(MSIP) (B0190-15-2013, Development of Access Technology Agnostic Next-Generation Networking Technology for Wired-Wireless Converged Networks).

8. REFERENCES

[1] Alexa - the web information company. http://www.alexa.com.

[2] LIWC statistics. http://www.liwc.net/descriptiontable3.php.

[3] A. Aizawa. An information-theoretic perspective of tf-idf measures. *Information Processing and Management*, 39(1):45–65, 2003.

[4] E. Bakshy, I. Rosenn, C. Marlow, and L. Adamic. The role of social networks in information diffusion. In *WWW*, 2012.

[5] C. Budak, D. Agrawal, and A. El Abbadi. Where the blogs tip: Connectors, mavens, salesmen and translators of the blogosphere. In *The Workshop on Social Media Analytics*, 2010.

[6] M. Cha, A. Mislove, and K. P. Gummadi. A measurement-driven analysis of information propagation in the flickr social network. In *WWW*, 2009.

[7] J. Cheng, L. Adamic, P. A. Dow, J. M. Kleinberg, and J. Leskovec. Can cascades be predicted? In *WWW*, 2014.

[8] C. Dagum. The generation and distribution of income, the Lorenz curve and the Gini ratio. *Economie Appliquée*, 33(2), 1980.

[9] S. Das and A. Lavoie. The effects of feedback on human behavior in social media: An inverse reinforcement learning model. In *The International Conference on Autonomous Agents and Multi-agent Systems*, 2014.

[10] M. De Choudhury and S. De. Mental Health Discourse on reddit: Self-disclosure, Social Support, and Anonymity. In *ICWSM*, 2014.

[11] E. Gilbert. Widespread underprovision on reddit. In *ACM CSCW*, 2013.

[12] S. Goel, A. Anderson, J. Hofman, and D. J. Watts. The structural virality of online diffusion. *Management Science*, 2015.

[13] S. Goel, D. J. Watts, and D. G. Goldstein. The structure of online diffusion networks. In *ACM Conference on Electronic Commerce*, 2012.

[14] V. Gómez, A. Kaltenbrunner, and V. López. Statistical analysis of the social network and discussion threads in slashdot. In *WWW*, 2008.

[15] R. Gunning. *The Technique of Clear Writing*. McGraw-Hill, 1952.

[16] J. Han, D. Choi, B.-G. Chun, T. Kwon, H.-C. Kim, and Y. Choi. Collecting, organizing, and sharing pins in pinterest: Interest-driven or social-driven? In *ACM SIGMETRICS*, 2014.

[17] G. Hsieh, Y. Hou, I. Chen, and K. N. Truong. "welcome!": Social and psychological predictors of volunteer socializers in online communities. In *ACM CSCW*, 2013.

[18] R. Kumar, M. Mahdian, and M. McGlohon. Dynamics of conversations. In *ACM KDD*, 2010.

[19] H. Lakkaraju, J. McAuley, and J. Leskovec. What's in a name? understanding the interplay between titles, content, and communities in social media. In *ICWSM*, 2013.

[20] D. Lazer, A. Pentland, L. Adamic, S. Aral, A.-L. Barabási, D. Brewer, N. Christakis, N. Contractor, J. Fowler, M. Gutmann, T. Jebara, G. King, M. Macy, D. Roy, and M. V. Alstyne. Social science: Computational social science. *Science*, 323(5915):721–723, February 2009.

[21] A. Leavitt and J. A. Clark. Upvoting hurricane sandy: Event-based news production processes on a social news site. In *ACM CHI*, 2014.

[22] M. Marcoccia. On-line polylogues: conversation structure and participation framework in internet newsgroups. *Journal of Pragmatics*, 36(1):115–145, 2004.

[23] E. Mayfield, D. Adamson, and C. P. Rosé. Hierarchical conversation structure prediction in multi-party chat. In *The 13th Annual Meeting of the Special Interest Group on Discourse and Dialogue*, 2012.

[24] L. Rossi and M. Magnani. Conversation practices and network structure in twitter. In *ICWSM*, 2012.

[25] P. Singer, F. Flöck, C. Meinhart, E. Zeitfogel, and M. Strohmaier. Evolution of reddit: From the front page of the internet to a self-referential community? In *WWW Companion*, 2014.

[26] C. Wang, M. Ye, and B. A. Huberman. From user comments to on-line conversations. In *ACM KDD*, 2012.

[27] T. Weninger. An exploration of submissions and discussions in social news: mining collective intelligence of reddit. *Social Network Analysis and Mining*, 4(1), 2014.

Sharing Topics in Pinterest:
Understanding Content Creation and Diffusion Behaviors

Jinyoung Han[1], Daejin Choi[2], A-Young Choi[3], Jiwon Choi[4], Taejoong Chung[2]
Ted "Taekyoung" Kwon[2], Jong-Youn Rha[4], Chen-Nee Chuah[1]

Dept. of Electrical & Computer Engineering, University of California, Davis[1]
Dept. of Computer Science & Engineering, Seoul National University[2]
Business School, Sungkyunkwan University[3], Dept. of Consumer Science, Seoul National University[4]

rghan@ucdavis.edu, djchoi@mmlab.snu.ac.kr, {cay0908, jiwon}@snu.ac.kr,
tjchung@mmlab.snu.ac.kr, {tkkwon, jrha}@snu.ac.kr, chuah@ucdavis.edu

ABSTRACT

Pinterest provides a social curation service where people can collect, organize, and share content (pins in Pinterest) that reflect their interests. This paper investigates (1) the differences in pinning (i.e., the act of posting a pin) and repinning (i.e., the act of sharing other user's pin) behaviors by topics and user gender, and (2) the relations among topics in Pinterest. We conduct a measurement study using a large-scale dataset (1.6 M pins shared by 1.1 M users) in Pinterest. We show that there is a notable discrepancy between pinning and repinning behaviors on different topics. We also show that male and female users show different behaviors on different topics in terms of dedication, responsiveness, and sentiment. By introducing the notion of a *Topic Network (TN)* whose nodes are topics and are linked if they share common users, we analyze how topics are related to one another, which can give a valuable implication on topic demand forecasting or cross-topic advertisement. Lastly, we explore the implications of our findings for predicting a user's interests and behavioral patterns in Pinterest.

Categories and Subject Descriptors

H.3.5 [**Online Information Services**]: Web-based services; J.4 [**Computer Applications**]: Social and behavioral sciences

Keywords

Pinterest; Online Social Network; Social Curation; User Behavior; Pinning; Repinning; Gender Differences; Topic Relation

1. INTRODUCTION

Over the past decade, online social networks (OSNs) have become platforms to create and maintain social relation-ships, disseminate content, exchange opinions, share news or images, and conduct political campaigns. This in turn has led researchers to examine how interests are shared among users [5,10], revealing valuable insights into understanding users and their interests. Such studies form a fertile ground for industry to develop new online services or to grow their businesses by identifying potential consumers who may be willing to use their services, or by recommending useful goods/services [5,10,12,23]. A recent New York Times article reported that traditional retailers like Target and Walmart have started to recognize the importance of such endeavors and sought their partners among OSN companies [11].

Recently, *Pinterest*, an emerging OSN, has been reported to become the fastest growing web site to reach 10 million visitors [6] and the third most popular OSN in the United States, behind Facebook and Twitter [16]. Pinterest provides a social curation service where people can collect, organize, and share content that reflect their tastes or interests [9,10,25]. Each content in Pinterest is called a pin, and a pinboard is a collection of pins organized by a user, each of which belongs to one of the 33 categories (or topics[1]) defined by Pinterest, varying from "food & drink" to "travel".

The great upsurge and popularity of Pinterest has spurred research into its usage patterns [4,9,10,13,25], revealing valuable insights into the characteristics of Pinterest. One of the unique properties of Pinterest is that interests (or topics) drive user activities and connectivities (among users or their pins) in Pinterest [10,22], in contrast to other OSNs such as Facebook. However, relatively little attention was paid to how different *"topics"* in Pinterest are shared by (i) *pinning* (i.e., the act of posting a pin) and *repinning* (i.e., the act of sharing other user's pin) behaviors, and (ii) gender differences in such behaviors, which might be the key to understanding what attracts the users to post and to interact with one another in Pinterest in the first place.

We believe investigating 'which' users post/share 'what' content, and 'with whom' those content are shared can provide valuable information for online retailers to enhance their marketing strategies. From consumer perspectives, content posting/sharing behaviors of users can be interpreted as behaviors that reflect the latent factors such as their needs, interests, and desires. In this sense, understanding

COSN'15, November 2–3, 2015, Palo Alto, California, USA.
© 2015 ACM. ISBN 978-1-4503-3951-3/15/11 ...$15.00.
DOI: http://dx.doi.org/10.1145/2817946.2817961

---

[1]In this paper, we regard a Pinterest category (e.g., "history" or "travel") as a particular topic (see Table 1).

users' posting/sharing behaviors can shed light on users' interests beyond their words, which in turn can be used to better satisfy them. By using Pinterest as a research context, we set out to investigate pinning (or posting) and repinning (or sharing) behaviors that can be construed as information creation and diffusion behaviors, respectively [18]. It has been reported that information creation and diffusion behaviors may happen due to the different motivations of users, the former requiring more efforts and dedication than the latter [18].

In this paper, we strive to shed light on such issues by performing a large-scale trace-driven analysis on topics shared by users in Pinterest and users' pinning/repinning behaviors. In particular, we seek to answer the following three questions:

- **Q1 - Topic Curated/Shared:** How are different topics shared by pinning/repinning behaviors and by male/female users? Are there any similarities or differences in user behaviors across different topics?

- **Q2 - Topic Relation:** How are topics related to each other? Can those topics be clustered into groups, and how?

- **Q3 - Application:** What would be the potential applications of the observed user behaviors on different topics? Can we forecast the topic usage/curation pattern of each user in Pinterest?

To address the above questions, we first build a bipartite network consisting of two types of nodes: (i) topics and (ii) users interested in those topics (Figure 1). If a user has a pin in a particular topic, there is a link between the user and its corresponding topic in the bipartite network. Projecting [26] a topics-users bipartite network into the topic space results in a *Topic Network (TN)*, whose nodes are topics and are linked if they share at least one common user (Figure 1). The rationale behind the proposed method is that two topics linked in the TN are likely to be shared by common users who are interested in both topics. This TN model has great utility in resource allocation of online retailers, e.g., via topic demand forecasting or cross-topic advertisement.

We conduct a measurement study using a dataset (1.6 M pins shared by 1.1 M users) that we collected by crawling web pages from Pinterest. We fetched the web information of all the newly-posted (i.e., pinning) and shared (i.e., repinning) pins in each category (i.e., topic) of Pinterest from June 5 to July 18, 2013. Using the dataset, we analyze: (1) the differences in the pinning and repinning behaviors by topic characteristics and user characteristics (gender), and (2) the relations among topics in Pinterest. In addition, we explore the implications of our findings to predict a user's interests and behavioral patterns in Pinterest.

We highlight the main contributions and key findings of our work as follows:

- **Topic Curated/Shared:** We comprehensively investigate how different topics in Pinterest are curated (and shared) from the perspectives of (i) pinning and repinning behaviors and (ii) gender differences in such behaviors, which shows completely different patterns in terms of dedication, responsiveness, and sentiment.

We find female users play more roles in repinning (disseminating the existing content) than pinning (creating a new content) whereas male users play more roles in pinning than repinning. We observe the notable differences in the pinning and repinning behaviors: (1) users' efforts on pinning are likely to be more skewed in some topics than repinning, and (2) repinning users (or *repinners*[2]) tend to show more positive sentiments than pinning users (or *pinners*), implying that users who engage in diffusing content tend to be more amiable. We believe this analysis can provide valuable implication on what attracts users to post/share content and to interact with one another in Pinterest-like social curation service.

- **Topic Relation:** To model the relations among topics, we apply a network-theoretic approach and propose the notion of a *Topic Network (TN)*. Based on the TN model, we analyze (i) how topics are related to one another, and (ii) how topics are clustered into groups (or communities), which can be used in identifying hidden (but important) links among the topics (or interests) towards topic demand forecasting or cross-topic advertisement. We find some topics (e.g., "animals", "film, music & books", or "travel") have more links (to other topics) than the others, each of which plays a role as a hub (or a portal) among the topics in the TN. We also identify which topics belong to which communities (e.g., "food & drink", "health & fitness", or "hair & beauty" belong to the same community), which can give valuable implications for online retailers to develop targeted-advertisement or cross-selling services.

- **Application:** We explore the implications of our findings for predicting which topics a user will be interested in the future. Our trace-driven study for predicting topic consumption patterns in Pinterest demonstrates that the proposed TN model (that reflects the collective opinions of other like-minded users) is useful in accurately predicting a user's interest and behavioral pattern.

The rest of this paper is organized as follows. After reviewing the related work in Section 2, we describe our measurement methodology in Section 3. We then present our results on how different topics are shared by pinning/repinning behaviors and by male/female users, and how topics are related to one another in Sections 4 and 5, respectively. We finally suggest prediction models to forecast how topics are shared in Pinterest in Section 6.

2. RELATED WORK

Despite its young age, Pinterest has attracted great attention [6, 16]. The huge popularity of Pinterest is attributed to its unique properties [6]. First, it is reported that over 80% of Pinterest users are female [4, 9, 10], which exhibits a different demographic distribution compared to other OSNs such as Facebook or Twitter. This allows researchers to investigate the gender differences in Pinterest [4, 9, 10, 15]. Ottoni *et al.* observed that female users are more active and invest more efforts in bi-directional social links than male

---

[2]In this paper, pinning and repinning users are referred to as *pinners* and *repinners*, respectively.

users in Pinterest [15]. Gilbert *et al.* showed that female users share more pins but have fewer followers than male users [9]. Han *et al.* observed different preferences of male and female users on different topics (or categories) in Pinterest; the portions of male and female users are significantly different across different topics [10]. Chang *et al.* investigated which topics are popular to male and female users in Pinterest, and showed that male and female users differ in collecting content across different topics [4]. We go one step further; while previous work (e.g., [10] or [4]) showed general preferences of male and female users on different topics, we perform an in-depth analysis on topics shared by male and female users with *different motivations* (i.e., (i) pinning; content creation, and (ii) repinning; content diffusion). This analysis may shed light on what attracts users to post/share content and to interact with one another in Pinterest-like social curation services.

Second, Pinterest supports a social curation service that allows users to collect, organize, and share content that reflect their tastes or interests [4, 10, 24, 25]. A growing number of popular Internet services have started to support *"curation"*, which is a process of searching and collecting information, organizing the collected information in meaningful or personal ways, and creating values beyond the sum of assets. A variety of valuable information on the Internet has made curation one of central elements for innovation and creativity [13, 19]. Pinterest provides a curation platform with social functionalities which is called *"social curation"*: users can follow other curators whose content they find interesting [4, 10, 13, 25]. Linder, Snodgrass, and Kerne conducted an interview with twenty Pinterest users and found that social curation allows users to engage in the process of everyday ideation; they use collected digital objects as creative resources to develop ideas for shaping their lives [13]. Han *et al.* investigated how Pinterest curators collect and curate pins in terms of number of pins, boards, categories, and followings/followers, and showed that the curators' efforts on pinning are skewed in a few categories [10]. Zhong *et al.* showed that curators with consistent activities and diverse interests attract more followers [25]. Chang *et al.* also found that sharing diverse types of content increases the number of followers up to a certain point [4]. Zhong *et al.* investigated how Pinterest (as a new social curation platform) can benefit from social bootstrapping by copying links from already established OSNs like Facebook [24]. Ottoni *et al.* analyzed cross-OSN user behaviors between Pinterest and Twitter, and showed that users are likely to generate new content in Pinterest, and then spread it in Twitter [14]. We analyze how Pinterest curators show different behaviors in content creation (i.e., pinning) and diffusion (i.e., repinning) on different topics. In addition, we apply the insights learned from our study to develop models for predicting which topics an individual Pinterest curator will be interested in.

Based on the curator behaviors and content properties, some studies have tried to predict users' future activities in Pinterest [10, 12, 23]. Kamath *et al.* proposed a supervised model for board recommendation in Pinterest, and showed that using social signals such as 'likes' can achieve a higher recommendation quality [12]. Han *et al.* showed that the properties of pins (e.g., category or source) are more important factors than those of users (e.g., number of followers a user has) in predicting which pins an individual user will be

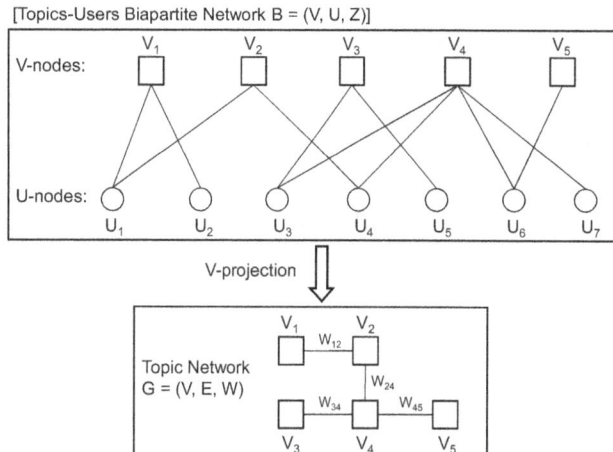

Figure 1: An example of a topics-users bipartite network B, as well as its V projection, is illustrated. V represents the set of topics and U is the set of users associated in those topics. An undirected weighted graph $G = (V, E, W)$ represents a notion of topic network (TN) where V is the set of topics, and E is the set of (undirected) edges between two topics.

interested in the future [10]. Zhong *et al.* proposed models to predict whether a user will be interested in repinning the given pin [23]. Given a user and an image repinned by her, they also suggested models for predicting which category she will repin the image into [23]. We introduce a new notion — a topic network — that represents the relations among topics in forecasting 'which topics' an individual user will be interested in, which might have an important implication on topic demand forecasting or cross-topic advertisement.

Lastly, another interesting property of Pinterest is that interests drive user activities or connectivities in Pinterest [10, 22], in contrast to other popular OSNs such as Facebook. Zarro, Hall, and Forte reported that one participant in the interview mentioned that Pinterest was about *what* they enjoyed, not about *who* they were [22]. Han *et al.* showed that sharing pins in Pinterest is mostly driven by pin's properties like its topic, not by users' characteristics such as the number of followers [10]. This was confirmed by Gelley and John [8], who showed that following is not significantly utilized in content sharing in Pinterest. We focus on 'what' topics (or interests) are shared in Pinterest, and characterizes user behaviors on different topics in terms of dedication, responsiveness, and sentiment. We further investigate the relations among topics (or interests) established by (i) different levels of dedication and (ii) gender differences, which can be used in capturing common interests of users in Pinterest.

3. METHODOLOGY

In this section, we first illustrate how to model topics and their associated users. We also explain our measurement methodology for data collection, and describe the dataset used in this paper.

3.1 The Model: Topics & Users

To describe topics and users in Pinterest, we first consider a topics-users bipartite network $B = (V, U, Z)$ whose nodes

1	diy & crafts	2	food & drink	3	education	4	animals	5	health & fitness
6	design	7	architecture	8	products	9	art	10	home decor
11	film, music & books	12	women's fashion	13	humor	14	quotes	15	men's fashion
16	gardening	17	hair & beauty	18	science & nature	19	technology	20	travel
21	cars & motorcycles	22	geek	23	shop	24	weddings	25	outdoors
26	celebrities	27	tattoos	28	photography	29	illustrations & posters	30	kids
31	history	32	sports	33	holidays & events				

Table 1: Pinterest categories (topics) with indexes are summarized.

are divided into two disjoint sets V and U, such that every edge in Z connects a node in V to one in U [26] (Figure 1). Here, V and U represent the sets of topics and users, respectively. If a user has pin(s) in a particular topic, there is a link in Z between the user (in U) and its corresponding topic (in V) in the topics-users bipartite network. Prior work reported male and female users show different characteristics in terms of user activities or connectivities in Pinterest [4, 9, 10, 15]. We conjecture that male and female users may also have different tastes for different topics, and hence we consider two divided user sets in the model for male and female users: U_{male} and U_{female}. We also conjecture that pinning and repinning may happen due to different motivations of users; i.e., pinning is likely to create content while repinning is likely to share or distribute content. Rha [18] reported that two information-related activities (i.e., (i) information creation; pinning in our case, and (ii) information diffusion; repinning in our case) show different characteristics, e.g., level of dedication. Thus, we consider two ways to connect a node in V to another in U: Z_{pin} and Z_{repin}. Finally, we build four topics-users bipartite networks: (i) $B_{male,pin} = (V, U_{male}, Z_{pin})$ to model pinning of male users, (ii) $B_{female,pin} = (V, U_{female}, Z_{pin})$ for female users' pinning, (iii) $B_{male,repin} = (V, U_{male}, Z_{repin})$ for male users' repinning, and (iv) $B_{female,repin} = (V, U_{female}, Z_{repin})$ for female users' repinning.

To show the relations in a particular set of nodes (i.e., V or U), bipartite networks can be compressed by one-mode projection [26]. That is, the one-mode projection onto V (V projection for short) results in a network that consists of nodes only in V where the nodes are connected if they have at least one common node (i.e., user) in U. See Figure 1 as an illustrative example of a bipartite network B and its V projection. We assume that an undirected weighted graph $G = (V, E, W)$ resulted from the V projection represents a notion of a topic network (TN) where V is the set of topics and E is the set of (undirected) edges between two topics. An edge $E_{i,j}$ in a TN exists between two topics V_i and V_j if there is at least one user who has pins both in V_i and in V_j. The rationale behind the proposed method of abstraction is that, if two topics are related to each other, they will have common users (who are interested in both topics). To understand the (statistically) meaningful relations among topics, we only consider the edges (in the TN) that have more users than the ones in the uniform case where each edge has the same number users (i.e., users are uniformly distributed in the edges of the TN). In transforming from a bipartite network into a one-mode projection, there can be a loss of information; *weighted projection* is one way to remedy this problem [26]. To this end, we define the weight $W_{i,j}$ of a given edge $E_{i,j}$ as the Jaccard coefficient between two topics V_i and V_j, $\frac{|U(V_i) \cap U(V_j)|}{|U(V_i) \cup U(V_j)|}$, where $U(V_i)$ and $U(V_i)$ are the sets

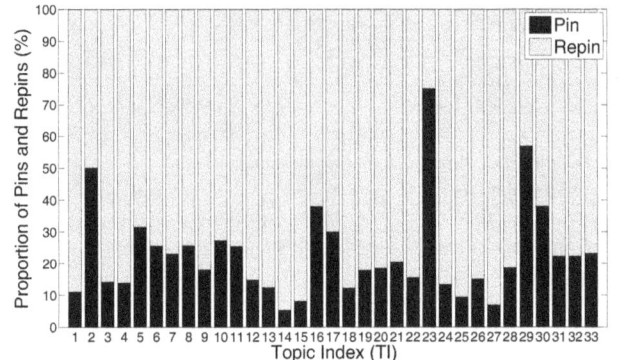

Figure 2: Proportion of pins and repins across different topics are plotted.

of users which are associated with topics V_i and V_j, respectively. Projecting [26] our four topics-users bipartite networks $B_{male,pin}$, $B_{female,pin}$, $B_{male,repin}$, and $B_{female,repin}$, into the topic space, we finally obtain four topic networks: (i) $TN_{male,pin}$, (ii) $TN_{female,pin}$, (iii) $TN_{male,repin}$, and (iv) $TN_{female,repin}$, respectively.

3.2 Data Collection and Dataset

Data Collection. Since Pinterest does not provide an official API for data collection, we developed web crawling software. Our crawling software fetched web pages in Pinterest, from which the relevant information is extracted; for instance, the data about each pin can be extracted. At the moment of our data collection, we found that Pinterest shows all the recent activities including pinning, repinning, and commenting in the menu of each category in the chronological order. To capture all the pinning activities, we fetched 10 recent web pages periodically (every five minutes) from the menu of each category not to miss any newly posted pins. If user B shares an original pin from user A, Pinterest provides a link of user B's pinboard to the original pin page (of user A); hence we could find and fetch the corresponding (shared) pin pages by user B. Whenever a pin of a user is shared by another user, we obtained the corresponding shared pin information (i.e., its category, description, and comments) as well as the corresponding user information (i.e., his/her description, gender, number of followers, number of pins, etc.). In this way, we could capture nearly all the pinning and repinning activities of users for each topic during our measurement period. To identify the gender of users, we used external links to Facebook and Twitter, which can be found in the profile pages of users. By querying Facebook and Twitter through their APIs, we could obtain the gender information of Pinterest users if available.

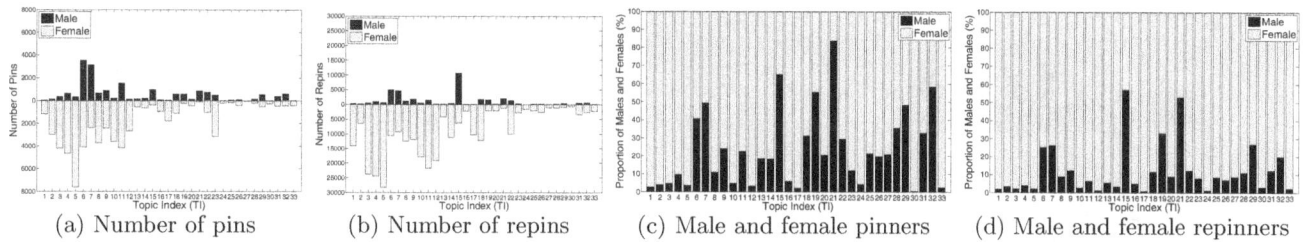

| (a) Number of pins | (b) Number of repins | (c) Male and female pinners | (d) Male and female repinners |

Figure 3: Numbers and Proportions of pins/repins and male/female users across different topics are plotted, respectively.

Dataset. We had collected the dataset for 44 days from June 5 to July 18, 2013, which contains 346,305 (original) pins and their 1,215,054 repins, shared by 1,051,054 users. The user dataset collectively contains 2,908,107,606 pins, 595,489,616 followers, 182,381,056 followings, 708,657 Facebook links, and 104,308 Twitter links. We obtained the gender information of 225,382 users. The numbers of male and female users are 23,215 and 202,167, respectively. Table 1 summarizes the Pinterest topics with their indexes, which are sorted in terms of the number of corresponding pins/repins. In addition to the 32 Pinterest topics, we investigate one more special menu in Pinterest, *"shop"*, which is directly related to online stores. Note that pins in the shop menu contain the prices of the corresponding items as well as links to the websites of the online stores.

4. TOPIC SHARING PATTERN

In this section, we discuss our observations on the differences in pinning and repinning behaviors in terms of topics and gender, to answer the first question, *Q1 – Topic Curated/Shared.* We first investigate the ratio of the number of pins (or repins) to the sum of numbers of pins and repins in each topic in Figure 2. In most cases, the portion of repins is higher than that of pins; the average portion of repins across the 33 topics is 77%. However, the portions of pins are higher than those of repins in "food & drink" (Topic Index (TI) 2), "shop" (TI 23), and "illustration & posters" (TI 29); users in those topics tend to upload new content more than share them. For example, designers may want to upload their own paintings in "illustration & posters" (TI 29); online retailers may be just interested in uploading their products in "shop" (TI 23).

We next examine the numbers of pins and repins by male and female users across different topics in Figures 3(a) and 3(b), respectively. We also plot the portions of male and female users in pinning and repinning in each topic in Figures 3(c) and 3(d), respectively. Overall, female users tend to post and share more pins than male users as shown in Figures 3(a) and 3(b). Note that the sample size for "kids" (TI 30) by male pinner is not significant, hence we exclude it in the following analyses. When we look at Figures 3(c) and 3(d), we find that male and female users play different roles in pinning (creating a new content) and repinning (disseminating the existing content) across different topics in Pinterest. We observe that the portions of male users in pinning are higher than those in repinning, which implies that male users play more roles in pinning than repinning. The portions of male users in "design" (TI 6), "architecture" (TI 7), "men's fashion" (TI 15), "technology" (TI 19),

"cars & motorcycles" (TI 21), "illustration & posters" (TI 29), and "sports" (TI 32) are higher than the ones in the other topics both in pinning and repinning. In particular, the portions of male users in "men's fashion" (TI 15) and "cars & motorcycles" (TI 21) are even higher than 50% both in pinning and repinning, meaning that those two topics are male-dominant. On the other hand, "sports" (TI 32) shows an interesting pattern; while the portion of male users in pinning is higher than 50%, the portion of male users in repinning is less than 20%. This indicates that content in "sports" (TI 32) are likely to be uploaded by male users but (mostly) shared by female users. Some topics show female-dominant characteristics; for example, the portions of female users in "women's fashion" (TI 12) and "weddings" (TI 24) are 99% in repinning; the portions of female users in "hair & beauty" (TI 17) are around 99% both in pinning and repinning. Interestingly, "weddings" (TI 24) is the topic that might be generally relevant to both male and female users, but male users are not interested in uploading or sharing content in the topic.

4.1 Pinning: Creating a New Content

We now analyze users' pinning behaviors on different topics. We first investigate the distribution of the numbers of pins among users in each topic by calculating the *Gini coefficient of pins*, a well-known indicator to evaluate the disparity of the income distribution in Economics [7]. The Gini coefficient is within the range of [0, 1], where 0 and 1 indicate a perfect uniform distribution (where all values are the same, e.g., everyone has the same income (or pins)) and an extremely skewed distribution (e.g., only one person has all the income (or pins), and all the others have none), respectively [7]. Figure 4 shows the Gini coefficient of pins in each topic, each of which (for a particular topic) is calculated based on the distribution of the numbers of pins each male or female user has posted on the topic. As shown in Figure 4, the Gini coefficients of pins in many topics are lower than 0.5, which signifies that most of Pinterest users contribute to posting pins without substantial disparity. Note that the "food & drink" (TI 2) shows the lowest Gini coefficient (< 0.1); users tend to evenly contribute to posting pins on that topic. The Gini coefficients of pins posted by female users are mostly lower than those posted by male users, implying that female users tend to contribute more evenly in pinning. Interestingly, some topics contributed by male users (e.g., "technology" (TI 19) and "history" (TI 32)) show relatively skewed distributions; a small portion of male users on those topics may be specialists on such topics, and are likely to post pins much more than the others. Note that the Gini coefficient of pins posted by male users in "kids" (TI 30)

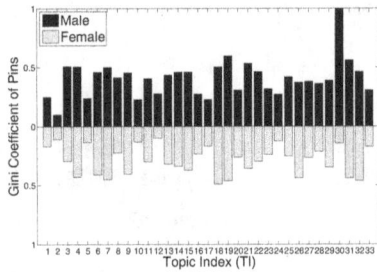

Figure 4: Gini coefficients of pins are plotted on each topic.

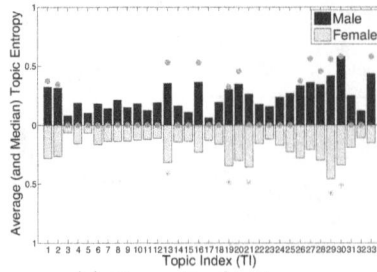

(a) Normalized entropy

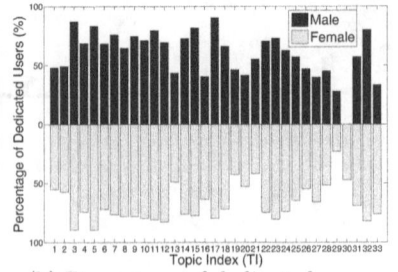

(b) Percentage of dedicated users

Figure 5: Topic concentration in pinning is explored in terms of topic entropy and percentage of dedicated users for each topic.

is 1.0 since there is only one male pinner in "kids" (TI 30). Likewise, a small portion of female users on particular topics (e.g., "science & nature" (TI 18), "technology" (TI 19), "history" (TI 31), and "sports" (TI 32)) are likely to post most pins; although those topics are not female-dominant ones, there may exist female specialists on such topics.

We also examine whether users' pinning efforts are skewed in some topics or evenly distributed across many topics. To this end, we adopt the Shannon's entropy [21], a well-known measure of variety. We calculate the normalized version of entropy for user u as follows:

$$TopicEntropy(u) = -\sum_{i=1}^{T_u} \frac{p_i^u \ln p_i^u}{\ln T_u} \quad (1)$$

where T_u is the number of topics that user u has, and p_i^u is the relative portion of the pins in the ith topic of u. The topic entropy of a user is one if she has pinned the equal share of content across the topics that she has, and is zero if all of her pins are pinned in a single topic.

The bar plots in Figure 5(a) show the average topic entropy of male and female users for each topic. Note that a circle and a star indicate the median values for male and female users in each topic, respectively. In our dataset, we observe that users are interested in pinning up to five topics. As shown in Figure 5(a), the topics which users are interested in are skewed since all the average and median topic entropy values are below 0.6. Average and median topic entropy values in "education" (TI 3), "health & fitness" (TI 5), "hair & beauty" (TI 17), and "sports" (TI 32) are even lower than 0.2, implying that users pinning on those topics are highly likely to focus on the particular topics. Interestingly, female users show lower entropy values than male users in pinning, which indicates that pinning efforts by female users tend to be skewed in less topics.

We further plot the percentage of dedicated users who post pins only on a single topic in Figure 5(b). For instance, 95% of male users in "hair & beauty" (TI 17) post pins only on that topic. Overall, female users tend to have higher portions of dedicated users than male users in pinning, which indicates pinning efforts by female users are likely to be dedicated to a particular topic. The percentages of dedicated users in "education" (TI 3), "health & fitness" (TI 5), and "hair & beauty" (TI 17) are over 90% both for male and female pinners, which signifies a high topic concentration. On the other hand, the percentages of dedicated users in "illustrations & posters" (TI 29) are lower than those in the other topics, meaning that users who are interested in the topic tend to have interests in other topics as well.

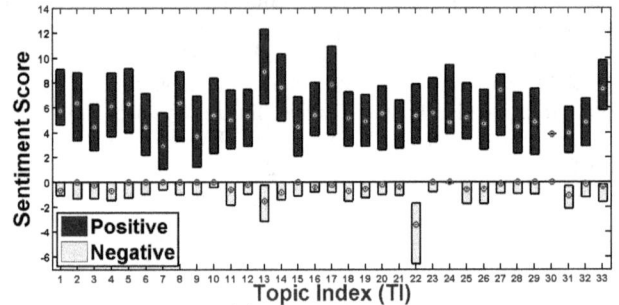

(a) Male pinners

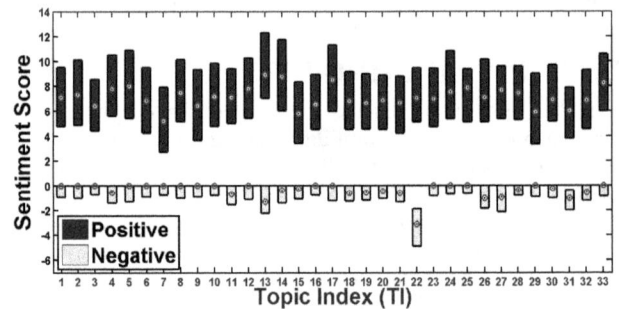

(b) Female pinners

Figure 6: Positive and negative sentiment scores of pinners on each topic are plotted.

We then investigate how strong emotions are exhibited depending on topics. We perform a sentiment analysis by using LIWC (Linguistic Inquiry and Word Count), a transparent text analysis program that counts words into psychologically meaningful categories [17]. For a given text, the LIWC tool provides a positive and a negative emotion scores, each of which is calculated as the relative frequency of the words in the given sentiment category (i.e., positive and negative emotions) on a percentile scale, out of all the words in the text. For example, the words "love" and "sweet" belong to the positive emotion category while "hurt" and "nasty" belong to the negative emotion category.

We collect all the texts a user has written including her descriptions and titles/texts/comments for her pins/boards, and then calculate the positive and negative sentiment scores for each user using LIWC. Figure 6 shows the distributions of sentiment scores for (a) male and (b) female users, who have been pinned in each topic, respectively. Note that the

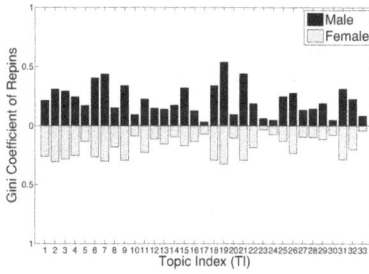

Figure 8: Gini coefficients of repins are plotted on each topic.

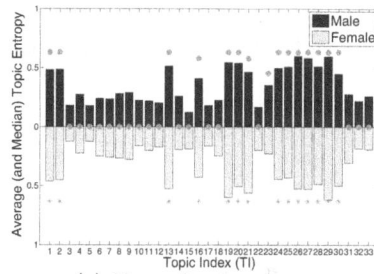

(a) Normalized entropy (b) Percentage of dedicated users

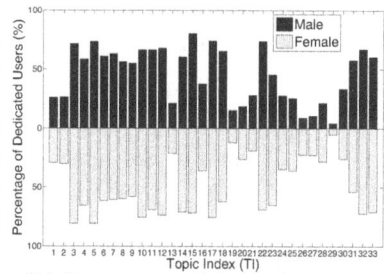

Figure 9: Topic concentration in repinning is explored in terms of topic entropy and percentage of dedicated users for each topic.

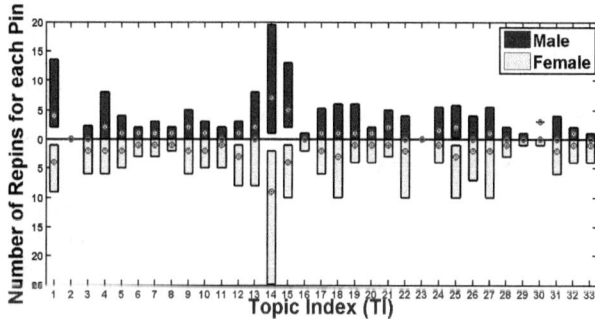

(a) Number of repins

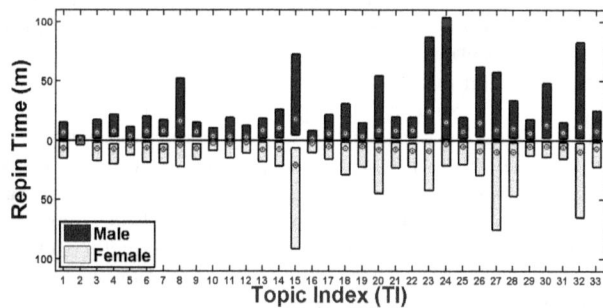

(b) Repin time

Figure 7: Repinning behaviors are analyzed in terms of the number of repins (for each pin) and repin time (in minute) on each topic.

(a) Male repinners

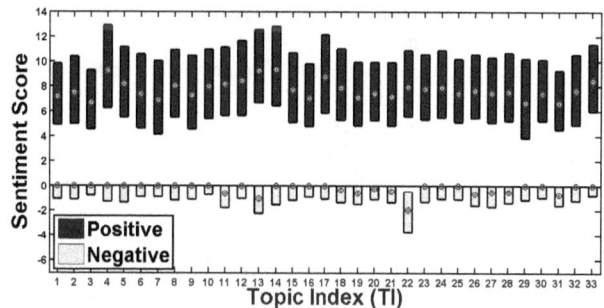

(b) Female repinners

Figure 10: Positive and negative sentiment scores of repinners are plotted on each topic.

bottom and top of the box in Figure 6 are the first (25th) and third (75th) quartiles, respectively, and the circle inside the box is the second quartile (the median). Overall, positive emotions are much stronger than negative ones in most cases, revealing that Pinterest users generally exhibit positive emotions, which is in line with the Pollyanna hypothesis that suggests a universal positivity bias in human communications [3]. Also, female users show higher positive scores and lower negative scores than male users on average. The "humor" (TI 13) shows the most positive score while the "geek" (TI 22) shows the most negative score, which is interesting since those two topics are related in the sense that funny things are shared, but the users who are interested in those topics show the opposite emotions. The positive emotions in "humor" (TI 13), "quotes" (TI 14), and "hair & beauty" (TI 17) are stronger than the ones in other topics both for male and female pinners. On the other hand, the

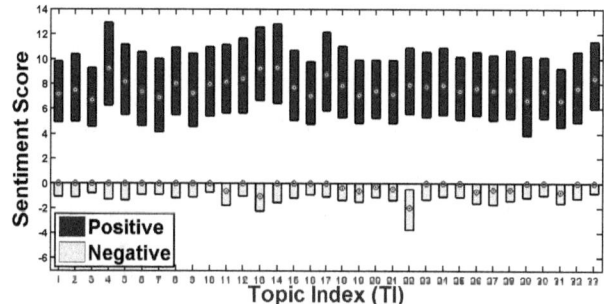

negative emotion for male pinners in "weddings" (TI 24) is almost zero; male pinners are likely to have negligible negative emotions on family-related topics like weddings. Interestingly, the absolute values of both positive and negative scores in "architecture" (TI 7) are relatively low, meaning that users interested in that topic tend to be calm.

4.2 Repinning: Disseminating the Existing Content

We now turn our attention to users' repinning behaviors on different topics. We first investigate how many pins are repinned and how fast users share pins in each topic. Figures 7(a) and 7(b) plot the distributions of number of repins for each pin and repin times (in minutes) in each topic, respectively. As shown in Figure 7(a), the number of repins in "quotes" (TI 14) is higher than those of the other topics; popular quotations are usually spread more widely both by male and female repinners. However, some topics show different patterns depending on male and female repinners. For instance, pins in "education" (TI 3), "women's fashion" (TI 12), "science & nature" (TI 18), "geek" (TI 22), "outdoors" (TI 25), or "tattoos" (TI 27) are likely to be repinned many times by female users but a few times by male users, while the number of repins by male users is much higher than that of female users in "diy & crafts" (TI 1) or "animals" (TI 4).

Figure 7(b) shows the distributions of repin times of content across the topics; note that a repin time is an interval between pinning and the 1st repinning or two consecutive repinning moments (of the same pin). The repin time of male users is mostly higher than that of female users, meaning that female users tend to spread content more quickly; note that the numbers of repins by gender are not so different mostly as shown in Figure 7(a). The repin times of "food & drink" (TI 2), "health & fitness" (TI 5), "home decor" (TI 10), "gardening" (TI 16), "illustrations & posters" (TI 29), and "history" (TI 31) are much lower than those of the other topics, which implies that users interested in those topics tend to react quickly or check frequently. Note that content in "food & drink" (TI 2) are shared in four minutes on average. On the other hand, the repin times of "men's fashion" (TI 15), "travel" (TI 20), "shop" (TI 23), "weddings" (TI 24), "tattoos" (TI 27), and "sports" (TI 32) are much higher than those of other topics. Interestingly, a significantly different pattern is observed between male- and female-dominant topics. For example, in the male-dominant topic, "men's fashion" (TI 15), the average repin time of a female user is higher than that of a male user. A similar pattern can be found in the female-dominant topic, "weddings" (TI 24); the repin time of a male user is much higher than that of a female user.

Figure 8 shows the distribution of the numbers of repins among users in each topic by calculating the *Gini coefficient of repins*. The Gini coefficients of repins of female users in most cases are lower than those of male users, which indicates that female users tend to contribute more evenly in repinning. The "hair & beauty" (TI 17), "weddings" (TI 24), and "kids" (TI 30) show the lowest Gini coefficients (< 0.05) of repins for male users while the "outdoors" (TI 23) and "holidays & events" (TI 33) show the lowest Gini coefficients (< 0.05) of repins for female users. Note that the "technology" (TI 19) shows the relatively skewed distributions both for male and female repinners; a small portion of users who are interested in that topic are more actively repinning than the others. From Figures 4 and 8, we find that the Gini coefficients of repins are lower than those of pins in many cases, meaning that repinners tend to more evenly contribute than pinners.

We also examine whether users' efforts on repinning are skewed in some topics or evenly distributed across multiple topics. Figures 9(a) and 9(b) show the average (and median) topic entropy of repinners and percentage of dedicated users who only share (or repin) pins of a single topic, respectively. Note that users are interested in repinning up to twelve topics in our dataset. Pinning the less topics (i.e., up to five) than repinning (i.e., up to twelve) may be due to the fact that information creation behaviors (i.e., pinning) require more efforts and dedication than information diffusion behaviors (i.e., repinning) [18]. Figures 5(a) and 9(a) reveal that most of topic entropy values in pinning are lower than those in repinning, which indicates that users tend to concentrate on less topics in pinning compared to repinning.

Similarly, the percentage of dedicated users in repinning is lower than the one in pinning as shown in Figures 5(b) and 9(b), meaning that pinners tend to focus more on a particular topic than repinners. The topic entropy values in "education" (TI 3) and "health & fitness" (TI 5) are lower than 0.2, implying that users who are interested in those topics are highly likely to focus only on a single topic. On the other hand, users' efforts on repinning in "illustrations & posters" (TI 29) are likely to be evenly distributed across multiple topics.

We finally investigate whether users show distinct emotions in sharing different topics. Figure 10 shows the distributions of positive/negative sentiment scores for (a) male and (b) female users, who have been repinned in each topic, respectively. As shown in Figure 10, like the pinning case in Figure 6, the "geek" (TI 22) shows the most negative score. From Figures 6 and 10, we find that repinners tend to show more positive scores than pinners, implying that users who engage in diffusing content tend to be more amiable.

5. TOPIC NETWORK

In this section, we seek answers for the second question, *Q2 – Topic Relation*, by analyzing the four topic networks (defined in Section 3): (i) $TN_{male,pin}$, (ii) $TN_{female,pin}$, (iii) $TN_{male,repin}$, and (iv) $TN_{female,repin}$, respectively.

5.1 How are topics related?

To investigate relations among topics in the TNs, we plot the graph models, whose nodes and edges represent topics and common users in two topics, respectively, in Figure 11. For illustration purposes, the thickness of an edge indicates the weight (defined in the methodology section). A larger circle indicates a node with a higher degree, and the same color of nodes indicates the same community, which will be explained later. As shown in Figure 11, relations among topics are significantly different across the TNs. For example, while "diy & crafts" (TI 1) and "products" (TI 8) are strongly tied together (i.e., having a relation with high weight) in $TN_{female,repin}$, there is no direct link between them in $TN_{male,pin}$. The top 3 related topics (in terms of weight) of "shop" (TI 23) in $TN_{male,repin}$ are "technology" (TI 19), "products" (TI 8), and "food & drink" (TI 2) while the ones in $TN_{female,repin}$ are "products" (TI 8), "diy & crafts" (TI 1), and "design" (TI 6), which might provide important implications for online retailers to develop their marketing strategies. As to the "hair & beauty" (TI 17), which is a female-dominant topic as shown in Figure 3, the related topics of "hair & beauty" (TI 17) by male users are "weddings" (TI 24) and "holidays & events" (TI 33), implying that male users interested in "hair & beauty" may have a particular motivation, e.g., preparing their weddings.

We next examine the degree of each topic in the four TNs. The degree of a topic indicates how many topics have relations with the given topic. If a particular topic has a large degree, the topic may play a role as a *hub* among topics. The average degrees of the nodes in $TN_{male,pin}$, $TN_{female,pin}$, $TN_{male,repin}$, and $TN_{female,repin}$ are 11.03, 10.48, 11.21, and 12.25, respectively. We observe that the degree of each topic is significantly different across the TNs. For example, "celebrities" (TI 26) is connected to many other topics in $TN_{female,repin}$, but it is connected to much less topics (i.e., small degree) in $TN_{female,pin}$. The topics of "products" (TI 8), "cars & motorcycles" (TI 21), and "history" (TI 31) in

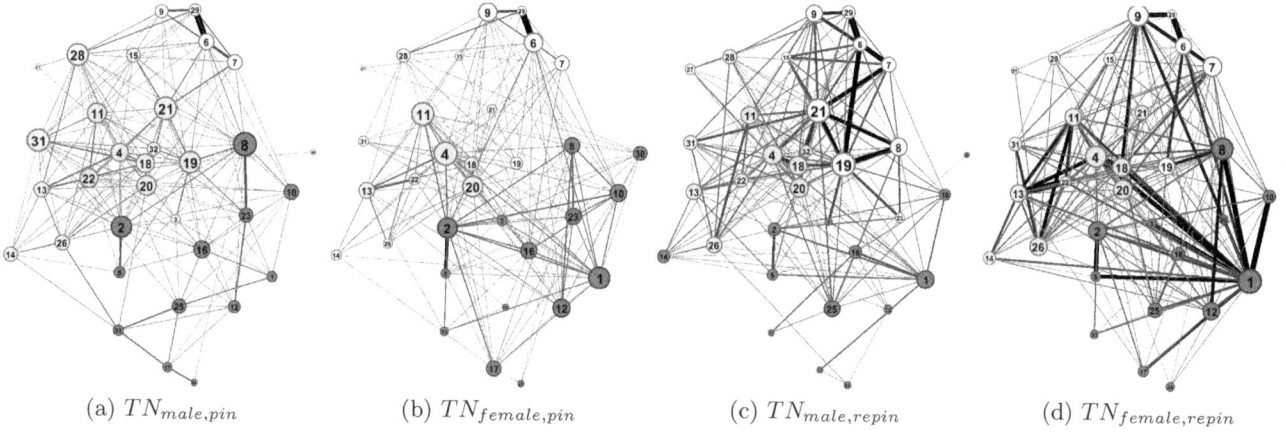

(a) $TN_{male,pin}$ (b) $TN_{female,pin}$ (c) $TN_{male,repin}$ (d) $TN_{female,repin}$

Figure 11: Graph models of four TNs are illustrated. The thickness of an edge indicates the weight (defined in Section 3). A larger circle indicates a node with a higher degree, and the same color of nodes indicates the same community.

TN	C	Member Topics
$TN_{m,p}$	1	education(3), animals(4), film,music&books(11), humor(13), quotes(14), men's fashion(15), science&nature(18), technology(19), travel(20), cars&motorcycles(21), geek(22), celebrities(26), kids(30), history(31), sports(32)
	2	design(6), architecture(7), art(9), tattoos(27), photography(28), illustrations&posters(29)
	3	diy&crafts(1), food&drink(2), health&fitness(5), products(8), home decor(10), women's fashion(12), gardening(16), hair&beauty(17), shop(23), weddings(24), outdoors(25), holidays&events(33)
$TN_{f,p}$	1	animals(4), film,music&books(11), humor(13), quotes(14), science&nature(18), travel(20), cars&motorcycles(21), geek(22), celebrities(26), history(31), sports(32)
	2	design(6), architecture(7), art(9), men's fashion(15), technology(19), tattoos(27), photography(28), illustrations&posters(29)
	3	diy&crafts(1), food&drink(2), education(3), health&fitness(5), products(8), home decor(10), women's fashion(12), gardening(16), hair&beauty(17), shop(23), weddings(24), outdoors(25), kids(30), holidays&events(33)
$TN_{m,r}$	1	animals(4), film,music&books(11), humor(13), science&nature(18), travel(20), geek(22), celebrities(26), tattoos(27), photography(28), history(31), sports(32)
	2	design(6), architecture(7), products(8), art(9), men's fashion(15), technology(19), cars&motorcycles(21), shop(23), illustrations&posters(29)
	3	diy&crafts(1), food&drink(2), education(3), health&fitness(5), home decor(10), women's fashion(12), quotes(14), gardening(16), hair&beauty(17), weddings(24), outdoors(25), kids(30), holidays&events(33)
$TN_{f,r}$	1	animals(4), film,music&books(11), humor(13), quotes(14), science&nature(18), travel(20), cars&motorcycles(21), geek(22), celebrities(26), tattoos(27), history(31), sports(32)
	2	design(6), architecture(7), art(9), men's fashion(15), technology(19), photography(28), illustrations&posters(29)
	3	diy&crafts(1), food&drink(2), education(3), health&fitness(5), products(8), home decor(10), women's fashion(12), gardening(16), hair&beauty(17), shop(23), weddings(24), outdoors(25), holidays&events(33)
	4	kids(30)

Table 2: The topics in each community (C) are identified in each TN: $TN_{male,pin}$, $TN_{female,pin}$, $TN_{male,repin}$, and $TN_{female,repin}$.

$TN_{male,pin}$, "animals" (TI 4) and "film, music & books" (TI 11) in $TN_{female,pin}$, "technology" (TI 19) and "cars & motorcycles" (TI 21) in $TN_{male,repin}$, and "animals" (TI 4), "products" (TI 8), and "art" (TI 9) in $TN_{female,repin}$ show the highest degrees, meaning that those topics have relations with many other topics and play roles as hubs, respectively. The degrees of "animals" (TI 4), "film, music & books" (TI 11), and "travel" (TI 20) are substantially high across the four TNs, which implies that those topics generally contain common interests with other topics. On the other hand, the degrees of "weddings" (TI 24), "tattoos" (TI 27), "kids" (TI 30), and "holidays & events" (TI 33) are generally lower than those of others, which means users interested in those topics tend to focus on the topics. From business perspectives, it may be more effective to identify the users who mostly focus on a particular set of topics for resource allocation in targeted marketing.

5.2 How are topics clustered into groups?

We now examine how topics in the TN are clustered into groups (or communities). Here, a community is a group of

topics, within which edges are denser, but between which edges are sparser. We identify communities of the four TNs using the Louvain method [2], a well-known fast community detection algorithm that maximizes the ratio of the number of edges within communities to that of edges between communities. We use the weighted version of Louvain method. Recall that the same color of nodes in Figure 11 indicates the same community.

Table 2 lists the topics in each of the identified communities in the four TNs. In $TN_{male,pin}$, there are three communities, and the member topics in the second community are related to fine arts or design. $TN_{male,repin}$ also has three communities but their members are somewhat different from $TN_{male,pin}$. For example, in addition to topics related to fine arts or design, "men's fashion" (TI 15) and "technology" (TI 19) are also members in the second community of $TN_{male,repin}$, which implies that "men's fashion" (TI 15) and "technology" (TI 19) are somewhat linked to the topics related to fine arts or design for male repinners. While "tattoos" (TI 27) is the member of the second community in both $TN_{male,pin}$ and $TN_{female,pin}$, it belongs to the first community in $TN_{male,repin}$ and $TN_{female,repin}$, respectively. This indicates that "tattoos" (TI 27) is connected to design-related topics in pinning, but is more closely linked to light-hearted topics such as "humor" (TI 13) or "geek" (TI 22) in repinning. When we look at $TN_{female,repin}$, there are four communities. The "kids" topic (TI 30) is the only member in the fourth community in $TN_{female,repin}$, meaning that female repinners are interested in the "kids" solely.

Overall, some particular topics generally belong to the same community; for instance, "diy & crafts" (TI 1), "food & drink" (TI 2), "health & fitness" (TI 5), "women's fashion" (TI 12), "gardening" (TI 16), and "hair & beauty" (TI 17) belong to the third community across the TNs. This implies that (users of) those topics share common interests regardless of genders or pinning/repinning behaviors. On the other hand, some topics (e.g., "shop" (TI 23) or "kids" (TI 30)) belong to the different communities depending on the TNs, which may give valuable implications for online retainers to develop targeted-advertisement or cross-selling services.

We believe our analysis on the four TNs can be used in identifying hidden (but important) links among the topics (or interests). One of well known examples of the hidden links is the association between beer and diapers [1]. The identification of such links can be applied to promotion strategies such as cross-product advertisement, bundling, or product-pairing. For example, in $TN_{male,pinner}$, we observe that there are close relations among "technology", "product", "sports", and "men's fashion". If products related to these topics are displayed together (in a department store or an online store), *relevant* products are exposed together to consumers, which might help to increase sales.

6. PREDICTING WHICH TOPIC A USER WILL BE INTERESTED IN

In this section, we strive to answer the third question, *Q3 – Application*: can we predict which topic a user will be interested in? To answer the question, we propose and evaluate the following prediction methods:

- *Popularity − based* selects the most popular topic, among the topics which a user has not been interested in. This method is suggested for comparison purposes.

- *CF − based* adopts the *(item-to-item) collaborative filtering (CF)* technique [20], a well-known recommendation algorithm, whose basic idea is to find the most similar topic that other users tend to consume together. For this, we define a topic vector whose elements are users who pin/repin the pins of the topic; the dimension of the vector is the number of entire users. The similarity between two topics is calculated by the cosine similarity of two topic vectors. If the selected topic has already been consumed by the target user, we select the next most similar topic.

- *TN − neighbor − based* uses the relation information of topics in the TN which the target user belongs to (based on her gender information and pinning/repinning preferences). This method first finds topic A, which the target user has been most interested in, and selects the topic that has the strongest relation (i.e., the highest weight in the TN) with A. If the selected topic has

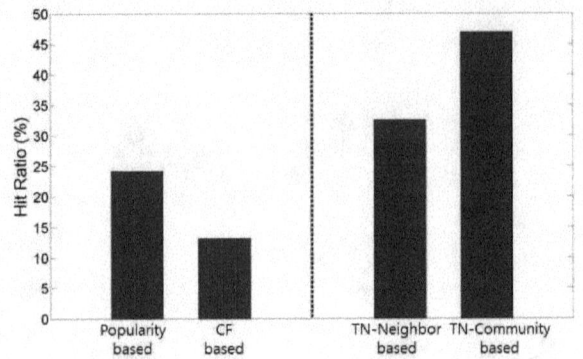

Figure 12: Hit ratios of the proposed prediction methods are plotted; $TN − community − based$ prediction performs the best.

already been consumed by the target user, we choose the topic which has the next strongest relation with A.

- *TN − community − based* further utilizes the community information of the TN which a user belongs to (based on her gender information and pinning/repinning preferences). We first find a corresponding community that contains the largest number of the topics (which the target user has been interested in), and select a topic (which the target user has not been interested in) from the same community. If there are multiple candidate topics in the community, we choose the topic that has the strongest relation with the one which the target user has been most interested in. The basic idea of this method is to find a similar topic based on the collective opinions of other like-minded users.

To evaluate the proposed prediction methods, we first select 1,913 target users satisfying two criteria: (i) her gender information is available, and (ii) she has at least 10 pins. Based on the proposed methods, as of Jul. 18th, 2013, we choose a candidate topic that may be consumed by each target user in the future. To validate whether the predicted topic is actually shared by each target user after 125 days, we collected another dataset (for 10 days, from Nov. 20th to 30th, 2013) that contains the target users' pins and their corresponding topic information. For the purpose of evaluation, we measure the hit ratio of each method, by calculating the ratio of the number of users who actually consume the predicted topic to the total number of target users.

Figure 12 shows the hit ratios of the four proposed prediction methods: *popularity − based*, *CF − based*, *TN − neighbor − based*, and *TN − community − based*. As shown in Figure 12, the prediction methods utilizing the TN information ($TN − neighbor − based$ and $TN − community − based$) perform better than *popularity − based* and *CF − based*, which indicates the relations among topics is useful in predicting a user's interested topic in the future. $TN − community − based$ outperforms the others (i.e., the hit ratio is close to 50%), implying that the community information (of the TN) that reflects the collective opinions of other like-minded users is an important predictor in predicting which topic a user will be interested in. We believe this can give important implications on topic demand forecasting or cross-topic advertisement in Pinterest-like social curation services.

7. CONCLUSION

This paper analyzed (1) the differences in pinning and re-pinning behaviors by topics and user gender, and (2) the relations among topics in Pinterest. We summarize three main contributions as follows. First, we investigated how different topics are shared from the perspectives of (i) pinning/repinning behaviors and (ii) gender differences in such behaviors, which shows significantly different patterns in terms of dedication, responsiveness, and sentiment. Second, by introducing the notion of topic networks, we analyzed (i) how topics are related to one another, and (ii) what topics are clustered into the same community, which can provide a valuable implication on topic demand forecasting or cross-topic advertisement. Lastly, we explored the implications of our findings for predicting which topics a user will be interested in later. We demonstrated that the notion of topic networks (that reflect the collective opinions of other like-minded users) is useful in accurately predicting a user's interest and behavioral pattern in Pinterest.

8. ACKNOWLEDGMENTS

We would like to thank our shepherd Dr. Virgilio Almeida and the anonymous reviewers for their valuable feedback. This work is supported in part by National Science Foundation CNS-1302691 grant, Institute for Information & communications Technology Promotion (IITP) grant funded by the Korea government (MSIP) (B0190-15-2013, Development of Access Technology Agnostic Next-Generation Networking Technology for Wired-Wireless Converged Networks), and Seoul National University Big Data Institute through the Data Science Research Project 2015.

9. REFERENCES

[1] M. J. Berry and G. S. Linoff. *Data mining techniques: for marketing, sales, and customer support*. John Wiley & Sons, Inc., 1997.

[2] V. D. Blondel, J.-L. Guillaume, R. Lambiotte, and E. Lefebvre. Fast unfolding of communities in large networks. *Journal of Statistical Mechanics: Theory and Experiment*, 2008(10), 2008.

[3] J. Boucher and C. E. Osgood. The pollyanna hypothesis. *Journal of Verbal Learning and Verbal Behavior*, 8(1):1–8, 1969.

[4] S. Chang, V. Kumar, E. Gilbert, and L. G. Terveen. Specialization, homophily, and gender in a social curation site: Findings from pinterest. In *ACM CSCW*, 2014.

[5] J. Chen, R. Nairn, L. Nelson, M. Bernstein, and E. Chi. Short and tweet: Experiments on recommending content from information streams. In *ACM CHI*, 2010.

[6] J. Constine. Pinterest hits 10 million u.s. monthly uniques faster than any standalone site ever -comscore. TechCrunch, 2012. http://goo.gl/EZFftf.

[7] C. Dagum. The generation and distribution of income, the Lorenz curve and the Gini ratio. *Economie Appliquée*, 33(2), 1980.

[8] B. Gelley and A. John. Do i need to follow you?: Examining the utility of the pinterest follow mechanism. In *ACM CSCW*, 2015.

[9] E. Gilbert, S. Bakhshi, S. Chang, and L. Terveen. "i need to try this!": A statistical overview of pinterest. In *ACM CHI*, 2013.

[10] J. Han, D. Choi, B.-G. Chun, T. T. Kwon, H.-C. Kim, and Y. Choi. Collecting, organizing, and sharing pins in pinterest: Interest-driven or social-driven? In *ACM SIGMETRICS*, 2014.

[11] E. A. Harris. Retailers seek partners in social networks. The New York Times, 2013. http://goo.gl/gzaKng.

[12] K. Y. Kamath, A.-M. Popescu, and J. Caverlee. Board recommendation in pinterest. In *Conference on User Modeling, Adaptation and Personalization*, 2013.

[13] R. Linder, C. Snodgrass, and A. Kerne. Everyday ideation: All of my ideas are on pinterest. In *ACM CHI*, 2014.

[14] R. Ottoni, D. L. Casas, J. P. Pesce, W. Meira Jr., C. Wilson, A. Mislove, and V. Almeida. Of Pins and Tweets: Investigating how users behave across image- and text-based social networks. In *ICWSM*, 2014.

[15] R. Ottoni, J. P. Pesce, D. Las Casas, G. Franciscani Jr, W. Meira Jr, P. Kumaraguru, and V. Almeida. Ladies first: Analyzing gender roles and behaviors in pinterest. In *ICWSM*, 2013.

[16] C. Palis. Pinterest traffic growth soars to new heights: Experian report. The Huffington Post, 2012. http://goo.gl/yMJCiG.

[17] J. W. Pennebaker, M. R. Mehl, and K. Niederhoffer. Psychological Aspects of Natural Language Use: Our Words, Ourselves. *Annual Review of Psychology*, 54:547–577, 2003.

[18] J.-Y. Rha. Consumers' usage of online social networks: application of use-diffusion model. *Journal of Consumer Studies*, 21(2):443–470, 2010.

[19] S. Rosenbaum. *Curation Nation: How to Win in a World Where Consumers are Creators*. McGraw-Hill, 2011.

[20] B. Sarwar, G. Karypis, J. Konstan, and J. Riedl. Item-based collaborative filtering recommendation algorithms. In *ACM WWW*, 2001.

[21] C. E. Shannon. Prediction and entropy of printed english. *Bell System Technical Journal*, 30(1):50–64, 1951.

[22] M. Zarro, C. Hall, and A. Forte. Wedding dresses and wanted criminals: Pinterest.com as an infrastructure for repository building. In *ICWSM*, 2013.

[23] C. Zhong, D. Karamshuk, and N. Sastry. Predicting pinterest: Automating a distributed human computation. In *ACM WWW*, 2015.

[24] C. Zhong, M. Salehi, S. Shah, M. Cobzarenco, N. Sastry, and M. Cha. Social bootstrapping: How pinterest and last.fm social communities benefit by borrowing links from facebook. In *ACM WWW*, 2014.

[25] C. Zhong, S. Shah, K. Sundaravadivelan, and N. Sastry. Sharing the loves: Understanding the how and why of online content curation. In *ICWSM*, 2013.

[26] T. Zhou, J. Ren, M. Medo, and Y. C. Zhang. Bipartite network projection and personal recommendation. *Physical Review E (Statistical, Nonlinear, and Soft Matter Physics)*, 76(4):046115+, 2007.

Team Formation Dynamics: A Study Using Online Learning Data

Milad Eftekhar
Department of Computer
Science
University of Toronto
Toronto, ON, Canada
milad@cs.toronto.edu

Farnaz Ronaghi[*]
Department of Management
Science and Engineering
Stanford University
Palo Alto, CA, USA
farnaaz@stanford.edu

Amin Saberi
Department of Management
Science and Engineering
Stanford University
Palo Alto, CA, USA
saberi@stanford.edu

ABSTRACT

Using data from online courses, we study the dynamics of team formation in online environments. In particular, we observe that the teams formed by online students for completing course projects are homogeneous in terms of age, location and education level but diverse in terms of primary skill. Motivated by the data, we propose a *coalitional game* that captures the teaming preferences of individuals and show that the core of the resulting game is always nonempty. Even though our proof is constructive, it does not always yield a polynomial-time algorithm. We show that it is NP-hard to find a solution in the core in the general case and propose polynomial-time algorithms for natural special cases motivated by observations of online course data.

Categories and Subject Descriptors

H.2.8 [**Database Management**]: Database Applications–Data Mining; K.3.1 [**Computers and Education**]: Computer Uses in Education – Collaborative Learning; I.2.11 [**Artificial Intelligence**]: Distributed Artificial Intelligence – Multiagent Systems; J.4 [**Social and Behavioral Sciences**]: Economics

General Terms

Algorithms, Measurement, Theory

Keywords

Team Formation; Online Education; Social Learning; Core of Collaborative Games

1. INTRODUCTION

In addition to increasing access to education at global scale, the emergence of Massive Open Online Courses (MOOCs)

---

*This work was done while authors were at NovoEd Inc.

has given us a new view into how people learn, interact, and collaborate. The availability of the MOOC data across research institutions, their scale and granularity, as well as their reach across countries and cultures make them an invaluable source for research.

This paper focuses on the dynamics of team formation in an online environment. We studied team formation in 11 online courses with about 50 thousand participants from over 150 different countries. The courses were offered on NovoEd, where teamwork and collaboration are an integral part of the coursework. Students were asked to form teams to work on a business project. The teams were organic; participants could search and browse each other's profiles and join each other's teams.

We studied the teams formed by students and reviewed the joint distribution of characteristics, e.g., age, location, gender, and education level. We observed a high degree of homogeneity across age, location, and education level but surprisingly not across gender. This was consistent across the courses as well as across different segments of the population. The tendency of individuals to associate with similar others - dubbed as *homophily* - is discovered in a vast array of studies about social networks.

The more interesting observation here is that among successful organic teams (teams that possess a high fraction of members who acquired a statement of accomplishment at the end of the course), we also observed a high degree of diversity (*heterophily*) in terms of participants' primary skill sets. In other words, multidisciplinary teams with more diverse skill sets were more successful than the rest: they sought to form multidisciplinary teams by seeking teammates with complementary skills. Homophily (across age, location, and education level) and heterophily (across skill set) proved to be an effective strategy, leading to more successful teams. Section 3 provides a detailed description of our observations.

Based on the observations, we proposed a simple game theoretic model to capture the preferences of individuals and their dynamics. In our model, each individual (or "agent") was endowed with a vector of characteristics, like age, location, or skill set. We partitioned agents into teams of a certain size and assumed that team success depended on the characteristics of the individuals present in that team. Obviously, every agent would seek a team with the highest quality but would have to be accepted into the team, as well. To capture this, we used the notion of a coalitional game core [10]. We define a partition of agents into teams as begin is in the core if no subset of agents could improve its score function by deviating from the proposed partition and forming its own team.

A few aspects of this model merit comment. First, the notion of core is a natural generalization of pairwise stability used in the context of widely studied stable marriage problems [20]. Instead of pairwise stability, we focus on the stability of groups of size larger than two. Second, like the stable marriage problem, we do not allow coalition to compensate each other with side payments. More precisely, we use the notion of core in a game with non-transferable payoff.

The most important distinction of the games studied here is that all team members benefit equally from the union. In other words, the utility of an agent in the team equals the value or quality score of that team. This is a natural assumption in our setting since all students in a team receive the same grade for a joint project. But our model is applicable elsewhere, too. For example, members of a group benefit in a similar way when they form teams to undertake a project that supports a community (like building a park, library or school) or when there are social norms against differentiation (like specifying authors in a theory paper).

We prove that under general assumptions, and as long as members of a team equally benefit from its value, the core of the game is non-empty. In other words, it is always possible to partition agents into sets such that no subset has an incentive to secede. Our proof (presented in Section 5) is constructive, but it does not always lead to a polynomial-time algorithm. In fact, we prove that it is NP-hard to find a stable partition in most cases. Section 6 offers polynomial time algorithms for natural special cases motivated by observations in Section 3.

2. RELATED WORK

The impact of homogeneity or diversity on team effectiveness has been studied extensively. In homogeneous teams, members share similar characteristics which results in easier collaboration, positive reactions, and extensive engagement [17,23]. In diverse teams, the existence of varied abilities and ideas sparks creativity and helps achieve a higher final performance [18]. Another detailed study of team composition (including personalities, skills, team size, roles, etc.) and its impact on team performance is found in Senior and Swailes [21].

A specific line of related research focuses on the impact of a founding team's composition on the performance of firms and ventures [5,7–9].

The team formation problem has been studied extensively for scenarios that aim to form a single team for each existing task. Having a set of users and one or multiple tasks, the goal is to find a team that contains all required skills to complete the task. The problem has been studied in operations research [25] and revisited in computer science by adding compatibility constraints (in the form of communication overhead over a social network of users) [15], cost constraints (the cost associated with adding each user to a team) [3,19], and time constraints (task work permitted only during free time) [11]. Another extension of the problem considers a time-series of arriving tasks whereby users are assigned to each task with a fair task allocation [4,16].

The concept of teams and forums performing *collaborative learning* in MOOCs has been studied more recently [13,

24]. In one work, users are assumed to have a vector of characteristics, and the goal is to group users into teams with an upper-bound size such that team members have identical values on all characteristics [6].

Another interesting line of work [1,2] considers the variance in individual ability. Assuming the ability of a group of users is the average of the ability levels of its members, the goal is to partition users into groups such that the number of users with an ability level less than that of their team is maximized. In our context, users have complete control over whom they choose to accept into their teams, therefore, we chose game-theoretic modeling instead of optimization. Combining the approach of the two papers poses an interesting open problem.

The structure of teams as coalitions has been studied as a network formation game in [22] and [12], where the strength of a coalition is defined as the strength of the social network structure creating it in a hedonic coalition formation game. In many network coalition games, the network is used to determine payoffs, or even network creation is considered as a strategic process [14]. Studying the team formation problem as a network formation game, one where network structure affects the utility functions of agents, offers an interesting future direction for our work. This paper defines the utility function of a team based on the characteristics of its members.

3. DATA OBSERVATIONS

This section describes the data, our methodology for measuring homogeneity and diversity in teams, and our analysis.

3.1 Teams

NovoEd is a social learning platform used to offer experiential and collaborative online classes of varying sizes. In many courses offered on NovoEd, team work and collaboration form an integral part of coursework.

The learning platform supports two types of team formation processes: algorithmic and organic. *Algorithmic teams* are formed automatically based on criteria set by the instructor (e.g., size of the team and geographical location of the members), and are often transient, being formed around a particular assignment and dissolved afterwards. *Organic teams* are formed by learners themselves and may persist throughout the course, although students can leave one team and join another at any time. Students find each other through searching submitted assignments, answers to course profile questions, locations and keywords in the profile. They may be invited to join a team by the team leader or individually ask to join a team.

This paper focuses on organic teams formed by the students, analyzes student preferences when selecting a team, and identifies success factors in these teams.

3.2 Dataset

Our dataset includes 11 courses offered in the summer of 2014. Enrollments ranged from 200 students to more than 25,000 students per course. These courses were four- to eight-weeks long and covered various business topics. Three of the analyzed courses had tens of *active students* (students who had done some course activities e.g., submitting an assignment), five had hundreds of them and three had thousands.

Each student had a profile that included age, education, gender, and location. Instructors could choose to introduce extra profile questions such as those regarding skills. Profile question responses were the main mechanism for searching out team members.

3.3 Measuring Homogeneity and Diversity in a Team

We propose a framework to determine whether students prefer to work with others similar to them (i.e., *homogeneity* is preferred) or with a diverse group (i.e., *diversity* is preferred). We describe this analytical framework by studying age diversity in organic teams.

Students are required to select their age range in their profile. Provided options are: $18-20$, $21-25$, $26-30$, $31-35$, $36-40$, $41-45$, $46-50$, Over 50. The age range selected is not shown on their profiles and is not searchable by other students, but it could be inferred from student profile pictures and biographies.

We calculate the number of pairs of students in one team that belong to age groups X and Y. To remove size bias, we normalize this number by the total number of possible pairs that could have been created from members of age group X with members of age group Y (students are not uniformly distributed in age groups). Let $n(X)$ represent the number of students in age group X and $pair(X,Y)$ represent the number of pairs with one student from age group X and one student from age group Y. Let $temp(X,Y) = \frac{pair(X,Y)}{n(X) \times n(Y)}$. For the special case of $X = Y$, the number of possible pairs is $\binom{n(X)}{2}$. Hence, we define $temp(X,X) = \frac{pair(X,X)}{\binom{n(X)}{2}}$.

Consequently, we define a metric to measure the preference of students from age groups X and Y to be in one team as:

$$pref(X,Y) = \frac{temp(X,Y)}{average(\sum_Z temp(X,Z), \sum_Z temp(Y,Z))}$$

Figure 1 shows age preferences in forming teams for a typical course.[1] Darker colors represent larger values, showing age groups that prefer to be in the same team. We observe that cells on the diagonal (or close to it) have larger values. This suggests a preference for age-homogeneous team creation. Students under 20 or students over 50 show a strong preference to join same-age teams (viz., dark colors on the bottom left and top right cells), while students between 26-40 show more flexibility in age groups when forming teams.

Student profiles in our dataset also include education level (i.e., Some high school, Graduated high school or equivalent, Some college or university, Graduated with an associate degree, Graduated with a bachelor's degree, Graduated with a master's degree, Graduated with a doctorate degree); gender (male, female); location (latitude-longitude pair); and skill set. Skill set, a course-specific question, may have different values in different courses. For example, skill set options defined by the instructor in a business class included: Aerospace, Finance, Machinery, Architecture, Chemicals - Materials, Consumer products, Other manufacturing, Telecommunications, Publishing- Schools, Service primary secondary, Energy - Electric utilities, Software - Internet - Mobile, Drugs - Biotech - Medical devices, Management and finance consulting, Electronics - Computers, Law - Accounting - other business services, Other services.

---

[1]We observed consistent behavior across all courses.

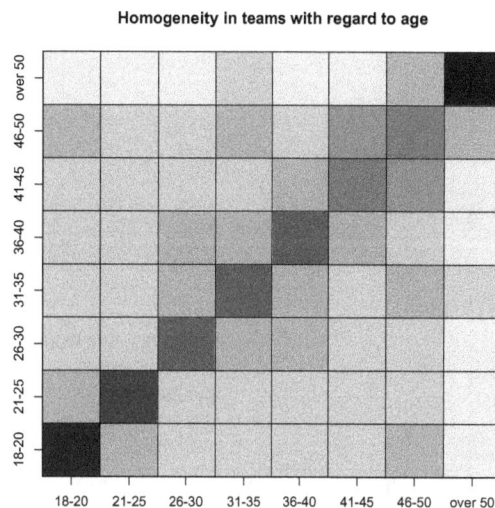

Figure 1: Students prefer to form teams with those of the same age group.

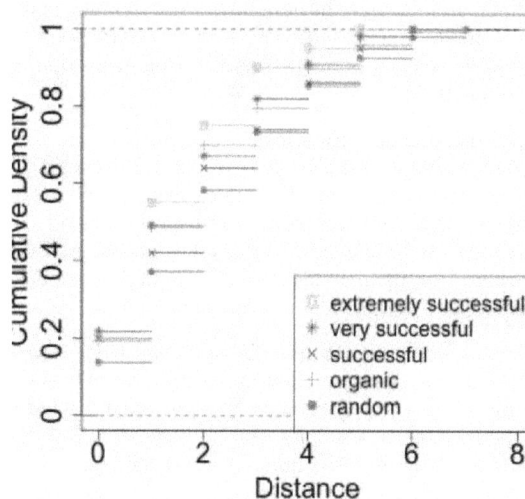

Figure 2: Preference for age-homogeneous team membership

We look deeper into team formation and analyze homogeneity preferences across different profile questions utilizing the following analytical framework. For each profile question, we plot the cumulative distribution of distances between responses given by team members in organic teams and compare it to the same distribution in teams that could be built completely at random. We consider all students who responded to each of the profile questions in this analysis. Profile questions can be represented as *numerical* (location [latitude, longitude] and gender [0,1]), *ordinal* (age and education), and *categorical* (skill set). We define pairwise distances between two data points for each profile question as follows:

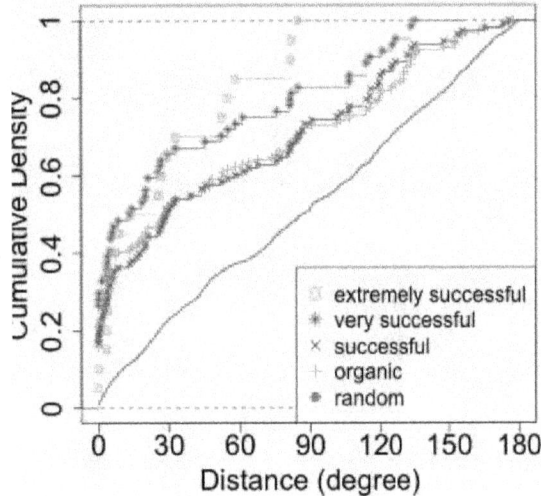

Figure 3: Preference for longitude-homogeneous team membership

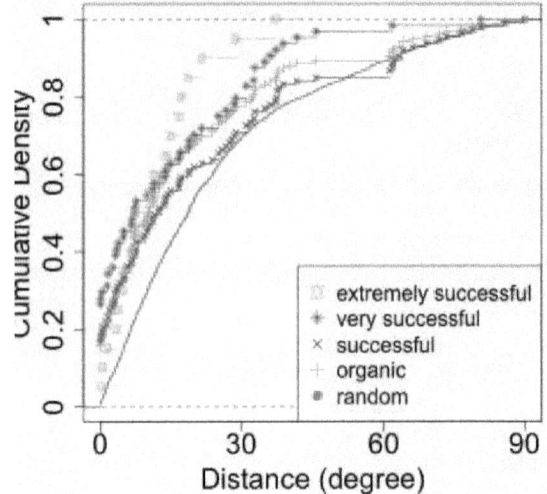

Figure 4: Preference for latitude-homogeneous team membership

- **Numerical profile questions:** Location is defined by two numeric values: latitude and longitude. Age is defined as an integer by assigning binary values to male and female. Pairwise distances of two data points for age and location is defined as the Euclidean distance between them.

- **Ordinal profile questions:** Ordinal features, such as age range and education level, are represented with consecutive categories. We define the pairwise distance between two data points as the distance between the categories to which they belong. For example, for education, the distance between "Some high school" and "Graduated high school or equivalent" is 1.

- **Categorical profile questions:** We utilize entropy to define the distance between categorical values. Entropy in a team is defined as $\sum_{i=1}^{m} p_i \log(p_i)$, where p_i is the fraction of students who have selected i as their response, and m is the number of categories.

3.4 Homogeneous and Diverse Teaming Preferences

We calculate cumulative distribution functions for pairwise distances of student profile data in teams formed organically and compare them to random teams. Organic teams are homogeneous with respect to a profile question if the CDF of pairwise distances of team members for that profile question appears higher than the same CDF for random teams.

We also study the impact of homogeneity on the success of students in organic teams by comparing the pairwise distance CDFs for all organic teams with the CDFs for the organic teams that contain at least 50% ("successful"), 75% ("very successful"), and 100% ("extremely successful") successful team members. A *successful student* is one who has completed the course and received a statement of accomplishment. Criteria for receiving a statement of accomplishment are highly dependent on the course instructor.

As explained in the following subsections, we observe that students prefer homogeneity with regard to location, distance, age range and education level. Interestingly, however, students do not have any preference concerning the gender of their team members. We also observe that students tend to prefer heterogeneous skill sets in successful organic teams.

3.4.1 Homogeneous Teaming Preferences

Figure 2 shows the CDF of pairwise distances for age range in a course. The CDF curve for the organic teams is always above the CDF for the random case, attesting to the preference for age-homogeneity in team formation. This result was reproduced consistently across all eleven courses in our dataset.

Figures 3-6 show CDF curves for longitude (time zone), latitude, geographical distance, and education level. The CDF for organic teams appears above the CDF for random teams for all these features consistently across all courses – even for courses with *supportive teams* (i.e., students who discuss assignments in teams but write answers individually). Teams show greater homogeneity with regard to longitude than latitude: longitude represents time zone, and our results show that students organically form teams with those in similar time zones.

We also reviewed invitations extended by team leaders when they are growing their teams and observed similar homogeneous preferences for team invitations. This provides us with a second resource to confirm that students prefer to work with those with characteristic similar to their own.

We analyzed team formation preferences for successful organic teams with regard to age, education, and location and reproduced the same homogeneous preferences for these teams compared to the random case. However, it is important to note that increasing homogeneity in a team does not necessarily translate into making individual students more successful in that team. In fact, in some courses we observed that teams with more successful students depict a more diverse distribution compared to all other organic teams. This

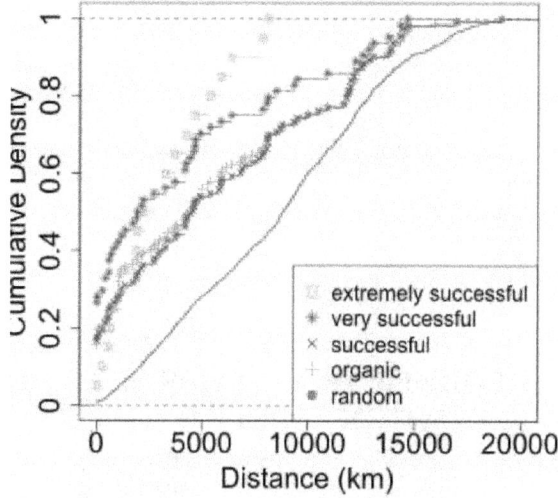

Figure 5: Preference for distance-homogeneous team membership

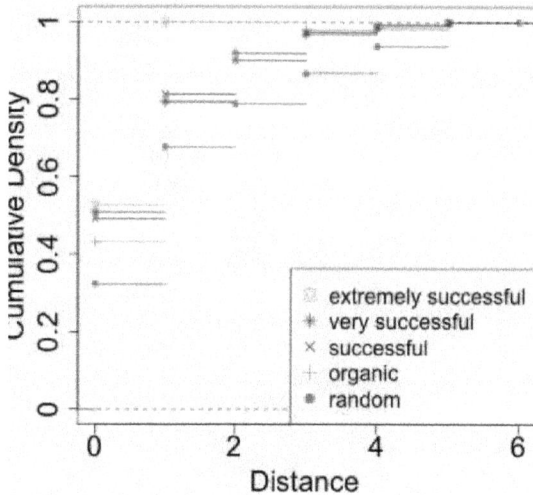

Figure 6: Preference for education-level-homogeneous team membership

suggests that teams with many successful students are more homogeneous than random teams but not necessarily more homogeneous than other organic teams.

We also analyzed teaming preferences with regard to gender. We didn't find any statistically significant result that is consistent across all courses.

3.4.2 Diverse Teaming Preferences

Finally, we analyzed skill diversity CDF curves for organic teams and for successful organic teams. Figure 7 shows that the CDF curves for the organic teams with many successful members are lower than the CDF curves for all organic teams. Higher skill set entropy in a team is equivalent to

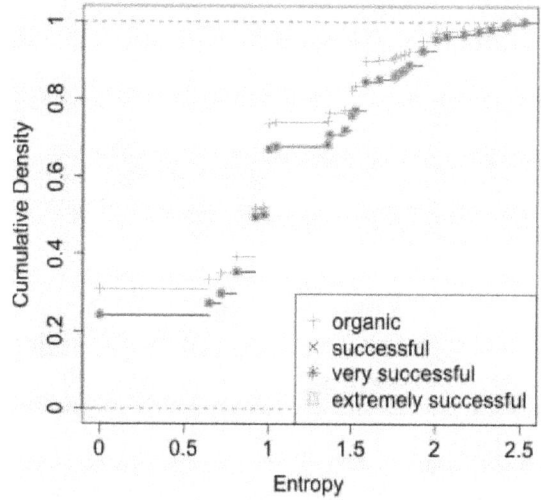

Figure 7: Skill diversity in high-profile organic teams versus all organic teams

higher skill set diversity among that team's members. Teams with more successful members have diverse skill sets. This result is consistent across all courses. Therefore, students depict diverse teaming preferences with regard to skill set and other similar profile questions (e.g., background, career sector, and professional interests).

4. MODELING

Our observations in Section 3 suggest two main criteria to consider when forming teams. Individuals prefer to form teams with those who are in the same timezone and have a similar location, age range and education level. We also observed that members of teams with more diverse skill sets achieve better learning outcomes in online courses.

To better understand the dynamics of team formation, we employ tools and solution concepts from cooperative game theory. This is appropriate because in our setting individuals have agency over team formation by choosing their own teammates. Moreover, they benefit directly from the success of their team and strive to form teams that have the highest probability of success.

Let A be a set of n agents (e.g., students). Let $c : A \to \mathbb{Z}^\ell$ map each agent to a vector of l characteristics with discrete values like age, education level, latitude, and longitude.[2] For each $a \in A$ and $1 \le j \le \ell$, $c_j(a)$ denotes the j-th characteristic of a.

In addition, we assume that each agent has a primary skill $s : A \to S$, where $S = \{s_1, ..., s_m\}$.

Team and Team Allocation. Given a number k and a set of predetermined thresholds $\{\delta_j\}_{1 \le j \le \ell} \ge 0$, a set $T \subseteq A$ is a team if $1 \le |T| \le k$, and for each $a, b \in A$ and $1 \le j \le \ell$,

$$|c_j(a) - c_j(b)| \le \delta_j.$$

We consider the above constraints as the *homogeneity* constraints, and we call $\{\delta_j\}$ the *homogeneity thresholds*. Here,

---

[2]Without loss of generality, we assume the difference between two continuous values is 1 and the values are in $\mathbb{Z}$.

k introduces a size constraint to avoid making very large teams, and homogeneity constraints are introduced in accordance with the observations in Section 3.4. We use $\mathcal{T} \subseteq 2^A$ to denote the set of all possible teams of agents. A *team allocation* $\mathcal{P}$ is a partition of A into teams.

Value Function of a Team. The *value function*, $v : 2^A \to \mathbb{R}_+$, assigns a non-negative value to each set $B \subseteq A$. One can think of $v(T)$ as the quality score or the likelihood of success of a team T. We assume that $v(B)$ is a monotone increasing function of the skill set present in B. In other words, we assume there exists a function $g : 2^S \to \mathbb{R}_+$ such that for any $B \subseteq A$,

$$v(B) = g \left(\cup_{a \in B} s(a) \right).$$

These assumptions simplify the problem significantly. In a sense, we reduce each person to a vector of characteristics and each team to a skill set. Obviously, the reality is far more complex; many other factors affect the decision of individuals to form a team and whether the resulting team is successful. On the other hand, in many situations, including team formation in an online course, individuals must form teams with limited information about each other. Our Section 3 observations indicate that the diversity of skill set and homogeneity of basic characteristics do play a strong role in both formation and success of teams and hence the validity of our assumptions.

Utility function. The utility of every agent is equal to the value function or quality score of the team to which he or she belongs. More formally, for any agent $a \in T$ of a partition $\mathcal{P}$,

$$u_\mathcal{P}(a) = v(T).$$

In our model, utility function assumes that all members benefit equally from the value created by the team. In other words, team members cannot distribute the value freely or compensate each other with side payments. This model applies to a variety of settings. The most immediate example is in the context of online courses, where all team members receive the same grade for finishing the project. Other scenarios include those where a large group benefits almost equally from some projects, such as building a museum, park, or school. Our model also applies tp situations where it is against social norms to differentiate explicitly between contributors (e.g., as when writing a paper in a theory conference).

4.1 Stable Solutions and Core of a Cooperative Game

Core of a game is a simple and intuitive notion defined in cooperative game theory to study the stability of groups or coalitions. The core consists of all configurations of agents and payoff allocations that cannot be improved upon by a coalition of agents. This means that once an agreement in the core has been reached, no coalition has an incentive to secede.

In our context, a team allocation $\mathcal{P}$ is *stable* ($\mathcal{P} \in$ core) if and only if for all $T \in \mathcal{T}$, there exists an agent $a \in T$ such that[3]

$$v(T) \leq u_\mathcal{P}(a).$$

This means that for all possible teams T, the utility of at least one agent (we call it a) under the current team allo-

---

[3]Please recall that $\mathcal{T}$ denotes the set of all possible teams.

cation $\mathcal{P}$ is not less than its utility when it secedes from $\mathcal{P}$ and forms team T. Hence, a is not willing to secede, and $\mathcal{P}$ is stable.

Our goal is to identify a team allocation in which: (1) the size of each team is at most k, (2) homogeneity constraints are respected, and (3) the solution is in the core. In particular, after forming the teams, there is no group of agents that could improve its utility by leaving its team and forming a new team.

PROBLEM 1. *Given a set of agents, A, a value function $v : 2^A \to \mathbb{R}_+$, a set of homogeneity thresholds $\{\delta_j\}_{1 \leq j \leq \ell} \geq 0$, and a size limit k, find a team allocation $\mathcal{P}$ that is in the core.*

5. THEORETICAL ANALYSIS OF THE TEAM ALLOCATION PROBLEM

This section partially answers Problem 1.[4] We start by showing that there is always a team allocation $\mathcal{P}$ in the core. Consider the following optimization problem.

PROBLEM 2. *Given a set of agents, A, a value function $v : 2^A \to \mathbb{R}_+$ and a set of homogeneity thresholds $\{\delta_j\}_{1 \leq j \leq \ell} \geq 0$, find a team $T \in \mathcal{T}$ such that*

$$v(T) \geq v(T')$$

for all $T' \in \mathcal{T}$.

Our first theorem shows that, given access to an oracle that solves Problem 2, there is an algorithm that can find a team allocation in the core in polynomial time. Then, we show that Problem 1 is equivalent to Problem 2 (up to a linear loss in $|A|$). We continue by discussing the fact that Problem 2 is NP-hard for an adversarially chosen value function. This suggests that Problem 1 is also NP-hard. We continue by constructing a team allocation for a special family of value functions.

THEOREM 1. *For any set of agents A, any value function $v : 2^A \to \mathbb{R}_+$, and thresholds $\{\delta_j\}_{1 \leq j \leq \ell} \geq 0$, core $\neq \emptyset$. Furthermore, given access to an oracle of Problem 2, there is a polynomial time algorithm that finds $\mathcal{P} \in$ core.*

PROOF. We propose a simple algorithm. First, we use an oracle of Problem 2 to find a team T with maximum value. We add T to $\mathcal{P}$, remove its members from A, and repeat the procedure on the remaining set. The algorithm terminates when A is empty. See Algorithm 1 for details.

Algorithm 1 Team Allocation Algorithm

---

while $|A| > 0$ **do**

    Use an oracle of Problem 2 to find $T \in \mathcal{T}$ (where $T \subseteq A$) of maximum value.

    Add T to $\mathcal{P}$ and remove T from A, $A = A \setminus T$.

end while

Return $\mathcal{P}$.

Let $\mathcal{P}$ be the output. For the sake of contradiction, assume there is a team $T \in \mathcal{T}$ such that for all $a \in T$,

$$u_\mathcal{P}(a) < v(T).$$

---

[4]A complete answer would be provided in the next sections.

Let a be the first agent in T that is assigned to another team by the algorithm, and let T' represent that team. Note that

$$v(T') = u_{\mathcal{P}}(a) < v(T).$$

By the definition of a, when T' is constructed, all members of T were available, so T was also a feasible team at that time. Since the oracle returned T, we must have

$$v(T') \geq v(T),$$

which is a contradiction. Hence, $\mathcal{P} \in$ core. $\square$

Observe that Algorithm 1 runs in polynomial time if the oracle of Problem 2 runs in polynomial time. Unfortunately, even where there is no homogeneity constraint and $v(.)$ is a submodular function, Problem 2 is NP-hard. In the following theorem, we show that this is not a limitation of Algorithm 1 because Problem 1 is equivalent to Problem 2.

THEOREM 2. *Problems 1 and 2 are reducible to each other in polynomial time.*

PROOF. Theorem 1 shows one direction: if we can solve Problem 2 in polynomial time, Algorithm 1 solves Problem 1.

Conversely, given a polynomial time algorithm for Problem 1, let $\mathcal{P}$ be the output of this algorithm. Let $T \in \mathcal{P}$ be the team with maximum value,

$$v(T) \geq v(T'),$$

for all $T' \in \mathcal{P}$. We return T as the solution of Problem 2. If T is not an optimal solution, there is a team T' such that $v(T') > v(T)$. But then $\mathcal{P}$ is not in the core because if all agents of T' withdraw from their allocated teams in $\mathcal{P}$ and form T', they receive a higher utility. $\square$

Even without the homogeneity constraints, finding a set of cardinality k maximizing a monotone function, even under submodularity or supermodularity assumption, is NP-hard. Therefore, Problem 1 is NP-hard.

COROLLARY 1. *It is NP-hard to find a team allocation in the core.*

With a more intricate construction employing homogenity constraints, we can also show that the maximization problem is NP-hard even when v is linear in the number of skills present in the set. However, we leave that proof for a more extensive version of this article.

6. TEAM ALLOCATION UNDER WEAKLY SEPARABLE VALUE FUNCTIONS

Given Theorem 1, we focus on a specific class of value functions. The following is a natural special case that admits polynomial time algorithms.

DEFINITION 1 (WEAKLY SEPARABLE FUNCTIONS). *A function* $g : 2^S \to \mathbb{R}_+$ *is weakly separable if for any* $B \subseteq A$ *and* $a, b \in A$ *such that*

$$g(B \cup \{a\}) \geq g(B \cup \{b\}),$$

the following holds: For all $B' \supset B$ *such that* $a, b \notin B'$,

$$g(B' \cup \{a\}) \geq g(B' \cup \{b\}).$$

We say that a value function $v : 2^A \to \mathbb{R}_+$ *is weakly separable if there is a weakly separable function* $g : 2^S \to \mathbb{R}_+$ *such that for any* $B \subseteq A$,

$$v(B) = g(\cup_{a \in B} s(a)).$$

EXAMPLE 1. *The following functions are weakly separable:*

- $g(V) = (|V|)^2$
- $g(V) = \sqrt{|V|}$
- *For any* $w : S \to \mathbb{R}_+$, $g(V) = \prod_{s \in V} w(s)$

The rest of this section assumes that the value function is monotone increasing and weakly separable. For each skill s, we define the weight of s, $w(s)$, to be the value of the singleton containing s,

$$w(s) = g(\{s\}).$$

First, we give a simple polynomial time algorithm for Problem 1 when there is no homogeneity constraint. In Subsections 6.1 and 6.2, we show that Problem 1 is polynomial time solvable in the number of agents and the homogeneity thresholds.

THEOREM 3. *If there is no homogeneity constraint and the value function is weakly separable, then Problem 1 is polynomial time solvable.*

PROOF. By Algorithm 1, we need only solve Problem 2 in polynomial time. Without loss of generality, assume that there is at most one agent in A having each skill in S (if more than one, keep one and remove the rest) and that $|A| \geq k$ (if $|A| < k$, return A as the solution). Let $A = \{a_1, \ldots, a_n\}$ such that

$$w(s(a_1)) \geq w(s(a_2)) \geq \cdots \geq w(s(a_n)).$$

We show $\{a_1, \ldots, a_k\}$ is the optimum of Problem 2.

First, note that by monotonicity, the optimum set has size k. Fix a set $\{b_1, \ldots, b_k\}$ such that

$$w(s(b_1)) \geq \cdots \geq w(s(b_k)).$$

By definition of $\{a_1, \ldots, a_k\}$, for all $1 \leq i \leq k$,

$$w(s(a_i)) \geq w(s(b_i)).$$

Therefore,

$$v(\{b_1, \ldots, b_k\}) \leq v(\{b_1, \ldots, b_{k-1}, a_k\})$$

since $w(s(a_k)) \geq w(s(b_k))$ and $v(.)$ is weakly separable. Similarly,

$$v(\{b_1, \ldots, b_{k-1}, a_k\}) \leq v(\{b_1, \ldots, b_{k-2}, a_{k-1}, a_k\}).$$

Repeating this k times, we conclude that

$$v(\{b_1, \ldots, b_k\}) \leq v(\{a_1, \ldots, a_k\}),$$

as desired. $\square$

Algorithm 2 outputs a team allocation in the core when the value function is weakly separable and no homogeneity constraint exists. It is easy to see that the algorithm runs in time $O((|S| + |A|) \log(|S| + |A|))$.

Building on the above analysis, Theorem 4 characterizes all team allocations in the core of Problem 1 when no homogeneity constraint exists and the value function is weakly separable.

Algorithm 2 Team Allocation Algorithm for weakly separable value functions and no homogeneity constraint

1: Sort the skills in the decreasing order of weights, i.e.,

$$w(s_1) \geq w(s_2) \geq \cdots \geq w(s_m).$$

Assume there is at least one agent with each skill.

2: **while** $|A| > 0$ **do**
3:     Construct a new team T of size k by selecting one agent from each of the highest weight k skills (if less than k skills remain in the sequence, choose one agent for each of them).
4:     Add T to $\mathcal{P}$ and remove its agents from A. If there are no more agents with skill s_i, remove s_i from the sequence.
5: **end while**
6: **Return** $\mathcal{P}$.

THEOREM 4. [5] *Consider a team allocation solution $\mathcal{P}$. Let u_i be the minimum utility an agent with skill s_i receives in $\mathcal{P}$. Rename u values to u' such that $u'_1 \geq ... \geq u'_m$.*

Team allocation $\mathcal{P}$ is in core if and only if there exists a permutation of skills $\hat{s}_1, ..., \hat{s}_m$ such that for all $1 \leq j \leq m$:

$$u'_j \geq g(A_j \setminus B_j),$$

where $A_j = \bigcup_{i=1}^{\min(k+j-1,m)} \{s_i\}$, $B_j = \bigcup_{i=1}^{j-1} \{\hat{s}_i\}$, and $\setminus$ is the set difference operator.[6]

EXAMPLE 2. *Consider a class of 15 students $A = \{a_1, \cdots, a_{15}\}$ and 4 skills $\{s_1, s_2, s_3, s_4\}$. Students $a_1 - a_3$ have the primary skill s_1, $a_4 - a_8$ have skill s_2, $a_9 - a_{12}$ have skill s_3, and $a_{13} - a_{15}$ have skill s_4. Students are allowed to form teams of size at most $k = 3$. Moreover, $g(V) = |V|$.*

Consider the following team allocation $\mathcal{P}$:
$T_1 = \{a_1, a_4, a_9\}, T_2 = \{a_2, a_5, a_{10}\}, T_3 = \{a_3, a_{11}, a_{13}\},$
$T_4 = \{a_6, a_{12}, a_{14}\}, T_5 = \{a_7, a_{15}\}, T_6 = \{a_8\}.$

The minimum utility of any student with skill s_1 is $u_1 = 3$. Similarly, $u_2 = 1, u_3 = 3$, and $u_4 = 2$. By sorting and renaming u_i values we get: $u'_1 = u_1 = 3 \geq u'_2 = u_3 = 3 \geq u'_3 = u_4 = 2 \geq u'_4 = u_2 = 1$.

Consider the following permutation of skills ($\hat{s}_1 = s_1, \hat{s}_2 = s_3, \hat{s}_3 = s_4, \hat{s}_4 = s_2$). The team allocation $\mathcal{P}$ is in core because
$u'_1 = 3 \geq g(\{s_1, s_2, s_3\} \setminus \{\}) = 3,$
$u'_2 = 3 \geq g(\{s_1, s_2, s_3, s_4\} \setminus \{\hat{s}_1\}) = 3,$
$u'_3 = 2 \geq g(\{s_1, s_2, s_3, s_4\} \setminus \{\hat{s}_1, \hat{s}_2\}) = 3$, and
$u'_4 = 1 \geq g(\{s_1, s_2, s_3, s_4\} \setminus \{\hat{s}_1, \hat{s}_2, \hat{s}_3\}) = 3.$

The following theorem gives a second approach to characterizing team allocations in the core.

THEOREM 5. *Let $u'_1, ..., u'_m$ be sorted minimum utilities for different skills in a team allocation $\mathcal{P}$. Let $s'_1, ..., s'_m$ be the corresponding skills. Solution $\mathcal{P}$ is in core if and only if for all $1 \leq i \leq m$*

$$g(\{s'_i, s'_{i+1}, ..., s'_{\min(i+k-1,m)}\}) \leq u'_i.$$

EXAMPLE 3. *Consider the setting in Example 2: 15 students, 4 skills, $k = 3$, and $g(V) = |V|$.*

---

[5]We discuss more complicated proofs, in the extended version of this article.
[6]Recall that without loss of generality, we assume that $w(s_1) \geq \cdots \geq w(s_m)$.

---

*Let team allocation $\mathcal{P}$ be: $T_1 = \{a_1, a_2, a_4\}, T_2 = \{a_3, a_5, a_6\},$
$T_3 = \{a_7, a_8, a_{12}\}, T_4 = \{a_9, a_{10}, a_{11}\}$, and $T_5 = \{a_{13}, a_{14}, a_{15}\}.$
We want to examine if $\mathcal{P}$ is in core.*

The minimum utilities are $u_1 = 2, u_2 = 2, u_3 = 1, u_4 = 1$. u_i values are already sorted; hence $u'_1 = u_1, u'_2 = u_2, u'_3 = u_3, u'_4 = u_4$ and $s'_1 = s_1, s'_2 = s_2, s'_3 = s_3, s'_4 = s_4$.

$\mathcal{P}$ is not in core because $u'_1 = 2 < g(\{s'_1, s'_2, s'_3\}) = 3$.

6.1 Team Allocation Problem under One Homogeneity Constraint

This subsection extends Theorem 3 to the setting where exactly one homogeneity constraint exists, i.e., we are looking for a team allocation $\mathcal{P}$ such that for any team T,

$$\max_{a,b \in T} |c(a) - c(b)| \leq \delta.$$

Note that we are dropping the indices because there is just one homogeneity constraint and, as usual, δ is the homogeneity threshold.

We prove the following theorem.

THEOREM 6. *If v is a weakly separable value function and there is exactly one homogeneity constraint, then Algorithm 3 finds a team allocation in the core in time polynomial in $|A|, |c_{\max} - c_{\min}|$, where $c_{\min} = \min_a c(a)$ and $c_{\max} = \max_a c(a)$.*

PROOF. First, observe that an agent a can join agents $b \in A$ only where $c(b) \in [c(a) - \delta, c(a) + \delta]$. So, for any team T, there exists an integer $i \in [c_{\min}, c_{\max}]$ such that for all $a \in T$,

$$c(a) \in [i, i + \delta].$$

Without loss of generality, assume $c_{\max} - c_{\min} > \delta$. For any $i \in [c_{\min}, c_{\max} - \delta]$, let

$$A_i := \{a : i \leq c(a) \leq i + \delta\}.$$

As before, we need only solve Problem 2. For each i, we find a team $T_i \subseteq A_i$ of maximum value using Algorithm 2. Then, among all T_i, we simply return the one with the maximum value T_i^* such that

$$i^* = \text{argmax}_i v(T_i).$$

Such a set satisfies the homogeneity constraint and obviously has the maximum weight among all teams. $\square$

Algorithm 3 finds a team allocation in the core when there is only one homogeneity constraint and the value function is weakly separable.

Algorithm 3 Team Allocation Algorithm for weakly separable value functions under one homogeneity constraint

1: For each $i \in [c_{\min}, c_{\max} - \delta]$, let

$$A_i = \{a : i \leq c(a) \leq i + \delta\}.$$

2: **while** $|A| > 0$ **do**
3:     **for** $i = c_{\min} \rightarrow c_{\max} - \delta$ **do**
4:         Let T_i be the output of Algorithm 2 on A_i.
5:     **end for**
6:     Let T^* be the T_i with maximum weight.
7:     Add T^* to $\mathcal{P}$ and remove it from A and all A_i.
8: **end while**
9: **Return** $\mathcal{P}$.

The following theorem is immediate.

THEOREM 7. *A team allocation $\mathcal{P}$ is in core if and only if Theorem 5 holds for all sets $A_i = \{a : i \leq c(a) \leq i + \delta\}$ where $c_{\min} \leq i \leq c_{\max} - \delta$.*

6.2 Team Allocation under Multiple Homogeneity Constraints

Finally, we proceed to the case where l homogeneity constraints are present. For $1 \leq j \leq l$,

$$\forall \text{ Team } T, \quad \max_{a,b \in T} |c_j(a) - c_j(b)| \leq \delta_j.$$

To identify a team allocation in core, again it is sufficient to solve Problem 2 for this generalized case. We generalize the approach described in the previous section. In particular, we create an l-dimensional cube based on c_j values. The cube contains $e_1 \times \cdots \times e_l$ cells, where e_j is the number of possible integer values for characteristic c_j between $c_{j_{\min}}$ and $c_{j_{\max}} - \delta_j$:

$$e_j = (c_{j_{\max}} - \delta_j) - (c_{j_{\min}}) + 1,$$

where $c_{j_{\min}} = \min_a c_j(a)$ and $c_{j_{\max}} = \max_a c_j(a)$.

For any i_j $(1 \leq j \leq \ell)$ where $c_{j_{\min}} \leq i_j \leq c_{j_{\max}} - \delta_j$, we construct a subset of A, denoted by $A_{i_1,\ldots,i_\ell}$ (that corresponds to a cell in the cube), as follows:

$$A_{i_1,\ldots,i_\ell} = \{u \in A : \vee\, 1 \leq j \leq \ell, i_j \leq c_j(u) \leq i_j + \delta_j\}.$$

We use Algorithm 2 to find the team with maximum weight in each set $A_{i_1,\ldots,i_\ell}$ and return the team with the maximum weight among all as the solution of Problem 2. The following theorem follows.

THEOREM 8. *If v is a weakly separable value function, then the above algorithm finds a team allocation in the core in time $O(|A| \cdot |S| \cdot \prod_{1 \leq j \leq \ell}(c_{j_{\max}} - c_{j_{\min}} - \delta_j))$.*

7. IMPLEMENTATION

Our algorithm builds teams based on teaming preferences and δ parameters observed in organic teams. Algorithmic teams can be used by instructors for brainstorming exercises, case study discussions, and negotiation simulations. Students are placed into teams to accomplish a collective goal in a short period of time. The quality of suggested teams has an immediate impact on learning outcomes in these activities.

Organic teams are the main mechanism for creating an intimate network of peers and learners in online courses. Organic team formation requires students to search for teams they can join or to find new members to join their current team. Both activities are time-consuming. Our algorithm can suggest new team members to small teams and to students without teams. This algorithm can implement a recommendation engine to reduce barriers of creating organic teams and to increase the probability of success in resulting teams.

This section describes how we implemented our proposed algorithm and compares its stability and performance to two baseline algorithms, Random and Exhaustive-Greedy. The *Random algorithm* groups users randomly considering the cardinality and homogeneity constraints. A student is randomly selected and added to a team if homogeneity and size constraints are satisfied. The *Exhaustive-Greedy algorithm* creates teams as follows. It starts with an empty set. In each step, it adds the student that maximizes the set's value to

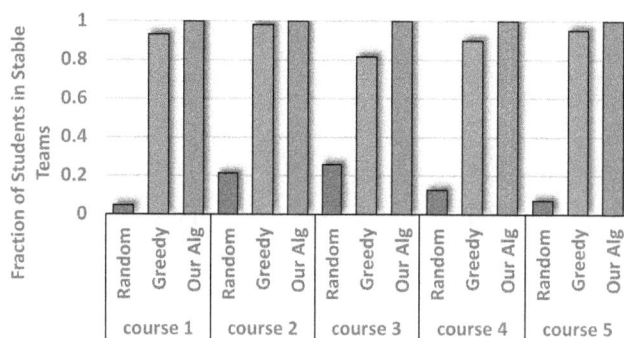

Figure 8: Fraction of students in stable teams formed by Random, Exhaustive-Greedy, and our algorithms

this set as long as size and homogeneity constraints are satisfied. A new empty set is created when the current set has k members or when no other student can be added to it without violating homogeneity constraints.

The run time of each algorithm is measured on a Mac-Book Air with 8GB of RAM and a 1.7 GHz Intel Core i7 cpu running OS X version 10.9.5. The algorithms are implemented with R and are single-threaded. The stability of the resulting teams formed by each algorithm is measured by computing the fraction of students in stable teams as defined in Section 4.

We compared the performance of Random and Exhaustive-Greedy algorithms with our algorithm for all courses, with different values for key parameters. We reproduced consistent results across courses and parameters. We report stability and performance comparisons for creating teams with maximum size constraint of $k = 4$ and two homogeneity constraints on age and education level, with parameters $\delta_{age} = 3$ and $\delta_{education} = 4$. The selected δ values for age and education are observed as the maximum difference between team members' ages and education levels, respectively, in 80% of all organic teams across eleven courses present in our database.

Figure 8 shows the stability of the three algorithms for four different courses. We observe that the quality of the teams formed by the Random algorithm is very low, with a stability fraction of about 0.1. The Exhaustive-Greedy algorithm provides teams with much higher quality than the Random algorithm, with an average stability fraction of about 0.9. Our algorithm forms the highest quality teams, with a stability fraction of 1. Figure 9 graphs the running time in milliseconds displayed in logarithmic scale, demonstrating the efficiency of our algorithm.

8. CONCLUSION AND FUTURE WORK

Teams are increasingly indispensable across organizations. Whether in a large company or startup, a foundation, or a research organization, interdisciplinary teams are essential for solving problems or performing new and sophisticated tasks. Despite our increasing dependency on high functioning teams, our understanding of the dynamics of team formation, people's biases in choosing teammates, and the composition of successful teams remains quite limited. This

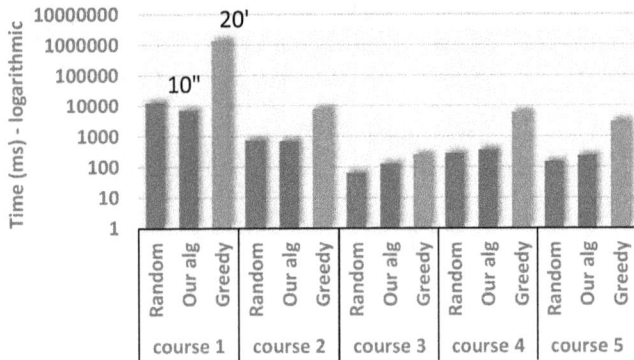

Figure 9: Run time of Random, Exhaustive-Greedy, and our algorithms for different courses

paper takes a small step towards using existing data to promote a better understanding of team formation dynamics and success.

By studying 11 MOOCs and analyzing students' preferences, we observed that students prefer to form teams that are homogeneous across age, education level, distance and time zone, but teams that are diverse with regard to skill set. The same results hold for high-performance teams (teams with many successful members). Our observations suggest a strong positive correlation between skill diversity and team success.

We proposed a game theoretic model for the team formation problem based on these observations. In particular, having a set of students with multiple characteristics and skills, we defined the automatic team formation problem as the partitioning of students into stable teams that fulfill predetermined homogeneity and cardinality constraints. The problem was modeled as a collaborative game with nontransferable utility, and the concept of core was utilized to model stability. We showed that the core of the defined coalitional game is always non-empty and proposed a polynomial time algorithm to form stable teams for a natural category of value functions. A set of experiments were conducted that show the performance and quality of our proposed algorithm compared to random and greedy baseline algorithms.

An interesting direction of future work would be to study the team formation problem when student history information is present. Specifically, we are interested in considering information on how students formed teams and how well they performed in previous assignments and courses. This data could help us define a proficiency score for students across different skills and topics. This is a generalization of [2], where students may have different proficiency levels on different subjects considered together with profile question constraints (such as age, education, and location). It would be interesting to discover whether teams were homogeneous or heterogeneous across proficiency levels and whether teams with more homogeneous proficiency levels were more successful.

We are also interested in considering social connections between users and whether these connections affect students' preferences to form teams, generalizing our model based on these observations.

Another interesting direction would generalize the problem for a dynamic setting, where the goal is to make recommendations to users to join teams or invite others and update the recommendations if users decline.

Finally, we would like to observe how teams evolve over time, how users behave in teams, when users leave their team or get asked to leave, and how new members are selected.

9. REFERENCES

[1] R. Agrawal, B. Golshan, and E. Terzi. Forming beneficial teams of students in massive online classes. In *Proceedings of the 1st ACM Conference on Learning@ scale*, pages 155–156. ACM, 2014.

[2] R. Agrawal, B. Golshan, and E. Terzi. Grouping students in educational settings. In *Proceedings of the 20th ACM SIGKDD International Conference on Knowledge Discovery and Data Mining*, pages 1017–1026. ACM, 2014.

[3] A. An, M. Kargar, and M. ZiHayat. Finding affordable and collaborative teams from a network of experts. In *Proceedings of the 2013 SIAM International Conference on Data Mining*, pages 587–595, 2013.

[4] A. Anagnostopoulos, L. Becchetti, C. Castillo, A. Gionis, and S. Leonardi. Online team formation in social networks. In *Proceedings of the 21st International World Wide Web Conference*, pages 839–848. ACM, 2012.

[5] C. M. Beckman. The influence of founding team company affiliations on firm behavior. *Academy of Management Journal*, 49(4):741–758, 2006.

[6] R. Bredereck, T. Köhler, A. Nichterlein, R. Niedermeier, and G. Philip. Using patterns to form homogeneous teams. *Algorithmica*, pages 1–22, 2013.

[7] C. E. Eesley, D. H. Hsu, and E. B. Roberts. The contingent effects of top management teams on venture performance: Aligning founding team composition with innovation strategy and commercialization environment. *Strategic Management Journal*, 35(12):1798–1817, 2014.

[8] K. M. Eisenhardt and C. B. Schoonhoven. Organizational growth: Linking founding team, strategy, environment, and growth among U.S. semiconductor ventures, 1978-1988. *Administrative Science Quarterly*, pages 504–529, 1990.

[9] D. P. Forbes, P. S. Borchert, M. E. Zellmer-Bruhn, and H. J. Sapienza. Entrepreneurial team formation: An exploration of new member addition. *Entrepreneurship Theory and Practice*, 30(2):225–248, 2006.

[10] D. B. Gillies. Solutions to general non-zero-sum games. *Contributions to the Theory of Games*, 4(40):47–85, 1959.

[11] X. Han, Y. Liu, X. Guo, X. Wu, and X. Song. Time constraint-based team formation in social networks. In *Proceedings of the 2013 International Conference on Mechatronic Sciences, Electric Engineering and Computer (MEC)*, pages 1600–1604. IEEE, 2013.

[12] M. Hoefer, D. Váz, and L. Wagner. Hedonic coalition formation in networks. In *Proceedings of the 29th AAAI Conference on Artificial Intelligence*, 2014.

[13] J. Huang, A. Dasgupta, A. Ghosh, J. Manning, and M. Sanders. Superposter behavior in mooc forums. In *Proceedings of the 1st ACM conference on Learning@ scale*, pages 117–126. ACM, 2014.

[14] M. O. Jackson et al. *Social and economic networks*, volume 3. Princeton University Press, 2008.

[15] T. Lappas, K. Liu, and E. Terzi. Finding a team of experts in social networks. In *Proceedings of the 15th ACM SIGKDD International Conference on Knowledge Discovery and Data Mining*, pages 467–476. ACM, 2009.

[16] A. Majumder, S. Datta, and K. Naidu. Capacitated team formation problem on social networks. In *Proceedings of the 18th ACM SIGKDD International Conference on Knowledge Discovery and Data Mining*, pages 1005–1013. ACM, 2012.

[17] L. L. Martins, L. L. Gilson, and M. T. Maynard. Virtual teams: What do we know and where do we go from here? *Journal of Management*, 30(6):805–835, 2004.

[18] A. S. Mello and M. E. Ruckes. Team composition. *The Journal of Business*, 79(3):1019–1039, 2006.

[19] S. S. Rangapuram, T. Bühler, and M. Hein. Towards realistic team formation in social networks based on densest subgraphs. In *Proceedings of the 22nd International World Wide Web Conference*, pages 1077–1088. International World Wide Web Conferences Steering Committee, 2013.

[20] A. E. Roth and M. A. O. Sotomayor. *Two-sided matching: A study in game-theoretic modeling and analysis*. Number 18. Cambridge University Press, 1992.

[21] B. Senior and S. Swailes. The dimensions of management team performance: a repertory grid study. *International Journal of Productivity and Performance Management*, 53(4):317–333, 2004.

[22] L. Sless, N. Hazon, S. Kraus, and M. Wooldridge. Forming coalitions and facilitating relationships for completing tasks in social networks. In *Proceedings of the 2014 International Conference on Autonomous Agents and Multi-agent Systems*, pages 261–268. International Foundation for Autonomous Agents and Multi-agent Systems, 2014.

[23] W. E. Watson, K. Kumar, and L. K. Michaelsen. Cultural diversity's impact on interaction process and performance: Comparing homogeneous and diverse task groups. *Academy of Management Journal*, 36(3):590–602, 1993.

[24] B. A. Williams. Peers in moocs: Lessons based on the education production function, collective action, and an experiment. In *Proceedings of the 2nd ACM Conference on Learning@ Scale*, pages 287–292. ACM, 2015.

[25] A. Zzkarian and A. Kusiak. Forming teams: an analytical approach. *IIE Transactions*, 31(1):85–97, 1999.

Author Index